✱ definition g worship (s sacramental purpose / participation -
  p 86

p. 241 - at issue between RC & Prot principle

now RC view g Eucharistic Sacrifice - p 272

Diff between Praise & Dogma - p 282

Moment g consecration; p. 329

Earliest date g Christian Christmas   p. 375

p. 376 Christianity & cultural adaptation. (Problems -
                                    attempted solutions

Summary g distinction between
     Sacred & secular   p. 405 ff.

Church + decisions g politics / justice - p 425 ff

meaning g 'intercession' p 40 3 parts.

Power g Sac   p. 121

Brief hist. g 'liturgical movement' p 334 ff.

'Euch. as Memorial' p 337 ff. ✱ (anamnasis & } together
                                      maranatha }

p 455 Summary g book's ✱
    intent & methodology. also p. 456

DOXOLOGY

DOXOLOGY

*The Praise of God
in Worship, Doctrine and Life*

A SYSTEMATIC THEOLOGY

GEOFFREY WAINWRIGHT

New York
OXFORD UNIVERSITY PRESS
1980

First published in Great Britain in 1980
by Epworth Press, Methodist Publishing House,
Wellington Road, Wimbledon, London SW19 8EU

First published in the United States in 1980
by Oxford University Press, New York

Library of Congress Cataloging in Publication Data

Wainwright, Geoffrey, 1939-
Doxology: the praise of God in worship, doctrine
and life.
Bibliography: p.
Includes indexes.
1. Theology, Doctrinal. 2. Liturgics. I. Title.
BT75.2.W34 1980 230 80-11886
ISBN 0-19-520192-2

Printed in the United States of America

CONTENTS

PART THREE
CONTEXTUAL QUESTIONS

Contents

PREFACE

THIS book may be taken in two ways. It is primarily intended as a systematic theology written from a liturgical perspective. It can also be considered as a theology of worship. My conviction is that the relations between doctrine and worship are deeper rooted and further reaching than many theologians and liturgists have appeared to recognize in their writings. In recent years there has indeed been a growing awareness of the links between worship and doctrine, but writers have still usually stopped short after a paragraph or two on the subject. Certainly I know of no complete systematic theology deliberately composed with these links in mind. By giving more substance to something which is in the air I hope that this essay may encourage other systematic theologians to make more sustained use of this approach. Meanwhile, readers with no taste for prolegomena may begin at page 15 and return to the introduction only when they start to feel the need of a theoretical account of what is going on.

The book was conceived in 1971 and had been a twinkle in my eye for five years before that. It developed in manuscript form only in 1977–78. My appointment by the Fernley-Hartley trustees to the lectureship at the Methodist Conference of 1979 has induced its birth into print. My thanks are also due to my colleague William Jardine Grisbrooke, who put his expert knowledge of liturgical history at my disposal. Several other friends have helped with occasional references and remarks. John Vickers compiled the indexes, and Albert Jakeway has been a co-operative publisher. The work is dedicated to John Macquarrie, who has done me many kindnesses.

Any systematic theology is bound to contain mistakes of judgment. In addition, a work which roams as widely as the present one will almost inevitably commit errors of fact. In either case I should be glad to hear from readers and, where it is a question of fact, to receive reference to the correct information. I also invite news of any other attempts at doing theology in the perspective adopted in this book.

The Queen's College, Birmingham   GEOFFREY WAINWRIGHT
Advent, 1978

ACKNOWLEDGMENTS

EXTENDED quotations from the following works are used with permission, which is here gratefully acknowledged: F. W. Beare, *The First Epistle of Peter*, Blackwell; J. H. Cone, article in *Theology Today*; G. J. Cuming, *Hippolytus: A Text for Students*, Grove Books; G. Dix, *The Shape of the Liturgy*, Dacre Press/A. & C. Black; J. D. C. Fisher, *Christian Initiation: The Reformation Period*, SPCK; M. E. Glasswell and E. W. Fasholé-Luke (eds.), *New Testament Christianity for Africa and the World*, SPCK; G. Gutiérrez, *A Theology of Liberation*, SCM; B. Hebblethwaite, article in *The Heythrop Journal*; J. H. Hick (ed.), *The Myth of God Incarnate*, SCM; L. Hodgson, *The Doctrine of the Trinity*, Nisbet; J. Kent and R. Murray (eds.), *Intercommunion and Church Membership*, DLT; J. McIntyre, *The Shape of Christology*, SCM; H. Ott, *Theology and Preaching*, Lutterworth; N. Pittenger, *Life as Eucharist*, Eerdmans; Pope Pius XII, *Christian Worship* ('*Mediator Dei*'), Catholic Truth Society; E. C. Ratcliff, *Liturgical Studies*, SPCK; N. Smart, *The Concept of Worship*, Macmillan; A. Squire, *Asking the Fathers*, SPCK; W. P. Stephens, *Christians Conferring*, Epworth; T. F. Torrance, *God and Rationality*, Oxford University Press; E. C. Whitaker, *Documents of the Baptismal Liturgy*, SPCK; B. Wicker, *Culture and Liturgy*, Sheed & Ward; M. F. Wiles, *The Making of Christian Doctrine*, Cambridge University Press.

ABBREVIATIONS

AAS	*Acta Apostolicae Sedis*
AV	Authorized Version
CSEL	Corpus Scriptorum Ecclesiasticorum Latinorum
DLT	Darton, Longman & Todd, publishers
DS	H. Denzinger – A. Schönmetzer, *Enchiridion Symbolorum*
ET	English translation
MHB	Methodist Hymn Book (London, 1933)
NEB	New English Bible
OUP	Oxford University Press
PG	Patrologia Graeca (Migne)
PL	Patrologia Latina (Migne)
PS	Patrologia Syriaca
RSV	Revised Standard Version
RV	Revised Version
SCM	Student Christian Movement, publishers
SPCK	Society for Promoting Christian Knowledge, publishers
WCC	World Council of Churches

INTRODUCTION

Tasks

1. *Vision and reality*

THEOLOGY is an intellectual activity. Yet the sources and resources of theology are richer than the human intellect. Theology is intellectual reflexion on all the dealings between God and humanity. In so far as the theologian is a believer, his thinking cannot be disengaged from his faith. His faith engages him as a total person, so that even his intellectual reflexion *upon* his faith is, dialectically and within the unity of his personality, still an activity *of* faith. Theology itself therefore is part and parcel of the dealings between God and humanity. The theologian is telling how he sees, from the viewpoint of a particular participant, the whole history of God with humanity. His intellect is at the service of his existential vision and commitment [note 1].

Such an understanding of the status and function of theology would, I surmise, command the support of Anders Jeffner, who brings to his consideration of the theologian's task a sharply analytical mind [note 2]. The Swedish thinker considers a systematic theology to be the articulation of a personal vision of faith which includes the insights of worship and carries ethical incidences. Logical argument continues to play a part in the coherent formulation of theology, but the total vision has other roots in life and experience. My own vision of faith is firmly shaped and strongly coloured by the Christian liturgy. It is this comprehensive vision which the present book seeks to express in the genre of a systematic theology. I am trying on a broader canvas the 'liturgical way of doing theology' which I attempted in my *Eucharist and Eschatology*. The resultant picture has for the most part the rough contours of a sketch, although in places the detail is

1

more refined. Such unevenness is a sign of further work to be done in worship, doctrine and life. I hope that I am right in judging the picture sufficiently advanced for public viewing. The point is to indicate a perspective in which theology can also be carried out by others [note 3].

The book is neither philosophy nor apologetics. I therefore consider myself dispensed from supplying a detailed theoretical epistemology. It is written from faith to faith and will, I trust, find echoes in the experience of Christians who seek to praise God in worship, doctrine and life. But since this expectation is itself making an epistemological claim, it may be useful immediately to give a brief statement of the implied epistemology. The rest of the book will be its practical illustration. Put simply, the claim is that a historical community, in this case the Christian Church, can transmit a vision of reality which helps decisively in the interpretation of life and the world. In one sense, the checking of the claim is easy: very many people will testify that the Christian vision has in fact determined their deepest understanding of things. In another sense, the testing of the claim poses all the problems which people of a culture imbued with the spirit of the natural sciences experience in face of all statements which purport to be about reality but which are not subject to instrumental measurement. Religious statements are in a worse case even than ethical or aesthetic claims, for religion deliberately refers to a transcendent dimension and asserts the ultimacy of the values which it claims to be grounded in the transcendent. As to transcendence, for my part I can do no more than propose the living experience of worship as evidence of the rootage of created reality in a creative Reality and declare that I remain unpersuaded by reductionist interpretations which allow psychology or sociology to explain away that irreducible experience [note 4]. As regards the ultimacy of values, the Christian vision includes a teleological tendency of reality towards 'the kingdom of God'. The believer therefore expects that the Christian values will 'one day' be incontestably and abidingly established as what is most real. Meanwhile it is quite proper that the Christian should be challenged for indications that reality is in fact being transformed in this direction. The reader must await the later chapters for more detailed suggestions about how the perspective adopted in this book can help in this matter [note 5].

Individual theologians present their version of the Christian vision. This book presents my version. It is inescapably individual, but it is not individualistic. It is held within the Christian community. That community of which I am part is both diachronic and synchronic: its history so far stretches over twenty centuries, and it exists today in variegated forms. I shall return in a while to the problems which arise in connexion with its diachronic and synchronic identity. Meanwhile I observe further that the Christian community itself is always set within the wider human community. The individual theologian is therefore operating within both the Christian and the human community. This communal location of the theologian may be seen in respect of worship, doctrine, and life, all three.

It is the Christian community that transmits the vision which the theologian, as an individual human being, has seen and believed. As a believer, the theologian is committed to serving the Christian community in the transmission and spread of the vision among humanity. *Worship* is the place in which that vision comes to a sharp focus, a concentrated expression, and it is here that the vision has often been found to be at its most appealing. The theologian's thinking therefore properly draws on the worship of the Christian community and is in duty bound to contribute to it. The specific task of the theologian lies in the realm of *doctrine*. He is aiming at a coherent intellectual expression of the Christian vision. He should examine the liturgy from that angle, both in order to learn from it and in order to propose to the worshipping community any corrections or improvements which he judges necessary. In his doctrinal task the theologian will, like the Christian community itself, be using in a dialectical relationship both Christian language and the language of the wider human community which has not yet accepted the Christian vision but to which the vision is being commended. The vision must also be tested in everyday *life*. As a believer, the theologian is a participant in the Christian community's application of its vision to interpret and change the world of humanity. The theologian's intellectual task calls him to measure up the vision and the application in order to propose to the Christian community the most effective ways of allowing its vision to illuminate and transform reality to the advantage of all humanity.

In saying, then, that this book is written from faith to faith, I am in the first place saying that it is written within the community of belief and counts on the agreement of readers within the community that the Christian vision, of which it offers a more or less adequate version, does correspond to reality. But I am also saying that I should like the book to serve the eliciting of faith, at least in the indirect sense of making a theologian's contribution to the clarification of the Church's vision and so to the more effective application of that vision and its further spread among the human community as a whole.

Let me now explain the structure of the book, which departs from the more customary ways of setting out a systematic theology. It matches my understanding of the theologian's task as I have just outlined it. It recognizes the focal position and function of worship in Christianity, a position and function which I will seek to justify immediately after sketching the structure of the book.

2. *Structure*

To set out the structure will be already to give a preliminary survey of the contents.

The book is organized in three main parts: substantial matters; traditional means; contextual questions. The first part sketches the Christian vision as I perceive it at this time and place within the historic Christian community. This is my immediate account of the substance of Christianity. It always presupposes an inheritance from the past and sometimes describes how that inheritance accumulated; but it does not give much theoretical consideration to the means by which the vision has been transmitted. Likewise, the first part of the book implicitly or explicitly responds to certain questions posed by the Christian and human context in which the vision is perceived; but it does not give much theoretical consideration to the effect which the context has on the perception.

The second part of the book turns to a formal examination of the instruments of Christian tradition, the means by which the vision is transmitted through time. Naturally, the material examples by which the process of tradition is illustrated have a substantial interest in their own right, and it is questions posed by the Christian and human context which necessitate a deliberate examination of the means by which the vision is transmitted; but the emphasis in this second part of the book falls on the nature and operation of the traditional means and the interaction among them.

In the third part, direct attention is given to questions posed by the Christian and human context in which the vision is expressed. Certain types of question are raised perennially by the context, and some theoretical account can be given of the range of possible ways of response. The acuity and precise form of the questions naturally vary with the context, and the attempt is here made to deal with those questions which are presently put most sharply and in the form which they take in our time and place. They affect the received picture and so inevitably involve us in matters of substance and in the appreciation of tradition and its means.

The conclusion of the book brings out the orientation towards the future which has underlain the study throughout. It is suggested that there are rewards for theology and for the whole life of the Church in doing the theological task in a liturgical perspective: the substance of the Christian vision is clarified, an effective vehicle of its transmission is recognized, and the history of the Church and of humanity is consciously kept in relation to God's final purpose. Since God's kingdom and human salvation can be described as true worship, every improvement in the quality of the liturgy by which our present Christian life is focally expressed can be considered to imply its own reward.

Now that the relations among the main parts of the book have been explained, it will be useful to explain the internal structure of each part.

When the substance of Christianity is being described in part one, the opening chapter states as simply as possible the relationship which it is believed God intends should obtain between humanity and himself. The divine purpose for humanity is fundamental to the whole Christian vision. This relationship and purpose is here expounded according to the traditional notion of the 'image of God', a notion from which cultic associations are never far distant. Since, in Christian eyes, Jesus Christ is the embodiment of the relationship and purpose summarized in the notion of 'image of God', the second chapter sharpens the focus on Christ. Occupying a central place and function in the Christian cult, he is seen as a recipient of worship, a mediator in worship, and a pattern for worship. It is in this perspective that the classical questions of the person and work of Christ are discussed. In the third chapter, the Holy Spirit appears as the divine enabler of a worship in conformity with the pattern of Christ. To talk of the Spirit is to acknowledge the divine work of transformation which is required if human beings are freely to enter into God's purposes for them. The communal character of humanity in God's purpose is given thematic attention in the fourth chapter, which is ecclesiological. Christian worship is seen to give ritual expression to the eschatological tension which marks the Church on the way to the achievement of God's purpose. The structure of this first part as a whole is governed by the scriptural and traditional understanding of Christian worship as the Church's worship of God through Christ in the Spirit. The order in which the themes are unfolded reflects the sequence of the classical creeds: God the creator, Christ, Spirit, Church, the last things [note 6].

The second part begins with a chapter (V) on the principal 'liturgical book' of the Church, the holy Scriptures. The cultic element in the original composition of the Bible is shown to make worship the connatural context for the continuing interpretation of the Church's foundational document. In the next chapter (VI), creeds are presented as summary confessions of faith and as hermeneutical grids through which believers interpret both the ampler witness of Scripture and the Church and also their own religious stance. Their use raises from various angles the question of Christian 'identity'. In virtue of their greater flexibility, hymns fulfil a complementary function to creeds; they also allow the expression of 'ecstatic reason'. The two remaining chapters (VII and VIII) bring out more sharply than the previous two chapters the dialectical relationship between Scripture and the continuing tradition of the Church. It is a matter of plain history that there has been a 'catholic' tendency to let liturgical and devotional practice lead in the 'development' of doctrine, although the magisterium has maintained a right of control. On the other hand, the critical principle of 'protestantism' has sought to bring both worship and dogma to a doctrinal bar that is more directly scriptural.

The third part of the book places the present-day Church and its worship in the context of Christian and human history. The chapter on ecumenism (IX) illustrates the irenical mood which now obtains in the treatment of hitherto polemically argued questions concerning Christian substance and its transmission. Worship is seen as a proper mode of attaining and expressing agreement in the Church's doctrine and community life. The chapter on liturgical revision (X) examines the tensions which the passage of ecclesiastical and cultural time necessarily introduces into the Church's vision of God. The suggestion is made that the current correction, enrichment and updating in favour of a more intimate relationship between God and the world represents a genuine return to the original Christian vision. In the chapter on culture (XI), liturgical examples are taken to epitomize the various attitudes which Christians have historically adopted towards human culture as a whole. It is argued that the view of worship presented in this book gives a proper place within the purpose of God to human culture in all its unity and variety, its failures and its achievements. The last chapter (XII) explores the ethical and political incidences of worship: presuppositions as well as consequences. It is maintained that Christian liturgy has an evangelistic and missionary part to play in the transformation of humanity and the world. In sum, the themes of the four chapters in this third part will be

seen on closer inspection to correspond to the four notes of
the Church confessed in the creed: unity, holiness, catholicity,
apostolicity.

3. *Worship, doctrine and life*

The survey of contents will have given some indication of
the ways in which the book enters into the three areas of
interest mentioned in the sub-title: worship, doctrine and
life. This tripartite division is not new. One may think, for
instance, of Newman's distinction between the devotional,
the dogmatical, and the practical [note 7]. But at the least the
three areas overlap, and it may be that their relationship is
better not conceived in terms of discrete areas at all.

Worship is better seen as the point of concentration at
which the whole of the Christian life comes to ritual focus.
It must be made clear from the start that I am not using
'ritual' in the pejorative sense of 'mere ritual' which it sometimes bears among Protestants. I mean ritual in the descriptive
sense of regular patterns of behaviour invested with symbolic
significance and efficacy. On my sense of the word, even those
communities which pride themselves on their freedom from
'ritual' will generally be found to use ritual; only they will
not be aware of it, and so will be unable either to enjoy its
pleasures to the full or to be properly vigilant about its
dangers. Similarly it may be important to state that liturgy (and,
much less often, cult) is here used of the public worship of the
Church, with liturgical (and cultic) as convenient adjectives.
Liturgy leaves room within itself for those spontaneous or
extemporaneous forms of worship which some Protestants
favour as an alternative to what they class as 'liturgical'. If
the word liturgy is allowed to retain from its etymology the
sense of 'the work of the people', it hints at the focal place
and function which I ascribe to worship in the Christian life
as a whole. Into the liturgy the people bring their entire
existence so that it may be gathered up in praise. From the
liturgy the people depart with a renewed vision of the value-
patterns of God's kingdom, by the more effective practice
of which they intend to glorify God in their whole life.

In the sub-title, doctrine is intended in a fairly broad

sense. Throughout the book, faith, doctrine, and theology are often used singly to cover a whole range of meanings within which it is sometimes necessary to make distinctions. When the three words are being used in a specific rather than the comprehensive sense, the following differences will become obvious. Faith then refers to the most fundamental and immediate belief, whether the substance (*fides quae creditur*) or the act (*fides quâ creditur*). Doctrine or dogma refers to official formulations of the faith which have become classical but which are conceivably not the only ways of stating the faith. Theology refers to the more individual but still ecclesial activity of reflecting on faith and doctrine with a view to their intellectual clarification. For all the usefulness of this threefold distinction, there is naturally overlap and interplay among faith, doctrine and theology. It is their mutual involvement which in fact makes possible the comprehensive use of any one of the terms on its own. Doctrine, in a comprehensive sense, both draws on and contributes to worship. Worship is a locus for the reception and transmission of the vision which is believed, formulated and reflected on. Because of the interlocking of that liturgical vision with life as a whole, doctrine also draws on and contributes to the dealings between God and humanity throughout human existence.

It may be wondered how my 'worship, doctrine, and life' relate to the 'six dimensions' which Ninian Smart introduced into the consideration of religion and whose use has become widespread: the ritual, the mythological, the doctrinal, the ethical, the social, and the experiential dimensions [note 8]. My 'worship' certainly includes Smart's 'ritual' and 'mythological', although instead of myth I have usually preferred to talk of vision or story. We are agreed that doctrine, on its theological side, has to do with intellectual clarity, coherence and system. Smart's social dimension becomes, in the Christian case, 'ecclesiology', which can take on considerable doctrinal significance and is ritually expressed in the liturgy. My 'life' is meant to have a strongly ethical component, but I would hold to a more intimate connexion between ethics and both worship and doctrine than Smart makes apparent in his theoretical account. Smart's 'experience' I would locate in worship, in life, and even in doctrine, in so far as theology is also an activity *of* faith [note 9].

I see Christian worship, doctrine and life as conjoined in a common 'upwards' and 'forwards' direction towards God and the achievement of his purpose, which includes human salvation. They intend God's praise. His glory is that he is already present and within to enable our transformation into his likeness, which means participation in himself and his kingdom.

4. *Identity*

In a number of ways I have already hinted at an underlying theme of this book: Christian identity. Identity is both posited and problematic whenever we try to describe the Christian vision and community across time and space. The question of continuing and changing identity is also raised by the whole transformationist thrust which the 'achievement of God's purpose for humanity' gives to the Christian vision. Further, the individual but not individualistic nature of systematic theology brings up the personal identity of the theologian within the community. For this last reason we may begin this section with a brief autobiographical paragraph.

Born (in 1939) and brought up in British Methodism, I am now a Methodist minister. Having acquired some linguistic, biblical and historical skills at Cambridge, I trained for the ministry under Raymond George, whose twin interests in systematic theology and liturgics appealed to me [note 10]. I undertook further study in Geneva, where I particularly appreciated the sacramental and eschatological orientation of F. J. Leenhardt, professor of New Testament, and of Nikos Nissiotis, the Orthodox director at the Ecumenical Institute. I exercised a brief pastoral ministry in Liverpool, at an early Anglican-Methodist partnership on the outskirts of the city. A year was spent in post-conciliar Rome, where I was welcomed among the early Protestant visitors but where I experienced also the life of the small Waldensian faculty of theology. For six years I taught systematic theology at the Protestant faculty in Yaoundé, Cameroon, which serves all the main churches of French-speaking Africa. In Yaoundé I also ministered in the interdenominational and multi-cultural anglophone parish. Since 1973 I have taught first biblical studies and then systematic theology at the ecumenical Queen's College, Birmingham [note 11]. Since returning to Europe I have been active in 'faith and order' affairs at the national and World Council of Churches levels and have travelled fairly extensively for international conferences and consultations. Throughout my studies, ministry and teaching I have had close relations with Roman Catholic institutions and individuals, always in a good and open spirit. These facts should suffice to suggest the eyes through which I have perceived the vision presented in this book and the purposes which I should like the book to serve.

Now for the diachronic and synchronic identity of the Christian vision and community. Diachronically, the question is posed by the developments and vicissitudes of ecclesiastical and cultural history. It is a matter of discerning an abiding identity through all the failures in quality and all the adaptations which have taken place in changed circumstances. It is a matter of discerning, ever again and with whatever continuity is possible, the true expressions of the original and normative vision centred on Jesus Christ. Synchronically, the difficulty is to decide where, at any given time, the line should be drawn between the diversity of different but symphonic voices and the clash of contradictions which becomes cacophony. It is a matter of deciding where a unilateral emphasis amounts to a distortion; where additions are enrichments, where dilutions; where simplification is purification, where truncation. It is a matter of deciding where tentative exploration opens up new vistas and where it misses its way and passes into error or nothingness. It is this question of diachronic and synchronic identity which inspires both the 'linear' history in this book and the 'comparative' evaluation of the varieties of Christianity in past epochs and at the present.

Finally, the question of identity is raised by the dynamic of transformation which is inherent in the Christian vision itself. The Christian vision is not meant merely to interpret a statically conceived world but rather to assist in a transformation of reality which it itself describes as the achievement of God's purpose. The Christian vision aims at a change for the better, or rather for the best of all. The change from sin to saintliness means death and resurrection. Christian identity is achieved only dialectically, through a self-surrender which becomes a reception of the self from the Other. That is to participate in God. My hope is that this book will assist both author and reader to enter into that rather mysterious process [note 12].

PART ONE

Substantial Matters

I

Image of God

1. *Creator and creature*

LUDWIG Feuerbach held that theology could be dissolved without remainder into anthropology: 'God' is the projection of ideal humanity. Rudolf Bultmann admitted that all talk about God is *also* talk about humanity: it is only as those upon whom God impinges by means of his Word that human beings can talk of God. Karl Barth affirmed that God's self-revelation allowed the believer to speak of God by the 'analogy of faith': the relationship of faith, in which the believer is set and maintained by grace, allows such a person to speak of his divine benefactor [note 13]. According to Karl Rahner, human self-transcendence is grounded in and oriented towards the divine Transcendence as its source and term: God is the 'formal cause' of humanity, a constitutive principle intrinsic to his human creature [note 14]. With their varied intentions, the atheistic philosopher, the two very different theologians of the Word, and the Jesuit dogmatician are all circling round the theme of the image as an expression of the relationship between humanity and God [note 15]. For Feuerbach, the making of God in the human image was the mistaken outcome of a noble aspiration which instead needed release into action within this world. For the Christian, however, Feuerbach's phantom deity would represent a yielding to the temptation of idolatry: the worship of the Creator would have been replaced by the worship of the creature, ultimately indeed by the worship of the human self. The exchange needs to be reversed. The worship of a lie must give way to the worship of the true God [note 16]. A barthian emphasis would fall on the fact that the *true God*, of whom we now have the image in Jesus

15

Christ, is the proper recipient of human worship. A bult-mannian accent would stress that it is *within the human situation* that God is addressed as well as expressed. Rahner holds that the movement of humanity into the divine Mystery is a movement of *adoration*.

The biblical and traditional view of humanity made in the image of God expresses a relationship [note 17]. This relationship between humanity and God is not, however, symmetrical. It is the relationship between creature and Creator. Outside this relationship, humanity would cease to be. God himself transcends his creation and therefore transcends also this relationship. The proper relationship between creature and Creator is, in Christian eyes, the relationship of worship. In order to understand the meaning of humanity's being made in the image of God, it will therefore be helpful to examine the Christian *practice* of worship, the liturgy of the Church. Christian worship will certainly show us the Christian view of humanity. It will also show us the Christian view of God; and, in so far as the faith is adequate to its object, God will thereby be revealed. (When I say 'object', I am of course using the word in a grammatical sense, with no thought of reifying the living God who is the gracious initiator of our personal relationship with himself [note 18].) God himself remains inexhaustible by his creature, or he would cease to be God [note 19].

In biblical exegesis and traditional hermeneutics, there are three main strands in the understanding of humanity's being made in the image of God. All three strands are woven into Christian worship [note 20]. The three strands are these: the human vocation to communion with God; the human task upon God's earth; the constitution of humanity as social being [note 21].

2. *Communion with God*

The proverb says that like communes with like. The first meaning of humanity's being made in the image of God is that God has made humanity sufficiently like himself for communion between God and human beings to be possible. Following Irenaeus, the Greek Fathers made an exegetically improbable but doctrinally valuable distinction between 'image' and 'likeness' in Genesis 1:26: the 'image' expresses the ontological or structural *possibility* of human communion with God; the 'likeness' stands for the existential or moral similarity with God into which humanity is to *grow* as it actually lives in communion with God. God's gracious calling of humanity to communion with himself includes the initial and fundamental capacity, the aided progress in time, and the final and eternal realization.

The eschatological goal of the human vocation is enunciated in strongly liturgical terms in the opening question and answer of the Westminster Shorter Catechism (1647–48):

What is the chief end of man?
Man's chief end is to glorify God, and to enjoy him for ever [note 22].

Glory is a heavily charged word in biblical and liturgical vocabulary [note 23]. Mainly predicated of God, it denotes both his character and his reputation. Upon earth, it is the sign of his active presence. Believers may *render* God glory by a kind of reflexion, as they are changed into his likeness, 'from glory into glory' (cf. 2 Corinthians 3:18). They glorify God as they grow in conformity with his character. They themselves thereby become glorified. The glorious bodies hoped for in the final resurrection bespeak this ultimate realization of the human vocation. God will thereby be glorified because his intention will have been achieved. Communion with God, the transformation of the human character according to God's own character: this is experienced as the *enjoyment* of God. The bodily anchorage of the language is not narrowly connected with sex but has more broadly to do with taste. It is on the will of God, which expresses his character, that the believer feeds. The Deuteronomist declared that 'man does not live by bread alone but by every word that proceeds from the mouth of God'. In his praise of the divine *torah*, the Psalmist confessed that God's words were 'sweeter than honey to my mouth' (Psalm 119:103). The invitation from another Psalm, 'O taste and see that the Lord is good', was echoed in two New Testament passages in which modern scholars have discovered reference to the initiatory sacraments of the Christian faith:

> Those who have been enlightened, who have tasted the heavenly gift, and have become partakers of the Holy Spirit, and have tasted the goodness of the word of God and the powers of the age to come . . .
>
> (Hebrews 6:4f)

> Like newborn babes, long for the pure spiritual milk, that by it you may grow up to salvation; for you have tasted the kindness of the Lord.
>
> (1 Peter 2:2f)

'Man is what he eats' was Feuerbach's aphorism [note 24]. By feeding on the word of God, the believer is changed according to God's character. 'My meat,' said the johannine Christ, 'is to do my Father's will' (John 4:32–34). The obedience of the cross was both Jesus's glorification of the Father and his own glorification (John 17:1–5). We shall return shortly to Jesus as the paradigm of worship. But first we shall look at the fundamental modalities of human communion with God.

It is in their life as a whole that human beings have the God-given capacity for communion with their Creator. But human life has both an inward and an outward aspect: it is both an inner awareness and experience and also an active bodily presence in the world. The link is the word. The Greeks used *logos* for both thought (*logos endiathetos*) and speech (*logos prophorikos*). The Hebrews took the potential for exteriorization even further: *dabar* could mean also thing, action, event. An important patristic interpretation identified the divine image in humanity with *logos*: God also had *logos*; indeed he was the source of *logos* in human beings. In both God and humans, *logos* is performative: it expresses being and engages the person. It is the basis for communication and therefore the means of communion [note 25]. A brief examination of the use of language in worship will help us to understand the meaning of communion between humanity and God.

Besides the sciences of language proper, philosophy and social anthropology have also in our century devoted great attention to language as a characteristic of humanity. Theologians may draw insights from these secular disciplines which will help them to appreciate the functions of language in worship, and hence the meaning of communion between humanity and God [note 26]. Three examples will be in order here. First: there is the notion of a 'universe of discourse'. Users of a common language presuppose the existence of a shared world of beliefs, ideas and experiences which enables words and phrases to convey intended meaning between speaker and hearer. Christian worshippers share with one another *and with God* a common history focused in Jesus Christ and a common interest in the continuing battle of grace against sin. A 'universe of discourse' is thereby constituted, which permits communion between human beings and God by means of the word. By divine grace, human words become the expression and vehicles of the traffic between humanity and God in which communion consists. God spoke through the prophetic message of the Old Testament, 'Thus saith the Lord'; now the divine Word has been made flesh (John 1:14), and in these last days God has spoken to us through a Son (Hebrews 1:1f). The continued reading of the scriptures in church keeps the vocabulary, grammar and syntax of the biblical revelation before the people. With the aid of the preacher as interpreter of scripture, the people's ears become attuned to hearing the voice of God speak to them in their present circumstances. In the other direction, the Bible also presents God as listening to the words of men and women who call upon him, and in the New Testament this prayer is made 'through Jesus Christ' (Romans 1:8; 2 Corinthians 1:20) or 'in his name' (Matthew 18:19f; John 16:23f). With the help of the skilled liturgist who is both obedient to the biblical pattern of prayer exemplified in Jesus and sensitive to the faith of his contemporaries, the people's voice is intelligently directed towards God from within the present circumstances. Thus the 'shared world' which God graciously sets up with mankind comes to expression in the language of worship where God and human beings each give and receive in an exchange which is their mutual communion.

The second example of an insight derived from the secular disciplines is the notion of 'language games'. There are many language games. The games have their own rules, techniques and aims. In Christian worship, we are not playing the game of scientific description or of everyday social exchange, nor even the game of theological discourse, but we are playing rather the game of the community's conversation with the God who is the creator and redeemer. This game has its ontological rules, at the level of the objective difference and relation between humanity and God. It includes technical 'moves' whose efficacy has been proved in past play. The present delight and permanent 'point' of the game lie in a growing communion of human beings with God.

The third insight from the secular disciplines coincides with the physical consistency of *dabar* in Hebrew [note 27]. Gestures, actions and the use of natural or cultural objects may also express being and engage the person. They may serve as communicative signs. They have a linguistic quality in relation to embodied humanity. There is a 'logic of action' (J. R. Lucas), 'un langage gestuel' (F. J. Leenhardt) [note 28]. Israel experienced the saving presence of God in the historical *events* of the exodus from Egypt and the return from Babylon. The prophets often proclaimed the Lord's message through symbolic *acts*. The deeds of Jesus were part of his announcement of the kingdom: he made the blind see, the deaf hear, the dumb talk, the lame walk; he ate and drank with sinners. Christian worship uses sacraments and sacramentals, rituals in which *gesture* and *movement* and *material objects* play a significant part. In all these cases, the action is accompanied by verbal interpretation and takes place within a framework of understanding. The body is the fundamental communicative sign of the human person; speech is the most supple sign, which allows precision in the expression of intention. It is an embodied humanity endowed with speech that God calls into communion with himself.

This communion with God, symbolically focused in

liturgy, is the primary locus of religious language for the Christian [note 29]. *Theological* language belongs to the second order: it is the language of reflexion upon the primary experience. The language of worship mediates the substance on which theologians reflect; without that substance, theological talk would have no referent. Yet the 'architectonic' and 'critical' functions of theological reasoning, secondary though that reasoning is in relation to substantial communion with God, play a proper part in shaping and pruning the continuing primary experience [note 30]. For *reflective* reason is part of God's endowment to humanity and must therefore be included in the total picture of human communion with God. The second-order activity of theology is therefore, at its own level, properly doxological: the theologian is truly theologian when, in his very theologizing, he is listening for the 'echo of a voice' and is contributing, even if indirectly, to the human praise of God [note 31]. It is indeed a traditional dictum in Eastern Christianity that the true theologian is the person who prays [note 32].

We are thus brought back to Jesus as the paradigm of worship. Contrary to all later tendencies towards Apollinarianism, the synoptic gospels present Jesus as fully human to the very depths of his being. The expression of this is the fact that he *prays*. 'He rose and went out to a lonely place, and there he prayed' (Mark 1:35). 'He went into the hills to pray' (Mark 6:46=Matthew 14:23). He agonized in prayer in the Garden of Gethsemane (Mark 14:35–41=Matthew 26:39–45, Luke 22:41–46). (For other instances, see Luke 5:16; 6:12; 9:28f; 23:24,46. John 11:41f may well raise suspicions, but John 17 reveals that by then the prayer of Jesus had been set in the trinitarian perspective of the incarnate Son [cf. also perhaps Matthew 11:25–27, Luke 10:21f]; the discussion of this is reserved until later [note 33].) There are three features in particular which I wish at this point to stress in the paradigm which Jesus presents for worship understood as human communion with God.

The first centres on the word 'Abba'. J. Jeremias has called attention to the high significance of this name by which Jesus characteristically addressed God [note 34]. Its authenticity is virtually guaranteed both by the so-called criterion of dissimilarity (if Jeremias cannot quite prove that its use as an address to God was unique to Jesus in Judaism, yet Jesus' use of it is certainly unusual and striking) and by the multiple attestation afforded by its traces in all the main strands of the gospel tradition (Mark 14:36; Matthew 6:9 par. Luke 11:2; Matthew 11:25f par. Luke 10:21; Matthew 26:42(M); Luke 23:34, 46 (L); John 11:41; 12:27f; 17:1, 5, 11, 21, 24, 25) [note 35]. It was the word used from child to parent, from disciple to rabbi; it combines intimacy and respect, familiarity and esteem, affection and reverence. Jesus used the word to address *God*. Christians have the same privilege in worship (Romans 8:15f; Galatians 4:6). The word characterizes the whole relationship to which God is calling humanity and which believers already know. The mighty Creator also provides and cares for his creatures with a parent's love; the sovereign Lord wants children, not slaves.

The second feature is the Lord's Prayer, which is given as the pattern for Christian prayer. It begins with 'Abba', and it brings out, in the fourth, fifth and sixth petitions, the fact that God is the provider, preserver and redeemer of his children. The opening clauses reveal that the glory of God involves the achievement of his will, the coming of his kingdom. For humanity, this *means salvation*; for that is precisely God's intention for mankind. On the human side, the active aspect of salvation is obedience to God: 'Thy will be done'. To echo the Book of Common Prayer, this 'service' is 'perfect freedom', for humanity is thus achieving its vocation and fulfilling its nature [note 36]. When the believer says with performative intent the words of the Methodist Covenant Service: 'I am no longer my own, but Thine', he is surrendering himself to God and thereby finding himself (cf. Mark 8:34f) [note 37].

The third paradigmatic feature of Jesus is, therefore, sacrifice [note 38]. His obedience to God meant taking up his cross. His self-surrender to God was total. 'Not my will but Thine' was the climactic expression of a life of complete openness to God (Mark 14:36). In Schleiermacher's christology, it was Jesus' 'God-consciousness' which constituted his divinity [note 39]. On a kenotic version of incarnational christology, the self-emptying of the Son began when he limited himself to the 'measures' of humanity in Jesus (*heauton ekenōse*, 'he emptied himself', Philippians 2:7); on the human plane, the self-emptying continued as Jesus 'gave himself up' (Galatians 1:4; Ephesians 5:2), ultimately to the point of death on the cross. At this culmination of a life spent in perfect transparency to God, Jesus could be confessed as 'son of God' (Mark 15:39). In Christian eyes, *this* sacrifice stands at the heart of the communion between humanity and God; it may even correspond, within the sphere of time, to that eternal *perichōrēsis* by which, according to highly developed trinitarian theology, the divine Persons empty themselves into each other and receive each other's fulness. At any rate, the classical movement of Christian worship has always meant a participatory entrance into Christ's self-offering to the Father and correlatively being filled with the divine life. The Christian liturgy appears once more as the symbolic focus of communion with God.

3. *The earthly task*

In the ancient near east, it was a custom of rulers to erect statues of themselves in distant provinces in order to assert their claim to sovereignty over the country [note 40]. A second strand in the interpretation of humanity as made in the image of God has considered humanity as God's viceroy upon the earth. At one stage in recent theological writing, the command of Genesis 1:28 to 'subdue and have dominion' was invoked to explain historically the rise of technology in a Western society where a biblically de-divinized nature had been set free for human use; further, the text was invoked morally to justify the exploitation of the earth's resources. With growing awareness of the modern ecological crisis [note 41], theologians turned rather to the other creation story in Genesis: the human task is to 'till the earth and *keep* it' (2:15), and the power to 'name' the non-human creation (2:19f) is less the right to exploit it than the duty to give it meaning. The job of humanity is to use God's gift of the natural creation properly, with responsibility to the Maker of

both human and non-human creation. The rest of creation
with which we have to do thus becomes the scene, and on
occasion the instrument, of humanity's growth into communion with God. God's creatures are 'good' (Old Testament
scholars state that the nuance of *tob* in the context of Genesis 1
is *zweckmässig*, 'meeting its purpose') [note 42], when they
are 'received with thanksgiving' (1 Timothy 4:3–5). As gifts,
they convey the divine blessing; they allow people to respond
with gratitude. Their use thereby becomes the means of
communion between humanity and God. That is their
meaning and destiny. Albeit less directly, the same is true
when the earth is more simply the scene, and less clearly
the instrument, of human communion with God. According
to St Paul, the destiny of the cosmos is in one sense dependent
on the destiny of humanity (Romans 8:19–23). The apostle

may well be developing the prophetic picture of a peace
which will embrace the whole zoological realm as well as
the human (Isaiah 11:1–9). Elsewhere in the scriptures also
the peace and justice which are both divine kingdom and also
human salvation appear to involve new heavens and a new
earth (2 Peter 3:13; cf. Isaiah 65:17–25).

The role of the material in the Christian sacraments constitutes a paradigm for the proper use of the non-human
creation in the communion between humanity and God. In
baptism, the water is used more or less *brut*. In the sacramental
oils, cultivation and manufacture come to the fore. The
prayers of the Roman Missal strikingly combine the parts
played by nature and culture in the provision of the materials
for the eucharist, the whole being set within the context of
God's creation:

> Blessed are you, Lord, God of all creation. Through your good-
> ness we have this bread to offer, which earth has given and
> human hands have made. It will become for us the bread of life.

> Blessed are you, Lord, God of all creation. Through your good-
> ness we have this wine to offer, fruit of the vine and work of
> human hands. It will become our spiritual drink [note 43].

In the sacraments, as foreshadowed already in Jesus' feeding
of the multitudes [note 44], the material creation becomes

the means by which God conveys to us not only our natural life but also the enhanced life of salvation in his kingdom; the proper human response is expressed in thanksgiving. When human beings administer the earth as the means of divine blessing, they are fulfilling a royal function on behalf of God; when they give God thanks and praise, they are fulfilling a priestly function on behalf of creation. The sacramental paradigm of divine provision and human gratitude has consequences in the area of social ethics, for the pattern of true life is to be stamped on the whole of our existence. These consequences will be drawn out later [note 45].

The prayers just quoted from the Roman Missal mention the part played by human labour in the process by which the material creation becomes the means of communion with God. Work is thus taken up into prayer; it becomes the stuff of prayer. Conversely, the attitude of prayer should inform our daily work. In the words of George Herbert which figure in many hymn-books:

> Teach me, my God and King,
> In all things Thee to see;
> And what I do in anything,
> To do it as for Thee.

> A man that looks on glass,
> On it may stay his eye;
> Or if he pleaseth, through it pass,
> And then the heaven espy.

> All may of Thee partake:
> Nothing can be so mean,
> Which with this tincture: For Thy sake,
> Will not grow bright and clean.

> A servant with this clause
> Makes drudgery divine;
> Who sweeps a room, as for Thy laws,
> Makes that and the action fine.

> This is the famous stone
> That turneth all to gold:
> For that which God doth touch and own,
> Cannot for less be told.

In this way, the adage becomes true: *laborare est orare*, to work is to pray [note 46].

It is Christian experience, however, that the adage can also be reversed: to pray is to work. The Hebrew word *'abad* (to serve) is used for both work and worship. Our word 'liturgy' contains the Greek *ergon* (work). The early Fathers called prayer a *kopos*, a hard task [note 47]. Work is energy directed towards a goal. The offering of ourselves in worship is the active direction of our whole personal being towards God.

Successful work results also in a product. Both work and worship are constructive in intention. In them human beings have the opportunity of sharing with God in the achievement of his design and the shaping of his kingdom. Due proportions kept, humanity becomes co-creative with God [note 48]. Our communion with God moulds us into the persons God intends us to be in his eschatological purpose. It also clarifies our vision concerning the place of our world in God's intention and so helps us to perform our everyday work upon the material creation conformably with God's purpose. 'My Father is working still, and I am working', said the johannine Christ (John 5:17). Human beings have a chance to participate in that work of bringing the world into its fulfilment in the purpose of God [note 49].

Work is not, however, the only model for the relationship between God and creation in the achievement of its destiny. The Old Testament creation stories speak of the sabbath rest of God, and the Letter to the Hebrews uses the same notion in an eschatological context. For God, work and rest are not ultimately opposed, as the context of the johannine saying just quoted makes clear. The Wisdom literature provides a hint of a playful attitude on God's part towards creation: his wisdom sports on the earth, taking delight in humanity (Proverbs 8:30f). It may be that play is the resolution of a dialectic between work and rest.

If humanity is, in Huizinga's phrase, *homo ludens*, then human play may be a facet of humanity's being made in the image of God [note 50]. Worship can be seen as the explicitly religious form of play. Worship may possibly be experienced as an island of rest on a working day; it may possibly be experienced as a bout of labour on a day of rest [note 51]. But it will be best experienced as the resolution of work and rest in play. It will then be genuinely re-creation. Romano Guardini wrote of the 'playfulness of the liturgy' [note 52]. J. J. von Allmen called worship an 'eschatological game' [note 53]. Harvey Cox saw Christian celebration as a 'feast of fools' [note 54]. The *gratuitous* character of worship understood as play may perhaps placate those who feared that my earlier linking of worship and work veered, despite my stress on the priority of *God's* work, towards the human earning of salvation. The gratuity of worship expresses the character of salvation as gift: a gift to be actively enjoyed [note 55].

Closely related to worship as an activity in which work is transmuted into play is another enterprise in which humanity may be considered to image God in relation to creation: artistic creativity [note 56]. The distinction must be made between the divine *creatio ex nihilo* and human works of art which presuppose the existence of human beings and the world. Nevertheless, the human artist also transcends his material in a certain sense; and, on the other hand, the divine Creator also continues to shape what he has once brought into being. It remains appropriate, therefore, to consider artistic creativity, properly exercised, as a participation in the creative activity of God. As is well known from paleontology and anthropology, the rise of the arts took place largely within the religious context. In the centuries of 'Christian civilization' also, the arts flourished chiefly in relation to the liturgy of the Church: they were exercised in providing the sacred building, the sacred pictures, the sacred vestments, the sacred utensils, the sacred books, sacred poetry and sacred music. From the Renaissance and particularly from the Enlightenment onwards, as the pace of secularization quickened in politics and the sciences (understanding secularization as freedom from Church control), so also the arts came to assert their autonomy. Paul Tillich affirmed a continuing 'religious dimension' in all artistic creativity; yet he was aware that the religious could take on demonic character [note 57]. That is a point to which we shall return when we consider human misuse of humanity's image relationship to God. But the doxological potential of artistic creativity remains.

There is another kind of exercise linked with worship which also expresses the transcendence of humanity over the material to which human being is related: it is ascesis. The earthly existence of humanity is embodied existence. The body is the fundamental means of human presence: the body is the fundamental sign for human communication [note 58]: the body takes in air and food from the material creation as support for human existence, and it is through the body that human beings work externally upon the material creation. Fundamental as the body is, it is the conviction of Christianity that human existence transcends the body and material creation in general. The body and material creation in general have 'spiritual' value as the vehicle and context by and in which human being may grow into communion with God [note 59]. The 'goods' of the earthly creation are indeed *good* if they are 'received with thanksgiving', yet they are relativized by the ultimate destiny to which humanity is called. Jesus placed heavenly treasures before earthly (Matthew 6:19–21, 24–34; Luke 12:13–21, 32–34). It is in this permanent perspective, and not simply in the context of the expectation of an imminent End, that Paul's teaching is to be understood concerning the use of earthly goods 'as if not' (*hōs mē*; I Corinthians 7). The sacraments provide a paradigm for the spiritual use of the material creation and thereby give the lie to any charge that accuses Christianity of a 'manichaean' depreciation of matter. Such ascetical practices as fasting may likewise serve as a kind of 'negative sacrament' against the abuse of the body or of the material creation in general. They positively affirm the transcendence of humanity over matter. It is significant that fasting and prayer are often joined (Matthew 6:5–18; 17:21; Acts 14:23, etc.). In the monastic life, ascesis goes with a devotion to the divine office: they are both expressions of the transcendent calling of humanity to communion with God.

4. *Social being*

In Genesis 1:26, when God decides to create humanity, he speaks in the first person plural: 'Let us make man in our image, after our likeness.' It is more than a royal plural. The background is that of the heavenly court where God is accompanied by the spiritual beings who may also be called *'elohim*. This picture, together with the use of the plural *'Elohim* for God himself, may testify to an earlier polytheistic history. Certainly the Israelite conception of God in the Old Testament period contained an element of plurality. The developing hypostatization of Word, Wisdom and Law prolonged this line [note 60]. The exegesis of the Church Fathers went so far as to give a trinitarian interpretation of the plural in Genesis 1:26. More recently, Leonard Hodgson proposed a rather 'social' model of God in his book on *The Doctrine of the Trinity* (1943), seeing in return the divine trinity as a pattern for the social peace of a culturally differentiated humanity [note 61]. Karl Barth [note 62] called attention to Genesis 1:27: 'So God created man in his own image, in the image of God he created him; male and female he created them.' Upon this scriptural basis, Barth argued for an analogy between the Trinity and the social constitution of a humanity characterized by sexuality. The heart of society, whether human or divine, is love. The image of God in humanity is then the God-given capacity to love. In so far as the love *between* God and humanity, humanity and God, is concerned, this interpretation of the image relationship rejoins the interpretation we examined first: the human vocation to communion with God. But divine love for humanity and human love for God have always been seen by Christianity to imply the love of human beings for one another. It is chiefly to this love on the human plane that I shall now seek to relate Christian worship.

Baptism is the sacrament of entry into a new set of family relationships. Rebirth as sons and daughters of God implies the acquisition of new brothers and sisters in the persons of all the Father's children. This is the basis of that 'love of the brethren' (*philadelphia*) in which Paul encourages Christians to continue (Romans 12:10; 1 Thessalonians 4:9ff; cf. 1 Peter

3:8). Refusal of love to the brother or sister is a denial of one's own filial relationship to the loving Father (1 John 3, particularly vv. 10, 14–17; 4:7–12, 20f). The New Testament epistles generally restrict the brotherhood to the circle of believers. But all human beings, made in the divine image, are called to filial communion with God and should therefore be considered by Christians as *future* brothers and sisters at the least. This would appear to match both Jesus' injunction to love the—temporary—enemy (Matthew 5:43–48) and his vision of the neighbour to be loved as any person in need (Luke 10:25–37). It would also be in harmony with Jesus' creative action in sharing table-fellowship with sinners (Mark 2:15–17 = Matthew 9:10–13 = Luke 5:29–32; Matthew 11:19 = Luke 7:34; Luke 15:1f; 19:1–10).

The internal practice of the Christian assembly should obviously evidence brotherly and sisterly love. The Letter of James castigates those who pay special attention to 'the man with gold rings and in fine clothing' when he comes into the assembly, while they dishonour 'the poor man in shabby clothing' (2:1ff). Whatever may be the details concerning the disorders in the Corinthian assembly, they clearly included feasting by some while others went hungry; and for Paul, that was to 'despise the church of God' (1 Corinthians 11:22). The Letter of Jude speaks of people who 'are blemishes on your love feasts, as they boldly carouse together, looking after themselves' (v. 12). On the more positive side, we find care deliberately taken to feed the widows, though even that was not without its troubles (Acts 6:1ff). Tertullian describes a meal by which the poor were helped (*Apology*, 39, PL 1, 474–8); and the *Apostolic Tradition* of Hippolytus gives the following instruction in connexion with an agape [note 63]: 'If you are invited all to eat together, eat sufficiently, but so that there remain something over that your host may send it to whomsoever he wills, as the superfluity of the Saints, and he to whom it is sent may rejoice with what is left over.' There is evidence that Christians also celebrated funeral meals at which the poor were fed. The love feast has had a chequered history from its very beginning [note 64], and from the fourth century conciliar action was taken to regulate

abuses. The agape eventually disappeared from the main
stream of Christian practice. Vestiges remain, for instance, in
the Orthodox practice of distributing blessed but unconsecrated bread after the eucharist. Otherwise the practice
has until lately been revived only among 'enthusiastic' or
'purist' groups such as the Paulicians, the Moravians, the
Mennonites, the German Baptist Brethren (the Dunkers),
and the early Methodists [note 65]. It appears sadly to be the
case that the love feast makes too strenuous demands in
personal relationships even upon many Christians who have
heard the call to 'love one another'. Very early on, a separation
took place between the agape and the sacramental eucharist
(they were closely linked in 1 Corinthians 11, but it was
probably the kind of abuse there described that necessitated
their separation). The sacramental eucharist, its character
as a meal having been reduced to exiguous proportions, has
for most of its history been left to bear the weight of symbolically expressing the brotherly and sisterly love to which
those who address God as 'Abba' are called.

   In this connexion, one significant opportunity in the
classical eucharistic rites has been the Peace. The 'holy kiss'
was practised already in apostolic times (Romans 16:16;
1 Corinthians 16:20; 2 Corinthians 13:12; 1 Thessalonians
5:26; 1 Peter 5:14). In the eucharist, it came to symbolize
that peace with the brethren which the Lord required before
the bringing of a gift for the altar (Matthew 5:23f; cf. Didache
14). The natural place for the kiss of peace was the 'offertory',
as Irenaeus (*Adv. Haer.* IV, 18, 1) and Cyril of Jerusalem
(Myst. Cat. V, 3) make plain. In the Roman rite, the gesture
was postponed and linked rather with the Lord's Prayer
('as we forgive those who trespass against us') and the
communion. In the East, the Peace eventually became reduced
to an exchange of greeting between the priest and the congregation before the great eucharistic prayer; in the West,
it became limited to the accolade exchanged by the ministers
before communion. One of the most significant features of
modern liturgical revision has been the reintroduction,
beginning perhaps from the Church of South India, of an
exchange of the Peace, in culturally appropriate forms, among

the whole assembly. It is not easy to be indifferent or hostile towards a brother or sister with whom one has exchanged a a personal token of love.

The other particularly creative moment in the liturgy for human fellowship is of course the communion itself. Eucharistic history became for many centuries a tale of lost opportunities in this respect: from the fourth century onwards popular communion largely declined to an annual event (the causes included the increase of a particular type of 'religious awe' in face of the 'mystery' and the 'real presence', and also the dilution in the quality of Christian profession with the 'conversion of the Empire' and the superficial evangelization of the northern peoples); and the form which the eucharistic celebration took became only vaguely reminiscent of a meal. Again, one of the most significant features of the modern liturgical renewal has been the increased frequency of communion and the recovery of the meal symbolism. (The latter feature had been anticipated in the Reformation at Zurich, where Zwingli, whatever the inadequacies of his eucharistic theology, had at least valued the Lord's Supper as an expression of communion among Christians [note 66]. In the Netherlands also, the Reformed Church has always gathered the people around a real table for communion.) Because the symbolic character of the eucharist itself virtually demands a certain stylization in the form of the celebration, the sacrament is now sometimes once again linked to what the Germans call a 'satisfying meal' (*Sättigungsmahl*): the 'parish breakfast', for instance. This close connexion keeps the meal character of the eucharist in mind. In other cases, the form in which the sacrament itself is celebrated has been brought closer to a meal. In these ways, the eucharist has a better chance of serving as a paradigm for social ethics not only within the Christian community but also in the relations between the Christian community and its natural and human environment. Participation in the eucharist implies a commitment to the proper use of the earth's resources to the benefit of all people.

Up to this point, the emphasis has fallen on the *similarity* between God and humanity: there is the similarity implied in the calling of humanity to communion with God; there is the similarity implied in the task of humanity to administer the earth on God's behalf; there is the similarity implied in the human vocation to imitate the loving character of God. I have nevertheless been careful to maintain the asymmetrical nature of the relation between Creator and creature. The time has now come to develop the *distinction* between God and humanity. We needed the similarity if we were to talk at all about God and the relation of humanity to him, but the similarity does not abolish the fundamental distinction [note 67].

5. *God and humanity distinct*

There is a strong strand in the biblical traditions which prohibits humanity, on its side, from fabricating any likeness to God. The second commandment is written deeply on the Jewish (and Islamic) mind, and the story of the golden calf in Exodus 32 serves as a permanent warning [note 68]. In Christian worship, the matter appears (as we shall see) rather differently on account of the belief in the incarnation, but Christian history also includes the activity of the iconoclasts in the eighth century and the *bilderstürmer* in the sixteenth [note 69]. Nothing *within* creation can depict God in so far as he, the creator, is transcendent *over* creation.

The non-representability of God is matched by his invisibility. What Ninian Smart calls 'the covered gaze' is a recurrent feature of religious ritual [note 70]. The bowing of the head, the shutting of the eyes, the screening of the holy are known also by Christianity. On a primitive understanding, to be seen by another is to lose power to the other, and the numen retains its numinosity by remaining mysterious. Within Christianity, there is the persistent theme of the hidden God (*Deus absconditus*). The divine invisibility is another expression of God's transcendence over his creation.

Yet the religions which know the transcendent creator possess also, in some form, a notion of revelation. In one way or another, God 'draws back the veil'. As St Paul put it, God's very handiwork in creation discloses at least the power of his divinity (Romans 1:20). On occasion, God may reveal himself in a more precise and personal way. In Israelite religion, the experience of these more particular disclosures is predominantly in the auditory mode, and so the invisibility of transcendence is safeguarded. Yet the prophet may *see* 'the word of the Lord' (Amos 1:1; 7:1,7; 8:1); even more directly, Moses is granted a glimpse of at least God's back (Exodus 33:23); and Isaiah distantly sees through the smoke of the temple the high and exalted God (Isaiah 6). When the apocalyptic literature is reached, there is less reticence about seeing God (Daniel 7:13). Within Christianity, St Paul speaks of seeing now 'through a glass darkly', but the *chiaroscuro* of the present will eventually give way to seeing face-to-face (1 Corinthians 13:12). The Christian tradition has conceived ultimate bliss as *visio Dei* [note 71], and the liturgical visions of the author of the Christian Apocalypse are an anticipation of the final kingdom in which saved humanity will worship God 'with open face' (to borrow a phrase from eschatologically oriented prayers in the Eastern liturgies.)

The notion of revelation maintains the superiority of God: if he reveals himself, it is by grace. In the biblical religions, the divine self-revelation is intended to benefit humanity. God wishes to *share* his glory. This very generosity is indeed his own greater glory. Thus creation, and a creation destined to receive and render God's glory, is ultimately *ad majorem Dei gloriam*. Yet the creating of something other than himself, and particularly the creating of a humanity endowed with a relative freedom, must have involved for God, at least 'provisionally', a certain self-limitation. He 'needed time' to bring creation through to its salvation which is also his kingdom. From the human side, the matter was put in the following way by the Orthodox theologian Olivier Clément: Time is the God-given opportunity to learn to love [note 72].

The making of humanity in the divine image means that humanity has the potential to reveal God. That capacity will be realized when, through communion with God in response to the divine vocation, human beings grow into his existential and moral 'likeness'. But the making of humanity in the divine image was also dangerous. It gives human beings the opportunity to mistake *themselves* for God. The distinction between Creator and creature is then left out of consideration. Instead of being gratefully received as a gift, the human similarity to God is asserted as a right. That is the meaning of the *temptation*: 'You shall be like God' (Genesis 3:5) The potential for creativity which humanity derives from God becomes devoted to the manufacture of idols. Herein lies the demonic possibility of art, to which reference was made earlier. Idols are in the last resort a form of human self-worship: *I* give value to what *I* choose. The God-given capacity to love turns in upon the self and becomes human self-love: *homo incurvatus in se* (Luther) [note 73]. Human beings thus let by the opportunities for that communion with God to which they are called.

6. *Firstborn Son and last Adam*

Nevertheless God does not revoke his calling. He persists in his intention that humanity shall find its true and saving destiny in communion with himself. The effective token of that continuing purpose is Jesus Christ. Accepting the two natures and the single person of traditional christology, it is possible to view Jesus Christ as being in himself the image of God from both the divine and the human perspectives. From the divine side, he is 'the image of the invisible God, first-born before all creation' (Colossians 1:15), he 'radiates the glory of God and bears the very stamp of his nature' (Hebrews 1:3). From the human side, he is 'the eschatological Adam' (1 Corinthians 15:45; cf. Romans 5:12–21), fulfilling, as we saw earlier, the human vocation to communion with God, to the right use of God's creation, and to love of one's fellows [note 74]. Or in terms of a christology, such as J.A.T. Robinson's, which is less wedded to pre-existence and incarnation: Jesus' transparency to God is such that he is 'a window into God'; his face is 'the human face of God'; he is at the same time 'the man for others' [note 75]. Or again: E. Schillebeeckx more recently makes Jesus, 'aspectually', *both* the definitive parable of God *and* the definitive paradigm of humanity [note 76].

A concrete example of image christology is found in the *ikon*, which occupies a characteristic place in the worship of the Orthodox churches [note 77]. At the most obvious level the ikon of Christ is, in Ninian Smart's phrase, a 'phenomenological focus' of worship: people bow down before the ikon, they kiss it, they light candles in front of it [note 78]. But what we may call the 'noumenal focus' of worship is Christ himself: for, according to the principle of participation by resemblance which is ingrained in religion and indeed in the whole of human life, the ikon is believed to 'represent' Christ in such a way that he is present in it. There is, however, yet a third depth: for Christ is the image of God; so God, 'represented' in the human form of Christ, is the *ultimate* Focus of the believer's worship as he worships before the ikon [note 79].

The Orthodox ikon encourages the transition from christology to soteriology. To look upon the ikon-Christ-God is to open oneself to transformation into the likeness of the object of contemplation. Such a belief in the transformative power of contemplation is widespread in religion and indeed in more mundane affairs. It finds some biblical sanction in 2 Corinthians 3:18, where it is by *beholding* the Lord that believers are changed from glory into glory, reflecting his likeness [note 80]. Elsewhere in the New Testament, the renewal of humanity 'after the image of God' is explicitly given an active ethical component (Colossians 3:10; cf. Ephesians 5:1f). The crucifix, on which the gaze of Western Christians has been focused, makes clear that the *imitatio Christi* includes treading the *via crucis*. The procession of the Stations of the Cross is the ritual recognition that following Christ means taking the way of self-surrender, of sacrificial love (Mark 8:34f). As St John's usage of the verb *doxazō* shows, the cross and the glory are only apparent opposites: the eye of faith discerns *sub contraria specie* (Luther's phrase) the glory of the self-giving Lord. Human salvation is the change of character into a love of that quality.

Another christological and soteriological model located in the context of worship is the one proposed in an earlier book by E. Schillebeeckx under the title *Christ the Sacrament of Encounter with God* [note 81]. On the basis of a traditional God-man christology, Christ himself is seen as the fundamental Sacrament, the primordial meeting between the human and the divine. Christian worship, which takes place 'in Christ', is the locus of saving encounter between humanity and God in a derived and analogous sacramental mode. Further investigation of this model is reserved for the chapter on christology. Here it is sufficient to note the value of 'meeting' as a category which permits the distinction between God and humanity to be preserved, while yet allowing for a creative effect upon the character of a humanity thus brought into touch with God. This *encounter* (distinction) may produce in the human partner *convergence* with the moral and spiritual character of God (asymmetric assimiliation).

The remaining task of this chapter is to show how the various moods and attitudes characteristic of Christian worship express the multiple aspects of the *personal* relationship, both dynamic and purposive, between God and humanity which is entailed in the making of humanity in the divine image.

7. *A personal relationship*

The character of God, his intention for humanity, his action to achieve his purpose, the human response to God's vocation: all these are expressed, by words and gestures, in the various 'moods' of the Christian liturgy. I will here list eight 'attitudes' which typically occur in Christian worship and which express various facets of the personal relationship between God and humanity.

(a) *Adoration.* Adoration is an acknowledgment of God's transcendence made possible by the fact that he is also self-giving. The original religious impulse to prostrate oneself upon the sudden appearance of the overwhelming Numen is ritualized into bows and genuflexions in the context of cultic repetition [note 82]. In biblical religion, the experience of the *mysterium tremendum et fascinosum* has taken on a personal and ethical character. The Wholly Other has become the transcendent Creator: 'Come let us worship and bow down, let us kneel before the Lord our Maker' (Psalm 95:6). If he inspires fear, it is on account of his power and his purity; if he attracts, it is by his creating love and his redeeming grace.

4

If the creature feels fear, it is on account of his own weakness and sin; if he is drawn towards God, it is because the love that made him will not let him go: 'Thou hast made us for thyself, and our hearts are restless till they find their rest in thee' [note 83]. We can go farther: God's power shows itself *as* love for the creature; God's purity shows itself *as* grace to transform the sinner. Love casts out fear: Christians are no longer craven slaves but have become sons and daughters. Whether in power and purity or in love and grace, there is nevertheless an irreducible majesty about God: worshippers can do no more than tautologously ascribe 'holiness' to him [note 84]. When in the liturgy we cry 'Holy, holy, holy', we say that we are joining our voices to the ceaseless songs of the angelic hosts. That is further symbolic recognition of God's transcendence. His majesty is sometimes indirectly indicated by the description of his entourage of heavenly beings. That is the case in the following Syrian Jacobite preface:

> It is very meet and right that we should give thanks unto thee; that we should adore, glorify, laud, exalt, honour, hymn with praises, bless and sanctify the one majesty of the Holy Trinity. . . . Not indeed that thy majesty requires our praise, nor that thou hast need of our thanksgiving. For those who praise thee are numberless: high authorities infinite, the clustering cherubim, thousands of bright seraphim and a countless host; multitudes and armies without number; ranks upon ranks of devouring flame; marvellous powers of burning coal, hidden legions which bear up the chariot of the cherubim, the revolutions of whose wheels are infinite; troops of seraphim which by the throb of their wings move the threshold; a shining galaxy which out of the midst of the burning coal is discerned by its own movements; thousand thousands who stand before thee and myriads of myriads who praise thy being. And with one clear voice and one loving harmony, with sweet song and ethereal tongue, they cry the one to the other and raise their voices in eternal praise saying 'Holy, holy, holy . . .' [note 85].

The language of adoration pays homage to the surpassing majesty of God and sings his amazing love for his creatures and his unexampled grace for sinners. At times, adoration

will pass over the linguistic horizon into silence [note 86].
Even that silence is directed towards God, and it is qualified
by what the stammering tongue has been straining to say
[note 87].

(b) *Confession of sin.* At various points in this chapter, it has
been necessary to speak of failed potential and missed opportunities. God's vocation of humanity to communion with
himself calls for free personal response; the human task upon
God's earth demands the free exercise of responsibility; the
constitution of humanity as social being requires free mutual
responsiveness among human beings. Yet in their mysterious
freedom, human beings turn their back on God, their hand
against the earth, their face from their fellows. We idolize
ourselves. When we return to God, there is therefore penitence
in our hearts and the confession of sin upon our lips. We
seek to be opened to the forgiving grace of God and his
renewing love.

(c) *Proclamation and thanksgiving.* The address of proclamation
is to the world; the address of thanksgiving is to God. Yet
proclamation and thanksgiving are closely related, as the
biblical use of the verb *exhomologein* shows [note 88]. Both
proclamation and thanksgiving typically recite the mighty
acts of God on behalf of humanity and his benefits bestowed
on us. Christians thank God 'for our creation, preservation,
and all the blessings of this life, but above all for thine inestimable love in the redemption of the world by Christ Jesus our
Lord, for the means of grace and the hope of glory' [note 89].
Christians proclaim before the world the mighty deeds or
excellencies, *aretai*, of the God who called them out of
darkness into his marvellous light (1 Peter 2:9). The opening
part of the great eucharistic prayer is called, in the Western
tradition, the preface: the word *praefatio*, from *prae* and *fari*,
to speak before (hearers), had been used in Roman times in
both religious and political spheres for a public proclamation
[note 90]. To 'eat this bread' and 'drink this cup' is to 'proclaim the Lord's death until he come' (1 Corinthians 11:26).
Both thanksgiving to God and proclamation before the
world are confession of faith (*exhomologein* can also mean
'confess'): they declare our belief that we are included in the

scope of God's action and have been touched by it. It is not surprising that creeds also, as confessions of faith, should include some narrative recital of the mighty acts of God on behalf of humanity [note 91].

(d) *Commitment*. The confession of faith is also an act of commitment. When we turn from idols and commit ourselves to this God, we are offering ourselves to him in obedience for his service, which is perfect freedom. In the Byzantine and some other rites of baptism, this new orientation is dramatically enacted by a westward-facing renunciation of Satan's service (*apotaxis*) and an eastward-facing engagement in the service of Christ and the Holy Trinity (*syntaxis*). In those forms of Christian worship where the believers' subjectivity is allowed ample expression (hymns, personal prayers), the dedication of the will and the direction of the feelings to God are put in the language of the deepest personal relationships: trust, yielding, clasping, giving and receiving. Here language assumes a strongly performative function: as these things are spoken, they happen; until they are spoken, they are not fully real. Such surrender to God entails sharing also in *God's* commitment to the world. That is the context of the attitude of intercession in Christian worship.

(e) *Intercession*. God's commitment to the world is shown by his very creation of it, by his continuing preservation of it, by his redemption of it through Jesus Christ, and by his purpose to bring it to ultimate salvation in his kingdom. Human intercession cannot therefore be a matter of changing God's fundamental will with regard to the world. Particular intercessions are addressed to God from within situations in which it appears, at least to human eyes, that the divine will for the well-being of the creatures is suffering frustration. We here confront the mystery of human freedom and the problem of evil (not only moral but also physical). As far as intercession is concerned, its character as a plea for the triumph of the divine purpose in spite of contrary appearances, and perhaps actualities, is itself an increase in free human commitment to the purpose of God and may therefore be allowed, in the mystery of grace, somehow to contribute to the achievement of the world's salvation [note 92].

(f) *Expectation*. I will lift up my eyes (Psalm 121). Lift up your hearts (*Sursum corda*). Look up and raise your heads, because your redemption is drawing near (Luke 21:28). When the believer looks to God, he is looking for salvation, either immediate or ultimate or both. He is expecting God to come to him from the transcendence of heaven or of the future. Salvation must continue to come to human beings 'from beyond': its source is God. That remains true, even though the human appropriation is such that the recipients are themselves being transformed in their inmost being in moral and spiritual assimilation to God. The motif of feeding allows an appropriate expression of the divine giving and the active human reception. The Psalmist confesses:

> The eyes of all look to thee,
>   and thou givest them their food in due season.
> Thou openest thy hand,
>   thou satisfiest the desire of every living thing.
>   (Psalm 145:15f)

In the Fourth Gospel, the divine giver puts so much of himself into his gift that the believers may be said to feed on Christ (John 6). The eating and drinking of the eucharistic bread and wine is the sacrament *par excellence* in which Christians have experienced the taking into themselves of God's giving of himself, both giver and gift. God enters into the very marrow of our being yet remains inexhaustible. The eucharist is an anticipatory concretion of that heavenly feast under which the Bible most often pictures the divine kingdom and human salvation [note 93]. Our expectation is increased precisely because we already have the promise, the pledge, the earnest, the taste. We have started to enjoy God.

There remain two moods or attitudes which, in the nature of the case, are less characteristic of the public liturgy of the Church and which yet recur particularly in an individual's more private experience with God. These experiences are also important in the question of the personal relationship between God and humanity. I refer first to the sense of God's absence and second to prayer as wrestling with God.

(g) *Absence* [note 94]. The sense of God's absence implies a relationship: it presupposes what has been, or it anticipates what might become, a divine presence 'for us'; it remembers a taste or betokens a desire not yet satisfied. The no-longer or not-yet of God's saving presence is a sign that the transcendent God remains his own, to give or to withhold himself. If we are bold enough to seek the rational motivation of this exercise of God's freedom in his relationship with humanity, it may be well to ponder two factors which both have to do with *human* freedom. If, first, God creates humanity at what John Hick calls an 'epistemic distance' from God himself, in order to give human beings room freely to grow into the love of their Creator, who would otherwise overwhelm them [note 95]: then there is the possibility that human beings will misuse their freedom and turn away from God. The absence of God would then be simply the counterpart—the other side of the coin, as it were—of the human refusal of God's invitation to communion with himself. In that case, a human awareness of the absence of God-in-relationship might be the first motion towards the search for God and a positive response to his call.

Second: it may be that God himself exploits the 'epistemic distance' for positive pedagogic purposes, in order to 'teach us that we must live as people who can get along very well without him'. Dietrich Bonhoeffer was there speaking paradoxically, as his next sentence made clear: 'The God who makes us live in this world without using him as a working hypothesis is the God before whom we are ever standing' [note 96]. It may be that the absence of the sense of God is a necessary stage in human growth towards a maturity and a responsibility which eventually enhance the character of the free and personal communion with God which he himself desires us to enjoy. Some may be able, in the 'secret discipline' of which Bonhoeffer spoke, to maintain a private sense of God's presence even when such a sense is lacking in the surrounding culture. But others may find themselves sharing in their own being the sense of god-forsakenness expressed in Jesus' cry on the cross: 'My God, my God, why hast Thou forsaken me?' The cross, however, was in fact the supreme moment of free human surrender to God. And there, too, God was present in all the profundity of his self-giving love for humanity. This was communion between God and humanity *sub contraria specie*. 'It behoved the Christ to suffer these things and enter into his glory' (Luke 24:26). The resurrection and ascension signify a communion in open glory: paradox gives way to plain *doxa*. There are many indications in the New Testament that this is the pattern which believers must and may expect. Apparent god-forsakenness, of which suffering is the sharpest sign, may in fact be a moment of growth in communion with the God who is never really absent from a creation which he never ceases to love. The final expectation, however, is of open communion, face to face, in visible glory.

The public liturgy of the Church is celebrated in the tension, of which the sacramental mode is characteristic, between the already and the not-yet of salvation: it is therefore not entirely a stranger to the dialectic of God's (apparent) absence and his presence. The public liturgy includes the themes of sin and forgiveness, of judgment and renewal [note 97]. More typically, however, the Church's sense of itself as the eschatological community moving through history will cause the official liturgy to stress the sureness of the goal and therefore also the certainty of God's accompanying presence along the saving way. This communal assurance will often support the individual member who may be more acutely aware, in private experience, of God's apparent absence and his own lack of sense of God-in-relationship-to-himself.

(h) *Wrestling*. The last, and strangest, attitude to be mentioned is human wrestling with God in prayer. Depth psychology has hinted how close love and hate are to one another. A fight may signify not only conflict but also affection between people. There is a powerful literary example of this in the naked wrestling of Rupert and Gerald before the open fire in D. H. Lawrence's *Women in Love*, but the phenomenon is as widespread as lovers' quarrels. The Christian tradition has spoken of sin as hostility to God (Romans 5:10), often with the further precision of rebellion against the due authority of God. This view of the matter properly safeguards the sovereignty of God. Yet the mysterious story of Jacob's night-long wrestling with the unnamed divine adversary at Penuel (*The Face of God*) and his own acquisition of the new name of Israel (*He who strives with God*, or *God strives*) has continued to haunt the religious imagination and to provide the language for describing many a personal experience in prayer (Genesis 32:22–32). A Freudian interpretation might make connexions with patricide and sibling rivalry. Exegetically, Jacob's holding firm, if not indeed his victory, may be seen as the test or proof of his election. On the wider theological and anthropological front, the theme may be that of a necessary temporary opposition between God and humanity, if humanity is to show its mettle as an eventually co-operating partner in God's design for creation (including humanity itself). The 'scandal of God's *defeat*'— if R. Barthes [note 98] is right to understand the Jacob story as a defeat for God—points, theologically, to the 'scandalous' divine self-giving represented first by creation and then by the Cross. Jacob's limp may serve as a reminder of the divine superiority. But in the divine kingdom which is final human salvation, that reminder will apparently no longer be needed, for 'the lame shall walk'. Only the mutual love between God and humanity will remain, the initiating graciousness of God being now unquestioned [note 99].

At several points in this chapter on humanity in the image of God, we had occasion to refer in various ways to Jesus Christ. Sometimes the reference was explicit, sometimes implicit. Following on these preparatory sightings, the next chapter looks directly to Jesus Christ as the central figure in the Christian faith.

II

Christ

1. *The place of Christ*

SOME of the most noticed writing in English theology in the 1970s was marked by a strong christological interest. Not that any large-scale constructive christology was produced. Rather, such theologians as M. F. Wiles, J. H. Hick and G. W. H. Lampe have been re-examining the inherited Christian views on the relation of Jesus to God, on the relation of Jesus to humanity, and on the broadest question of how God relates at all to the world and to history [note 100]. In the exercise of what Wiles calls 'doctrinal criticism' [note 101], these theologians in their various ways have radically questioned the incarnational model of the relation between Jesus and God, the revelatory and redemptive uniqueness of Jesus in the context of a religiously and culturally pluralist humanity (this is most explicit in the case of Hick), and the whole interventionist understanding of God's dealings with the world. Because it raises perennial issues for Christian thinking, the recent debate on christology is of more than contemporary interest.

Wiles' concern, and the others mentioned would not perhaps dissent in their own cases, is for coherence and economy in the expression of truth (he admits that his more traditional opponents might prefer to describe him as rationalist and reductionist) [note 102]. But coherence, perhaps, and economy certainly, are not the most obvious characteristics of worship, even Christian worship. It will therefore be interesting and important to relate the theological reflexion of these doctrinal critics to the first-order activity of worship. The subject of christology offers a vital example, both historically and systematically, of the interaction between worship, doctrine and theology.

It is plain that Jesus Christ has been a central figure in the Church's worship ever since the earliest days of Christianity [note 103]. Jesus Christ was the *content* of the primitive Church's preaching: the Proclaimer had, in Bultmann's celebrated phrase, become the Proclaimed. Converts were baptized 'in the name of the Lord Jesus Christ' (Acts 2:38; 8:16; 10:48; 19:5) or 'into Christ' (Romans 6:3; Galatians 3:27): it does not matter for our present purpose whether these texts reflect an actual christological *formula* used in the performance of baptism or not; the christological *reference* is enough. When the believers gathered for worship (the expressions 'come together' and 'in one place' have strong cultic connotations in the New Testament and in the post-apostolic writings), they assembled 'in his name' and he was there 'in the midst' of them (Matthew 18:20). It was 'the Lord's supper' which they ate, with the bread and the wine as signs of his body and his covenant-blood, and this was a proclamation of the Lord's death until he should come (1 Corinthians 11:17–26).

The central place of Jesus Christ in Christian worship having thus been established as a basic fact from the beginning [note 104], we must now try to specify more closely the precise value which has there been ascribed to him, the precise function which he has there occupied, his precise role in the dealings between God and humanity as these come to expression in worship. We shall begin with that point in Christian worship which corresponds to the neuralgic point in contemporary theological discussion, namely the question of Christ's divinity. Liturgically, the matter to be discussed is: Christ as object of worship.

2. *Object of worship*

The title 'Lord' (in Aramaic, *mar*; in Greek, *kyrios*) was, in the appropriate context, simply a title of respect that could be exchanged between two human beings. But by the time Thomas, in the Fourth Gospel (John 20:28), hailed Jesus as 'My Lord and my God', the title had clearly been filled, when applied to Jesus, with the divine resonances that *mar* and *kyrios* could also carry with them in suitable circumstances [note 105]. And when the Evangelists show Jesus being addressed as *kyrie* during the course of his ministry, we may properly see this stereoscopically as both a vocative of respect to a man and, by later light, a confession of his more-than-human sovereignty. In the realm of gestures, the act of *proskunēsis* may similarly be seen at two levels, when the Evangelists, particularly Matthew, report that people bowed down or prostrated themselves before Jesus: Matthew 2:2, 8, 11; 8:2; 9:18; 14:13; 15:35; 20:20; 28:9, 17; Mark 1:40; 5:6, 22; 10:17; 15:19 (ironically); Luke 5:12; 8:41; 17:16; 24:52; John 9:38; 11:32; 18:6. In the Old Testament the verb *shāḫāh* covers both an oriental homage to one's human superiors (Genesis 27:29; 1 Samuel 25:23; 2 Samuel 14:33; 24:20) *and* the attitude of reverence towards the Lord God (Genesis 24:52; 2 Chronicles 7:3; 29:29) [note 106]. The point is that between the ministry of Jesus and the writing of the Evangelists there had occurred what Christian tradition calls the resurrection of Jesus. The New Testament frequently connects the resurrection and the lordship of Christ. Thus there is a significant pauline turn of phrase: 'God raised the Lord Jesus' (1 Corinthians 6:14; 2 Corinthians 4:14); and the apostle quotes two apparently fixed formulas as equivalent: to 'confess with your lips that Jesus is Lord' and to 'believe in your heart that God raised him from the dead' (Romans 10:9). The death of Jesus was in some sense followed by God's exaltation of him to lordship (Acts 2:36; Philippians 2:8–11).

There is no doubt that worship constituted the primary locus of Christ's recognition as Lord by Christian believers. He was *confessed* as Lord at baptism: the baptismal stamp of Romans 10:8–13 is unmistakable (1 Corinthians 12:3 may represent an echo of baptism in the context of subsequent persecution). He was *invoked* as Lord in the Christian assembly: so much is clear, whatever the detailed exegesis concerning *maranatha* at 1 Corinthians 16:22 (see also Revelation 22:20). He was already *worshipped* as Lord by Christians, in anticipation of the day when every knee should bow: that is reflected in the probably pre-pauline hymn of Philippians 2:5–11 (in the passage from which the hymn quotes, Isaiah 45:18–25, Yahweh had uncompromisingly declared his own uniqueness as Lord) [note 107]. Individuals *prayed* for his help as Lord in time of need (Acts 7:59; 2 Corinthians 12:8). The ethical acknowledgment of Christ's sovereignty in everyday living is secondary to the religiously primary acknowledgment of Christ as Lord in the context of worship.

This very early feature of Christian worship was fundamental to the formation and development of christological doctrine and thought. The cautious A. M. Hunter puts it in terms of likelihood: 'It is altogether likely that the primitive church worshipped Jesus as the exalted Messiah and Lord; that this presupposes a cultus (i.e. a properly religious devotion) of Christ; and that, in this confession and cultus of Jesus as the exalted Lord and Christ, lay the essential elements of all later Christology' [note 108]. H. E. W. Turner boldly states: 'That Jesus was Lord and therefore to be worshipped is the "given", more fundamental than any doctrine, from which Christology starts, but in the long run it required a doctrine to explain and support it' [note 109]. At the level of doctrinal history Maurice Wiles fully recognizes, already in the New Testament and then beyond, 'the important role played by worship in the development of christological ideas': 'The continuing practice of invoking the name of Jesus in worship helped to ensure that when the time came for more precise doctrinal definition of his person it would be in terms which did not fall short of the manner of his address in worship.' This is what Wiles calls the 'more creative' role played by worship in addition to its 'conservative' function as 'an effective medium for giving memorable expression to the ideas of one place or one generation and transmitting them to other people and subsequent generations' [note 110].

While it was from the very earliest days of the Church that the title Lord was applied to Jesus with a divine charge and used of him in the context of worship, it appears to have taken rather longer for him to be called God. R. Bultmann held that John 20:28 was the only certain case in the New Testament: and it is perhaps significant that Thomas' confession 'My Lord and my God' is placed in the quasi-cultic setting of a Sunday meeting of Jesus' disciples. In all other possible instances, there are textual, grammatical, syntactical or exegetical difficulties about the direct application of the word God to Jesus. Nevertheless, R. E. Brown has, in a more recent re-examination of the question, added what he considers two other 'certain' cases (John 1:1; Hebrews 1:8f) and five further 'probable' ones (John 1:18; Romans 9:5; Titus 2:13; 1 John 5:20; 2 Peter 1:1) [note 111]. It is interesting that two of these instances come from the prologue to the Fourth Gospel, where there is strong rhythmic and structural evidence in favour of this passage having at its base a hymn of some kind [note 112]. Hebrews 1:8f is the quotation of a psalm, and it is likely that the psalms were employed, probably with christological meaning (note especially the use of Psalm 110 in the New Testament), in Christian worship [note 113]. Romans 9:5, if so punctuated, would be the application to Christ of a Jewish form of 'blessing' God. B. M. Metzger has presented a formidable internal case for this interpretation of Romans 9:5 [note 114]; but many scholars have considered the Letter to the Romans as too early a date for such a 'blessing' of Christ. By the time of 2 Timothy 4:18 possibly, and of 2 Peter 3:18 and Revelation 1:5f and 5:13 certainly, Christ was the recipient of a doxology appropriate to God. This is confirmed by Pliny's evidence, for what it is worth: *carmen Christo quasi deo dicere* [note 115]. In this matter, then, of calling Christ God, Christian worship appears to have constituted a primary formative context.

In another category of material presented by the New Testament, more of an initiating role may have been played by theological speculation, with worship functioning in a rather more secondary way as a means of expression and transmission. I refer to the hymns or hymn-like passages which speak of Christ's part in creation [note 116]. Even here, the rootage in religious experience should not be dismissed. Somewhat as Israel appears to have reached its understanding of Yahweh as universal creator by way of an experience of him as national redeemer, so will present experience of Christ as Lord and Saviour—and in some sense divine—have been the route by which Christians came to ascribe to him pre-existence and a part in the creation of the universe which also finds in him its end. Fragments of hymns ascribing pre-existence and agency in creation to Christ may well be embedded in 1 Corinthians 8:6 and Hebrews 1:2f, for example. The clearest case of all is Colossians 1:15–20, which has been the object of much recent detailed study. In some hymns, Christ's pre-existence figures as the starting-point of a movement that passes through abasement/incarnation/death to re-exaltation/glorification. In 1 Timothy 3:16, the starting-point is merely adumbrated: 'He *(some read:* God) was manifested in the flesh . . . taken up in glory.' The pattern is most fully developed in Philippians 2:5–11. This passage, with its underlying pre-pauline hymn, has been most thoroughly studied by R. P. Martin under the title *Carmen Christi* [note 117].

The letters of Ignatius of Antioch, written about the year 110, contain hymns in praise of Christ which predicate things of him in the third person. This follows the New Testament pattern. In Ignatius' letter to the Ephesians, 19:2f, Christ is praised as the new star at whose appearance all the other stars gathered round in chorus [note 118]. Ephesians 18:2 seems to take up a baptismal hymn or confession, when it says of 'our God, Jesus the Christ' that 'he was born, and was baptized, that by himself submitting (*or* by his suffering) he might purify the water'. That fragment praises Christ by recalling events in his life: it is thus making what R. Deichgräber, following C. Westermann's terminology, calls a 'deed-predication' or 'narrative praise' [note 119]. The hymn in Ephesians 7:2, however, predicates titles and properties of Christ; it is 'descriptive praise', a style which became more common in the second century:

> There is one Physician,
> who is both flesh and spirit,
> born and yet not man,
> true life in death,
> both of Mary and of God,
> first passible and then impassible,
> Jesus Christ our Lord.

In the second and third centuries, the practice grew of addressing hymns directly to Christ in the second person [note 120]. M. F. Wiles stresses the popular character of such piety. He also points out that it seems to have been most common in circles associated with Gnostic teaching. 'It is not surprising,' he writes, 'that Gnostic piety should have taken such forms. The Gnostic Christ was a denizen exclusively of the spiritual world and more naturally, therefore, one to whom prayer was to be addressed. Moreover, effective hymnody requires a measure of free play on the part of the poetic imagination which came more naturally to the Gnostic mind.' That a hymn addressed to Christ should have been composed, or at least adopted, by Clement of Alexandria is not surprising in view of the way in which he 'takes over and baptizes into orthodox Christianity ways of thought and expression whose natural home was in Gnosticism' [note 121]. Clement places this hymn at the end of his *Paidagogos*:

> King of Saints, almighty Word
> Of the Father, highest Lord;
> Wisdom's head and chief;
> Assuagement of all grief;
> Lord of all time and space,
> Jesus, Saviour of our race.

The *Phōs hilaron* is an evening hymn which goes back to the same period and is best known to English-speaking Christians in John Keble's version:

> Hail gladdening Light, of His pure glory poured
> Who is the immortal Father, heavenly, blest,
> Holiest of Holies, Jesus Christ, our Lord!

In popular circles, the distinction between 'orthodoxy' and 'gnosticism' may not have been too finely drawn [note 122]. It is in any case certain, as Wiles says, that this worship of Christ in popular piety 'had a considerable influence on the developing theology of the Church'.

In the effort to save monotheism, early theologians explored the two avenues which modern historians of doctrine have called modalist and dynamic monarchianism [note 123]. Modalism might appear to fit well with the worship of Christ, but its lifting of the distinction between Father and Son ran counter to much else in scripture and in Christian experience. A dynamist such as Paul of Samosata took the other route and denied Christ's divinity: as bishop he is reported to have 'put a stop to psalms addressed to our Lord Jesus Christ on the ground that they are modern and the compositions of modern men' [note 124]. The similar views of Artemon on christology ran up against the claim that they contradicted 'all the psalms or songs written from the beginning by faithful brethren, which celebrate the Word of God, even Christ, and speak of him as God' [note 125]. Origen's solution [note 126] was to distinguish between prayer in the strict sense of the term (*kyriolexia*), which should be offered only to the Father, and prayer which is offered in a secondary sense (*katachrēstikōs*) to Christ as the high priest who will convey it to the Father. This matches the distinction which Origen drew between the Father, who is God in the absolute sense of the word, and the Son, to whom the word applies in a relative sense. Origen's strong subordinationism was several decades later hardened by Arius—who abandoned Origen's teaching on the *eternal generation* of the Son—into a view which made the Son a *creature* of the Father. Athanasius argued that the cardinal error of arianism was that it would thus turn Christians into creature-worshippers [note 127]. The eventual victory of nicene orthodoxy was accompanied by the growth of major prayers addressed directly to the Son in the public liturgy of the Church. The heavily predominant pattern in earlier practice—and Origen's treatise *On Prayer* had argued in its own pre-nicene and origenistic (strongly subordinationist) way for the theological propriety of this pattern—had been to address the official liturgy of the Church to God the Father *through* Christ. The triumph of the *homoousion* opened the way for even the liturgical president's prayers to be addressed to the Son. The frequency of collects addressed to the Son in surviving gallican and mozarabic texts indicates a keenness on the part of Catholics to score against the persistent arianism of the visigothic rulers in Gaul and Spain.

In the East [note 128], the tendency to address liturgical prayer to the Son was increased both by the weighting of trinitarian doctrine in favour of threefoldness (in contrast with the 'augustinian' stress on the divine unity in the West) and by a certain 'monophysite' trend in the matter of Christ's person and natures. After Chalcedon, even the great euchar- istic prayer or anaphora could be addressed to Christ in the worship of the monophysite churches [note 129]. Although the Byzantines did not go as far as that, they introduced the hymn *Monogenēs*, attributed to the emperor Justinian, into the enarxis or opening part of the Orthodox liturgy:

> Only-begotten Son and Word of God, who being immortal yet didst deign for our salvation to be incarnate of the holy Mother of God and Ever-Virgin Mary, and without change didst become man and wast crucified, Christ our God, and by death didst overcome death, being One of the Holy Trinity and glorified together with the Father and the Holy Spirit: Save us.

The lessons in the Orthodox liturgy are preceded by a further hymn which dates at latest from the fifth century and whose original intention was christological:

> Holy God, Holy and Strong, Holy and Immortal, have mercy upon us [note 130].

East and West share the *Gloria in excelsis*, which dates from the fourth century and whose address in the second part is to the Son [note 131]. The use of this canticle in the Western churches is in the eucharistic liturgy; in the East, it serves rather as the climax of matins in the Byzantine office. Western matins includes the *Te Deum*, which also dates from the fourth century and whose address in the second section is likewise to the Son:

> Thou art the King of Glory, O Christ:
>   thou art the everlasting Son of the Father.
> When thou tookest upon thee to deliver man:
>   thou didst not abhor the Virgin's womb.

5

When thou hadst overcome the sharpness of death:
  thou didst open the Kingdom of Heaven to all
  believers.
Thou sittest at the right hand of God:
  in the glory of the Father.
We believe that thou shalt come to be our Judge.
We therefore pray thee, help thy servants:
  whom thou hast redeemed with thy precious blood.
Make them to be numbered with thy saints:
  in glory everlasting [note 132].

Throughout the middle ages the worship of Christ as the divine Son, the Second Person of the Trinity, continued to be expressed in these and other ways in the official liturgy of the Church [note 133], even though the canon of the mass adhered fundamentally to the classical pattern of addressing God the Father through Christ; and both practices have remained to this day. The later middle ages, however, witnessed another, and superficially contradictory, development in popular devotion: the devotion to the human Jesus on the cross. This devotion never made its mark on the central texts of the official liturgy, unless it be in the later masses of the Sacred Heart of Jesus, the Sacred Crown of Thorns of our Lord Jesus Christ, the Lance and the Nails, the Sacred Shroud, the Five Wounds. More characteristically, it found expression in para-liturgical hymns, prayers and processions. I shall be suggesting later that devotion to Jesus in his suffering humanity is in fact by no means unimportant for our deeper understanding of lordship and godhead and of the nature and destiny of humanity.

At the end of a chapter devoted to the part played by worship as *one* of the factors in 'the making of Christian doctrine', Maurice Wiles implicitly raised a systematic question which pointed beyond the primarily historical scope of his 'study in the principles of early doctrinal development'. He wrote at that point: 'Undoubtedly the practice of prayer has had its effect on doctrine; undoubtedly the practice of prayer *should* have its effect on doctrine. But that is not to say that the effect which prayer has actually had is at every point precisely the effect which it should have had' [note 134].

In the course of his chapter, Wiles had drawn further examples from the trinitarian and marian areas in order to illustrate the historical relations between worship and doctrine. We shall ourselves be returning to these fields later in this book. But it is clearly the christological question which most interests Wiles from a systematic point of view: it is to the example of christology that he returns when, in the final chapter of *The Making of Christian Doctrine*, he edges 'towards a doctrine of development'. He writes: 'At the point where the worship of Christ was of decisive significance for the development of doctrine, it was a question of popular devotion rather than formal liturgical worship. Popular devotion is not without significance but it is no infallible guide. Its history is full of examples of confusion between the medium and the ultimate object of worship, between the image and the reality. It is not clear that we are in a position to rule out the possibility of something of the same kind having happened in this case also' [note 135]. And again [note 136]: 'It is never enough . . . to show that later doctrine is a development of earlier. Our search is for criteria which will enable us to say why one development is true and another false, or even why one development is in some respects truer than another. In the case of Nicene orthodoxy it is tempting to suggest that it was the true development because it gave the "highest" account of the person of Christ, because it took most seriously the worshipping tradition of the Church. But such a criterion is clearly unreliable. It was just such an approach which was responsible for the conviction of Eutyches and the Monophysites that their teaching must be the true expression of the faith.'

There are hints here of how Wiles would apply the principles of 'doctrinal criticism' to worship both as a creative factor in the earlier formation of doctrine and as a continuing mode of maintaining and transmitting it. In the nature of the case, we needed to begin with historical description. We can now pursue in more systematic terms our discussion of the relations between worship, doctrine and theology, taking Wiles as our principal partner in dialogue. At the moment we remain with the sensitive area of Christ's divinity.

From the outset, it must be granted that it is a legitimate and indeed salutary task to apply critical theological reason to the realm of Christian worship. There are hints in the New Testament that such criticism was already necessary in the early days of Christianity. Let us take a number of examples that cluster round a single theme. Daniel von Allmen has argued persuasively that the pauline author of Colossians did not leave unaltered the christological hymn quoted in 1:15–20 [note 137]. In particular, his addition of 'marginal notes' at verse 18 ('the head of the body, *the church*') and verse 20 ('*by the blood of his cross*') is intended to correct any tendency on the part of the Colossians to remove the centre of soteriology from the plane of human history into a superior cosmic realm to which triumphalistic imaginations might easily resort in order to escape the painful facts of our world. Paul's 'theology of the cross' has similarly been brought to bear, von Allmen also argues, on the tendency of Hellenistic Christians to understand baptism, in the manner of the pagan mysteries, as *already* their own resurrection [note 138]. In Romans 6 Paul is refuting a simple parallelism between 'Christ has died and is risen' and 'You have died and are risen'. He keeps the believers' resurrection in the domain of promise (future tense in v.8) and unfinished task (subjunctive mood in v.4). In Colossians 2 and 3 the formal parallel between Christ's death and resurrection on the one hand and the mystical experience of the believer in baptism on the other ('You have been raised with Christ', 3:1) is in fact qualified by a measure of the not-yet (3:4) and by the need for ethical exhortation (3:5ff). Yet again: the cross is recalled, and the note of 'eschatological reserve' struck, in connexion with the over-enthusiastic Corinthian celebration of heavenly bliss ('and another is drunk', 1 Corinthians 11:20) at the eucharist: the Lord's *death* is proclaimed *until he come* (11:26) [note 139].

The Reformation provides many obvious examples of a theological critique being applied at a later period to current worship practice and the doctrine it appeared to express: we shall return to the Reformation in chapter VIII. The question now arises, whether our contemporary 'doctrinal critics' wish to set to work upon the Church's liturgy in the matter of Christ's divinity. Both Wiles and Hick state or imply that they (still) consider the use of 'divine' language about (and to?) Christ appropriate in the context of worship, whatever dissatisfaction they may feel with incarnational and trinitarian language at the level of theological reflexion [note 140]. But this view of the matter raises a number of questions, three of which may be mentioned here.

In the first place, there is the question of how language and belief inside the Christian liturgy are related to Christian language and belief outside the liturgy. Wiles and Hick associate worship with poetry [note 141]. In comparison with the language of theological reflexion, liturgical language is indeed typically and appropriately more poetic, more affective. But this is hardly licence for holding that one may be a trinitarian within the charmed circle of the liturgy and a unitarian in the academic study. There needs to be at least a consistency, if not an identity, between the belief expressed in worship and the belief expressed in the forms of reflective theology. This is necessary on two scores: first, because worship and theology are both 'intending' a single object, namely the truth of God; and second, because worship and theology are each occupations which engage the person of the one who practises both. To acquiesce in less than a positive correspondence between liturgy and theology would thus be to accept internal contradiction in both the content and the act of belief, both the *fides quae creditur* and the *fides quâ creditur*. At any one time, a particular believer may in his theological reflexion consider (let us say) unitarianism to be intellectually preferable to trinitarianism because it appears to him to satisfy better his criteria of rationality and economy—yet he may simultaneously desire, on important grounds of history, culture, aesthetics or fellowship, to remain within the community of believers who express their worship in trinitarian terms. He may as an individual be prepared to live provisionally with that personal contradiction; but his integrity will require him to seek ways of establishing some kind of congruity of content between his own belief and the belief that is expressed in the liturgy in which he participates.

If he is convinced of the truth of his own position, he may seek to alter the worship, and thereby the belief, of the community with which he is associated. Such reformers, let alone revolutionaries, have been rare in the history of the Church, though they are not absent from it: in chapter VIII we shall look at cases from the sixteenth century. On the other hand, the individual may judge it wiser to let the inherited and continuing pattern of the community's worship and belief impress itself 'correctively' on his own tentative position. Whether in the one direction or the other, it is clear that integrity requires a movement towards congruity. In certain situations of social, cultural or intellectual change within and outside the Church, it may be that a whole community finds itself, through the agency of a fairly coherent group of its articulate members, re-interpreting its inherited belief in such a way that theological reformulation and liturgical revision go hand in hand and retain their congruous relationship. In chapter X, we shall ask how far this is happening in the life of the contemporary Church. The whole issue of the 'traditional' character of Christianity, or of the relations between identity, development, change and correction, is thereby raised. That will be a point also at which to discuss further the category of 'myth', which some at least of the contributors to *The Myth of God Incarnate* may wish to exploit in order to relate the language used inside the liturgy to theological language outside it [note 142].

The second question to be raised at this stage is the question of idolatry. In connexion with worship addressed to Christ, Maurice Wiles talked of a possible 'confusion' having occurred between the image and the reality, between the medium (Christ) and the ultimate object of worship (God). The deep drift of Wiles's thinking would appear to be towards ending the confusion by abandoning the worship of Christ. The movement of Athanasius' argument was the precise reverse. The Church's worship of Christ was there the accepted fact, and the conclusion was drawn that since the worship of a creature would be intolerably idolatrous, the Son *must be* 'homoousios' with the Father. Let us, however, try a tack which avoids Wiles's religiously unsatisfactory drift towards

unitarianism or even deism while ourselves approaching
Athanasius' finishing-point rather more indirectly than
Athanasius himself did.

The phenomenon of different intensities of worship
directed towards divinities of different magnitudes is widespread in the religions of the world. Because of its own
anchorage in the monotheism of the Old Testament prophets
and in a certain Greek philosophical tradition for which the
'simplicity' of God was axiomatic, Christian theology has
tended to dismiss this phenomenon as 'pagan'. Religiously,
however, a similar pattern has (re)asserted itself over large
areas of Christianity. Despite the iconoclasts of the eighth
century and the *bilderstürmer* of the sixteenth, and despite
persistent Protestant suspicion, the veneration of images and
of saints has remained a feature of the broad Christian tradition. The dangers of this practice are real, and the periodic
attacks and the constant questioning are therefore valuable
and even necessary in view of sinful humanity's propensity
to erect more 'congenial' idols in place of the true God. Yet
theology has in fact managed to suggest an understanding
which in principle purges this religious pattern of its polytheistic origins and potentially idolatrous content by turning
the worship in the direction of the true God who may be
encountered *in* his saints or *in* given symbols. My fellow
Protestants will charge me with admitting the mediation of
the saints in worship (I will return to the question later). But
all Protestants share in the fundamental acceptance of *Christ*
precisely as *mediator*: and I shall be showing shortly how
this is his principal role, according to both scripture and
classical tradition, in Christian worship.

As I hinted earlier in talking about the ikon, the appropriate
way to view the matter is stereoscopically. Christian worship
is directed towards God the Father as its ultimate Focus,
but it passes 'through' Christ. Lest it be feared that the
function of Christ be thereby reduced to mere transparency,
let it be said that the Christian understanding is that he
mediates *actively* by assuming our imperfect worship into his
perfect service of the Father. It is doubtless because of this
redemptive role of his that our worship may sometimes

appear to 'stop short' at Christ himself as already the sufficient object of our devotion. But even worship addressed to Christ must in the last resort be destined for God the Father. That, at least, appears to be the biblical view of the matter, even where the appreciation of Christ's lordship is at its highest. So Philippians 2:9–11:

> Therefore God has highly exalted him and bestowed on him the name which is above every name, that at the name of Jesus every knee should bow, in heaven and on earth and under the earth, and every tongue confess that Jesus Christ is Lord, *to the glory of God the Father.*

The same principle is expressed in *temporal* terms in 1 Corinthians 15:24–28, where the lordship of Christ or 'the Son' is *pen*ultimate in relation to the final kingdom where God will be all in all. On these lines, the worship addressed to Christ *is* therefore addressed *katachrēstikōs* even when it is offered to him in his divinity (I will speak of his humanity in a moment)—in so far as it is not offered directly to the Father. But that need not carry the arian implication of 'worship of a creature'. It could properly fit either with that measure of subordinationism which has its place in orthodox trinitarian doctrine, where the Father remains 'the fount of deity' [note 143], or with a bultmannian willingness [note 144] to confess the saving Christ as God *pro me* while refusing to go beyond his value or his function into the ontology of his person. To take the ontological risk: I myself go for 'subordinationism'. I understand that the Son is *God as self-given* (the divine self-giving takes incarnate form in Christ), while the Father is *God as inexhaustibly self-giving.* This may not be so far removed from Athanasius' position that the Son is God in all things, except that he is not the Father [note 145].

The third question in our present series is whether worship of Christ is worship of a (mere) human being. Such is the accusation which Jews and Muslims have brought against Christianity. A Chalcedonian reply would invoke the dual principle of the simultaneous indivisibility and distinction of Christ's divine and human natures: it would be argued that, in accordance with the *communicatio idiomatum* of the one Person, the worship accorded to Christ in virtue of his divinity could also be ascribed to him as human without implying any worship of 'mere' humanity. In less incarnationalist and more eschatological terms, it may be said that no humanity is ever 'mere' humanity: it is always humanity called to a destiny of communion with God. This vocation to glory is such that a strong stream in the Christian tradition had been prepared to speak of 'divinization', *theopoiēsis*. The heart of divinization lies in the transformation of human character into that self-giving love which is moral and spiritual likeness to God. Jesus, the 'last Adam', already displays that character to perfection. God has set the highest value upon him ('has super-exalted him', Philippians 2:9). If God might almost be said to 'worship' Jesus Christ as his life-companion, then it is hardly surprising that human beings should set such high value upon the one in whose footsteps they hope to follow. Medieval and later devotion to Christ's 'suffering humanity' may be considered a true religious recognition of him as the embodiment of self-giving love. This way of viewing the matter does not *require* the incarnation of a pre-existent divine Person: it would fit the 'adoptionist' view of Jesus which has left its traces in the New Testament and which runs secretly through the history of christology on its antiochene side [note 146]. But neither does it *exclude* an incarnationalist view of Christ, if it be held that only such 'direct' and 'personal' divine action in revelation and redemption could advance God's purpose (the question of whether *such* divinity is 'required' of the historical Saviour will recur in the next section). The patristic notion that 'the Son of God became man in order that men might become sons of God' would need, by our modern sensibility, to be understood on the kenotic model that is already clearly expressed in some parts of the New Testament: 'Though he was rich, yet for your sake he became poor, so that by his poverty you might become rich' (2 Corinthians 8:9). On this understanding, the Son lived, in human form and within the conditions of humanity, the divine life of self-giving love. Enriched by that life and love, human beings are enabled to grow into the divine likeness by living 'likewise'. A strongly kenotic hymn by Charles Wesley praises 'our God contracted to a span' in these terms:

> He deigns in flesh to appear,
>   Widest extremes to join;
> To bring our vileness near,
>   And make us all divine:
> And we the life of God shall know,
> For God is manifest below.
>
> (MHB 142)

To return to the principal theme of chapter I, the image of God. From the human side, Jesus fulfilled perfectly in his own life the vocation that is adumbrated in the making of humanity in the image of God. From the divine side, the character of God and, I believe, the very being of God were embodied in the human being named Jesus [note 147].

In these last paragraphs we have already been approaching the theme of the next section: the function of Christ in worship. It will be argued, from scripture and tradition, that his function is characteristically mediatorial.

3. *Mediator in worship*

In speaking of prayer and God's universal purpose of salvation, 1 Timothy 2 states that 'there is one mediator between God and men, the man Christ Jesus'. The dominant christological theme in the Letter to the Hebrews is Christ the high priest, appointed by God from among his brethren (2:11–18; 3:1f; 5:1–10) and now, having made the sacrifice of obedience (10:9f), appearing in heaven as our forerunner (6:19f): so we are able to 'draw near' to God *through* Christ (7:25; 10:19–22; 13:15). Again, according to Ephesians 2:18 it is *through* Christ that we 'have access' to the Father. Our worship is thus offered to God not only on account of what Christ has already done but also by his present mediation (*dia* with genitive, Romans 1:8; 16:27; 2 Corinthians 1:20; 1 Peter 2:5; 4:11; and the passages quoted from Ephesians and Hebrews) [note 148].

In a definitive study of *The Place of Christ in Liturgical Prayer* [note 149], J. A. Jungmann demonstrated that this understanding of Christ's role as a mediatorial one governed the solemn prayer of the Church from the earliest days, as is specially clear from the (often doxological) formulae of conclusion. In the Didache we already find:

> For Thine is the glory and the power through Jesus Christ for ever.

In the account of Polycarp's martyrdom, the bishop's last words appear to echo the liturgy:

> For this and all benefits, I praise thee, I bless thee, I glorify thee through the eternal and heavenly high priest, Jesus Christ, thy beloved Son, through whom be to thee glory, now and for all the ages to come. Amen.

Jungmann further showed how anti-arian motives eventually came to shift the emphasis from the human Christ, or the incarnate Son in his continuing mediatorial function, to the Son as the Second Person of the Trinity and therefore himself a recipient of worship. The transition may be reflected in the mixed style of the extant conclusion of the eucharistic prayer in the so-called *Apostolic Tradition* of Hippolytus:

> That we may praise and glorify thee through thy child Jesus Christ, *through whom glory and honour is unto thee, the Father and the Son with the Holy Spirit*, in thy holy Church, now and in eternity.

Jungmann thought that the trinitarian phrase in this particular example might be the personal addition of Hippolytus, but it is more likely the result of later anti-arian tinkering. However the case may be with that text, Jungmann proved conclusively from later liturgies that the liturgical result of the arian controversy in both East and West was that 'stress was now placed not on what unites us to God (Christ as one of us in his human nature, Christ as our brother), but on what separates us from God (God's infinite majesty)' [note 150].

In the East, the tendency towards monophysitism, to which reference has already been made, betokened a further weakening in the mediatorial understanding of Christ's place in liturgical prayer. Nevertheless, the continuing influence of Cyril of Alexandria, a father revered by Monophysites and Chalcedonians alike, must have helped to keep the old pattern alive. As T. F. Torrance has shown, Cyril's theology ascribed an important role to the human mind of Christ as that which allows him to take up the Church's worship into his own worship of the Father [note 151]. In the West, the old *per Jesum Christum Dominum nostrum* remained, particularly in the conservative Roman rite, as a continuing reminder of the earliest pattern. It is remarkable that the liturgies produced by the modern Liturgical Movement in the West follow closely the pattern of addressing the Father through Christ [note 152]. An important factor will have been the diffused influence of Jungmann's thesis, and there is no reason to think that the authors of these liturgies have wished to depart from inherited trinitarian orthodoxy. Nevertheless, the triumph of this pre-nicene pattern in contemporary liturgical worship may offer some encouragement to those who feel that the search for a christology more attuned to the contemporary spirit may profitably go back behind Chalcedon and Nicaea [note 153].

It is not only as mediating human worship to God that Christ figures in the liturgy: he also figures as the mediator of divine blessings to humanity. Already in the New Testament, Christians give thanks to God on account of what he had done for them in Christ (Ephesians 1:3–14; 1 Peter 1:3). This theme finds expression in the christological thanksgiving series which dominates the great eucharistic prayer of the *Apostolic Tradition* and which, after suffering mixed fortunes in later liturgies, has been finely reintroduced into many modern compositions. In the *Apostolic Tradition* the relevant part of the prayer runs as follows:

We render thanks to you, O God, through your beloved child Jesus Christ, whom in the last times you sent to us as saviour and redeemer and angel of your will; who is your inseparable Word, through whom you made all things, and in whom you were well pleased. You sent him from heaven into the Virgin's womb; and, conceived in the womb, he was made flesh and was manifested as your Son, being born of the Holy Spirit and the Virgin. Fulfilling your will and gaining for you a holy people, he stretched out his hands when he should suffer, that he might release from suffering those who have believed in you. And when he was delivered to voluntary suffering, that he might destroy death, and break the bonds of the devil, and tread down hell, and shine upon the righteous, and fix the limit, and manifest the resurrection, he took bread . . .

A sober modern example may be taken from the British Methodist *Sunday Service* where the rehearsal of Christ's saving activity reads in this way [note 154]:

Father, all-powerful and ever-living God, it is indeed right, it is our joy and our salvation, always and everywhere to give you thanks and praise through Jesus Christ your Son our Lord. You created all things and made us in your own image. When we had fallen into sin, you gave your only Son to be our Saviour.
He shared our human nature, and died on the cross. You raised him from the dead, and exalted him to your right hand in glory, where he lives for ever to pray for us. Through him you have sent your holy and life giving Spirit and made us your people, a royal priesthood, to stand before you to proclaim your glory and celebrate your mighty acts. And so with all the company of heaven we join in the unending hymn of praise . . .

It is not only for Christ's saving work in the past that we give thanks: the Methodist prayer already points to Christ as the *continuing* mediator of the divine blessings to us. Christ's present function in this direction has generally been felt to receive strongest sacramental expression in the act of holy communion. But more generally Christ is traditionally seen as the principal minister of all the sacraments. In Augustine's words: 'It is Christ who baptizes . . .' [note 155]. As to the *future*: the eucharist in particular, traditionally understood as an anticipation of Christ's parousia and as a foretaste of the messianic banquet, expects Christ to keep his role as the mediator of God's blessings to humanity [note 156].

The most characteristic function of Christ in Christian worship, then, is understood to be mediation: he mediates human worship to God, and he mediates salvation from God to humanity. If this view of the matter is accepted, modern 'doctrinal critics' may nevertheless raise questions concerning two positions that have traditionally appeared as concomitants to it. First: need such a mediator himself be divine? Is his divinity required for the coherence of the total picture? And second: is Christ the only such mediator? Some attention must now be given to these two questions.

In the Christian tradition, the profoundest views of revelation and redemption have always, in one way or another, let God appear as the loving God who saves his erring creation at great personal cost. The self-giving God spends himself for the sake of winning sinners into the communion with himself which has always been his intention for his creatures. The death of Jesus is felt to show that the winning of sinners requires love *unto death*. But could *God* die? [note 157]. It is not merely an allegedly abstract philosophical notion of the impassibility of God which causes the problem: it would on any view appear absurd that the living God, upon whom all other life uninterruptedly depends, should die. Yet God must himself be involved in the redemption of his world and must himself pay the price. Trinitarian, or at least binitarian, doctrine may have arisen partly as an answer to this problem [note 158]. God did not spare 'his Son' (Romans 8:32; cf. 5:8, 10). The Father experienced at least com-passion with the Son in his suffering and death. It is not merely 'in his human nature' that the incarnate Son suffers: the deepest religious sensibilities have been willing to exploit to the full, in the terminology of a two-nature christology, the principle of the *communicatio idiomatum*, in order to speak, with Luther, Wesley and now Moltmann, of a 'crucified God' [note 159]. The one who became the object of worship as exalted Lord was accorded this highest value by both God and human beings precisely because ('therefore', Philippians 2:8f) he had embodied on the cross the ultimate in God's self-giving for the love of humanity. It is to that 'foolishness of God' [note 160] that the *graffito* from the Palatine palace in

Rome bears ironic witness: a man kneels before a crucified figure whose head is the head of an ass, and the legend reads 'Alexamenus worships his god'. In that perspective, we may say this concerning the question of Jesus Christ's divinity as mediator of revelation and redemption: in so far as God in some sense identified himself with humanity in Jesus Christ, *to that same extent* and *in that same sense* Jesus Christ *is* God. Whether he 'needed' to be can scarcely be answered in the abstract. The affirmation of his divinity is, at the least, congruous with a generative step on God's part in the process of overcoming human alienation from God and the conformation of humanity to God's moral and spiritual likeness [note 161]. In traditional trinitarian terms, the nomenclature of *Son* expresses on the divine side his mediating function between 'the Fount of Divinity' and humanity. That such a mediator was, and needed to be, human is hardly an issue in modern christological thinking, and we shall spend little time on it. The fact of Christ's humanity is not in question; and if humanity's need of redemption is at all admitted, then assent will now certainly be given to the principle formulated by Gregory Nazianzen in an anti-apollinarian context: 'What Christ had not assumed he would not have healed' [note 162]. We have already noted the importance of Jesus as our human forerunner into the presence of God.

The second question is: is Christ the *only* mediator in the sense which has emerged? The Christian tradition has no difficulty in allowing that God has revealed himself, in some sense and to some degree, through other people than Jesus, at different times and places. It admits this for the people of the Old Testament and would claim it for the history of the Church. In both cases, some kind of reference is made to Christ. With regard to the Old Testament, the divine revelation will be understood as a typological anticipation of the coming Christ or as the work of the pre-existent Christ [note 163]. With regard to the history of the Church, God's revelation through the lives of the saints will be through lives lived 'in Christ', lives in which 'Christ lives'. Where Christians have found a saving presence and action of God in people living in other religious and cultural traditions than the biblical, they have usually kept the christological reference in play in some way [note 164]. Justin Martyr already recognized as Christians *avant la lettre* those Greeks who had lived 'according to the Logos' [note 165]. Now K. Rahner speaks of 'anonymous Christians', and R. Panikkar of 'the unknown Christ of Hinduism' [note 166]. The claim of the johannine Christ that 'no one comes to the Father but by me', and even the cyprianic dictum 'no salvation outside the Church', are given an inclusive rather than an exclusive sense. John Hick, however, would consider such claims to be acts of Christian imperialism [note 167]. In his new map of the universe of faiths, it is *God*, in the strict sense, who is at the centre; Christ is no longer the *unique* mediator but is joined by other figures from the world religions. It is noticeable that Hick's own view of humanity, sin and salvation does not appear to require an 'objective' work of redemption after the manner of most theories of the atonement in Christian theology. In Hick's theodicy, *Evil and the God of Love*, humanity was 'created as a fallen being', sin is thereby de-radicalized, and God is exculpated through his provision of universal salvation in the end [note 168]. Hick's view of human history as the opportunity to discover God by faith and to grow in love towards him does, however, leave room for an abelardian view of the atonement. This would also, incidentally, strengthen his theodicy in so far as God himself is seen, in the perspective indicated above, to love humanity to the point of suffering and death. In this way, too, the road may be opened to an understanding of Christ as mediator which maintains the deep-rooted Christian insistence on Christ's uniqueness while yet avoiding the dangers of both culture-bound exclusivism and imperialistic inclusivism. We will try to put it as follows.

Christians may look upon Jesus Christ as the *ultimate* revelation of God in the sense that Christ loved humanity 'to the end', that is, unto death [note 169]. There *is* no greater love than to lay down one's life for . . . one's enemies (cf. Romans 5:6–10). Such is the divine love. *Wherever* self-giving love is shown by human beings in any degree at all, God must be said to be present in the transformation of human character into God's own moral and spiritual likeness. There *redemption* is happening, as people are being set free from self-regard and self-interest. There *salvation* is being tasted, for salvation is precisely growth into that self-giving which is also God's character and which is exercised in communion between God and humanity and among human beings. No matter where they see manifestations of self-giving love, Christians cannot avoid seeing reflexions of Christ, for it is in the case of Christ that they see this pattern displayed with such primordial clarity and such final intensity that this person becomes the focal point of reference for all other instances. This view of the matter would claim for Christ a uniqueness of the pattern-setting or criteriological kind, transcending the 'exclusive/inclusive' or 'culture-bound/imperialist' alternatives. It would certainly allow Christians to continue seeing Christ as the mediator of all God's blessings to them in revelation and redemption, and of their own worship to God. It may even be possible to say that every human life lived, every deed performed, every prayer offered in a spirit of self-giving love, is lived, performed and offered 'after the character of Christ'. 'After the character of Christ' captures at least part of the rich meaning of the biblical and traditional phrase 'in the name of Christ' [note 170]. Even where the name of Christ is not confessed, it may be legitimate for Christians to see lives and deeds and prayers taken up by Christ into his own offering to the Father—and that without impugning the human authenticity of persons who are living within other religious and cultural traditions than the Christian.

It might be said that the function of Christian worship *within the world* is to bear symbolic witness to the Christ-pattern. In so far as the Christ-pattern impresses itself upon human life, the kingdom of God is being established. Consequently, the witness which authentic Christian worship makes before the world is itself doxological. I want now to develop the notion of Christ as the pattern for worship and therefore for life. The notion of Christ as pattern will help towards an understanding of God's way of dealing with humanity, and we shall then be able to draw some conclusions

6

concerning the objections of the 'doctrinal critics' against interventionism.

4. *Pattern for worship*

The nearest traditional equivalent to the notion of pattern as I want to develop it is the notion of sacrament. In traditional usage, the predominant linguistic location of the word sacrament is the cult: sacraments, in the plural, is a general name given to a number of regularly observed liturgical rites whose basic features remain recognizably constant amid considerable variation in the manner of overall performance. They are distinguished from less important rituals by their closer connexion with Christ: he is seen in one way or another as their author, their minister or even their content. On the one side, then, the notion of sacrament opens out to Christ himself. On the other side, the notion of sacrament opens out to the whole life and destiny of the Christian, the Church, and all humanity: by word, gesture and the use of natural elements or cultural artefacts, the various sacraments show forth the character of Christian existence in the present and give promise of what may be hoped for in the future by all who respond to the divine vocation. The sacraments may therefore be seen as the ritual expression of a pattern which is set by Christ and whose intended scope is nothing less than the universal divine kingdom.

In a widely influential book first published in 1953, Edward Schillebeeckx turned what had become the primarily *ritual* category of sacrament into a major concept for *christology* [note 171]. The Flemish Dominican presented Christ himself as the great, original, primary Sacrament (*Ursakrament*), the personal embodiment of the meeting between God and humanity. The mystery of God, or God's design for all humanity, had been made flesh in Jesus Christ. The active incorporation of individual human beings into that mystery, or the realization of that design on a widening scale, now takes place in the Church through the sacraments. 'Sacrament' is in fact the Latin equivalent of *mysterion*, which is both a New Testament word for God's ultimate purpose and also the term used in the Greek tradition for baptism, eucharist

and the rest. In all this, Schillebeeckx was developing a line
of thought that had been present in the Fathers. Witness
the dictum of Leo the Great: *quod Redemptoris nostri conspicuum
fuit in sacramenta transivit*, what was revealed in our Redeemer
has passed over into the sacraments [note 172]. This line of
thought had also been implied whenever theologians appealed
either to the person of Christ, in order to understand the
relation between God and man in the sacraments, or to the
sacraments, usually the eucharist, in order to understand
the relation between God and man in the person of Christ
[note 173]. But it is precisely at this point that questions
arise. Schillebeeckx's use of the category of sacrament to
link Christ, the Church and the Christian is undoubtedly
attractive and stimulating, but it must be asked whether a
single category may properly subsume what may in fact be
rather different relationships or 'meetings' between God and
humanity in Christ, the Church, the Christian, and the
sacraments respectively. It would, for example, be possible
to detect a common *tendency* in all of the following: a chalcedonian christology interpreted from the alexandrine side
[note 174], a lofty ontological view of the Church as an
'extension of the incarnation', a high doctrine of the transforming work of grace in a humanity destined for divinization,
and a transubstantiationist understanding of the eucharist;
and this *tendency* is in fact present in Schillebeeckx. Yet an
orthodox Roman Catholic, and Schillebeeckx certainly intended to be that, must also *distinguish*, in essence and not
merely in degree, between the 'unique' hypostatic union of
divinity and humanity in Christ, on the one hand, and the
meeting between God and humanity in the Church, the
Christian or the sacraments, on the other [note 175]. It might
be that a more adoptionist view would allow for greater
consistency all along the line: the man Jesus was 'taken up'
into the purposes of God in fundamentally the same way—
even though he alone, so far, is perfect in degree—as God
intends for all humanity, and indeed for the whole material
creation (of whose final destiny the use of the elements in
the sacraments is a pledge). Yet in that case, the objection
may be forcefully made that the christology does not do

justice to the radical self-engagement of God with and in the world, to which the traditional incarnational doctrine of Christ gives expression. I myself judge that a 'high' doctrine of the incarnation, *kenotically* conceived, is in fact the best safeguard against anthropological or ecclesiological triumphalism: God gives himself in order to bring us to self-giving [note 176].

A further complication in the use of the category of sacrament lies in the fact that the Christian tradition has lacked unanimity as to which rites should be included in this general class. The Eastern churches have commonly been reluctant to specify a number or give a definition. The Roman tradition sticks by the list drawn up at the Second Council of Lyons in 1274: baptism, confirmation, penance, eucharist, ordination, marriage, unction of the sick. Protestants have usually limited the name of sacrament to those two which appear most clearly from the gospels to have been instituted by Christ: baptism and the Lord's supper or eucharist. Even if the list is restricted to those two, and Roman Catholics have been willing to consider baptism and eucharist as the 'principal' or 'major' sacraments [note 177], the manner of Christ's presence and activity is usually understood differently in baptism on the one hand and in the eucharist on the other. Except perhaps in the Zwinglian tradition, Christ has been held to be more intimately present and active in the sacrament of eating and drinking than in the sacrament of washing; his relation to the bread and wine is more 'internal' than his relation to the water [note 178]. The variety will be even greater if the other 'sacraments' are included. In view of this variety, different conclusions can be read back upon the person and work of Christ if the sacraments are taken as clues to christology and soteriology. I myself welcome the variety afforded by the sacramental models for christology and soteriology. In the area of soteriology [note 179], the various sacraments allow expression to varied views of humanity's nature, predicament and destiny and, correspondingly, of Christ's redeeming work. In the area of christology, the various sacraments allow expression to varied views of the whole relation between God and humanity, and particu-

larly of the case of the one whom Christians have confessed
as the God-Man. Sometimes the variety is evidence of a rich
and harmonious complexity. Where, however, the variety
bespeaks tension and even contradiction among views, the use
of the traditional sacraments as models allows us to keep our
anthropological, christological and soteriological options open,
while yet remaining within the recognizably Christian tradition.

Let us now therefore run briefly through various instances
of the Christ-pattern as this has come to expression in the
principal rites of the Church. It should be said at the outset
that it matters little whether these rites, or which of them,
are called sacraments on any precise definition of a category.
The question of dominical institution has been re-opened on
two fronts: first, by the modern critical debate on the historicity of the 'institution narratives' of (even) baptism and the
eucharist [note 180]; and second, by the willingness of modern
exegesis to see baptismal and eucharistic reflexions in other
words and deeds reported of Jesus in the gospels (and if
baptism and eucharist can be grounded in this wider way
in the gospel texts, judgment being reserved on the historicity
of particular instances [note 181], then the case becomes stronger
for allowing, say, a sacrament of healing the same sort of
dominical backing). The important thing is that the rites of the
Church should display in certain vital respects the Christ-
pattern of the relation and dealings between God and humanity
to which the fundamental scriptural documents bear witness.

(a) *Baptism* [note 182]. The profoundest significance of
baptism is expressed in St Paul's interpretation of it in the
Letter to the Romans as entrance into Christ's death and
resurrection. Baptism's proper result and counterpart in the
continuing existence of the believer is, according to St Paul,
death to sin and the living of a life of righteousness unto
God (6:1–23). Its christological and soteriological pre-
supposition is Christ as the representative man who lived to
the end a life of perfect obedience towards God (5:12–23).
Yet this one man who broke the otherwise universal reign of
sin and death could himself only be the gift of the loving
God to humanity, 'his Son' (5:6–11). Moreover, the new life
that now comes to believers 'in Christ' is itself a free gift of

God. Hence baptism can only be received (baptismal verbs are often in the passive voice in the New Testament). Yet the gift must be actively appropriated: hence the active ethical imperatives which St Paul grounds upon baptism. Baptism as the sacrament of death and resurrection thus symbolizes the radical reorientation and transformation which humanity needs, which only God can bring about, and which humanity must then make its own [note 183]. The next most powerful strand of baptismal language in the New Testament centres on regeneration or rebirth. Again, it is a change which God must operate *for us*, and yet which opens into a new life which *we* must actively live. The new life can be described in terms of 'sonship' to God: Christ turns out to be 'the firstborn of many brethren' (Romans 8:29f), believers become *filii in Filio* (cf. John 3:3–7; Romans 8:14–17; Galatians 3:26ff; Titus 3:4–7), and many sons will thus have been brought to glory (Hebrews 2:10). Christ, as the *pattern-setter*, needed to be human, if human beings were to be able to follow him in his obedience to God; yet as the *pattern-setter*, he must have been in some profound sense the gift of God, if the divine self-giving love was to communicate itself to humanity and to start transforming human beings into its own likeness.

(b) *Confirmation* [note 184]. The emergence of confirmation as an independent sacrament in the Western Church is a complicated and adventitious affair, and the vicissitudes of its later history suggest that confirmation has remained a rite in search of a meaning. The commonest idea in the Western Catholic tradition has been that confirmation is a strength-giving unction of the Spirit. Combative imagery has been associated with it in order to express either resistance to evil or courage in witness. From the New Testament there is evidence that St Paul pictured the Christian as engaged in 'fighting the good fight' (Romans 8:37; 1 Corinthians 9:26; Ephesians 6:10ff; 1 Timothy 6:12; 2 Timothy 4:7). At the christological and soteriological level, this corresponds to that *Christus victor* view of the work of Christ, the importance of which Gustav Aulén has taught us to recognize in the New Testament and in the history of Christian thought

[note 185]. Just as the fight against sin and evil is ours to
fight and yet we cannot win without the strength of God, so
in the primordial victory of Christ on the cross we see the
battle of 'the proper Man', who was at the least the one 'whom
God himself had bidden', and perhaps even 'the Lord Sabaoth's
Son'. For it may be that no less than God's personal Word was
and remains needed in order to fell the enemy [note 186].

(c) *Penance* [note 187]. The First Letter of John enunciates
the principle that 'no one born of God commits sin' (3:9),
yet the same epistle realistically admits that Christians do in
fact commit sin (1:8f; 2:1). For St Paul, sin stands in such
contradiction to the baptismal life that he can only express
his perplexity through the rhetorical questions of a *reductio
ad absurdum* rebuke (Romans 6:1ff; 1 Corinthians 1:10–13),
yet Luther was not entirely wrong to find in Paul the recognition that even the justified believer remains in this life a
sinner. The early Church had the greatest difficulty in coming
to terms with the need to restore the lapsed. The Letter to the
Hebrews had declared that 'it is impossible to restore again
to repentance those who have once been enlightened, if they
then commit apostasy' (6:4–6) [note 188]. Gradually, however,
a system evolved whereby the gravity of the sin committed
was matched by the penance to be done and by the period of
excommunication to be suffered. Eventually, the sacrament of
penance emerged as the regular means of dealing with post-
baptismal sin in the life of every Christian. Although the
Protestant churches have rejected sacramental penance
(Luther at first retained it), their services of worship nevertheless include the confession of sin. The soteriological
themes to which penance bears witness are forgiveness and
reconciliation. In the restoration of communion between
God and sinning humanity, the initiative lies with God's
forgiveness: Jesus 'blasphemously' pronounced the divine
forgiveness, and the scribes' question 'Who can forgive sins
but God alone?' is a piece of ironic christology (Mark 2:1–12);
the stories of Jesus' sharing table-fellowship with sinners
are the evangelists' counterpart to St Paul's 'God was in
Christ reconciling the world to himself' (2 Corinthians 5:18f).
The sacrificial language used in connexion with re'onciliation

in this and other passages has seemed to some to conflict with the idea of God's free forgiveness which precedes any move from the human side. Yet must it surely be admitted that the restoration of relationships requires not only forgiveness on the part of the offended but also the penitent willingness to be forgiven on the part of the offender. Thus R. C. Moberly interpreted the sacrifice of Christ in terms of the offering of perfect penitence by Jesus as the inclusive representative of all humanity [note 189]. The notion of inclusive representation responds to the need for a universal objective atonement. Some theologians will find this difficult and unnecessary, but certainly God's forgiveness comes alive for every sinner when he turns to God in penitence. The sign and effect of our willingness to be forgiven by God is our willingness to forgive others: the prayer 'Forgive us our trespasses as we forgive those who trespass against us' implies that the lesson of the parable of the unforgiving servant has been learnt (Matthew 18:21–35). To forgive those who have wounded us is to grow into the moral and spiritual likeness of God. 'Be merciful, even as your Father is merciful' (Luke 6:35–38): that is a translation of 'perfection' (compare Matthew 5:48 in its context).

(d) *Unction of the sick* [note 190]. The gospels present Jesus as a healer. He ordered his apostles to heal the sick (Matthew 10:1, 8; Luke 9:1f, 10:9). The primitive Church continued to do so 'in his name' (Acts 3:1–10; 4:30; 5:14–16; 28:8f; 1 Corinthians 12:9, 28, 30; cf. Mark 16:18). The Letter of James speaks of an anointing of the sick which accompanies prayer by the elders (5:14–16). The Orthodox and Catholic churches practise a sacramental unction of the sick; Pentecostals and others pray for sick persons with the laying on of hands; all churches include the sick in their intercessions. Two points of soteriological and christological importance may be made in this connexion. First, the gospels see sickness as a sign of the human predicament, and healing as a sign of salvation. In any given context, the verb *sōzō* may carry resonances of both 'to heal' and 'to save'. Eschatological salvation can be presented as 'the healing of the nations' (Revelation 22:2). Second: although Jesus apparently con-

sidered the healings which he performed to be signs of the
messianic kingdom of salvation (Matthew 11:2–6), their
performance was not restricted to himself; they constituted
a pattern into which his followers could actively enter. Hence
the early record of healings 'in the name of Jesus' (e.g.
Acts 3:6); hence also the continuing sacramental and medical
work of the Church [note 191]. In the light of the significance
with which Christ invested healing, it is possible to read *all*
healing, whatever the human instrumentality, as a sign of
the divine kingdom, evidence of God at work to achieve
his salvific intention for humanity.

(e) *Orders* [note 192]. Ordination is essentially to ministry.
Wherever the leaders in the Church have domineered over
their fellow Christians, they have failed to follow the pattern
of their common Lord who exercised his sovereignty in free
service. 'Whoever would be first among you must be slave of
all. For the Son of Man also came not to be served but to
serve' (Mark 10:42–45). 'Let the greatest among you become
as the youngest, and the leader as one who serves. For which
is the greater, one who sits at table, or one who serves? Is it
not the one who sits at table? But I am among you as one
who serves' (Luke 22:24–27). 'If I then, your teacher and
lord, have washed your feet, you also ought to wash one
another's feet. For I have given you an example, *hypodeigma*,
that you also should do as I have done to you' (John 13:12ff).
Whatever redemptive uniqueness may be attributed to Jesus
when he is seen as a 'ransom for many' (Mark 10:45b) [note
193], his giving of himself for others appears in the gospels
as a *pattern* for his followers. The vocation of the ordained
ministry is to be a personal reminder to the whole Church
of the mutual service to which all the followers of Jesus are
called. That is the value in the Roman Catholic notion of
ordination as 'conformation' to Christ, although the value
of that notion diminishes whenever it is forgotten that the
special calling of the ordained ministry is precisely to lead *all*
the baptized into growing conformity to Christ. Freedom
for the selfless service of God and of fellow human beings
is the true liberation which following Jesus brings.

(f) *Marriage* [note 194]. There has always been an obvious

problem when dominical institution has been sought for the sake of the sacramental status of marriage. The better way is to notice how first the Old Testament dignifies marriage by using it to illustrate the relationship between God and his people, and then the New Testament goes even further by proposing, in return, the relationship between Christ and his Church as the model for the relationship between husband and wife (Ephesians 5:21–33). While superficially the passage in Ephesians might be used to buttress male superiority, its most profound point is the responsibility which each marriage partner must exercise towards the other if they are to emulate the self-giving love of Christ; the forms of that responsibility may vary with the culture. The couple is the basic unit of socially constituted humanity, and Christ thus sets the pattern for proper personal relationships within it. The immediate extension of that pattern in time concerns the relationships between parents and children, and again the Letter to the Ephesians shows mutual responsibility in love to be the order of the day, if attitudes and behaviour are to be 'in the Lord' (6:1–4). The way for humanity to attain the vocation implied in its constitution as social being is the way of the self-giving love displayed in Christ.

(g) *Eucharist* [note 195]. The eucharist has been reserved until last, because it has traditionally been considered the crown of the sacraments, and it brings together many of the subjects associated in a particular way with the other rites [note 196]. The themes of the great eucharistic prayer indicate both creation and redemption as the gifts of God to humanity, and its form precisely as thanksgiving expresses the proper human response. The bread and wine of the communion are the present concretion of God's gifts of creation and redemption, and our acceptance of them commits us to living according to what may be called an ethic of gratitude (see chapter XII). In the eucharistic prayer, Christ appears as God's supreme gift to us, 'his own Son' [note 197]; and, in response, the eucharistic prayer itself is a memorial thank-offering for that gift of Christ *in illo tempore*. In the communion, Christ comes to us again as God's gift *hic et nunc* and we are enabled in response to offer ourselves to God, in the terms of the old Anglican prayer of oblation, as a 'reasonable, holy and lively sacrifice' (cf. Romans 12:1). From the side of God, Christ appears as the most personal of all God's gift's to us, and it is in his light that we are able to discern all the other benefaction of God towards us. Perhaps this is the best existential interpretation of the New Testament notion of creation 'through Christ' and the Roman canon's *per quem haec omnia, Domine, semper bona creas, sanctificas, vivificas, benedicis, et praestas nobis* [note 198]. From the side of humanity, Christ's total surrender of himself in love towards God and towards friend, neighbour and enemy ('Father, forgive them') defines a movement into which we may enter—and must, if we are to fulfil the human vocation to communion with God and among ourselves. Our self-identification with this movement of Christ's is the best existential translation of traditional liturgical phrases concerning our offering Christ (the *offerimus* of the eucharistic oblation). Whatever may be the case with Jesus' self-sacrifice understood as meeting the need for a universal objective atonement, it is obvious that atonement becomes effective in the lives of other human beings only when they give themselves to God and to the achievement of his purpose for humanity.

In our discussion of christology in sacramental terms, and then of the sacraments themselves, we have had at the back of our mind the whole question of God's relationship to the world and to humanity and his manner of dealing with them. In particular, we have been aware of the difficulties which many modern theologians find with an interventionist understanding of God's action. The final section of this chapter will now take up these questions and difficulties explicitly.

5. *God's presence and action in the world*

Upon further consideration, it might appear that the difficulty of many modern theologians over interventionism was a difficulty of their own making. Having removed God from the world and set him in a somewhat deistic relation to it, they are then obliged to see any alleged 'post-creational' action of God in respect of the world as 'intervention'. This they reject as both unworthy of a perfect Creator and, nearer

the bone, incompatible with 'the modern scientific view'.
It was, in fact, largely the elevation to *dogmatic* status of the
methodological concentration of the sciences on secondary
causes (as they were called on an older view), which led to
the removal of God from the world in the first place. The
case of R. Bultmann is typical, and is particularly interesting
for us in so far as the sacraments are mentioned in his argument. In the name of 'the modern scientific world-view',
Bultmann dismisses the sacraments, at least as they appear
to him to have been anciently conceived: that is, as 'magical
forces', 'influences upon God', 'material means of feeding
man's spiritual life' [note 199]. But the difficulty he has in
defining the meaning of God as acting in respect of humanity
without intervention in the chain of natural, historical and even
psychological events is such that he rarely returns to the
sacraments in order to give them a positive re-interpretation.
Other theologians, however, have questioned whether 'the
modern "scientific" world-view' is a philosophically necessary
consequence of a proper regard for the natural sciences. Such
diverse examples may be mentioned as the Process Theology
deriving from A. N. Whitehead [note 200], or T. F. Torrance's
Theological Science [note 201], or J. Macquarrie's plea for a
more 'organic' view of the relations between God and the
world [note 202].

The underlying question for theology is the classical
question of the *concursus divinus* [note 203]. The Chalcedonian
Definition recognized a *concursus* between the divine and
human natures of Christ (*suntrechontes*). On a wider scale,
it is a matter of the relative autonomy of humanity and the
world. The freedom of the creature is required for personhood
(what 'freedom' might mean for other than intelligent and
moral creatures, say sub-atomic particles, is not our immediate
concern; but the Christian cannot ultimately divorce any
level of creation from the purposes of God, and humanity has
a part to play, at least as far as its earthly habitat is concerned),
and yet the creation must continue to depend on God, who has
indeed his purposes for it and is generally supposed by Christians
to be in some sense 'leading' his creatures to the goals he
intends for them. How are we to conceive the concursive

operation between God and humanity? Or, in terms which, superficially at least, stress presence rather than action: it is the question of the transcendence and the immanence of God.

In this connexion, Ninian Smart offers some linguistic considerations that will clear the decks for an attempt to draw help from our previous discussion of the sacraments as we now search for ways of conceiving the presence and action of God in the world. He writes [note 204]:

> The main sense that one can give to the thought that God has a place in some sense 'beyond' the cosmos is that he exists, without spatial predicates attaching to him, in such a way that he is different from the cosmos and 'behind' it—that is, the force which makes and sustains it, so that from this point of view the doctrine of transcendence is strongly connected to the doctrine of creation. The idea, however, has a consequence, which is not immediately apparent. Since it involves treating 'behind' and 'beyond' as spatial analogies and not as literal places, the *trans-* which introduces the concept of transcendence must suffer the same fate. Its Latin origin has no magical properties to defend it. Then one begins to ask a question or two about the supposedly contrasted idea of immanence. I realise that loosely the immanent refers to the particularities through which God manifests himself, while the transcendent represents the way in which God lies beyond these particularities. But leaving aside this so to say 'vulgar' contrast between the two ideas, and considering the other contrast sometimes attempted—where the immanent refers to God's working in the world, e.g. through his preserving power, providentiality and so on—then one asks whether the distinction between this sense of the term and transcendence can be maintained. The reason is a simple one and can be put simply and crudely thus: When you say that God is in all things and when you say that God is beyond or behind all things, you appear to be saying two different things; but how can you be, considering that 'in', 'behind' and 'beyond' are analogical, not literal? . . . Thus there is no strong reason to differentiate between transcendence and immanence. Indeed there are some reasons of a doctrinal sort to encourage the identification of the two locations of God: for instance, because God's creative activity is not confined to his being there at the moment of creation; but he is present at the continuous creation of the world every day and every minute

working thus in all things. . . . Inasmuch as God is a dynamic being his presence means work, and his being present everywhere thus means that he is working everywhere.

Couple with that Smart's point that the omnipresent God may also be 'multipresent', and 'present in varying degrees', in 'degrees of special presence': and one has a religious-philosophical basis upon which to learn the lessons of the sacraments in order to avoid the kind of interventionism which has helped to render the notion of incarnation unacceptable to some modern theologians [note 205].

If, then, God intervenes, he intervenes not as a stranger to his own creation, but 'from within'. Standing on that general basis, we may develop from our discussion of the sacraments two more particular points which take us even further towards a more acceptable conception of God's presence and action than that of naïve interventions *ab extra.* The first point is that the sacraments are *interpersonal events,* meetings between God and humanity for the purpose of advancing the communion with God to which humanity is called by God as its destiny [note 206]. The sacraments are thus not capricious interferences by divine powers, such as seem to be envisaged when Bultmann apparently rejects them as irretrievably mythological. They are rather the 'appointed ways' (that is what lies behind the traditional concern for their dominical institution [note 207]) by which the permanent cause of God and humanity is furthered. They express the pattern of God's set purpose of communion between humanity and himself, and in so doing they promote its success. That is precisely what Jesus, the *Ursakrament,* did; and there is no need to understand the presence and action of God in a more crudely interventionist way in his case than in the case of the sacraments. The greater the *personal* character of God's presence and action, the more in fact the problem of God's self-involvement is eased. Notice, then, the personal character of the functions performed both in the case of Jesus and in the case of the sacraments: giving, redeeming, saving, regenerating, enlightening, strengthening, forgiving, reconciling, healing, serving, loving, offering.

The action of God is, then, to be conceived *within* an

existing relationship, namely the enduring relationship between God and a world which continues to depend on God as its creator and for which God has a purpose. Here we arrive at the second point which the sacraments may contribute. They enable us to conceive of God's action less in spatial terms ('intervention') and more in terms of values. The definitive values are those of the divine kingdom, which is also human salvation: love, peace, justice, joy. . . . In the sacraments, present realities are evaluated in relation to the ultimate values—and are either rejected, or purified, or affirmed, or enhanced, or transformed, in the sacramental action. Thus all that is 'sin' is 'put behind' in baptism and penance. The anointing of the sick is the sacrament of restoration to health. Ordination reinterprets authority as service. In marriage, human love is affirmed and socially constituted humanity is shown the demands of its calling to mutual responsibility. In the eucharist, we experience the enhancement of all that the body of believers have so far learnt in the way of positive human community, the right use of the earth's resources, and saving fellowship with God. In all sacramental action, God is present to transform into his own moral and spiritual likeness those who consent to the values of his kingdom. The sacraments are but focal instances within the continuing relationship between God and his creatures which is directed towards God's kingdom. As effective displays of the ultimate values, neither they nor Jesus himself as the *Ursakrament* require a divine intervention 'from without': they occur *within* a continuing goal-directed personal relationship between God and humanity.

Within the framework of such a conception of God's presence and action in relation to the world, there is still room for a variety of views on the respective parts played by God and by humanity in the achievement of their common cause of divine rule and human salvation. This variety shows itself in the answers given to two classical and related questions. The first is the question of grace and freedom [note 208]. All answers here should fall within the limits of the following principle: In the one direction, human freedom is most truly expressed in the service of God; in the other direction (and this is really the primary movement), divine grace is most truly itself when it is enabling human freedom. God is both the source and goal of human freedom. When God and humanity are thus not conflicting but concurring, any thought of competition between them is out of place [note 209]. Both extreme augustinianism and full pelagianism are thereby excluded [note 210], but there is room for a variety of accents in between. With the exception of baptism as administered to infants, all the sacraments bring into play both divine grace and human freedom: the variety of the possible interplay between divine grace and human freedom is reflected in the variety of the sacraments, ranging perhaps from a strong emphasis on divine grace in the sacrament of healing to a strong emphasis on human freedom in the case of marriage [note 211].

The second question centres on the presence and work of the Holy Spirit in the believer. The matter may be put in terms of the medieval debate on sanctification. One tendency favoured the simple identification which Peter Lombard made between the indwelling Holy Spirit and charity: 'The Holy Spirit is the love or charity by which we love God and the neighbour.' The other tendency went towards the separation between the Holy Spirit and his gifts which Abelard countenanced. The high scholastics sought a middle way with their notion of 'created grace': as *forma transformans*, the Holy Spirit produces in man a *forma transformata* (so the *Summa Halensis*). While approving this last solution to the problem, a modern study by G. Philips prefers to express the central position in terms of 'participation', an idea which the author considers to be at once more biblical (e.g. 2 Corinthians 13:13; 1 John 1:3; 2 Peter 1:4), more patristic and more supple [note 212]. Philips is concerned to avoid the *chosification* of grace and to preserve the fully personal character of the believer's relation to God: adoptive sonship to the Father through a growing conformity with the Son produced and enabled by the Spirit. After our previous discussion it will not be difficult to see baptism as the sacrament of the start of this relationship and eucharistic communion as the sacrament of its continuance and progress.

It remains to ask whether these two issues—of grace and

freedom, and of sanctification—cast any light on christology. Certainly D. M. Baillie found in the—paradoxical—experience of grace the clue to christology (1 Corinthians 15:10 was his scriptural text) [note 213]. I should myself wish to exploit christologically the variety of ways in which grace and freedom, or the process of sanctification, are experienced and understood by Christians. Provided both God and humanity are all along kept in concursive play, there is nothing to be regretted in the *tensions* which have characterized the history of reflexion on Christ and salvation: adoptionism *versus* incarnation, the antiochene *versus* the alexandrine school of christology, the pelagian stress on human freedom *versus* the augustinian emphasis on divine grace, true humanization *versus* divinization as the destiny of humanity in the purpose of God. Such tensions in understanding are probably inevitable as long as we creatures have not yet arrived at the fulness of communion with himself to which our Creator calls us. The tensions keep us open to the future and their resolution [note 214]. Christians have always believed that in Jesus Christ himself that future was already present: he was the image of God both from the side of God and from the side of humanity, both the true revelation of God among humanity and the true human response to the divine vocation, God-in-man and man-in-God (as P. Schoonenberg might say).

With an approach from the divine side, W. R. Matthews 'dynamized' the notion of image into that of a 'moving pattern' [note 215]:

> I contend then that there is no contradiction or absurdity in holding that the moving pattern of the will of God could be also the moving pattern of the behaviour-events which constitute the temporal and historical aspects of a human life. The scale on which the pattern is manifested makes no essential difference. A personal life of which it could be said that it is of the same pattern as the temporal will of God would be the supreme revelation of God; it would be God manifest 'in the flesh'.

A complementary approach 'from below' would present the 'moving pattern' of Jesus' life as the proper human *response* to God's purpose and invitation. The notion of 'moving pattern' happily combines two categories which have traditionally been employed both in christology and, more widely, in the whole matter of the relationship and dealings between God and humanity: Logos as meaning and coherence, and Spirit as energy and direction. Furthermore, the notion of 'moving pattern' can also be fittingly applied to ritual: the mental, verbal and dramatic signs of Christian worship are kinetic expressions of the constant purpose of God on its way to achievement among his responding creation.

   In the discussion of God, humanity and Christ, occasional mention has been made of the Spirit. It would have been possible to make the pneumatological dimension much more explicit, as will become evident when the Spirit is brought thematically to the fore in the next chapter. Because of the central place of Christ in Christianity and the corresponding importance of the theme of the present chapter, it may meanwhile be useful, by way of exception and emphasis, to summarize the position here preferred. First: God has given himself so personally to the world in Jesus that Jesus may be considered, in trinitarian terms, as the second person of the Godhead incarnate, 'the Son' in human form. He is rightly the object of worship. Worship is addressed to him primarily in his divinity. Because the man Jesus is inseparable from God, he may be the object of worship even in his humanity. Indeed the worship of him as a human being points to the value which God has set on the human race as the object of his creating and saving love. Second: Jesus Christ, the same yesterday, today and for ever, mediates God's blessing to us. It is through his remembered, experienced and anticipated presence, concentrated in worship, that God reaches us. Jesus embodies not only the divine initiative but also the human response, not only God's grace but also man's freedom. He prays for us and includes the motion of our attempted self-offering in his own. For, third: the God who made us without ourselves will not save us without ourselves [note 216]. God enables us from within actively to follow the pattern of the self-giving which Jesus revealed the divine nature to be and whose reciprocation he exemplified from the human side in a creative anticipation of our final destiny.

III

Spirit

1. *Broad and narrow uses*

SPIRIT is one of the most subtle words in the Bible, in Christian thinking, and indeed in the languages of all cultures that have been marked by the Christian tradition. Leaving aside secular and secularized uses of the word, there are two distinct but related areas of use which are of religious and theological importance in the Christian tradition. In the broader of these two, spirit is a characteristic or quality of both God and humanity. It appertains to God in the first place, and then to humanity in its openness to God. The background in the history of religions may well be animistic, dynamistic; and this is still the impression sometimes made by biblical and later Christian usage. But already in the Bible and then in the Christian usage a moral and personal content has also been given to the concept, so that it may now serve much the same function as the notion of humanity's being made in the image of God. A definite affinity between the divine Spirit and the human spirit is therefore assumed in Christian thought, the priority of the Spirit of God being always granted [note 217]. The variety and intricacy of the relations between God and humanity, all of which come to symbolic expression in the cult, are reflected in the complexity, ambiguity and, at worst, confusion of the broad religious and theological usage of our word.

The second and more restricted area of Christian use concerns the third person of the Trinity. In developed Christian doctrine, the Holy Spirit has been the name reserved for the third divine *hypostasis*. The development towards full trinitarianism was slower in the case of the third person than in the case of the second. In the latter case, the third-century shift from Word to Son as the major model [note 218] was symptomatic of a growing hypostatic distinction which had in any case been rendered easier from the start by the obviously 'personal' character of Jesus Christ. But just as the johannine 'only Son' developed into the full-blown 'God the Son', the nicene 'God from God', so also the johannine 'other Paraclete' eventually developed into 'the Holy Spirit, the Lord, the giver of life, who proceeds from the Father (and the Son), who with the Father and the Son together is worshipped and glorified' [note 219].

In the history of trinitarian thought, it is in the case of the Holy Spirit that the hesitation is most apparent between considering the divine *hypostaseis* as distinct 'modes of being', or even 'centres of consciousness', in God (immanent or essential trinitarianism) and considering them simply as God's 'modes of operation' towards creation (economic trinitarianism). The former tendency reaches its climax when worship or prayer is addressed to the distinctly or even separately named Holy Spirit, i.e. when the Holy Spirit is named as one of the Trinity or even without mention of the other persons. On the other hand, economic trinitarianism forswears more knowledge of God's being than is minimally required by the experience that he works within humanity for its sanctification. This practically amounts to a return to the broader usage of the divine Spirit in relation with the human spirit [note 220].

There has already been a hint at the close connexion between the doctrine of the Spirit and the place of the Spirit in worship. We now turn to a historical exploration of that connexion. Thereafter we shall look, from a liturgical angle, at the importance of pneumatology for a number of questions concerning the doctrines of salvation and the Church.

2. *New Testament evidence*

The Fourth Gospel records one saying which, if taken in isolation, is a clear instance of the broader use already mentioned. Jesus said to the Samaritan woman: 'God is Spirit, and those who worship him must worship in spirit and truth' (John 4:24). In general terms, this appears to be calling for an authentic use of the human capacity, itself no doubt God-given, to worship God. But the particular context is in fact strongly christological. Jesus claims to be the expected Messiah (v.25f), and the possibility of true worship is connected with his 'hour': 'The hour is coming, and now is, when the true worshippers will worship the Father in spirit and truth, for such the Father seeks to worship him' (v.23). In the Fourth Gospel, the 'hour' of Jesus is the hour of his crucifixion, which made possible the gift of the Spirit (7:39; ?19:30; 20:22). Just as Jesus himself was 'the truth' (14:6; compare his self-designation as 'the true bread', 'the true vine', and so on), so the Paraclete who comes after his exaltation is 'the Spirit of truth' (14:17; 15:26; 16:13) [note 221]. For St John, therefore, the sayings of 4:23f will already be oriented in the direction of the more precise pneumatology of 'the Holy Spirit'. It is the revelation brought by the Christ ('he will show us all things', 4:25), and the Spirit released by his death, which henceforth make possible the true worship which supersedes the worship offered either by the Samaritans on Mount Gerizim or even by the Jews in the Jerusalem Temple (4:19–22; cf. 2:13–22). In any theological evaluation of St John on the matter of true worship, we should have to allow for the Fourth Gospel's polemic against 'the Jews', at least of the generation which 'did not receive' the Messiah. We should need also to note St John's claim that Jesus is the sole way to the Father ('No one comes to the Father but by me', 14:6), a claim whose exclusive sound is qualified by the universally inclusive promise of 12:32; 'And I, when I am lifted up from the earth, will draw all men to myself.'

When St Paul is writing on ethical matters, it is not always easy for exegetes to decide whether his references to spirit merit a small or a capital S (compare, for example, translations of Romans 8:1–11). In such cases his language presupposes the most general use of the word to indicate the human potential for openness to God. In 1 Corinthians 2:9–13, the apostle draws an analogy which rather more precisely makes the divine Spirit and the human spirit constituent faculties of God and human beings respectively. The background to the analogy is the 'extension of personality' which, according to the biblical writers, can characterize not only human

beings but God [note 222]. St Paul may, however, be going
further in this passage: he appears to be edging towards what
A. W. Wainwright calls the characteristically Christian idea
of 'interaction' within the extended divine personality. When
that idea is fully developed, it means not only that the Spirit
may 'leave' God in order to bring revelation to us (such is
the main thrust of 1 Corinthians 2:9–13, and in this respect
the passage scarcely goes beyond Old Testament notions);
it means also that the Spirit may, as it were, join us on the
human side and 'interact' with 'God'.

Such is the picture in a worship passage which, whatever
the difficulties of detail, is clear in this main respect:

> The Spirit helps us in our weakness; for we do not know how to
> pray as we ought, but the Spirit himself intercedes for us with
> sighs too deep for words. And he who searches the hearts of men
> knows what is the mind of the Spirit, because the Spirit intercedes
> for the saints according to the will of God.
> (Romans 8:26f RSV) [note 223]

This picture may already be envisaged a few verses earlier,
where St Paul writes:

> When we cry, 'Abba! Father!' it is the Spirit himself bearing
> witness with our spirit that we are children of God. . . . (8:15f
> RSV)

The word cry, *krazomen*, is the word used for a solemn
proclamation, as made by the town-crier, and the reference
may therefore be to the public worship of the Church [note
224]. The same would be true if the other possible sense,
namely, 'violent shout', were to suggest the 'pentecostal'
assembly presupposed by 1 Corinthians 14. It appears, then,
that the witness of the Spirit is borne *before God*. (This particular interpretation of Romans 8:15f, which places the Spirit,
as in 8:26f, on our side of the dialogue with God, would of
course fail if it were thought necessary to translate *auto to
Pneuma sunmarturei tōi pneumati hēmōn*, as some have done,
by 'the Spirit himself bears witness *to* our spirit'.)

The general view of St Paul is certainly that the Spirit

enables our worship. The characteristic preposition is *en*: *in* or *by* the Spirit [note 225]. An alternative construction of Romans 8:15f to the one just given would probably provide an instance of this use:

> You have received the Spirit of sonship, *in which* we cry 'Abba! Father!' The Spirit himself bears witness. . . .

The fact that some translators may write 'spirit of sonship' with a small s serves to show that the work of the Spirit upon the human spirit is a transforming work. The Spirit in fact operates from first to last throughout the process of the gospel's coming, its reception and its confirmation in the believer; and that process is often presented in liturgical and sacramental terms. The preaching of the gospel comes 'in power *kai en Pneumati hagiōi*' (1 Thessalonians 1:5). The confession that Jesus is Lord is made *en Pneumati hagiōi* (1 Corinthians 12:3). It is *en heni Pneumati* that believers are baptized; and they are made to drink *hen Pneuma* (1 Corinthians 12:13) [note 226]. It is in or by (*en*) the Holy Spirit of God that we are sealed for the day of redemption (Ephesians 4:30; cf. 1:13f and 2 Corinthians 1:22) [note 227]. As a minister, *leitourgos*, of Jesus Christ, the apostle Paul sees his preaching of the gospel as a priestly service, *hierourgountos*, which makes the Gentiles into an acceptable offering sanctified *en Pneumati hagiōi* (Romans 15:16). It is *en heni Pneumati* that we have access through Christ to the Father (Ephesians 2:18). As we have seen and shall see again, this verse from Ephesians expresses exactly a classic pattern in the history of Christian worship.

Another classic pattern, however, will address worship to all three persons of the Trinity on the same footing. In the last chapter we investigated worship addressed to Christ. It must now be asked: Does the New Testament already provide examples of worship addressed *to the Spirit*? Two passages in St Paul demand consideration [note 228]. The first is:

> For we are the circumcision, who worship by the Spirit of God, and glory in Christ Jesus, and have no confidence in the flesh.
> (Philippians 3:3 RV)

Since in Greek the object of the verb *latreuein* is expressed in the dative case, it is possible to translate *hoi Pneumati Theou latreuontes* as 'who worship the Spirit of God'. Augustine, in *de Trinitate* I 13, took the text in that way. But when the whole context is borne in mind, the contrast which St Paul is making with 'the flesh' makes it preferable to construe the dative as a dative of instrument. The translation then runs: 'who worship by the Spirit of God' (as in the RV). Philippians 3:3 thus becomes a further example of the pauline teaching that the Spirit enables our worship. The RSV takes advantage of the weakly attested variant *Theōi* for *Theou* and translates 'who worship God in spirit'. Here, too, there must be the temptation to write 'Spirit' on account of the way in which the human spirit of believers is qualified by the Spirit (compare the hesitations about capitals in Romans 8:1–11 and John 4:23f). But we are brought no nearer to the Spirit as an *object* of worship [note 229].

In the other passage the argument is ethical but the imagery liturgical:

> Do you not know that your body is a temple of the Holy Spirit within you, which you have from God? You are not your own; you were bought with a price. So glorify God in your body.
>
> (1 Corinthians 6:19f, RSV)

For *doxasate dē ton Theon en tōi sōmati humōn* Augustine's Latin translation read *glorificate ergo Deum in corpore vestro*, and he interpreted this as 'glorify therefore the God in your body', i.e. 'the Holy Spirit which is in you' (*de Trinitate* I 13). The Latin allows 'in your body' to be taken as adjectival to God: '(the) God (which is) in your body'. But the original Greek will in fact support only an adverbial sense of instrument or location: glorify God 'with your body' or 'in your body' [note 230]. An earlier Latin reading might appear to support Augustine in his mistake: Marcion, Tertullian, the Old Latin manuscript g, and the Vulgate all have *glorificate ET POR-TATE Deum in corpore vestro*. But it can be clearly shown that this variant is due to scribal errors [note 231]. Once more, therefore, the examination proves negative. So we may conclude that there is no case in which the Spirit figures as an object of worship in the New Testament writings.

3. *Later developments*

Continuing now our historical exploration beyond the New Testament, we discover three distinct pneumatological patterns in worship. Two of them were already present in the New Testament. The third we have just failed to find there. As to the first: the use of Isaiah 11:2 in, say, confirmation kept alive the broad understanding whereby the affinity between the divine Spirit and the human spirit allowed communication between God and human beings and, consequently, the shaping of human character and conduct according to the divine model and purpose. The Spirit of the Lord is expected to act transformingly upon the spirit of the believer, so that it is difficult to decide whether to write a capital or a small s when the sevenfold gift is enumerated. Take, for instance, the confirmation prayers in the Anglican *Book of Common Prayer*:

> Strengthen them, we beseech thee, O Lord, with the Holy Ghost the Comforter, and daily increase in them thy manifold gifts of grace: the spirit of wisdom and understanding; the spirit of counsel and ghostly strength; the spirit of knowledge and true godliness; and fill them, O Lord, with the spirit of thy holy fear, now and for ever.

> Defend, O Lord, this thy child (servant) with thy heavenly grace, that he may continue thine for ever; and daily increase in thy Holy Spirit more and more, until he come unto thy everlasting kingdom.

In prayers of ordination also, the Spirit of God is expected to work with enabling effect upon the human spirit. The ancient Roman prayer at the ordination of bishops includes the following petitions [note 232]:

> Hallow them with the dew of heavenly unction. May it flow down, O Lord, richly upon their head; may it run down below the mouth; may it descend to the furthest parts of the whole body,

so that the power of thy Spirit may both fill them within and surround them without. Let there abound in them constancy of faith, purity of love, sincerity of peace.

And for presbyters:

Renew in their inward parts the spirit of holiness.

And for deacons:

Send upon them, O Lord, we beseech thee, thy Holy Spirit, through whom, faithfully accomplishing the work of ministering, they may be strengthened by the gift of thy sevenfold grace. Let the pattern of every virtue abound in them: discreet authority, unfailing modesty, purity of innocence, and the observance of spiritual discipline.

And finally a prayer at the ordination of a bishop, from the Leofric Missal used at Exeter in Anglo-Saxon times:

Let thy Holy Spirit, bestower of heavenly gifts, be with this man, so that, as that chosen teacher of the gentiles taught, he may be in justice not wanting, in kindness strong, in hospitality rich. . . .

As was already starting to happen in the New Testament writings, this work of God upon the human spirit is more or less clearly attributed to 'the Holy Spirit' in the sense of the third divine hypostasis [note 233].

In the second pneumatological pattern, the Holy Spirit is seen to be specifically the enabler of worship: worship takes place 'in the Holy Spirit'. Origen, it will be remembered, taught that worship and prayer should properly be addressed to the Father, through Christ, *in the Holy Spirit*. Those who attacked St Basil's use of a 'co-ordinated' form of the doxology —a matter to which we shall shortly return—were able to claim that the normal practice was to give praise to the Father through the Son *in the Holy Spirit*. The eucharistic prayer in Sarapion's *Euchologion* ends up: 'through your only-begotten Jesus Christ in holy Spirit'; and the prayer at the blessing of the font asks that the baptized may be enabled to worship according to that same pattern. Furthermore, J. A. Jungmann argued convincingly that the phrase *in unitate Spiritus Sancti* in the very ancient concluding doxology of the Roman canon is likewise to be understood along the lines of 'in the Holy Spirit' [note 234]. The precise thought is of the Spirit as the ground of the Church's unity (compare Ephesians 4:3; and early prayers occasionally mention the Church as the locus of doxology, as it appears in Ephesians 3:21). It is only in later Latin prayers that 'in the unity of the Holy Spirit' is construed, as by Fulgentius (†533), so as to make the 'reigning' Holy Spirit virtually a co-recipient of the doxology: 'through Jesus Christ your Son our Lord, who lives and reigns with you *in the unity of the Holy Spirit.* . . .' Jungmann demonstrated that the tendency to 'elevate' the Holy Spirit to the position of recipient of worship rather than its mere medium or locus was encouraged by anti-arian motives, just as it was felt necessary to make clear that Christ was not only a mediator of worship to the Father but also its proper recipient along with the Father.

It is again interesting to ask whether the tendency in modern liturgical revision to revert to an earlier pattern of pneumatology is to be explained as fidelity to scripture, liturgical antiquarianism, or a theological unease in the face of fully developed trinitarian doctrine. Notice, for instance, the concluding doxology of the Church of England's Series 3 eucharist [note 235]:

> With him (your Son, Jesus Christ our Lord), and in him, and through him, by the power of the Holy Spirit, with all who stand before you in earth and heaven, we worship you, Father Almighty, in songs of everlasting praise: Blessing and honour and glory and power be yours for ever and ever.   Amen.

If this is how worshippers conceive the activity in which they engage, it is clear that there is, in the traditional terms of doctrinal history, a certain element of 'subordinationism' in their faith. Subordinationism has never, of course, been simply equivalent to 'arianism'. Instead of framing the discussion in terms of the patristic debates, however, it may be better to see worship as once more inviting the theologians to re-think the doctrine of God. The matter is complicated by the fact that deliberate liturgical compositions are themselves the work of theologically self-conscious writers. More will be heard of this question in chapters VI, VIII and X.

Incidental mention has already been made of the third pneumatological pattern. This is the pattern whereby worship or prayer is addressed *to the Spirit*, whether with the other persons of the Trinity or separately. We shall investigate the former case first. It must be stated at once that the address of praise and glory to the three divine *hypostaseis* together in fact antedated the arian controversy. This is not, of course, to deny that anti-arian motives then greatly encouraged the development of the practice in contexts where it had not been customary. St Basil of Caesarea (†379) was accused by the Pneumatomachians of 'innovation' when he used a 'co-ordinated' form of doxology:

> Glory to God the Father with (*meta*) the Son with (*sun*) the Holy Spirit,

instead of the usual 'sub-ordinated' form with *dia* and *en* [note 236]. When he defends himself in his treatise *On the Holy Spirit*, it can hardly be said that all the precedents Basil quotes are persuasive, but two cases are particularly interesting [note 237]. The first dates back to St Denis of Alexandria in the middle of the third century, and the Egyptian connexion may not be unimportant in view of G. Kretschmar's thesis concerning the Sanctus, to which I shall come in a moment. The Alexandrian bishop concludes a letter to his Roman namesake thus:

> Having received from the presbyters who went before us a form and rule, we conclude our present letter to you with those same words by which we, like them, make our (eucharistic) thanksgiving: To God the Father and the Son our Lord Jesus Christ with (*sun*) the Holy Spirit be glory and might for ever and ever. Amen [note 238].

Many historians of the liturgy hold that it was in Egypt that the Sanctus was first introduced into the eucharistic prayer. G. Kretschmar has proposed that the Christian use of Isaiah's vision was an important factor in the origin and growth of trinitarian worship and doctrine [note 239]. The two seraphs of the prophetic vision were identified as the Son and the Spirit. At first they were both considered to be mediators of worship to the Father. Notice, for instance, Justin Martyr's statements that the president of the eucharist 'offers praise and glory to the Father of all in the name of the Son and of the Holy Spirit', and that 'we bless the Maker of all things through his Son Jesus Christ and through the Holy Spirit over all that we receive' [note 240]. But later, helped perhaps by the triple 'holy' of the Sanctus, they became co-ordinate recipients of worship with the Father.

The other interesting case in Basil is his report that the Christians of Mesopotamia were obliged on linguistic grounds to 'offer the doxology by the syllable "and"' [note 241]. This matches other Syrian evidence. Aphraates, who died shortly after 345, used that form: 'Praise and glory to the Father and his Son and his living and holy Spirit from the lips of all' [note 242]. Theodore of Mopsuestia testifies that Diodore and Flavian introduced a translation of the Syriac formula 'Glory to the Father and the Son and the Holy Spirit' into the Greek psalmody of Antioch about the year 350 [note 243]. There were anti-arian motives at work here, but the Syrian pattern is certainly earlier than the fourth century, and its origin cannot therefore reside in anti-arian polemic, no matter how convenient it may later have proved in that connexion. Already the third-century *Didascalia Apostolorum* suggests the pattern: 'We (the apostles) have fixed and determined that you shall worship God [the Father] almighty and Jesus, [his Son] the Christ, and the Holy Spirit' [note 244]. There are hints that the earliest Syrian understanding of eucharistic consecration depended on the naming of the threefold name. The Syriac Acts of Thomas read: 'Bread . . . we name the name of the Father over thee; we name the name of the Son over thee; we name the name of the Spirit over thee, the exalted name that is hidden from all' [note 245]; and

Narsai († about 502) still appears to attach some 'consecratory' importance to the eucharistic fraction accompanied by
the words 'In the name of the Father and the Son and the
Spirit' [note 246]. Syria provides also the earliest testimony
to the use of the threefold name as a declaratory formula in
baptism [note 247]. According to Kretschmar, it is the
baptismal use which will have given the example for other
liturgical uses. None of this is meant to imply that second
and third century Syrian Christians held a full-blown niceno-
constantinopolitan doctrine of the Trinity *avant la lettre*. It
simply shows the firm liturgical entrenchment of the pattern
of three divine names linked by 'and'. This was soil in which
doctrinal reflexion might thrive.

   In other places than Syria, the earliest use in baptism seems
to have consisted of three distinct questions put to the
candidates concerning their belief in God the Father, in
Jesus Christ his Son our Lord, and in the Holy Spirit; and
upon each affirmative response the candidates were, according
to the so-called *Apostolic Tradition* of Hippolytus, 'baptized'.
This baptismal co-ordination of the three divine names,
found already at Matthew 28:19, will have everywhere, and
not just in Syria, played an important part in shaping doctrinal
consciousness. M. F. Wiles writes of the second and third
centuries that 'when little theological interest was shown in
the person of the Spirit, it was the continuing fact of baptismal practice which did most to keep alive the idea of the
Holy Spirit as a third alongside the Father and the Son'; and
then: 'it is to the baptismal formula that we are continually
driven back as the supremely significant influence in the
development of the doctrine of the Spirit' [note 248]. Already
Tertullian cites the baptismal practice of three immersions,
one at each several name, as evidence of belief in three
distinct persons when he is arguing against the modalist
'Praxeas'. On the other front, Athanasius and Basil invoke
the triple co-ordination of baptism against the fourth-century
Tropici and Macedonians who denied, not the distinctness,
but the full divinity of the Spirit [note 249].

   Granted, then, the historical facts of the doctrinal development, the theological question must be asked: Was the full

trinitarian doctrine either a necessary or a legitimate development from the baptismal practice? It can hardly be maintained that Matthew 28:19 was originally said or written with a constantinopolitan doctrine of the Trinity in mind. The author of the *Apostolic Constitutions*, arianizer as he seems to have been, was probably closer to the mind of the New Testament Church when he interpreted Matthew 28:19 as Christ's order 'to preach the gospel to all the world, and to make disciples of all nations, and to baptize them into his death by the authority of the God of the universe who is his Father and by the testimony of the Spirit who is his Paraclete' [note 250]. Linguistically, this would be quite possible in view of the very flexible semitic usage of 'in the name of', a phrase which may link a number of very disparate entities [note 251]. Theologically, the interpretation given in *Apostolic Constitutions* V 7 would fit well with the predominant New Testament view that just as worship is made to God through Christ in the Spirit so also God's blessings reach humanity through Christ in the Spirit. A modern exegete, Markus Barth, takes the matthaean text as an expansion of baptism 'in the name of Christ' (Acts 2:38; 8:16,37; 10:48; 19:5): and so the meaning is baptism 'in the name of Christ who was sent by God and who himself baptizes with the holy Spirit now being poured out upon all flesh' [note 252]. The triadic phraseology of Justin Martyr's account of baptism in the middle of the second century could still bear that kind of meaning, stopping short of three *substantially* co-ordinated divine persons: converts 'receive the washing with water in the name of God, the Father and Lord of the universe, and of our Saviour Jesus Christ, and of the Holy Spirit' [note 253].

But does not all this in the long run *imply* the position which Athanasius and Basil will make explicit? Athanasius and Basil were not so superficial as to rely on the outward form according to which three identical immersions corresponded to a recital of a co-ordinated threefold divine name. More profoundly, they argued that Christ *needed* to be divine in order to reveal and to redeem, and that the Holy Spirit *needed* to be divine in order to sanctify and to divinize [note

254]. As in christology, so in pneumatology, it was human salvation which was at stake. It is again the question we faced in chapter II. How far does God need to engage *himself* with the world in order to bring humanity to the kind of salvation he intends for us, namely personal communion with himself? How far *did* he engage himself with us in Jesus Christ? How far *does* he engage himself with us 'in the Spirit'? Only a deist would say that God *could not* and *cannot* so personally engage himself with the world; but the deist's view of salvation differs from the traditional Christian view. (It might be thought that a deistic view safeguards better the 'autonomy' of humanity. But the traditional Christian view is not properly authoritarian. As we have seen, God's Spirit or grace is 'enabling', not coercive; and the service of God in which we find our freedom consists in the responsible exchange of love with the God who first loved us [note 255].)

To the extent that God engages *himself* with the world, it is legitimate to read back from his presence and action into his very being. If he appears to engage himself with the world *in different ways*, it will to that extent be legitimate to trace a certain plurality into God himself. If the 'economy' is read and experienced in a trinitarian way, then there is so much grounding for 'immanent trinitarianism', though it must be remembered that the best traditional trinitarianism has always been sensitive to its own inadequacy in face of the unfathomable God [note 256]. That is the degree of legitimacy in Tertullian's use of baptismal words and practice as an argument for the distinction of three divine persons. St Basil's theological use of the liturgical doxology is more complex.

St Basil allows that the doxology with *dia* and *en* is the more suitable form in a context of thanksgiving [note 257]. He is recognizing that just as God's blessing comes to us through Christ 'the Son' in the Holy Spirit, so our thanks are properly returned by that 'route' [note 258]. But this reading of the economy does not lead, in Basil's view, to any 'arianizing' subordinationism *within* God. He defends the doxology with *meta* and *sun* as the more suitable form in 'contemplation', i.e. as the more fitted to God as he is in himself. The point is that Basil subscribes, even in his view of the economy, to the principle that will later be formulated as *operationes Trinitatis ad extra indivisae sunt*. Because of the axiomatic indivisibility of God, his operations in relation to the world may indeed be 'appropriated' to one or another hypostasis but never *in separation from* the other hypostaseis. Correspondingly: in the inner life of God, the three hypostaseis mutually co-inhere. Worship is therefore finally directed simultaneously to three mutually indwelling persons. Nevertheless the use of *meta/sun*, as distinct this time from the 'Syrian' *and/and*, may testify to the Cappadocian sense that the Father alone is the 'fount of godhead', and hence to a persistent, and *proper*, element of subordinationism within the Trinity. Its propriety resides in its reflection of the fact that God the transcendent creator is 'more and greater than' (the *hypostaseis* which mediate) his relations with his creation —though these are truly and essentially 'himself' [note 259].

The one remaining historical point is the question of worship or prayer addressed *particularly* to the Spirit or Holy Spirit. As we shall see, the classic form of the eucharistic epiclesis in the Eastern churches asks the Father to send the Holy Spirit. There are, however, early traces—in gnostically inclined circles—of a direct invocation of the Holy Spirit. Thus the third-century Acts of Thomas contain, in connexion with the unction of initiation, an invocation of a female divine power which ends:

> Come, Holy Spirit, and purify their reins
> and their heart,
> And give them the added seal in the name of
> the Father and Son and Holy Spirit [note 260].

But in orthodox circles, the particular address of worship or prayer to the Holy Spirit appears to be a later development. It has never become very common, and it occurs characteristically in hymns. In a passage in which it is to the advantage of his thesis to discover such occurrences, L. Hodgson gives the following six examples from the English Hymnal: *Basileu ouranie, Paraklēte* (No. 454), from about the eighth century; *Veni Creator Spiritus* (No. 154), from before the

tenth century; *Veni sancte Spiritus* (No. 155), from the thirteenth century; Cosin's 'Come, Holy Ghost, our souls inspire'
(No. 153), Dryden's 'Creator Spirit, by whose aid' (No. 156),
and Coffin's 'O Holy Spirit, Lord of grace' (No. 453), from
the seventeenth and eighteenth centuries [note 261]. Hodgson
seems to have missed 'Come down, O Love divine' (No. 152),
by Bianco da Siena (†1434). From the Methodist Hymn
Book we might add 'Come, Holy Spirit, heavenly Dove' by
Isaac Watts (No. 292), and a number of strong hymns by
Charles Wesley:

> Come, Holy Ghost, all-quickening fire (No. 299)
> Come, Holy Ghost, our hearts inspire (No. 305)
> Spirit of faith, come down (No. 363)
> Come, Holy Ghost, all-quickening fire (No. 553)
> O come and dwell in me (No. 554)
> Come, Thou everlasting Spirit (No. 765)
> Come, Holy Ghost, Thine influence shed (No. 767).

Even so, the hymns of Charles Wesley addressed directly to
the Holy Spirit are relatively few, considering the Wesleys'
undoubted stress on sanctification. It is the nineteenth
century which appears to make the largest and most widespread contribution of such hymns. For example:

> F. W. Faber: 'Spirit of wisdom, turn our eyes' (No. 282)
> C. Wordsworth: 'Gracious Spirit, Holy Ghost' (No. 290)
> S. Longfellow: 'Holy Spirit, truth divine' (No. 288)
> E. Hatch: 'Breathe on me, Breath of God' (No. 300)
> T. B. Pollock: 'Spirit blest, who art adored' (No. 295)
> T. T. Lynch: 'Gracious Spirit, dwell with me' (No. 291)
> A. Reed: 'Spirit divine, attend our prayers' (No. 289)
> A. H. Vine: 'O Breath of God, breathe on us now' (No. 285).

How is the paucity and lateness of the development to be
interpreted? In the early centuries it strikes but the feeblest
echo to the development of worship and prayer addressed
particularly to Christ. The reason may be that the Holy
Spirit has always proved far less easy to 'personalize', in a
modern sense of 'person', than either God 'the Father' or
Christ as 'Lord' or 'Son'. The 'place' of the Holy Spirit in
the Trinity, in terms both of divinity and of personality (in a
technical trinitarian sense), was recognized less by popular

devotion than by theological reflexion; and it may be that the notorious cinderella position of pneumatology even in theology is due to the relatively poor place occupied by the Holy Spirit as an object of living worship. (Would things have gone differently if the feminizing of the Holy Spirit found in Syrian gnosticism had made its way more widely?) On the other hand, the presence of a less-easy-to-personalize Holy Spirit in the Trinity may have saved trinitarianism from developing into tritheism: Leonard Hodgson's *Doctrine of the Trinity*, for instance, moves a certain way in that direction [note 262]. When hymns begin to be addressed to the Holy Spirit, they often follow the lines of the 'sevenfold gift', which, as we saw, inclines to the broader use of Spirit/spirit to categorize the relation between God and humanity. The tendency to the broader use certainly characterizes several examples from the nineteenth-century flowering of Spirit-hymns. Perhaps the culmination of the tendency is found in Percy Dearmer's hymn 'O Holy Spirit, God, all loveliness is thine', where Holy Spirit becomes a simple synonym of God in his immanence or even of an immanent God.

With that we have arrived at the first of seven theological questions which, following on our historical survey of the liturgical links between pneumatology and trinitarian doctrine, I now wish to consider more systematically. We shall see how the Spirit dimension in worship affects four matters in the area of soteriology and three in the area of ecclesiology. The first question in soteriology concerns the identity of the God who saves.

4. *The identity of the Saviour: the Spirit, Christ and God*

While spirit/Spirit may be used in a rather general way to speak of communion between humanity and God, we have observed a tendency in the Church's worship, from the New Testament onwards, to give a strong christological colouring to pneumatology. The Spirit of Christian worship is the messianic Spirit which 'descended' upon Jesus at his baptism and then was 'released' more widely by his death and exaltation. This principle, recognized by all Christians, comes to expression in the 'epiclesis' or invocation of the Holy Spirit

which has been particularly prized in the liturgies of the
Eastern churches [note 263].

In the baptismal prayers, the pneumatology often carries
an after-taste of animism: the Holy Spirit is to chase away
the evil spirits which infest the water and any which may
remain in the exorcized candidates; but the reference to the
Christian Messiah is made specific by the mention of the
'power of the Cross' and the crosswise signations of the water.
Take, for example, the Byzantine rite:

> ... Thou didst sanctify the waves of Jordan, thou didst send down
> thy Holy Spirit from heaven and crush the heads of the serpents
> that lurked there. Therefore do thou, our loving king, be present
> now in the visitation of thy Holy Spirit and sanctify this water . . .
> May all the enemy powers be crushed down by the sign of the
> type of the cross of thy Christ. May all aerial and unseen shapes
> depart from us, may no dark demon lie hidden in this water: and
> we pray thee, Lord, let no evil spirit go down with him at his
> baptism to bring darkness of counsel and confusion of mind. But
> do thou, maker of all things, declare this water to be a water of
> rest, water of redemption, water of sanctification, a cleansing of
> the pollution of the body and soul, a loosening of chains, forgive-
> ness of sins, enlightenment of souls, washing of rebirth, grace of
> adoption, raiment of immortality, renewal of spirit, fount of life.
> For thou, Lord, hast said, *Wash you and make you clean* (Isa. 1:16).
> Take away the wickedness from our souls. Thou hast given us the
> new birth from above by water and Spirit. Be present, Lord, in
> this water and grant that those who are baptized therein may be
> refashioned, so that they may *put off the old man, which is corrupt*
> *according to the deceitful lusts* (Eph. 4:22), and *put on the new man,*
> *which is restored after the image of him that created him* (Col. 3:10):
> that being *planted together in the likeness of the death* (Rom. 6:5) of
> thy Only-Begotten Son, through baptism, they may share also
> in his resurrection: and guarding the gift of thy Holy Spirit, and
> increasing the store of grace, they may receive *the prize of the high*
> *calling* (Phil. 3:14) and be numbered among *the first-born who are*
> *written in heaven* (Heb. 12:23) in Christ Jesus our Lord. . . [note
> 264].

By the end of this prayer, the existential and ethical implications of baptism have come to be expressed according to the

personalist understanding of 'image' which we established in chapter I, and it has become clear that the sanctifying work of the Spirit signified by baptism is the renewal of human beings through their conformation to Jesus Christ.

The eucharistic epiclesis usually makes the same christological and soteriological points more concisely. The verbal forms and arrangement vary, but the eucharistic epiclesis characteristically enumerates two themes, the one being the (theo)logical precondition of the other. God is asked to send the Holy Spirit: (1) in order to 'make' or 'show' the bread and wine to be the body and blood of Christ; (2) in order that those who share in them may receive the blessings of salvation. The material creatures of bread and wine are not treated in isolation. The work of the Holy Spirit in relation to them is for the purpose of the divinely initiated communion between God and humanity in which human salvation consists. That communion is somehow qualified by the Christ who gave his life to God and for humanity. Christians have felt their communion with God to be mediated in this meal by the presence of Jesus Christ as both host and food (Zwingli's phrase, *hospes et epulum* [note 265]). The eucharistic presence of Christ is a coming 'in the Holy Spirit', the 'other Paraclete' (John 14:16–21). Taking up a theme from the 'Clementine liturgy', John and Charles Wesley provided the following 'epiclesis' in their *Hymns on the Lord's Supper* [note 266]:

> Come, Thou everlasting Spirit,
>   Bring to every thankful mind
> All the Saviour's dying merit,
>   All His sufferings for mankind.
>
> True Recorder of His passion,
>   Now the living faith impart,
> Now reveal His great salvation,
>   Preach His gospel to our heart.
>
> Come, Thou Witness of His dying;
>   Come, Remembrancer divine,
> Let us feel Thy power, applying
>   Christ to every soul, and mine [note 267].

A vital role is thus recognized to the Spirit in that 'dynamic

memorial' which biblical scholars now reckon to be characteristic of worship in the scriptures. In Calvin's terminology,
it is a function of the Holy Spirit to 'join', *lier*, heaven and
earth at the Lord's supper [note 268].

The liturgical association of the Holy Spirit with Jesus
Christ raises again the question of the sense in which we may
properly interpret the Christian claim concerning the 'uniqueness' of Jesus Christ [note 269]. If the Holy Spirit now 'bears
the imprint' or 'character' of Jesus, is true worship limited
to communities in which the 'memorial' of Jesus Christ is
made by name? Or is there true communion between the
divine Spirit and the human spirit wherever the 'spirit of
Jesus' is displayed by worshippers even in other historical
traditions than the Christian? But if the spirit of Jesus is at
all discernible in the worship of the other traditions, must
we not conclude that the *S*pirit of Jesus is present and active
there? That is to say: the Spirit which rested upon Jesus
would also be at work there. It may be a happy providence
that Christian liturgical practice has never really taken to
invoking 'the Holy Spirit' directly 'by name' as the furthest
developments of trinitarian thought would allow. To address
'the third person of the Trinity' is to give maximum value
to the line which doctrinal development factually took in the
historical and cultural tradition of Christianity. The liturgical
practice of addressing prayer for the Spirit to *God* has perhaps
helped to keep open the possibility of recognizing that the
divine Spirit may be present in worship on a plane wider
than historic Christianity. Since God is one and his purpose is
constant, the God whom the worshippers meet cannot, on
Christian belief, be other than the God who has revealed
himself in Jesus Christ; and this must hold good even where
the names of Christ and of 'the Holy Spirit' are not named.
Christians have, therefore, an ethical test of the Spirit's
presence in worship, in whatever religious tradition: it is the
worshippers' growth in conformity to Christ in his self-giving
love towards God and humanity. Outward appearances of a
pneumatic presence in worship remain empty and worthless
without the 'charity' which seeks the good of all (1 Corinthians
11:17–14:40).

It has already been hinted that true worship is impossible without the aid of the divine Spirit, and this is the next point to be developed.

5. *The gift of the Spirit*

True worship implies, as we have just seen, self-giving love on the part of the worshippers who are thus responsively reflecting the self-giving love which God displayed towards humanity in the gift of Jesus Christ and which Christ himself displayed in his relations both with 'the Father' and with his fellow human beings. According to the apostle Paul, the human response is made possible 'because God's love has been poured into our hearts through the Holy Spirit which has been given to us' (Romans 5:1–11). It is the gift of the Spirit which enables human beings to love and therefore to worship [note 270].

In several ways the Christian liturgy makes explicit the fact that God's gift of the Spirit is the prerequisite for the saving communion with God which comes to ritual expression in worship. Water-baptism is the sacrament of Spirit-baptism [note 271], and it is a strong tradition that only the baptized may participate in the other sacraments. There was an early understanding that the imposition of hands in the reconciliation of penitents 'restored' to the returning sinners the Spirit which had departed from them in their schism, heresy or crime. Ordination prayers recognize that the special enablement of the Spirit is needed for those who are to minister in the life and worship of the Church. The eucharistic epiclesis testifies to the fact that every communion is a divine gift. In the Anglican tradition the communion service is begun by a prayer which acknowledges that it is only 'by the inspiration of thy Holy Spirit' that 'we may perfectly love thee and worthily magnify thy holy name'. It is common practice also in less formal worship to call for the aid of the Spirit.

The detailed phrasing of the prayers on these occasions will reflect varying views on the relation between the human asking and the divine giving. It is again the question of grace and freedom, which we have already discussed in chapter II. Whatever the particular emphasis, the help of the divine

Spirit 'on our side' is considered indispensable for true worship. Though it needs active human appropriation, salvation is and remains a divine gift, and the place of the Spirit in worship expresses this [note 272].

6. *The seal of the Spirit*

Human salvation is part of the definitive purpose of God which will reach completion in the final kingdom. In the understanding of Acts 2:17, the abundant outpouring of God's Spirit belongs to 'the last days'. The presence of the Spirit in worship indicates that God's purpose is coming closer to achievement. This can be maintained despite the delay of the 'parousia' expected by the New Testament writers and perhaps by Jesus. For if our lives and our history bear at all a cumulative character, every occasion of communion with God will have become an ineradicable part of those who experienced it. True worship does not leave us unchanged. In so far as we have been thus transformed into the likeness of God, his kingdom is now so much nearer. These ideas, which are quite independent of the *length* of time the transformation takes, are pictorially expressed when the pauline writings say that we 'have been sealed by the Holy Spirit of God unto a day of redemption' (Ephesians 4:30), we 'have been sealed by the promised Holy Spirit, which is the earnest of our inheritance' (Ephesians 1:13f). Or again: 'God has put his seal upon us and given us his Spirit in our hearts as a guarantee' (2 Corinthians 1:22). As to our future communion with God in the final state (2 Corinthians 4:14ff): 'He who has prepared us for this very thing is God, who has given us the Spirit as a guarantee' (5:5) [note 273]. The 'sealing' is spoken of as a single event in the past. Exegetes take this to be a reference to Christian initiation. It matters little for our present purpose whether the reference is to baptism, or to a distinguishable imposition of hands or anointing (an embryonic 'confirmation'), or to an inner experience of which the rites are a sacramental expression. Once given, the Spirit continues with believers as a 'guarantee' or 'earnest', *arrabōn*. The prospect is glory, and of this the Spirit is, in another image, the 'firstfruits', *aparchē* (Romans 8:23). This image is drawn from Old Testament worship: the firstfruits are the promise and anticipation of the whole. As Israel returned to God the firstfruits of his gifts to the people, so God's gift of the Spirit enables the worshippers already to render God glory in anticipation of the final kingdom when God will be all in all. In my book *Eucharist and Eschatology*, I adduced ample evidence for the traditional view of the sacrament as pledge, prefiguration and taste of the kingdom. The eucharist is such 'in the Spirit'.

7. *The place of the saints*

The previous three sections provide the theological context for the particular place of the saints in the Christian tradition as it is focused in the liturgy. The saints are those who, by the gift of the Spirit at work in their lives, have reached an outstanding degree of conformity to Jesus Christ that the divine kingdom is considered to have come conspicuously close in their persons, and they themselves are considered to be already particularly near to God in anticipation of final salvation. Orthodox and Catholic worship has shown a strong sense of the place of the saints in the Church and in the whole purpose of God, but the Protestant Reformers objected to certain features of the medieval Western tradition in this matter, and by over-reaction the Protestant churches have allowed their awareness of the saints to wither [note 274]. Four points need attention in this contentious area.

First there is the question of veneration paid to the saints. It is true that the middle ages witnessed an unedifying scramble for relics, often valued for their thaumaturgical properties. Yet at the heart of the veneration of the saints stands an acknowledgment that the Holy Spirit was at work in their lives and persons. This is a Christian instance of the principle expressed in general religious terms by Ninian Smart: 'The holiness possessed by the holy man is derivative. . . . One can as it were worship God by reference to the saints, for they reflect God's holiness' [note 275]. The veneration of the saints is also, in Christianity, a plea for the coming of God's kingdom: it is to associate oneself with the impatient 'How long?' of the martyr saints whom the Apocalypse pictures under the heavenly altar (Revelation 6:9–11). It is a prayer for the final triumph of God in human lives and history: a triumph of which the victory of the saints is the sign and promise [note 276].

Second, there are the prayers of the saints. In the Roman Catholic 'litany of the saints', the saints are directly asked: *orate pro nobis*. This might be seen as no more and no less than asking fellow Christians on earth to pray for one. But sometimes prayer is made to God that he will grant requests at the intercession of particular saints on account of their 'merits': *quorum meritis precibusque*, in the Roman canon. The medieval abuses centring on the notion of a 'treasury of merits' evoked from the Protestant Reformers an insistence that the divine favour was always an undeserved gift, and Protestants characteristically appeal to the parable of the pharisee and the publican (Luke 18:10–14). Authentic Catholic teaching explains that talk of merit is to be understood in terms of 'God crowning his own gifts'. Scriptural Protestants will pay heed to the principle that 'the prayer of a righteous man availeth much' (James 5:16). The righteous person is one who is growing into conformity with Christ, and he will therefore be able to pray with insight Christ's prayer 'Thy will be done'; the Spirit will be enabling him to pray according to the will and purpose of God (Romans 8:26–30). Are the prayers of the saints in heaven likely to be less effective than the prayers of the saints on earth?

Third, the liturgy proposes the saints to us as examples of holy living. There is adequate scriptural basis for this in St Paul's injunction to the Corinthians: 'Be imitators of me, as I am of Christ' (1 Corinthians 11:1). A welcome sobriety has been restored to the readings from the biographies of the saints in the post-Vatican II *Liturgy of the Hours*: 'to lie like a second nocturn' had remained proverbial since the middle ages, even though many legends had been removed by Pius V. Protestants can have no objections of principle to commemorations which allow the example of the Spirit's transforming work in people of the past to inspire Christian living in the present. It would be good if Methodists, for instance, could broaden their hagiography beyond the Wesleyan tradition and commemorate heroes of the faith from the broad span of Christian history. Such commemorations bear testimony to the constancy of God's saving purpose.

The fourth matter is the communion of the saints. There are many indications in tradition that the eucharist especially is considered to be a participation in the worship of heaven [note 277]. The Greek liturgy of *St James* makes it explicit that the heavenly assembly, in whose worship of God the earthly Church joins at the Sanctus, includes 'the spirits of just men and prophets, the souls of martyrs and apostles'. According to the Mozarabic Easter mass it is 'all the angels and *saints*' who do not cease from shouting 'Holy'. In the Byzantine liturgy, the eucharistic offering is made 'for' the saints (*huper*): Nicholas Cabasilas, in his classic fourteenth-century Commentary, explains that the earthly Church is thereby joining with the saints in their own praise of God for 'the glory and perfection which he has bestowed upon them' [note 278]. According to the Roman canon, the offering is made 'in communion with' the saints (*communicantes*), and the worshippers ask that, sinful servants though they are, they may be given 'some part and fellowship with the holy apostles and martyrs' (*nobis quoque*) [note 279]. In the Anglican *Book of Common Prayer*, the prayer for the Church militant ends by opening up the eschatological prospect of communion with the saints in the kingdom: 'And we also bless thy holy name for all thy servants departed this life in thy faith and fear, beseeching thee to give us grace so to follow their good example that with them we may be partakers of thy heavenly kingdom'. In the Wesleyan experience, the solidarity of earthly fellowship is such that it can scarcely be broken by death, as Charles Wesley's hymn makes clear [note 280]:

> Come, let us join our friends above
>   That have obtained the prize,
> And on the eagle wings of love
>   To joys celestial rise.
>
> Let all the saints terrestrial sing,
>   With those to glory gone;
> For all the servants of our King,
>   In earth and heaven, are one.

> One family we dwell in Him,
>   One Church, above, beneath,
> Though now divided by the stream,
>   The narrow stream of death.
>
> Ev'n now by faith we join our hands
>   With those that went before,
> And greet the blood-besprinkled bands
>   On the eternal shore.
>
> Our spirits too shall quickly join,
>   Like theirs with glory crowned,
> And shout to see our Captain's sign,
>   To hear His trumpet sound.
>
> O that we now might grasp our Guide!
>   O that the word were given!
> Come, Lord of hosts, the waves divide,
>   And land us all in heaven.

It may have been Karl Rahner who said that individual eschatology was a theological department whose door was at present marked 'shut for repairs' [note 281]. Worship is certainly the place in which Christians have had the closest sense of the communion of the saints: it is perhaps here that theological reflexion should begin again. The liturgy anticipates, in the one Spirit, a final state in which the *whole family of God* will glorify him and enjoy him for ever [note 282].

Our discussion of the place of the saints has made plain the link between soteriology and ecclesiology. The last three points to be made in this chapter will be directly ecclesiological, still arising from the function of the Holy Spirit in Christian worship.

8. *Institution and event* [note 283]

Obscurity surrounds the early history of the epiclesis in the eucharistic liturgy [note 284]. By the late fourth century, however, the liturgy of *Apostolic Constitutions* VIII was asking God to send down his Holy Spirit to 'show' or 'make' the bread and wine to be the body and blood of Christ for the purpose of communion and its benefits. The Byzantine liturgies have retained such a request, and indeed in the same position, i.e. after the recital of the institution narrative and the anamnesis-oblation in the great eucharistic prayer. The Orthodox have deployed the sanctifying power of the Holy Spirit as an argument for the Spirit's divinity, but they have remained content, like the arianizing or strongly conservative compiler of *Apostolic Constitutions* VIII, with a prayer addressed to God (the Father) in this liturgical connexion, rather than a direct address to the Holy Spirit. In the West, some gallican and mozarabic masses prayed God to send his Spirit upon the elements, but the Roman canon contained no overt pneumatological epiclesis [note 285]. In medieval and later Orthodox/Catholic controversy, this state of affairs allowed an argument to develop over the 'moment of consecration' [note 286]. The Romans held consecration to be effected by the 'instituting' words of Christ now spoken by the priest *in persona Christi*. The Byzantines considered consecration to be complete only when the prayer for the Spirit's descent had been added. The controversy is now outdated: the best modern theology of the eucharist has rejoined the more ancient view that it is the whole eucharistic prayer, if not indeed the whole sacramental action, which 'consecrates' [note 287]. Nevertheless the Orthodox were making a valuable point when they suggested that the lack of a pneumatological epiclesis in the Catholic rite was symptomatic of a more general undervaluing of the Spirit in Western thought and experience. The exclusive Catholic stress on the consecratory agency of Christ's words typified, in Orthodox eyes, the characteristically *Roman* juridicalism whereby transmitted authority operates by *fiat*. Isolated emphasis on the narrative corresponded to an excessively institutional view of the Church. A further obvious sign of this mentality was the 'rubricism' which Roman Catholic scholars now reckon to have disfigured the Tridentine liturgy [note 288]. The Byzantines insisted that the institution needs the vivifying and energizing power of the Spirit: and of this the prayer for the descent of the Holy Spirit in the eucharist is the liturgical sign. In the face of all tendencies to rigidity and uniformity, the Spirit is the principle of freedom and variety. The ancient institution comes alive in each new liturgical event. In the ecumenical twentieth century, the

Roman Catholic church has heard this Eastern voice. It is more than coincidental that the new eucharistic prayers of the Vatican II Missal of 1969–70 should include a pneumato-logical epiclesis and that greater freedom and variety should now mark both the liturgical and the general life of the Roman Catholic church [note 289].

The next two sections will discuss in a different context the proper relations between structure and liberty, between unity and plurality.

9. *Structure and liberty*

By the middle of the second century, Justin Martyr describes a Sunday morning service whose shape has remained, with many and various overlays, the classical shape of the eucharistic liturgy [note 290]. The heart of the first part of Justin's service is the reading from the written witness to Christ, with an exposition of its relevance to the situation of the hearers. This is followed by the common prayers of intercession. The ensuing sacramental meal consists of the presentation of the material elements, the prayer of thanksgiving for creation and redemption spoken by the president and con-cluded by a general 'Amen', and the sharing in the bread and wine over which thanks have been said [note 291]. Justin provides no texts of the prayers said. Indeed his phrase *hōsē dunamis autōi* is usually taken to mean that the eucharistic president prayed extempore, and we may assume that the common intercessions were also improvised. There is evidence that the improvisation of the main public prayers continued in places for centuries [note 292]. But by about the year 215, if we follow the conventional dating, the *Apostolic Tradition* of Hippolytus was providing at least a 'model' for the eucharistic president to follow in the great prayer of thanks-giving. The fourth century saw the origin of the ancient eucharistic rites which still survive, and from then onwards an increasing degree of verbal fixity prevailed, notwithstand-ing certain structural transpositions and elaborations. The desire for 'orthodoxy' was already a concern of the *Apostolic Tradition* ('only let his prayer be correct and orthodox'), and the same motive led some North African councils around the year 400 to discourage new compositions. Other factors making for fixity will have been the social need for formality in large assemblies, especially with the 'conversion of the Empire', and the psychological need for regularity on the part of the worshippers. Much later the invention of printing provided the technical means for imposing uniformity and central control which various seats of ecclesiastical (for example, Rome) and political (for example, the English crown [note 293]) authority found desirable in liturgical as in other matters. In parts, however, the Protestant Reformation began a return to greater verbal freedom in worship. In the Lutheran and Reformed traditions, there has been a tendency to propose outline structures and model prayers. In the 'radical Reformation' and among later 'Free Churches', an even greater liberty has been claimed, although here too a certain degree of fixity has resulted from the regular and corporate nature of worship, and, less laudably, from the laziness which takes refuge in mental and spiritual ruts.

The movement of the Holy Spirit experienced in the modern pentecostal and neo-charismatic movements has led many people to the greater use of improvisation in worship. The most striking sign of freedom from the constraints of received language is speaking in tongues. In a sympathetic study entitled *Charism and Sacrament*, D. L. Gelpi has valued this most 'elementary' of the special gifts of the Spirit as a sign that all worship is first of all a gift from above, a motion of the Spirit at the affective level which cannot be controlled rationalistically although it will call forth rational inferences, moral evaluations and practical decisions [note 294]. If public glossolalia is to pass the pauline test of communal edification, it will best be set within the tried structures of the liturgy, where the familiar witness to Christ will itself provide a context of interpretation. Starting from rather different presuppositions, the modern Liturgical Movement has found that its own concern for the clarification of the fundamental structures of liturgy has left room for a more relaxed approach to the details of celebration, so that improvisation and even glossolalia may properly clothe the bare bones of the rite. With the pneumatics it may be affirmed that 'where the Spirit is, there is liberty' (2 Corinthians 3:17). But equally, that liberty is *defined* by the character of Christ (John 8:31–36). In the other direction, a literal witness to Christ remains dead without the enlivening Spirit.

10. *Unity and pluralism*

According to St Paul, the Holy Spirit is a principle of both unity and diversity. The image of the body and the members shows that there is properly no contradiction here, but only complementarity. Special gifts of the Spirit are given to *each* for the common good of *all*: for it is by the *one* Spirit that all have been baptized into *one* body, and all have been made to drink of the *one* Spirit (1 Corinthians 12). Since there is only one body and one Spirit, the various gifts have been given for the building up of the whole in love (Ephesians 4).

Sacramentally, the one baptism which is administered to all is the sign of the things which all Christians have in common in the one body: the one God and Father, the one Lord, the one Spirit, the one faith, the one hope (Ephesians 4:1–6). Baptism is the outward sign of the fundamental unity which the Spirit gives. It is fitting that entry upon this basic and, in intention, universal and permanent unity should be marked by a single ritual sign: baptism. Within the body, however, there are many and varied 'service gifts' (D. L. Gelpi), which may be temporary and local in their exercise. These lend themselves less easily to signification by any permanent and universal rite; though D. L. Gelpi, from the viewpoint of the developed Roman Catholic sacramental system, allows to the historically 'extra' sacrament of confirmation the meaning of a 'public profession of personal readiness to respond to whatever gift(s) of service the Spirit may choose to give in the course of one's development as a converted Christian' [note 295].

In Christian tradition, the *ordained* ministry is related, in the one direction, to the universal and permanent unity signified by baptism and, in the other direction, to the various gifts of temporary and local service which usually remain unritualized. In intention, ordination has given a person a permanent place and function within the structures of the universal Church as constituted by baptism (though problems arise in connexion with both baptism and ordination, as we shall see in chapters IV and IX, on account of the factual failure of Christians to live the unity which the sacraments signify). The structural place and function of the ordained ministry within the Church may be stenographically character- ized as 'oversight' [note 296]. For this office a particular gift of the Spirit is required, as ordination prayers reveal; and, in turn, one of the most important expressions of 'oversight' is the co-ordination of the individual 'service gifts' for the edification of the total community. In the context of worship, oversight is exercised through presidency of the liturgical assembly [note 297]. In Justin Martyr's *First Apology*, 67, the eucharistic president is called *ho proestōs*, and this designation may cast light on the 'leadership' mentioned already in the New Testament at Romans 12:8 (*ho proistamenos*), 1 Thessa- lonians 5:12 (*tous proistamenous*) and 1 Timothy 5:17 (*hoi proestōtes presbyteroi*).

In the chapters on Christ and on the Spirit, we have inevitably tended to raise also matters of ecclesiology. On the christological and pneumatological foundations now laid, we turn in the next chapter to consider the Church more directly. The approach will once more be by way of worship.

IV

Church

1. *Eschatological tension*

IMAGE of God, Christ, Spirit: the previous three chapters in the first and 'substantial' part of this book lead with a certain inevitability to a fourth chapter on the Church. The human vocation to communion with God bears an inescapably social character: Christ attracted to himself a body of disciples whom he called communally to follow his way to the Father: the Spirit has continued to inspire and enable people to join in adopting the pattern defined by Christ for the achievement of the divine kingdom and human salvation. All three of these interwoven strands lead to the Church. Or at least to *a* Church. For there is a tension here. On the one hand, there is a human community as it is meant to be in the purposes of God and as it will be when God's intentions for humanity are fully realized: the ideal or eschatological Church. On the other hand, there is the Church as it is in historical fact, a society which both qualitatively and quantitatively falls short of God's intentions for humanity and which yet embodies those intentions to some degree. Christian living is marked by that tension, and the tension comes to ritual expression in worship. The rites also indicate the final resolution of that tension: they point the historical Church towards a closer approximation to the Church as it is meant to be [note 298].

This chapter will begin with an 'anthropology of signs', showing briefly how and where the rites of Christian worship situate the historical Church in the purposes of God. The central sections of the chapter will then examine, in the light of worship, the four 'notes' or 'marks' by which the Nicene Creed characterizes the Church: unity, holiness, catholicity, apostolicity. Finally we shall return in a more concentrated way to three questions concerning the composition of the Church, still viewing them from the perspective of the liturgy.

2. *Ritual signification* [note 299]

In the twentieth century, the human sciences have given considerable attention to the category of 'signs'. Cultural anthropologists have demonstrated the role of ritual activity in maintaining order within a social universe. The historians of religion have been particularly interested in the deliverances of cultural anthropology and have contributed to their interpretation: witness the writings of Mircea Eliade in the realm of 'myth and ritual' [note 300]. Furthermore psychologists and philosophers have recognized the importance of both verbal and non-verbal symbols (images, objects, actions) in the business of expression and communication. The philosophers of religion have set to work interpreting these symbolic forms: witness the writings of Paul Ricoeur on the 'hermeneutic of symbols'. A Christian theology of worship needs to draw on all these disciplines, though it will synthesize their insights according to its own criteria and will work on material furnished by an existing Church tradition of practice and understanding that is part 'spontaneous', part 'reflected'.

A recurrent function of religious ritual is to put successive generations in dramatic touch with an archetypal story which accounts for the present order of the people or the world [note 301]. Representation, by word and deed, of a primal event asserts the foundational value of that event and allows later-comers to participate in its benefits and commit themselves to the maintenance of the established order. Where that order is threatened or disrupted, a specifically apotropaic or reconciliatory rite may be performed; but in any case the positive rehearsal of the original creative event is needed for the continuance of well-being. We have to do here with the 'myth of the eternal return'. On a cyclical view of time, salvation is by way of a perpetual recovery of the 'good beginning', a perennial re-assertion of the fixed pattern. In many religions, ritual is closely tied in with the annual rhythms of nature and culture, and the primal events commemorated are dateless mythical events among the gods.

A nomadic or agricultural basis can be found for most of the festivals in ancient Israel, but the striking feature of the Old Testament in this connexion is the degree to which it 'historicizes' the cultic observances so that they become commemorations of Yahweh's mighty deeds in history on Israel's behalf: the exodus from Egypt, the giving of the covenant law, the entry into the promised land, and so on. This historical anchorage, this insertion of the 'primal' events into human time, allows a more open attitude towards the future, especially where enemy forces or the people's own failings presently mar the original promise. Instead of permanent repetition there comes the expectation of a *new* deliverance which will certainly be patterned after the first but will nevertheless be historically novel. Passover commemorates the exodus under Moses and looks forward to an even greater deliverance under the messiah. In Jewish apocalyptic expectations, the 'age to come' will be qualitatively superior to the present age [note 302].

It is into this historical context that Jesus came, and the early Christians, particularly in the light of Easter, saw in him 'the beginning of the end'. The divine kingdom was dawning. In and through Jesus God had inaugurated the new covenant. God had now started to pour out his Spirit on all mankind. In the interval before the universal and incontestable establishment of God's rule, the Christian ritual would chiefly and characteristically consist of baptism and the Lord's supper. Jesus himself had become the founding event, and baptism was performed 'in his name' and the meal was celebrated at his command ('Do this'). Even more: in their worship the earliest Christians felt the continuing presence of the once crucified but now risen and living Lord Jesus. This presence also bespoke the future, for the coming of the definitive kingdom of God would be marked by Christ's *parousia*. Baptism was the sacrament of entry upon 'life in Christ'. This was a new life which by its ethical quality secretly anticipated the life of glory to be opened by the final resurrection (Romans 6:1–23; Colossians 3:1–17; 1 John 3:2).

The Lord's supper, prolongation of the meals with the earthly Jesus and anticipation of the expected messianic banquet in the final kingdom, provided a taste of the communion with God which table-fellowship with Christ had signified and which was pictured for the future as the marriage feast of the Lamb. When celebrated by a community that lives accordingly, these sacraments express ritually the fact that the historical Church is definitely on the way to that perfect glorification and enjoyment of God which is God's purpose for humanity. When an ethical or religious gap arises between the actual life of the celebrating community and the values signified by the sacraments, the sacraments assume, as we shall see, an aspect of judgment but also convey an offer of forgiveness. *(faith.)*

Ritual signs play an important part in the expression and communication of meaning. They are the solemn way by which a community formulates its common mind on the meaning of life and of the world, and by which it transmits its vision of the truth to new generations and to those who come to it from outside. For the Christian community, meaning does not reside in a once-given world-order which needs only to be maintained; and its most characteristic rituals are not therefore of a predominantly preservative kind. For the Christian community, meaning is in the making: life is oriented towards God's ultimate purpose, and history-making is the way to the attainment of that purpose for both individuals and humanity as a whole; the most characteristic Christian rituals are therefore predominantly transformative in character, actions that signify divine grace coming to begin and continue the shaping of active recipients into the people God is calling them to become.

Christian ritual is thus marked by eschatological tension. It brings to focus the character of the historical Church as a pilgrim community on its way to becoming the people of God's final kingdom. In its liturgical creed the Church confesses itself to be 'one, holy, catholic and apostolic'. The application of these four adjectives to the Church is also marked by tension. The four qualities are enjoyed by the historical Church only in an imperfect way. They apply fully only to the Church as it ideally is and eschatologically will be. We shall be examining more closely the place of creeds in worship in chapter VI. Taking up the thought of J. J. von Allmen that the true face of the Church is revealed in its worship, we here and now look at how the four 'notes' of the Church's self-description in the Nicene Creed come to expression in liturgical practice [note 303]. It will be proper to bear in mind in our own way the christological criterion set by von Allmen: 'Worship is indeed for the Church, while it waits for the Kingdom, the time and place *par excellence* at which it finds its own deep identity; the time and place at which the Church becomes what it is. . . . (Yet) worship is not the time and place at which the Church becomes aware of its own identity in the sense that it might be the time and place at which the Church might discover in a purifying mirror its own image cleansed of every spot and wrinkle. It is not by looking at itself, even washed clean, that the Church learns what it is. What makes the Church first glimpse, and then see clearly, its true face is meeting with Christ and learning *from him* what sort of Bride it is that he loves. It is on Christ's face that the Church learns who it is.'

3. *Unity*

If Christ is the revelation of self-giving love, the body of his followers must be expected to exhibit a unity in which the members are bound to one another by the ties of mutual self-giving love. Unity belongs to the Church's calling:

> I therefore, a prisoner for the Lord, beg you to lead a life worthy of the calling to which you have been called, with all lowliness and meekness, with patience, forbearing one another in love, eager to maintain the unity of the Spirit in the bond of peace. There is one body and one Spirit, just as you were called to the one hope that belongs to your call, one Lord, one faith, one baptism, one God and Father of us all, who is above all and through all and in all.
>
> (Ephesians 4:1–6)

The christological and soteriological grounding of Christian unity is expressed with polemical sharpness in the rhetorical questions which St Paul poses in face of the absurdity of divisions:

> Is Christ divided? Was Paul crucified for you?
> Or were you baptized in the name of Paul?
> (1 Corinthians 1:13)

The apostle returns to the charge in 1 Corinthians 12:13:

> By one Spirit we were all baptized into one
> body . . . and all were made to drink of one Spirit.

It is notable that in all these three passages baptism appears as a ritual sign of Christian unity, and to this point we shall return shortly. But the tone of exhortation and even of rebuke in the passages quoted is sufficient to show that unity among Christians has been existentially problematical even from the earliest days. In the course of history, the difficulties of living in Christian love have proved so acute that from time to time schisms have arisen in contradiction to the deepest nature of the Church.

In the absurd situation of disunity among Christians, baptism has inevitably become a focus of controversy. Baptism is the ritual sign of a christologically, soteriologically and pneumatologically grounded unity. Yet groups separated from one another continue to perform the rite which signifies unity. A dilemma is thereby posed. Can it possibly still be 'the one baptism' which they are severally celebrating? But if it is maintained that it remains 'the one baptism' even when performed in communities divided from one another, how can such communities continue living in separation? The theological response to the dilemma has taken two contradictory directions. The first line was classically argued by St Cyprian of Carthage when dealing with 'Novatianists' in the middle of the third century [note 304]. Cyprian held that his was the continuing indivisible Church; that alleged baptisms performed by schismatic groups outside the Church were in fact empty charades; and that a person coming into the Church from a schismatic group needed to receive baptism by the Church (it was not rebaptism, since the 'baptism' received in schism was no baptism at all). This line was modified by St Augustine in his dealings with the Donatists in the first decades of the fifth century [note 305]. The bishop of Hippo did not require converts from schism to undergo baptism at Catholic hands, but he held that their earlier baptism became 'fruitful' only when they entered the Catholic fold. Baptism given in schism remained 'the baptism of Christ': that is the ground of its non-repetition (we shall come later to the matter of baptism's unrepeatability). But baptism received in schism was either unprofitable in its very performance or at once became unprofitable because of the baptized person's persistence in schism. The difficulty with the cyprianic view and its augustinian modification is its supposition that only one party can be 'in the right' in any dispute, and that only one side can with justice be seen as the continuing body after a division. But hindsight, or even a less impassioned contemporary observer, can often discern both positive and negative values on each side of a dispute, and the positive Christian values do not simply disappear from one group or the other immediately upon a division.

The other main theological direction has been most clearly taken by modern Protestantism. Protestants have held that the various confessionally and institutionally divided groups together constitute the Church on earth at any one time. It is the saving presence of the Lord which gives saving value to any community, but the Lord does not entirely withdraw his saving presence even when human institutions embody his gospel with only imperfect truth and purity. Even most of the sixteenth-century Reformers did not completely deny the name of Church to the papal communion despite their attack on the corruptions in its life which seemed to disqualify it from being 'a community in which the gospel is preached purely and the sacraments are administered rightly' [note 306]. Later Protestants have tended to increasing generosity in their evaluation of the churchliness of other communities than their own. They have not questioned baptism as performed in all the various communities [note 307]. The problem here is that of too easy an acquiescence in a continuing disunity of life, when the recognition of 'the one baptism' throughout the several communities ought to be pressing divided Christians towards a closer correspondence between actual existence and the rite which signifies unity.

Modern Roman Catholicism appears to be approximating to this second general position. Thus Vatican II recognized that the 'separated communities', i.e. the communities separated *from* the Roman Catholic church, are 'not without significance in the mystery of salvation'. Nevertheless the council also made the claim that *all* Christian values, whether at the individual or at the communal level, really belong, even when found 'outside' the Roman Catholic church, to the one true Church which 'subsists in' the Roman Catholic church [note 308]. The Roman tendency to a generous recognition of baptism in its quality as the fundamental sacrament of salvation may date back to Cyprian's contemporary, pope Stephen. At least, Cyprian and his supporter, Firmilian of Caesarea, understood Stephen's position to be that 'whoever is baptized in the name of Christ, no matter where, immediately obtains the grace of Christ' [note 309]. Nevertheless a massively exclusivist position was typified by Boniface VIII's bull *Unam sanctam* of 1302: 'There is one holy catholic and apostolic Church, and outside this Church there is neither salvation nor remission of sins. . . . It is altogether necessary to salvation for every human creature to be subject to the Roman pontiff' [note 310]. In 1547, however, the Council of Trent anathematized anyone who should deny that baptism given by heretics in the name of the Trinity and with the intention of doing what the Church does was 'true baptism' [note 311]. For a long time, doubt concerning Protestant 'intentions' led Roman Catholics to give 'conditional baptism' or even (re)baptism to converts from Protestantism; but the modern ecumenical movement has almost brought this practice to an end, and it is on the basis of a recognition of their baptism that the Roman Catholic church first recognized other Christians *individually* as 'separated brothers', and then the presence of baptism in other Christian communities became one of the factors which led

the Roman Catholic church to attribute some saving significance to them even as *communities* [note 312]. As we saw, this
is coming nearer to the Protestant view of the matter. Yet
static tolerance of a persisting division in life among those
who are considered to be sacramentally united in baptism
would be to sanction an insupportable gap between rite and
life. The dynamic of baptismal recognition should lead the
divided Christian communities towards a closer overall
approximation to the unity which belongs to the Church's
vocation.

The christological criterion comes into more detailed play
at two points which have so far received only passing mention
in our discussion of the problems posed by the contradiction
between disunity among would-be Christians and the Church's
vocation to unity—problems typically encountered in connexion with baptism. The points at issue are the unrepeatability of baptism and the importance of 'intention' in the
performance of the rite. All parties have agreed that baptism
is unrepeatable: the question is whether baptism administered
'in schism' (or, when the question is raised by (Ana)baptists,
in infancy) is baptism at all; if it is, then it should never be
repeated. This unanimity is grounded in a felt correlation
between a once-for-all-ness of baptism and the once-for-all-
ness of Christ's death and resurrection (e.g. Romans 6), so
that to repeat the act by which a person is once made a
sharer in Christ's death and resurrection would strike at the
sufficiency of the death once accomplished by Christ for his
redemption or be tantamount to crucifying Christ afresh
(so, for instance, John Damascene [note 313]). The stronger
the view of the decisiveness of Christ for human salvation,
the greater is likely to be the insistence both on the need for
baptism (and to this we shall come in the last section of this
chapter) and on its unrepeatability.

There is also a christological implication in the 'intention'
of baptism. The tridentine mention of an intention 'to do
what the Church does' makes an important point. If an
impersonal automatism of the rite is to be avoided, both the
minister and the recipient must be presumed to hold a
Christian intention (supporters of infant baptism have to be

satisfied with the absence of a counter-intention on the part of the candidate: *non ponens obicem*) [note 314]. Ecumenical recognition of baptism acknowledges that other communities than one's own have a sufficient doctrinal and practical grasp of Christianity for them to be considered essentially Christian. This implies, particularly in modern times, a rather wide drawing of the limits of permissible variety. The unity towards which the ecumenical movement is directed is likely to bear a markedly pluralist character. This is explicable if the God who acted in Christ and who acts in Christian baptisms is greater than our understandings of him, and if our existential appreciation of him is, as yet, imperfect. If and when communion with him increases, our improved understandings will more easily harmonize with one another, though we may doubt whether they will ever—granted the varied human component—become monotonously identical [note 315]. It is only the dissonances of sin that will disappear: and thereby we arrive at the second 'note' of the Church, its holiness [note 316].

4. Holiness

According to the New Testament writings, the Church is holy on three counts: it is the people of God; it is the body of Christ; it is indwelt by the Holy Spirit [note 317]. Baptism is the fundamental ritual sign of the Church's holiness. The baptismal echoes are unmistakable in 1 Corinthians 6:11:

> You were washed, you were sanctified (*hēgiasthēte*), you were justified in the name of the Lord Jesus Christ and in the Spirit of our God [note 318];

and in Ephesians 5:25–27:

> Christ loved the Church and gave himself up for her that he might sanctify her (*hagiasēi*), having cleansed her by the washing of water with the word, . . . that she might be holy (*hagia*) and without blemish.

The imagery of washing is used in other baptismal passages also: Titus 3:5–7; Hebrews 10:22. The idea is that God has cleansed the baptized of their past sin and that henceforth they are expected to live a life of corresponding purity. There is thus an inescapable ethical side to holiness. The context of the baptismal reference in Titus 3 makes this plain:

> We ourselves were once foolish, disobedient, led astray, slaves to various passions and pleasures, passing our days in malice and envy, hated by men and hating one another. . . .

Then comes the reference to the saving action of God in Christ, whose appropriation has been signified by baptism. And the writer continues:

> I desire you to insist on these things, so that those who have believed in God may be careful to apply themselves to good deeds (*or*: enter honorable occupations). . . . But avoid. . . .

Similarly in 1 Corinthians 6:

> Do you not know that the unrighteous will not inherit the kingdom of God? . . . And such were some of you.

Then comes the reference to baptismal sanctification, and the ethical consequences are listed:

> Shun immorality. . . . Do you not know that your body is a temple of the Holy Spirit within you, which you have from God? You are not your own; you were bought with a price. So glorify God in your body.

The rhetorical questions ('Do you not know. . . ?') show that St Paul is at a loss in the face of post-baptismal sin. Its absurdity is indicated in a similar way in Romans 6:

> What shall we say then? Are we to continue in sin that grace may abound? God forbid! How can we who died to sin still live in it? Do you not know that all of us who have been baptized into Christ Jesus were baptized into his death? We were buried therefore with him by baptism into death, so that as Christ was raised from the dead by the glory of the Father, we too might walk in newness of life.

Again the reference to baptism. The rest of chapter 6 goes on to stress the ethical content of the 'new life'. The thought-pattern is similar in Colossians 3 (Colossians 2:12ff shows the baptismal connexion): 'You have put off the old nature with its practices (cf. Romans 6:6: Our old self was crucified with him), and you have put on the new nature, which is being renewed in knowledge after the image of its Creator.' Colossians 3:1 goes so far as to say that 'you have been raised with Christ', but there remains a note of reserve in both Romans 6 and Colossians 3. In Romans 6:5 and 6:8 the reference to our resurrection takes a future tense, and according to Colossians 3:3f 'your life is hid with Christ in God' and *awaits* its glorious revelation. In both Romans 6 and Colossians 3 ethical *exhortation* is required:

> You also must consider yourselves dead to sin and alive to God in Christ Jesus. Let not sin therefore reign in your mortal bodies. ... Do not yield your members to sin as instruments of wickedness, but yield yourselves to God as men who have been brought from death to life, and your members to God as instruments of righteousness ... Yield your members to righteousness for sanctification.

> ... Seek the things that are above. ... Set your minds on things that are above, not on things that are on earth. ... Put to death therefore what is earthly in you: immorality, impurity, passion, evil desire, and covetousness, which is idolatry. ... But now put them all away: anger, wrath, malice, slander, and foul talk from your mouth. ... Put on then, as God's chosen ones, holy and beloved, compassion, kindness, lowliness, meekness, and patience. ... As the Lord has forgiven you, so also you must forgive. And above all these things put on love, which binds everything together in perfect harmony. And let the peace of Christ rule in your hearts, to which indeed you were called in the one body. ... Let the word of Christ dwell in you richly. ... And whatever you do, in word or deed, do everything in the name of the Lord Jesus, giving thanks to God the Father through him.

These passages reveal an eschatological tension: holiness, or the new life, is a gift of God already given, and yet its realization still has to be striven for, because the power of sin for the present remains such that there is danger of a relapse into the ways of the old eon that is now passing away. The passage from Colossians 3 was quoted at length in order to show that there is, according to New Testament thought, a christological test and example for the conduct appropriate to the new age: it is to this that Christians should direct their behaviour. It is by the imitation of God in Christ that the human character is shaped for the final kingdom of God (compare Ephesians 4:17–5:20, where the theme of imitation and likeness leads the whole argument and the eschatological dimension shines through).

But relapses not only threaten, they also occur. Is it possible to give some theological account of this practical fact? According to C. F. D. Moule in a New Testament essay on 'the judgment theme in the sacraments', submission to baptism is voluntary submission to the judgment of God upon sin; it is so because baptism is the sacrament of participation in the death by which Christ bore the divine condemnation merited by human sin [note 319]. Theological opinion will vary as to whether the 'theory of atonement' by which Moule grounds his point is found in the New Testament or is in any case tolerable; but his insight that baptism means the acceptance of God's verdict on sin appears to be correct in the light of what we have seen so far in this section. It becomes interesting therefore that Moule should go on to argue that the eucharist is the pre-eminent occasion for a Christian self-judgment by which the baptismal judgment is renewed. He supports his case by a detailed exegesis of 1 Corinthians 11:17–34, paying particular attention to the verb *krinein* and its compounds. In an exegesis of the same passage, E. Käsemann had elucidated the pauline view that salvation, when spurned, turns to condemnation [note 320]. Moule now stresses the positive opportunity which the eucharist offers for repeated repentance . . . and forgiveness. A soteriological grounding could be found in the fact that to drink the eucharistic cup is to drink the cup over which Jesus, according to St Matthew, said: 'Drink of it, all of you; for this is my blood of the (new) covenant, which is poured out for many for the forgiveness of sins' (Matthew 26:28).

If the eucharist may properly be viewed as the renewal of a judgment and forgiveness decisively signified by baptism, we are on our way to being able to give a theological account of the 'absurd' but undeniable fact that the baptized continue to sin.

We must not get there too quickly, however, if we are to reflect the point that the early Church recognized the fact of post-baptismal sin only with extreme reluctance [note 321]. From a lapse as grave as apostasy the Letter to the Hebrews allows to the baptized no 'renewal of repentance', no 'second conversion' (Hebrews 6:1–8). The First Letter of John declares that 'no-one born of God commits sin' (3:9). Nevertheless St John saw himself obliged to say: 'I am writing this to you that you may not sin; but if any one does sin, we have an advocate with the Father, Jesus Christ the righteous' (1 John 2:1). The 'sin' which the Letter envisages appears to be either the denial of a fundamental christological confession (Jesus the Christ has come in the flesh) or the refusal of the fundamental pattern of Christian behaviour (love). There is no suggestion that one may *go on* sinning with impunity. In the middle of the second century, the Shepherd of Hermas allows only one restoration after a grave sin. The patristic Church evolved a penitential discipline whereby those who committed grave sins could be readmitted to communion only after a long period of excommunication and public penance [note 322]. Nevertheless there was an early recognition that sin is not limited to the more flagrant and spectacular crimes. It must be with this in mind that the *Didache* orders: 'On the Lord's day, come together, break bread, and give thanks, having first confessed your transgressions, that your sacrifice may be pure. But let none who has a quarrel with his companion join with you until they have been reconciled, that your sacrifice may not be defiled' (14:1–2). The teaching of the Sermon on the Mount supposes that there are sins of the heart which may never come to practical expression. It is into such a situation that the practice of private penance and absolution fits, as well as the more general confessions of sin and unworthiness which figure in the later liturgies (and with particular frequency in the churches of the Reformation) [note 323].

A theological account of post-baptismal sin must therefore be on the lines of *simul justus et peccator* [note 324]. This is better not taken in the form in which it is found in some Lutheran theologians, i.e. as an extreme and continuing paradox, as though the believer became one hundred per cent justified while remaining one hundred per cent sinner. Resignation to the 'inevitability' of sin risks making it innocuous and thereby opens the door to antinomianism. Rather the believer must be seen as engaged, with the help of God, in quelling the remains of his old nature in a process of real personal transformation. This takes seriously the historical process as a time, in Olivier Clément's phrase, of learning to love. The continuance of God's enabling grace is pre-eminently signified in the eucharistic communion. It is also signified in the sacraments of penance and of healing, the latter being understood in the broad sense of applying to the whole personality as in the Orthodox tradition. The link between penance and healing is made in an embryonic reference in the Letter of James: 'Confess your sins to one another, and pray for one another, that you may be healed' (James 5:13–16).

In the search for the ending of divisions among Christian communities, I suggest that there is a place for the mutual administration and reception of sacramental penance and healing by representatives of each community. Such acts would commit all penitent parties to the mercy of God's forgiveness and would effectively help the healing of personal and institutional wounds. Reconciliation would be signified by the kiss of peace and eucharistic concelebration. Not only would the historical Church thereby come closer to unity and holiness: its catholicity would also be visibly enhanced [note 325].

5. Catholicity

The johannine Christ promised that when he was lifted up from the earth on the cross, he would draw all to himself (John 12:32). The hymn of Philippians 2 proclaims that God has exalted Jesus to the heights and given him the name above every name, so that he should receive the worship of all as universal Lord. If these are the christological and soteriological claims made by Christians, the implied vocation of the Church is to catholicity. The ultimate scope of the Church cannot properly be less than universal. Within the Church, moreover, there can properly be no divisive distinctions based on human differences. The central acts of Christian ritual make clear this intended catholicity grounded in the universal Saviour and Lord.

The story of Cornelius' baptism encapsulates the earliest Church's realization that God does indeed mean to pour out his Spirit on all flesh (Acts 10–11; cf. 2:17). Henceforth the Church's mission will be to make all nations Christ's disciples, baptizing them in the name of the Father and of the Son and of the Holy Spirit (Matthew 28:18–20; cf. Acts 1:8). In a baptismal passage, St Paul argues that life in Christ transcends all differences of race, culture, social state, and sex: 'As many of you as were baptized into Christ have put on Christ. There is neither Jew nor Greek, there is neither slave nor free, there is neither male nor female; for you are all one in Christ Jesus' (Galatians 3:27f). We shall see in a moment that this transcendent baptismal unity by no means implies an undifferentiated uniformity; it rather provides a basis for variegated diversity in place of unreconciled divisions.

The eucharistic cup contains 'my blood of the (new) covenant, which is poured out for many' (Mark 14:24; Matthew 26:28). On the basis of semitic idiom, J. Jeremias has convincingly argued that 'many' here bears an inclusive sense: *not* 'many but not all', but rather 'all, who are many' [note 326]. A johannine equivalent is found in the eucharistic saying of John 6:51c: 'The bread which I shall give *for the life of the world* is my flesh.' The Christian eucharist is the sign and taste of the feasting by which the Bible pictures human salvation in the final kingdom of God: 'On this mountain the Lord of hosts will make *for all peoples* a feast. . . .' (Isaiah 25:6–9); 'I tell you, *many* will come from east and west and sit at table with Abraham, Isaac, and Jacob in the kingdom of heaven' (Matthew 8:11; cf. Luke 13:29); 'Blessed are those who are invited to the marriage supper of the Lamb' (Revelation 19:9). The many meal-words and meal-deeds which stud the teaching and activity of Jesus according to the gospels are to be interpreted in this light: the sayings, the parables, the feedings, the table-fellowship with sinners, the post-resurrection meals. The eucharist is the sacramental continuance and anticipation of the 'messianic banquet' inaugurated by the companionship of Jesus during his earthly ministry and to be consummated when he 'drinks the wine new with his friends in his Father's kingdom' (Matthew 26:29). This is the most powerful sign of salvation in our human existence: to take into ourselves with thanksgiving the good gifts of the God who in Christ gives his very self to us. The offer is for all, and 'whosoever will may come' [note 327]. Corresponding behaviour is expected of all who accept the invitation. Any divisiveness among the guests reduces 'the Lord's supper' to 'your own supper', and the result is disastrous (1 Corinthians 11:17–34).

Now the question of variegated unity, of harmonic diversity. The differences which nature provides in the matters of sex and race have often been hardened and distorted by culture to produce division and conflict. The catholicity of the Church's calling gives room and encouragement for both sexes and all races to place themselves under the sovereignty of Christ, which means, when expressed on the social plane, the gift of self for the good of others and of all. The sexually differentiated contributions which men and women make to the whole Christian community will vary according to psychological and social circumstances, which appear themselves to depend on a mixture of biological and cultural factors. In the modern West, the judgment is growing that it is wrong to schematize the properly diverse contributions of the sexes by restricting the eucharistic presidency and the more general oversight of the Church to male Christians. The exclusion of women from these focal offices is now widely felt to be untrue to the Church's vocation to catholicity. In the matter of race and nation, the modern development of weaponry and communications has brought to world level the problem of rivalry that has often been locally explosive; but modern technology has also brought to our awareness the great variety of positive cultural achievement among the races and nations and at the same time provided the means for a truly universal civilization. Some of these themes will be treated in chapter XI: Culture. At present it is enough to state that Christian ritual, as the symbolic focus of the life of the Church and (potentially) of humanity, must seek to combine the universal and the particular in such ways that the sovereignty of Christ may there come to expression. The relations between the liturgy and 'social condition' ('neither slave nor free') will be discussed in chapter XII: Ethics.

If I may be permitted to close this section with a personal illustration, I will mention my six years of ministering in the English-speaking congregation of Yaoundé, Cameroon (1967–1973). It is obvious that some options close one set of possibilities while opening others: the use of English had drawbacks in an area where French was literally the *lingua franca*, but in compensation the language brought together Christians from West Cameroon, Nigeria, Ghana, Liberia, the U.S.A., Canada and the British Isles. The worshipping congregation included cabinet ministers, house servants, ambassadors, schoolchildren, unemployed people, teachers, civil servants, technicians. Their denominational allegiance varied through Presbyterian, Baptist, Anglican, Methodist, Roman Catholic. In a strong liturgical life, a particular contribution would be made from time to time from one cultural or ecclesiastical tradition. In numerous cases, fellowship in this congregation permitted mutual help and the settling of quarrels. It was for me a striking instance, from many angles, of the catholicity of the Church, and to preside at the eucharist of such a body was a satisfying ministry.

6. *Apostolicity*

The apostolicity of the Church is ultimately grounded in God's mission to the world. Christians see in Jesus the supreme instance of God's mission to humanity (e.g. Hebrews 1:1f): Jesus himself is held to have sent out the apostles to proclaim further the gospel of Christ (e.g. Matthew 28:19f; Acts 1:8). The words of the johannine Christ express the Christian view of the divine mission: 'As the Father has sent me, even so I send you' (John 20:21). The Church will not consider its apostolic task complete as long as there are those to whom the gospel must still be preached.

The continuing apostolicity of the Church involves both message and messengers. It is the gospel, the message of God in Christ, which must be preached if the Church is to be true to the divine mission. The closest original witness we have to Jesus and the events surrounding him is contained in those documents which the early Church came to receive as its New Testament scriptures because it judged their substance to derive directly or indirectly from Jesus himself or from the apostles he commissioned to bear him witness. The New Testament scriptures do not stand alone as an expression of the message. On the one hand, the cultural shifts brought by history or geography necessitate the *interpretation* of the New Testament if the original message is to reach different times and places. The seriousness with which the Church undertakes this task is a measure of its belief in the universal validity of the revelation of God in Jesus. On the other hand, there are also the classical summaries of the faith known as *creeds*, which may be partly derived from the scriptures but which may also have had to some extent an independent parallel existence in the Church from the earliest days; and these, again, need interpretation. These questions of scriptures, creeds, and their interpretation will occupy us throughout part two of this book: traditional means; and we shall examine them from the angle of Christian worship. I shall say no more about them at this point. But the transmission and interpretation of the original message raises also the question of the messengers, and this must at least be touched upon in a consideration of the apostolicity of the Church.

The personal 'location' of the apostolic succession has been controversial in Christian history [note 328]. It would generally be agreed that in a broad sense all the baptized have a responsibility to transmit, interpret and apply the Christian message within their own circumstances. It would also be agreed, at least as a matter of historical and sociological experience and even perhaps as corresponding to some divine disposition, that a more limited number of members of the community articulate the message with particular authority. This authority is usually held to be grounded in a particular call of God, who also gives the necessary gifts for preaching and teaching. Yet tensions may start to appear. From time to time, powerful figures arise claiming insights into the Christian message which the Church of the day is neglecting or distorting. The reformers may run into conflict with a substantial proportion of the community and its officially appointed teaching authorities. A breach of communion may result between those who accept the reformers' teaching and those who stand by the received state of affairs. It becomes difficult to decide where Christian 'identity' is more faithfully expressed. Is it on the side of the reformers, who usually claim to get behind inherited and current abuses and restore a more primitive and authentic Christianity? Or is it on the side of those who claim that only a continuous chain of transmission and interpretation down the generations can preserve the identity of the message? Sometimes the reformers may judge that a 'negative sign' of *dis*continuity is needed, and they may then, in their appointment of preachers and teachers in their own community, deliberately break with the inherited lines of appointment to official ministry. This will be seen on the conservative side as 'loss of the apostolic succession', but the reformers will have been motivated by an intended fidelity to the original apostles. My description has been coloured by *the* Reformation of the sixteenth century [note 329], but certain features of the pattern can also be recognized in the origins of the Waldensians and the Methodists, for example.

Once such reformed communities have become established, they themselves usually seek to maintain internal continuity of preaching and teaching, to which they give ritual expression in ordination. They thus rediscover a 'conservative' practice which is appropriate enough when the message is being faithfully transmitted and interpreted. In these circumstances, ordinations signify at least three things. First: the imposition of hands by existing bishops and presbyters signifies the aggregation of new ministers to the continuing ministerial college. Second: the lay recognition of those who are to exercise official ministry in the continuing community is signified, for instance, by popular acclamations ('They are worthy!'), by imposition of lay hands (in the Congregational tradition), or at the least by silent acquiescence when objections to the impending ordinations are invited. Third: the ordination prayer and invocation of the Holy Spirit signifies the dependence of (even!) the official ministry upon the gift of God. Where the gifts of God are properly received and used, there should be no opposition between official ministries and less formal ministries [note 330].

Having seen how the liturgy reflects the Church's eschatological tension towards unity, holiness, catholicity and the fulfilment of the apostolic task, we may close this chapter by examining, once more in liturgical terms, three questions concerning the composition of the Church. The third question returns to a matter which was adumbrated when we talked of catholicity but which remained unstressed in our discussion of apostolicity, namely the scope, constituency or destination of the Church's missionary proclamation. These last three sections on the Church can be arranged according to the three 'theological virtues', the three gifts of God which 'remain': faith, love, hope.

7. *Justification by faith*

There can be no doubt that the heart of the primitive Christian message was a summons to active faith in the God who had effectively revealed his saving design in and through Jesus Christ. In and through their response to God's gracious initiative, men and women entered upon the communion with God which was the divine intention for humanity: they passed from death to life, they became sons and daughters of God, they tasted the joy of the Holy Spirit. All this was the gift of God, a gift consciously appropriated. In one of St Paul's dominant images, it was 'justification by grace through faith'.

The decisive ritual sign of justification is baptism. In the New Testament writings baptism appears, in W. F. Flemington's apt phrase, as 'the kerygma in action', the gracious application of the gospel message [note 331]. It might also be said that baptism in the New Testament is the acted *response* to the kerygma: Flemington shows how often baptism follows upon 'hearing the word' or 'believing'. Baptism is thus the sign of both grace and faith, the divine and human 'sides' of justification. In the biblical perspective it is obvious that there is no thought of a bargain struck between equal partners: the 'covenant' is God's gift inviting human acceptance.

Down the centuries the question has repeatedly arisen whether infants are proper subjects of baptism. The historical evidence concerning practice in this matter during the apostolic period is scant and ambiguous [note 332]. Infants were certainly baptized by the late second century, and the overwhelming custom ever since has been to baptize infants of Christian parents. The constant motive may generally be described as a family solidarity by which the same saving benefits are claimed for the children as the parents enjoy. The more precise theological coloration which this motive long took will be discussed in chapter VII. When the practice of infant baptism has come under theological challenge, its supporters have often claimed it to be a striking sign of the prevenient grace of God, who acted first for man's redemption in Jesus Christ and who is at work from the start to bring individuals to salvation. Those who contest the propriety of infant baptism argue that baptism, on the New Testament pattern, is the decisive sign not only of grace but also of faith, and that the justification which baptism signifies is 'by grace *through faith*'; the celebration of the sign ought therefore to await the faith by which the person responds to God's gracious initiative.

The defenders of infant baptism have usually felt obliged to make an association of some sort between such baptism and faith. Four main tacks have been tried. First, faith has been equated with the absence of any obstacle put in the way of God's grace (*non ponens obicem*). But this is altogether too vacuous a view of faith by New Testament standards. Faith may be 'receptivity', but it is not a purely passive reception [note 333].

Second, it has been supposed that infants may already have an active faith. This is the implication of addressing the baptismal interrogations to the infants, for whom the sponsors serve simply as mouthpiece, just as they would, according to a rubric in the Greek rite, for dumb people and barbarians also. Or it has been supposed that infants may be given an active faith by baptism. Luther noted the case of the unborn John who leapt in Elizabeth's womb when confronted by the embryonic Word at Mary's Visitation, Luke 1:41 [note 334]. But these two variants make light of the intelligibility of a gospel message addressed to rational and moral creatures. While surpassing human understanding, the gospel mystery yet includes it. Nor is it proper to extrapolate from the case of those who are congenitally deprived of reason by a fault on the plane of nature to the case of those who will become capable of an intelligent decision in response to the preaching of the gospel. The special care which God doubtless takes of the naturally handicapped does not lessen the element of challenge in the invitation which God addresses to the well endowed.

The third tack has been to ascribe substitutive value to a *fides aliena* on the part of the infant's sponsors and the Church as a whole [note 335]. Appeal is sometimes made to the healing stories in the gospels, where the cure was preceded by the faith of others [note 336]. But while we may all be aided by the faith of others, it may be argued that the very essence of salvation requires the personal appropriation of God's self-gift [note 337].

On these lines, it is the fourth approach which in my judgment best relates infant baptism to faith. It is suggested that the infant is baptized with a view to his future coming to faith. If we may trust the texts and the grammatical competence of the scribes, there is a hint of this in the Bobbio Missal (about 700 A.D.), where the sponsor replies 'May he believe (*credat*)', and in some manuscripts of the Spanish *Liber Ordinum*, where the response is 'He shall believe (*credet*)' [note 338]. The 1662 *Book of Common Prayer* of the Church of England also looks to the future: 'until he come of age to take it upon himself'. In place of the traditional baptismal interrogations many modern Protestant services ask the parents or sponsors rather for a promise to provide such an upbringing for the child that he may come one day to profess his own faith. This forward look is now written into the revised Roman Catholic *Ordo baptismi parvulorum* of 1969.

With regard to the composition of the Church, the question is whether the infants of Christian believers are *part of* the Church. My own view is that the grace of family solidarity is properly and sufficiently expressed by saying that the children of Christian parents have a 'provisional place' in the Church until such time as they responsibly take up their place or decline it. The best ritual correspondence to this view is a solemn admission of such infants to the catechumenate in the hope of their future baptism [note 339]. They will 'learn the faith' in ways appropriate to their age and growth, until they freely ask, it is hoped, for baptism. As far as the 'boundaries' of the Church are concerned, I would rather have the 'positive' indefiniteness brought by the idea of a provisional place for the children of believers than the 'negative' penumbra of baptized unbelievers resulting from the failure of many millions baptized in infancy to arrive at personal commitment. In other words, any fringe had better be composed of those hopefully 'on their way in' than of those apparently 'on their way out'. The matter is set in a broader perspective by the issues to be treated in the last section of this chapter.

It may finally be noted that in our day the question of infant baptism has taken on a clearly cultural and even political dimension. Karl Barth suspected that opposition to the recovery of the biblically and theologically preferable practice of baptism solely upon profession of faith sprang from an ecclesiastical desire to retain a 'constantinian' status in European society. In the German Federal Republic, non-Christian opposition to infant baptism has alleged that the ecclesiastical practice infringes the freedom of religion which the civil constitution guarantees to every individual; and even Christian thinkers argue that the churches, by baptizing infants, are favouring oppression instead of self-determination. I myself would uphold the aim of a 'Christian society' as a penultimate approximation to the divine kingdom, in something like Bonhoeffer's sense of penultimate. But I consider that the freedom which is an essential characteristic of that kingdom is best respected and most clearly signified by a baptism freely decided on by its subject.

8. *Love of the brethren*

The second point about the composition of the Church may be made very briefly. It is that the liturgy makes manifest the *community* nature of the Church.

The Christian religion is neither an atomistic affair of isolated individuals nor yet a totalitarian collectivism in which individual identities and responsibilities are submerged. It is rather a case of members integrated into a body. New believers are baptized 'into Christ', and the communal dimension of that incorporation continues to be expressed in the eucharist, where common participation in the one loaf properly keeps the many individual members united in the one body (1 Corinthians 10:16f). On the one hand, individuality is respected. In the Fourth Gospel, the benefits of the eucharist are promised to each individual who 'eats my flesh and drinks my blood' (John 6:54–58). In St Paul's view of the Lord's supper, it is each person who needs to examine himself lest salvation turn to judgment (1 Corinthians 11:27–32). According to Zwingli, a sacrament is an oath, *sacramentum* in Latin, which each Christian swears to his Master.

On the other hand, no Christian sacrament is celebrated by an individual acting singly. At least two people are required for them all, and the communal nature of the Church is thereby underlined. In connexion with the Lord's supper, St Paul speaks of the Corinthians as 'coming together as a church (*en ekklesiai*)' and 'coming together to eat' (1 Corinthians 11:17f,33f): 'to come together' and the noun *synaxis* became technical terms for the liturgical gathering (cf. 1 Corinthians 14:23; Ignatius, *ad Eph.* 13:1; Didache 14:1; Justin, *First Apology*, 67). The liturgical assembly is an occasion for Christians to 'glorify God with one heart and one voice, *homothumadon en heni stomati*' (Romans 15:5f). J. Gelineau has stressed the unifying force of rhythm and melody in religious ritual as in other cultural contexts: 'Singing together both manifests and constitutes a community. . . . Song in common signifies the community so well because it affords man an opportunity to express himself in a way that is at once fully personal and yet essentially social'; and the same author goes on to show how appropriate this is in the worship of a 'community of love' [note 340]. In the Christian liturgy the kiss of peace is the ritual hinge between social ethics and common praise (cf. Matthew 5:23f): it is suitably placed before the great eucharistic prayer, as in the Byzantine rites and most modern revisions. In its Roman position as a prelude to communion, the *pax* may be seen as highlighting the social presuppositions and consequences of table fellowship.

As a 'sacrament of assembly' (N. Afanasiev), the eucharist manifests the internal structure of the Christian community [note 341]. Vatican II spoke of the liturgical assembly as *praecipua manifestatio Ecclesiae*, and the Constitution on the Sacred Liturgy pictures 'the full active participation of all God's holy people in the same liturgical celebrations, especially in the same eucharist, in a single prayer at one altar, at which there presides the bishop surrounded by his college of priests and ministers' (41). The modern Liturgical Movement has had a fair measure of success in ending the isolation of the Catholic priest at his altar and the Protestant preacher in his pulpit. There is a growing understanding of differentiated contributions to a liturgy guided by the appointed president of the assembly. On the Roman Catholic side, this tendency was bewailed by Archbishop Lefebvre as the 'democratization of the mass', while Nicholas Lash has greeted the same re-structuring as a better model for the exercise of authority in the Church [note 342]. In Protestant churches, the Liturgical Movement may eventually lead to a rethinking of the role of the preacher-theologian who has long dominated the whole service of worship. Here again there are questions concerning authority, and this theme will recur throughout part two of this book.

9. *Hope for the world*

The third point concerning the composition of the Church is its limits and their relation to the field of its witness. That is the ecclesiological version of the general question about the relation of Christianity to other religions and world-views. Christologically, it is a matter of the soteriological uniqueness which Christians have traditionally proclaimed in connexion with Jesus. The sharpest ritual expression of the question asks: Is baptism necessary for salvation? Urgent consideration of the matter in some form or other is being made inescapable by the growth of a universal civilization, the reduction of the world to a 'global village' [note 343].

In the history of Christian thought and practice on the matter, two contradictory tendencies may be detected: the exclusivist and the inclusivist. First: the exclusivist attitude. It is found in Tertullian's irreducible opposition between Athens and Jerusalem. In medieval Europe Boniface VIII claimed that 'there is one holy catholic and apostolic Church, outside of which there is neither salvation nor remission of sins', and that 'it is altogether necessary to salvation for every human creature to be subject to the Roman pontiff' [note 344]. Much missionary work has been motivated by the concern not to leave pagans to perish eternally in their heathen night. The exclusivist attitude seems blind to the existence of religious and human values outside Christianity, which appear *prima facie* to signal the saving presence of God among those who enjoy them. Furthermore, the missionary drive may look like an attempt at aggressive self-expansion on the part of an ecclesiastical institution whose own moral and spiritual imperfections must diminish any claim to absolute authority. Finally, the exclusivist attitude evokes a feeling of repugnance in face of a God who would consign the unevangelized multitudes to damnation.

Then: the inclusivist attitude. It is found as early as Justin Martyr, who held that wise Greeks who had lived 'according to the Logos' were in fact Christians *avant la lettre*. In our own day it has been represented by Paul Tillich's 'latent Church', Karl Rahner's 'anonymous Christianity', and Raymond Panikkar's 'unknown Christ of Hinduism' [note 345]. For all their generosity, such views still strike even well-disposed adherents of other faiths as Christian imperialism by dint of unwanted annexation.

From within Christianity, John Hick has redrawn the map

of the religious universe so as to put God himself at the centre, rather than the Christian religion or even a Christ not tied to institutional Christianity [note 346]. Hick's proposal raises the fundamental question of the relation of Christ to God, as we saw in chapter II. Many Christians will consider that Hick does not do justice to what they confess as the 'definitiveness' of Jesus Christ [note 347]. Here I may simply recall my suggestion of a criteriological christology, made in chapter II: Jesus Christ is the pattern by which we may discern the presence and activity of God among and within humanity [note 348]. The more adequate we hold the 'ostensive definition' embodied in Jesus Christ to be, the nearer shall we situate him to the heart of God (cf. John 1:18, NEB).

In this light, baptism is seen as a non-exclusive promise. When it is administered, it signifies that here at least, in this individual person and in this community, God is actively at work for salvation. The pattern of the salvation is the self-giving love embodied in Jesus Christ, and the baptismal themes express this: dying to sin and self; living for God and for fellow human beings; filial growth into the moral likeness of the Creator; openness to the transforming Spirit. Wherever we see that pattern being enacted, we may discern by faith the saving presence and action of God—and that is ground for hope that the divine kingdom is on the way. But that is not to say that the Church should immediately 'baptize' all such situations even metaphorically, let alone ritually. If baptism is a *non-exclusive* promise, the door may be open—without a concomitant rejection of the unbaptized to a position beyond the pale of salvation—for a sharpening of its signifying power by administering it only in cases where a voluntary request is accompanied by the clear beginnings of faith and the conversion of manners. It would then make a more powerful contribution than is possible in a situation of 'indiscriminate' administration to the firm witness which it is the Church's particular calling to make to the way of God in Christ. This witness is needed *both* for the encouragement of people to personal commitment in a context sympathetically disposed towards the message *and* for warning in a social and cultural environment that is at the time hostile to the universal purposes of God as they are revealed in Christ. The paradox is only superficial: to give the Church a somewhat sharper contour would not in fact diminish the prospective universality of the divine kingdom; it would allow the Church to function more effectively as a 'sacrament of the world's salvation' [note 349].

As a final note to this chapter, it may be useful to commend the further application of the method which we ourselves are applying to Christianity: to examine the rituals of other religions and world-views as a focal expression of their teaching and behaviour. Christian theologians should find this helpful as they look for evidence of God's saving presence and activity beyond the bounds of Christianity. Global surveys by historians of religion may be found, for instance, in Geoffrey Parrinder's *Worship in the World's Religions* and Ninian Smart's *The Religious Experience of Mankind*. John Hick makes a modest theological start with such material in support of his own theses. But much more investigative work and theological reflexion is needed, and we may be grateful for such beginnings as J. S. Mbiti has made in his *Concepts of God in Africa* and his *Prayers of African Religion* [note 250]. We shall return to this issue in chapter XI.

PART TWO

Traditional Means

V

Scripture

1. *A holy book*

THE Church has its sacred book, the holy Bible. The special character of the scriptures is given ritual recognition in various ways. In the Byzantine liturgy, the 'lesser entrance' with the book of the gospel for reading is made with a dignity second only to the 'greater entrance' with the bread and wine prepared for the eucharist. In the Roman Catholic mass, the gospel may be censed and kissed at its reading. In the Reformed tradition, the bringing of the Bible into the church may constitute the ceremonial beginning of the service, though it is also a common custom to leave an open Bible on the Lord's table at all times. In all churches, the scriptures are read with solemnity [note 351]. In the mausoleum of Galla Placidia at Ravenna, a fifth-century mosaic depicts the cupboard in which the gospel texts were kept. Such special housing of the sacred writings prolongs an institution as old as the 'ark of the covenant' which served as a repository for the engraved decalogue in the wilderness and then in the first temple; the place given to the scroll of Torah in the architecture of the synagogue continues the line on the Jewish side. Similar reverence is shown for 'the book' in other 'scriptural' religions: the Qur'ān in the Islamic mosque, the Granth in the Sikh gurdwara.

Both in its resting position and even more in its liturgical use, the Bible as an actual book serves as some kind of sacrament of the Word of God. To borrow the scholastic categories: the printed and bound object is the *sacramentum tantum*, the external sign, like the bread and wine at the eucharist; the substantial or ideational content of the Bible is the *sacramentum et res*, the thing as signified, like the eucharistic

149

body and blood of Christ; the *res sacramenti*, the purpose or fruit, is in both cases the communion of the Church with the God who gives himself to us in Christ [note 352]. In the case of the Bible, the medium of communion is words: communion takes the particular form of 'communication'. In and through the reading of the scriptures, the Church hears God's voice and message, and from its own side the Church speaks its response to God in prayer. In this more or less 'naïve' reality of the Church's liturgical experience, the holiness of the scriptures is derived from both their source and their function: they *mediate* the word of *God*. God is considered to be in some sense their author; and he is further considered to assist our understanding and application of them. In historical terms: the scriptures come to us from the past as witnessing to a revelation of God which is believed definitive; it is by their means that the definitive revelation is able to qualify our present. It is a task of theology to help the Church interpret the more or less raw experience of its use of the scriptures in the liturgy. It is obvious that theology in our day must employ for this task the tools of biblical criticism, hermeneutical theory, doctrinal history, sociological analysis, psychological science, cultural anthropology, and so on. In the other direction, it is equally important that the Church's experience of scripture in the liturgy should set one of the perspectives from which the scriptures are considered by the biblical scholar as he seeks their meaning and by the systematic theologian as he seeks to build the scriptural component into his thinking.

Such themes will be treated in the latter part of this chapter, when we face in more detail some of the issues raised by the presence of the scriptures in the liturgy. In the meantime, however, we shall be dealing with the presence of the liturgy in the scriptures. Formally, the approach will be largely historical; but it will not be without theological importance to have shown the part played by worship in the formation of the foundation documents of Christianity. We shall look at the liturgical material in the Old and New Testaments separately, and then at the decisive contribution of liturgical practice to the establishment and definition of the scriptural canon.

2. *The liturgical element in the Old Testament*

My purpose at this point is simply to remind systematic theologians of the ways in which modern biblical scholars allow a very considerable part to the cult in the formation, formulation and transmission of the material that came to be deposited in the Old Testament [note 353]. For our purposes it is not the details of any particular theory which count: the important thing is the widespread agreement that the cultic hypothesis has proved illuminating in so many cases. Examples may be given from the Law, the Prophets, and the Writings.

For a large-scale theory we may mention G. von Rad's account of the structure of 'the hexateuch' [note 354]. Beneath admittedly later expansions and phraseology, von Rad detected in Deuteronomy 26:5–9 (cf. 6:20–24 and Joshua 24:2–13) an ancient liturgical confession, whose four principal 'moments' had supplied the Yahwist (J) with his outline for the composition of the hexateuch in its first form: (1) the ancestral beginnings ('A wandering Aramean was my father'); (2) the time in Egypt; (3) the Lord's deliverance of the people from Egyptian bondage; (4) the entry into the promised land. The Yahwist added a preface which set Israel in the context of universal history (the J material in Genesis 2–11); he expanded the patriarchal sagas in order to take in the traditions of all the various tribes; he inserted material concerning Sinai and the Law, which in von Rad's opinion belonged to a separate strand of tradition from that represented by the very ancient credo. According to von Rad, the original *sitz im leben* of the liturgical confession of faith was the annual feast of weeks at the shrine of Gilgal. He further noted that its present structure resembles in part the cultic genre of the 'individual thanksgiving', which we meet in the Psalms (distress: appeal: deliverance), and that this type may itself be very old (cf. 1 Samuel 12:6–8). The content of the ancient confession was woven into the later liturgical practice in Psalms 78, 135, 136, and its substance became the ground of prophetic appeals in Amos 2:9f and Micah 6:3–5. Even more, the old credo was finally extended to become, if but the outlines of von Rad's theory are correct, the very Torah which continues at the heart of the Jewish cult and religion. This development may properly be seen, from the theological angle, as a faithful generalization of the original purpose of the ancient liturgical confession. Notice the theological point which von Rad makes in connexion with the 'harvest festival' setting of Deuteronomy 26:5ff: 'In verse 9 the recital of the historical events comes to an end. With verse 10 the speech becomes quite personal, for the speaker now puts himself into the situation of which he has just recounted the historical background. The fruits he has to offer come from "the ground which thou, O Lord, hast given *me*". With these words the speaker has taken his place in the story of salvation and, in a splendid foreshortening of time, has acknowledged himself to be a direct recipient of the act of salvation which was the gift of the promised land.' The same principle holds good when in Joshua 24 the confession of faith is set in the context of the annual 'covenant renewal' festival at Shechem [note 355].

In our own terms, the theological point may be expressed in the following way. The cult brought into focus the continuing benefits of an earlier and foundational act of salvation: it allowed the people to thank God for the original act and for the blessings which by his doing continued to flow from it (in the case of the harvest, the first fruits are representative of the whole crop); it allowed the people to commit themselves afresh to this God and to a style of life which corresponded to his character and will (cf. Deuteronomy 26:10b–19; Joshua 24:14–28). It was the function of the narrative recital, and eventually of the scriptures into which it became incorporated, to recall the inaugural saving event. Some modern scholars have said that this original event was understood to 'become present' again and again through the cult (*Vergegenwärtigung*) [note 356]. It may be clearer to say that the matter was understood in terms of the continuing identity of God and the people: the same God who once brought the people into the promised land then continued to give its blessings to their successive generations; if they were to retain their identity as the favoured people, the succeeding generations had for their part to renew the commitment which their ancestors made to the God of their salvation. The liturgy was, and *mutatis mutandis* remains for us, the locus in which the story of the constitutive events is retold in order to elicit an appropriate response in worship and ethics to the God who remains faithful to the purposes which his earlier acts declared. As the book in which the original stories have been deposited, developed, and classically defined, the scriptures subserve that continuing function of the liturgy.

That this understanding of the liturgy obtained from post-Exodus days in Israel's religion may be shown also from the example of the passover. This example would itself prove our point, even if von Rad's grand theory concerning the hexateuch as a whole did not carry conviction. The annual passover liturgy allowed the succeeding generations to 're-live' in ritual form the original deliverance from the bondage in Egypt. In the material finally deposited as scripture in Exodus 12–13, there is a certain oscillation between the events of the first passover night itself and the later memorial observance of passover and unleavened bread. By commemorating the great Exodus, the annual ritual transmitted 'throughout the generations' a belief in, almost an experience of, the saving power of the Lord who 'by a strong hand brought us out of Egypt'. The identity of the favoured people is maintained from generation to generation:

> And when your children say to you, 'What do you mean by this service?' you shall say, 'It is the sacrifice of the Lord's passover, for he passed over the houses of the people of Israel in Egypt, when he slew the Egyptians but spared our houses.'

Because the Lord remains true to his own identity and purposes, the Exodus from Egypt could later serve as a model for the hoped-for deliverance from Babylon: Isaiah 43:15–21; 48:20f; 51:9–11; Jeremiah 23:7f. At the time of Jesus and the Roman occupation, the passover season, and particularly the paschal night itself, was the time when Jewish messianic expectations reached their highest [note 357]. Christians believe that a mighty deliverance, with universal significance, did in fact take place through the death and resurrection of

Jesus the Christ at the season of the Jewish passover. In the early centuries of Christianity the paschal sense of expectancy was maintained, now transposed to the awaited final parousia of Jesus Christ at Easter time [note 358]. Moreover, there are hints that the early Christians saw their eucharist as the successor of the Jewish passover, and this will account in part for the eschatologically charged atmosphere which surrounded the Christian sacrament from the first and which has never entirely disappeared [note 359].

Returning to the Old Testament, we find recent scholarship also ready to make positive and direct connexions between the cult and the prophets. Earlier scholars, especially among Protestants, had emphasized the prophetic critique of the official priestly cultus. There are indeed numerous passages in which the canonical prophets attack the sacrificial worship of their day: one need only look at, say, Isaiah 1:10–17 or Amos 5:21–24. However, it is now widely held that the target of the prophetic criticism was not sacrificial worship as such, but rather a sacrificial cult which was adulterated by pagan elements and which found no backing in social righteousness. On both these counts Yahweh was being mocked, not honoured, by his people's worship. The only place in which the very existence of the sacrificial system comes under question is Jeremiah 7:21ff, where the prophet looks back with nostalgia to the time in the wilderness ostensibly before the institution of 'burnt offerings and sacrifices'. It is as though the prophet, at a time when Israel had apparently descended to human sacrifice (7:30ff), judged the whole sacrificial system irredeemably 'Canaanite', whereas the 'official' view, eventually deposited above all in Leviticus, was doubtless that the sacrificial system (though hardly human sacrifice!) had originally been instituted by Yahweh through Moses. On the other hand, recent scholars have noted that Samuel and Elijah among the 'former prophets' performed sacrificial functions (1 Samuel 7:9; 9:13; 1 Kings 18:30ff). Furthermore it is now widely held, following the work of Hölscher, Mowinckel, and A. R. Johnson, that there were 'cultic prophets' associated with the priests in the service of the Jerusalem temple [note 360]. Prophets and priests are linked in connexion with the temple at Jeremiah 23:11 and Lamentations 2:20, for instance. Some of the Psalms make good sense when interpreted as a medley of prayers and oracles in which cultic prophets could have taken part, although inevitably the case falls short of proof. Of the 'later prophets' it has been suggested that Amos and even Jeremiah were cultic prophets, but these suggestions go far beyond the evidence and may even be contrary to some of it. Much more noteworthy is the prominent place of the temple in Ezekiel's vision of the restored homeland. The hymnic forms in deutero-Isaiah may have liturgical origins. Among the minor prophetic books preserved in the canon, Joel, Obadiah, Nahum, Habakkuk and Zephaniah have all been held, with varying degrees of plausibility, actually to be 'cultic liturgies', or at least to be strongly influenced by liturgical forms [note 361]. The certain thing is that the prophetic messages of judgment and hope from earlier times were preserved through their reading in the worship of the synagogue.

If the part of the cultic prophets in the composition and use of the Psalms remains conjectural (and it has also been surmised that the cultic prophets ended up as the temple singers of the Chronicler's day), it is not in serious doubt that many of the Psalms had liturgical origins. Using form-critical methods, H. Gunkel and S. Mowinckel were able to make illuminating classifications of the Psalms: the types included hymns of praise, individual thanksgivings and laments, pilgrimage songs, royal psalms, and enthronement psalms [note 362]. It is much more difficult to situate the particular psalms in their precise ritual context, and the results of scholarly imagination have been various. One of the most striking theories—proposed by S. Mowinckel in the light of Babylonian models—associated the enthronement psalms with an autumn new-year festival in which both the human ruler and the divine Monarch whom he represented were annually re-enthroned (Psalms 47; 93; 95–100) [note 363]. Whatever the early historical and liturgical details about the Psalms, the most significant fact for our purposes is that the Jewish and Christian communities have continued to find in the Psalter a rich treasury of material for direct and indirect use in their praise and supplication of God [note 364]. The use of the Psalter may for various reasons need to be selective, but that is part of the more general question of canonicity, to which we shall return [note 365].

3. *The liturgical element in the New Testament*

The New Testament has been characterized as 'the Church's oldest extant collection of sermons'. In calling the New Testament documents sermons, W. Marxsen is picking on the fact that they are adaptations and applications of earlier traditions made necessary by the passage of time and by differences in cultural circumstances [note 366]. Within the New Testament itself, the process can be illustrated from the way in which Mark's gospel is 're-written' by Luke (the delay in the expected parousia obliges him to place 'the Church' in 'salvation history') and by Matthew (in order to reach the special problems of his Jewish-Christian context), or from the development of the pauline theology in Paul's successive letters and on into the deutero-paulines. That process of preaching the Christian message in terms appropriate to particular situations had already begun before any of our New Testament documents were written down. For behind the period of *Redaktionsgeschichte* lay the period treated by *Formgeschichte*. Form-criticism helped us to see that many of the pericopes now included in the gospels had already been used in the earliest preaching of the Church [note 367]. This broadly 'liturgical' character of the New Testament material means that there is a fundamental identity of purpose between the 'oldest collection of sermons'—which acquired scriptural status—and all the Church's subsequent preaching in its worship. This fact will afford help both when we seek to understand the normative function of the scriptures and also when we state a theology of preaching.

Formgeschichte and *Redaktionsgeschichte* have also detected other types of liturgical material embedded in the New Testament and shown how it was used by the authors of our documents. The most basic form is doubtless the brief acclamatory confession which the writers introduce by the verb *homologein*:

> If you confess with your lips that Jesus is Lord . . .
>
> (Romans 10:9f)
>
> Whoever confesses that Jesus is the Son of God . . .
>
> (1 John 4:15)

The forms in which the evangelists report Peter's confession may also reflect liturgical usage:

> You are the Christ (Mark 8:29)
>
> You are the Christ, the Son of the living God
>
> (Matthew 16:16)
>
> The Christ of God (Luke 9:20)

The confession 'Jesus is Lord, *Kurios Jēsous*' may have been most characteristic of Gentile Christians: it is found not only at Romans 10:9 but also at 1 Corinthians 12:3. Scholarly opinion is divided in its preference for a liturgical or a juridical locus for this confession. Certainly the verb *homologein* can carry a juridical flavour (Matthew 10:32f; Luke 12:8), and the disciples of Christ could expect to have to bear witness to him before human tribunals (Matthew 10:17–20; Mark 13:9–11). Yet the context in Romans might suggest a baptismal locus for the confession *Kurios Jēsous*, and in 1 Corinthians the worship assembly. The liturgical and the juridical possibilities are not in fact mutually exclusive. Pliny's letter to Trajan shows that the appearance before the imperial authorities could itself take on a 'liturgical' complexion [note 368]: Pliny's test for alleged Christians upon arrest comprised 'reciting a prayer to the gods', 'making supplications with incense and wine before the emperor's statue' (we know the rival confession 'Caesar is Lord'), and 'cursing Christ' (1 Corinthians 12:3 mentions '*Anathema Jēsous*') [note 369]. Besides the brief acclamatory confession centred on the person of Jesus, scholars have distinguished a potentially longer and more 'creedal' form, which Paul in Romans 10:9 introduces by the verb *pisteuein* and which fills out some of the 'work' of Christ:

And if you believe in your heart that God raised him from the dead. . . .

Deposits from this kind of 'creed' may perhaps be found in such places as Romans 1:3f; 4:25; 1 Corinthians 15:3–5; 1 Timothy 3:16—although some scholars might wish to assign the 1 Corinthians 15 passage to a special context of teaching-transmission (*paradidonai*/*paralambanein*: the later dual ceremony of the *traditio* and *redditio* of the creed suffices however to show that the teaching and responsive confession of the faith are simply the two sides of a single coin [note 370]); and some might class 1 Timothy 3:16 as a hymn. Whether in acclamatory or creedal form, the confession is made not only to God but also to the world. Concerning the New Testament confessions, H. Conzelmann writes: 'The Christian community declares publicly who is its Lord. The confession not only demands a decision but has the power to produce one . . . Christ's rule is confessed before the world because his domain is not only the Church but the world. This the Church knows, whereas it is hidden from the unbelieving world. Therefore the Church must go on disclosing to the world the truth about itself' [note 371]. While it may be necessary to nuance this distinction between the Church and the world, Conzelmann's statement may properly be applied to the continuing confession of Christ in the Church beyond New Testament times. There is thus once more a fundamental identity of purpose between the confessions now deposited as New Testament scripture and the later liturgy of the Church as it repeats and interprets them: they are to express and elicit the acknowledgment of God in Christ.

Another liturgical form which modern scholarship has re-discovered in the New Testament is the hymn. We have already referred to New Testament hymns in connexion with christology in chapter II [note 372], and in chapter VI we shall treat the question of hymns in more detail. At this juncture it is sufficient to make three remarks. First: the New Testament writers find it valuable to draw on the known hymns of the Christian community when they are themselves establishing points of doctrine. Whether the New Testament writers are viewed as 'apostolic authorities' or as 'early theologians', their practice in this matter sets a precedent for later ecclesiastical authorities and theologians. Second: the New Testament writers do not take over the apparently more or less spontaneous, unreflected hymnic material of the community uncritically. We saw, for instance, grounds for thinking that modification had been made to the hymn quoted in Colossians 1:15–20. This suggests that later ecclesiastical authorities and theologians may also be expected to operate critically with respect to the poetic expressions of popular piety. Third: the combination of the two previous points should invite Christians with poetic gifts and theological awareness to use their imagination and understanding in the service of the Church's liturgy. We shall be looking in the next chapter at some outstanding contributions from the past.

The next type of liturgical material to be found in the New Testament is prayers. We have already looked in chapter I at the Lord's Prayer as a paradigm for Christian worship. Here we will mention only the New Testament reflexions of a style of prayer which must have been common in the primitive Church: Jews frequently 'blessed' God on account of his manifold mercies, and the Church took over this style in order to 'bless' God particularly for his saving acts in Jesus Christ [note 373]. The Jewish *berakoth* did not constitute a uniform liturgical genre, but recent scholarship has established beyond doubt that the Christian *eucharistia* developed from that broad family pattern of prayers, and a strong case can be made for the particular influence of the Jewish table-prayer, *birkat ha-mazon*. Despite attempts to find subtle differences between the verbs *eulogein* and *eucharistein* in the various New Testament accounts of meals, it is probably sufficient to take 'thank' as simply a Greek translation of the Semitic 'bless'. Epistolary adaptations of the blessing type of prayer are found at various places:

> Blessed be the God and Father of our Lord Jesus Christ, the Father of mercies and God of all comfort, who comforts us in all our affliction. . . .   (2 Corinthians 1:3ff)

Blessed be the God and Father of our Lord Jesus Christ, who
has blessed us in Christ with every spiritual blessing in the
heavenly places. . . .   (Ephesians 1:3ff)

Blessed be the God and Father of our Lord Jesus Christ! By
his great mercy we have been born anew to a living hope through
the resurrection of Jesus Christ from the dead. . . .
                                                (1 Peter 1:3ff)

In several other cases the pauline letters begin with a first-
person thanksgiving indirectly addressed to God: Romans
1:8; 1 Corinthians 1:4; Philippians 1:3; Colossians 1:3;
1 Thessalonians 1:2; 2 Thessalonians 1:3; 2 Timothy 1:3;
Philemon 4. This regular pattern of letter opening, with
'blessing' and 'thanksgiving' as apparent alternatives, suggests
that a liturgical type is being used to transform an ancient
epistolary convention in a Christian sense. A similar thing
happens with initial and final greetings in the New Testament
letters [note 374]. When the writers pass over at times into
doxology, the link becomes even more apparent between
'doing theology' and 'teaching ethics', on the one hand, and
the worship of God on the other: Romans 11:33–36; 16:25–
27; Ephesians 3:20f; 1 Timothy 1:17; 6:16; Jude 24f. Here
again is a model for later attitudes.

Other liturgical material in the New Testament is provided
by the norms which are given for various liturgical occasions.
Several baptisms are reported in a brief descriptive way in
the Acts of the Apostles: 2:37–41; 8:35–39; 9:18; 10:46–48;
16:29–34; 19:1–7. It is not impossible that the author is here
supplying a 'paradigm' which is equivalent in its own way
to the matthaean 'institution narrative' (Matthew 28:19).
From 1 Corinthians 11:17–34 and 14:1–40 it is possible to
put together a fairly substantial picture of the Corinthian
assemblies. It is important to notice in this case that St Paul,
whether as apostle or as theologian, is quite definitely setting
out corrective guidelines for liturgical practice. The spontaneous assembly requires a certain authoritative control.
Before they were used for pastoral teaching by St Paul, and
for 'history' by the synoptic evangelists, the 'eucharistic

institution narratives' probably served as agreed 'rubrics' for the celebration of the Lord's supper. Without prejudice to the historical question of whether Jesus 'instituted the eucharist' at a Last Supper, it may be said that New Testament scholars have found a number of indications that the 'canonical' forms of the narratives have been influenced by earlier liturgical practice [note 375]. Our present point is that worship requires certain practical, and ultimately doctrinal, norms. This is already apparent in New Testament times, and it continues to be the case in the later worship of the Church. The added factor in subsequent history is that the New Testament writings have now become 'scripture' and themselves constitute a permanent part of the authority pattern in which later and contemporary teachers, both pastoral and theological, also figure. In the other direction, it is equally important to notice that the New Testament writers find it valuable to draw upon the recognized liturgical practice of the community—just as we saw them drawing upon hymns—when they are themselves establishing points of doctrine or giving ethical teaching. We need only recall the use which St Paul makes of baptism: Romans 6; 1 Corinthians 1:13; 12:12f; Galatians 3:26–29; cf. Ephesians 4:5; Colossians 2:12; Titus 3:3–7. This matter of doctrine and liturgy as correlative norms will be treated thematically in chapters VII and VIII, although it might almost have been possible to entitle the whole book *Lex orandi, lex credendi.*

Before ending this survey of liturgical material in the New Testament, brief mention must be made of theories that resemble von Rad's on the hexateuch, though on a rather less ambitious scale. It has been suggested of a number of complete New Testament writings that they were in fact originally liturgical texts or were shaped in their entirety by a liturgical context. Again, there is here no question of evaluating particular theories. The point is to illustrate the way in which respectable modern scholars have been willing to contemplate a very considerable formative role for worship in the making of the New Testament writings.

Thus twentieth-century scholarship has long recognized the baptismal connexion of 1 *Peter*. The first suggestion was that the document was, in whole or in part, a baptismal homily [note 376]. In 1951 H. Preisker, a German Protestant exegete, detected more precisely the elements of a baptismal service composed largely of hymns, prayers and sermons. In 1954 F. L. Cross, a Catholic-minded Anglican student of the Fathers, saw in *1 Peter* an incomplete text of the celebrant's part in the paschal vigil service of baptism [note 377]. However fanciful the details of these divergent reconstructions, the ritual and theological themes of baptism are certainly dominant threads in the texture of our present epistle. Apart from the express mention of baptism at 3:20f, there is talk of rebirth at 1:3, 1:23 and 2:2, and of light at 2:9 ('enlightenment' was an early term for baptism: Justin, *Apol.* I, 61; cf. Hebrews 6:4; 10:32). The reference to milk at 2:2 may echo the early practice of giving milk and honey to the neophytes (attested by Tertullian, by Clement of Alexandria and by *The Apostolic Tradition* [note 378]), and the allusion in 2:3 to Psalm 34:8 may presage the later popularity of that verse as a communion text ('O taste and see that the Lord is good'). There is furthermore an interesting parallel between 3:3 and Hippolytus' instruction that women candidates for baptism should loose their hair and take off their gold ornaments [note 379]. A somewhat similar approach has been adopted by J. C. Kirby towards the enigmatic Letter to the Ephesians [note 380]. Showing links with a past baptism, the early style of eucharistic prayer, and a supposed Jewish-Christian version of the feast of Pentecost as covenant renewal, Kirby argued that *Ephesians* is fundamentally a prayer and liturgical discourse with epistolary additions and insertions [note 381].

Further examples of liturgical theses are provided by the lectionary approach to the gospels. In *The Fourth Gospel and Jewish Worship*, A. Guilding argues that the Evangelist arranged his material in such an order that the discourses supplied a thematic Christian commentary on the triennial cycle of readings from the Law and the Prophets which was established in Palestinian synagogue worship well before St John's time [note 382]. M. D. Goulder, in *Midrash and Lection in Matthew*, proposes that *St Matthew* should be understood as a midrashic expansion of *St Mark*, so ordered as to provide weekly and festal readings round a Jewish-Christian year, the discourses being seen as 'fulfilments' of the Jewish festivals [note 383]. Lectionary theses are difficult to evaluate in detail and hence arouse suspicion [note 384], but the anchorage which they suppose for the gospels in the liturgical life of the primitive Church is entirely plausible in a general way.

4. *The canon established and defined*

Despite the dangers of 'pan-liturgism' it is now generally agreed, at the least, that the Old and New Testaments contain much material, whether entire or fragmentary, which originated in the context of worship [note 385]. Many reputable scholars also accept the likelihood that the liturgy contributed decisively to the structuring of whole 'books', or series of books, in the Bible. It remains in the historical part of this chapter to consider briefly the part played by liturgical use in the establishment and definition of the scriptural canon.

Although the word canon was not used in this sense before the fourth century A.D., the Church had from the start been familiar with a corpus of authorized scripture. It inherited both the principle and the actual material of 'the Old Testament' from Judaism. New Testament writers mention the Law and the Prophets (Matthew 5:17; Matthew 11:13 = Luke 16:16; Matthew 22:40), or the Law and the Prophets and the Psalms (Luke 24:44f; cf. 24:27). The last-mentioned triad is significant, because these were precisely the categories of books unquestionably used in the public worship of the synagogue. Jewish doubts about certain other books, which eventually achieved canonical status as part of the third category, 'the Writings', were largely doubts about their suitability for use in public worship [note 386]. The earliest extant listing of *New* Testament books—the Muratorian fragment dating from the late second century—shows that it was again a question of books 'to be read in Church, *legi in ecclesia*'. In the reverse direction, it is highly probable that it was their being read in worship along with the 'Old Testament' scriptures that established the scriptural prestige of writings presumed to be apostolic [note 387]. Whether or not they were originally composed, as Guilding and Goulder have argued, with such a liturgical purpose in mind, the gospels were certainly read in worship by the time of Justin Martyr:

> And on the day called Sun-day an assembly is held in one place of all who live in town or country, and the records of the apostles (*elsewhere Justin refers to* the records composed by the apostles, which are called gospels) or writings of the prophets are read for as long as time allows . . . [note 388].

St Paul, or another, appears to have envisaged his epistles being read in the public assembly of the local church:

> And when this letter has been read among you, have it read also in the church of the Laodiceans; and see that you read also the letter from Laodicea.   (Colossians 4:16)

It has indeed been suggested that the pauline epistles, *Hebrews*, and *1 Peter* all display towards the end a fairly regular tripartite pattern, which may correspond to a sequence of events near the conclusion of the service at which the epistle was to be read: (a) prayer or praise to 'the God of peace'; (b) a kiss or greeting; (c) the 'grace' [note 389]. Such formal reading of the epistles would help to explain why the author of *2 Peter* could put the letters of 'our beloved brother Paul' on a par with 'the other scriptures' (2 Peter 3:15f).

The case of *Revelation* in the Eastern churches offers a counter-proof of the importance of liturgical use in matters of canonicity. The East hesitated long before accepting the Apocalypse of St John, doubtless because of the encouragement the writing could give to 'prophetism' of a montanist kind. Although the book eventually became officially part of the scriptural canon, it has never been much drawn upon by Eastern lectionaries, and Eastern theologians in consequence rarely quote it in doctrinal argument. Liturgical use thereby influences the effective doctrinal canon, in despite of conciliar recognition given to a particular book as scriptural. An example on the more positive side is provided by the long traditional popularity of *St Matthew* in all the churches over against *St Mark*. *St Matthew* predominated in classical liturgical use, doubtless because it provided a 'fuller record' than *St Mark*. Liturgical familiarity then influenced the theologians, before the rise of modern criticism, to quote by preference the matthaean version.

The major contribution of the liturgy to the content, composition, establishment, delimitation and doctrinal exploitation of the scriptures should now be clear. This historical case, coupled with the continuing 'religious' sense of the Bible as a 'holy book', constitutes a sufficient basis for the theological assertion that the liturgy is and remains the primary and 'connatural' context for the Church's understanding and use of the scriptures. Nevertheless, the rise of modern biblical scholarship, and the more general cultural desire to subject all things to rational scrutiny, mean that systematic theology cannot escape the need critically to justify the place occupied by the scriptures at the ritual heart of Christianity, and to show the conditions upon which the scriptures may properly continue to fulfil their liturgical role in present circumstances. In the rest of this chapter, therefore, we shall be examining a number of critical questions raised by modern biblical scholarship in their relation to the liturgy, and we shall be suggesting that the liturgy itself supplies an essential hermeneutical perspective for the biblical and doctrinal theologian. The following subjects will be treated in turn: the character of the scriptures as foundational and permanent witness; the unity of the Bible, and of the New Testament within itself; the liturgy as a hermeneutical continuum; the function of preaching as application of the message; the role of the scriptures in the mediation of communion between God and human beings, or the questions of scriptural 'inspiration' and of the divine presence through scripture.

5. *The scriptural witness*

The constant reading of the scriptures in worship bears testimony to the fact that Christianity considers itself a historical religion centred upon the revelation of God in Jesus Christ. One of the earliest major categories for interpreting Jesus saw him as the fulfilment of the promises made by

God to Israel and, through Israel, to the world. From the start, the Christians claimed the 'Old Testament' as their own scriptures, and its use in Christian worship signifies its original and continuing function of providing an interpretative framework for the history of Jesus. The earliest Christian interpretations of Jesus—both against the background of Israel and contemporary Judaism and against the complex background of Graeco-Roman culture—became deposited in the writings which eventually attained, as we saw, the status of New Testament scripture. By the time of the Muratorian fragment in the late second century, the chief formal criterion of a writing's acceptability for 'reading in church' was its supposed apostolic origin—either direct or, as in the case of *St Mark* and *St Luke*, virtual. This criterion of apostolicity was also being applied by Irenaeus and Tertullian to the line of bishops and to the teaching which they gave by the *regula fidei*. In the patristic period, the writings known as 'church orders' usually claimed the same apostolic sanction. Origen's defence of infant baptism appealed to the apostolic origin of the practice. It is clear, then, that the Church of the first centuries looked to the apostles for the authorized account and interpretation of the story of Jesus, his person, his teaching and the events surrounding him. This has been the continuing justification, more often implicit than explicit, for the reading of the New Testament in worship.

In the Church's traditional concern—to which the liturgical reading of scripture bears testimony—for the historical foundation of Christianity in Jesus, it is fair to distinguish two themes: the concern for who Jesus was, what he said, did and suffered, and the concern for the apostolic witness to him. The two are inseparably connected, for the second is a means of access to the first. Modern biblical scholarship has directly or indirectly raised a number of questions which must be faced if a satisfactory rationale is to be provided for the continuing liturgical practice. Thus the only New Testament documents to which an indisputably direct apostolic authorship is now attributed are some of the pauline letters: and St Paul himself has always, from his own days, occupied a problematical status in relation to 'the twelve' who traditionally constitute the apostolic nucleus; for he was certainly not 'one of the men who have accompanied us during all the time that the Lord Jesus went in and out among us' (Acts 1:21f), his own call came to him in his extraordinary experience on the Damascus road (cf. 1 Corinthians 15:8f), and his relations with Peter and the other pillars were not untroubled (Galatians 2). The remaining writings of the New Testament are usually ascribed to second and even third generation Christians, between say the years 65 and 125. In the intervening period since the days of Jesus, the Church had been affected not only by the normal passage of generations, itself a matter complicated in this case by the delay in the expected return of Christ, but also by its own great geographical and cultural expansion. The story of Jesus had already been told, interpreted and applied in (rapidly) changing circumstances before it was deposited in the writings which by, say, the middle of the second century were believed to be apostolic.

Consequences of four sorts need to be drawn concerning the liturgical use of the scriptures. First, the 'quest of the historical Jesus' must be pursued despite the varying degrees of uncertainty which will attach to particular features of the recovered character and story. This search is indispensable if, as we saw in chapter II, Jesus Christ is believed to be a definitive revelation of God and constitutes a focus for Christian worship. The New Testament scriptures supply, to speak simply at the historical level, our closest witness in time to Jesus and to the impression which he created. It is part of the ministry of teaching in the Church to help Christian worshippers listen with a discerning ear to the scripture readings in order at the very least to catch 'a whisper of his voice' and 'trace the outskirts of his ways' [note 390].

Second, we need a frank commitment to the source of scriptural authority. If the patristic Church was anxious that its approved scriptures should have apostolic authorship, the reason lay in the belief that the Lord Jesus himself had appointed the apostles to be his authorized witnesses (cf. Acts 1:8). If we for our part are greatly dubious about the apostolic origins of the New Testament scriptures, we must nevertheless trust God at the least to have overseen the provision of an adequate foundational record—however *chiaroscuro* in mode—of his self-revelation in Jesus. Otherwise the very notion of a definitive revelation is contradicted. To experience the religious effectiveness of the reading of the scriptures in the context of worship helps to confirm our trust that God has provided for us in this way. It is not possible to appeal to the Church itself, apart from the scriptures, as a kind of foundational witness; for the scriptures are precisely the scriptures of the Church.

The third consequence is, in fact, that the scriptures have a canonical function throughout the continuing history of the Church. In order to safeguard the substance of Christianity, the early Church decided, over a period of time, that these books, and these books alone, should be read with scriptural status in Church; and again, at least some minimal doctrine of divine providence is required with respect to this decision. As a result, the history of Christian theology can be read as the history of the interpretation of scripture. We shall see shortly that the liturgy provides a continuing context for the positive interpretation of scripture. Meanwhile we notice that the liturgy also keeps the 'original' scriptures before the attention in a way that is partly independent of current interpretation and application, so that there is always the possiblity of a critical challenge to the present-day Church, whether pastors, theologians or people, in the name of the primitive authenticity to which the scriptures bear witness. This will prove very important when we come, in chapters VII and VIII, to questions of the development and correction of doctrine.

The fourth consequence is that we must take seriously the dynamic component which is written into the New Testament canon. Certainly the New Testament is canonical in respect of the *substance* of Christianity. But it is no less canonical in respect of *method*. The New Testament writings show us in exemplary manner that the gospel is always to be preached into particular circumstances, where it will meet with a particular response according to the circumstances. Christian worship provides a focal context for that particular preaching and that particular response.

I think that we have by now justified the need and manifold

usefulness of the scriptures in the worship where Christianity comes to focal expression; and that we have done something to indicate an approach to some of the apparent difficulties raised by critical scholarship in this regard. But we are not yet out of the woods. For one of the urgent themes of recent biblical scholarship has been to detect in scripture a diversity amounting to contradictoriness. Diversity is precisely what we should expect in view of the particularity of the preaching and the response: but plain contradictions would call into question the coherence of the substance of Christianity, or the coherence of the scriptural canon at least. We need therefore to face the question of the unity of the Bible. We shall find that liturgical practice gives a nuanced view of the matter, a view which can in fact help the biblical and systematic theologians in their own problematic.

6. *The variegated unity of the Bible*

The broader question concerns the relation of the two Testaments, but we shall deal first with the question which is more acute for most contemporary Christian scholars: the narrower question of the internal coherence of the New Testament. Ernst Käsemann has treated the topic with characteristic sharpness, asserting that there are plain contradictions among the New Testament writings. He appears to imply that the only justification for such a 'mixed' canon is as a permanent warning to the Church, a 'documentation of the struggle between gospel and world'—which takes place even within the Church [note 391]. But we need to ask whether Käsemann's alleged contradictions are contradictions in fact. To take his prize example first: it must constantly be re-asserted, against all Lutheran tendencies to the contrary, that there is no 'irreconcilability, *Unvereinbarkeit*' between St Paul and St James on justification [note 392]. Both writers held that works are the expression and test of faith. The Church was not being inconsistent when it recommended its catechumens to study St James as well as St Paul [note 393]. Again: Käsemann detects an 'incongruity' between the matthaean and lucan motif of a Virgin Birth and the johannine picture of the Logos who is from the beginning in the bosom of the Father and can alone be the Revealer [note 394]. Neither the Nicene Creed nor the Christmas hymns of the Church find any such incongruity between the eternal generation of the Son and his human birth. If either the pre-existence or the virgin birth of Christ, or both of them, are rejected, the reason will not reside in the mutual incongruity of the two. Or a final example: Käsemann makes much of the divergent eschatologies of the New Testament, as between say the 'inaugurated eschatology' of the preaching of Jesus and the earliest Christians, its lucan replacement by 'salvation history', and the 'thoroughgoing elimination of the apocalyptic element' in favour of the *Christus praesens* in (Bultmann's edition of) the Fourth Gospel [note 395]. In the Church's eucharistic experience, the eschatologies are united in the present parousia of the One who came and who is to come. In all three cases, whether from the area of justification or christology or eschatology, some 'demythologization' may be needed in the circumstances of our culture, but it is unfair to lay the charge of contradictoriness at the door of the New Testament.

Granted that there is variety without fundamental contradictoriness in the New Testament, it may be shown that liturgical usage sets useful perspectives for the treatment of some issues in biblical and systematic theology concerning the complex unity of the New Testament. First: the binding theme of all the writings that are read as New Testament scripture indicates where the heart of Christianity is fixed. The one thing which these writings have in common is, in the words of C. F. D. Moule, 'devotion to the person of Jesus Christ, the historical Jesus acknowledged as Messiah and Lord' [note 396]. Luther's material canon for the New Testament scriptures was that they should 'advance Christ, *Christum treiben*'. This is also the task of biblical and systematic theologians in so far as they see themselves as Christians, and it provides a touchstone for their work.

Second: the liturgical distinction between Gospel and Epistle, together with the fact that readings are taken at the eucharist from *both* categories in all the traditional rites, indicates that Christianity needs both 'the story of Jesus' and a paradigm for the proclamation and application of the message in particular circumstances. This dual need is not halved by the modern (re)discovery of the perspectives of post-Resurrection proclamation in the gospels. The rediscovery simply means that the 'story of Jesus' will be seen stereoscopically as the 'questers' seek to penetrate to the figure Jesus was, while remaining aware that the impact he made was such as to lead some to belief and eventually to worship.

Third: the Church makes uneven use of the New Testament in its worship, some writings being noticeably more heavily drawn upon than others. There are thus, in practice, internal gradations within the category of canonicity. The liturgy thereby gives sanction to similar selective operation on the part of theologians. Theologians would be wise to pay respectful attention to the Church's more or less instinctive usage in the matter of proportionate weightings when it comes to the evaluation of the New Testament writings and to the shaping of their own thought. On the other hand, the theologians render service to the whole Church, if they keep a critical eye on the proportions of liturgical usage in the light of their judgments on matters of New Testament history (for the biblical scholars) and of their reading of the present-day cultural situation (for the systematicians).

Fourth: the fact that the whole of the New Testament canon nevertheless continues to be used in worship, unevenly though it be, has important implications on both the ecumenical and the cultural planes. Ecumenically: this fact points to a persistent sense of the 'wholeness' of the Christian tradition in despite of the partiality of restricted interpretations and limited applications which emphasize varying facets of the primitive deposit. Hans Küng was right to contend for the 'catholicity' of the New Testament over against Ernst Käsemann's championship of a single 'canon within the canon', though Küng himself would doubtless agree that the *Roman* Catholic use of the New Testament has often been just as partial as the Lutheran insistence upon the theme of justification [note 397]. Culturally: it is clear that certain parts of the New Testament have more appeal than others according to the social and historical circumstances. This is empirically confirmed by observation of the choices which 'new' African churches in practice make in connexion with the reading of the scriptures in worship [note 398]. But precisely because cultures change, it is important that the whole range of the New Testament be kept alive by the liturgy in the consciousness of the Church, against the day when historical shifts will favour the prominence of other parts of the gamut.

Fifth: the liturgy indulges in considerable 'cross-referencing' among the various New Testament writings. It does so at the readings by allowing the Epistle and the Gospel to comment on each other. Later Christian hymns draw promiscuously on the New Testament texts, as we shall see in chapter VI. Creeds and classical prayers blend the principal themes and images of the New Testament into a total pattern. All this constitutes a liturgical basis for the traditional principle of exegesis and interpretation according to which the passages of scripture should be allowed to illuminate one another. This unifying principle is particularly important at a time when an otherwise welcome scholarly recognition of the diversity of the scriptures (broadly corresponding to a contemporary awareness of cultural pluralism) risks becoming exaggerated into the complete dissolution of the unity which Christianity has traditionally sensed the scriptures to possess (corresponding to the 'reconciling' message of the gospel).

Curiously, a period as recent as the 1950s saw the heyday of a 'biblical theology' movement which stressed the unity of the whole Bible, Old and New Testaments. By 1970 one of its exponents, B. S. Childs, wrote a book under the title *Biblical Theology in Crisis* [note 399]. The movement unquestionably influenced the reintroduction of an Old Testament lesson into the eucharistic lectionaries of all the major Western Churches around the 1960s. A regular Old Testament lesson had been lacking in the eucharistic liturgies of both East and West for over a millennium. The original loss signified Christianity's forgetting of its Jewish origins as Christendom itself became an independent culture. Several points of theological importance may be made in connexion with the presence or absence of an Old Testament reading at the liturgical centre of Christianity.

First: the reading of the Old Testament scripture is a reminder of the religious and cultural background of the historical Jesus of Nazareth and may thus correct any tendency to see him as a docetic bolt from the blue. Moreover, some familiarity with the religious and cultural background which Jesus shared with a fair proportion of the primitive Church is necessary for our understanding of Jesus' message and of the primitive Church's proclamation concerning him. Second: the reading of the Old Testament scripture brings us into touch with the history of the God of Jesus with human beings over a far longer stretch of time than the New Testament alone is able to do. This longer vision gives us more of a chance as we seek to discern the hand of God in the movements of history: it gives us more of a sense by which to detect promise and fulfilment, judgment and mercy [note 400]. Third: the reading of these originally 'national' scriptures of the Old Testament brings home both the particularity and, despite the *prima facie* paradox, the universality of God's purposes for, and dealings with, humanity [note 401]. They are the scriptures of a people which, at its best, knew that it was in some sense 'for' all peoples; and the themes of, say, the primal stories in Genesis 1–11, the promise to Abraham in Genesis 12:2f, the rule of Yahweh in the Psalms, the servant songs in deutero-Isaiah, and the apocalyptic vision in Isaiah 25:6–9 make this universal scope explicit. Fourth: the reading of the Old Testament scriptures confronts the Church with both promise and judgment in the matter of the relations between Christianity and Judaism. It both opens the hope of reconciliation and also, and consequently, speaks judgment upon Christian hostility towards the Jews.

Those considerations favour the reading of the Old Testament in Christian worship. Nevertheless there are perhaps positive conclusions to be drawn from the fact that the Churches managed for a thousand years without an Old Testament lesson at the eucharist, so that we should hesitate now to consider such a lesson as 'indispensable'. First: the absence of an Old Testament lesson brings into relief the radical 'newness' of the Christian message. It is an unheard-of novelty that God should give himself in loving identification with humanity for the achievement of his saving purposes to the extent that Christians have confessed and proclaimed in the doctrine of the incarnation [note 402]. Second: the fact that the Old Testament lesson could be dispensed with speaks a warning, which the churches also need to hear, against any exclusive limitation of 'saving history' to a particular nation, race or culture (be the culture as wide as historical Christendom itself). The tendency to exclusivism, which appeared in classical Judaism and which keeps re-appearing in Christianity, needs correction in terms of the idea of non-exclusive promise or paradigm which we proposed in chapters II, III and IV [note 403]. That brings us to the third and last in this series of conclusions: the absence of an Old Testament lesson could be taken as leaving 'room' for at least an occasional (or, in some cultural situations, a more regular) reading from another religious tradition [note 404]. It would be difficult to allow readings which appeared plainly contradictory to the Christian message; but the tentative use of matter which appeared at first sight harmonious with, or complementary to, the Christian scriptures would make a contribution to that exploration of relations which the contemporary trends towards a universalization of culture seem to demand of the religions. If the Christian message concerning Jesus indeed bears certain 'new' or unique qualities, they should emerge in relation to other religious values which, from a Christian point of view, they will either (regrettably, in the end) contradict or (one must hope) fulfil. So much should be possible; on the other hand, it remains difficult to envisage that a fully committed Christian should so far reverse his perspective as to see the Christian values as simply complementary elements in a pattern which was basically set by either a single non-Christian religion or a programmatic religious relativism or a deliberate policy of syncretism.

A final point must be made in connexion with the 'novelty' of Christianity and the way in which it may nevertheless be said to 'fulfil' the Old Testament and, *mutatis mutandis*, the other religions. The Jesus of *St Matthew* claimed to have come not to abolish the Law but to fulfil it (Matthew 5:17). Jesus fulfilled the profound intentions of the Law in a way which Jewish practice had been powerless to achieve: this is the view which may underlie the apparent *double entendre* of St Paul in Romans 10:4, where he says that 'Christ is the end, *telos*, of the Law'; such a view seems in any case necessary in order to reconcile St Paul's positive appreciation of the Law (e.g. Romans 7:12; 13:8–10) and his more familiar recognition of its bankruptcy as an instrument whereby to achieve salvation [note 405]. The German word *Aufhebung* would allow us to make the point that there may be an 'abolition' which is also an 'assumption': the deep values of the Law are taken up into a new and efficacious reality by which their forms are transfigured. According to *Hebrews*, the animal sacrifices of the Old Covenant—divinely appointed, but 'shadows', and of limited effectiveness, 7:18f; 8:5f; 9:1–10:4—are fulfilled and transcended by the self-offering of Christ, 'who through the eternal Spirit offered himself without blemish to God' (9:14; cf. 10:5–10) and inaugurated a new and everlasting Covenant (7:22; 8:6–13; 9:15; 12:24). Believers now enter into the movement of their Forerunner and High Priest (6:20) and are summoned 'continually to offer up through him a sacrifice of praise to God' (13:15a). The Christian eucharist is traditionally called *sacrificium laudis* [note 406]. It focuses 'the tribute of lips'—and of lives (9:14; 10:24; 13:1–6; 13:16)—'that acknowledge God's name' (13:15b) [note 407]. In chapter XI we shall return to the dual theme of novelty and fulfilment, this time in relation to other religions also [note 408].

7. *The liturgy as hermeneutical continuum*
The way in which the liturgy acts as a hermeneutical continuum for the scriptures should be pretty clear by now, but five new or reformulated points may be made briefly here.

First: the liturgy has contributed in the most concrete way to the preservation and transmission of the biblical text. Until the invention of printing, it was largely in order to meet liturgical needs that manuscripts were copied [note 409].

Second: liturgical use sets the proper atmosphere for the

exegete and interpreter. The fundamental motivation of Christian exegesis and hermeneutics should be doxological.

Third: the liturgy also supplies thematic guidelines for the exegete and interpreter. It composes the multiple motifs of the scriptures into a coherent vision [note 410].

Fourth: the liturgy is the pre-eminent place in which the Church ponders and applies the scriptures [note 411]: it thus contributes creatively to the development of doctrine. More critically, the liturgy can also serve as a control on the untoward development of doctrine: since official liturgies are generally slow to change, they allow a breathing space while new popular or intellectual tendencies can be tried out unofficially without immediately affecting the standard worship and doctrine of the Church. Where doubtful developments have nevertheless eventually made their way into the worship and doctrine of the Church, the liturgy is the place from which doctrinal reform can radiate into the wider thinking of the Church. These issues will be faced in detail in chapters VII and VIII, when we treat the two-directional principle of *lex orandi, lex credendi*, and also in chapter X, in connexion with modern liturgical revision.

Fifth: some contemporary biblical scholars have recognized the contribution which the liturgy can make to surmounting the historico-cultural gulf between the ancient writings and the present community. James Barr writes:

> The liturgical or devotional use of the Bible . . . accentuate(s) the idea of its reapplicability to new situations, the notion of it as a treasury of imagery usable again and again, a sort of divinely-given poetry in which the church of all ages can express itself and understand itself [note 412].

And C. F. Evans:

> The effects (of cultural relativism) are commonly mitigated by the use of the Bible in liturgy, whether of the Word or Sacraments, where the congregation experiences some sense of continuity of discourse, and may find itself able to greet Abraham as its father [note 413].

Nevertheless, both these writers see this imagic continuity

as only a partial solution. The bridging of the historico-cultural gap demands serious interpretative work in theology and preaching [note 414]. With that we arrive at our next section.

8. *Preaching as application of the message* [note 415]
Those who put questions on behalf of the 'simple believer' often ask the professional theologian, with doubt in their voice, whether his theology 'can be preached'. The question is mistaken if it implies that there ought properly to be a simple equation between theology and preaching. But it is justified in so far as it requires that theology should serve the Church's proclamation. If it is permissible to take 'dogmatics' in rather a broad sense, the following passage from Heinrich Ott's *Dogmatik und Verkündigung* may be endorsed:

> It may be necessary to affirm that dogmatics is the conscience of preaching and that preaching, again, is the heart and soul of dogmatics. In order to be able to preach at all well, the preacher must engage in dogmatic reflection; while the dogmatic theologian, in order to teach dogma well and truly, must realize that he works with the intention of preaching and must constantly bear in mind the mission of preaching, even though he himself does not have to mount the pulpit Sunday by Sunday. That preacher who proposed to be nothing other than a preacher and to leave dogmatic thinking to the specialist in dogma would be a bad preacher, a preacher without heart and conscience. And the dogmatician who proposed to be nothing other than a dogmatician and to leave to the pastor the concern with the practical task of church preaching would be a bad church teacher; he again would be a dogmatician without heart and conscience. . . . We are faced then by the fact of reciprocal action: doctrine grows from the task of preaching incumbent upon the Church, and the 'needs' which this involves, and in turn it operates in a regulative way upon the actual fulfilment of this preaching mission. Thus preaching is at one and the same time an impulse of power and a criterion, and is itself both impelled and criticized by dogma [note 416].

The theologian's task is to help preaching to meet two tests. First, Christian preaching should be true to the discernible revelation of God in Jesus Christ; it should be a faithful reformulation of the 'definitive original' and a legitimate development of its implications. Second, Christian preaching should be both intelligible and pertinent to its present audience; these two qualities are demanded by the claim that the Christian message is indeed a 'revelation', and a revelation of universal importance. Thus the fundamental intention of R. Bultmann's programme of demythologizing, even though the word demythologization may not be satisfactory, as Bultmann himself admitted, is entirely correct. It is the message of *the New Testament* which must be preached in the present, since the New Testament is our best-provided access to Jesus and his impact (Bultmann oddly stressed the impact more than he stressed Jesus). It is *into the present* that the New Testament message must be preached (though there are other categories than those of Bultmann's heideggerian existentialism in which it may be made intelligible and pertinent). The reading of the New Testament scriptures allows something of a first-hand contact with the foundational myth, in the sense of the original story of God's decisive action in the world in and through Jesus Christ. The sermon's job is to 'apply' that story in such a way that the continuing action of God according to that paradigm may be detected and received in the contemporary world. It matters little whether the preacher begins with the scriptures and moves to the present or begins with the present human context and seeks to illuminate it from the scriptures. The two approaches may be combined to produce a constant oscillation between the scriptural text and the situation of the preacher and hearers. As G. Casalis has finely said: 'Que certains partent de l'Écriture et d'autres de l'enracinement dans ce temps m'importe peu, pourvu qu'ils tiennent ces deux pôles et qu'entre eux jaillisse l'étincelle, présence vivante du Christ dans l'histoire.' The question of 'the living presence' brings us to the final section of this chapter.

9. *Divine presence and inspiration*
We have already had cause to state that Christians must hold at least a minimal doctrine of divine guidance concerning the

composition and choice of the scriptures. Something of the same kind is clearly required in the case of the Church's preaching, as it seeks to interpret and apply the Christian message. With the scriptures it was a matter of establishing the foundation documents: with preaching it is a matter of adequate interpretation and application. Obviously the composition and choice of the permanent scriptures was a process of more importance than has been any particular sermon since; yet without the divine assistance the message will not 'come alive' in the particular circumstances of the ever-changing present. With regard to both scriptures and sermon, at their proper levels, it has been traditional to speak of 'divine inspiration'. This inspiration has been appropriately ascribed to the Holy Spirit. The presence of the Holy Spirit implies, in trinitarian terms, the presence of the God who revealed himself in Jesus Christ and the presence of 'the Lord' Jesus himself (cf. for example John 14:8–11, 15–23).

In its liturgy the Church has experienced the divine presence both in the reading of the scriptures and in the preaching. Let us listen first to St Augustine on the reading of the Gospel:

> So let us listen to the Gospel as though the Lord himself were present. And do not let us say: 'How fortunate were those who could see him!' For many of those who saw him also killed him, while many of us who have not seen him have also believed in him. The precious things that came from the mouth of the Lord were written down for us and kept for us and read aloud for us, and will be read by our children too, until the end of the world. The Lord is above, but the Lord of truth is here. The Lord's body in which he rose from the dead can be in one place only; but his truth is everywhere [note 417].

Fr Aelred Squire comments that 'there is implied in this passage a sense of the presence of God in the words of holy scripture which runs through the thought of the Fathers and continues at least into the early middle ages. If this kind of presence was gradually obscured by a special awareness of the rather different kind of presence of Christ in the sacrament of the altar, it is enough to read some of the things the earlier

writers have to say to see that these two kinds of presence
were by no means mutually exclusive, but rather intimately
interconnected in their minds.' Despite certain features that
will be particularly problematic to modern minds, the two
examples quoted by Fr Aelred are worth repeating [note 418].
First, from Origen:

> You who are accustomed to be present at the divine mysteries
> know how you receive the Lord's body with every care and rever-
> ence, lest the smallest crumb of the consecrated gift should be
> dropped. You would think, and think rightly, that you were
> culpable if something fell to the ground through your negligence.
> If you use, and rightly use, such care about his body, why do
> you think it less of a crime to be negligent about his word than
> his body? [note 419].

Then from the twelfth-century abbot Rupert of Deutz:

> As often as the Holy Spirit opens the mouths of apostles and
> prophets and even doctors, to preach the word of salvation, to
> unveil the mysteries of the scriptures, the Lord opens the gates
> of heaven to rain down manna for us to eat. As long as we are
> going through the desert of this world, as long as we are walking
> by faith and not by sight, we need these goods desperately. We
> are fed in our minds by reading and hearing the word of God,
> we are fed in our mouths by eating the bread of eternal life from
> the table of the Lord, and drinking the chalice of eternal salvation.
> But when we come to the land of the living, to the blessed Sion,
> where the God of gods is seen face to face, we shall not need
> the word of doctrine, nor shall we eat the bread of angels under
> the appearances of bread and wine, but in its own proper substance
> [note 420].

In its Constitution on the Sacred Liturgy, the Second Vatican
Council has returned to the multiple modes of Christ's
presence in the continuing work of salvation:

> To accomplish so great a work, Christ is always present in his
> Church, especially in its liturgical actions. He is present in the
> person of his minister, 'the same now offering, through the
> ministry of priests, who formerly offered himself on the cross',

but especially under the eucharistic species. By his power he is present in the sacraments, so that when a man baptizes it is really Christ himself who baptizes. He is present in his word, since it is he himself who speaks when the holy scriptures are read in church. He is present, lastly, when the Church prays and sings, for he promised: 'Where two or three are gathered together in my name, there am I in the midst of them.' Christ indeed always associates the Church with himself in this great work wherein God is perfectly glorified and men are sanctified. (§7)

It would be fair to say that classical Protestantism [note 421] has never lacked a strong sense of the presence of God in and through the reading and preaching of the Word—and in and through the sacraments at least as *verba visibilia* [note 422]. To authentically Christian preaching the word of St Paul may be applied: 'We are ambassadors for Christ, God making his appeal through us' (2 Corinthians 5:20) [note 423].

Critical scholarship has made it impossible for many people 'naïvely' (though the question of interpretation was never absent, of course) to hear the words of the Lord Jesus in the Gospels; but modern biblical and theological scholarship can also serve the preacher as he seeks to help contemporary believers hear the present word of the God who spoke in and through Jesus Christ. Nor need the contemporary believer hesitate to think in terms of the multiple modes of God's presence. As to multiplicity of modes: the scriptural awareness of varied 'extensions of personality' (word, messenger, gift, and so on) has been strikingly revived by modern phenomenological analyses of the supple notion of 'presence' in inter-personal relations [note 424]. As to the presence of *God*: we recall what we said in chapter II concerning transcendence, immanence, and the variable intensity of the divine.

VI

Creeds and Hymns

1. *Confession of faith*

CHRISTIANS confess their faith both before God and before their fellow human beings. The motive and purpose of their confession is both doxology and witness. The act of confession is part of a more ample movement, a broader sweep which takes its origin in God and comes to completion in God, having drawn humanity to salvation during its course. Faith is confessed in response to the preaching of a preacher who preaches God's word at God's call (Romans 10:8–17). In its witnessing capacity, the confession of faith itself becomes part of the extension of grace to more and more, so that the thanksgiving, *eucharistia*, may be increased to the glory of God (2 Corinthians 4:13–15) [note 425].

We have already seen how the earliest Christians expressed their faith through brief 'acclamations' and 'creeds' [note 426]. Here are the rudiments of the creeds with which we are familiar in our own worship, the Apostles' Creed and the Nicene Creed. The New Testament contains further material of the kind that was to be incorporated into our creeds, and again there is a liturgical feel about its form and context. Thus 1 Corinthians 8:4 makes confession of the uniqueness of God against all idolatry, harking back to the Jewish *sh⁼ma'* (Deuteronomy 6:4); and St Paul goes on apparently to quote some (liturgically) stereotyped phrases which anticipate the articulation of the first and second articles in our familiar creeds:

> For us there is one God, the Father, from whom are all things and for whom we exist, and one Lord, Jesus Christ, through whom are all things and through whom we exist.   (1 Corinthians 8:6)

Again, the christological and soteriological 'kerygma', whose outline C. H. Dodd reconstructed from the summary speeches in *Acts* and from stereotyped passages in the epistles, has clearly been fed into the second article of the later creeds [note 427]. There is also an obvious affinity between our creeds and some of the New Testament texts which modern scholars have designated as 'hymns', e.g. 1 Timothy 3:16:

> He was manifested in the flesh,
> vindicated in the Spirit,
> seen by angels,
> preached among the nations,
> believed on in the world,
> taken up in glory.

At its most characteristic, the Christian hymn may perhaps be considered as a sung confession of faith. For that reason, creeds and hymns are being treated in a single chapter, although it will also emerge that there are important differences between the two genres.

Dealing first with creeds, we shall take a historical look at their various functions in worship, both initiatory and recapitulatory. This will already hint at some of the questions concerning both the positive values and also the difficulties in the use of creeds, which we shall then be discussing in a more systematic vein.

2. *Initiatory use of creeds*

The primary setting of the early creeds was unquestionably baptism. This is the context from which all our earliest evidence concerning recognizable creeds is drawn. In *The Apostolic Tradition* it appears that an interrogatory creed, spoken at the very moment of baptism, constituted the 'form' of the sacrament, i.e. the central words essential to its performance:

> He who baptizes shall lay hand on him saying:
>   Do you believe in God the Father almighty?
> And he who is being baptized shall say:
>   I believe.
> And forthwith the giver, having his hand placed
> upon his head, shall baptize him once.
> And then he shall say:

> Do you believe in Christ Jesus, the Son of God,
> who was born from the Holy Spirit from the
>   Virgin Mary,
> and was crucified under Pontius Pilate, and died,
> and rose again on the third day alive from
>   the dead,
> and ascended into heaven,
> and sits at the right hand of the Father,
> and will come to judge the living and the dead?
> And when he has said, 'I believe', he shall be
> baptized again.
> And he shall say again:
>   Do you believe in the Holy Spirit and the holy
>   Church and the resurrection of the flesh?
> Then he who is being baptized shall say,
> 'I believe', and thus he shall be baptized
> a third time [note 428].

The use of an affirmative pronouncement by the minister during the baptismal act (*Ego te baptizo. . . . Baptizetai. . . .*) appears to be of later date, and it was doubtless its introduction which shifted the candidate's own confession of faith to a point *before* the baptismal act (the use of an affirmative pronouncement by the minister may itself have come in through the case of infant baptism). The declaratory form of the creed, 'I believe in . . .', as distinct from the interrogatory, 'Do you believe in . . . ?', may well spring from catechetical use. From the fourth century we have evidence of a ceremonial 'handing over' of the creed to the candidates some while before their baptism: the *traditio*. At a point nearer their baptism they then had to 'return' the creed they had learned: the *redditio*. Egeria's *Travel Diary* reveals that in Jerusalem, at the turn of the fourth and fifth centuries, the candidates had the creed explained to them clause by clause [note 429]. In Milan, the explanation of the creed apparently took place in the days immediately *after* baptism. In the catechetical and baptismal use of the creed we have to do with the faith that was received, learnt and confessed at entry into membership of the Church. The creeds express the faith that is fundamental to becoming and being a Christian. They are profoundly doxological, in that they express verbally the substance of the faith of those who, through baptism and beyond, surrender themselves to God in Christ in the life of believing obedience [note 430].

The substance of the faith may, however, be viewed not only from the angle of the people taught but also from the angle of those who teach. Certainly the apostolic writers could address the Church at large concerning the teaching it had *received*:

> You have become obedient from the heart to the pattern of teaching to which you were committed. . . .   (Romans 6:17)

> As therefore you received Christ Jesus the Lord, so live in him, rooted and built up in him and established in the faith, just as you were taught, abounding in thanksgiving. . . .
> (Colossians 2:6f)

> So then, brethren, stand firm and hold to the traditions which you were taught by us, either by word of mouth or by letter. . . .
> (2 Thessalonians 2:15)

Yet as time went on, it was also necessary to ensure that successive *teachers* transmitted to those in their charge 'the words of the faith and of good doctrine' (1 Timothy 4:6), 'the pattern of sound words' (2 Timothy 1:13), 'the good deposit' (1 Timothy 6:20; 2 Timothy 1:14). The impression is given that the *regula fidei* or *regula veritatis* to which Irenaeus and Tertullian refer existed in a pretty fixed form from early days. Irenaeus himself says that the 'rule' would have been sufficient for the transmission of the faith even if the Church had been left without scriptures by the apostles. According to Irenaeus, the successive bishops in each place were the guardians of the rule [note 431]. In the nature of the case, there must have been substantial identity between the 'rule' of the teachers and the 'creed' of the taught. When conciliar decisions concerning truth and heresy became necessary, it was therefore natural that bishops should be asked to submit the baptismal creed of their church, and that such a local creed should become the basis of the statement of faith by which the nicene bishops in 325 sought to exclude Arianism [note 432]. Several such statements were produced by various lesser councils in the next half-century, and they will sometimes have affected in their turn the creeds of the local churches through the intermediary of their bishops. In dealing with the macedonian heresy, the council of Constantinople in 381 probably blended its own additions into the third part of a local baptismal creed in order to affirm the divinity of the Holy Spirit against the 'Spirit fighters' [note 433]. In the form finally confirmed by the council of Chalcedon in 451, the 'Nicene-Constantinopolitan Creed' became the creed of the Orthodox East: the plural form ('We believe') is the conciliar form of the bishops; the singular form ('I believe') is the baptismal (and, as we shall see, eucharistic) form. The West, meanwhile, stuck to the developing Apostles' Creed as its baptismal creed [note 434]; and while conciliar statements of faith may have been used as tests of episcopal orthodoxy, the Nicene-Constantinopolitan Creed entered into strictly liturgical use only through Eastern influence, and that at the eucharist [note 435].

A creed thus expresses a church's faith: what its presiding minister teaches and what its members confess [note 436]. The central focus for teaching and the fundamental moment for confession is baptism. But the teaching and the confession continue, and we must now move from the initiatory to the recapitulatory use of creeds.

3. *Recapitulatory use of creeds*

The Nicene-Constantinopolitan Creed was introduced into the Byzantine eucharist during the patriarchate of Timothy (511–17), a bishop of monophysite tendencies [note 437]. This use quickly spread throughout the Eastern churches (though not, significantly, to the Nestorians of East Syria, who did indeed introduce a creed at the eucharist, but an old baptismal creed of their own). The Byzantine use may be seen as one of several liturgical innovations which exalted the divinity of Christ: the *Monogenēs* hymn and the *Holy God, Holy and Strong* date also from this period in which a monophysite ferment was at work. The original, anti-arian purpose of the Creed returned to the fore in its introduction into the eucharist in the West. This occurred in Spain, where liturgical influence from Byzantium was in any case present. The particular occasion, however, was the conversion of Reccared, king of the Visigoths, from Arianism to Catholicism in 589: the council of Toledo thereupon decided that the creed should be recited by the people at every mass. The eucharistic use reappears in the Frankish empire towards the end of the eighth century in the opposition to Adoptionism. The emperor Henry II was astonished to find the creed missing from the Roman mass when he visited the city in 1014. Pope Benedict VIII agreed that it should henceforth be recited on Sundays and major feasts. The local explanation for its absence hitherto was that the Roman church, never having been affected by heresy, did not need to repeat the creed so often.

The various positions of the creed in the course of the eucharistic liturgy illustrate the part it was intended to play in the maintenance of right teaching and confession. Its Byzantine position early in the eucharist proper seems to correspond to the place of an earlier *mystagogia* or summary of doctrine which, according to the *Testamentum Domini*, was recited on great festivals after the departure of the catechumens *ante oblationem, ante sanctam liturgiam* [note 438]. Its Spanish position, as ordered by the council of Toledo and still found in the mozarabic *Missale mixtum*, is before communion. This placing recalls the profession of faith before the reception of baptism: the council of Toledo says that it is for the purifying of the heart by (the right) faith before the reception of communion, and the priest's invitation in the mozarabic rite runs 'Let us say with our lips the faith we believe in our heart'. In its Roman position after the gospel (and, in the Missal of Paul VI, the homily), the creed expresses the congregation's renewed reception of the Christian message. In all these ways the baptismal faith is being 'recapitulated'. The purpose of 'orthodoxy' in continued teaching and confession is that God may be truly glorified and true witness borne to his gospel of salvation. The recitation of the creed is meant as doxology and testimony [note 439].

The daily repetition of the creed outside the eucharistic

liturgy serves the same ends. St Augustine recommended its private practice:

> Say the creed daily. When you rise, when you compose yourself to sleep, repeat your creed, render it to the Lord, remind yourself of it, be not irked to say it over [note 440].

'Render it to the Lord' expresses the directly doxological motif. The self-reminder is part of the shaping of a life which will bear faithful witness to the Lord before fellow human beings: the riches of the creed become, in Augustine's phrase, 'the daily clothing of your mind'. The introduction of the Apostles' Creed into the Western monastic office in the seventh and eighth centuries prolongs these lines of thought. Its inclusion in the morning and evening prayer of the Anglican *Book of Common Prayer* has brought the regular use of the Apostles' Creed into the lives of millions of Christians to the benefit of their worship and witness.

It might even be claimed that the Anglican communion has been the most 'creedal' of all communions in its public worship. The *Book of Common Prayer* made the Nicene Creed part of *every* communion service, and not just on high days, as in the Roman rite, and the Apostles' Creed became a daily part of morning and evening prayer. On thirteen occasions in the year, the so-called Athanasian Creed, borrowed from the monastic Prime, was to replace the Apostles' Creed at morning prayer. Although the *Quicunque vult* had never been a baptismal creed, it was thus, like the creeds, serving the causes of saving belief and confession ('Whosoever will be saved . . .'), orthodoxy ('And the Catholick Faith is this'), and doxology (the recital was concluded by the *Gloria Patri*, picking up the repeated theme that this is the God we *worship*). Nevertheless the Athanasian Creed has had a rough ride in the course of the Church of England's liturgical history: in the eighteenth century it was disliked on account of its 'westernity' by those with Eastern sympathies, on account of its trinitarianism by those with arian and unitarian sympathies, and on account of its length by the busy; in the nineteenth and twentieth centuries, the 'damnatory clauses' became the centre of attention [note 441]. The 1928 Prayer Book proposed making the use of the *Quicunque vult* optional. On the whole, the Nicene Creed had had an easier time of it, although it did not avoid attack in the deistic atmosphere of the eighteenth century. Until the twentieth century, the Apostles' Creed more or less entirely escaped adverse attention among Church people. 'Modernism' was liturgically content with a tacit and private re-interpretation of the clauses in the creeds which referred to the virgin birth, resurrection, ascension and second advent of Christ [note 442]: the 1938 report on *Doctrine in the Church of England* did not take the matter beyond this stage [note 443]. By the time of the 1976 report on *Christian Believing*, however, it was acknowledged that a serious body of Anglican opinion was ill at ease with the continuing use of the traditional creeds in public worship [note 444]. The Anglican contributions to *The Myth of God Incarnate* (1977) make clear that the difficulties lie not simply with the 'trappings' of the Christian story but with trinitarian and incarnational doctrine as such [note 445].

This recognition of the present situation in a sister church which has historically made great liturgical use of the traditional creeds leads us now to face systematically the question of the place of creeds in worship. Our historical survey has shown the valuable function which creeds have fulfilled in allowing Christians to bring their faith to verbal expression in summary form for the purpose of praise and witness. That some such creeds are needed may be taken for granted from the linguistic nature of man and from Christianity's belief in revelation as Word. But the question arises as to the continuing suitability of the *ancient and traditional* creeds for these purposes. In seeking to appreciate positively the continuing values of the traditional creeds, we shall come close to the heart of the problem that the 'creedal critics' are posing. Insight into this problem will face us with a creative task that needs to be accomplished. The key-word is identity—its achievement and maintenance.

4. *Creeds and identity*

The traditional creeds are the concise verbal forms of the

Christian community's identity in time and space. Diachronically, the use of creeds whose substance goes back to apostolic times and whose precise formulations go back to patristic times has allowed successive generations of Christians to find their identity in a Church to which its Founder is believed to have promised his abiding presence and support until the end of time. When the believer confesses his baptismal faith, he is being initiated into a people of God which has a historical identity undergirded by the Christ who is 'the same yesterday, today and for ever'. As long as the believer goes on recapitulating his confession, he may be assured of his own identity in the identity of the Christian people. The liturgical use of the traditional creeds is a sign that it is indeed the Church of Jesus Christ to which the believer belongs—a Church whose transcendence of time and death is experienced in faith's sense of the risen Lord's presence and (it may be) the communion of the saints as predecessors in the way. Synchronically, the use of common creeds is a sign of Christian identity throughout the inhabited earth. The believer is thereby enabled to find his ecumenical identity, his solidarity in the universal Church. His worship and witness become part of a world-wide liturgy and mission. The Eastern churches have no difficulty in acknowledging the Western Apostles' Creed as a proper baptismal creed. The Nicene-Constantinopolitan Creed is claimed, and in various ways used, by all the great ecclesiastical communities of both East and West. It is only a pity that the *filioque* clause should be a cause of dissension: the Western tradition ought to have the humility to drop it from official texts. Ecumenically, the Roman Catholic theologian Nicholas Lash has suggested that confession of the traditional creeds would constitute a sufficient agreement at the basic level of faith for proceeding now to reunion of the churches [note 446]. The achievement of Christian unity is in fact part of every Christian's finding his full identity.

Although it is impossible, as we shall presently admit, to make a divorce between 'the basic faith' and rational theology, it is fair to state that the place of creeds is on the basic level of faith: their baptismal origin and their regular liturgical use suffice to demonstrate that. They are fundamentally 'first-order' language, expressing with a somewhat naïve obviousness the heart of the religious belief. In this expression of the *fides quae creditur*, the force of the *fides quâ creditur* is firmly felt. The existential commitment is being brought to words in as direct a way as possible. Faith is saying as well as it can what it needs to say. It is not entering into more details than are required to prevent grave misunderstanding. A path can be traced at this basic level from the primitive 'Jesus is Lord' to the classical creeds, including, *à la rigueur*, the more metaphysical clauses of the Nicene Creed, for the whole reality of Jesus as *Saviour* was felt to be at stake in the arian controversy. In confessing his faith through the medium of a creed, the believer is expressing his deepest self. If I was stressing in the previous paragraph the communal quality of the believer's identity, I am now emphasizing its inalienably individual quality. The traditional creeds have allowed the single expression of the two interlocking qualities.

Faith and theology shade into one another: belief and reflexion each affect the coloration of the other. Yet the same creedal core can tolerate a certain range of theological explicitations; or, to put it the other way round, a certain variety of theological positions can all see in a single short creed their own condensation on the plane of faith. In the course of his ecumenical argument previously mentioned, Nicholas Lash showed that creedal unanimity *and theological pluriformity* had historically co-existed *within* a denomination (in his case the Roman Catholic church), and he proposed that this twofold principle should be extended to relations *between* the denominations in their search for unity. But the question of the *limits* of theological pluralism has now in fact taken on a broader aspect than it had in denominational *Kontroverstheologie* or in the modern search for unity among the divided churches. The question has been broadened by the difficulties which modern culture is now felt by Christians and would-be Christians to place in the way of Christian belief as such—or at least in the way of the Christian faith as it has been traditionally held and formulated. The 'plausibility structures' of contemporary society [note 447] are felt to militate against the ancient faith—or even to exclude it as a present possibility altogether. It is on those alternative 'ors' that the whole discussion turns. The maintenance of Christian faith-identity with the past appears to require the use of the traditional creeds: but how far can the limits of theological interpretation be stretched before the 'distance' between the new interpretation and the old formulation becomes intolerable? The achievement of honest identity in the present appears to require that a life-commitment, even if it went in some respects against the stream of contemporary culture, should nevertheless be verbalized in a way that was intelligible in that culture. Certainly the Christian notion of *witness* before the world would bring in that requirement. But the risk is that the new formulation will fail, by contradiction or inadequacy, to match the substance which the old formulation expressed. If that were the case, an honest contemporary identity might be achieved, but it would not be a *Christian* identity if the traditional creeds were a true expression of Christian identity.

The question may also be put in this way: How far, and in what sense, are the traditional creeds 'binding' upon the modern Christian or would-be Christian? A first answer would be: They are binding in so far as they summarize in words the primal revelation of God in Jesus Christ (to which the scriptures bear fuller verbal witness in the way set out in chapter V) and so enable the believer to declare his own life-commitment to *that same God* in the present. The binding quality of the traditional creeds lies in their provision of a *résumé* of the Christian faith. They have provided a hermeneutical grid through which the believer could interpret both the ampler witness of scripture and the Church and also his own religious stance. Maurice Wiles has perceptively suggested that it was the creeds, as a fixed point of reference, which helped many Christians of the nineteenth and early twentieth centuries to weather the storms of historical and rational criticism of the Bible [note 448]. But Wiles judges that historical and rational criticism of the creeds themselves has now in turn become inescapable in the contemporary intellectual climate, and indeed he sees it as his theological duty to engage in creedal criticism in order to provide a coherent and economical statement of Christianity that will be credible today. It is necessary to attend to the reasons which are advanced for the incapacity of the traditional creeds, in the eyes of many, to perform any longer their function as a statement of the Christian faith.

These reasons centre on the nature of human language as culturally conditioned. It is held that the language of the traditional creeds depends on an ancient metaphysic or perception of reality which the modern world has abandoned. The epistemological framework in which modern people set humanity, the world and, if at all, God, is no longer the framework which the old creeds presuppose. The main question we are facing concerning 'identity' may therefore be re-phrased yet again: How far is the Christian faith tied to the *language* of the traditional creeds? Although his focus was scripture rather than the narrower one of the creeds, this is essentially the same question as Bultmann was tackling when he was led to advocate 'demythologization'. Bultmann appears to have felt that it was possible to penetrate, through the language conditioned by the ancient *weltanschauung*, to the substance of the faith, and then to re-express the substance in a language intelligible by people holding a modern-view. The model is almost that of the kernel and the shell. It has been suggested, however, that the peeling of an onion offers a more appropriate model for the process of demythologization: one peels away each layer until finally there is nothing left, though one has cried a lot on the way. The onion *was* the onion. Probably, however, the relation between the faith and the ancient and traditional language of its expression is neither as extrinsic as Bultmann's understanding of demythologization seemed to imply nor yet as totally intrinsic as the onion model would suggest. Some of the contributors to *The Myth of God Incarnate* were on a better track when they hinted that poetry provides a clue to the functioning of the old language in religion. This line merits further exploration, and we shall return briefly to it in a moment. First, however, it is necessary to make a more general point about the history of thought.

The matter of shift in world-views is more complex than a simple contrast between 'the ancient world-view' and 'the modern world-view' would suggest. In facing the question of the continuing identity of the Christian faith in relation to general historico-cultural shift, E. Schillebeeckx has helpfully applied to the matter of world-view the model of the turning of concentric circles [note 449]. At the outer and superficial level of 'ephemeral history', the speed of change in our understanding is rapid, expressing itself in fleeting 'fashions'. Deeper and closer to the centre is 'conjunctural history', where the movement is slower, and longer 'periods' are detectable. The profoundest centre is 'structural history', where there is scarcely any change at all. In the last analysis, all this constitutes *one* history, which we experience as full of tensions on account of the different rhythms of change in the different areas of understanding and culture. The deepest structures show themselves only in and through 'conjuncturally', and even 'ephemerally', conditioned forms. This explains why the language of the New Testament and of the early creeds and doctrinal formulations can strike us, who live in a different 'period', as both meaningful and strange. In the tensions of history, the task of interpretation is always laid upon us if we would receive from other times and cultures; the possibility of interpretation is present in so far as a 'common humanity' is at all a recognizable reality [note 450]. With that we may return to the help which the example of poetry may give in understanding the functioning of the creeds.

5. Creeds and poetry

Poetry is able to 'speak' transhistorically, transculturally and transpersonally: this fact presupposes some common experience and understanding between the poet in his circumstances and us in ours. Yet the poem is also able to enlarge and enhance our experience and understanding: the poems which 'live on' do so precisely in virtue of this capacity which originates in the poet's primary and 'fresh' experience and understanding. The poem has a substantive referent, whether this lie in the external world or in the poet's private experience; the referent becomes accessible to the hearer through the poet's interpretation of it in his poem. The language of the poem is integral to the poem, yet poems can be translated with more or less success (and *all* human communication is a matter of more or less success!) into the language of another culture by persons who are themselves not only 'hearers' of poetry but also have some poetic gifts [note 451]. Poetry crtiics may perform a useful function in sharpening the naïve reader's appreciation of the poem; yet it is the poem itself which stands and lives on. *Mutatis mutandis*, similar points can be made in respect of the traditional creeds or, more diffusely, the New Testament scriptures. Their substantive referent is the revelation of God in Christ as this was perceived and interpreted by the early Christians. The primary and fresh experience of the first believers as linguistically transmitted has proved to have a life-enhancing capacity for successive generations. More or less 'literal' translations have been made, but these have been surrounded and supported by the work of theologians and preachers in their interpretative work between the primary texts and the later hearers. Successful interpretation has required knowledge (of the primary material and the present situation), reason (a scarcely-changing 'deep structure'), empathetic imagination (or human insight into both authors and audience), and (most profoundly of all) the experience of having had one's own existence 'opened up' by the early witness to the original revelation of God in Christ. When all has been said and done, however, it is the scriptures and the creeds which have 'lived on': it is they which possess the most intense vitality.

Some may object to my taking the scriptures and the ancient creeds together in this way. Are not the creeds secondary in relation to the primary scriptures? Could not the scriptures live on, while the creeds be allowed to die? The creeds are secondary only in the sense that they may be looked on as *summaries* of the New Testament scriptures. But we have seen that summary confession of faith is to be found *within* the New Testament writings and at their very heart. The classic creeds represent expansions in relation to

the very brief confessions recorded in the New Testament—
but they draw on material found in the New Testament or in
substantially identical parallel oral transmission *and* (unless
the anti-arian clauses in the Nicene Creed be held to represent
a qualitatively new degree of 'hellenization' in comparison
with anything in, say, the Fourth Gospel or the more 'hellenistic' parts of the *corpus paulinum*) they move in the same
'conjunctural' thought-world. From the viewpoints of both
material substance and cultural expression (in so far as the
two may be distinguished), the New Testament and the
ancient creeds stand or fall together.

But to return to the creeds and poetry. Just as a great and
original poet may start a 'tradition', so may the primal
Christian confessions serve as fountain-head to a stream of
subsequent confessions. It is in fact the hymnic element in
the primal confessions which has had the greatest following,
and we shall be considering shortly the place of the hymn in
the Christian tradition. Apart from the tumultuous period
of the fourth century, when doctrine was being made more
precise in the face of apparent misunderstandings which
seemed to sap the foundations, very few attempts have been
made to compose further baptismal creeds once the Apostles'
Creed and the Nicene-Constantinopolitan Creed had achieved
stable form [note 452]. This absence of new compositions
must be ascribed to satisfaction with the old creeds. In the
Reformation period, the *Bekenntnisschriften* re-affirmed the
classic creeds before going on to deal with contentious
matters. In the Roman Catholic church, the *de fide* dogmas of
1854, 1870 and 1950 were not added to the baptismal creed.
There are signs of a slight change in the more recent liturgical
revisions officially undertaken in the churches of the West.
Occasionally a shorter creed is supplied at baptism. Thus
the Church of England's Alternative Services Series 2 Baptism
and Confirmation gave the following interrogatory form
[note 453]:

> Do you believe and trust in God the Father,
> who made the world?
> *I believe and trust in him.*

Do you believe and trust in his Son Jesus Christ,
who redeemed mankind?
I believe and trust in him.

Do you believe and trust in his Holy Spirit,
who sanctifies the People of God?
I believe and trust in him.

Was this meant as a return to primitive or childlike simplicity? Primitive: note the interrogatory form. Childlike: the phrases echo the Prayer Book catechism which was chiefly intended for 'children, servants and prentices'. Was it intended to avoid what were taken to be the more obviously 'mythical' parts of the Apostles' Creed? A positive attempt at moderate 'demythologization' was made by the United Church of Canada in the following 'new creed'. We shall be returning in chapter X to the theological problems involved in modern liturgical revision, but the Canadian text is given here because of its appropriateness in our discussion of creeds [note 454]:

> We believe in God:
>   who has created and is creating,
>   who has come in the true man, Jesus,
>   to reconcile and make new,
>   who works in us and others by his Spirit.
> We trust him.
> He calls us to be his Church:
>   to celebrate his presence,
>   to love and serve others,
>   to seek justice and resist evil,
>   to proclaim Jesus, crucified and risen,
>   our judge and our hope.
> In life, in death, in life beyond death,
>   God is with us.
> We are not alone.
> Thanks be to God.

Particularly striking is the constant interweaving between the 'objective referent' and the 'existential' believing and doing of those who confess. The United Methodist Church of the U.S.A. recommends the use of this affirmation of faith

14

in its 'alternate' order for the Lord's Supper (1972). In my opinion, such compositions are worth testing in use alongside the classical creeds, as occasional alternatives rather than replacements. There is much to be said for a variety of 'alternate' confessions corresponding to the variety of culture(s) [note 455]. Their users will gradually tell whether they are acceptable as summary confessions of their faith. For them to be *Christian* confessions, they will need, through all the 'conjunctural' differences, to match the classic creeds at the level of deep structure. The decision concerning the adequacy of the match raises with some acuity the question of authority in the Church. That question underlies, more diffusely, much of this book, and it will be treated more thematically in chapter VIII. The more usual complements to the classical creeds in recapitulatory doxology and witness have been hymns of varying longevity. To these we now turn.

In order to prevent misunderstandings, however, a final word is needed about creeds and poetry. Use of the poetic model should not be taken to imply the view that the classic creeds are *mere* 'poetry'—with that word suffering the same kind of devaluation as the word 'myth' in popular speech or the word 'theology' in the discourses of politicians. There was a certain oscillation between the more technical and the popular senses of the word 'myth' in the book *The Myth of God Incarnate* [note 456]. When some of the contributors call creedal and liturgical language 'poetry', one becomes a little fearful for that word also.

6. *The place of hymns*

Although fairly easy to recognize, hymns are rather more difficult to define. St Augustine's definition has found wide acceptance. It looks for the combination of three characteristics: a hymn is *praise*; it is praise *of God*; it is the *sung* praise of God [note 457]. Each of the three points calls for elaboration or qualification. First: we should want to add, from our own perspective, that the public praise of God is *eo ipso* witness before the world also. By the same token, a hymn of witness must be allowed to count as praise. Moreover, praise must here include the various moods or attitudes we discussed in chapter I: confession of sin and prayer for forgiveness; self-offering and dedication; invocation of the divine help, presence, advent or rule. All these are doxologically motivated, even though they may not be so overtly 'praise'. Thus the *Agnus Dei* is clearly a 'hymn' [note 458], and so are Wesley's 'O Thou who camest from above' and 'Lo, He comes with clouds descending' [note 459]. Second: the praise must have God as its object, but the style of address may be in the second person (*Te Deum laudamus*) or in the third (*Ein' feste Burg ist unser Gott*) or may be quite oblique ('Come, let us join our friends above'). Furthermore, we have already seen hymns addressed to the Son and to the Holy Spirit as well as to God the Father or the undivided Trinity. A hymn that was not intended to praise *God* in whatever way would be idolatry. Third: the praise must be *sung*, but the variety of literary and musical forms is great. The hymn may range from the rhythmic prose of the *Sanctus*, the *Gloria in excelsis*, and the Eastern odes, to the regular metre, rhyme and strophe of the characteristic Western type, whether in Latin or in the modern languages. The Indian churches have developed their own 'lyrics' and the afro-americans their 'spirituals'. Moreover, the 'balance' in the singing between the word element and the music element is quite variable: sometimes the word will so predominate as to make the singing little more than rhythmic speaking; sometimes the musical elaboration will outweigh the verbal content; in the simpler species of Gregorian chant there can occur 'the perfect wedding of text to music', and the best 'congregational hymns' familiar to the Protestant churches also achieve an admirable balance between the two [note 460]. Finally, it should be said that there is no value in annexing into the category of hymn everything that may be 'sung' in the liturgy (e.g. collects, gospel, preface).

Singing is at home in the liturgy because worship bears, in Christianity as in other religions, the character of *drōmenon*, a complex 'drama' of words and actions in which music may help to bring mental and physical activity together in unity or counterpoint. The processional hymn allows the synchronization of mental and physical movement. The offertory procession in the open-air mass of the Catholic parish of Yaoundé-Melen, Cameroon, is an unforgettable experience: the gifts are brought step by step towards the altar in gradually mounting excitement to the accompaniment of the drum and the insistently repetitious chant of words of adoration [note 461]. Even in the more sedate worship familiar to Protestants, the hymn allows the union of mind and voice in rhythmic praise. In the temporal *déroulement* of the service, a hymn may constitute an act of praise in its own right, or it may allow the expression of response to the reading of scripture, or it may provide a meditative context for punctiliar acts such as the breaking of the bread by the eucharistic president or the reception of the bread and wine by successive communicants. The anthropological point that is of significance for theology is that singing clearly demonstrates worship—and therefore the divine kingdom and human salvation—to be an affair of the whole person, mind, heart, voice, body.

Singing is the most genuinely popular element in Christian worship. Familiar words and music, whether it be repeated response to biddings in a litany or the well-known phrases of a hymn, unite the whole assembly in active participation to a degree which is hardly true of any other component in the liturgy. The sociologist David Martin goes so far as to call the hymn 'the central feature of English religion' [note 462]. Descriptions of worship in the patristic period show that the experience is neither novel nor geographically isolated. Theologians should take the point that the blending of voices may express and strengthen the bonds of affection within the 'community of love' [note 463].

The memorability of hymns allows their substance to penetrate thought and life. Harnack suggested that they played a significant part from the first in the mission and expansion of Christianity [note 464]. Certainly [note 465] the early heretics—Bardesanes and Areios were real poets—had such success in writing songs according to popular models for the spread of their teaching that there was for some time after the middle of the third century an attempt in the Church to suppress all 'modern compositions' and limit singing to the biblical canticles (a few approved and established hymns such as the *Phōs hilaron* were for a time copied and transmitted among the 'orthodox' along with the biblical canticles) [note 466]. From the evidence of Arius' *Thalia* or 'Banquet', fragmentarily preserved in Athanasius' polemical writings and characterized by J. N. D. Kelly as 'a popular medley of prose and verse', it appears that the 'arch-heretic' used song for propaganda purposes [note 467]. Among the orthodox, Hilary of Poitiers wrote a 'book of hymns' but, according to Jerome, had little success among the Gauls on account of their ignorance in the matter of hymnody. Ambrose of Milan, author of *Splendor paternae gloriae*, and the Spaniard Prudentius Clemens, author of *Corde natus ex parentis*, appear to have had more popular appeal [note 468]; indeed the two hymns mentioned have persisted into modern hymn-books: 'O Splendour of God's glory bright' (translated by R. S. Bridges), and 'Of the Father's love begotten' (translated by J. M. Neale). The great hymns of the German Reformation helped to stamp the *sola fides* on the Protestant consciousness; the part still played by *Ein' feste Burg* in the Confessing Church of the 1930s is well documented. John Wesley's preaching [note 469] found an indispensable complement in the hymns of his brother Charles [note 470], who on occasion put the melodies and rhythms of street songs to the service of the gospel and bequeathed to Methodism what Wesley called in the preface to their 1780 hymn-book 'a little body of experimental and practical divinity'; through all the impoverishment and enrichment of its subsequent hymn-books, the spirit of Methodism is still most truly expressed in the best of the Wesleyan hymns which live on [note 471].

Wesley's preface to the *Collection of Hymns for the Use of the People called Methodists* sets out some principles that are of broader application in the theological evaluation of hymnody. We shall pick up three motifs from the following passage as we continue to analyse the place of the hymn:

(The Hymn Book) is large enough to contain all the important truths of our most holy religion, whether speculative or practical; yea, to illustrate them all, and to prove them both by Scripture and reason: and this is done in a regular order. The hymns are not carelessly jumbled together, but carefully ranged under proper heads, according to the experience of real Christians. So that this book is, in effect, a little body of experimental and practical divinity. . . . In what other publication of the kind have you so distinct and full an account of scriptural Christianity: such a declaration of the heights and depths of religion, speculative and practical: so strong cautions against the most plausible errors; particularly those that are now most prevalent? and so clear directions for making your calling and election sure; for perfecting holiness in the fear of God? . . . . That which is of infinitely more moment than the spirit of poetry, is the spirit of piety. And I trust, all persons of real judgment will find *this* breathing through the whole Collection. It is in this view chiefly that I would recommend it to every truly pious Reader, as a means of raising or quickening the spirit of devotion, of confirming his faith; of enlivening his hope; and of kindling and increasing his love to God and man. When Poetry thus keeps its place, as the handmaid of Piety, it shall attain, not a poor perishable wreath, but a crown that fadeth not away.

The first motif is the *doctrinal*. We shall return presently to the particular theme of hymns and scripture. Here I mean by doctrine the major truths to whose verbal formulation scripture, tradition, reason and experience have all contributed in a complex interplay. The Byzantine liturgy is rich in 'doctrinal' hymns, of which C. Northcott writes: 'The fine, steel-like objectivity of the Greek hymn rests in the revelation and attributes of God and makes little condescension to human motives or emotions' [note 472]. A celebrated example is the hymn *Monogenēs*, attributed to the Emperor Justinian and already quoted in chapter II. The elongated rhythms of the East are shaped to Western lines in T. A. Lacey's translation:

> O Word immortal of eternal God,
>> Only-begotten of the only Source
>> For our salvation stooping to the course
> Of human life, and born of Mary's blood;
> Sprung from the ever-virgin womanhood
>> Of her who bare thee, God immutable,
>> Incarnate, made as man with man to dwell,
> And condescending to the bitter Rood:

> Save us, O Christ our God, for thou hast died
>   To save thy people to the uttermost,
>   And dying tramplest death in victory;
>   One of the ever-blessèd Trinity,
>   In equal honour with the Holy Ghost,
> And with the eternal Father glorified.

From the medieval West the great eucharistic hymns of St Thomas Aquinas are fundamentally 'doctrinal' [note 473]:

> Lauda, Sion, Salvatorem. . . .
> Pange, lingua, gloriosi Corporis mysterium. . . .
> Verbum supernum prodiens, nec Patris. . . .

Here the subjective 'interest' of the worshippers is given more room, and this movement is carried further in some, though by no means all, of Charles Wesley's 'doctrinal' hymns [note 474]:

> With glorious clouds encompassed round,
>   Whom angels dimly see,
> Will the Unsearchable be found,
>   Or God appear to me?
>
> Will He forsake His throne above,
>   Himself to me impart?
> Answer, Thou Man of grief and love,
>   And speak it to my heart!
>
> In manifested love explain
>   Thy wonderful design;
> What meant the suffering Son of Man,
>   The streaming blood divine?
>
> Didst Thou not in our flesh appear,
>   And live and die below,
> That I may now perceive Thee near,
>   And my Redeemer know?
>
> Come then, and to my soul reveal
>   The heights and depths of grace,
> The wounds which all my sorrows heal,
>   That dear disfigured face.

> I view the Lamb in His own light,
>   Whom angels dimly see,
> And gaze, transported at the sight,
>   Through all eternity.
>
> (MHB 172)

We are thereby brought to the second motif: the *existential*. It is more than a matter of emotional expression. Wesley's preface is concerned that the hymns should assist the Christian in his growth in grace. So the 1780 Hymn Book is arranged according to overlapping phases and interlocking aspects of the Christian life. Thus the headings of the fourth part run: For believers rejoicing, for believers fighting, for believers praying, for believers watching, for believers working, for believers suffering, for believers seeking for full redemption, for believers saved, for believers interceding for the world. The personal engagement of the Christian is nowhere more strongly uttered than in the conclusion of Isaac Watts' 'When I survey the wondrous Cross':

> Were the whole realm of nature mine,
>   That were an offering far too small;
> Love so amazing, so divine,
>   Demands my soul, my life, my all.

The eschatological longing for the completion of the work of grace breathes through Charles Wesley's 'Love divine, all loves excelling':

> Finish then Thy new creation,
>   Pure and spotless let us be;
> Let us see Thy great salvation,
>   Perfectly restored in Thee;
> Changed from glory into glory,
>   Till in heaven we take our place,
> Till we cast our crowns before Thee,
>   Lost in wonder, love, and praise.
>
> (MHB 431)

These two hymns live on because they express so successfully the whole existential intention of the Christian life towards the divine kingdom which is also human salvation.

The third motif is the fusion of *poetry and piety*. It is towards poetry that the 'ecstatic reason', as some have called it, of the religious believer presses when it comes to speech [note 475]. The sharpest, most poignant expressions match the believer's amazement at being included in the revealed mystery of God's saving purpose, as in Charles Wesley's 'And can it be that I should gain':

> He left His Father's throne above—
> So free, so infinite His grace—
> Emptied Himself of all but love,
>   And bled for Adam's helpless race.
> 'Tis mercy all, immense and free;
> For, O my God, it found out me!
>   (MHB 371)

Or in another hymn:

> O Love divine! what hast Thou done?
>   The immortal God hath died for me!
> The Father's co-eternal Son
>   Bore all my sins upon the tree;
> The immortal God for me hath died!
> My Lord, my Love is crucified.
>   (MHB 186)

'The immortal God hath died': Wesley's language here reflects a deep theological conviction of the Christian faith and a connected christological principle. The theological conviction is that in the man Jesus Christ God has revealed himself *sub contraria specie*, 'under the opposite kind' and even 'counter to all appearance' [note 476]. The christological principle is the *communicatio idiomatum*: things which may be predicated of Christ in one of his natures may, in virtue of the unity of his person, be predicated of him in his other nature also. These points are important enough to merit some development.

7. Paradox and strange continuity

The paradox of the *sub contrario* and the strange continuity of the *communicatio idiomatum* depend on a view of Christ which is already adumbrated in the hymn of Philippians 2:5–11. The paradox began with the incarnation: he who 'was in the form of God' took 'the form of a slave, being born in the likeness of men'. The paradox was intensified by the crucifixion: 'being found in human form he humbled himself and became obedient unto death, even death on a cross.' But the 'slave' then received from God the Father the name of 'Lord'. Throughout the movement of *katabasis* and *anabasis*, through the self-emptying of incarnation and crucifixion and into the consequent exaltation, there is a single continuing Person: Christ. It is no accident that this view of Christ should from the earliest days of Christianity seek to express itself in *poetry*. Man as 'image of God' might be called to grow into the moral and spiritual likeness of his Maker: but that the ikonic relationship should, as it were, operate in reverse, and that the Maker should become man and should even go to death for the love of man—that astonishing thing evoked *rapturous praise* from believers.

Christmas and Good Friday hymns embody that rapturous praise. The paradox and the strange continuity occur in the old hymns of both East and West and in Wesleyan hymns for these occasions. The Greek canon for Christmas Day, by St Cosmas the Melodist (†760), is translated in J. M. Neale's *Hymns of the Eastern Church* [note 477]. His first ode makes use of Psalm 18:9:

> For the Maker, when His foe
> Wrought the creature death and woe,
> *Bow'd the Heav'ns, and came below,*
> And, in the Virgin's womb His dwelling making,
> Became true Man, man's very nature taking;
> For he hath triumphed gloriously!

According to the third and fifth odes, the eternally-begotten Son has now taken upon himself 'human clay' and raised it from corruption to a divine destiny:

> Thou, Jesus Christ, wast consubstantial
>   With this our perishable clay,
> And, by assuming earthly nature,
>   Exalted'st it to heav'nly day.   (Ode III)

'Midst Caesar's subjects Thou, at his decreeing,
  Obey'dst and was enroll'd: our mortal race,

To sin and Satan slave, from bondage freeing,
  Our poverty in all points didst embrace:
    And by that Union didst combine
    The earthly with the All-Divine.   (Ode V)*

The ninth ode begins, in literal translation:

Lo! a strange and paradoxic mystery: the Cave is heaven; the
Virgin is the Cherubic Throne; the Manger is the place wherein
is laid the Uncontainable, Christ the God, whom we magnify in
hymns.

Now all these themes—and more starkly kenotic—recur in
Charles Wesley. First from the *Methodist Hymn Book*, No. 134:

Glory be to God on high,
  And peace on earth descend:
God comes down, He bows the sky,
  And shows Himself our Friend. . . .

Emptied of His majesty,
  Of His dazzling glories shorn,
Being's source begins to be
  And God Himself is born!

Stand amazed, ye heavens at this:
  See the Lord of earth and skies;
Humbled to the dust He is,
  And in a manger lies. . . .

Knees and hearts to Him we bow;
  Of our flesh and of our bone,
Jesus is our Brother now,
  And God is all our own.

And from the *Methodist Hymn Book*, No. 142:

Our God contracted to a span,
  Incomprehensibly made man. . . .

He laid His glory by,
  He wrapped Him in our clay . . . .

---

*The last clause is literally.
And from that oneness and communion hast deified clay.

> He deigns in flesh to appear,
> Widest extremes to join;
> To bring our vileness near,
> And make us all divine:
> And we the life of God shall know,
> For God is manifest below.

And finally some lines which did not make their way into the hymn-book:

> Who gave all things to be,
> What a wonder to see
> Him born of His creature and nursed on her knee!
>   [note 478]

Among the Passion hymns, the *Vexilla regis prodeunt* of Venantius Fortunatus (*c.* 530–609) exploits an early Christian reading of Psalm 95(96):10 for the theme of 'God reigned from the tree' (*Dominus/Deus regnavit a ligno*) [note 479]. Gregory the Great's *Rex Christe, factor omnium* joins incarnation and passion in a single movement:

> Qui es creator siderum,
> Tegmen subisti carneum,
> Dignatus hanc vilissimam
> Pati doloris formulam. [note 480]

The 'crucified God' of Gregory Nazianzen and Martin Luther is known also to Charles Wesley: Calvary is 'that happiest place',

> Where saints in an ecstasy gaze,
> And hang on a crucified God.
>   (MHB 457) [note 481]

Wesley can speak of 'the streaming blood divine'. His hymn 'God of unexampled grace' takes us to the foot of the Cross:

> Endless scenes of wonder rise
> From that mysterious tree,
> Crucified before our eyes,
> Where we our Maker see:

Jesus, Lord, what hast Thou done?
  Publish we the death divine,
Stop, and gaze, and fall, and own
  Was never love like Thine!

Never love nor sorrow was
  Like that my Saviour showed:
See Him stretched on yonder Cross,
  And crushed beneath our load!
Now discern the Deity,
  Now His heavenly birth declare!
Faith cries out: 'Tis He, 'tis He,
  My God, that suffers there!

(MHB 191)

The connaturality between the *sub contrario* and the *communicatio idiomatum*, on the one hand, and poetic praise, on the other, is bound to raise the question: how much of this strange and paradoxical language is 'poetic licence'? Certainly antiochene christology, anxious for the immutability of God, found such language hard to take. Nestorius' objection to calling Mary 'God-bearer', *Theotokos*, typifies the problem. Yet the Antiochenes always had difficulty in giving a satisfactory account of the unity of the Saviour's person. The alexandrine school of christology, anxious precisely for the personal identity and continuity of the divine Saviour, used the language of the *communicatio idiomatum* in a more-than-figurative way; but even the Alexandrines, for the sake of God's impassibility, were driven to double, and thereby weaken, the paradox: 'He suffered impassibly, *apathōs epathen*'. Modern theologians with deistic or unitarian tendencies will obviously be unhappy with *sub contrario* and *communicatio idiomatum* language. But once such language has been used *religiously*, and the prayers and hymns of the liturgy display and continue that use, it is hard for the *worshipper* to be satisfied with a God who would be less committed to the world in self-giving love than the God who gave himself to the world in the incarnation and crucifixion of Jesus Christ. The God of the deists is less worthy of adoration than the God of Jesus Christ [note 482]. In terms of the God of Jesus Christ, the God of the deists is an idol, and his worship—if he attracts it—is idolatry. In the vigorous language of Luther: 'To seek God outside Jesus is the Devil' [note 483]. There is no doubt that a divine incarnation and crucifixion cause difficulty for a rational doctrine of God the creator and sustainer of the universe. Yet we are not completely stranded. In *The Crucified God*, J. Moltmann helpfully argued that the doctrine of the divine impassibility, inherited from Greek philosophy, was intended to save the *freedom* of God (from 'outside interference'); but the Christian God exercises his freedom in *love* for his creation, and love does not go without self-engagement and therefore vulnerability. In developing the theme of 'God as mystery of the world', E. Jüngel argued for the Cross as the starting-point of the *trinitarian* doctrine of God: the Easter faith sees in the Cross 'the unity of life and death to the advantage of life'; but that is precisely 'love', and the doctrine of the Trinity is the Christian explication of it [note 484]. We might say that the very essence of God is, in Christian eyes, *kenosis*: self-giving love extended also to his creatures for the sake of their salvation. Existentially we may get some understanding of that, even though rational difficulties remain. Before the God of Jesus Christ the believer worships:

> Where reason fails, with all her powers,
> There faith prevails and love adores [note 485].

8. *Hymns and scripture*

The Psalms from canonical scripture have been the staple diet of the Church's singing. Colossians 3:16 and Ephesians 5:19 might suggest that the Old Testament Psalms were sung by Christians from the earliest days:

> Let the word of Christ dwell in you richly, as you teach and admonish one another in all wisdom, and as you sing psalms and hymns and spiritual songs with thankfulness in your hearts to God.

> ... addressing one another in psalms and hymns and spiritual songs, singing and making melody to the Lord with all your heart.

But *psalmos* can bear a much more general meaning, and it may well be that improvised or ecstatic or at least specially composed songs are here in view, as seems to be the case in 1 Corinthians 14:26 (*psalmon echei*) [note 486] and as Tertullian reports for his own day [note 487]. Indeed B. Fischer has held that in the earliest times Christians did not *sing* 'the Psalms' but only *read* them as scriptural lessons [note 488]. However that may be, the singing of the Psalms occupied a central place once the daily office developed, both in its 'cathedral' and in its 'monastic' form [note 489]. Certain Psalms were suited to particular offices: the praise psalms went to morning lauds (Psalms 148–150), while Psalm 141 naturally fell to vespers: 'Let my prayer be counted as incense before thee, and the lifting up of my hands as an evening sacrifice'; compline claimed Psalms 4, 91 and 134. The monastic office, perhaps out of simple biblicism or out of a desire for 'perfection', ran through the whole Psalter over a variable period. The classical eucharistic liturgies drew on the Psalms for singing at various points: introit, between the lessons (especially between epistle and gospel), offertory, and communion (where Psalm 34 was favoured on account of verse 8: 'O taste and see'). Appropriate psalmody is often found in the occasional services also, particularly perhaps in the East: for baptism, Psalms 51 and 32; for marriage, Psalms 19 (see verse 5), 21 and 45 ('royal psalms'), and 128; for funerals, Psalms 42, 116 [note 490]. In the Protestant tradition, particularly on the Reformed side, the Psalms have been used as 'hymns' in the Word-service through the medium of metrical versions, notably the French of Clément Marot (taken up by Calvin and completed by Théodore de Bèze) and the Scots paraphrases; though the versions of Sternhold and Hopkins (1562), and then of Tate and Brady (1696), were popular also in England until 'hymn-books' started to take over in the eighteenth and nineteenth centuries [note 491].

Although some of the Old Testament Psalms stand in their own right as embodiments of perennial religious experience, the Christian Church has given the Psalter a christological and ecclesiological interpretation. The process began with the use of certain psalm-verses as christological 'proof-texts' in the New Testament itself: Psalms 2:7; 16:10; 22; 68:18; 69:21; 110:1, 4; 118:22 [note 492]. Not only did the Psalms help the primitive Church to interpret Christ, but also Christ in turn became the key for understanding the Psalms and the Old Testament as a whole [note 493]. Classical liturgical usage provided 'psalter-collects' to guide Christian use of the Psalms [note 494], and the practice has been taken up again in connexion with the Psalter of the French Jerusalem Bible, where J. Gelineau and D. Rimaud have supplied invitatories and concluding prayers for each Psalm. Typological exegesis and allegorical interpretation are very problematic areas, to which we cannot here devote attention. I simply give without commentary an ancient and a modern example of what I judge to be successful collects for Psalm 23. The first is ancient, Roman, and discreet; the second is modern, French, and more developed.

> Rege nos, Domine, suauibus tuae praeceptionis habenis:
> ut, aeterni tabernaculi habitatione percepta,
> plenitudine perennis poculi repleamur [note 495].

> Seigneur Jésus, Pasteur de ton Église,
> ceux que tu as fait renaître dans les eaux
>   du baptême
> tu les marques de ton Esprit par l'onction
>   de salut,
> et tu les invites à la table de ton Corps
>   et de ton Sang:
> Guide-nous au chemin de ta justice,
> pour qu'arrachés aux ténèbres et sans craindre
>   aucun mal,
> nous goûtions à jamais le repos dans la demeure
>   du Père [note 496].

Isaac Watts set out the theological principles on which he operated in his *Psalms of David imitated in New Testament Language* (1719):

It is necessary to divest David and Asaph, &c of every other character but that of a Psalmist and a Saint, and to make them always speak of the common sense of a Christian. . . . Where the

Psalmist describes religion by the Fear of God, I have often joined Faith and Love to it. . . . Where he talks of sacrificing goats or bullocks, I rather choose to mention the sacrifice of Christ, the Lamb of God. Where he attends the Ark with shouting in Zion, I sing the Ascension of my Saviour into Heaven, or his Presence in his Church on Earth [note 497].

Watts' famous '*Jesus* shall reign where'er the sun' is a case of putting his christological principle to work on Psalm 72.

In addition to the Psalms, the Church has from early centuries included directly into its worship certain other obvious 'canticles' from the Bible, notably the Song of the Three Children (*Benedicite*, from the expanded book of Daniel) and the three 'New Testament' canticles in Jewish style included in St Luke's gospel: *Benedictus* (used in the morning office: 'the day-spring from on high'), *Magnificat* and *Nunc Dimittis* [note 498]. We have already noted on several occasions that modern scholars have detected hymnic material in the New Testament documents. It is fragmentary and may in some cases have been worked over theologically by the writers who 'quote' it. Nevertheless, after lying 'hidden' for many centuries some of it is now being incorporated into contemporary revisions of the office. The hymn of Philippians 2:5–11 has found its way into the Roman *Liturgy of the Hours* [note 499] and the Series 3 Evening Prayer of the Church of England. The 'new songs' of the book of Revelation— doubtless reflecting in their time the worship of the seer's church—have long been matter for close imitation if not for direct use as hymns: see Revelation 4:8, 11; 5:9f, 12, 13; 7:10, 12; 11:15, 17f; 12:10–12; 15:3f; 19:1–8; 21:3f. The Roman *Liturgy of the Hours* and the Series 2 and Series 3 daily offices of the Church of England took into direct use Revelation 15:3f ('Great and wonderful') and the catena Revelation 4:11; 5:9, 10, 12 or 13b ('Worthy art thou'/'Glory and honour'). Roman Sunday vespers include Revelation 19:1,2,5–7.

The great hymn-writers of the Church have always woven the themes, images and phrases of scripture into their compositions. For tissues of texts take two examples from Charles Wesley:

15

Behold the servant of the Lord!	(Lk. 1:38)
I wait Thy guiding eye to feel,	(Ps. 32:8)
To hear and keep Thy every word,	(Jn. 14:23)
To prove and do Thy perfect will,	(Rom. 12:2)
Joyful from my own works to cease,	(Heb. 4:10)
Glad to fulfil all righteousness.	(Mt. 3:15)

And:

No man can truly say	
That Jesus is the Lord,	(1 Cor. 12:3)
Unless Thou take the veil away,	(2 Cor. 3:12–18)
And breathe the living word;	(Mt. 4:4; Jn. 20:22)
Then, only then, we feel	
Our interest in His blood,	
And cry, with joy unspeakable:	(1 Pet. 1:8)
Thou art my Lord, my God!	(Jn. 20:28)

The superior may cry 'biblicism'. The more discerning will recognize that by these means the deep patterns of the Christian faith are entering the memory and shaping the mind.

9. *Hymns complementary to creeds*

Enough has emerged in the course of this chapter to make clear the creedal character of the Christian hymn. Nevertheless there are differences of genre between hymns and the creeds, and these differences allow hymns to complement the doctrinally primary creeds. The special qualities of the hymn centre on its flexibility. The variability of the hymn brings the following benefits.

(a) *Freshness*: New individual and communal visions of the faith can come rapidly to liturgical expression in newly composed hymns. To be identifiably Christian, these new apprehensions will take place within the framework of the classical creeds; but they will doubtless highlight particular features of the faith and relate to particular contemporary circumstances. One thinks, for example, of the freedom songs among afro-american Christians. Hymns can take all the risks of exploration and particularity; and while many turn out to be ephemeral, some transcend their origins and live on to become part of the classical treasury. Whether or not the compositions prove durable, fresh composition is a sign of vitality in the faith.

(b) *Seasonal and occasional emphasis*: Hymns can serve a function similar to that of 'propers' in the case of prayer texts. They allow an appropriate emphasis to be made according to the season or the occasion. They do this within the overall context which the creeds, like the fixed texts and the stable ritual scheme, continue to recall. Granted the richness and 'depth' of the Christian mystery, it is fitting that the liturgy should envisage it from various angles; and the use of an ecclesiastical calendar, which not even the most 'puritanical' of reformers have been able to eradicate, testifies to a persistent sense of the propriety of this procedure [note 500]. Given also the variety of 'occasions' in individual and communal life, it is appropriate that particular liturgical offices and formulas should be composed to mark them. Seasonal hymns abound in Christian worship, but there are also hymns for occasions such as baptisms, weddings, and the consecration of new churches.

(c) *Ecumenical and cultural variety*: More will be said in chapters IX and XI about both ecumenism and culture in relation to worship. Here we simply note that hymns and music have often been the form in which ecclesiastical and cultural traditions have come to their most *popular* characteristic expression. Music has a strong thrust towards universality as an art form. It readily unites among themselves the members of a single social community, and it is at the same time a medium in which mutual borrowings easily take place across ecclesiastical and cultural frontiers. Modern hymnbooks in particular are most often historically, geographically, ecclesiastically and culturally variegated collections. Here multiform expressions are felt to cohere into an acceptable unity. Here is a counter-balance to the uniformity which an exclusive use of the classical creeds might threaten to impose.

10. *Heart, mind, life and voice*

There is a final cluster of problems to which attention must be at least briefly drawn—at this mid-point in the book—in connexion with the use of creeds and hymns in worship.

Creeds and hymns allow confession with the lips. The question is, first, the relation between what is confessed in words and what is believed in the heart and mind; and, second, the relation between what is confessed in words and what is lived in everyday life. In each case there is both a moral (we must risk the charge of 'moralizing') and a philosophical side to the question.

As to the relation between external confession and internal belief, the moral question concerns the sincerity-hypocrisy axis. Since language is the divine gift which allows self-expression, there should properly be a positive correspondence between lips and heart:

> If you confess with your lips that Jesus is Lord and believe in your heart that God raised him from the dead, you will be saved. For man believes with his heart and so is justified, and he confesses with his lips and so is saved. (Romans 10:9f)

Among human beings, however, words may be used to hide and deceive as well as to reveal and express. But God searches the heart (Jeremiah 17:10), and he is not mocked (Galatians 6:7). Hence the prophetic warnings to Israel concerning its cult (Isaiah 1:10–17; Jeremiah 7:1–34; Amos 5:21–27); hence also St Peter's warning to Simon Magus (Acts 8:18–23). Put in its benign form, the problem is that of interiorization: how the publicly professed belief and doctrine of the community becomes a faith that penetrates and shapes the heart and mind.

The philosophical question in the relation between internal belief and external confession is one of verbalization. How adequate are words to express the inner experience with God? The articulate mystics have insisted on ineffability. The simple believer may also consider that the words which overflow from the abundance of his heart are inadequate to his devotion.

As to the relation between liturgical confession and everyday living, the moral problem concerns the transition from word to action. The weakness introduced by sin may hinder the passage from what is heard and said in the liturgy to its accomplishment in behaviour. St James admonishes his readers that salvation and true religion require not being hearers of the word only, but also doers (James 1:21–27). The Jesus of 'Q', in a saying which may already by then carry the resonances of liturgical address, warns that 'not every one who says to me, "Lord, Lord", shall enter the kingdom of heaven, but he who does the will of my Father who is in heaven' (Matthew 7:21; cf. Luke 6:46).

The philosophical, or perhaps cultural, question in the relation between everyday living and liturgical confession is again one of verbalization: how to put into words the commitment which one acts? In our day, there are certainly those who aim to follow Jesus but find that the traditional doctrinal and liturgical language of the Church no longer easily express their practical intention. Where are they to get their words for worship?

There is another way of relating the three elements: what is confessed in words, what is believed in heart and mind, what is lived in everyday life. It is to say that belief and action meet in the liturgy. We may then talk in terms of opportunity rather than of problems. We can serve God because he first serves us. Understood first as God's service to us, the liturgy becomes a locus in which God's gracious self-giving promotes the interiorization of our faith, the articulation of our devotion, and the strengthening of our will for action. The anthropological medium through which God works is the assembled community in which mutual help is afforded among the members in the overcoming of the various difficulties mentioned [note 501]. The liturgical assembly mediates encouragement and strength on the moral plane; on the cultural plane, it may assist in the evolution of forms which allow the significant expression of the traditional faith in the midst of the contemporary world.

At the half-way stage in this book we have thus tied fairly closely together the three themes of the sub-title: worship, doctrine and life. As we start on the second half we shall at first allow the three strands to resume their intertwining in varying permutations, and then as we approach the end we shall once again knot them rather more tightly together.

VII

Lex Orandi

1. A Latin tag in modern use

THE Latin tag *lex orandi, lex credendi* [note 502] may be construed in two ways. The more usual way makes the rule of prayer a norm for belief: what is prayed indicates what may and must be believed. But from the grammatical point of view it is equally possible to reverse subject and predicate and so take the tag as meaning that the rule of faith is the norm for prayer: what must be believed governs what may and should be prayed. The linguistic ambiguity of the Latin tag corresponds to a material interplay which in fact takes place between worship and doctrine in Christian practice: worship influences doctrine, and doctrine worship. Much of the present book is taken up with explorations of that interplay. The emphasis in parts one and three is placed on the content of the substantial matters and contextual questions that are being examined in this perspective. In part two, however, the emphasis resides more formally with means. This is therefore the place to undertake a more theoretical examination of the interplay. According to what criteria is worship allowed to influence doctrine and *vice versa*? Chapter VII will treat chiefly the influence of worship on doctrine. Chapter VIII will treat chiefly the influence of doctrine on worship. In each case the chapter will begin historically, though already hinting strongly at systematic questions; it will gradually move into a more direct systematic discussion. Although the approach will be formal and theoretical, the cases taken as examples will naturally be of substantive interest.

A preliminary ecclesiastical point must be made. It is a fairly rare occurrence for the theme of *lex orandi, lex credendi* to be treated by a Protestant writer. In recent reading I have come across no more than a handful of Protestant theologians who have addressed themselves at all directly or at any length to the questions that are involved in the interplay of worship and doctrine which undeniably takes place even in Protestant churches. These few exceptions will be mentioned in the next chapter. Yet it was the policy of the Reformers to establish doctrinal control over worship, and the critical primacy of doctrine in relation to liturgy has remained characteristic of Protestantism. We shall therefore be drawing more heavily on Protestantism for important historical examples in the next chapter, when it is a matter of considering the influence of doctrine on worship. The theological neglect of the *lex orandi, lex credendi* theme among Protestant writers may in fact be due to the use which Roman Catholic theologians have made of the tag in predominantly the reverse direction: Catholics have appealed to past and present liturgical practice in order to justify doctrinal positions and developments which Protestants have considered unacceptable. One of my purposes in writing has been to rescue the interplay of worship and doctrine—with both its problems and its opportunities— as an area of interest for Protestant theology. Some critical questions must certainly be put to Roman Catholics concerning the use they have made of the movement from worship to doctrine. On the other hand, the Protestant practice of doctrine needs to recover a more explicit doxological dimension [note 503]. The liturgical perspective can help Protestant theology in this regard.

The modern Roman Catholic interest in *lex orandi, lex credendi* as a theological theme was prepared by the work of the great Latin liturgiologists of the seventeenth and eighteenth centuries in collecting the texts of Eastern rites for publication in the Western world. The doctrinal questions raised by the existence of these generally orthodox rites in the officially heterodox churches of the Monophysites and Nestorians did not escape the attention of the discerning [note 504]. The Oratorian E. Renaudot prefaced his *Liturgiarum orientalium collectio* (1716) with a theological essay in which he argued that Eastern liturgies, not being simply the words of the one great doctor to whom they might be attributed but having apostolic roots and having received the unanimous and uninterrupted approval of entire churches, possessed a value equal to the Latin and second only to the scriptures as witnesses to the tradition [note 505]. The Maronite J. A. Assemani, compiler of the *Codex liturgicus ecclesiae universae* (1749–66), followed Renaudot closely in insisting on the doctrinal authority attaching to liturgies 'in virtue of their use in the Churches' [note 506]. In his *Bibliotheca ritualis*, published in Rome in 1776, F. A. Zaccaria had a dissertation on 'the use of liturgical books in dogmatic matters'. He argued that universal agreement among Eastern and Western liturgies constituted a most solid argument in favour of a dogma, since the universal Church could not have fallen into error [note 507]. We shall have to evaluate such arguments in our systematic discussion.

Apart from the interest raised by the Eastern liturgies, several other occasions have given rise to the treatment of *lex orandi, lex credendi* by Roman Catholic writers in the nineteenth and twentieth centuries. First, there was the persistent tendency in Gallicanism—dating from the seventeenth century—to make alterations to the Roman liturgy on the ground that it contained 'much that is idle, profane, and foreign to true religion': that phrase is found in an episcopal letter accompanying the Meaux Missal of 1709, which itself did away with the 'secret' recitation of the canon of the mass and introduced people's responses into the canon. Guéranger saw in this a hint of the 'heresy' that the consecration was not effected by the priest alone but by him and the people together [note 508]. It was also a Gallican tendency to reduce the prominence of the cult of Mary in the liturgy. Those who defended the doctrinal credit of the Roman liturgy advanced arguments from its long-standing usage and from its explicit authorization by the magisterium: these are again points to which we shall return in our systematic discussion.

Second, the *lex orandi, lex credendi* theme figured in the Modernist controversy. On the one hand, the modernist George Tyrell had a lively sense of the role of worship in preserving the 'deposit of faith'. Thus he wrote:

The 'deposit' of faith is not merely a symbol or creed, but is a concrete religion left by Christ to his Church; it is perhaps in some sense more directly a *lex orandi* than a *lex credendi*; the creed is involved in the prayer, and has to be disentangled from it; and formularies are ever to be tested and explained by the concrete religion which they formulate. Not every devotion of Catholics is a Catholic devotion, and the Church needs to exercise her authority continually in checking the tendency to extravage, and in applying and enforcing the original *lex orandi*. In this work she is helped by a wise and temperate theology. But theology is not always wise and temperate; and has often to be brought to the *lex orandi* test. . . . Devotion and religion existed before theology, in the way that art existed before art-criticism; reasoning, before logic; speech, before grammar. Art-criticism, as far as it formulates and justifies the best work of the best artists, may dictate to and correct inferior workmen; and theology, as far as it formulates and justifies the devotion of the best Catholics, and as far as it is true to the life of faith and charity as actually lived, so far is it a law and corrective for all. But when it begins to contradict the facts of that spiritual life, it loses its reality and its authority; and needs itself to be corrected by the *lex orandi* [note 509].

On the other hand, the 'symbolism' and 'fideism' of the modernists were felt to threaten both the hard substance of the faith and the objective, external authority of the magisterium in interpreting it. A modernist appeal to worship would inevitably come under suspicion as a soft option allowing the 'believer' to take Christianity in a reduced or *merely* 'symbolic' sense [note 510].

The third occasion for the treatment of the *lex orandi, lex credendi* theme by modern Roman Catholic writers has been the Liturgical Movement [note 511]. On the one hand, the Liturgical Movement is greatly indebted to the leading liturgical scholar of the twentieth century, the Austrian Jesuit J. A. Jungmann, whose early and carefully documented book on *The Place of Christ in Liturgical Prayer* has impressed the pattern of prayer-address found in the classical liturgies on all official revisions and compositions: prayer is addressed to God the Father through Christ in the Holy Spirit. We have several times touched on the doctrinal and theological

importance of this pattern already. On the other hand, the
more speculative views of Dom Odo Casel, a monk of Maria
Laach and another mentor of the Liturgical Movement,
concerning the understanding of the liturgy in the early
Church as a mystery-memorial, *mysteriengedächtnis*, called forth
caution, though not condemnation, on the part of Pius XII
[note 512]. Whereas Casel saw in the pagan mysteries a kind
of *praeparatio evangelica*, some members of the 'history of
religions' school had earlier used the alleged similarities
between pagan mysteries and Christian sacraments in order
to discredit Christianity; and it was this fact, rather than any
barthian opposition of principle to a positive relation between
pagan mysteries and Christian sacraments, which accounted
for the papal caution [note 513].

Pius XII showed some reserve towards the Liturgical Movement for other reasons also. At an apparently superficial
level, there was the disciplinary challenge of unauthorized
innovations by 'private individuals' in the face of pope and
bishops [note 514]. More deeply, Pius XII saw that liturgical
'archeologism', as he called it [note 515], represented a threat
to the whole notion of *doctrinal development* [note 516]:

> The liturgy of the early ages is worthy of veneration; but an
> ancient custom is not to be considered better, either in itself or in
> relation to later times and circumstances, just because it has the
> flavour of antiquity. More recent liturgical rites are also worthy
> of reverence and respect, because they too have been introduced
> under the guidance of the Holy Spirit, who is with the Church
> in all ages even unto the consummation of the world. These too
> are means which the august Bride of Christ uses to stimulate and
> foster the holiness of men.

> To go back in mind and heart to the sources of the sacred liturgy
> is wise and praiseworthy. The study of liturgical origins enables
> us to understand better the significance of festivals and the
> meaning of liturgical formulas and ceremonies. But the desire
> to restore everything indiscriminately to its ancient condition
> is neither wise nor praiseworthy. It would be wrong, for example,
> to want the altar restored to its ancient form of table; to want
> black eliminated from the liturgical colours, and pictures and

statues excluded from our churches; to require crucifixes that do not represent the bitter sufferings of the divine Redeemer; to condemn polyphonic chants, even though they conform to the regulations of the Apostolic See.

No sincere Catholic could go so far, in his desire to revert to the ancient formularies used by the earlier Councils of the Church, as to repudiate the definitions of Christian doctrine which the Church, under the assistance and guidance of the Holy Spirit and with the most beneficial results, has drawn up and imposed upon the faithful in more recent times. No sincere Catholic, again, could disregard existing laws in order to revert to the decrees that are found in the most ancient sources of canon law. Similarly in regard to the liturgy, it is a zeal both unwise and misguided that would go back to ancient rites and customs and repudiate the new regulations which under God's wise Providence have been introduced to meet altered conditions.

This is a most significant passage from the pen of a pope who, three years after the encyclical on the liturgy, *Mediator Dei*, was to give dogmatic definition to the Assumption of the Blessed Virgin Mary. Not only is *development* affirmed, but the right of the magisterium to control the liturgy is also asserted. The question of *authority* is thus not merely disciplinary: the pope and the bishops have authority in liturgical matters because of the intimate linkage between liturgy and dogma. As an earlier passage in *Mediator Dei* puts it:

The sacred liturgy has a very close connexion with the chief doctrines that the Church teaches as most certainly true; it must therefore remain in perfect conformity with the pronouncements on the Catholic faith issued by the Church's supreme teaching authority to safeguard the integrity of revealed truth [note 517].

The encyclical takes *lex orandi, lex credendi* to include the sense that 'the law of our prayer is the law of our belief': 'Whenever some divinely revealed truth has to be defined, Popes and Councils have frequently used the liturgy as a theological source of arguments. Our Predecessor Pope Pius IX, for example, did this when he defined the Immaculate Conception of the Blessed Virgin. Similarly, whenever some doubtful question was under discussion, the Church and the Fathers have been accustomed to seek light also in the venerable and traditional sacred rites. This is the origin of the well-known and time-honoured principle: "Let the law of prayer establish the law of belief", *legem credendi lex statuat supplicandi'* [note 518]. But the fact that the liturgy has thus been used to 'provide important indications to decide some particular point of Catholic doctrine' demands as its counterpart that the reverse principle also be true: 'If we wanted to state quite clearly and absolutely the relation existing between the faith and the sacred liturgy we could rightly say that "the law of our faith must establish the law of our prayer", *lex credendi legem statuat supplicandi'* [note 519]. In other words: the liturgy is 'subject to the Church's supreme teaching authority' [note 520]. The two-way relation between worship and doctrine which these passages expound is grounded in the assumption, and requirement, that 'the whole liturgy contains the catholic faith, in as much as it is a public profession of the faith of the Church' [note 521].

The encyclical *Mediator Dei* raises several questions to which we shall return in our systematic discussions: for example, the relation between the authority of the worship of the Church as such and the authority of the teaching office in the Church; or the question of whether there is an exact correspondence between the worship of the Church and Christian truth: does the Church's worship contain the truth, the whole truth, and nothing but the truth? But for the moment we stay in the historical field. We note that the marian definitions of Pius IX and Pius XII, briefly mentioned just now, have provided the fourth occasion for modern Roman Catholic writers to treat the *lex orandi, lex credendi* theme; and to these cases we shall return [note 522]. Meanwhile, however, we take the hint of the encyclical's quotation of the original formula, *legem credendi lex statuat supplicandi*, in order to go further back into the history of our theme.

2. *Early use of the 'lex orandi' principle*

The axiom *legem credendi lex statuat supplicandi* derives from the so-called *capitula Coelestini* which were annexed to a letter of pope Celestine I (422–32) but which are now held to be the work of the lay monk, Prosper of Aquitaine, dating from between 435 and 442 [note 523]. A literary disciple and defender of St Augustine, Prosper is arguing against semi-pelagianism. His point is that the apostolic injunction to *pray* for the whole human race—which the Church obeys in its intercessions—proves the obligation to *believe*, with the holy see, that all faith, even the beginnings of good will as well as growth and perseverance, is from start to finish a work of grace. A parallel passage in the same author's *de vocatione omnium gentium* shows that the apostolic injunction in question is 1 Timothy 2:1–4 [note 524]. Both the eighth capitulum itself and the parallel passage are plainly quoting from liturgical prayers in setting out the argument, and a further text suggests that it is the daily intercessions at the eucharist which Prosper had in mind [note 525]. Capitulum VIII may be given in full, since it already includes the various strands that will constantly be woven into arguments 'proving' doctrine from the liturgy:

In inviolable decrees of the blessed apostolic see, our holy fathers have cast down the pride of this pestiferous novelty and taught us to ascribe to the grace of Christ the very beginnings of good will, the growth of noble efforts, and the perseverance in them to the end. In addition, let us look at the sacred testimony of priestly intercessions which have been transmitted from the apostles and which are uniformly celebrated throughout the world and in every catholic church; so that the law of prayer may establish a law for belief. For when the presidents of the holy congregations perform their duties, they plead the cause of the human race before the divine clemency and, joined by the sighs of the whole church, they beg and pray

> that grace may be given to unbelievers;
> that idolaters may be freed from the errors
>   of their impiety;
> that the Jews may have the veil removed
>   from their hearts and that the light of
>   truth may shine on them;
> that heretics may recover through acceptance
>   of the catholic faith;

that schismatics may receive afresh the spirit
　　of charity;
that the lapsed may be granted the remedy
　　of penitence;
and finally that the catechumens may be
　　brought to the sacrament of regeneration
　　and have the court of the heavenly mercy
　　opened to them.

That these things are not asked of the Lord lightly or uselessly is shown by the outcome. For God is pleased to draw many out of every kind of error, liberating them from the power of darkness and placing them in the kingdom of his beloved Son, turning them from vessels of wrath to vessels of mercy. This is felt to be so completely the work of God that the God who achieves it is always given thanks and praise for bringing such people to the light or truth.

There are several points to be noted about this argument. First, the argument from the practice of prayer is brought in parallel to the direct teaching of the papal see (*praeter*, besides): liturgy and magisterium are in substantial agreement on the point of doctrine and are therefore mutually confirmatory; there is, however, no suggestion that the liturgy receives its authority from the papal magisterium. Second, Prosper appeals to apostolic authority for the practice on which his argument is based, and the apostolic injunction in turn is, so the parallel passage in *de vocatione omnium gentium* argues, grounded in the dominical will. Third: neither the papal teaching (as a substantive parallel) nor the apostolic injunction (as the initial warrant for the practice) can, as relatively external factors, detract from the value which is ascribed by the argument to the worship practice *as such*. On the contrary, appeal is made to a number of features belonging perhaps more intrinsically to the worship practice itself: the practice is universal, *in toto mundo*, the same everywhere, *uniformiter*, and followed *in omni ecclesia catholica*; it is the practice of the gathered people of God, who are holy, *sancta plebs*, and are led in this 'by the Spirit of God' [note 526]; the practice expresses the mind of the whole Church, *sensus ecclesiae* [note 527]; the practice is demonstrably agreeable to

God, who in this case shows his pleasure by converting the people prayed for. Again, these are considerations which will come up for systematic discussion.

Before leaving Prosper's *capitula*, it only needs to be added that in chapter IX he advances a similar argument on the basis of a ritual act or gesture: the pre-baptismal exorcisms and exsufflations. As the universal and uniform practice of 'holy Church', they are adduced to show the need for grace from the very beginning. Doctrinal appeal is thus made not only to the word-content of prayers but also to a complex ritual act. If this kind of appeal is considered proper, an important principle is thereby established: it is recognized that the liturgy which may serve as a doctrinal locus is the liturgy understood as a total ritual event, not simply a liturgy reduced to its verbal components.

Although Prosper has the honour of having composed the historic formula *legem credendi lex statuat supplicandi*, his literary mentor Augustine had already made ample use of the doctrinal proof from the liturgy. Against Julian of Eclanum [note 528], who maintained that children are born without original sin, Augustine points to pre-baptismal exorcism and exsufflation as implying that, on the contrary, infants are until then in the power of the devil. He further appeals to the fact that baptism itself, which is administered for the remission of sins, is given also to infants, and that infants also receive communion 'in order that they may have eternal life': 'why have recourse to the remedy if the ailment is absent?' [note 529]. Against the semi-pelagian monks of Marseilles (in *De dono perseverantiae*) and against Vitalis (*Ep.* 217) [note 530], Augustine defends his doctrine of grace —its necessity in both conversion and perseverance—by reference to the Spirit-led *orationes ecclesiae* which pray both that unbelievers may be brought by God to the faith and that believers may continue in the faith of Christ without falling into temptation. Making a point whose theological importance transcends the *ad homines* form of the argument, Augustine stresses the significance of the people's Amen to the prayers: 'We will defend both ourselves and you, lest we be found to pray without cause and you to subscribe Amen without cause. Brethren, your Amen is your subscription, your consent, your agreement' [note 531]. Augustine turns to the memorial of the departed in the mass, and to the liturgy of death in general, in order to prove that there are differences in the fate of the dead in the after-life: the Church does not pray for the salvation of the damned, which shows that their condemnation is irrevocable; the commemoration of the martyrs is separate from that of the other departed, for the martyrs no longer need our help, but we theirs; nevertheless we can help the others, and it would be heretical to say that one may not offer for them; even if there were no scriptural proof in 2 Maccabees 12:43–46, the practice of the universal Church in commending the dead in prayer would carry 'no little authority' as a proof of purgatory [note 532]. More amusingly, Augustine uses the liturgical dates of Christmas and Epiphany to establish the historical dates of the birth of Jesus and the visit of the wise men [note 533].

It is not in fact only in controversial matters that Augustine finds doctrinal value in the liturgy. He often uses liturgical examples or illustrations in his sermons [note 534], and he recommends others to do the same [note 535]. The liturgy itself is eloquent to teach saving truth: its visible, physical, temporal figures, few and simple as they are, move the affection to things invisible, spiritual, eternal [note 536].

Such is the teaching power of the liturgy in respect of faith and morals that the bishop, while avoiding unnecessary disturbance, is advised by Augustine to correct any errors that may be present in it and to introduce features that will be profitable [note 537]. The regular doctrinal value of the liturgy is also evidenced in the practice of mystagogical catechesis, ancient examples of which are associated with Cyril of Jerusalem, Ambrose of Milan, John Chrysostom, and Theodore of Mopsuestia [note 538]. When the bishop explained to the neophytes the initiatory sacraments through which they had just passed [note 539], he was in fact inevitably instructing them in the fundamental doctrines of the Christian faith which came to ritual expression in those sacraments [note 540]. Ambrose, for example, takes the baptismal interrogations and responses as teaching the orthodox doctrine of the Trinity:

So you went down (into the water). Remember what you answered: that you believe in the Father, you believe in the Son, you believe in the Holy Spirit. It is not a case of: I believe in a greater, a lesser, and a least. But by the pledge of your own word you are bound to believe in the Son in the same way as you believe in the Father, and to believe in the Spirit in the same way as you believe in the Son; the only exception is that you profess the necessity of belief in the cross of the Lord Jesus alone [note 541].

This example from St Ambrose points us back to the use of liturgical evidence in doctrinal controversy: the bishop of Milan was also warning his neophytes against arian teaching on the Godhead. We find that the Arians themselves had been trying out a doctrinal proof from the liturgy. In the East, they sought support for their radical subordinationism in the traditional address of the doxology by the Church '*to* the Father *through* Christ the Son *in* the Holy Spirit'. While Basil's treatise *On the Holy Spirit* defends this form of the doxology in an 'orthodox' sense, it is also apparent from the treatise that some Nicenes had been provoked by arian attacks into switching from the 'subordinated' to the 'co-ordinated' form, which itself had traditional roots (*meta, sun*) and was the normal version in the Syriac-speaking churches (*and . . . and*) [note 542]. In the West (North Italy or the Danube), and from about the time of Ambrose, there is an anonymous arian treatise which plays off the 'catholic' liturgy against 'catholic' theological writings [note 543]:

In their writings they (the catholics) in no way put the Father before the Son and indeed they condemn all who put the Father before the Son, yet they themselves in their (?pre-baptismal) imposition of hands put the Father before the Son when they say 'God, supreme author and maker of the world, God and Father of our Lord Jesus Christ. . . .'
. . . They themselves in the creed put the Father before the Son when they say 'Do you believe in God the Father almighty, maker of heaven and earth? Do you also believe in Christ Jesus his Son?'
. . . They themselves in their blessings (?'confirmation') put the Father before the Son when they say 'May the God and Father

16

of our Lord Jesus Christ, who has given you the new birth through water, himself anoint you with the Holy Spirit. . . .'

. . . They themselves in their oblations put the Father before the Son by saying 'It is right and fitting that we should give thanks to you here and everywhere, holy Lord, almighty God; and there is no one through whom we can have access to you, pray to you, offer a sacrifice to you, except the one whom you sent to us' and 'It is right, proper and fitting that we should give thanks to you above all things, holy Lord, almighty Father, eternal God . . . asking you in your great and merciful kindness to accept this sacrifice which we offer you before the face of your divine goodness through Jesus Christ, our Lord and God, through whom we pray and ask. . . .'

In meeting arian arguments from the liturgy, Ambrose's method was not to 'correct' or change the catholic custom but rather to explain and defend such a practice as praying to the Father through the Son. Thus he writes to the emperor Gratian, with echoes of John 14:13f and 16:23:

> The Father wishes to be asked through the Son, the Son wishes the Father to be asked. . . . Whatever the Father does, the Son does the same and likewise. The Son does it likewise and the same, but he wishes the Father to be asked for what he himself will do, not that one may see therein a sign of his incapacity but rather a sign of their unity in power [note 544].

From about the same period we may pick up two further authors who also contribute to our theme. Jerome argues that a universal practice of the Church can be equivalent to an express biblical command:

> Are you unaware that it is a custom of the churches that hands should afterwards be laid on the baptized and the Holy Spirit be thus invoked? Do you ask where it is written? In the Acts of the Apostles. Even if no scriptural authority existed for it, the agreement of the whole world in the matter would have the value of a precept. For many other things which are observed by tradition in the churches have acquired the authority of a scriptural law [note 545].

The underlying train of thought may be that expressed by Augustine:

> A thing which is held by the universal Church and was not instituted by a council but has always been kept is rightly believed not to have been transmitted without apostolic authority [note 546].

Our other writer, Optatus of Milevis, whose seven books *contra Parmenianum Donatistam* were used by Augustine, puts a strong stress on catholicity as a mark of the true Church [note 547]. Another of his arguments is to allege a contradiction between donatist belief and donatist liturgical practice: even the 'holy' Donatists pray 'Forgive us our trespasses'. Optatus also adumbrates an argument which later Roman Catholic theology will use to support the infallibility of the Church, namely that God would not allow such false teaching to prevail as would lead the faithful astray: because the confession of the right faith on the part of the recipient is necessary to the efficacy of baptism, the Spirit of Truth protects the Church's liturgical formula (baptismal creed) in order to ensure that the divine grace is properly administered and may be properly received.

Further back, Cyprian also held that the efficacy of the sacraments is conditional upon right faith on the part of their minister and recipients [note 548]. When others allege a proof from liturgical custom, he opposes *consuetudo* with *ratio* and *veritas* [note 549]. For the 'truth of God' he turns—on the question, say, of the eucharistic elements—to the founding actions of Christ as recorded in scripture [note 550]. It must therefore be on the grounds of their truth, itself perhaps dependent on their dominical or apostolic origin, rather than on the grounds of their antiquity—'custom without truth is but old error' [note 551]—that Cyprian considers not only the baptism itself unalterable, but also the blessing of the water, the baptismal interrogations, the blessing of the oil and the anointing [note 552]. His reproaches to 'schismatics' include the alteration of the eucharistic prayer: *precem alteram inlicitis vocibus facere* [note 553]. He is prepared to argue from the unreflective practice of the Church, which he does not further seek to justify: the fact that the Church does not rebaptize those who have received clinical baptism shows that they have received grace and are full Christians [note 554]; and the fact that the Roman church imposes hands on converted heretics is held, in an *ad hominem* argument, to be an admission that the heretics had not earlier received the Spirit and that the Roman church should therefore 'repeat' the *whole* of the heretics' 'failed' initiation, including baptism itself [note 555].

Tertullian also was concerned with the dominical or apostolic origin and faithful transmission of the truth [note 556]. In his confrontation with heretics, he attaches great weight to the *regula fidei* as a summary statement of the Christian faith and a hermeneutical key to the scriptures. The single and catholic character of the *regula* is ascribed by Tertullian to its apostolic origin and its preservation by the Holy Spirit through the succession of bishops. In chapter VI we already pointed to the liturgical context and use of the *regula* in catechesis, baptism and preaching [note 557]. The other main contribution of Tertullian to our *lex orandi* theme consists in his appeal to sacraments and sacramentals against gnostic and other dualisms. Marcion had not dared to drop the eucharistic institution from his 'gospel' (or the eucharist from his practice): but the eucharist—in which Christ made the bread the 'figure' of his body—refuted any docetic view of Christ [note 558]. Matter is good, and the one good God is its creator. Tertullian establishes the point ironically:

> (Your 'superior God') has not up to now rejected the Creator's water, for in it he washes his own people; nor the oil with which he anoints them; nor the mixture of milk and honey on which he feeds his children; nor the bread by which he represents his own body. Even in his own 'sacraments' he needs things begged from the Creator [note 559].

In arguing for the resurrection of the body Tertullian points again to the sacraments, for in them the body is already the means by which the soul receives grace [note 560]:

The flesh (*caro*) is the hinge (*cardo*) of salvation. . . . The flesh is washed that the soul may be made clean; the flesh is anointed that the soul may be consecrated; the flesh is signed that the soul may be strengthened; the flesh is shadowed by the imposition of the hand, that the soul may be enlightened by the Spirit; the flesh feeds on the body and blood of Christ, that the soul may feast on God. Therefore the things that are joined together in work (i.e. body and soul) cannot be separated when it comes to the reward.

Against the gnostics Irenaeus likewise turns to the eucharist for 'proof' concerning not only the particular doctrine of the resurrection of the body but also the more general fact that the one God is both creator of the material world and Father of the Lord Jesus Christ:

We must make our oblation to God and in all things be found grateful to God the creator, offering the firstfruits of his own creatures with a pure mind and sincere faith, with firm hope and fervent love. And this oblation the Church alone offers pure to the creator, offering to him, with thanksgiving, from his creation. . . . How will they (the gnostics) allow that the bread over which thanksgiving has been said is the body of their Lord, and that the chalice is the chalice of his blood, if they do not say that he is the Son of the creator of the world; that is to say, his Word through whom the tree bears fruit and the fountains flow and the earth yields first the blade, then the ear, then the full corn in the ear? [note 561].

Since, then, the cup which is mixed and the bread which is made receive the Word of God and become the eucharist of the body and blood of Christ, and of them the substance of our flesh grows and subsists: how can they (the gnostics) deny that the flesh is capable of the gift of God which is eternal life, that flesh which is fed by the body and blood of the Lord and is a member of him? For blessed Paul says in his Letter to the Ephesians: 'We are members of his body, of his flesh and of his bones.' He does not say this of a spiritual and invisible sort of man (for a spirit has no flesh and bones), but of man in his real constitution of flesh and nerves and blood. It is this which receives nourishment from the cup which is his blood, and growth from the bread which is his body. And as the wood of the vine planted in the ground bears fruit in its season, and the grain of wheat falls into the ground and moulders and is raised manifold by the Spirit of God who upholds all things; and afterwards through the wisdom of God they come to be used by human beings, and having received the Word of God become the eucharist which is the body and blood of Christ: so also our bodies, nourished by the eucharist, and put into the ground, and dissolved therein, will rise in their season, the Word of God giving them resurrection to the glory of God the Father [note 562].

For Irenaeus there was thus a general coherence between sacramental worship and 'catholic' doctrine on creation, man, incarnation and resurrection: 'our doctrine agrees with the eucharist, and the eucharist confirms the doctrine' [note 563]. Doctrinal appeal can be made to the eucharist because in the eucharist the faith comes to focal expression. It is impossible to mistake this procedure as a method of argument— or indeed to deny the substantial force of Irenaeus' general case for the spiritual significance of matter, however uneasy we may feel concerning, say, his conception of the resurrection of the body [note 564].

The eucharist functions as a test against christological docetism already in the letters of Ignatius of Antioch. To the Smyrnaeans he writes that the heretics 'abstain from eucharist and prayer because they do not confess that the eucharist is the flesh of our Saviour Jesus Christ which suffered for our sins and which the Father raised' (7:1). The johannine notion that the final resurrection of believers will be a fruit of their participation in the eucharist cannot be far away when Ignatius continues: 'They, then, who deny the gift of God are perishing in their disputes; it would be better for them to have love, that they also may attain to the resurrection.' When Ignatius, in Ephesians 20:2, calls the eucharist a 'medicine of immortality', the phrase is therefore obviously not to be understood as excluding the final resurrection in a possibly 'docetic' way: participation in the eucharist is on the contrary a confession of the resurrection-hope (cf. John 6:53f). Docetic disparagement of the body, of which abstention from the eucharist is the (anti-)sacramental sign, comes to negative expression also in practical ethics: 'they are not concerned to show love for the widow, the orphan, the afflicted, the prisoner, the hungry or the thirsty' (Ignatius, *Smyrnaeans* 6:2). By contrast, Justin Martyr's description of the Sunday assembly reveals that diaconal service issued from the eucharist: 'And the wealthy who so desire give what they wish, as each chooses; and what is collected is deposited with the president. He helps orphans and widows, and those who through sickness or any other cause are in need, and those in prison, and strangers sojourning among us' (*Apology* I, 67, 6f).

An anti-dualist doctrinal argument appealing to prayer-practice (prayer of a category to which the eucharistic prayer is not a stranger) is found already in the New Testament [note 565]. 1 Timothy 4:1–5 warns against liars 'who forbid marriage and enjoin abstinence from foods which God created to be received with thanksgiving by those who believe and know the truth. For everything created by God is good, and nothing is to be rejected if it is received with thanksgiving; for then it is consecrated by the word of God and prayer.' In chapters II and V we saw other examples of New Testament writers drawing, though not uncritically, on existing worship practice in doctrinal argument.

If we had worked not backwards but forwards from Prosper of Aquitaine in our historical survey of the *legem credendi lex statuat supplicandi* principle, we should have been struck by the increasingly Roman turn which the arguments took. We shall look at a few examples of this as our route into the present and a modern systematic discussion.

3. *Characteristically Roman use*

Whereas Prosper had placed the universal liturgy and papal teaching in parallel, later Western versions of the argument from worship practice attach great weight to the Roman liturgy in particular, and indeed to the Roman liturgy as sanctioned by the magisterium [note 566]. Thus the Adoptionist controversy of the eighth and ninth centuries was largely conducted in terms of liturgical texts. When the Spanish Adoptionists appealed to the mozarabic liturgy in support of their position, Alcuin countered by adducing Roman prayers. Against Felix of Urgel he writes:

We desire the truth of our statement and our faith to be supported by Roman rather than by Spanish authority, although we do not reject the latter when it speaks in a catholic way. A person should know that he is wrong where he differs from the universal Church. The Roman church, which it is right that catholics and orthodox should follow, is accustomed to acknowledge the true Son of God both in the Mass and in all other writings or letters [note 567].

Alcuin then goes on to quote five prayers from the mass, three of which belong to the Gregorian sacramentary. In writing against Elipandus of Toledo, Alcuin looks critically at the prayers which have been quoted from the Spanish liturgy and himself appeals to pope Gregory:

You should know how greatly different were the prayers composed for Mass by blessed Gregory, a venerable and highly esteemed doctor of the catholic faith [note 568].

Alcuin again quotes four prayers from the mass, three of which are found in the Gregorian sacramentary [note 569].

In controversy with Protestantism, the council of Trent quoted the liturgy in support of the doctrine of a growth in justifying grace after the initial act of justification. The prayer cited was the Roman collect of the thirteenth Sunday after Pentecost: 'Holy Church prays for this increase of justice when it asks: Give us, Lord, an increase of faith, hope and love' [note 570]. For later Roman Catholic writers this becomes a favourite example of the use of the liturgy as a dogmatic locus by the conciliar magisterium [note 571]. The strength of a dual establishment of dogma, by both liturgy and magisterium, is stressed. The same point is made in connexion with the tridentine declaration that the Roman mass-canon is *ab omni errore purum*: this central prayer of the liturgy, its error-free status explicitly confirmed by the magisterium, can be the source of dogmatically *certain* conclusions [note 572]. Johannes Brinktrine, who makes the point concerning the certainty of dogmatic conclusions drawn from the canon of the mass, extends the argument even as far as the (post-tridentine) rubrics [note 573]: from the rubrics concerning genuflexion and adoration one may draw the certain dogmatic conclusion that the words of institution effect the consecration, and that any words which follow are not essential (this against the Eastern insistence on a subsequent epiclesis to complete the consecration). Admittedly, Brinktrine clothes his naked rubricism with the additional contention that it was impossible that an officially introduced rubric should daily lead countless priests and believers into formal idolatry, as would be the case if they worshipped the elements before consecration; but the atmosphere differs from that in which Thomas Aquinas had appealed to the doubtless more spontaneous elevation of the host for the people's adoration immediately after the word over the bread, in order to prove that the consecration of the bread was complete before the words were spoken over the wine [note 574]. The weight has shifted from the liturgical practice itself in favour of the official rubric 'governing' the practice [note 575].

Bossuet, bishop of Meaux (†1704), remained closer to the older sense when he wrote in refutation of 'false mystics' [note 576]:

> Le principal instrument de la tradition de l'Église est renfermé dans ses prières, et, soit qu'on regarde l'action de la liturgie et le sacrifice, ou qu'on repasse sur les hymnes, sur les collectes, sur les secrètes, sur les post-communions, il est remarquable qu'il ne s'en trouvera pas une seule qui ne soit accompagnée de demandes expresses; en quoi l'Église a obéi au commandement de saint Paul (Phil. 4:6). . . . La conclusion solennelle de toutes les oraisons de l'Église 'par Jésus Christ', et 'en l'unité du Saint-Esprit', fait voir la nécessité de la foi expresse en la Trinité, en l'incarnation et en la médiation du Fils de Dieu.

It was by this kind of appeal to the living practice of the liturgy itself that medieval theologians argued in marian matters. They certainly had a sense that the Church cannot importantly err in its worship practice; but 'the Church' had not been narrowed down in this connexion to the official magisterium, let alone the Congregation of Rites, founded only in 1588. Thus Bernard of Clairvaux and Thomas Aquinas both take the Church's celebration of Mary's Nativity as a holy day (8th September) to be proof of her sanctification before her birth:

> It is beyond doubt that the Mother of the Lord became holy before her birth. Holy Church is in no way mistaken in considering holy the day of her nativity and celebrating it with exultation every year throughout the world [note 577].

> It is said that the Blessed Virgin was not sanctified before her birth from the womb. . . . On the contrary, the Church celebrates the nativity of the Blessed Virgin. But a feast is not celebrated in the Church except for something holy. Therefore the Blessed Virgin was already holy at her nativity. Therefore she had been sanctified in the womb [note 578].

In the nineteenth and twentieth centuries, the definitions of the two special Roman dogmas of Mary's immaculate conception (1854) and her bodily assumption (1950) were preceded, accompanied and retrospectively justified by appeal to the worship practice of the (Roman Catholic) Church; but there was by now an explicit insistence on the fact that the quoted practices had been sanctioned or even introduced by the authority of the magisterium [note 579]. Prosper of Aquitaine had brought in the rather independent liturgical evidence as a conclusive argument *beyond* the papal teaching: in the last two centuries it is the papal authorization of appealed-to liturgical practices which serves to clinch the argument. It is not simply that 8th December (Immaculate Conception) and 15th August (Assumption) are 'spontaneously' celebrated as feasts by the Christian people, and that Mary is unreflectively called 'spotless' and 'queen of heaven' in Christian worship. Rather Pius IX himself wrote as follows in the bull *Ineffabilis Deus* of 8th December 1854. Among other things it will be noted that the pope gave a new twist to Prosper's dictum: a new *lex orandi* is seen by Pius to have been deliberately introduced by his papal predecessors in order to promote (that would seem to be the meaning here of establish) a particular doctrine [note 580].

> This doctrine (of Mary's purity from original sin) flourished from earliest times, being deeply implanted in the souls of believers.

It was wonderfully propagated throughout the catholic world by the care and attention of the holy bishops. This doctrine the Church itself showed forth most splendidly, when it did not hesitate to propose the conception of the Virgin as matter for the public worship and veneration of the faithful. . . . Nothing was dearer to the Roman Church than most eloquently to affirm, preserve, promote and defend the immaculate conception of the Virgin and its cult and doctrine. . . . Our predecessors counted it a special honour by virtue of their apostolic authority to institute the feast of the conception in the Roman Church [note 581]. They enriched and adorned the feast by a proper office and mass, in which Mary's privilege of preservation from original sin is most clearly declared; and they sought by every means to promote and spread the cult. . . . They were pleased to make the feast of her conception universal in the whole Church, with the same rank as the feast of her nativity, and to be celebrated with an octave. . . . Desiring to increase daily this doctrine of the immaculate conception in the souls of the faithful and to excite the people's devotion to the immaculately conceived Virgin, (the Roman pontiffs) most willingly granted that the immaculate conception of the Virgin should be mentioned in the litany of Loreto and even in the preface of the mass, so that 'the law of belief might be established by the law of prayer' [note 582]. . . . Since plainly worship is intimately bound to its object and cannot remain stable if its object is doubtful and ambiguous, our predecessors as Roman pontiffs took every care to foster the cult of the immaculate conception and strove zealously to explain and inculcate its object and doctrine.

The feast of Mary's assumption is older and apparently more popular in origin: it dates perhaps from the fourth century in the East [note 583], and in the West there is a prayer in the Gregorian Sacramentary for the feast *in quā sancta Dei Genetrix mortem subiit temporalem, nec tamen mortis nexibus deprimi portuit* [note 584]. In the seventeenth century, F. Suarez concluded the assumption of Mary from the liturgical texts of his day; but while the assumption would not, he declared, be called in doubt by a pious Catholic, and could not be denied without temerity, it was not (according to Suarez) *de fide*, because it had not been defined by the Church and the testimony from scripture and tradition was insufficient [note 585]. In the build-up to the dogmatic definition of 1950, however, the theologians add the factor of the magisterial sanction of existing liturgical texts. Philipp Oppenheim OSB, the author of a work entitled *Principia theologiae liturgicae*, argued as follows in a mariological work published in 1946 and again in 1952 [note 586]:

> The liturgy is the faithful deposit of almost two thousand years' experience by the Church; it is moreover a Spirit-inspired and Spirit-protected treasure of the faith. It is the official cultus of the Church; it rests upon the authority of the Church, with which it stands or falls, and its smallest details are regulated by the Church. Every text, every action is exactly prescribed and ordered by the highest ecclesiastical authority, the holy see itself; time and place and minister are unambiguously determined; everything is tied and subjected to the legislative power of ecclesiastical authority. . . . There can therefore be no doubt that the Church brings to expression in its liturgy the most profound truths concerning also the person and place of the Mother of God, and that the Church there sets up the norms according to which Mary should be given the honour which is her due. In this matter the Church itself has for centuries been the best guide and leader [note 587].

If Protestant readers have persisted with this section till now, they will be asking why the Roman magisterium did not curtail, rather than sanction and even encourage, popular devotion when it took an aberrant turn. In the next chapter we shall be looking more closely at the tendency of Protestant authorities to prune the liturgy. The marian examples have, however, clearly raised again the historically unavoidable question of 'development' in liturgy and doctrine and, with particular sharpness, the question of magisterial responsibility to and for the worship of the Church [note 588]. These questions, together with those raised in connexion with the earlier history of Prosper's principle, will now form part of our systematic discussion.

4. *Systematic questions at issue*

The systematic questions at issue may be grouped under four

heads: (a) What gives to the Church's worship any authority which it carries in matters of doctrine? (b) What is the relation between the doctrinal authority carried by worship and other instances of doctrinal authority in the Church? (c) Is the worship practice of the Church equally authoritative throughout, or are there rather internal gradations in its value as a doctrinal locus? (d) What is the role of worship in relation to the development of doctrine?

These are very much questions of authority, but it could scarcely be otherwise when we are dealing with the theme of '*lex*' *orandi*, '*lex*' *credendi*. Laws, however, may be either descriptive or prescriptive. In the question of worship and doctrine we are faced with the basic problem which arises in any discussion of the Church. On the one hand we may assume, in rather a Catholic manner, that the history of the Church has, under the divine guidance, taken the 'right' course: so that a description of the past is tantamount to a prescription for present and future. But what do we then do in face of the historical facts of liturgical and doctrinal disunity among people who all claim to be Christian? How do we decide which of the divergent groups has taken the right course? And what do we make of the history of the others? On the other hand, the contradictions of Christian history may speak to us, in rather a Protestant way, of the fragility and inadequacy of all human response to God. But where then do we find our prescription of how liturgy and doctrine ought to have gone and ought to go?

It is hard to see how we could have access to any entirely *extra*-historical standard by which to evaluate past developments and shape the present and future. There is, however, one point in history at which, Christians unitedly believe, God has visited humanity in a unique way (alexandrine style) or with a unique intensity (antiochene style). Jesus Christ— in his Palestinian existence (a Protestant emphasis) and as the intended centre, or focus, of continuing Christian worship (a Catholic emphasis)—is the *trans*-historical orientation-point by which we must try to judge the past course of liturgical and doctrinal history and take our bearings for the present and future. And this despite the cultural difficulties of our access to the historical Jesus and the spiritual difficulties of our discernment of Christ's presence in worship. The former kind of difficulties arise most acutely when a Protestant reliance on *sola scriptura* is coupled with an acceptance of the critical principles of modern biblical scholarship; but Protestants in dialogue with Catholics must not give up their insistence on the need for a scriptural test to be applied to Christian worship and doctrine, however difficult the application may be. The latter kind of difficulties—those concerning the discernment of Christ's presence in worship—require us precisely to seek help from the New Testament as our closest witness to the historical Jesus with whom the *Christus praesens* of the Church's worship must stand in personal continuity if *Jesus* is our Christ. I hope that the ensuing discussion of the four groups of questions will show that all this is more than a mere restatement of the basic problem.

First, then: (*a*) *What gives to the Church's worship any authority which it carries in matters of doctrine?* Since God as truth is the ultimate authority in matters of doctrine, it is of prime importance to hear a point which is made from experience in two such different parts of the Christian tradition as the Orthodox and the Lutheran. The point, in Orthodox terms, is that worship is first and foremost the 'presence and act of the trinitarian God': 'Worship is not primarily man's initiative but God's redeeming act in Christ through His Spirit. The eucharistic sacrifice as the centre of Christian worship implies the absolute priority of God and his act before man's "answer" and "acknowledgment", as we usually describe Christian worship' (N. A. Nissiotis) [note 589]. Or, in Lutheran terms: *Gottes-dienst* is God's service to us before it can be our service to God [note 590]; Luther charged the Roman church with having made the mass a human *sacrificium* directed towards God, whereas the gospel sacrament is a divine *beneficium* directed towards humanity [note 591], and our offering of praise and life can only be a response to God's gift. Worship, then, is a source of doctrine in so far as it is the place in which God makes himself known to humanity in a saving encounter. The human words and acts used in worship are a doctrinal locus in so far as either God makes them the vehicle of his self-communication or they are fitting responses to God's presence and action. It is difficult to measure the degree in which repeated liturgies or any particular occasions of worship satisfy these requirements, but a number of inter-dependent tests can be applied with varying exactitude and persuasiveness. One test is that of origin. Most weight will be given to ideas and practices which go back to Jesus. Prayers which treat God as 'Abba' and seek the coming of his kingdom *as Jesus preached it* will score heavily. Historical difficulties arise already with regard to the origins of eucharist and baptism. But in any case the post-Easter Church, as the first to feel the impact of the total event of Jesus, must be credited with an authority of historical origination second only to Jesus himself. Whatever the distribution of items between the earthly Jesus and the primitive Church, the exegetical and hermeneutical questions remain: what did the ideas and practices mean in their first context, and what do they mean in later contexts? But at least the New Testament texts, as our closest witnesses to the earthly Jesus and the primitive Church, continue in a fixed form and themselves impose certain limits on the way in which they are interpreted—and the practices which they originated are continued—by succeeding generations. We saw in chapter V that worship forms a connatural context for their interpretation.

Another test, itself twofold, is that of spread in both time and space. The closer a liturgical item comes to the universality of the vincentian *quod semper, quod ubique, quod ab omnibus* [note 592], the greater will be its importance as a doctrinal locus. Against the human possibility of universal error must be set at least a minimal trust in God's overruling guidance of his people: it is hard to believe that any practice approaching universality in the Christian tradition should be so far removed from the divine truth as to lack suitability as a source of doctrine. As J. H. Newman showed [note 593], the vincentian canon cannot be applied simplistically: the facts of internal reflexion within the Church, and of changing circumstances in the cultural context, point in the direction of some form of doctrinal development; and to this question we shall shortly return. At present, however, we must recognize the force of 'critical exceptions' to the near-universality of some liturgical practices. To take the example of infant baptism: in addition to the difficulty of historically establishing its apostolic origin, we must note the recurrent appearance within the Christian tradition of individuals who doubt its appropriateness and groups which abandon its practice. Their own motives may differ; but, negatively, their questioning of infant baptism weakens Augustine's use of the practice as a 'proof' for his doctrine of original sin (and has thereby helped to keep open the possibility of other thinking on the human predicament); and, positively, the advocacy and practice of baptism on profession of faith has called attention to the place of repentance, faith and personal commitment in human relations with God—themselves matters of doctrinal importance. Or to take another example of critical exceptions: the Quaker rejection of particular sacraments in favour of a sacramental view of the whole of human life. While it would be difficult to gainsay the propriety of making doctrinal use of the sacraments in their capacity as focal expressions of Christian faith and life, the Quaker practice enters a doctrinally valuable *caveat* against any narrow sacramental*ism* which fails to make the connexions between ritual and way of life [note 594]. From a sympathetic Catholic point of view it might be possible to see further examples of critical exceptions in the Protestant refusal of the marian cult and of the eucharistic sacrifice as Catholics have practised them; but we shall return to these two matters in the next chapter. Meanwhile it may certainly be said, from a Protestant angle, that the absence of the marian cult and of a sacrificial eucharist in a large swathe of the Christian tradition ought, even or precisely on Catholic terms, to give pause before the drawing of doctrinal conclusions from their presence in admittedly the greater part of Christendom. Obviously the numbers of worshippers involved are not absolutely decisive in the use of liturgy as a source of doctrine, and a sign of that is the existence and corrective value of minority positions. 'Purity' (the significant minorities are usually those that want to prune) and 'fulness' (which majorities may more easily embody) often stand in dialectical

tension. Nevertheless the approach to universality, in both
time and space, in items of liturgy is a matter of more than
phenomenological significance in discerning Christian doctrine. Description has prescriptive force—to the extent that
God is believed to have succeeded in guiding his people.

A third kind of test is thereby presaged. Augustine and
Prosper considered that the holiness of a Church indwelt and
led by the Holy Spirit gave authority to its liturgical practice
as a source of doctrine. At this point, the manner in which
the Fathers assume 'the Church', as distinct from 'heretical'
or 'schismatic' groups, to be holy tends to beg the question.
I should myself wish to stress the *ethical* component of
holiness. It is, for instance, the ethical reputation of Quakerism
which enjoins us to take seriously its liturgical practices of
avoiding particular sacraments for the sake of a wider sacramentality, waiting in communal silence for divine guidance,
and taking action only in accordance with 'the sense of the
Meeting'. In other words, it is the ethically tested holiness
of Quakers which gives some *authority* to their liturgical
practices—which themselves have certain doctrinal incidences.
(I have already mentioned the doctrinal incidences of Quakerism in the matter of sacraments: the reader will easily see
the doctrinal incidences of 'waiting upon God' and 'consensus'
also.) It is obvious that there is no simple one-to-one relationship between liturgy and ethics: other variables enter into the
situation on both sides of the relationship. Nevertheless a
liturgical practice which is matched with some directness by
holiness of life makes a weighty claim to be treated as a source
of doctrine; and any link that could be traced between a
liturgical practice and moral turpitude would to that extent
disqualify the liturgical practice as a source of doctrine [note
595]. Such a practice would fall victim to the apostolic irony:
Shall we continue in sin, that grace may abound? [note
596].

We have, then, looked at three kinds of test—those of
origin, of spread, and of ethical correspondence—that help
to determine when worship, in its intended capacity as a
meeting between humanity and God, can in fact properly be
drawn on as a doctrinal source. In doing so, we have

already started on our three remaining systematic questions, which each make more precise an aspect of the first question (*a*) and therefore compel us to sharpen up a part of our first attempt at an answer. The next question is: (*b*) *What is the relation between the doctrinal authority carried by worship and other instances of doctrinal authority in the Church?*

This second question brings particularly the scriptures and the magisterium or teaching office into play as other instances of doctrinal authority. In chapter V, and resumptively in the present discussion, we have shown how the scriptures, especially the New Testament, are our best witness to the originating person of Jesus and the events surrounding him, and how the worship of the later Church constitutes the connatural hermeneutical context for scriptural texts which were themselves doxologically shaped and which reciprocally continue to supply a permanent norm for the liturgy and doctrine of the Church. I shall therefore now concentrate rather on the relations between liturgy and magisterium.

It should first be recognized that the reality represented by the convenient Latin word *magisterium* is not limited to the Roman Catholic church: a teaching office is needed and is in fact present, however much or little recognized as such, in all streams of the Christian tradition, whether it be in the form of pope, councils, bishops, synods, (Methodist) conferences, preachers or theologians. The need and the reality are there because there is no *simple* way of reading off doctrine from the scriptures or from the intended encounter with God in worship, even though we have seen those two places—which themselves overlap—to be the proper sources of doctrine. Apart from the problems of scriptural exegesis, doctrinal debate is made inevitable by the need for fresh interpretation of inherited material in changing cultural contexts [note 597], and by the difficulties of evaluating current worship experience and translating it—so far as it is positive—into doctrinal form. The task of the magisterium is to identify the true faith, both by its own positive proclamation and by its exclusion of mistaken views. The magisterium has a responsibility *for* the liturgy as a doxological expression of the faith: it should actively promote liturgical forms which reflect the true faith, and it should nip in the bud any 'spontaneous' developments in worship which in its judgment distort the true faith. The magisterium also has a responsibility *to* the liturgy: it should draw on the experience of Christian worship, so that the doxological intention may spill over into doctrinal pronouncements, and dogma may be shaped by prayer.

It is this obligation of the magisterium itself to *learn* from the worship of the whole Christian people which properly makes impossible any over-sharp distinction between teachers and taught, any permanent categorization of magisterium and faithful into an *ecclesia docens* and an *ecclesia discens*. The human shape of the liturgical assembly may reflect differing patterns of authority, not least doctrinal authority, in the Church. The modern Liturgical Movement has put 'the president of the worship assembly' in the place that used to be occupied by the Protestant theologian-preacher in 'his' pulpit and the Catholic hierarch-priest at 'his' altar. An authoritarian pope such as Pius XII was understandably worried by some aspects of the Liturgical Movement. An authoritarian prelate such as Archbishop Lefebvre is understandably upset by the implications of post-Vatican II liturgy in the Roman Catholic church [note 598]:

It is obvious that this new rite is, if I may put it this way, of an opposing polarity, that it supposes a different conception of the Catholic religion, that it supposes a different religion. It is no longer the priest who offers the Holy Sacrifice of the Mass, it is the assembly. Now this is a complete programme. From now on it is also the assembly which will replace authority in the Church. . . . It is the weight of numbers which will give the orders from now on in the Holy Church. And all this is expressed in the Mass precisely because the assembly replaces the priest, to such an extent that now many priests no longer want to celebrate the Holy Mass if there is not an assembly there. Very quietly, it is the Protestant idea of the Mass which is creeping into Holy Church. And this is in accordance with the mentality of modern man, with the mentality of modernist man, completely in accordance, for it is the democratic ideal which is fundamentally the idea of modern man. That is to say that power is in the

assembly, authority is vested in men, *en masse*, and not in God. . . .
This Mass is no longer a hierarchic Mass, it is a democratic Mass.

Yves Congar remarks on the oddity of making the exercise
by the faithful of their baptismal priesthood equivalent to a
denial that power comes from God; he also maintains that
the liturgical 'presidency' in no way excludes the appointed
person from acting 'in persona Christi' *towards* the community
[note 599].

Drawing on Congar's own historical studies of changing
conceptions of ecclesiastical authority, Nicholas Lash has
welcomed the recent move away from the clerical authority
structure of the preceding generations, the liturgical embodiment of which was the mass celebrated by an individual
agent supplied with attendants and an audience. The vision
of the eucharistic assembly promoted by the Liturgical
Movement is characterized by the principle of 'distribution
of function' and is reflected in Vatican II's *Constitution on the
Liturgy* (article 28): 'In liturgical celebrations, whether as a
minister or as one of the faithful, each person should perform
his role by doing solely and totally what the nature of things
and liturgical norms require of him.' Lash comments: 'Article
28 of the *Constitution on the Liturgy*, for all its low-key abstrac-
tion, is important because it is one of a number of conciliar
texts that point to that recovery of a far richer, more ancient
and biblical vision of the church, which was one of the major
doctrinal achievements of the council. . . . A profound shift
in liturgical structures and self-understanding has both
stimulated and expressed an underlying shift in ecclesial
consciousness, the nature of which may be indicated by
speaking of the recovery of a functional model of ministry. . . .
The shift in catholic liturgical practice in recent decades has
brought about, or is bringing about, a corresponding shift
in the manner in which, pre-reflexively and informally,
authority in the church is experienced and understood.' All
this, says Lash, is in accordance with the 'principle of the
public accountability of office-holders', which is important
for the healthy exercise of authority in any society: 'they are
answerable to the community for their stewardship'; in terms

of the Church and theology, it represents a recovery of 'the ancient doctrine of the consent of the church, the *consensus ecclesiae*' [note 600].

The discernment of the true faith amid the historical flux of the Christian tradition is obviously a complex and difficult task. Sometimes a move may begin 'spontaneously' in the worshipping community. It is then the business of the magisterium sensitively to evaluate its appropriateness in relation to the best available understanding of the scriptures, to what is sensed to be the best in Christian tradition, and to the cultural context; and then either to encourage or to discourage it accordingly. But what if the community at large does not 'receive' the decision of the magisterium? Or if hindsight reveals that the magisterium judged badly? At other times, the initiative may come from the magisterium. The magisterium may judge it timely that a neglected truth or a new insight should find liturgical expression; or it may seek to correct past aberrations or replace outdated forms. But what if the magisterium miss its opportunities? Or if the community at large refuse its guidance? We are approaching the third and fourth of our main systematic questions: (*c*) *Is the worship practice of the Church equally authoritative throughout, or are there rather internal gradations in its value as a doctrinal locus?* And: (*d*) *What is the role of worship in relation to the development of doctrine?* It is also becoming clearer that the most fundamental question of all is that of the (in)fallibility of the Church.

It is by now obvious that there must be gradations in the value of the Church's worship as a doctrinal locus, and that we shall be seeking to measure any particular feature of the liturgy in a complex way on a number of different scales. There is the question of dominical, apostolic and scriptural institution. There are the matters of universal extension and of critical exceptions. There is the measure of ethical congruence. There is the degree of magisterial control and of community initiative or consent. There is the passage of cultural time which can require re-evaluations and reformulations. All these criteria have already been mentioned. The new point to be made is that the siting of any particular feature of worship in terms of this complex of co-ordinates adiaphora?

can only be approximate. It is hard therefore to see how absolute certainty could attach to any doctrinal conclusion drawn from the worship of the Church. Such conclusions will possess varying degrees of probability and must remain open to revision. But that is the case, I suspect, with all doctrinal statements. The question of (in)fallibility emerges again.

Openness to revision is the critical side of the coin whose other and more confident face is inscribed 'doctrinal development' [note 601]. To come to our fourth systematic question: (d) *What is the role of worship in relation to the development of doctrine?* In chapter II we saw the contribution made by worship to the doctrinal recognition of Christ's divinity. In chapter III we observed the part played by the threefold pattern of baptism in the shaping of trinitarian doctrine. In the present chapter we noticed that the marian dogmas of the Roman Catholic church had a base in popular devotion. In all three cases, worship practice was in advance of doctrinal decision. Yet it is also clear, whether in christology or trinitarian theology or mariology, that magisterial influence has been brought to bear on the liturgy for the sake of establishing a developing or developed doctrine—sometimes before, sometimes after formal definition. Popes sanctioned or even introduced marian feasts long before the definitions of Pius IX and Pius XII. Bishops were shifting to trinitarian doxologies of a 'co-ordinated' type ahead of the first council of Constantinople. And, as we shall see again in chapter VIII, liturgical devices continued to be adopted in order to combat recurrent arianism on behalf of the nicene orthodoxy concerning Christ. The reverse question is whether a developing, or a developed and even defined, doctrine can be undone by a withering in public devotion or by the deliberate intervention of a differently advised or constituted magisterium. Or can change in cultural circumstances call forth a new understanding and a new formulation which in fact amount to a contradiction of earlier liturgy and doctrine? [note 602]. The question of the (in)fallibility of the Church is now inescapable. It will be more directly faced in the next chapter.

VIII

Lex Credendi

1. Catholics and Protestants

ROMAN Catholicism characteristically appeals to existing liturgical practice for proof in matters of doctrine. There *lex orandi, lex credendi* is most readily taken to make the (descriptive) pattern of prayer a (prescriptive) norm for belief, so that what is prayed indicates what may and must be believed. Protestantism characteristically emphasizes the primacy of doctrine over the liturgy. The phrase *lex orandi, lex credendi* is not well known among Protestants, but they would most easily take the dogmatic norm of belief as setting a rule for prayer, so that what must be believed governs what may and should be prayed. (May: in critical distinction from what may *not*. Should: Protestantism also desires positively to promote true worship.) Although such a distinction can properly be made between the directions in which Catholicism and Protestantism characteristically see the relations between worship and doctrine, yet Catholicism and Protestantism each know also the reverse relationship between the two. Catholicism also seeks to control the liturgy doctrinally. It is difficult, if not impossible, for official Catholicism to conceive that the magisterium might have sanctioned or might still sanction any considerable doctrinal error in the worship of the Church. On the positive side, the Catholic magisterium values the power of the liturgy to educate the community in the true faith. Nor is it unknown that Protestants—in a way which runs counter to their more characteristic view of the relations between worship and doctrine—should turn to the liturgy to illustrate, and perhaps even to re-inforce, an item of doctrine. Nevertheless the differences remain. It is rare that the Roman Catholic church prunes its liturgy in

251

any doctrinally substantial way. On the other hand, the origins of Protestantism lie in a critical confrontation with existing liturgy and doctrine, and the original Protestant search for purity of worship and belief is prolonged in the notion of *ecclesia semper reformanda*. Protestantism does not consider its worship or its doctrine infallible, whereas the Roman Catholic church makes that claim for its dogma and, in essentials, its liturgy. The agreement and the difference may be put as follows. Both Catholicism and Protestantism consider that there is properly a complementary and harmonious relation between worship and doctrine, and that it is the business of worship and doctrine to express the Christian truth. They tend to differ on the question of which of the two, doctrine or worship, should set the pace, and they differ profoundly on the question of whether either or both—the Church's worship or its doctrine—may fall into error.

In the last chapter we presented and discussed numerous examples from the early Church of doctrinal argument from the liturgy. We found great approval among Roman Catholic theologians for such use of the liturgy as a doctrinal locus. It is a procedure which the magisterium of the Roman Catholic church has itself employed in recent centuries. Towards the end of the present chapter we shall look at some Protestant cases of this use. The bulk of the chapter, however, will be devoted to an examination of the reverse relationship: doctrinal control over worship. We shall look first at the early Church, secondly at some Roman Catholic examples, and thirdly at the Reformation. Our treatment of the Reformers will broaden into a systematic discussion of the eucharistic sacrifice. The chapter will close with a presentation and critique of the few significant modern considerations by Protestant writers of aspects of the *lex orandi, lex credendi* theme.

2. *Doctrinal control over liturgy in the early Church*
From the New Testament itself we have already had occasion to mention cases in which a hymn has been quoted, as part of an epistolary argument or exhortation, in a doctrinally 'corrected' form: Colossians 1:15–20; Philippians 2:5–11. We

do not know whether these 'improvements' ever found their way into actual liturgical practice [note 603]. It is certain, however, that St Paul sought on doctrinal grounds to control the worship practice of the Corinthian church. The criteria he sets in 1 Corinthians 14 for the conduct of the charismatic assembly are theological: the intelligibility of the Christian message; the priority of edifying the church; and finally, 'God is not a God of confusion but of peace'. The instructions he gives in 1 Corinthians 11 concerning the Lord's supper are based in soteriology and eschatology: 'As often as you eat this bread and drink the cup, you proclaim the Lord's death until he comes.' Modern exegesis sees the apostle engaged in combating an over-realized eschatology on the part of the 'enthusiasts' ('another is drunk'). In the not-yet before the final *parousia*, Christian life still stands under the banner of Christ's death. H. Lietzmann even argued that St Paul's teaching changed the whole character of the Church's euchar-ist from the joyful meal of the post-resurrection Jerusalem church into a solemn memorial of the Lord's redemptive death. It is more likely that the themes of death and resur-rection commingled in the eucharist from the first, as they did in the earliest Christian proclamation [note 604]. It is, however, clear that St Paul saw himself obliged, in the circumstances of Corinth, to bring out the *ecclesiological* and *ethical* consequences of the grounding of the new covenant in Christ's *death*, and of the fact that the Lord is both a saviour and a judge who is still *to come* [note 605].

When we move beyond the New Testament period, an interesting and important example of doctrinal control over liturgy is furnished by the great prayer of thanksgiving, which gave its name to the eucharist. After the Lord's prayer itself, which was the prayer *kat' exochēn* of the Church and the model and standard of all Christian prayer [note 606], the great eucharistic prayer was inevitably, in virtue of its place at the heart of the Sunday sacrament, the principal prayer of the Church. It was suggested by some earlier scholars that the Lord's prayer was the oldest form of eucharistic prayer [note 607], but today it is generally recognized that the origins of the Christian *eucharistia* are to be found rather in the prayers of the Jewish table, especially the *birkat ha-mazon*, now transformed by the belief that Jesus was the Messiah [note 608]. The argument is based on the earliest extant versions of the Christian *eucharistia*. From the account given by Justin Martyr in the middle of the second century, however, it appears that the president of the assembly improvised the eucharistic prayer: he prayed *hosē dunamis autōi* (*Apology* I, 67). The probability therefore is that the president used his liberty of expression within the bounds of an accepted shape or structure of prayer [note 609]. This matches the picture suggested by Hippolytus, in the work we know as his *Apostolic Tradition*, when he sets out our earliest known *eucharistia* and then continues: 'The bishop shall give thanks according to the aforesaid models. It is not altogether (*or*: at all) necessary for him to recite the very same words which we gave before as though studying to say them by heart in his thanksgiving to God; but let each one pray according to his own ability. If indeed he is able to pray suitably with a grand and elevated prayer, this is a good thing. But if on the other hand he should pray and recite a prayer according to a fixed form (*or*: with moderation), no one shall prevent him. Only let his prayer be correct and right in doctrine' [note 610]. From the record of a conference between Origen and some bishops in Arabia about the year 246 it appears that there were conventions, *sunthēkai*, within which the president was expected to remain, and Origen pleaded with the bishops not to introduce their own eccentric ideas into the eucharistic prayer [note 611]. About ten years later, Cyprian denounced the novatianist bishops for making the (eucharistic) *prex* with illicit words, *illicitis vocibus* [note 612]. It was the danger of 'heretical' formulations even 'within the Church' which led to stricter doctrinal control and the eventual disappearance of extemporization at the central prayer of the eucharist [note 613]. North African councils supply evidence from the turn of the fourth and fifth centuries. The following enactments come in turn from the council of Hippo (393) and the council of Milevis (402):

> Let no one in the prayers name the Father in place of the Son, or the Son in place of the Father. At the altar, prayer should

always be directed to the Father. And if any one should copy prayers from elsewhere, he should not use them unless he has first conferred with the more instructed brethren about them.

It was decided that prayers or orations or masses which had been approved in council should be used by all, whether prefaces, commendations or hand-layings, and that others contrary to the faith should not be proffered at all, but that only those collected by the more judicious should be said.

For a time, presbyters in the West were forbidden to preach [note 614].

It is certain that those who eventually became recognized as 'heretics' both altered the prayers and practices of the catholic Church and introduced their own compositions in order to promote their own version of the Christian faith. Tertullian reports that the gnostic Valentinus wrote hymns [note 615]. So did Paul of Samosata in the third century and Apollinarius in the fourth [note 616]. In the face of such activity, the council of Laodicea forbade the singing of 'psalms composed by private individuals' (canon 59). Arius had written hymns, and Sozomen records that at the time of John Chrysostom, the constantinopolitan Arians were still singing hymns in which the Trinity was defamed [note 617]. We have already noticed Cyprian's charge that the Novatianists made the eucharistic prayer 'with illicit words'. Paul of Samosata is alleged to have tampered with prayers which expressed Christ's divinity [note 618].

A special christological significance was from some date given to the use of water at the eucharist: it signified the humanity of Christ. St Irenaeus relates that the Ebionites rejected wine and used only water at the eucharist:

The Ebionites [who do not believe in the divinity of Christ] reject the mixture of heavenly wine and desire only to be an earthly water by not accepting that God should be mixed with them [note 619].

Could the ebionite practice even be the origin of the *positive* orthodox association of Christ's humanity with the water of a

cup that had been 'mixed' at least as early as Justin Martyr?
[note 620]. Later on, the monophysite Armenians refused to
add water to the wine, and they saw the mixture as a sign of
'the chalcedonian error', whereas the Chalcedonians in turn,
both Byzantine and Roman, have treated the Armenian
refusal as the token of a defective recognition of Christ's
humanity [note 621]. A rather different symbolism, which
may also be implicit in Irenaeus' remark, becomes explicit
at least with St Cyprian. He sees in the mixture of wine and
water at the eucharist the union of Christ and the Church:

> If any one offers only wine, the blood of Christ is there without
> us. If it is water alone, the people is there without Christ [note 622].

This theme was repeated and amplified in the middle ages.
Having been taken as a sign that both Christ and the Church
were offered at mass, the mixed cup was viewed unfavourably
by Luther, who would not allow any soteriological addition
from the human side to the work of God in Christ: 'Nothing
has been poured out for us save the blood of Christ only,
unmixed with ours, of which we make commemoration
here' [note 623]. In defence, the council of Trent anathematizes
any who should say that water ought not to be mixed with the
wine [note 624]; among scriptural texts appeal is made to
Revelation 17:1, 15, where the designation of the peoples as
'waters' is taken to give biblical support to an understanding
of the eucharistic mixture as 'a representation of the union
of the faithful people with Christ their head' [note 625].

It was not only 'heretics' who changed words and practices
in the liturgy during the earlier centuries. The Church's
liturgy was also adapted in order to *exclude* positions judged
heretical and to *promote* the orthodox doctrine in contra-
distinction to heresy. From the fifth century onwards, the
collects in the Latin sacramentaries appear sometimes to have
been deliberately phrased in opposition to pelagianism and
semi-pelagianism:

> In order that you may give what they desire to those who ask,
> make them ask for things which are agreeable to you.
>
> (old *Missale romanum*, Pentecost IX)

We ask, Lord, that your grace may always both precede and
follow us and constantly keep us intent on good works.

(old *Missale romanum*, Pentecost XVI)

The same motive may account for the invocation at the
beginning of the divine office, dating from about the sixth
century: 'O God, make speed to save me: O Lord, make
haste to help me.' It has been suggested that Leo I's
addition of *sanctum sacrificium*, at the '*supra quae*' in the canon
of the mass, was directed against the manichaean depreciation of the sacramental matter, particularly the wine [note
626].

It was, however, the anti-arian motif, as J. A. Jungmann
insisted, which had the profoundest effects on the Church's
liturgy [note 627]. We have several times had occasion to
note the contribution of worship to the doctrinal recognition
of Christ's divinity. After the fourth-century councils of
Nicaea and Constantinople had excluded arianism and
affirmed a fully trinitarian doctrine of the Son and the Spirit,
the liturgy of the Church began to show the consequences
of developed trinitarianism [note 628]. Prayers became more
regularly addressed to the Son (a trend which gathered
strength in circles inclined to christological monophysitism),
and eventually to the Holy Spirit. From the late fourth
century onwards, the classical pattern became established in
the East, whereby an epiclesis for the descent of the Holy
Spirit 'completes' the consecration of the eucharistic bread and
wine begun by the Lord's words of institution [note 629].
This same contribution by the Holy Spirit to the 'completion'
of the divine work of salvation received ritual expression
also when, from about the same time onwards [note 630], an
earlier rather varied Eastern pattern of initiation finally
settled into associating the 'seal of the Spirit' with post-
baptismal unction [note 631]. In the West, arianism persisted
among the Goths who had been converted to Christianity in
that form. Orthodox baptismal practice became deliberately
anti-arian in Gaul and Spain. Because the Arians used the
three immersions to 'rend the unity of the Godhead', Catholics
in Spain were encouraged to employ a single immersion [note

632]. In the *Missale Gallicanum vetus* the baptismal interrogations run as follows [note 633]:

> Do you believe the Father and the Son and the Holy Spirit to be of one virtue? *I believe.*
> Do you believe the Father and the Son and the Holy Spirit to be of the same power? *I believe.*
> Do you believe the Father and the Son and the Holy Spirit of threefold truth, yet remaining of one substance, to be perfect God? *I believe.*

The formula of administration in the Bobbio Missal reads [note 634]:

> I baptize you in the Name of the Father and of the Son and of the Holy Spirit, which have one substance, that you may have a part with the saints in everlasting life.

In both East and West, victory went to the 'co-ordinated' form of doxology, by which glory was given equally to the three persons of the Trinity. The fifth canon of the council of Vaison (529) reveals that the addition of *sicut erat in principio et nunc et semper et in saecula saeculorum* to the *Gloria Patri et Filio et Spiritui sancto* was made in order to refute the Arians, *propter haereticorum astutiam*, who 'blasphemously' held that the Son 'had a beginning' rather than 'having been with the Father always' [note 635]. Our 'Nicene Creed' results from the work of the councils of Nicaea and Constantinople in having inserted anti-arian clauses on the Son and the Holy Spirit respectively into local baptismal creeds in order to provide a universal doctrinal test [note 636]. The 'Nicene Creed' in turn became the baptismal creed throughout the Byzantine East and beyond and was introduced into the eucharist [note 637] at Constantinople (by the monophysitically inclined patriarch Timothy, 511–17), in Spain (when the Visigothic king Reccared renounced Arianism 589), in Charlemagne's Aix (in face of the Adoptionism of Elipandus and Felix), and in Rome (in 1014 at the instance of the emperor Henry II, though the Roman clergy had explained to him that the Roman church had no need to confess its faith very often since it had never been touched by heresy). Once introduced into the

Roman mass, its use was limited to Sundays and to feasts 'mentioned in the creed'. J. A. Jungmann comments that the Roman church thereby 'followed a middle course between a combative zeal for the true faith'—which had marked the introduction of the creed into mass in countries where christological heresies were being fought—'and the quiet devotion of prayer addressed to God. This solution manifests the serenity with which the Roman church, which never ceased to be attentive to the purity of the faith, yet avoided in its worship any noisy protestation against heresy, in such matters also as the concluding formulae of prayers' [note 638]. Jungmann's comment conveniently brings us to a discussion of Roman practice in the doctrinal control over liturgy.

3. *Doctrinal control over liturgy in the Roman church*

In the last chapter we already came across Roman Catholic theologians drawing doctrinal conclusions from earlier liturgical practices and texts on the grounds that those practices and texts had been allowed, authorized or even introduced by the Roman teaching authority. Such doctrinal control over the liturgy as the argument envisages might be seen rather passively as an assurance that nothing untoward would ever have been allowed by the magisterium to develop in the Church's worship (though we shall see that the Reformers judged the magisterium to have failed in this duty and even to have abetted error). Or the doctrinal control might take the active form of deliberately using the liturgy to promote a teaching on the grounds of its truth and its spiritual value.

Let us look first at some characteristic Roman examples of the deliberate use of the liturgy to promote teaching. In the last chapter [note 639] we already found Pius IX affirming that 'nothing was dearer to the Roman church than most eloquently to affirm, preserve, promote and defend the immaculate conception of the Virgin and its cult and doctrine. Our predecessors counted it a special honour by virtue of their apostolic power to introduce the feast of the conception into the Roman church. They marked the feast by a proper office and mass, in which Mary's privilege of preservation from original sin is clearly expressed. They sought by every means to promote and spread the already existing cult. . . . They were inspired by the desire to anchor daily more firmly this doctrine of the immaculate conception in the hearts of the faithful and to increase the people's devotion to the immaculately conceived Virgin.'

Another example from medieval western Catholicism is the feast of Corpus Christi. Both at the popular and at the theological level, the early middle ages witnessed an increasingly 'realistic' understanding of the presence of Christ in the eucharistic elements [note 640]. In ninth-century terms, the future lay with Paschasius Radbert rather than with Ratramnus. In 1059 the Roman magisterium imposed on Berengar of Tours a profession of faith which sounds distinctly 'capernaite' in its crudity (cf. John 6:52, 59f): 'The bread and wine after consecration are the real body and blood of our Lord Jesus Christ, not merely the sacrament thereof; and that body is sensibly, not merely sacramentally, but in reality, *sensualiter, non solum sacramento, sed in veritate*, handled by the priests' hands and crushed by the teeth of the faithful.' Although 'transubstantiation'—the doctrine declared by the fourth Lateran council in 1215 and confirmed by the council of Trent—has been for most Protestants the badge of an exaggeratedly realistic understanding of Christ's presence in the sacrament, Catholic theologians insist that its profound intention has always been to reject a crudely materialistic conversion at the level of appearances, the *species*, and to place the change rather on the metaphysical level of the inner reality or *substance* [note 641]. St Thomas Aquinas, who taught transubstantiation, is credited with being, at papal invitation, the author of the propers for the office and mass of Corpus Christi, instituted as a universal feast by Urban IV in 1264. Was the official feast therefore an attempt to correct, purify *and then* encourage a popular devotion to the sacramental Christ which had taken the form of adoration and processions and which had spread from the Low Countries? [note 642]. Or was the papal action simply an inclination before the popular ritual counterpart of a materialistic conception of the eucharistic presence that had indeed already once before found the highest magisterial sanction in the profession of faith imposed on Berengar? Certainly the Protestant Reformers, including the Lutherans, who had the 'strongest' doctrine of the presence, rejected Corpus Christi and its complex of associations [note 643]. The natural meaning of the Anglican Articles of Religion is that such practices are *contrary* to Christ's intention, when they state that 'the Sacrament of the Lord's Supper was not by Christ's ordinance reserved, carried about, lifted up, or worshipped'. In turn, there may be an anti-Protestant animus in the Counter-Reformation magnification of the cult of the reserved sacrament, which reached such a pitch that J. A. Jungmann could see in the sun-shaped monstrance the symbol of a whole period in which liturgical life was marked by 'a move towards the periphery' [note 644].

A modern example of Roman use of the liturgy to promote teaching is the feast of Christ the King, instituted by Pius XI in 1925 for the last Sunday in October [note 645] and moved in the 1969 *Calendarium romanum* to the Sunday before Advent. The intention is to bring home to the present time the theme of Christ's universal rule. The 1969 Calendar makes the Sunday after Christmas the feast of the Holy Family: there is a teaching intention motivated by pastoral concern for the values of family life threatened in contemporary society. In the case of neither feast is there doctrinal development or innovation. It is in both cases a matter of impressing traditional values upon the modern world.

To revert to confessionally controverted doctrine. While the Roman magisterium has been willing to sanction, adopt and promote certain developments in worship and doctrine, it has on other occasions sought to protect the liturgy from change [note 646]. First against the Wycliffites and Hussites and then against the Protestants the councils of Constance and Trent forbade that current sacramental rites and practices be disregarded, omitted or altered [note 647]. The tridentine canons on the sacrifice of the mass include the following:

> If any one should say that the ceremonies, vestments and outward signs used by the Catholic Church in the celebration of Mass are

18

an incitement to impiety rather than an aid to piety: let him be anathema.

If any one should say that Masses in which the priest alone receives sacramental communion are unlawful and ought therefore to be abolished: let him be anathema.

If any one should say that the rite of the Roman Church, in which a part of the canon and the words of consecration are spoken in a low voice, should be condemned; or that the Mass should be celebrated only in the vulgar tongue; or that water should not be mixed with the wine which is to be offered in the chalice, as being contrary to Christ's institution: let him be anathema.

The tridentine suspicion of the vernacular depended partly on a fear of doctrinal adulteration. A formulation of August 1562 read: 'The Latin language, which is used for the celebration of Mass in the Western Church, is in the highest degree appropriate, seeing that it is common to many nations. . . . There would also be great danger of various errors arising in many translations, with the result that the mysteries of our faith, which are in fact one, would seem rather to differ' [note 648]. As late as 1947, Pius XII argued similarly in his encyclical on the sacred liturgy, *Mediator Dei*: 'The use of the Latin language prevailing in a great part of the Church affords at once an imposing sign of unity and an effective safeguard against the corruption of true doctrine' [note 649]. The thrust towards universality in liturgy and doctrine accords well with the universal claims of the one gospel, but it could be argued that precisely this universal scope of the gospel requires that verbal and ritual expressions be found for it that fit each local culture in its distinctiveness. In the sixteenth century, Latin was still the international language of educated Western culture; but even by then a genuinely popular liturgy required the use of the vernacular, a language 'understanded of the people', to borrow the phrase of the Anglican Articles. In the twentieth century or, in the Roman Catholic church, at least since Vatican II, there has been an increasing recognition of the desirability of pluralism in liturgical expression and doctrinal formulation. Such pluralism is necessary to the rootage of Christianity in the varied cultures. Nevertheless, the question of the limits of pluralism must be faced if the faith is to retain some recognizably consistent identity. Since Vatican II, the Roman magisterium keeps some control over local translations and adaptations of the *Missa normativa*, but there is also a tolerance of experimentation which was undreamt of only a generation ago [note 650]. The post-tridentine period had in fact been dominated by the Roman Congregation of Rites, founded in 1588, which exercised such a tight rein in the details of ceremonial and (Latin) language that histories of the liturgy can characterize it as a period of 'rigid unification' and 'rubricism' (T. Klauser), 'unyielding uniformity' and 'timelessness' (J. A. Jungmann) [note 651].

We have already noticed *en passant* some Protestant reactions to the ways in which the Catholic magisterium controlled, or failed to control, the liturgy. Let us now look more thematically at attitudes and practices among the Reformers in the matter of doctrinal control over the liturgy.

4. *Doctrine and worship among the Reformers*

The Protestant Reformers sought a root-and-branch cleansing of medieval western doctrine and its liturgical expression. They returned to the scriptures and, to a less extent, the patristic Church [note 652], in order to recover the original gospel for both teaching and worship. In the liturgy, they operated both at the level of ceremony, where the pruning was severe, and at the level of the ritual structures and texts, where they set about a drastic re-shaping and re-formulation. We shall look first at the ceremonies.

There was first of all the question of unity and uniformity in ceremony. Mindful of the changes which the Lutherans had made, the peace-seeking authors of the Augsburg Confession told the Catholics that 'it is not necessary for the true unity of the Christian Church that ceremonies, instituted by men, should be observed uniformly in all places'. The *Confutatio pontificia* replied that ceremonial uniformity was both historically demonstrable and indeed necessary to the Church's unity. Besides re-applying Colossians 2:16ff, the Lutheran

Apology in turn produced evidence from the early Church and from the Eastern churches in order to prove that 'a difference in human observances does not harm the unity of faith' [note 653]. Nevertheless the Reformers were aware that ceremony *could* be doctrinally significant [note 654]. Changes were not made needlessly, but the Protestants did not hesistate to remove ceremonies which they considered to bear doctrinally erroneous meaning. The matter was clearly put in the preface to the Elizabethan *Book of Common Prayer*, where it speaks 'of ceremonies, why some be abolished, and some retained' [note 655]:

> Of such ceremonies as be used in the Church, and have had their beginning by the institution of men, some at the first were of godly intent and purpose devised, and yet at length turned to vanity and superstition; some entered into the Church by undiscreet devotion, and such a zeal as was without knowledge; and for because they were winked at in the beginning, they grew daily to more and more abuses, which not only for their unprofitableness, but also because they have much blinded the people, and obscured the glory of God, are worthy to be cut away, and clean rejected: other there be, which although they have been devised by man, yet it is thought good to reserve them still, as well for a decent order in the Church, (for the which they were first devised) as because they pertain to edification, whereunto all things done in the Church (as the Apostle teacheth) ought to be referred.

In connexion with the eucharist, the ceremonies which the Church of England abolished were chiefly those which fell foul of the position expressed in Article 28, dating from 1553: 'The Sacrament of the Lord's Supper was not by Christ's ordinance reserved, carried about, lifted up, or worshipped.' It is this position which accounts for the famous 'black rubric', introduced in 1552, dropped in 1559, and restored in 1662 (in slightly modified form): the kneeling reception of communion is declared *not* to mean 'that any adoration is done (1662: intended), or ought to be done, either unto the sacramental bread or wine there bodily received, or unto any real and essential (1662: corporal) presence there being of Christ's natural flesh and blood'. On the other hand, Lutheran doctrine on the presence could tolerate the continuance of elevating the consecrated bread and cup (so in both the *Formula missae* of 1523 and the *Deutsche Messe* of 1526) [note 656].

Protestant churches were willing to allow variety of ceremony *among themselves*, provided the doctrine was sound. Thus Polish Lutherans, Polish Calvinists and the Bohemian Brethren agreed in the consensus of Sandomierz (1570): 'We leave the rites and ceremonies of each church free by this concord. For it does not matter much what rites are observed, as long as the doctrine itself and the foundation of our faith and salvation are kept intact and incorrupt' [note 657]. It was with an eye to sister churches in Protestant Europe that the Elizabethan Anglicans declared at the conclusion of their statement on ceremonies: 'And in these our doings we condemn no other Nations, nor prescribe any thing but to our own people only: For we think it convenient that every Country should use such Ceremonies as they shall think best to the setting forth of God's honour and glory, and to the reducing of the people to a most perfect and godly living, without error or superstition: and that they should put away other things, which from time to time they perceive to be most abused, as in men's ordinances it often chanceth diversly in divers countries.'

Yet *within* the realm of England, 'uniformity' in ceremony was required for the sake of 'common order' and 'quiet discipline'. The conservatives are told some ceremonies have been abolished on account of their burdensomeness ('Christ's gospel is not a ceremonial law') or the superstitions and abuses associated with them. The 'new-fangled' are told that the ceremonies retained are venerable for their antiquity, useful, and clear in meaning ('apt to stir up the dull mind of man to the remembrance of his duty to God, by some notable signification, whereby he might be edified'). All are reminded of the need for 'a decent order and godly discipline'. It may be that some limited uniformity, even in ceremony, is after all required as a safeguard for unity of doctrine. Later Anglicans have sometimes argued that the Prayer Book tradition, with its closely related 1662 and Scottish-American ('1549') branches, has defined the *liturgico-doctrinal* identity of Anglicanism and set the limits within which a plurality of merely *theological* tendencies can exist in a single communion [note 658]. As we shall see in chapters IX and X, divergences in modern liturgical revision in the various provinces may be symptoms, if not causes, of strain upon the coherence of the Anglican communion [note 659]. With that, we are moving from the ceremonial point to the broader question of ritual structures and texts. It is these which pose more explicitly the interpretative context within which the otherwise often ambiguous ceremonies gain significance. The transition will be made by way of a paragraph on Calvin's attitude and practice in the reformation of worship.

Among the mainstream Reformation churches, it was the Calvinists who were most severe in the pruning of ceremony. All the Reformers eventually abandoned, say, the use of oil in the liturgy (in baptism, confirmation, ordination, and the sacrament of the sick) [note 660], but it was Calvin who most strongly associated secondary (dare one simply say: material?) ceremony with devilry and idolatry. This is what he says at the end of the baptismal service in the *Forme des prières* (1542):

We know that elsewhere many other ceremonies are used, which we do not deny to have been very ancient; but because they have been invented at will, or at least for some slight consideration, whatever it may be, since they have not been founded upon the word of God: and furthermore seeing that so many superstitions have arisen out of them, we have had no hesitation in abolishing them, so that there might be no more impediment to prevent the people from going directly to Jesus Christ. First with regard to what is not commanded us by God we are free to choose. Again all that serves in no way to edification must not be received in the church: and if it has been introduced, it must be cast out. For a much stronger reason *all that only serves to give offence and is the means of idolatry and false opinions, must not be tolerated at all. But it is certain that the chrism, candle and other such pomps are not of God's ordinance, but have been added by men: and finally they have come to this, that people are more attracted by them and hold them in greater esteem than the ordinances of Jesus Christ.* At least we have such a form of baptism as Jesus Christ has ordered, as the apostles have preserved and followed, as the primitive church has used, and we cannot be criticized on any point, save that *we do not wish to be wiser than God himself* [note 661].

This passage from Calvin, and similar ones from John Knox [note 662], illustrate the chief positive principles of all the Reformers in the reform of worship, even though the practical execution was ceremonially more drastic in Calvinism than elsewhere. The Reformers were keen to return 'directly to Jesus Christ', and the liturgical method of doing so was to concentrate on the apparently simple rites which the gospels showed him to have 'instituted': baptism in water, and the meal with bread and wine. These were held to be God-given through the sole mediation of Jesus Christ. Purely human additions were always prone to superstitions and even to idolatry, which is ultimately a worship of self by those who presume to be 'wiser than God himself'. The only human words required are those which set forth the gospel as the word of God and as the context in which the dominical sacraments are to be used. Right preaching of the gospel and proper administration of the sacraments become the crucial elements in Reformation ecclesiology.

There is undoubtedly a strong streak of didacticism in the reformed rites. A. H. Couratin cruelly called them 'anti-liturgies' because, by his definition, liturgies 'arise spontaneously from the life of the worshipping community', whereas the Protestant orders of service were 'deliberately framed by removing from the traditional rites those features which were dogmatically objectionable' [note 663]. The Protestant rites can be more sympathetically seen as an attempt, by action and word, to shape the people's faith more closely according to the gospel pattern. It was an exercise in magisterial control over the liturgy by prophets who critically opposed current understanding and use in the name of a renewed vision of the gospel. The 'remarkable creative achievement' of a Cranmer has been appreciated by E. C. Ratcliff [note 664], particularly in relation to the Second Prayer Book: 'Cranmer's purpose was to give an exact liturgical expression to the fulfilment of the command, "Do this in remembrance of me". The liturgical action of the Lord's Supper, according to Cranmer's later conception of it, consists in the eating of bread and drinking of wine in thankful remembrance of Christ's death. It is possible to reject this conception as inadequate or mistaken; but rejection neither requires nor justifies refusal to acknowledge the skill and felicity with which the rite embodying the conception is constructed. The several parts of the rite succeed each other in a logically inevitable order which deserves the admiration of all students of liturgy.' It may be a further compliment to Cranmer that a Roman Catholic writer should have singled out the 1552 words at the administration of communion as his example from among the sixteenth-century 'innovators' of the way in which 'heretics' also control the liturgy for their own purposes: 'Take and eat this in remembrance . . .' [note 665].

The Reformers differed among themselves on the question of the presence of Christ in the eucharist, from the 'consubstantiationism' of Luther through the 'spiritual parallelism' of Calvin to the 'memoralism' of Zwingli [note 666]. They were, however, at one in their rejection of the sacrificial character of the Roman mass. Luther saw this as the root of all false understandings and practical abuses in connexion with the sacrament: mechanical conceptions of the *opus operatum*, mass-stipends, multiplication of private masses, especially 'for the dead', infrequent communion, and so on. In the light of Luther's radical insistence on redemption through the cross of Christ alone and his radical doctrine of justification through faith alone, the sacrifice of the mass appeared as an expression of works-righteousness which threatened the all-sufficiency of Calvary. According to Luther, the mass was nothing but a 'work of men, even wicked fellows, by which one may reconcile oneself and others with God and earn and merit forgiveness of sins and grace'. And again: 'In the mass the papist priests do nothing but repeat ceaselessly such words as "We offer, we offer" and "These gifts, these gifts"; and they never say anything about the sacrifice which Christ himself performed, they do not thank him, indeed they despise and deny his sacrifice and want to come before God themselves with their own sacrifice' [note 667].

Luther therefore set about removing the 'dogmatically objectionable' features of the human *sacrificium* and turning the sacrament more clearly into a divine *beneficium*. His ritual measures were accomplished in two stages, the *Formula missae et communionis* of 1523 and the *Deutsche Messe* of 1526. Zwingli and Cranmer also needed two steps to depart from the Roman rite and complete their own structure: Zwingli's *De canone missae epicheiresis* of 1523 was followed by the *Action oder Bruch des Nachtmals* of 1525; Cranmer's two Prayer Books came in 1549 and 1552. Calvin's Genevan rite of 1542 drew upon Bucer's Strasbourg rite [note 668].

From the start, the 'little canon' which had grown up around the 'offertory' was removed by all the Reformers. In dealing with the canon itself, Luther's method was to excise the sacrificial prayers. In the *Formula missae* he retained only the *Sursum corda*, part of the preface, the institution narrative, and the *Sanctus* and *Benedictus*. In the *Deutsche Messe* the institution narrative alone is left, with the bread being distributed after the bread-word, and the wine after the cup-word; the *Sanctus* and the *Agnus Dei* may be sung in German during the distributions. Of later Lutheran rites, some followed Luther's first model, others the second. In 1523 Zwingli retained the *Sursum corda*, the preface and the *Sanctus*, but replaced the canon from the *Te igitur* by four prayers and the institution narrative. The prayers turn around the twin themes of a memorial thanksgiving and a spiritual feeding on Christ through faith. In Zwingli's 1525 service, only the institution narrative is left. All later zwinglian rites have followed this pattern. In Calvin's rite, the institution narrative is isolated as a 'warrant' and is followed by instruction and exhortation addressed to the people rather than by prayer addressed to God. Calvinist worship has remained the most didactic form of Protestant worship.

In 1549, Cranmer stuck far closer to the structure of the Roman canon than any of the other Reformers had done, keeping *Sursum corda*, preface, *Sanctus*, *Benedictus*, intercessions

(with commemoration of the saints and commendation of
the faithful departed), 'epiclesis' (*ut nobis fiat*), institution,
anamnesis, 'oblation', petition for benefits, and doxology.
But he introduced, between the intercessions and the epiclesis,
an emphatic statement of the all-sufficiency of Christ's
historical sacrifice on the cross:

> O God, heavenly Father, which of thy tender mercy didst give
> thine only Son Jesus Christ to suffer death upon the cross for
> our redemption; who made there (by his one oblation once
> offered) a full, perfect, and sufficient sacrifice, oblation, and
> satisfaction, for the sins of the whole world; and did institute,
> and in his holy gospel command us to celebrate a perpetual
> memory of that his precious death, until his coming again: hear
> us (O merciful Father) we beseech thee; and with thy Holy
> Spirit and word. . . .

In the final part of the prayer, the oblation theme occurs
thrice, interwoven with petition for the benefits of Christ's
completed work. Although some (partly displaced) Roman
phraseology is used, the sense has been altered in accordance
with Cranmer's understanding of Christ's work [note 669]:

> . . . entirely desiring thy fatherly goodness mercifully to accept
> this our sacrifice of praise and thanksgiving (*sacrificium laudis*);
>
> and here we offer and present unto thee (O Lord) our self, our
> souls and bodies, to be a reasonable, holy and lively sacrifice
> unto thee (*oblationem rationabilem . . . sanctum sacrificium . . .*);
>
> and although we be unworthy (through our manifold sins) to
> offer unto thee any sacrifice, yet we beseech thee to accept this
> our bounden duty and service (*haec munera*), and command these
> our prayers and supplications, by the ministry of thy holy angels
> to be brought into thy holy tabernacle, before the sight of thy
> divine majesty (*jube haec perferri per manus sancti angeli tui . . .*).

In the Roman understanding, it is Christ who is being offered.
In Cranmer's text, it is our praise, our prayers, our selves.
Following Bucer's *Censura* of Cranmer's First Prayer Book
and Gardiner's 'catholic' misinterpretations [note 670], the
Book of 1552 took the further step of removing the oblation

of praise, prayer and self to a place after communion. Other re-locations and excisions left intact only the statement of the sufficiency of Calvary (still in prayer form), a prayer for the benefits of communion according to Christ's institution, and finally the institution narrative itself. Some Anglican rites have followed the 1552 pattern, others the 1549.

5. Eucharistic sacrifice

The 'eucharistic sacrifice' has remained a focal point of controversy between Protestants and Catholics. Some *rapprochement* has, however, taken place in the twentieth century. It became fashionable, particularly among 'catholic' Anglicans, to excuse the 'excesses' of the Reformers by saying that they were reacting against popular misconceptions and abuses which in the later middle ages obscured the true Catholic doctrine of the mass. A blow was dealt to this account of the matter by the book of Francis Clark, SJ, *Eucharistic Sacrifice and the Reformation* (1960) [note 671]. Clark produced ample evidence to show the constant presence, in late medieval and early sixteenth-century Catholic theology, of the doctrine finally canonized by Trent, namely that the sacrifice of the mass and the sacrifice of Calvary are *one and the same sacrifice*— so that there can be no question of repetition or addition of a pelagian or works-righteousness kind. Clark showed, moreover, that the Reformers were well aware of *this* doctrine— and rejected it with open eyes. Clark's fellow Catholic, Nicholas Lash, charged him with greatly underestimating the complexity of the relationship between verbal orthodoxy and the practical context:

> If what the church is doing, in the concrete, can reasonably be said to be significantly different from what she ought to be doing [Clark admits the practical abuses prevalent in the late medieval period], then the theory according to which she interprets her activity may be calculated to mislead, even if that same theory, when employed as the interpretation of a more adequate state of concrete activity, were irreproachable [note 672].

Lash's point, with the supporting argument he takes from J. F. McCue, is crucial, especially when we are dealing with a church which on other occasions will make positive use of existing worship practice in order to draw doctrinal conclusions. A more irenic way of putting the sixteenth-century sacrificial controversy would be to regret that Catholic theologians had no adequate conceptual framework in which to explain their affirmation that the mass and Calvary are one and the same sacrifice. As will be seen in chapter X [note 673], the rediscovery of the dynamic biblical view of *anamnesis* and the application of ritual phenomenology to the Christian sacraments have led our contemporary theology to a better understanding in this matter. Even then, however, the Protestant still balks at 'we offer Christ', while as late a text as Eucharistic Prayer IV of the 1970 Roman Missal can say, with a starkness unparalleled in liturgical history, *offerimus tibi eius corpus et sanguinem*. Are Catholics and Protestants as far apart as ever?

Protestants can be encouraged by such a book as L. Dussaut's *L'eucharistie, pâques de toute la vie* [note 674]. After fresh exegetical work, the Catholic author presents the eucharist as allowing men and women, in the time of the Church, to share the life and destiny of Jesus Christ in surrender to God; it provides a 'ritual' focus of the 'personal' sacrifice of Christ and of the Church. This more personal and ethical view of the eucharistic sacrifice ought to attract those Protestants who have readily allowed the sacrament to be 'a sacrifice of praise and thanksgiving' for the work of Christ and an offering of 'ourselves, our souls and bodies'. But does not this Cranmerian formulation itself run the risk, directly against the author's intention, of 'pelagianism'? When Luther was prepared, in an explanatory rather than a directly liturgical text, to talk of Christians offering themselves to God in the eucharist, he was careful to state it was 'Christ offering us' to the Father as we 'entrust ourselves to Christ with a firm faith in his testament' [note 675]. Could not the contentious notion 'we offer Christ' paradoxically be seen as antipelagian? It could be an acknowledgment that we have nothing else to offer. It could be the equivalent of the publican's cry in the parable, 'God be merciful to me, a sinner'. Or even:

> Nothing in my hand I bring,
> Simply to thy cross I cling [note 676].

It is this *pleading* of the sacrifice of Christ which the Wesleys intend in their *Hymns on the Lord's Supper*: 'we present our Saviour's death', we 'offer up the Lamb to God' (hymn 118, verses 3 and 4), 'we again to thee present / the blood that speaks our sins forgiven' (hymn 121, verse 1), and (hymn 125, verse 2):

> With solemn faith we offer up,
> And spread before thy glorious eyes,
> That only ground of all our hope,
> That precious, bleeding sacrifice.

Precisely the reference to the 'bleeding sacrifice' shows that we are pleading Calvary, not repeating it. When in the eucharist we 'set forth' Christ's sacrifice before God, this is a sacramental action on earth corresponding to the fact that Christ is even now 'showing' himself, the once Crucified, to God in heaven on our behalf. There must, of course, be no opposition between Father and Son, either in the sacrifice of Christ or in his intercession. In the words of Cyril of Alexandria, the Father 'anticipates the petition of the Mediator' [note 677]. All is done out of the divine philanthropy which characterizes the whole Trinity.

Sacrifice is the loving surrender of self to the Other, from whom one receives back one's life. Eberhard Jüngel has described love, and God, as a 'unity of life and death to the advantage of life' [note 678]. To achieve 'the image of God', we must enter into this sacrificial movement and find its pattern reproduced in ourselves and our relationships. Christians have described this experience as 'I live, yet not I, but Christ lives in me' (cf. Galatians 2:20). To say 'we offer Christ' may then become a bold way of acknowledging the the transforming presence and work of Christ within us. Again, paradoxically, it could thus be the very opposite of pelagianism. A pleading of Christ and an acknowledgment of his work of sanctification: it may be that neither of these two complementary attempts to understand 'we offer Christ' will persuade many Protestants to use this paradoxical expression themselves; but they may perhaps now find it less 'dogmatically objectionable' on Catholic lips.

After that extended discussion of a material issue, we may now return to our formal question of doctrinal control over liturgy. We take the opportunity to discuss the few significant considerations of the *lex orandi, lex credendi* theme in modern Protestant writing. The chief substantial examples will be christological.

6. *Modern Protestant discussions*

In the summer semester of 1933 Dietrich Bonhoeffer gave a course at Berlin on christology; it has been reconstructed by Eberhard Bethge from students' notes [note 679]. Bonhoeffer began with 'the present Christ', he moved on to 'the historical Christ', he never reached his intended third part on 'the eternal Christ'. His starting point is important in the context of our discussion: 'Jesus is the Christ present as the Crucified and Risen One. . . . "Present" is to be understood in a temporal and spatial sense, *hic et nunc*. So it is part of the definition of the person. . . . Christ is present in the church as a person. . . . Only because Christ is present can we enquire of him. . . . Only because preaching and sacrament take place in the church can Christ be sought after. The understanding of his presence opens the way for the understanding of the person.' Belief in the presence of the risen Christ is at the heart of Christian faith (Bonhoeffer quotes 1 Corinthians 15:17). Christ is present in and as the spoken word of preaching addressed to me. In and as the sacrament, the embodied Word reaches me in my corporeal nature. Christ is present in and as his new creature, the community. In Bonhoeffer's thought, the Lutheran *pro me* thus takes a distinctly liturgical form. Worship becomes the starting point and criterion for the theologian's task of christological investigation and reflection. That (Jesus) Christ becomes *geschichtlich* for me in worship is the ground of my 'interest' in Jesus (Christ) as *historisch* [note 680]. My knowledge of him in worship as *pro me* is held to be the clue to the personal nucleus of Jesus

Christ as precisely the one who is *pro me*. His being present in worship carries the ontological implication of his unity as God-man: only because Jesus Christ is man is he present in the limits of time and place; only because Jesus Christ is God is he always contemporaneous with us everywhere.

Bonhoeffer's fragmentary insights are pursued by another Lutheran, Regin Prenter, both in respect of historical investigation and in respect of ontological understanding concerning Jesus Christ. In his little-known *Connaître Christ* (1966), the Danish theologian begins by setting out his 'method' in christology [note 681]. He holds that christology has two 'sources': the written tradition of the Church concerning Jesus, preserved in the scriptures, and its oral tradition concerning Jesus, which is Christian worship, with its preaching, prayer and praise, its baptism and its eucharist. The two traditions 'can never come into conflict', because 'they have the same content'. Only their functions differ: 'The written tradition is historical witness to a past confession. The oral tradition, in the form of a living and present confession, is the continuation of the confession of the primitive community to which the written tradition bears historical witness. The written tradition is the oral tradition's criterion of authenticity. And the oral tradition is the written tradition's interpretative guide. The two forms of the tradition about Jesus of Nazareth are correlative and therefore inseparable.' Prenter holds that 'the true oral tradition (particularly baptism and the eucharist) is clearly described in the written tradition', and that contrariwise 'every baptism and every celebration of the eucharist are the uninterrupted continuation, within the Church, of the cultic acts instituted by Jesus himself'. While admitting verbal variation in baptism and eucharist at a (trivial) linguistic level, Prenter asserts that 'their meaning always remains the same'. Confident in these assumptions, he tackles the substance of christology on the basis, first, of 'the christological confession' (pp. 39–74), which is equated with 'the oral tradition concerning Jesus', and then of the written tradition, where the chapters are entitled 'the man Jesus of Nazareth' (pp. 75–98) and 'Jesus Christ the Lord' (pp. 99–149). The humanity of Jesus and his 'divinity', in a sense to be explained, correspond to what we may learn about him from baptism and eucharist respectively. Only the co-ordination of the two forms of tradition, written and oral, allows us to 'preserve the unity of the person of Jesus Christ, who is both a historical personality and a living object of faith'.

Prenter begins with the oral tradition on the grounds that it remains existentially prior to the written tradition in the Church; but *chemin faisant* he must also have recourse to the written tradition as the oral tradition's dogmatic norm, in order to ensure authentic comprehension of the details of the oral tradition. In both baptism and eucharist, the Church believes in the presence of the risen Christ, but according to Prenter it considers his presence in two very different manners. In baptism, the Church sees Jesus at the door of the church, on the boundary between Church and world; he is a royal figure, our brother, the Son of Man, the 'justice' of all human beings in the sight of God. In the eucharist, the Church sees Jesus in the sanctuary, away from this world and close to heaven; he is a sacrificial figure, the Servant of Yahweh, the Son of God pouring himself out in love for us so that we as believers can follow him through the death of self into eternal life. Tension-laden as it is, this dual witness of baptism and eucharist to Jesus Christ helps—by its very dynamism— to overcome the difficulties which Prenter sees to be involved in the 'static ontology' of traditional christology: 'For there is no reason why a human life lived for others in the sight of God and a divine act of salvation could not meet in a single historical event. Without affront to logic, one can consider Jesus of Nazareth as a true man and as the event of God's love among men' [p. 149) [note 682].

In *The Shape of Christology* (1966), the Edinburgh theologian John McIntyre argues for a proper complexity of method in christology [note 683]. The 'liturgical element' will condition christological method: 'When the christological subject-matter is approached, it has to be borne in mind that we are dealing with a person towards whom the proper attitude is not one of scientific curiosity, or detached inquisitiveness, but ultimately one of worship and adoration, trust and obedience. . . . We shall not be satisfied with any christological analysis which eliminates from its conception of who he is all valid basis for an attitude of worship to him. It is on this very score that humanistic interpretations of the person of Jesus Christ fail, that they present to us someone who cannot sustain human *worship*; admiration, perhaps, even a sense of wonder at the courage he had in the face of danger and death, but never worship. That is given only to God. The questions with which the liturgical interest will always tax any christo-logical analysis will, therefore, be: How easily does the analysis integrate with a living situation in which the believer trusts, loves and obeys Jesus Christ? To what degree is the analysis organically united with the worship of Christ, so that it may finally come to inform, to deepen and enrich the worship of Christ?' McIntyre recognizes that the christologian must be able to 'stand back, as it were, and critically review the documents, the literary forms, the narratives, the hymns, the confessions of faith, in order to determine their authenticity and their veracity'. He even admits that, at one point or another in history, the 'liturgical element' may have become distortingly absolutized in relation to other constituents in christological method, so that 'the liturgist constructed christology solely in relation to the worship of the Christian Church, hoping to save it from the humiliation of bitter controversy'. Nevertheless the 'more questioning attitude' appears in McIntyre's intention to be finally subject to the attitude of worship.

In the matter of christology, Bonhoeffer, Prenter and McIntyre all fundamentally accept what they take to be the constant experience of the Church in worship. With greater or less explicitness or reinterpretation, they all stand in the dogmatic tradition of the God-man, which has been trans-mitted notably in the liturgy and which has served in turn to shape the experience of Christian worship and its interpreta-tion. This whole liturgico-dogmatic tradition has recently been subjected to an attack whose boldness is matched only by its brevity. I refer to D. Cupitt's fifteen-page contribution to *The Myth of God Incarnate* [note 684]. Cupitt (all but) equates the worship of Christ with idolatry. He claims that the conciliar dogmas and the anti-arian address of prayer direct to Christ are part and parcel of an extensive paganization of Christianity which took place under the influence of political needs and pressures. 'The entire imperial cult and ideology was refocused on Christ, while in return Christ crowned his earthly deputy and validated his rule. . . . Early Christianity had repudiated the Emperor-cult, but now conciliar Christianity came increasingly to be modelled on the Emperor-cult. It is scarcely surprising that the Emperors saw the correct definition of the dogma of Christ as a matter of high political importance; and when it was defined to their satisfaction they enforced it with all the power of the State, establishing a political order which in one form and another lingered on until the First World War.' In face of the Byzantine *Christos pantocrator*, all Cupitt's sympathies lie with the defeated iconoclasts. By legitimizing the pictorial representation of the supposedly 'divine', ikons of Christ cleared the way for the eventual portrayal—'barbarous anthropomorphism'—even of God the Father. This 'blasphemy' entails the loss of God's transcendence and finally produces atheism. Chalcedonian christology is made out to be 'a remote ancestor of modern unbelief, by beginning the process of shifting the focus of devotion from God to man. It could not put up any resistance to the focusing of piety upon the glory of the incarnate Lord rather than the glory of God, and then upon the humanity of Christ, and then upon humanity in general. On the contrary, it appeared to legitimate a cult of humanity.'

It is difficult to know where to begin answering Cupitt's (at best) lopsided thesis. Historically, his thesis ignores the fact that a cult of Christ, 'Jesus is Lord', dates from the earliest days; it was in the name of *this cult* that earliest Christianity rejected the 'lordship' of Caesar [note 685]. His thesis further ignores the fact that *Christos pantocrator* is also *judge*: the medieval iconography of the final judgment critically relativizes all earthly authorities. Theologically, incarnational doctrine may be used not only conservatively to 'sacralize' whatever is, and so to establish authoritarian patterns: it may also, and more properly, become the ground of a revolution in favour of the disadvantaged, with whom Christ identified himself in an ontological kenosis and an existential solidarity.

Ad hominem, it might be argued that it was precisely excessive *transcendentalism* which paved the way for 'modern unbelief' by making communion with God impossible. Furthermore, the 'cult of humanity', which Cupitt deprecates, might be seen as an expression of the *great value* which the incarnation recognized to human beings in the sight of God; in its atheistic form, the 'cult of humanity' could be parasitic upon the notion that the loving Creator calls us to a high destiny of communion with himself and has personally, 'in his Son', visited us in order to advance its achievement [note 686].

M. F. Wiles, another contributor to *The Myth of God Incarnate*, has been much gentler in his questioning of the liturgico-dogmatic tradition of Christ's divinity. In *The Making of Christian Doctrine* (1967), Wiles clearly recognized the very early contribution of devotion to the eventual dogmatic definition of Christ's divinity: he then calmly asked whether 'the effect which prayer has actually had is at every point precisely the effect which it should have had'. The 'should' both recognizes the propriety of *some* influence of prayer on doctrine and rightly claims that this influence is in turn properly subject to critical examination. Whether Wiles' own criteria of 'coherence' and 'economy', or at least his particular use of them, are appropriate to this examination, may itself be open to question [note 687]. There is a delicate relationship between coherence and mystery: the latter is not necessarily equivalent to obfuscation. Nor must economy be allowed to make a generous God parsimonious: Occam's razor ought not to shave away the very beard of Aaron down which the oil of divine bounty may flow. Wiles may be admitting these points when he expresses, in later writings, a willingness to retain in *worship* the language of incarnation and divinity in connexion with Christ, even though his *critical reason* apparently rejects such language. The question then becomes: how is his liturgical 'poetry' related to his doctrinal/theological prose? We thereby come close to a discussion which other Protestant theologians have conducted in recent years, though from rather different starting points [note 688].

E. Schlink's investigation of the relation between doxology

and dogma sprang from his experience in the modern ecumenical movement [note 689]. He observed that 'members of divided Churches find it much easier to pray and witness together than to formulate common dogmatic statements'. Schlink sought to account for this by the category shift which takes place when the content stated in prayer and preaching is translated into the structures of dogma. In worship and witness, we face God and our fellow human beings more directly, even when we use third-person language (third-person language signifies the self-surrender of the worshipping and witnessing 'I' and operates within the context of our encounter with the divine 'Thou' whom we worship and with the 'thou' of our fellow human-beings to whom witness is borne). In dogmatic statements, however, we are *talking about* (the proper way to) worship and witness. We are *teaching* about God, his acts, and the human response. The risk is that the teacher withdraws to 'a neutral position from which (the) encounter between God and man may be observed, described and be cast into didactic formulas'. Problems arise when 'attention moves away from the experience of salvation which comes through the gospel and is concentrated instead on giving a theoretical definition of the relationship between the divine and human contributions in redemption'. Schlink holds the 'structural change' from doxology to doctrine responsible for some of the most persistent dogmatic problems in Western Christendom. For example, with an eye to Augustine and Calvin: 'It is one thing for the believer to confess that he has been saved by the gospel alone, but quite another to teach that God's grace operates irresistibly. . . . The most radical effect of a structural shift may be seen in the history of the doctrine of predestination. Instead of a thankful recognition of the abundance of God's grace, which alone can save, and instead of God's eternal loving decree, we are confronted with the problem of determinism, in the face of whose awful logic the voice of doxology is put to silence' [note 690]. Or again (and here Schlink, himself a Lutheran, shows himself sensitive to the problems posed by the misuse of a Luther slogan): 'The statement *simul peccator justus* can be found throughout

Not a definition of —
only a description of the Christian.

almost the whole of Christendom as a statement of existential confession of sin and faith. As such it may even be found within the Roman Church. But the same statement must appear as a denial of recreating grace, and especially of baptismal regeneration, if it is misunderstood as an onto- logical and metaphysical definition of the Christian' [note 691].

Schlink is not so naïve as to suppose that dogma is un- necessary. It is needed in the debates with philosophy and with heresy. It is needed if prayer is not to be dissolved into individualism; if redemptive history is not to be reduced to existentialism; if actualistic missionary proclamation is not to lose the identity of the message. Yet dogma's tendency towards general and theoretical statements must not rob the faith of its particular and concrete qualities, which are experienced ever afresh in the confession of worship and witness, and *from which* dogma itself takes its origin. The particular and concrete origins of dogma are shown in the *variety* of confessional statements found in the New Testament and allowed in the first three centuries. Uniformity was an imperial imposition; and even then, the more doxological form of the Nicene Creed rightly came to find a happier home in worship than the more doctrinal Chalcedonian Definition ('We *teach* that it ought to be confessed . . .') or the 'Athana- sian Creed' ('Whosoever will be saved: before all things it is necessary that he hold the Catholic Faith. Which Faith except every one do keep whole and undefiled: without doubt he shall perish everlastingly. And the Catholic Faith is this: That we worship . . .') [note 692]. In modern ecumenism, Schlink contends, the need is for mutual recognition of a variety of dogmatic statements among the churches (and *a fortiori*, we should add, the tolerance of varied positions among merely individual theologians within the churches). This recognition will become easier, Schlink appears to say, when it is admitted that dogma, though irreducible and necessary, is finally a second-order activity and subject to marked historical and anthropological conditioning. Dogma and theology properly reflect the variety in human perception of God's ways and response to his will. When the underlying confession made in the structures of worship and witness is examined, Schlink promises the discovery of both a unity and a fulness which differences in doctrinal statements had obscured [note 693].

In his contribution to a *festschrift* in honour of Schlink, W. Pannenberg approached some of the latter's concerns by way of a confrontation with the notion of analogy [note 694]. In religious language, the transfer is not from human language to the being of God, but from everyday statements to liturgical and theological statements. Pannenberg understands the 'sacrifice of praise' in a strong sense: we *surrender* our words to God and so open them to be filled by him. Doxology is well grounded when it is founded on an historical experience of God's activity. Epithets thus predicated upon God in worship, however, do not properly constitute a basis for drawing out 'logical' consequences concerning the divine ontology. 'The humility of adoration protects it against becoming the overweening pride of having comprehended the eternal truth of God by means of human words.' The very fact that we use 'personal' language of God is a tribute to his 'non-manipulability'. The possibility of Christian speech about God is given by God's self-disclosure, self-demonstration, self-commitment in Jesus. There God 'owned' (the expression is itself metaphorical) some metaphors of human speech about himself: 'The metaphorical character of our speech about God, which Jesus also shared when he spoke of God as father, is at the same time taken up by God himself, in so far as he raised Jesus and thus gave his acknowledgment to him.' Just as the resurrection of Jesus is a *prolepsis* of salvation for all who believe in him, but *only* a prolepsis: so also, and in consequence, our doxology, our adoring speech about God, 'points ahead' to the *doxa* of God's ultimate and universal self-revelation when our knowledge of God's love will be complete. In its provisionality, our doxology is both valid (in so far as it is grounded in the act of God in Jesus Christ) and limited (by the eschatological proviso) [note 695].

Like Schlink, Pannenberg concludes that the provisionality opens up room for an ecumenically important '*plurality* of formulations of what happened in Jesus Christ'. More explicitly than Schlink or Pannenberg, we ourselves should conclude to the room left for *error* in both liturgical and theological formulation by the present incompleteness [note 696]. Nevertheless, it is in the perspective of intention and hope that questions of (in)fallibility can most profitably be considered. Christian worship is stretched between the already and the not-yet of the eschatological prospect. In the conclusion of this book, it will be claimed that one of the rewards of our study has been the light shed on the (in)fallibility question. Meanwhile, the next two chapters in particular look more 'ecumenically' at some of the issues that have been treated rather 'controversially' in chapters VII and VIII.

PART THREE

Contextual Questions

IX

Ecumenism

1. *Communicatio in sacris?*

CANON 33 of the fourth-century council of Laodicea enacts that 'no one shall join in prayers with heretics or schismatics' [note 697]. Before Vatican II my memory is that the sharing of Roman Catholics in prayer with other Christians was usually limited to a recitation of the Our Father. Common worship has flourished since Vatican II, but it remains the official position of the Roman Catholic church that eucharistic communion must wait to seal the achievement of ecclesiastical unity. An apparently growing number of Catholic theologians nevertheless consider that eucharistic sharing could have a part to play even now in the advance towards full unity. In the modern ecumenical movement, the Orthodox were quicker to allow common prayer. They invoked the mitigating principle of 'economy' to permit what 'strictness' forbade [note 698]. But, with rare exceptions among individual theologians, the Orthodox find it incomprehensible that eucharistic communion could be viewed not only as the end but already as a means on the way [note 699]. The difficulties and qualified possibilities of *communicatio in sacris* among divided bodies bear further testimony to the intimate linkage between worship and doctrine. Where doctrinal differences exist among Christians, it is ultimately the conception of God which is at stake. Can it be one and the same God whom doctrinally divided Christians are worshipping? If it is a different God, how can they worship together? Or if *per contra* there is a sense in which 'the walls of separation do not reach up to heaven', what contribution can common worship make to breaking down the earthly partitions? Can the living experience of worship help to bring doctrinal harmony?

The difficulty of *communicatio in sacris* is still felt by some modern Protestant theologians also. At the end of his book *Il problema del cattolicesimo* (1962), the Waldensian Vittorio Subilia, one of my own teachers, hinted darkly that the fundamental problem between Catholicism and classical Protestantism lay in their different conceptions of God [note 700]. The Catholic view of the Church as *alter Christus* or *totus Christus* is held by Subilia to betoken a view of God in which the divine reality is irreversibly, exhaustively and corporeally present in history and in the world. In the Reformation view, God retains his holy sovereignty, his mystery and his eternity, his freedom to reveal himself and to hide himself, to speak and to keep silence; he remains the one who elects and judges; he is not dissolved into human words, sentiments or institutions. Subilia developed his 'Protestant' doctrine of God at greater length in *I tempi di Dio* (1970) [note 701]; and then, at the beginning of *Presenza e assenza di Dio nella coscienza moderna* (1976), he explicitly faced the question of *communicatio in sacris* [note 702]. He respects common prayer in so far as it expresses an awareness that no theological conceptions, of whatever confession, are adequate to God, and in so far as it springs from the conviction that God alone is able to make manifest the unity which ecclesiastically divided Christians have in him and which in the midst of their divisions they can only 'believe'. Yet Subilia remains uneasy in the face of common worship between Catholics and Protestants. If Catholics and Protestants are not (yet) able to confess a common faith, how dare they appear together in 'pre-confessional ambiguity' before the living God?

The Waldensian theologian returns to alleged differences in the conception of God and of his presence. It is suggested that the Catholic insistence on the Sacrament corresponds to a sedentary conception of God, objectivized in the tabernacle and in the ecclesiastical institution [note 703]. The Protestant accent on the preached Word would express rather a conception of God as a God in movement, who manifests himself in event and is recognized only in faith and hope. If Catholics will meet Protestants only in the exchange of preachers and in services of the Word, Subilia seemingly wonders whether they are not being disloyal to their own conception of God. Might it not rather be that Catholics are regaining, perhaps with Protestant help, some insight into those very characteristics of the God of the Word which Subilia himself wants to stress? If, contrariwise, Catholics were able to discover among Protestants a more lively aware- ness of the God who has *committed himself* to the world in and through the sacraments, might the Catholic church not then be more willing to practise sacramental sharing with Protestant churches? Could Catholics perhaps help many Protestants to a greater sacramental awareness? I suggest that this is already taking place and has been made easier by two factors: first, the purified and enriched celebration of the sacraments brought about by the Liturgical Movement, which was largely Catholic in origin and inspiration [note 704]; and second, the strong tendency in contemporary Catholic theology to reconceive the sacraments in terms of dynamic events, personal encounters with the living God [note 705].

Practical participation in the worship of the other con- fessions, as fully as respective disciplines and consciences allow, has been proved in the experience of recent times to draw divided Christians and churches closer together. Before ourselves trying to give some theological account of this fact, we may listen to the personal testimony of some veterans in the ecumenical movement. In the third edition of *Confessions in Dialogue* (1975), reflexions on their own experience are offered by E. Schlink (Lutheran), W. R. Cannon (Methodist), N. A. Nissiotis (Orthodox), J. C. McLelland (Presbyterian), and Y. Congar (Roman Catholic) [note 706].

Fr Congar recalls the early conversations in the 1930s between French Catholics and Protestants: 'One only really knew the others when one had seen and heard them praying, for it is only in God's presence and in living relationship with him that a Christian can fully express himself and truly be himself. We realized already then that theology needs a doxological soil, a climate of prayer and praise, if it is to unfold, blossom and bear fruit. In our meetings and conversa- tions, therefore, it was not just a matter of academic exercises. We met together as Christians in obedience to the Lord who

prayed for the unity of all who believe in him. It is *he* who
reunites us. And when the purpose of dialogue is not simply
to exchange information and to reach theoretical conclusions,
but to build up our unity in Christ, discussion alone is not
enough; we must also pray together.' The Dominican goes
on to describe the celebrated Groupe des Dombes, in which
French-speaking Catholics and Protestants have met since
1937 and which has produced a number of remarkable
'agreed statements': 'The hallmark of their method is the
integration of theological discussion and prayer, and the
fecundity of the Groupe is due to this interaction. When you
have prayed together, your discussion takes on a new quality.
You are changed by prayer. More than once at the Dombes
meetings an impasse has been reached in the discussion, but
then after we have prayed together again a way forward has
opened up. A level is attained at which the spirit of self-
justification and rivalry disappears. One of the dangers of
intellectual work, and even more of engaging in theological
dialogue, is that we become trapped in an attitude of self-
assertion. Prayer delivers us from this. For here a third factor,
beyond myself and the other, a factor which is Reality and
not pure idea, and which is shared by us both, is disclosing
possibilities which we had failed to perceive. As we dispose
ourselves humbly in God's presence and before others, we
prepare ourselves to receive the illumination and secret
anointing of one and the same Holy Spirit. Theologians like
to affirm that this Spirit is the same in Christ as in his members:
it is he who establishes the unity of the body. And it is also
in him that all glory is rendered back to the Father: *in unitate
Spiritus Sancti*. Doxology is at the beginning and at the end
of all striving for unity. It also accompanies it at every stage
of the way' [note 707].

Nikos Nissiotis recalls his time as director of the Ecumenical
Institute at Bossey, and particularly the annual Easter seminar
on the worship and theology of Eastern Orthodoxy for non-
Orthodox students: 'It is impossible to convey the spirit of
Orthodoxy merely by means of a theoretical presentation in
the classroom. But I have observed time and time again how
a liturgical theology grounded in the worship life of the

Church, coupled with attendance at Orthodox parish services, can render the Orthodox position understandable and familiar and, in the end, make it a source of joy and spiritual enrichment.' More generally, Nissiotis observes that 'inter-confessional worship is filling the gulf created by the past separation between church traditions. . . . It urges those who participate in dialogues to engage in a strenuous effort of sharing in the most intimate experience of the partner.' Nevertheless, a 'genuine ecumenical spirituality' has not yet been achieved. By this Nissiotis means 'a real commitment to enter into a new relationship with the partner as joint members of the one historic Christian community. It means a thorough-going transformation of one's whole existence, a radical change of heart and mind including all the preconceived ideas about one's own identity and tradition as well as those of the partner' [note 708].

E. Schlink raises the same theme of divine judgment and renewal, mediated at least in part by liturgical encounter with other traditions. Schlink also finds in worship a methodological paradigm for the whole ecumenical dialogue. In chapter VIII we saw him urging the restitution of dogmatic statements to their doxological basis in the hope and expectation that doctrinal differences would thereby lose their antagonistic character and even be eliminated. Now, 'the same is true for statements of church law. Church law has its origin in the order of worship. In the first place it is meant to serve the event of Divine Service: in its rules for admission to baptism and eucharist and thus for church membership; for the leadership of the church; for the relation of the local church to the regional and universal church, etc. In the history of church law, this origin has fallen more and more into the background and the individual legal rules have obtained a momentum of their own. For example, if one compares in the different churches the canonical and dogmatic statements on the ministries, the apostolic succession, and the relation of bishop to presbyter, one finds immense differences; and an ecumenical dialogue which limits itself to a comparison of these statements will remain stuck in fruitless confrontations. These differences, however, appear in another light and can be largely eliminated, if one considers the service which is actually carried out through those ministries and relates it to the service committed to the apostles. Only if they are translated back into the elementary functions of church life, can canonical rules be compared in a fruitful dialogue. For those elementary functions have their centre in the worshipping community.'

My own theological account of the legitimacy and effectiveness of common worship among divided Christians can be formulated in terms of *intention* and *purpose*. The objective intention of all would-be Christian worship is, by definition, 'the God and Father of our Lord Jesus Christ'. The love which God has shown us through Jesus Christ attracts from us a response whose focus and channel is in turn the same Jesus Christ. This common direction of our worship is sufficient justification for our worshipping together. But our subjective intentions may differ, at least in formulation and perhaps in the very content we give to our responses to God's loving initiative. By worshipping together we are all exposing our intentions to the corrective judgment of God and imploring his gracious enrichment. The correction and enrichment have often proven to be mediated by our partners' traditions. Sometimes, in the modern ecumenical and liturgical movements, God appears to have done an unaccountably new thing in the midst of all the traditions. The teleological or eschatological perspective set by the purpose of God for humanity is also, I believe, the right one in which to consider the delicate question of intercommunion and communion; and to this most sensitive instance of *communicatio in sacris* I will devote a fuller discussion later in the chapter. Meanwhile we shall examine some contemporary attempts to achieve greater ecumenical agreement of understanding and practice in matters of worship. These are attempts to harmonize the doctrinal formulation and ritual expression, and so the substantive content, of our subjective intentions in our worship of God.

2. *Consensus in liturgical doctrine and practice?*

Many of the first documents in the recent series of ecumenically 'agreed statements' were devoted to questions that may be broadly designated liturgical. The World Council of Churches text on *One Baptism, one Eucharist, and a mutually recognized Ministry* (1975) provisionally summed up almost fifty years' work in the Faith and Order movement [note 709]. In bilateral conversations, the Anglican/Roman Catholic International Commission produced texts on the eucharist (Windsor 1971) and on ministry and ordination (Canterbury 1973). Lutherans and Roman Catholics in the USA composed statements on 'the status of the Nicene creed as dogma of the Church' (1965), 'one baptism for the remission of sins' (1966), 'the eucharist as sacrifice' (1967), 'eucharist and ministry' (1970). Lutheran and Reformed theologians in Germany formulated the Arnoldshain theses on the Lord's supper (1957) [note 710]; and at the level of official church life, agreement on sacraments and ministry figured largely in the Leuenberg concordat which established pulpit and table fellowship among all willing Lutheran and Reformed churches in Europe (1974) [note 711]. The list of subjects treated by the Dombes group numbers many themes of Church, ministry and sacraments, and recent texts showing 'elements of agreement' include *Vers une même foi eucharistique?* (1972), *Pour une réconciliation des ministères* (1973), and *Le ministère épiscopal* (1976). It would be a superficial judgment to claim that the churches and the theologians had thereby been occupying themselves with secondary questions rather than 'larger matters' of faith and praxis. The reader of this book should be in no doubt that questions of worship and sacraments bring into focus all the major themes of theology: God, humanity, Christ, Spirit, scripture, tradition, and (largely still to come) the place of the Church in human history and the wider world.

To the question of *doctrinal* consensus, with which the 'agreed statements' are mainly concerned, we shall come in a moment. But first we should look at progress towards agreement in *ritual*. Especially in a reflective community, rites presuppose and express doctrine. But there is still a sense in which the rite and its accompanying 'story' constitute a pre-reflexive matrix in which doctrine takes shape or develops. We became aware of that two-way relationship in the chapters on *lex orandi, lex credendi*. In the modern discussion, recognition of existing agreement in ritual and 'story' has been interpreted in favour of implicit agreement in faith and doctrine; and, looking ahead, the deliberate encouragement of convergence in ritual has been seen as a contribution to the achievement of even greater and more explicit unity in faith and doctrine.

The modern Liturgical Movement has brought the churches closer together both in the structure of their rites and also, though rather less completely, in their understanding of the nature of ritual and its function in Christianity [note 712]. Historians of the Liturgical Movement rightly place its creative beginnings in the Roman Catholic church [note 713]: with Dom Prosper Guéranger at the abbey of Solesmes in nineteenth-century France, with Dom Lambert Beauduin in Belgium at the beginning of the twentieth century [note 714], with Abbot Herwegen and Dom Odo Casel at Maria Laach in the 1920s and 1930s, with the Centre de Pastorale Liturgique in Paris from the 1940s. The Catholic pioneers went to the worship of the early Church to relearn two things: first, the basic outline of rites that had since become structurally distorted and overlaid with secondary detail; and second, the understanding of the liturgy as participation in 'the mystery of Christ' [note 715]. Pastorally (and pastoral concern was a major motive even in the *retour aux sources*), the Catholic liturgists sought to recover (for these things had been present in early history) the intelligent and active cooperation of the whole people in the rites. Intelligibility required at least the use of the vernacular language and a contemporary catechesis. Active cooperation required the appropriate distribution of functions among the various 'orders' within the assembly, and above all full lay participation, at the heart of which stands regular eucharistic communion. Protestants came at the matter from rather different angles, varying both from Rome and among themselves. But it can be fairly said that Lutherans, Reformed, Anglicans and Methodists have all experienced the Liturgical Movement in the form of a sacramental revival within variable areas of their respective traditions.

As we shall see in more detail in the next chapter [note 716], the Liturgical Movement has borne fruit in the large-scale revision and composition of liturgies in all parts of Roman and Protestant Christianity. Here we note the remarkable convergence of ritual structures which is apparent in revised and new liturgies of the eucharist. There would now be practically universal acceptance of the service-structure outlined by the semi-official Joint Liturgical Group, whose membership is drawn from the Roman Catholic, Anglican, Reformed, Methodist and Baptist Churches in Britain [note 717]. This same sequence of principal events in the *déroulement* of the eucharist is displayed in new service-books throughout the world: OT reading; NT reading(s); sermon; intercessions; presentation and taking of the bread and wine; eucharistic prayer; fraction and communion. While the homily has been reinstated in the *Ordo missae* of the Roman Catholic church, Protestant churches increasingly recognize that 'the worship of the Church is the offering of praise and prayer in which God's Word is read and preached, and *in its fullness it includes the Lord's Supper*' (British Methodist *Sunday Service*, 1974). Ecumenical collaboration on lectionaries is a sign of agreement on the original 'story' which is being told in the rite. This may be illustrated again by the widespread adoption among British churches of the work of the Joint Liturgical Group on 'calendar and lectionary' [note 718], or by the action of some Lutheran churches in taking up the new Roman lectionary of 1970.

There is even considerable ecumenical agreement on the structure of the eucharistic prayer which *in nuce* recites the activity of God for which our praise and thanks are being offered, and which implores the continuance of God's blessings into the present and their completion in the future. Many eucharistic prayers in revised service books will be found to follow more or less exactly the structure which W. J. Grisbrooke obtained when he arranged in a 'logical' order the elements he drew from an examination of ancient anaphoras: (1) introductory dialogue; (2) preface or (first part of the) thanksgiving; (3) Sanctus; a transition which may either (4) continue the thanksgiving, or (5) take the form of a preliminary epiclesis, if not both; (6) narrative of the institution; (7) anamnesis-oblation; (8) epiclesis; (9) intercessions; (10) concluding doxology and Amen [note 719]. It is to this central or 'great' prayer that one looks for a statement, in doxological form, of the meaning which the worshippers intend in the rite as a whole. Subtle variations of wording, particularly in the epiclesis and even more in the anamnesis-oblation, often betray different understandings of what is happening in the eucharistic action. How, or in what sense, is the eucharistic rite expressing and effecting, embodying and affecting, the relations between God and the worshippers? In the terms of classical controversy, the questions are those of presence and sacrifice. What part do the eucharistic bread and wine play in mediating Christ to the worshippers and enabling them to enjoy communion with God through Christ in the Holy Spirit? What part does the eucharistic action play in the worshippers' entry into Christ's offering of himself in love to the Father through the Holy Spirit? What range of understandings was left open by the first epiclesis of the Church of England's Series 3 Holy Communion?

> As we follow his example and obey his command, grant that by the power of your Spirit these gifts of bread and wine may be to us his body and his blood; for in the same night. . . .

What range of intentions can be gathered in the anamnesis-oblation (and second epiclesis?) of the same service?

> Therefore, heavenly Father, with this bread and this cup we do this in remembrance of him: we celebrate and proclaim his perfect sacrifice made once for all upon the cross, his resurrection from the dead, and his ascension into heaven; and we look for his coming in glory. Accept through him, our great high priest, this our sacrifice of thanks and praise; and as we eat and drink these holy gifts in the presence of your divine majesty, renew us by your Spirit, inspire us with your love, and unite us in the body of your Son, Jesus Christ our Lord.

Do such an epiclesis and such an anamnesis-oblation say too much, or too little, or the wrong thing? Is what they say clear, unhappily ambiguous, or happily polyvalent? I deliber-

ately give an Anglican example because modern liturgiographers in that tradition have avowedly to accommodate
both 'catholics' and 'evangelicals' [note 720]. Are differences
over presence and sacrifice differences of fundamental faith,
or official doctrine, or private theology? How much do they
matter?

It is to the exploration of such questions, both of substance
and of evaluation, that *doctrinal* conversations between the
churches have been devoted. What agreement can be reached
on the nature and function of the eucharist? On what plane
is such agreement situated (faith or doctrine or theology)?
How important are the remaining differences? We may take
as a first example the Windsor statement on the eucharist
by the Anglican/Roman Catholic International Commission
(ARCIC). The commission was composed of bishops and
theologians officially appointed by each communion, but its
statements have not yet been ratified by the respective
church authorities. ARCIC was convinced that it had 'reached
agreement on essential points of eucharistic doctrine', and
that 'though no attempt was made to present a fully comprehensive treatment of the subject, nothing essential has
been omitted'. Their declared intention, which they apparently
see themselves as having fulfilled, was 'to reach a consensus
at the level of faith, so that all of us might be able to say,
within the limits of the Statement: this is the Christian faith
of the eucharist'.

The key categories in the ARCIC statement are 'effectual
proclamation' and 'effectual signification'. The sacrificial
controversy is unlocked by the notion of a dynamic *anamnesis*,
'the making effective in the present of an event in the past':
'In the eucharistic prayer the Church continues to make a
perpetual memorial of Christ's death, and his members,
united with God and one another, give thanks for all his
mercies, entreat the benefits of his passion on behalf of the
whole Church, participate in these benefits and enter into
the movement of his self-offering.' It is noteworthy that the
language of 'we offer Christ' is avoided. Indeed there is a
strong use of 'offer' in the other direction. Three times Christ
is said to 'offer' the 'special gift of himself' to his people in

the sacrament. Concerning the controversial question of the presence of Christ in relation to the bread and wine, the mysterious action of the Holy Spirit is stressed, and the 'change' is expressed by the verb 'become' without further qualification [note 721]. Christ's sacramental presence, though not dependent on individual faith, is described in terms of a gracious 'personal relationship' with the believer, and the benefits of this 'lifegiving encounter' to the faithful include a deepening of our relationship with God as our Father and with one another as his children, in anticipation of the joys of the age to come.

An interesting index of ecumenicity is the way in which the ARCIC statement echoes, perhaps unwittingly, many of the themes in the eucharistic theology of, say, the Reformed theologian F. J. Leenhardt [note 722]. Another of my own teachers, the Geneva professor was among the first to exploit for eucharistic purposes the rediscovery of the dynamic character of 'remembrance' according to the Bible. In good calvinist tradition, he was always aware of the pneumatological dimension of the Lord's supper, in which the Holy Spirit served as 'link' between the believing communicant and Christ, between earth and heaven, where 'our hearts are lifted'. Leenhardt contributed to the recovery of the eschatological prospect: to share a cup was to share a destiny, and participation in the eucharist 'gave rendez-vous' with Christ in the final kingdom. He reversed the emphasis in the eucharistic sacrifice, making it first and foremost the self-offering of Christ to the welcoming believer. Most strikingly of all, perhaps, Leenhardt stands at the fountain-head of contemporary Roman Catholic attempts to rethink transubstantiation in terms of transsignification and transfinalization [note 723]: when Christ gives the bread with the words 'This is my body', the bread *is* no longer, in its deepest constitution, what the baker made it but what the Word has made it, namely the vehicle of his presence. Many of Leenhardt's themes, with various colorations, have in fact become common ecumenical property, as can be seen from our second agreed statement: the WCC Faith and Order text on 'one eucharist'.

The text on 'one eucharist' was formulated by the Faith

and Order Commission meeting at Accra in 1974. As part of *One baptism, one eucharist and a mutually recognized ministry*, it was sent upon authority of the 1975 Nairobi Assembly of the WCC for the comment and response of the churches. The text on the eucharist used many of the notions that had become familiar during the half-century of the Faith and Order movement's existence; much of its language was direct repetition from the Faith and Order meetings of 1963 (Montreal) and 1967 (Bristol). The statement was therefore the fruit of labours in which theologians from all the major traditions had taken part, and its ideas were not new to the churches. The text will be revised in the light of the replies from the churches, and it is hoped that the revised statement may then be commended by the next Assembly of the WCC for 'a new and larger response from the churches'. A process is under way whereby documents agreed by theologians find acceptance among the churches and an 'ecumenical consensus' is built.

The Accra document records a 'wide and growing agreement' on many aspects of the eucharist. Instituted by Christ, 'this meal of bread and wine is the sacrament, the effective sign and assurance of the presence of Christ himself, who sacrificed his life for all men and who gave himself to them as the bread of life'. The meaning of the eucharist is expounded according to a trinitarian pattern. The eucharist is, first, a 'thanksgiving to the Father': the Church speaks a great sacrifice of praise on behalf of the whole creation for all God's benefits, past, present and future. The eucharist is, next, an 'anamnesis or memorial of Christ': Christ is present and active in and through the Church's 'effective proclamation' of all the mighty acts which God has accomplished and will accomplish in him. The eucharist is, finally, 'invocation and gift of the Spirit': the whole action of the eucharist depends on the work of the Holy Spirit who comes to renew the Church and give it a foretaste of the final kingdom. Ecclesiologically, the eucharist is a sign of 'communion within the body of Christ': division of all kinds makes a mockery of the eucharist. While such liturgical diversity as is compatible with a common eucharistic faith should be recognized as a

healthy and enriching fact, the churches are summoned to
re-examine their liturgies in the light of such ecumenical
agreement as has already been attained in liturgical and doctrinal matters. Practice also needs attention if the churches
are to achieve 'unity in eucharistic celebration and communion'. Protestants are surely in view when it is recommended that 'as the eucharist is the new liturgical service
Christ has given to the Church, it seems normal that it should
be celebrated not less frequently than every Sunday, or once
a week'. Likewise, eyes are on the Orthodox when it is
recommended that 'as the eucharist is the new sacramental
meal of the people of God, it also seems normal that every
Christian should receive communion at every celebration.'

What is the status and function of the two 'agreed statements' which we have taken as examples? As is hardly
surprising in view of the broad sweep of denominations
involved in the wcc, the Faith and Order statement sees
itself as less far advanced on the road to full agreement
concerning the eucharist. It is helpful first to bear in mind
the metaphor used earlier by Lukas Vischer to indicate the
function of Faith and Order conference reports: 'Verbal
agreement defines to a certain extent the *area* within which
the churches with their differing conceptions have to meet
together. Although it does not represent a genuine consensus
and must not be misunderstood as such, it nevertheless
represents a certain *framework* within which the conversation
can be continued' [note 724]. To this must be added the
recognition of new *perspectives* within which old controversies
may be freshly illuminated and perhaps resolved. Thus the
Accra statement hopes that the historical controversies over
sacrifice may be reconsidered in the perspective of anamnesis;
that many of the difficulties concerning 'the real presence of
Christ' may be overcome by recognition of the role of the
Holy Spirit in bringing about the presence; and that problems
over a special moment of consecration may be surmounted
by a recovery of the epicletic character of the whole prayer-
action. At the practical level, it is recommended that differences
over the reservation and disposal of the consecrated elements
be treated in the light of the fact that the elements remain

the sacramental reality which they have become for the sake of being consumed [note 725]. *– but still deserve reverential* *regard?* *afterward* *LC view*

Clearly, the Accra statement admits that important differences still exist between the churches and need to be overcome; it sees itself as helping in the process. The ARCIC statement makes bolder claims: 'We believe that we have reached substantial agreement on the doctrine of the eucharist. . . . We are convinced that if there are any remaining points of disagreement they can be resolved on the principles here established.' In view of the earlier claim that 'nothing essential has been omitted', any remaining differences must be non-essential. If the church authorities adopt the Windsor statement, the churches will have achieved the 'substantial consensus on the purpose and meaning of the eucharist' which is 'an important stage in progress towards organic unity': 'It is our hope that, in view of the agreement which we have reached on eucharistic faith, this doctrine will no longer constitute an obstacle to the unity we seek.' The Windsor statement is meant to be more than 'a framework within which the conversation can be continued' or even the setting of 'perspectives within which old controversies may be freshly illuminated and perhaps resolved'. It behoves us to examine more closely the question of 'substantial agreement' and its expression in words.

3. *Verbal or substantial agreement?*

Lukas Vischer was prepared to admit that there may be 'verbal agreement' which falls short of 'agreement in the matter itself'. The deepest reason for this lies in the nature and function of human language. There is rarely a 'mathematical' correspondence between the way we speak of things and the way things are. Both language and reality are in flux. Synchronically, every linguistic unit has meaning only within a larger context: words within a sentence, sentences within a paragraph, paragraphs within a story, and so on; and the possibility for different combinations of the units at every level is virtually infinite. Diachronically, every language has its history, being subject to change through internal developments and through interaction with other languages. Reality itself is complex, nor does it stand still. Language and reality 'meet' in human beings who perceive reality and talk about it. But human perception varies according to factors of several different orders: physiological, psychological, socio-cultural. Mastery of the resources of language is variable. In addition to any epistemological gap between the *ding an sich* and the perception of it, there is also a communicational gap between people trying to describe reality: it is due to the variability of their perceptions and the variability of the associations carried for the interlocutors by the language they use. The wonder is that we succeed in communicating at all [note 726]. The greater our existential engagement in a matter, the more we sense the inadequacy of our linguistic attempts to share it.

Despite all the difficulties, it is by means of words and language that we reach, recognize and express agreement in substance. Precisely in connexion with eucharistic doctrine, Nicholas Lash warns against over-scrupulosity in the assessment of verbal agreement [note 727]. Since, first, any set of words is capable of more than one interpretation, the securing of agreement 'beyond' one formula would require another interpretative formula, and so on *ad infinitum*. Second, Lash quotes Karl Rahner to telling effect:

> An agreement about truth always takes place between human beings in a sociological milieu and when it is attained *there*, it is, none the less, attained. But it is attained there when it is attained in words and propositions (i.e. *verbally*, if you like) as used by men who pay attention to what they hear and think about what they say. There is a danger that, particularly in controversial theology, a neurotic fear that we are perhaps not 'really', not 'in our furthest depths' at one, may destroy such unity as might exist. . . . In order to have the right to live in separate Churches, we should have to be certain (to put it in broad general terms) that we were unmistakably disunited about the truth, and not merely be slightly uncertain whether we were really entirely at one. . . . We should not, then, say at once of every formula of agreement: Oh, yes, but go a little deeper into it and discrepancies will soon appear; the general terms in which it is stated are simply hiding them! As though we could not have the very same suspicion about all the unity within the Catholic Church! [note 728].

Thirdly, Lash suggests that the degree of doctrinal agreement or disagreement can be tested by an examination of the forms of worship employed by the various parties: 'If one party is worshipping in a way which seems to indicate that he understands the doctrinal formula, by which he interprets his action, in a manner which is radically different from that of his partner in the dialogue then certainly a further mutual examination of the meaning of the formula would be entirely in order.'

Besides serving in that way as a critical test of claimed doctrinal agreement, liturgy may perhaps function more positively as a primary medium in which substantial agreement is expressed. Let us take up again the earlier hints from Edmund Schlink on those lines, as we now broaden our discussion from doctrinal agreement on the sacraments to the wider areas of doctrine in which ecumenical consensus is also sought. Recognition that consensus is needed over a wider area of doctrine does not contradict in any way our claim that worship, and particularly the sacraments, bring into focus all the major doctrinal themes. On the contrary, it is the focal position of liturgy and sacraments in the wider field that both requires the treatment of the other doctrines which they assume and imply and also makes possible our treatment of the other doctrines from the standpoint of the doctrine and practice of the liturgy and the sacraments [note 729].

4. *Wider doctrinal agreement, liturgically formulated?*

Creeds are the genre in which the faith professed and the doctrine taught come to dense and co-terminous expression. They owe this character to the baptismal and catechetical matrix in which they developed, as we saw in chapter VI. In Edmund Schlink's terminology [note 730], 'confession' is the concentration of both 'prayer' before God and 'witness' before fellow human beings. The most 'objective' type of prayer is 'doxology', and 'doctrine' is the most 'objective' form of witness. Our traditional creeds are instances of confession in a strongly objective style. In our traditional creeds, the 'I' of the professing believer is subsumed and preserved in the 'we' of the teaching and worshipping Church. Neither the 'I' nor the 'we' are the object of attention, however: attention is turned on God and his whole work of salvation. In my judgment, this objective intention of the creeds makes them highly suitable as a form in which to seek and express ecumenical agreement, for it leads us correctively away from subjective preoccupations towards the God we are all aiming to serve. Moreover, our traditional creeds intend to encompass the whole work of salvation, from creation to the final kingdom, and so they cover succinctly the whole area in which substantial agreement could possibly be required between the churches. Finally, our traditional creeds already exist: they need only to be appropriated or re-appropriated by all the churches in their unifying ecumenical significance.

As a Roman Catholic theologian, Nicholas Lash has in fact suggested that affirmation of 'the Creed' is evidence of sufficient agreement in belief for all who make that affirmation to be considered as belonging to a single community of belief (and so not justified in keeping 'separate tables') [note 731]. As we should expect from our earlier encounter with his thinking on these questions, Lash is well aware that basic statements may be diversely interpreted, and that contrariwise the use of different formulations does not exclude the sharing of belief. To these two questions we shall ourselves return. For the moment, the important point ecumenically is that for Lash 'the Creed' is sufficiently expressed and exemplified by the Apostles' and Nicene Creeds. These are primary, and primarily doxological, statements; they are what Newman called 'rudimental', and the features and function by which they exclude false teaching are secondary. On the other hand, the (improperly called) Creed of Pius IV, as a summary of tridentine teaching, is primarily of a 'controversial' nature; and, once doctrinal process has ceased to be seen simply as a uni-directional, deductive 'unfolding' of the implicit content of divinely revealed premises, the marian and papal dogmas are bound to rank lower than creedal matters in what Vatican II calls the 'hierarchy of truths' [note 732]. None of the tridentine or later differences is judged by Lash to constitute so grave a divergence in belief as to prevent eucharistic fellowship. He considers the Apostles' and Nicene Creeds to be equivalents, since they each attempt to 'give verbal expression to the *entire* Christian mystery'. On those grounds, the Roman and the Protestant churches may already be considered a single community of belief. Nor do the Eastern churches find difficulty in recognizing the Apostles' Creed of the West. In an ecumenical gesture the Western churches might drop the *filioque* from their version of the Nicene Creed [note 733]: the clause is a later and unilateral expansion, somewhat 'deductive' in nature and certainly 'controversial' in function (anti-arian); on the intimate point of inner-trinitarian theology, it is possible to recognize the more characteristically Western and Eastern views as tolerable variants within a broader area of agreement [note 734].

The creeds were late-comers into eucharistic worship. Nor do they stand there alone. As J. P. Jossua remarks: 'True, the creeds as a specific form made their way only very late into the celebration. But long before then, the eucharistic anaphora itself was a profession of faith, very close to the baptismal formulae' [note 735]. The nineteenth-century scholar Ferdinand Probst insisted on the substantial identity between the eucharistic 'canon' of the early Church and the 'rule' of truth, *regula veritatis*, which guided its missionary preaching and was reflected in the baptismal profession of converts. Both 'embody the kernel and quintessence of Christian doctrine', the one in 'didactic' form, the other in 'hymnic' [note 736]. More recent scholars have also remarked on the broadly triadic pattern of early eucharistic anaphoras, which is reminiscent of the tripartite structure of the creeds: praise of God (the Father), anamnesis of Christ, epiclesis of the Spirit [note 737]. While this pattern may have been reinforced in late fourth-century 'Byzantine' anaphoras for anti-arian reasons, it was already present in the eucharistic prayer of chapter 4 of *The Apostolic Tradition*, where there is no compelling cause to doubt the authenticity of the Spirit-epiclesis [note 738]. Certainly there was some kind of trinitarian *understanding* of eucharistic prayer as early as Justin Martyr, and there is no reason to limit the verbal expression of that understanding to a concluding doxology: 'The president offers praise and glory to the Father of all in the name of the

Son and of the Holy Spirit.' 'We bless the Maker of all things through his Son Jesus Christ and through the Holy Spirit' [note 739].

On the ecumenical front, the Roman Catholic theologian H. J. Schulz has recently argued that an adequate 'unity in faith' can be drawn from the ancient eucharistic tradition which the divided churches have retained or restored [note 740]. The words, actions and celebration of the eucharistic rites, and particularly the great eucharistic prayer, provide sufficient expression of trinitarian faith, and of doctrine concerning Church, sacraments and ministry [note 741]. It is to relations between the Roman and the Eastern churches that Schulz devotes most attention [note 742], but he sees positive prospects also for reconciliation with the churches of the Reformation by this route. Indubitably, many Protestant churches have drawn deeply on ancient tradition in their recent liturgical revisions, and the excessively sacrificial emphasis of the Roman canon has been corrected in the new Roman eucharistic prayers inspired by early sources. Most significant of all, perhaps, is the collaboration of Catholic and Protestant liturgiographers in the composition of 'ecumenical rites', and particularly eucharistic prayers. In Britain, the Joint Liturgical Group has produced an 'ecumenical canon', whose boldest feature is a reinforcement of the dominical anchorage by the use of the first part of the Lord's Prayer to join the hallowing of the Father's name in the Sanctus with the prayer for heavenly bread in the first epiclesis:

> Heavenly Father,
> we offer you this praise
> through Jesus Christ, your only Son, our Lord,
> who hallowed your name,
> accomplished your will,
> established your kingdom,
> and gave himself to be our spiritual food.
> And now we pray that by the power of your Holy Spirit
> these gifts of bread and wine
> may be to us his body and his blood.
> For on the night . . . [note 743].

This canon 'is primarily intended for use on ecumenical occasions', although its unifying capacity would be enhanced if the churches in Britain would endorse its use as at least an alternative text in denominational worship. Such adoption is happening in the U.S.A. in the case of the 'common eucharistic prayer' composed in 1975 by an unofficial committee. The prayer draws heavily on the 'Eastern-style' fourth eucharistic prayer of the 1970 Roman missal, though it makes the sacrificial language more circumlocutory. It has now been included for optional use in the *Book of Common Prayer* of the Episcopal Church (1976).

A Methodist will perhaps be pardoned for calling attention to one other possible locus of 'wider doctrinal agreement, liturgically formulated', namely hymns. In his *Mary, Mother of the Redemption*, Edward Schillebeeckx O.P. blamed the marian inadequacies of Protestantism on the inadequacy of Protestant doctrine concerning the incarnation: 'The basic reason for the difference between the Protestant and the Catholic attitudes towards Mary in the sphere of worship is undoubtedly to be found in the different dogmatic views of Christ and in the fact that we, as Catholics, do not hesitate to call our Lady the mother of the redeeming God in humanity. Our Protestant brothers in faith, on the other hand, do not appear to grasp the deep and fundamental meaning of this great reality, "God in humanity", and consequently fail to fathom the full depths of Mary's motherhood.' [note 744]. Whatever may be the truth about the marian connexion [note 745], it would be hard to find a stronger expression of the christological doctrine of the council of Ephesus than this couplet from one of Charles Wesley's Christmas hymns:

> Being's source begins to be,
> And God Himself is born.
>   (MHB 134).

Or consider the view of divine incarnation and human destiny expressed in another of Wesley's hymns (MHB, No. 142), already quoted in part (p. 207f) [note 746]. Methodists are delighted to discover Wesley's compositions finding their way into modern Catholic hymn-books [note 747].

Two final values may be noted in the liturgy as a locus of doctrinal agreement. Nicholas Lash rightly remarks that 'agreement and disagreement are not patient of quasi-mathematical demonstration. There is always a penumbra of uncertainty surrounding any agreement that we judge to have been reached. And the search for agreement has no end. People change, situations change, meanings change. Agreement is constantly sought for, more or less successfully achieved, only to be sought for again' [note 748]. I suggest, first, that the (notoriously) conservative character of liturgy provides a welcome factor of stability in a restless search which might otherwise be completely subject to cultural shift or, worse, the fluctuations of theological fashion. Second, I think that the 'penumbra of uncertainty' which surrounds agreements attained on the intellectual plane can well be contained within the mysterious and multi-dimensional framework of doxology.

It seems that the search for agreement among the denominational churches has been leading up to some kind of *mutual recognition* at the least. We must now examine this explicitly or implicitly recurrent idea. What could it mean more concretely? Would its attainment adequately embody the note of unity?

5. *Mutual recognition?*

The most basic instance of mutual recognition appears to occur in connexion with baptism [note 749]. The matter proves to be much more complex than is realized by the jack-in-a-box optimists who keep emerging in the modern ecumenical movement to tell us that our 'common baptism' is one of the things that still (or already) unite us across denominational boundaries. To speak of our common baptism is to beg a number of important questions, as any conversation between a Baptist and an Orthodox or a Roman Catholic quickly reveals. For baptism puts at stake the whole doctrine of the Church and the whole understanding of ritual activity (in a Christian context: sacramental activity). Both the ecclesiological and the anthropological or sacramental question are ultimately facets of the even more fundamental question of God's saving dealings with humanity. Doctrinal and practical agreement on baptism, and any ensuing mutual recognition of baptisms as 'our common baptism', would therefore have far-reaching consequences in the search for unity. Let us at this point look for signs of progress on the part of denominational churches which come to the matter from various angles.

The Orthodox remain closest to cyprianic exclusivism; but if they nevertheless do not baptize converts who have already received water baptism in other trinitarian communities, they are at the least suspending judgment on the value of such baptisms, even though the implication may be that conversion to Orthodoxy is necessary for their 'activation'. If the chrismation given to converts is regarded (merely) as reconciliation, their earlier confirmation is being regarded in the same way as their earlier baptism; if their Orthodox chrismation is regarded as strictly initiatory, the implication is that any earlier confirmation was either totally absent or irretrievably faulty. In earlier centuries the Roman Catholic church largely took the augustinian view that baptism (and confirmation) administered outside the Roman church was valid (and therefore not repeatable) but was not efficacious for salvation until the baptized person joined the Roman church. The baptism which the council of Trent affirmed as 'true baptism' was performed with water, in the name of the Trinity, and with 'the intention of doing what the Church does'. Fears concerning defect of intention were partly responsible for the Roman practice of giving (conditional) baptism to converts from Protestantism [note 750]. But this practice has now almost ceased, and we shall ourselves return to the question of intention shortly. When, in modern times, baptism (correctly) administered outside the Roman communion began to be seen more generously as both valid *and* efficacious [note 751], the Roman generosity was based on the notion that such baptism substantially belonged to the one (Roman Catholic) Church; such baptism was a *vestigium ecclesiae*. Unity required the 'reintegration' of 'separated brethren' into the Roman Catholic church: 'brethren' they were by (properly Roman) baptism, but 'separated' they remained until their 'restoration' to Roman communion. They were, individually, Christians *in spite of* their denominational allegiances [note 752]. However, Vatican II gave, perhaps dialectically, some kind of ecclesiological recognition to other 'churches and churchly communities', including communions stemming from the Reformation, when the decree on ecumenism declared them to be *as communities* 'not devoid of meaning and value in the mystery of salvation'. Despite hints of other ecclesiological perspectives in the Vatican II documents, however, the council's dominant ecclesiology remained, in Avery Dulles' terms, 'substantialist', though of the 'inclusivist' rather than the exclusivist sub-type: the other communities benefit from 'endowments' of the one and only Church of Jesus Christ which 'subsists in [*subsistit in*, albeit not *est*] the Catholic Church' [note 753].

In Protestant ecclesiology, on the other hand, schisms are usually seen to be *within* the (universal) Church. The Church itself is divided. Baptism and (in whatever sense) confirmation are taken to relate a person both to a 'denomination' and to 'the Church'. I judge this to be a realistic acknowledgment of the tension between eschatological calling and actual historical dividedness. The Protestant temptation, however, appears to be a too ready acquiescence in division which takes the form of denominational*ism*. Can it (also) be 'the one baptism' when it is (also) baptism 'into' a denomination which is divided from others? Is there not here an anomaly which can only be resolved by the ending of denominations and the achievement of full unity?

The immediately preceding discussion appears to assume agreement on the salvific significance of baptism for the person, even though the enjoyment of its ecclesial benefits may be, at least in part, frustrated. The existence of Baptists, however, reminds us that once again the matter is not so simple. Strict or closed Baptists maintain a simple cyprianic exclusivism in ecclesiology. But complexity becomes apparent when open Baptists give some ecclesiological recognition to *believers* from other denominations by admitting them to occasional communion, or even permanent membership, without requiring baptism upon profession of faith. Either some degree of recognition is being accorded to the infant baptism practised in paedobaptist denominations, or believers are being admitted *in spite of* their (infant/lack of) baptism. To the extent that Baptists maintain 'inter-church' relations with paedobaptist denominations, they also give ecclesiological recognition to those denominations as *communities of faith*. Although touched by the generosity of the open Baptists, many in other denominations will consider that the Baptists are, in one way or another, showing a curious lack of appreciation of the significance of baptism. In reality we are once more being brought up against the problematic nature of 'the one baptism'. Can it be—even from a paedobaptist point of view, let alone a Baptist—one and the same baptism which Baptists give only to believers, and not to all of them, and which other churches give, apparently without distinction, to believing adults and to infants? But again: 'apparently without distinction' itself needs investigation. Some churches which give baptism to infants distinguish explicitly between baptismal membership and the 'full' membership which comes only upon profession of personal faith, whether in confirmation or otherwise. This is clear in Methodism and in parts of other traditions, even Lutheran, Reformed and Anglican, which have been touched by what their detractors call pietism, intellectualism, voluntaryism or adultism. But all churches, even the Roman Catholic, which baptize infants but give communion only 'at the years of discretion', are by their practice making an implicit distinction between baptism as given to infants and baptism as given upon profession of faith, whatever their protests to the contrary.

In view of such difficulties, it is not surprising that an ecumenical consensus on baptism is still in the process of being sought after. That is clearly the case in the Accra Faith and Order statement on *One Baptism* and in the responses of the churches to that statement. As I evaluate the present stage [note 754], the churches are in tolerably sufficient agreement both about what constitutes the basic theological referent of baptism, namely the saving acts of God in Jesus Christ, and also about what constitutes the broader existential referent of baptism, namely the human salvation which may be described as forgiveness of sin, rebirth, new life in the Spirit, and so on. The churches differ, however, on the precise place and function of baptism in the process by which God's saving acts take effect in the salvation of particular human beings. In other words, they differ on *how* baptism 'refers' to God's saving activity, and on *how* baptism 'refers' to the human appropriation of that activity. I suspect that some of the deepest divisions in the area of Christian initiation concern the anthropology and theology of *ritual signs*. How far does the performance of signs *produce* the reality which they signify? How far is any such production instantaneous, and how far is it spread over a future time-span? How far, on the other hand, does the performance of signs *presuppose* already the existence of the reality signified? In what measure must the reality be present before the signs are allowed to express it? There is, moreover, a close connexion—undoubtedly with two-way traffic—between the theological understanding of initiation and its ecclesial practice. There is obviously a relation between the understanding of initiation and, on the other hand, the stage or stages in the individual's life at which it is deemed appropriate for the rite or rites to take place. If it is maintained that there is nevertheless 'one baptism' common to all, the implication is that baptism itself is somehow greater than even the major circumstances of its performance (i.e. the understanding on which it is performed, and the point at which it is performed). This is an extremely far-reaching claim, and at this juncture it is important to mention again, first as a warning and then as an encouragement, the principle of intention. The warning is that some notion of intention, however minimal, is required if the Christian sacraments are not to degenerate into magic. The hope is that some general intention, such as the promotion of human salvation in Christ, may be accepted by all the churches as sufficiently covering what each does when it baptizes, without requiring that all agree on the precise way in which baptism contributes to this end.

In my judgment, variety in the understanding and practice of initiation rites need be no bar to mutual recognition, provided the intention remains within the generous limits of the promotion of human salvation in Christ. Indeed variety of understanding and practice is not only tolerable but welcome. It is the outcome of varying experiences of God's gracious operation, and in turn it helps to keep human beings open to discern and respond to the approach of God in all his manifold resourcefulness. The baptism of infants, for instance, signifies the loving purpose of God for the whole of a person's existence, while baptism upon profession of faith signifies the mysterious interplay between God's enablement and active human response [note 755].

Many churches already implicitly 'recognize' the baptism administered in or by other churches. It would be a service to unity if they would make such recognition explicit. Possible actions include a church-to-church declaration of baptismal recognition, the use of a common baptismal certificate, and the encouragement of participation by ministers and sponsors across denominational lines. It is only as mutual recognition of baptisms is thus enacted that it can become the model, as Edmund Schlink suggests it should, for mutual recognition of eucharists and ministries [note 756]. It is only when baptisms are mutually recognized that a real basis exists for the operation of what the Accra Faith and Order statement sees as the *baptismal dynamic* towards 'eucharistic sharing', 'common witness' and all the components of 'full visible union' [note 757].

When baptism administered in other churches than one's own is 'recognized', it is recognized as 'the one baptism', Christian baptism, the baptism of Christ. In what sense and to what extent, if at all, is such baptismal recognition (also) an ecclesiological recognition of the baptizing church? We are inevitably brought to a discussion of the value and limits of the denominational phenomenon. As is known, the Roman Catholic church has traditionally made a close if not total identification between itself and 'the Church' and it would therefore not see itself as a 'denomination' among others; it has nevertheless begun in recent times to see other communities as 'not devoid of meaning and value in the mystery of salvation'. On the other hand, Protestant churches have tended to acquiesce more easily in a situation of denominational pluralism, and in so far as they have given ecclesiological recognition to Roman Catholicism, they have seen the Roman Catholic church as 'a denomination'; it has nevertheless been the Protestant churches which made the running in the modern ecumenical movement towards visible ecclesiastical unity. Granted these shifts on the part of both Catholicism and Protestantism, it is now conceivable that agreement could be reached in a way which would acknowledge the positive values of 'the denominations' while yet confessing their provisionality in relation to the goal of a full unity in which the negative features of denominational*ism* will have been overcome. The next two sections will be devoted to elaborating such a view.

6. *Confessional pluriformity?*

It is from the Roman Catholic side that one of the most promising suggestions has been put forward for a positive recognition of denominational values. Jan Willebrands, cardinal president of the Roman Secretariat for Promoting Christian Unity, has propounded the notion of ecclesiastical *typoi* [note 758]. Reflecting perhaps the example of the Eastern uniat churches which are in communion with Rome [note 759], Willebrands hints at an extended pattern whereby ecclesial communities, while retaining and enjoying their distinctive and coherent style of life in liturgy, spirituality, discipline and theology, might be rejoined in faith, doctrine and eucharistic communion to the primatial see of Rome, whose own Latin or Western style had come to predominate in the churches which accepted its authority [note 760]. The distinctiveness of the uniat churches is, we note, largely *geographico-cultural* in basis and expression. Could the model ever serve to regulate future relations between 'non-Roman' *confessional* types and Rome? Could the Lutheran, Anglican, Reformed, Methodist and Baptist families or communions find unity in faith and doctrine with Rome and, directly or indirectly, with each other, while recognizably keeping their 'typical' character in worship, devotion, discipline and theology? It is a path worth exploring [note 761].

As far as worship, faith, doctrine and theology are concerned, all the issues raised in this chapter and the previous
two come into play. Doctrinal consensus must be pursued
and mutual recognition achieved. Although plain contradictions cannot be integrated, 'typical' emphases must be
prepared to receive both the correction and the enhancement
that may come from being included in a larger and still
coherent picture. Our previous discussion suggests that
consensus and recognition will be promoted by collaboration
in the liturgical field. Churches will probably find that here
they are already closer together in faith and doctrine than
would appear when their doctrines are stated in a non-
liturgical context and terminology. This may be a surprising
claim, since worship is an area in which a church is felt to be
at its most 'typical'. The paradox is more apparent than real:
the differences will, I am persuaded, turn out to be more of
style than of substance. Churches should nevertheless examine
their typical liturgies in the light of the emergent ecumenical
consensus and should submit them to a friendly critique by
others. A living style of worship should be able to benefit
from critical examination without losing its identity. Good
must be expected also from the creation of ecumenical
liturgies for regular use in united worship and for occasional
use within a denomination.

As long as the *typoi* retain a separate identity which falls
short of the full visible unity which is being sought, the
churches remain in a *pre-conciliar* relationship with one
another. This is to take up a notion which began to be
explored in the ecumenical movement after the Uppsala
Assembly of the WCC in 1968 had summoned the churches to
'work for the time when a genuinely universal council may
once more speak for all Christians' [note 762]. Building upon
the description of 'the unity we seek' given by the New
Delhi Assembly in 1961 [note 763], a Faith and Order consultation at Salamanca in 1973 proposed the following
'vision' [note 764], which was then adopted by the Nairobi
Assembly of the WCC in 1975:

Jesus Christ founded one Church. Today we live in diverse

churches divided from one another. Yet our vision of the future is that we shall once again live as brothers and sisters in one undivided Church. How can this goal be described? We offer the following description to the churches for their consideration: The one Church is to be envisioned as a *conciliar fellowship* of local churches which are themselves truly united. In this conciliar fellowship each local church possesses, in communion with the others, the fulness of catholicity, witnesses to the same apostolic faith and therefore recognizes the others as belonging to the same Church of Christ and guided by the same Spirit. As the New Delhi Assembly pointed out, they are bound together because they have received the same baptism and share in the same eucharist; they recognize each other's members and ministries. They are one in their common commitment to confess the Gospel of Christ by proclamation and service to the world. To this end each church aims at maintaining sustained and sustaining relationships with her sister churches, expressed in conciliar gatherings whenever required for the fulfilment of their common calling.

The Salamanca document used the term 'pre-conciliar' of the 'the councils of divided churches (e.g. the World Council of Churches, National Councils, etc.) which have come into existence in the ecumenical movement as instruments to promote the search for unity and common witness'. The same word would still apply to a situation in which world confessional families or communions 'recognized' each other in baptism, eucharist and ministry while yet falling short of full unity in structure and the exercise of authority. The prefix 'pre' in 'pre-conciliar' is of course restrictive, but on the other hand it is also forward-looking in a positive sense. It is an indication of the fact that we have already been granted, even while in some respects divided, a partial anticipation of the conciliar life in which all Christians should be united. The gift also imposes a task: we have to work, in the strength of the gift, for the fuller realization of the common life. The goal itself, in the manner of a 'final cause', draws us on.

It is within the context of pre-conciliarity that one should see the so-called 'inter-communion' debate which has taken place from the beginning of the modern ecumenical movement [note 765]. On the one hand, there have been those who reject the implications of the prefix 'inter' on the ground that eucharistic communion among the churches must await the achievement of complete unity in all matters of faith and life. On the other hand, there have been those who reject the implications of the prefix 'inter' on the ground that the table is the Lord's, and that he already invites all Christians to gather round it together, irrespectively of their divisions. Between the proponents of these extreme positions the conversation has often been a dialogue of the deaf. The more hopeful discussion has taken place on a middle ground where the conversationalists have tried to gauge the point at which the divided communities (will) have reached a sufficient measure of unity for eucharistic communion *both* to express a certain substantial reality of existing fellowship and *also* to foster the increase of that measure of unity towards full achievement. *Inter*-communion is or would be an admission of the persisting degree of disunity. Inter-*communion* is or would be the expression of an achieved degree of unity and a creative anticipation of the final fulness. Roman Catholic theologians have fought shy of the term inter-communion; but the practice it describes becomes a clear possibility for the Roman Catholic church also, in a post-Vatican II climate in which Roman Catholic theologians readily speak of other churches as being 'in imperfect communion' with the Roman Catholic church [note 766]. They intend that phrase primarily in a positive, forward-looking sense similar to the hopeful sense of 'pre-conciliar', although we note its 'typical' Rome-centredness in comparison with an 'inter-communion' which tends to place the churches on an equal footing.

In order to encourage the Roman Catholic church towards intercommunion as the next step in ecumenical progress, it may be helpful to start our case from a principle familiar to Roman Catholics and accepted by them. According to pope Innocent III, the eucharist *significat et efficit unitatem ecclesiasticam* [note 767]. This adage sums up a view of the eucharist which was held from the earliest days. The biblical and patristic teaching is that the eucharist both *expresses* an existing unity of the Church and *produces* such unity. The question to be faced is: how are the expressive and the productive functions of the eucharist properly related, particularly at a stage when divided Christian communities are seeking unity?

To celebrate the eucharist together clearly requires some measure of existing unity. Complete disunity makes a common celebration improper if not unthinkable. The Lord's words in Matthew 5:23f are recalled in many liturgies. When Augustine taught that fractious church-members give the lie to the 'Amen' which they say in response to the words *corpus Christi* as they receive communion, he was re-expressing the warning which St Paul gave to the Corinthians (1 Corinthians 11:17–34; cf. 1:10–17; 10:16f) [note 768]. On the other hand, the relation between history and eschatology is such that it would be quite unrealistic to expect Christians to be already in perfect harmony with one another. Christian truth can only be perceived in love, and an increase in mutual love is necessary if Christians are to come closer to one another in the truth. That is where the productive function of the eucharist comes into play. The eucharist not only seals an existing unity brought from the past: it also 'leads forward' the communicants into a future where the unity will be greater. The eucharist *effects*. It is a means of *grace*. As a creative anticipation of the future, a present 'taste' which whets the appetite for the messianic banquet in the completed kingdom, the eucharist is fulfilling an eschatological function in history. Granted the final superiority of eschatology over history, the eucharist is more important for *what it makes of us* than for what it expresses as being true of us. It is the future which takes precedence.

I suggest that all this is relevant not only *within* ecclesial communities but also *among* them. We should be ready to let common participation in the eucharist promote reconciliation among partially disunited communities which are seeking to overcome existing differences and so come to a closer companionship in the progress towards the kingdom. As a 'pro-jection' of the Lord's final *parousia*, the eucharist is an occasion when the Lord may exercise his eschatological functions of casting out from us in judgment what is amiss in us, of uniting us closer to himself in divine fellowship, and of joining us together in common enjoyment of his presence and gifts. It is when it is celebrated ecumenically that the eucharist can most truly fulfil its character as an effective sacrament of reconciliation and renewal [note 769].

The following are examples of cases in which inter-communion would be appropriate among the mainstream churches and denominational families. First, mixed marriages should be seen as promises of the future, as 'domestic churches' with a creative part to play in stimulating the wider ecclesial communities towards greater unity. For the deepening of their married love and for the sake of the witness which their unity can make to the churches, the couple should be allowed regularly to communicate together in each of their churches [note 770]. Second, eucharistic hospitality should be offered and accepted in the normal circumstances of visiting. Without waiting for the emergency of the prison-camp or the jungle, it should be an open practice that individual Christians share in eucharistic fellowship wherever their travels take them [note 771]. When visits of whole congregations are arranged, the two churches should communicate sacramentally together. Third: when representatives of divided churches meet officially together in 'pre-conciliar' fashion, the circumstances are sufficient for a common eucharist to promote the cause of unity to which they are committed. Fourthly, churches which join in a covenant towards unity should include intercommunion as part of their growing together [note 772].

If the churches or denominations achieved mutual recognition and inter-communion, it must be asked what further structural changes, if any, would be necessary before visible unity was attained. We shall tackle that question now.

7. Local and universal unity?

For some, the final test of visible unity is a matter of ecclesiastical government and authority. The problem is sometimes put in terms of overlapping jurisdictions. Protestants are tempted to ask whether the Orthodox and Catholic principle of unity in each place under the bishop is not contradicted by the practice of geographically overlapping jurisdictions

among the linguistically or culturally diverse groups of
Orthodox in the Western diaspora or in the case of uniat and
'Latin' communities among Roman Catholics. Catholics can,
in reply, point to the integrative function of the pope as
universal 'bishop of the Catholic Church'. Indeed Protestants
might be challenged to see that the more they propose a
communion of confessional families as the model, the greater
the need appears for some kind of universal ministry of
vigilance and unity [note 773]. But to return to the local
level: the problem is how to express proper *cultural* variety
(which is sometimes, at least temporarily, linguistic), and in
future perhaps *confessional* variety, in each place in a way
which respects and, if possible, even positively displays
fundamental unity in worship and in church government.
(Worship and church government are brought to a common
focus in the question of the presidency of the liturgical
assembly.) Over-emphasis on cultural or confessional pluralism, it is feared for instance by Lesslie Newbigin, could lead
to an 'all of each sort' pattern that missed the goal of 'all in
each place' [note 774]. Yet 'place' itself, we need to recognize,
is a complex notion amid the mobility of our contemporary
world [note 775]; and the communicational networks which
increasingly turn the earth into a 'global village' may constitute another summons to create or accept an integrative
ministry of vigilance and unity in the universal Church (as
Roman Catholics have seen in the pope) [note 776]. Within
each socially constituted but geographically recognizable
zone humaine, the churches might develop a corporate 'episco-
pate' in which cultural, and perhaps confessional, variety was
represented, while liturgical and governmental unity found
expression in common decisions and, at least occasionally,
interchanged or shared presidency of the liturgical assembly.
On the confessional plane, this pattern could begin as soon
as mutual recognition was attained; it would, one may hope,
develop in such ways that mere 'mutual recognition' was no
longer an adequate description of the unity which was taking
shape [note 777].

    The ecumenical movement that is conveniently dated from
'Edinburgh 1910' has found expression in two outstanding

cases of 'organic union': the Church of South India and the
Church of North India. It is particularly on account of his
experience as a bishop in the CSI that Lesslie Newbigin's
views command respect, even though we must not ignore
the new data which have been introduced by the entrance of
the Roman Catholic church into the ecumenical movement,
namely an immediate access of 'universality' and the consequent convenience of dialogue among 'world confessional
families' [note 778]. The Church of South India came into
being in 1947 [note 779] and unites the Anglican, Congregational, Methodist and Presbyterian traditions. Earlier comity
arrangements among the missionary societies had to some
degree kept the traditions geographically apart at district
level, so that in many cases there has been no immediate need
for 'static' congregations to meet the other traditions. Nevertheless all observers agree that there has taken place a real
growth into unity within the structural framework of the
united church. One unifying factor has been church government, the liturgical incidences of which we should not
forget; the second important factor has been the liturgical
pattern embodied in the *Book of Common Worship* [note 780].
The South Indian book includes elements from the constituent
traditions within service-shapes recovered by the Liturgical
Movement; it has also had the courage to borrow from Syrian
liturgy of the long-established Thomas Christians; it shows
some signs of sensitivity to the broader cultural traditions of
India.

In North India, the denominational spread was broadened
by the participation also of believer-baptists, both Baptists
and Brethren, in unity negotiations [note 781]. This made
the attainment of union in 1970 all the more remarkable.
The North Indian example provides an encouragement to
others elsewhere who seek, first, mutual recognition of
initiation rites, and then perhaps a deliberately pluriform
pattern in a united church. In North India, the union plan
from early days provided for the practice of two patterns of
complete initiation as *equivalent alternatives*: the one being
(a) infant baptism, (b) Christian nurture, (c) public confession
of faith, (d) participation in communion; the other (a) infant

dedication, (b) Christian nurture, (c) baptism upon profession of faith; (d) participation in communion. The form of 'admission into communicant membership', whether of those baptized as infants or of those baptized as believers, was to include prayer for the gift of the Holy Spirit and the laying-on of hands by the bishop or presbyter. It was at this service also that persons baptized in infancy would make their public profession of faith, affirm their acceptance of the baptism administered to them in infancy, and 'recognize in that baptism the outward visible sign of the regenerating grace of God'.

For several years, however, union was held up by the delicate question of possible requests for a 'second baptism' when persons baptized in infancy might come to believe that they should receive baptism upon profession of faith. In the eyes of paedobaptists, the granting of such a request would strike at infant baptism in general and would contravene the traditional tenet that baptism is unrepeatable in the life of any one person. Believer-baptists argued the need to respect such a person's conscientious desire for baptism upon profession of faith, just as believer-baptists would themselves be respecting the conscience of paedobaptists by agreeing to a pattern of initiation dictated by infant baptism as one of the two alternative patterns in the united church. Eventually the question was shelved for resolution after union. Requests for a 'second baptism' have so far proved very rare.

I should not myself wish to exclude the possibility of 'second baptism' in difficult cases [note 782]. But the more normal solution will perhaps be found by using an opportunity which more and more churches are now offering in order to meet a rather more widespread need. In many places the need is felt to 'renew' a baptism whose permanency is not in question. Historically, baptism has been commemorated or renewed by such diverse provisions as the *Asperges* before Sunday mass [note 783] and the annual covenant service of the Methodists [note 784]. The Roman revision of the Holy Week liturgy in 1955 introduced the renewal of baptismal vows by the whole congregation during the paschal vigil. The practice has spread and is now included, for instance, in the *Book of Common Prayer* (1977) of the Episcopal Church in the U.S.A. and in the *Alternative Service Book* (1980) of the Church of England. In the U.S.A., the United Methodist, Episcopal and Lutheran churches have all introduced a repeatable service for the 'renewal' or '(re)affirmation' of baptism. In the Methodist 'alternate text' for *Baptism, Confirmation and Renewal* (1976), confirmation appears as 'the first renewal of baptismal faith', and 'other renewals of the baptismal covenant' may take place on individual or congregational occasions: reaffirmation of faith on the part of hitherto inactive persons; transfer of membership from other congregations or denominations, or the establishment of associate membership; public testimony and thanksgiving by 'persons who have reached a new level of commitment or a heightened awareness of God's grace'; or annually by the congregation at Easter or on the feast of the Lord's Baptism. Hands are imposed on individuals, and in the case of individuals or entire congregations 'water may be sprinkled toward all persons being confirmed or making other renewal of their baptismal faith'. The *Lutheran Book of Worship* (1978) includes confirmation, reception into membership from other denominations, and restoration of membership under the single title *Affirmation of Baptism*. Hands are imposed only at confirmation, although the earlier draft in *Contemporary Worship 8* (1974) had tried to abandon the idea of an unrepeatable quasi-sacramental confirmation. The final Lutheran pattern closely resembles that of the Episcopal *Book of Common Prayer* (1977) at 'confirmation, reception, or reaffirmation'.

In this chapter we have made several cross-references between the ecumenical movement and the liturgical movement. In the next, we look more directly at liturgical revision.

X

Revision

1. *Repristination or aggiornamento?*

WHENEVER the revision of the Church's worship is deliberately undertaken, liturgical experts may find themselves stretched between two potentially conflicting poles of demand. Revision is called for when existing forms of worship are felt to be inadequate, but the sense of inadequacy may arise in two distinct ways. On the one hand, a gap may be perceived between a degenerate current practice and the practice of an earlier and classical period. In that case, the demand will be for a return to the sources. If the degeneration has lain in impoverishment, a restoration of the pristine fulness will be required. If the degeneration has lain in adulteration, it is the former purity which will need to be restored. On the other hand, the gap may emerge between inherited or imported forms of worship and the requirements of worshippers in a changed cultural situation. In that case, the demand will be for updating or adaptation: updating, where the cultural shift has been temporal; adaptation, where the cultural change has been geographical. Questions of geographical adaptation will receive more attention in the next chapter. In the present chapter we shall concentrate on the European tradition which has so far been dominant in the history of Christianity.

In the European situation, the demands for a *retour aux sources* and for updating can easily appear at first blush to be contradictory. It is probable that a certain tension must always remain between them. But that tension may be the healthy tension of a community seeking to maintain its diachronic identity. Or in theological as distinct from socio-logical terms: the Church is seeking to keep alive, in worship, its vision of God. The Church believes its vision to be true: it believes its vision to have been decisively revealed in and through Jesus Christ: the envisaged God is believed to have a universal and lasting concern for humanity. For these reasons the Church seeks for its liturgy *both* substantial identity through time *and* culturally appropriate forms which vary with human history. The intimate link between substance and form makes difficult the adjudication of substantial continuity amid formal change. Yet substance can also be lost through formal rigidity, when outdated forms no longer enkindle the vision. Nor, as we said, is it only cultural change which necessitates a liturgical revision which will retain the substance. Re-vision is also needed when a degeneration of vision on the Church's part has resulted in the impoverishment or adulteration of its worship.

In our century, both the qualitative and the cultural type of gap have been perceived, and the call has been both for a return to the sources and for updating. Provided the possibility be allowed of substantial identity amid formal variety, there need be no contradiction between the two demands, despite the tensions which result from the difficulties of adjudication in the relationship between form and substance. This is not to prejudge the success or failure of any actual attempts that have been made simultaneously to meet both demands. The central part of this chapter will be a discussion of such attempts. But before that, we shall look at some past examples of liturgical revision in order to bring out more clearly the issues which have just been presented rather abstractly. First we shall look at the Reformers, and briefly at Trent, from that angle; then at cases from the eighteenth century and, as a transition to contemporary attempts, at some revisions in the early part of our century.

2. *Reformation?*

The Reformers perceived both a qualitative and a cultural gap. The cultural gap was most obviously linguistic, and the Reformers filled it by vernacular liturgies which have in large measure continued to serve as the vehicles of Protestant worship into the twentieth century. The medieval content of

22

some concepts was changed by the Reformers, the most notable example being the concept of sacrifice [note 785]. On the whole, however, words and images, even when translated from Latin into the vernaculars, retained the meaning they had held in earlier liturgy and culture. In more recent centuries, the biblical and liturgical tincture in general European culture has for several reasons become more and more dilute: it is this which has gradually made the churches aware, and sharply since the secularization debate of the 1960s, of a new cultural gap between the language of their worship and the language of everyday society in which the worshippers, ex-worshippers, or would-be worshippers also participate [note 786]. The linguistic problem for liturgists is now both deeper and more complex, as we shall see again later in the chapter.

When the Reformers re-introduced the vernacular, they were contributing also to the closure of the qualitative gap which they had perceived between current practice and the worship of the primitive and early Church. Intelligent popular participation required the use of a language 'understanded of the people'. This fact had clearly been recognized in former days [note 787]. The earliest Aramaic-speaking Christians seem to have worshipped in their own tongue, as may be gathered from the passage of some of their key words even into Greek-speaking Christianity: *Abba* (Romans 8:15f; Galatians 4:6), *Maranatha* (1 Corinthians 16:22; Didache 10:6) [note 788]. When Christianity spread round the Mediterranean basin, the language of worship was Greek in the Hellenistic areas, and apparently Latin in Roman North Africa. In the third- and fourth-century church in Rome, the social shift from Greek to Latin preponderance was followed before too long by a corresponding change in the liturgical language [note 789]. The early Church also used Syriac, Coptic, Armenian, Georgian, and Ge'ez in worship in the respective linguistic localities. In the late ninth century, pope John VIII approved the use of 'the Slavonic language' in the Byzantine liturgy in the regions evangelized by St Cyril and St Methodius. The Reformers were therefore reverting to a principle inherent in the character of Christianity from the start: an intelligible gospel requiring a deliberate response [note 790].

A second way in which the Reformers sought to close a qualitative gap was also connected with popular participation: they tried to encourage more frequent communion. New Testament and pre-nicene Christians had communicated daily or weekly. A daily gathering for communion can be understood from Acts 2:42, 46f. Tertullian and Cyprian record that the faithful took bread home from the Sunday eucharist for communion during the week [note 791]. According to Justin, the Sunday eucharist brought all Christians together from 'the towns or the country' [note 792]. And, as Gregory Dix observed: 'In the first three centuries, to be present at the eucharist virtually meant being a communicant' [note 793]. It was in the fourth and fifth centuries that the eucharistic assembly started to lose its character as the domestic gathering of the household of God for the Lord's Supper. Dix again remarked: 'It was the indiscriminate admission to baptism . . . of the infant children of christian parents when all society began to turn nominally christian which was at the root of that decline of lay communion which set in during the fourth and fifth centuries.' Furthermore, the later fourth century saw the emergence of a new feature in eucharistic worship which appears to have deterred communicants. This sense of 'fear and awe attaching to the eucharistic service' [note 794] may have sprung in part from an anti-arian emphasis upon the divinity of the Presence [note 795]. First witnessed in the East, it spread to the West where, at least from St Ambrose onwards, there appears to have grown up an increasingly 'realistic' identification between Christ and the consecrated elements. In both East and West, lay communion almost faded away. From the ninth century, a Western rule ordered annual communion at Easter, but this minimum appears to have been lacking in the East.

The Reformers tried by various means to increase the frequency of communion. Inspired by the Acts of the Apostles, both Luther and Calvin aimed at a frequent celebration of the Lord's supper in its entirety [note 796]. In 1520 Luther wanted it 'daily throughout Christendom', although by 1523 he ordered a celebration only on Sundays, unless there were those who wished to receive more often. Calvin called the custom of a merely annual communion 'an invention of the devil', part and parcel of 'the abomination of the mass set up by Satan'. He desired a return to apostolic practice, with 'the Lord's Supper celebrated in the Christian congregation once a week at the very least'. But the Genevan magistrates never allowed Calvin to establish more than a quarterly communion. Whatever Zwingli's reasons, his more modest plans for the Lord's Supper four times a year appear more feasible in the Reformers' context of a multitudinist *corpus christianum*. The English Reformers resorted, by the 1552 Prayer Book, to making triannual communion an obligation upon parishioners and therefore a statutory duty of citizens. Dix suggests a reason of some theological significance for the practically universal failure of the laity between the fifth and the nineteenth centuries to respond to the exhortations which the clergy never entirely ceased to make to them to communicate more often: 'The *domestic* character of eucharistic worship, which had been lost to sight by the officials of a church long dominant in social life, continued obscurely to assert itself in the feeling of the laity that communion was somehow not intended to be "for everybody". And since "everybody" was now equally qualified in theory by having received baptism. . . , the only line of demarcation which remained was that between clergy and laity. Between the seventh century and the nineteenth all over christendom the clergy were normally the only really frequent communicants. The dechristianization of society in general in the nineteenth and twentieth centuries has once more marked out the practising christian laity as members of "the household of God", and so included them again within that "exclusiveness" which the eucharist has always been instinctively felt to demand' [note 797]. We thereby return to matters which were discussed under the limits and mission of the Church in chapter IV and which will recur in chapter XI.

A third type of qualitative gap perceived by the Reformers concerned doctrinal content or theological understanding,

both of the faith as a whole and of worship as its focal
expression. To close this gap, the Bible was translated and
then read in lengthy portions in public worship; expository
preaching was practised by the great figures and encouraged
among the clergy. Catechisms were written to teach the true
faith and explain the sacraments correctly. We saw in chapter
VIII how the Reformers removed from the eucharistic liturgy
what they considered to be false ideas concerning sacrifice. In
their attempts to purify worship they sometimes, ironically,
remained prisoners of medievalism. Take the structural
prominence given to the eucharistic institution narrative.
In Luther's *Formula missae*, it alone remains of the canon,
sandwiched between the exiguous common preface and the
Sanctus; in the *Deutsche Messe*, it alone 'consecrates', its
recitation (now in the gospel tone, as 'promise') is divided
into two by the administration of the bread after the bread-
word, while the cup follows on the cup-word. In the Reformed
tradition, the institution may be read as an initial 'warrant'
(Calvin) or at the distribution (Zwingli, Bucer); the Westminster Directory in fact prescribes its use both at the beginning of the 'setting apart and sanctification' and at the fraction
and distribution. But as Pierre Benoit said in connexion with
the New Testament period itself: 'On ne récite pas une
rubrique, on l'exécute' [note 798]. And there is scholarly
controversy as to when the institution narrative was introduced into the eucharistic prayer: the anaphora of Addai and
Mari may indeed have lacked it [note 799]. Certainly the
isolated stress on the institution narrative is neither primitive
nor early patristic: it is the consequence of that interest in a
'moment of consecration' which took off in the late fourth
century and which eventually led to the ceremonial highlighting of the *Hoc est enim corpus meum* in the middle ages. So
close, in their desired return to the dominical and the primitive,
did the Reformers ritually remain to what, theologically,
they would themselves have considered hocus-pocus. On the
whole, the Reformers respected the Fathers [note 800]. In
their selective use of Augustine, for instance, some of them
took up the notion of the sacraments as 'visible words'. But
their knowledge of early and Eastern *liturgies* was generally

not good enough to furnish them with richer models for a reconstruction of eucharistic worship in which medieval Roman distortions could have been corrected within a more satisfactory framework [note 801].

A further instance of the Reformers' medieval captivity is found in initiation. True, they got rid of salt, spittle, oils and candle, although some at least of these in fact originated in the patristic period before the rot was supposed to have really set in. But the Reformers did not tackle the major difficulties in initiation practice, perhaps because the deeper nature and full extent of the existing divergence from the primitive remained hidden from them. They inherited the pattern whereby both confirmation and communion were usually separated by several years from a baptism administered in infancy. They made 'confirmation', in so far as they kept it, the occasion of catechesis, profession of faith, and admission to communion. Where confirmation retained a sacramental nuance (as with Bucer and in the English Prayer Books), it was the occasion also of solemn prayer for the Spirit. The Reformers thus retained, and probably exaggerated, the various problems posed by the temporal disintegration of initiation in the medieval West [note 802]. What, from the angles of faith professed and Spirit received, was the relationship between baptism and confirmation? Why were the baptized for several years excluded from communion for a fault no graver than the lack of capacities whose absence had not impeded the administration of baptism? How, more radically, could the Reformers square the continuance of infant baptism with their rediscovery of justification by faith? [note 803]. Only the Baptists went the whole hog and removed the notions of presumed, provisional or substitutive faith from infants altogether. For all his *post factum* theological defence based on the covenant and circumcision, would Calvin have retained infant baptism if he had not (mistakenly) supposed in primitive Christianity the existence of formal post-baptismal catechesis for those who had been baptized in an infancy when they had been incapable of professing faith? For all his *post factum* appeal to the leaping of the embryonic John in Elizabeth's womb at the Visitation as a scriptural example of infant faith [note 804], would Luther have retained infant baptism if he had not assumed the strictly *primitive* character of the inherited practice of sponsors answering the baptismal interrogations directly as the infant's mouthpiece? [note 805]. Or perhaps the baptism of infants would after all have been preserved under the pressure of the weightiest inheritance of all from the middle ages: the *corpus christianum*. It was apparently the threat posed to the identification of Church and civil community by the possible abandonment of infant baptism which finally drove Zwingli, theologically the most 'adultist' of the classical Reformers, nevertheless to suppress the early Baptists [note 806].

Although the Protestants aimed at repristination and remained in some respects curiously medieval, they were seen by Catholics as 'innovators'. The sacramental and liturgical measures at and after the council of Trent were marked by defensive reaction [note 807]. Although the tridentine anathemas were directed against those who said that the mass should be celebrated *only* in the vernacular, at the other extreme the Roman mass itself remained *only* in Latin, for fear that *any* use of the vernacular would appear as a capitulation to the Protestants [note 808]. Communion continued to be given to lay people in one kind only, for fear of apparent surrender in face of the Reformers' appeal to the Lord's example and command concerning the cup (a let-out was found in the medieval principle of concomitance, whereby the whole Christ was held to be present under each species). The Protestant threat to the medieval Roman understanding of the sacrifice was met in part by the declaration that the canon of the mass was free from error [note 809]; and the firm, in fact rigidly anti-Protestant, doctrinal statements of Trent concerning the eucharistic sacrifice henceforward dictated the interpretation of the prayers. The mass was to be restored *ad pristinam sanctorum Patrum normam ac ritum*: this repristination was hampered by the undeveloped state of liturgical science and failed to get back beyond the 'Gregorian' sacramentary to Gregory the Great himself, let alone to an earlier period [note 810]. In any case, the principal aim appears to have been the imposition of a central standard from Rome.

The printed missal of Pius V (1570) 'corrected' the variations developed in the medieval manuscript tradition. More seriously, the suppression of any *rite* which could not prove an uninterrupted history of two hundred years (so that only some religious orders and a few dioceses kept their own divergent use) effectively stifled any future local developments or 'adaptations' to local culture also [note 811]. So it remained in the Roman Catholic church until Vatican II, although that council's Constitution on the Liturgy was of course made possible by certain acquisitions of sacramental theology in the twentieth century and by the achievements of the Liturgical Movement.

3. *Enlightenment?*

By the eighteenth century, liturgical science was making considerable growth. Among the first to use it for liturgical revision were the Anglican Non-Jurors in their rite of 1718 and the Scottish Episcopalians in the 1764 liturgy [note 812]. R. F. Buxton traces two distinct traditions of Anglican eucharistic theology in this period [note 813]. The first is associated with the rite of 1662, and its characteristics are a (weakish) memorialist view of the eucharistic sacrifice, a 'real receptionist' view of the presence, and the view that consecration is effected by a prayer that must include the institution narrative. The other school's motto might have been *ex orientalibus lux*. It was much influenced by Eastern Fathers and rites, notably the 'Clementine' liturgy of *Apostolic Constitutions*. It was characterized, in Buxton's words, by 'a belief that the eucharist is an objective Godward pleading of Christ's sacrifice, that the essential consecratory part of the eucharistic prayer is the institution narrative-oblation-epiclesis sequence, and that there is an objective and permanent real presence associated with the elements and brought about by the Holy Spirit making the bread and wine to be in power, virtue, and effect the body and blood of Christ'. This school (re)interpreted Cranmer's rite of 1549 and the Scottish episcopal rite of 1637 [note 814] accordingly. With these earlier English rites and with further Eastern models and ideas in mind, the rites of 1718 and 1764 became 'the designed liturgical expression of this school of Anglican eucharistic theology'. Here was an attempt at repristination which cut back behind the limitations and distortions of both the Roman and the Protestant West in order to recapture an earlier balance and fulness which the Byzantine and some other Eastern churches had preserved. Very shortly we shall see the modern Liturgical Movement taking the same path, benefiting now from even better knowledge of the early sources.

The eighteenth century was, however, also the age of 'the Enlightenment'. Among German Protestants we find some notable examples of revision in the sense of *aggiornamento*. One K. R. Lang recommended the following formula at the distribution of the eucharistic elements: 'Enjoy this bread. May the Spirit of devotion rest upon you with its full blessing. Enjoy a little wine. The power of virtue does not lie in this wine but in yourselves, in religious instruction, and in God.' William Nagel quotes some sermon themes of the period [note 815]. On the first Sunday in Advent, with the gospel of Matthew 21:1–11, one might preach 'on the stealing of wood' ('and others cut branches from the trees'), or 'on the value of human expressions of good wishes' (Hosanna!). On Christmas Day, with the gospel of Luke 2:1–20, the sermon might be 'on the hardiness of shepherds and a warning against the use of fur-caps'. Easter Monday's Emmaus-story could inspire a message 'on going for walks' (Sermons for Hypochondriacs, Gotha 1788). Nor did the Roman Catholic church in Germany escape such rationalism, moralism, individualism, anthropocentrism; but, as A. L. Mayer describes, there was also a liturgical movement in favour of genuine simplicity, intelligent participation, and edifying concentration on the heart of the matter, with a corresponding battle against the exaggeration of exorcisms and blessings, against the misuse of votive processions and pilgrimages, and against the fragmentation of piety on peripheral devotions [note 816].

In the nineteenth century, the Church of England showed some discreet signs of a desire for *aggiornamento*, if only in the removal of features that offended enlightened intellects and sensibilities [note 817]. The Prayer Book ordered the recitation of the *Quicunque vult*, inherited from Roman prime, at morning prayer on thirteen occasions in the year, including the major feasts. Ever since the eighteenth century and its widespread inclinations to arianism, unitarianism and even deism, the use of the Athanasian Creed had been under attack [note 818]. After the F. D. Maurice controversy, its damnatory clauses in particular could not fail to attract further attention. Nevertheless, the 'creed' had its defenders among those of both evangelical and anglo-catholic sympathies, and its use survived the Shortened Services Act of 1872. The 1928 Prayer Book revised the translation and would have made the saying of it optional. However, the more obvious direction of attempted revision of the Prayer Book and Anglican liturgical practice in the nineteenth and early twentieth centuries was towards a 'repristination' that had at first been inspired by a 'Romantic' interest in the middle ages on the part of the Ecclesiologists [note 819] but was then increasingly mediated by the living model of Roman Catholicism [note 820]. Ornaments, vestments and ceremony were the patent concern of 'the Ritualists', although it was eucharistic reservation which longest remained the object of controversy. In the rite itself, Anglo-Catholics made unofficial borrowings from contemporary Roman Catholicism. Official Anglican revisions in the first half of the twentieth century generally moved in a gently 'catholic' direction, while continuing to use a largely cranmerian phraseology which by now positively allowed but still did not actually require an interpretation in the style of Tract XC [note 821]. In England, it was chiefly the Evangelicals who blocked the passage of the 1927–28 Prayer Book through Parliament. In several countries where the Anglican church was not by law established, the 'upward' revision of the Prayer Book was legally achieved, notably in South Africa, the West Indies, and in dioceses served by anglo-catholic missions [note 822]. With that we are on the verge of the modern Liturgical Movement, which began roughly with our century but whose first full compositions appeared only after the second world war.

4. *Archaeology or ephemerality?*

If Dom P. Guéranger and the abbey of Solesmes are reckoned as precursors of the Liturgical Movement [note 823], the Movement will appear to some to have been attended from its beginnings by the threat of antiquarianism: one of Guéranger's interests lay in the restoration of plainsong. If the liberal Protestant johnny-come-latelys, who are its most recent converts, stand as the Movement's representatives, the Liturgical Movement will appear to have run into the shifting sands of contemporary cultural fashion: Harvey Cox has made the 'only half-facetious' suggestion that 'the next step in liturgical reform, after the kiss of peace, might be the introduction into church congregations of some form of massage' [note 824]. In between, however, the Movement has married sound history with pastoral care for the modern world. Sometimes the accent has fallen in one place, sometimes in the other, but the belief has usually been that repristination and *aggiornamento* meet in the desire for Christian authenticity. Dom Lambert Beauduin, who is honoured as the founder of a Movement conventionally dated from his address to the Malines congress in 1909, came to the work after ten years of pastoral experience in a Belgian industrial parish and never became a 'liturgiologist' [note 825]. Seeing the mass as *the* prayer of the Church, his prime objective was intelligent popular participation and the best execution of Pius X's call to frequent communion. At Maria Laach, the Movement found in Odo Casel a historical theologian who, for all the controversial character of his historical interpretations, provided the fundamental theological perspective of liturgy as participation in the mystery of Christ. The finest flower of the Movement in France has been the *Centre de pastorale liturgique*, founded in 1940: its journal, *La Maison-Dieu*, is characterized by a fusion of historical scholarship with psychological and sociological research as they impinge on worship today. An individual embodiment of the Movement is found in the Austrian Jesuit J. A. Jungmann, whose technical skill in the history and theology of the liturgy was accompanied by a strong practical concern for preaching and catechetics. Among Anglican and Protestants, the Liturgical Movement has

drawn heavily on biblical scholarship and has itself contributed
to the 'rediscovery of the Church', its vocation to unity, and
its awareness of its setting and role within society.

It is with the return to the biblical and patristic sources
that we may begin our thematic consideration of the modern
Liturgical Movement. This return has been perhaps the most
striking characteristic of official revisions and compositions
in the area of service-books. For the Roman Catholic church
the return has meant a purification. Ritual, ceremonial and
calendrical excrescences have been docked in a great process
of simplification. Roman unilateralisms have been corrected
by being set within a geographically wider patristic context
and a more scriptural context of interpretation. The 'new
mass' illustrates all this. The earliest known Roman ritual
structure of the whole Sunday service, that attested by Justin
Martyr, now stands out clearly as the backbone of the mass:
readings, sermon, prayers, the taking of the elements, the
eucharistic prayer, communion. The earliest known Roman
eucharistic prayer, if that is indeed supplied by *The Apostolic
Tradition*, now constitutes the basis of the concise second
canon. The third eucharistic prayer draws on gallican and
mozarabic sources, the fourth is Eastern in inspiration [note
826]. The mass is still a sacrifice (and the strongly sacrificial
first canon remains), but the understanding of sacrifice is no
longer confined to the narrow and polemical statements of
Trent: the second and fourth eucharistic prayers open up
early and Eastern perspectives, which themselves fit more
easily, as we shall see, in the biblical category of *anamnesis*.
Protestants also have exploited the category of *anamnesis*, and
for them the rediscovery of patristic structures and themes
has contributed not so much a purification as an enrichment.

We noted in chapter IX how the primitive and early Church
had become a meeting-ground for churches today. A further
example of growing ecumenical agreement achieved by the
ritual route is the recognition, in the liturgical revision of
many churches, of the normative character of the full initiation
of believers. The Roman *Ordo initiationis christianae adultorum*
of 1972 is one of the most splendid achievements of the
Liturgical Movement [note 827]. It stretches from the first

stages of evangelization and pre-catechumenate, through the catechumenate proper and the proximate preparation, to the sacrament of baptism upon profession of faith, confirmation and first communion, being rounded off by 'mystagogical' instruction on the sacraments just received and their continuing significance. The classical pattern of the early Christian centuries is thereby relived. It was from the 'mission fields' that the initial pressure came for the restoration, but the full initiation of adults is becoming a more usual occurrence in Europe also, now that the fading of the *corpus christianum* is reducing the practice of infant baptism. Restoration is thereby at the service of *aggiornamento*. In Anglican and Protestant revisions also, the primary rite is in most cases clearly the full rite for admitting believers, and the baptism of infants is the 'derived' rite (it need matter little which rite is actually printed first in the service-books). This fact is important ecumenically: it is in the case of the initiation of believers that the churches are likely to come closest to one another in their doctrine and understanding of baptism; or, at the least, a unified pattern of initiation is more able to accommodate a diversity of understandings that are felt in a split pattern to be intolerable. The debate about infant baptism then becomes a debate about a secondary or exceptional matter [note 828].

The scriptures guard their secrets on the question of infant baptism [note 829], but they have yielded light on another matter which has proved to be of great importance both for liturgical revision and for ecumenical convergence. I refer to work on the biblical notion of memorial which, in respect of the eucharist in particular, has freshly illuminated the controversial questions of presence and sacrifice. Since the 1920s, Odo Casel had been drawing inspiration largely from hellenistic religion for his idea of the Christian sacraments as 'mystery-memorials'. According to Casel, the mass was a cultically enacted commemoration of the sacrifice of Christ on the cross (and the resurrection which is inseparable from it), here made 'really present' not 'historically' but 'in a mystery' [note 830]. Controversial already in the Roman Catholic church, Casel was unlikely to gain a great hearing from a barthian Protestantism suspicious of all 'religion' and ever ready to scent paganism. In 1959, however, Max Thurian, sub-prior of Taizé, provided a bridge into Protestantism for a living and powerful view of the 'eucharistic memorial' (to borrow the title given to the English translation of his book, *L'eucharistie: mémorial du Seigneur, sacrifice d'action de grâce et d'intercession*). By dint of exegetical work which has since been broadly confirmed by independent Old Testament specialists, Thurian called attention to the dynamic value of memorial in Hebrew thinking [note 831]. Memory provokes action, and the cult serves to 'remind' God. God is thanked for his saving work in the past and is asked to prolong it into the present. By God's gracious disposition, ritual 'memorial' may make present, if not a mighty deed of God from the past, then at least the salutary benefits which it secured. This interpretation of the biblical evidence concerning the efficacy of worship in both Old and New Testaments would stand in a general way, even if J. Jeremias' precise thesis concerning 'Do this in remembrance of me' did not carry complete conviction. According to Jeremias, God was being asked to remember the messiah (i.e. Jesus, who had already begun the work of salvation) by bringing in the kingdom through the parousia [note 832]. Jeremias' thesis of the Godward memorial would fit nicely with the primitive *maranatha*, of which Paul's eucharistic 'until he come' may be an echo (1 Corinthians 11:26). The 'Come, Lord Jesus' of Revelation 22:20 makes it most likely that the *maranatha* of 1 Corinthians 16:22 and Didache 10:6 is to be taken as an invocation for Christ to make his parousia now—if not eschatologically, then at least liturgically, according to the pattern of Matthew 18:20 and the post-resurrection meals [note 833].

Taken closely together, anamnesis and maranatha set a biblical context in which Catholics and Protestants can come closer to a common understanding on the controversial matters of sacrifice and presence. The Christ who makes himself present in the eucharist is the one whose character and action is to give himself sacrificially to God and for humanity. As we receive him among us and into ourselves, he enables us to make a grateful surrender of ourselves to

God in and through him. Protestants have readily allowed
the eucharist to be a 'sacrifice of praise and thanksgiving'
and an offering of 'ourselves, our souls and bodies'. They
should therefore be able to appreciate those recent Catholic
writers who have brought out the personal and ethical
character of the eucharistic sacrifice through the notion of a
present participation by Christians in the Christ who for our
sake offered himself to God on the cross and was received
into glory. In *L'Eucharistie, pâque de l'Église*, the Dominican
theologian J. M. R. Tillard presents the eucharist as the
Church's sacramental participation in Christ's 'Passover': the
eucharist embodies the Church's continuing passage from
sin to newness of life. This approach is taken even further in
L. Dussaut's study, *L'Eucharistie, pâques de toute la vie* [note
834]. Here it is held that the (pauline) emphasis on death and
resurrection is too narrow: the eucharist is rather (in the
perspective of the Fourth Gospel and of Hebrews) the memorial of the *whole* of Christ's life, with all that is thereby implied
in the way of ethical example. Dussaut capitalizes on the
bi-polar character of the Last Supper, where the action with
the bread started the meal and the action with the wine took
place 'after supper'. In the eucharist, the bread, the sign of
the body, signifies the incarnation, and the wine, sign of the
blood, signifies the passion. The whole of Christ's life was a
'sacrificial meal': a sacrifice to God for humanity, a meal
bringing men and women into fellowship with God. The
eucharist allows people, in the time of the Church, to share
the life and destiny of Christ in surrender to God. It provides
a ritual focus for the personal sacrifice of Christ and of the
Church.

In both Catholic and Protestant revision of eucharistic
liturgies, the old concentration on the cross has in fact been
broadened to include the other mighty acts of God in Christ
within the memorial [note 835]. The thanksgiving series in
the preface or post-Sanctus of the eucharistic prayer is
expanded to take in the whole christological economy of
salvation. Often the technical anamnesis, coming after the
institution narrative, will mention incarnation, death, resurrection and ascension, and the expectation of Christ's final

advent may be declared: *praestolantes alterum eius adventum/ exspectantes ipsius adventum in gloria* (to quote only the new Roman eucharistic prayers III and IV). Indeed the twentieth-century rediscovery of eschatology in both biblical and systematic theology has led the liturgiographers to reintroduce the imagery of the messianic banquet, whereas it had failed to be exploited over large tracts of Western liturgical history [note 836]. The *nobis quoque* of the canon and some of the old post-communions had just managed to keep the eschatological prospect open in the Roman rite; it was precisely at those points that the British Methodist *Sunday Service* of 1974 opened up the eschatological vision:

> Accept us as we offer ourselves to be a living sacrifice, and bring us with the whole creation to your heavenly kingdom.

> We thank you, Lord,
> that you have fed us in this sacrament,
> united us with Christ,
> and given us a foretaste of the heavenly banquet
>   prepared for all mankind.

Another Western rediscovery has taken place in the realm of pneumatology, and it again has affected liturgiography. Reference to the Holy Spirit has been strengthened in many rites, the focus being the single or double epiclesis introduced into the eucharistic prayer. Where the notion of consecrating the elements is directly combined with praying for fruitful communion, the single epiclesis is usually placed after the institution narrative. Sometimes, however, a '(pre)conse-cratory' epiclesis precedes the institution narrative, and prayer for the Spirit-given benefits of communion rather follows it. These variable procedures reflect old controversies between Byzantium and Rome about the 'moment of consecration': the important thing is that almost all Western rites now recognize the pneumatological dimension of the eucharist with a liturgical explicitness that had earlier been confined to the calvinist tradition and the Wesleys' *Hymns on the Lord's Supper*. Pneumatology in fact provides the category of a divine continuum in which 'efficacious memorial' can occur and the past, present and future of salvation-history can be held together. In an image taken up from the epiclesis of *Apostolic Constitutions* VIII, *ton martyra tōn pathēmatōn tou Kuriou Iēsou*, the Wesleys call the Holy Spirit the 'true Recorder' of Christ's passion, the 'Witness of his dying', and invoke him:

> Come, Remembrancer divine,
> Let us feel thy power, applying
> Christ to every soul, and mine.

It is 'in the Spirit' that the glorified Christ holds sacramental fellowship with his Church. The Spirit is the 'firstfruits' and 'earnest' of final salvation (Romans 8:23; 2 Corinthians 1:22; 5:5; Ephesians 1:13f): it is by virtue of the Spirit's operation that the eucharistic communion can appear, in the ancient post-communion prayers and in the Wesleyan hymns, as the pledge, *pignus*, of heaven [note 837].

To talk of 'the mighty acts of God' and of 'salvation-history', to allow eschatology to include a future prospect, even perhaps to talk of the Spirit in the way we have just talked: all this would be judged by, say, J. L. Houlden to remain imprisoned in an 'historical-cum-mythological approach'. It is with this failing that Houlden taxed the Church of England's Series 3 eucharist [note 838]. The same accusation may easily be levelled by him and other 'modern theologians' against the whole work of official liturgical revision which has been taking place in the main Western churches since the second world war. The 'new' liturgies are said to be already out of date because, in Houlden's phrase, they lag far behind 'current theology'. This charge needs examination.

It is true that post-war liturgical revision owes much to the 'biblical theology' which had its hey-day in the 1940s, 50s and early 60s. It is also true that 'biblical theology' then found itself 'in crisis', to borrow the title of a later book by one of its earlier exponents (B. S. Childs). One factor in the crisis was a rediscovery of the diversity within the Bible, and

23

even within the New Testament alone [note 839]. In chapter V I have already argued that the liturgy provides a needed unifying framework within which it is possible both to emphasize the central core of the New Testament message and also to hold together the diverse scriptural witnesses to Jesus Christ. These arguments suffice to justify our liturgical revisers when charged with a harmonization that has become unfashionable in biblical scholarship.

A more serious factor in the crisis is the realization that the *whole* of the Bible is culturally conditioned. The cultural conditioning of the Bible becomes more obvious and more problematical when it is perceived that the biblical myths, world-views and understandings of history are no longer shared by contemporary culture. In Europe this change has been part of what is called secularization [note 840]. Outside 'christendom' the gap has always existed between the Bible and the culture by which the local Christians are surrounded. But the surrounding cultures have usually possessed 'myths' which expressed ultimate meanings and values and have usually practised sacred 'rituals' by which the myths were enacted, transmitted, and entered into. The striking problem for Christianity in secularized Europe is that any such notion of myth and ritual may now have become existentially implausible. One aspect of the problem lies in the extent to which awareness of cultural relativities has called into question the notion of human history as a single whole for which the one 'story' focused on Jesus Christ can serve as meaning-giver and value-setter [note 841]. This is not a specifically liturgical problem, however. In so far as Jesus Christ fails to be accepted as giving meaning and setting values, it is the Christian faith as a whole which is diminished. No amount of liturgical reformulation will put that right, if by reformulation is meant an acquiescence in the loss of the ultimacy and universality which has hitherto been recognized by Christians, not least in their worship, to the meaning and values revealed in Jesus Christ. If the Christian faith is to maintain its identity, the only legitimate liturgical revision of the *aggiornamento* kind would be one which, perhaps by a renewal of images and concepts, reasserts the meaning and values in all their ultimacy and universality. For all the fragmentation of human history highlighted by the relativists, it might be that such potentially ultimate and universal images and concepts are already available, or at least remain possible. Certainly marxism, from some points of view the rival of Christianity, makes the claim to ultimate and universal meaning and values, and marxism has found images and concepts which succeed in making its appeal acceptable to a very large proportion of the world's population. In social thinking, some Christians have been willing to reintegrate the biblical elements which have found a (temporary) home in marxism [note 842]. It may be that liturgists also should turn to marxism for help in the renewal of the great themes of alienation, liberation, work, distribution, community, the equitable society.

Liturgy would need to give to these ideas the distinctively biblical and Christian dimensions which have been lost or distorted in marxism. Some humane marxist thinkers have in fact started to appreciate the question of a true 'transcendence' and the need for 'grace' [note 843]. It would be ironic if, acceding to the desire of those theologians who wish to remove myth from Christianity, the liturgy were now to be reformulated in such a way as to exclude the idea of God acting in history. Unlike the deistically inclined demythologizers in British theology, even Bultmann felt obliged to spare the notion of 'God acting' from the axe of demythologization [note 844]. Bultmann's restriction of the action of God to the individual existence in the present would not satisfy the aspirations for grace and transcendence on the part of marxists who bring a strong sense of the social and of the future. A stronger attraction would be the messianic banquet, sacramentalized in the eucharist, in which the future and permanent goal of humanity can be creatively anticipated and brought closer. Here is the traditional ritual focus in Christianity for present grace and transcendent hope. In chapter XII we shall be bringing out the ethical incidences of Christian liturgy. Meanwhile we simply note that the traditional liturgy, possibly with *aggiornamento* in images and ritual styles but without the reductions which some would operate on it in the name of contemporary culture, remains capable of serving both the interpretation and the transformation of the world.

The warning against reductionism brings us back again to Houlden's complaints against a liturgy trapped in the 'historical-cum-mythological' and lagging far behind 'current theology'. But *which* current theology? Worship will necessarily express a theology, or at least will allow a not unlimited range of theological interpretations. But the Church's worship must not be tied to one particular theological school or be reduced to the limits set by passing theological fashions. A certain ephemerality is natural to theology as it seeks to do its work in today's rapidly changing cultural context. It also seems that many contemporary theologians are taking the way of reduction as they attempt to expound the faith intelligibly and credibly in and to our world (although it is by no means certain that *aggiornamento* does not require rather a transposition of the faith in all its richness). At this time, therefore, it is important that official liturgical revision should err on the conservative side, if the faith is to be transmitted through a period of reductionism into a time when an adequate reformulation of its substance may take place. It is never the function of *avant-garde* theologians to control the public worship of the Church. The 'theology' expressed in official worship must be acceptable to the broadest possible range in the present Christian community and must be as faithful as possible to what is sensed to be authentic in the past. That is because the liturgy is a public act by which the worshippers identify themselves with a continuing community and enter into the 'story' of that community. *Après coup*, some of the ideas of formerly 'advanced' theologians may prove themselves authentic to the diachronic identity of the Church, and even some of the seeming 'reductions' may turn out to have served the causes of purification and concentration on essentials. Then will be the time to apply them to the liturgy. What must be affirmed at the present juncture is that any liturgy which re-focused the encounter between God and humanity elsewhere than in Jesus Christ, to whom the scriptures bear witness, would be other than Christian worship.

Unofficial experimentation in worship has made bold

attempts, both in actions and in words, to renew images and experience. American Protestants have perhaps been the most adventurous. The extent of the attempted renewal of forms can be gauged from J. Killinger's 'handbook for experimental worship', *Leave it to the Spirit* (1971). For convenience I quote from the (rather mocking) review which the book received in *Theology* (March 1972) [note 845]:

Since the Spirit no longer works through existing liturgical forms, and because 'most people born since 1940 require a maximal freedom to respond to stimuli in their own way and not according to any controlled or prearranged plan', the author recommends a spontaneous do-it-yourself approach to worship. . . . 'What we ought to be doing' in church is something like this. 'The congregation enters in complete silence and remains seated without speaking or looking around. After a few minutes of this, a man somewhere near the front of the congregation stands up and begins to remove his clothes. He may stop at his shorts or an athletic strap. Someone . . . begins to write aggression or resentment phrases on him. . . .' Later, other people including women and 'the ministers' strip too. Eventually, everyone begins 'to race about the room crying and screaming. . . . During the melee a figure in white robes walks quietly down the centre aisle to the altar and begins to disrobe. . . . He may be painted . . . in black and white waves emanating and swirling out from his navel. . . .' As a setting for this kind of thing, Dr Killinger 'would like to see a church designed in the shape of a hornet's nest'. Why? Because it is like a womb, of course. In it there should be 'maximal freedom for parishioners to move about and dance their religious feelings' so that people *'can believe the creed with their bodies'* [author's italics]. Meanwhile, 'paper bags are passed out to the congregation. Everyone inflates one and pops it. Confetti is thrown around the room. The music is speeded up to double or triple time. There is a screech and the lights go out.'
I am not surprised. If I were there, which God forbid, I should screech the house down, and emulate the lights.

The reviewer wondered 'whether "the Spirit" referred to in the title is the Spirit of God or the spirit of trendy American youth, 1971 vintage'. Coincident with the *aggiornamento*, however, there may lie hidden a two-stage repristination—via early Christianity to the Garden of Eden. The amount of divesting recalls Epiphanius' description of the fourth-century Adamites, who worshipped in the nude inside their heated church or 'Paradise' [note 846]. Nor need the eschatological dimension be lacking: *Urzeit gleicht Endzeit* [note 847]. Nevertheless, the obvious danger, despite Killinger's reference to 'believing the creed', is that worship of the kind he advocates, if it became staple practice, would lose its grip on the recognizable substance of Christianity in the flurry of ephemeral forms.

Unofficial Catholic experimentation has been much more cautious. The continuing ritual structure of the mass has been the framework for the renewal of images at the linguistic level attempted by Huub Oosterhuis [note 848]. The Dutch poet writes from his faith experience, which is a contemporary human experience. He avoids the worn words of cult and dogma. His eucharistic prayers are 'table prayers'. The language appropriate to liturgy 'is not a language of having and understanding, but a language of groping and naming', 'a language of playing and superfluity, of finger painting and free association'. Oosterhuis is constantly aware of the seeming impossibility of meeting an 'absent' God. Yet 'God's word is near', concentrated in the *mitmenschlichkeit* of Jesus the suffering servant, 'the living parable of God':

> In him your grace was said to be transparent,
> your gentle, constant way.
> In him, we were told,
> once for all there came to light
> what you are really like:
> the selfless, defenceless
> servant of people.
> He was the way we all would want to be:
> a man of God, a friend,
> a light, a shepherd. . . .

The institution narrative can be paraphrased thus:

> . . . Jesus of Nazareth,
> who on the night of his suffering and death

took bread, saying,
'I want to be your food,
I want to share what I am
with you, my neighbour, and with every man.'

Oosterhuis moves away from the 'objective' proclamatory
praise of the classical anaphora and 'more in the direction
of interior monologue or an address toward the assembly':
his table prayers are 'part of the ongoing faith dialectic whose
expression proceeds in a zig-zag manner [faith is a "to-and-fro
between yes and no"]. The build-up is not directed so much
toward praising God, but rather toward getting ready to
participate in the sign of the bread left by that man from
Nazareth. Participation in this bread and wine is commitment
to what Jesus, the revelation of God, proclaimed in his
lifetime' (J. B. Ryan). The praise of God is pulled up short:

> God and Father
> source of life
> voice and heart
> our maker
> you—or was it not
> you who made us
> to look out for and support each other?

The attributes of God can be praised obliquely in what is
formally petition, thus concretizing God in relation to the
community:

> Be restless in us
> be clear light in us
> be insight in us, knowledge, tireless patience.
> Be thirst in us which nothing can allay
> for justice and for peace.

The quotations from Oosterhuis [note 849] express a religious
'feel' which is clearly distinct from the texture of any of
the classical liturgies. The prayers of Oosterhuis have found
echoes among many contemporary Christians in Europe
and North America, and they are an indication of the shift

which is apparently taking place in our understanding of God, humanity, and the relations between God and humanity. It is this shift which is the deep dimension of the linguistic tensions which are experienced in both official and unofficial liturgical revision and composition. Official revisions tend to be drawn one way in the polarity, unofficial compositions in the other way.

Today, in fact, we face the problems of maintaining a number of bipolar tensions between legitimate *desiderata* in liturgical language:

Traditional and contemporary. Christianity has a history and a memory, and the psychological power of traditional associations is great; but archaisms in liturgy threaten intelligibility. Christianity intends to actualize the gospel in every situation; but worship should not fall into the language of barber's-shop conversation. Official revisions incline to the traditional, unofficial compositions incline to the contemporary.

Sacred and secular. Christianity has its specialized vocabulary because of its particular experience of God's acts in the world and the linguistic 'registers' of worship are in part determined also by the fact that the awe-inspiring God is a partner in the conversation. But God is claiming *the whole world* for his kingdom, and in Christian worship human beings in Christ are exercising the human role as priest of *all creation*, as the Orthodox theologians are fond of saying [note 850]. In 'post-Christian' or in unevangelized areas, how much notice should be taken, linguistically, of the 'fringe-attender' (cf. 1 Corinthians 14:23ff)? Official revisions incline to sacral language, unofficial compositions often move towards the secular.

Plural and common. Varied levels and styles of education, and the variety of social and cultural experience, make it difficult to find a common vocabulary which is rich enough for the purposes of worship and yet does not preclude understanding on the part of particular social or cultural sections [note 851]. This responsibility lies most heavily on official revisions; unofficial compositions tend to be made and used among socio-culturally homogeneous groups or within situations where people are united by a common interest.

Fixed and free. According to Justin Martyr, the liturgical president extemporized the great eucharistic prayer, but various North African councils around 400 A.D. document the fact that later moves towards complete fixity were due at least in part to the need to ensure the doctrinal orthodoxy of new prayers even when written down. Other factors making for fixity are the social need for formality in large assemblies and the psychological need for the regularity which confirms relationships [note 852]. But what is the place for improvisation in the Spirit? For use at other than 'the principal Sunday or weekly celebration', the *Book of Common Prayer* of the Episcopal Church in the U.S.A. (1977) has bravely supplied a merely outline 'order for celebrating the holy eucharist', and improvisation of praise, thanksgiving and petition is there allowed even within the great eucharistic prayer. The U.S.A. provides further instances of new official favour towards a kind of 'directory', whereby basic structures and fundamental themes are supplied, but not fixed and invariable prayer-texts: so, for example, *Word and Table: a basic pattern of Sunday worship for United Methodists* (1976), and *Word, Bread, Cup* (1978), produced by COCU (Consultation on Church Union) [note 853].

5. Greater immanence?

It is, then, the unofficial compositions which have up to now most strongly reflected a certain shift in the understanding of many contemporary Western Christians concerning God, humanity, and the relations between God and humanity [note 854]. 'Immanence' is probably the best single word to indicate the direction of the move. In philosophical and systematic theology, one expression of the movement is found in the 'process theology' associated with the names of A. N. Whitehead, C. Hartshorne, J. B. Cobb, Jr., and S. M. Ogden [note 855]. One of the popularizers of process theology, N. Pittenger, has shown how the eucharist may be 're-conceived' in this perspective [note 856]. Against the false transcendence of a 'remote, separated God, entirely outside and beyond the world', Pittenger wishes to reinstate a 'more biblical picture of God as distinct from, yet ceaselessly involved in, the world, a picture that stresses movement, relationship, and identity as faithfulness of purpose through changing adaptations to circumstance, . . . a "model" of God as present in the world, really affected by it, and enormously concerned for all its changes and chances, yet consistently himself in the integrity of his character and will.' The conception of God as 'active Love' is considered to 'fit' our contemporary sense of reality as dynamism, energy, event, interrelation, aim. When God and all reality are viewed in this way, sacraments are not appropriately spoken of in the language of 'substance' or 'things'. Pittenger concludes his *Life as Eucharist* with the following interpretation of what is meant by calling the bread and wine 'the spiritual food of Christ's body and blood': 'We mean that the universal cosmic Love that is personified as God himself—and not by our theorizing but by the very fact of love's personalizing quality—has been brought near to us and dwelt among us in the human loving that was Jesus. We mean that this same Jesus is made present in his very innermost reality, his "very self", to his faithful people as they "do this in remembrance" of him. We mean that his disciples live in him and he in them. And we mean that by this participation they are empowered as God's children to become the lovers God intends them to become.'

Although not himself a process theologian, John Macquarrie has many times argued for a more 'organic' or 'intimate' conception of God and the world [note 857]. He considers Christian thinking, particularly in the West, to have been too much under the domination of the 'monarchical' model of God and the world that is most characteristic of the Old Testament: 'God is a self-sufficient and transcendent being who by an act of will creates the world external to himself.' Correction is needed from the more emanationist side of Greek thought, in which God and the world are not so sharply separated [note 858]. In his *Principles of Christian Theology*, Macquarrie speaks of the participation of 'beings' in 'holy Being'. He rejects the 'personal encounter' model of revelation as misleading and goes so far as to deny that God is *a* being, even 'the greatest among beings' [note 859]. In

NB

the matter of Old Testament interpretation, one might question Macquarrie's picture of the happy survival of some elements of baalist naturalism which temper the dominant monarchic transcendentalism [note 860]. The strong, central vision in the Old Testament is rather that of a sovereign creator who continues to give life and show care to the creation in which he delights. Psalm 104 is an excellent example of this view, and it can be matched in many other places [note 861]. The notion of a personal Creator has remained integral to Jewish worship and also to Christian worship in both East and West. Fortunately, John Macquarrie sees the appropriateness of 'personal' language in liturgy and remains willing to use it in his own writing on word, sacraments and prayer [note 862]. If we are allowed to take this use at its maximum value without a hidden and undermining obligation to translate it into a system where God is Being but not a being, we may then learn much from the way in which Macquarrie speaks of worship at the heart of a 'participatory' movement from creation through redemption to consummation 'in God'.

My own inclination is to welcome the move towards greater 'immanence' in the conception of the relations between God and the world. It seems to me the appropriate speculative counterpart to the liturgical datum of a worship whose proper address is to 'Abba'. This address expresses the proximity between God and humanity in terms of a personal relationship. The personal relationship also allows us to conceive God's *transcendence* in a way which avoids false remoteness. Speculatively, transcendence should not be taken to imply that the infinite begins only where the finite ends and ends where the finite begins. More personally, God upholds and transforms his creation from within. In that he upholds and transforms, he is transcendent. In that he does it from within, he is immanent. In the terms of personal relationship by which Christian worship is unashamedly characterized, the transcendent immanence or immanent transcendence of God expresses itself as God's love for his creatures. This love is self-gift, self-limitation, self-realization: all three, in a dialectical process. The act of creation is God's self-gift: the gift of reality from the sole self-subsisting Reality. That self-gift is also self-limitation in so far as God respects the integrity (which means freedom) of a creature other than himself which is yet upheld by him. God's self-limitation was still more radically expressed in the kenotic gift of himself, in the person of Jesus, to his human creation [note 863]. When human beings freely requite the self-effacing love of God thus shown them, the self-realization of God is taking place in this sense: the achievement of the project which must be initially implied in his creating. All this is properly called love on God's part, because it is for the sake of the creature. From the human side, any self-limitation which may appear, from outside the relationship of responsive love, to be entailed in the giving of self to God is in fact experienced, inside the relationship, as the very opposite. The gift of self to God is experienced as self-realization in the free service of a God whose glory includes human salvation. *Gloria Dei vivens homo.* To take Irenaeus' words in a dynamic, teleological sense: the flourishing of human life, the well-being of humanity, is God's glory.

Liturgy is the ritual focus of our love for the one who first, and always, loves us. That worship takes place 'in the Spirit' is a sign of the closeness of a God who can be immanent without forfeiting his transcendence. He is among and within us to transform us into his moral likeness as love, which is the best worship we can give him. This is to become 'sharers in the divine nature' (2 Peter 1:4). The participation which he affords us in himself makes us partners in his enterprise for the whole world. The evangelistic and ethical incidences of worship will be sketched in the last section of this chapter and then described more fully in chapters XI and XII. Meanwhile we must notice one other linguistic factor in current liturgical revision which has theological and anthropological importance and may not be unrelated to the question of immanence.

6. *Male or female?*

In North America in the 1970s, efforts were begun, both

unofficially and officially, to remove 'sexist' language from worship [note 864]. This policy included not only the avoidance of generic masculines in reference to humanity but also the non-use of masculine pronouns and images in reference to God. In commenting on the WCC statement on *One Baptism*, an American group objected to the sexist character of the traditional baptismal formula: in the name of the Father and of the Son and of the Holy Spirit [note 865]. Sometimes, the final trinitarian blessing now comes from 'almighty God, Creator, Redeemer, and Sustainer' (the noun-endings presumably having lost any masculine character which once attached to them). Sometimes an inclusive noun is used on the human plane: 'our parents' in place of 'our fathers'. Sometimes the two sexes are mentioned in their differences: 'our mothers and fathers'. The last style may also be adopted with respect to God: 'Father and Mother God'.

Part and parcel of the feminist movement, these changes in the language of worship have at the least had the effect of challenging the often unconscious assumptions of male superiority which many women have consciously begun to find offensive and oppressive. The changes must be applauded in so far as they express and foster the non-discrimiratory relationship between men and women which St Paul declared to obtain in the unity of Christ Jesus (Galatians 3:28). Certain problems occur in connexion with the changes so far proposed when the reference is to God. The constant use of 'Creator, Redeemer, Sustainer' might push the understanding of the Trinity in an unacceptably modalist or economic direction [note 866]. Forfeiture of sexual language is to risk falling into an impersonal neuter. A better solution might lie in the development of deliberately feminine imagery to be used of God alongside masculine imagery. John Macquarrie writes: 'God has no sex, but transcends both sexes. . . . God transcends rather by inclusion and by bringing both roles to a higher level than by the exclusion of sheer sexlessness' [note 867]. Certainly, C. G. Jung taught that every balanced human personality includes both masculine and feminine elements. There are certain difficulties here. In part, masculinity and femininity have a biochemical and physiological basis and form, but our ideas of male and female are also partly conditioned by culture, and a sinful distortion may be involved. Subject to any correction which may be needed on those grounds, we may sympathize with John Macquarrie when he calls attention to the rather unilateral character of the traditional Christian understanding of God in terms of God's 'farther side': transcendence, majesty, rationality, immutability, masculinity. In Macquarrie's opinion, a renewal of the doctrine of the Holy Spirit would bring out the more 'feminine' characteristics of God's 'nearer' side: immanence, humility, accessibility, openness and love [note 868]. Obviously this would in no way run counter to the revelation of God in the Jesus who himself said 'O Jerusalem, Jerusalem . . . how often would I have gathered your children together as a hen gathers her brood under her wings, and you would not' (Matthew 23:37) [note 869]. Worship may be the sphere in which such a renewal of vision and imagery can best take place [note 870].

7. *Visio Dei?*

Revision of the forms of worship is meant to express and kindle a renewed vision of God. Our vision of God affects, and is affected by, our character and our lives. It is to the pure in heart that the sight of God is promised (Matthew 5:8). It is by beholding the glory of the Lord that we are enabled to reflect it in ourselves (2 Corinthians 3:18). Revision of liturgy and revision of life are mutually conditioning. From his side, God is of purer eyes than to behold iniquity (Habakkuk 1:13). He acts transformingly upon those who repent. The Church's worship and its vocation to holiness cannot be separated. Holiness means growing into the moral and spiritual likeness of God. Without holiness no one will see the Lord. Our vision now is 'through a glass, darkly': one day we shall see 'face to face'. Liturgical revision should serve the clarification and enrichment both of the Church's vision of God and of its own life. It should in turn be sensitive to such clarification and enrichment as come to the Church's vision and life in areas which are not directly liturgical. Only so will the liturgy be able to meet its focal functions of both informing and resuming the Church's being and activity.

The Church's vision of God is at the origin of its evangelistic mission. The God who revealed himself in Jesus Christ is believed to have a saving purpose for all humanity. His character and his purpose need to be proclaimed, because his purpose is to bring human beings to conscious and active participation in the love which characterizes God himself. The Church's concern for the spread of the gospel—for the sake of God's kingdom and human salvation—is ritually expressed in intercession for the world. All intercession for the world must be governed by the prayer 'Thy kingdom come', because the values of the divine kingdom are, for human beings, salvation: love is concretized as justice, peace, health, freedom, life. At this point, the task of liturgical revision is to encourage informed and sensitive prayer for the establishment of these values in precise historical situations. There is a place for freely formulated biddings in most contemporary revisions.

The test of sincere intercession is the commitment to corresponding action. If the liturgy is an assembly-point, it is also a dispersal-point [note 871], and the prayer at the end of the Church of England's Series 2 eucharist expressed the link which at least the post-1945 liturgical movement has made between 'worship and mission' (to borrow the title of a book by J. G. Davies [note 872]):

> Almighty God,
> we offer thee our souls and bodies,
> to be a living sacrifice,
> through Jesus Christ our Lord.
> Send us out into the world
> in the power of thy Spirit,
> to live and work
> to thy praise and glory [note 873].

That prayer recognizes that the dispersed witness of Christians takes place in 'life and work'. Worshippers may glimpse the character and purposes of God and learn and experience the value-pattern of his kingdom in the Christian assembly. Their testimony is then to be borne in word and deed before their fellow human beings. Chapter XI explores the catholic scope of the gospel message. Chapter XII brings out the ethical dimension of the apostolic task.

XI

Culture

1. *Universal or particular?*

ONE of the most striking features of Western culture in recent times has been the recognition of cultural relativity. Eighteenth-century literature produced the disingenuous device of the *ingénu*, the visitor from another and ostensibly more primitive culture, who voiced with apparent naïvety the ironic comments of the author concerning a European society which considered itself to be in the van of human civilization [note 874]. Since then, Western anthropologists and historians of ideas have made abundantly plain the cultural conditioning of the customs, rituals and thoughts of people in other places and past times. They have often been less aware than the eighteenth-century ironists of the culturally conditioned character of their own modern Western standpoint. In practice, Western scientific observers of culture have implicitly claimed at least part exemption from cultural conditionedness in the case of their own observations. The dilemma has been that their science requires neutrality on the part of the observer, yet *ex hypothesi* the observers themselves are culturally conditioned. How far indeed has their view of science itself been culturally conditioned? Most fundamentally, the 'sociology of knowledge' approach has erected cultural relativity into an epistemological principle whose tendency is to deny any possibility of 'absolute' knowledge (a German word for absolute is 'unconditioned', *unbedingt*). But again: how far is a relativist epistemology of this kind itself free from cultural conditioning? There are tensions here which must also be borne in mind when Christianity is challenged by the cultural relativizers.

As the maker of claims for the universal validity of the

Christian vision of reality, Christianity has naturally been a target for relativizing attack. Two extreme responses should be avoided. On the one hand, it is not necessary to succumb to relativism as though the attackers were themselves on unquestionably solid ground, and as though their missiles were not sometimes aimed at men of straw or aunt sallies of their own fabrication. On the other hand, and lest the military metaphors be damagingly taken to betoken a defensiveness arising from psychological insecurity, it is not necessary to suppose that Christianity cannot benefit from a serious consideration of the questions addressed to it by cultural and epistemological relativists. Avoiding those two extremes, the following four series of remarks are intended as replies in a dialogue.

First, there is nothing in principle impossible about a claim to possess a universally valid vision of reality, as long as all contenders agree that the envisaged reality constitutes a coherent whole and the only question is to decide, in case of conflict, which vision of it is true. Given those conditions: if a vision is true, it will be universally true in respect of the entire reality envisaged. However, radical relativism in epistemology denies, or at least remains agnostic about, the coherence of reality. Again: there is nothing in principle impossible about all humanity being able to *see* a universally valid vision of reality, as long as it is agreed that there are capacities of intellectual or spiritual perception common to humanity. The more radical the cultural relativism, however, the more meagre the content one can give to the notion of common humanity. Paradoxically for the relativists, the investigation of different cultures has disclosed a general sentiment among the cultures that reality is one (however much the interpretation of the one reality may vary from culture to culture), and that humanity is a recognizable whole (however odd the figure cut by strangers). *Weltanschauungen*, then, strive to be all-embracing.

The Christian vision of reality has the grounds for its own universal claim written into it. It pictures a single consistent Creator with a constant purpose for all humanity (and indeed for the whole universe). The divine purpose for humanity is growth into the likeness of God as self-giving love (and God's purpose for other parts of creation must match that in appropriately transposed forms) [note 875]. When God's purpose for humanity is thus simply expressed, it is hard to credit that it cannot be grasped by the simplest human spirit or intelligence. In the nature of the case (it is a matter of self-giving love), acceptance of that purpose can only be by free response. Again, the ways in which the existential response is given will naturally vary according to human circumstances [note 876]. When the response is reflected on, the form which the response has taken will affect the way in which the original vision is *post factum* described. A natural variety in the forms of response will therefore lead to variety in statements of the vision. The community aids the individual by means of 'classical' statements of the vision which help the individual to see the vision in the first place, and then to test by reference to other people the restatement which he makes on the basis of his own experience. Ever since the days of the New Testament, the Church has recognized that there are variant versions of a vision which remains recognizably one. The major doctrinal controversies in Christian history can be seen as the process of deciding the limits beyond which the vision becomes distorted past recognition or totally denatured. In our century, the broader question has been raised in a way almost unknown since the second century: can the Christian vision of reality be descried outside the bounds of historic Christianity? That question brings us to the second series of remarks.

Second, then, we face what Gerhard Kittel called 'the scandal of particularity' [note 877]. If God has revealed himself and his purpose with especial clarity at certain points in human history, the very nature of human history in time and space means that these revelations are 'particular'. In the case of the Christian claim, this particularity is heightened by the attribution to Jesus of uniqueness in a strong sense. Leaving aside the question of whether Jesus of Nazareth was the second person of the Trinity incarnate (although if the question is put in those terms, I myself would rather affirm that contention than deny it), I suggested in chapter II that,

functionally, the uniqueness of Jesus could properly be seen
as a criteriological uniqueness [note 878]. If there is to be
within history a revelation of God and his purpose which
serves as the decisive test by which to judge all other claimed
visions of the final truth about things, it could only happen
at one time and place and in the cultural form appropriate to
that time and place. In that sense, the revelation of God in
Jesus is 'culturally relative'. That very limitation is in fact
necessary to there being a *historical* test by which to judge
claimed revelations at any and all points in history. 'Culturally
relative' can thus be given a positive and universal sense: the
particular man Jesus is—criteriologically—related to all
culture and history. Such is the Christian claim. Whether or
not it be true, its universal scope cannot be said to be in
principle contradicted by its particular reference to one man
in a single time and place, Jesus of Nazareth. The difficulties
of transcultural measurement for correspondence to the divine
revelation given in Jesus cannot be blinked at, but the
possibility of such measurement is excluded only to the extent
that a common humanity is denied [note 879]. The admitted
difficulties bring us to the third series of remarks.

Third, then, the difficulty of measuring substantial congruence between any claimed version of the truth, on the one
hand, and God's purpose as it was embodied in the words,
life and death of the man Jesus, on the other, constitutes a
standing warning to Christians in any time or place against
taking their own version of the Christian vision as 'absolute'.
The difficulties of measurement apply not only between
Jesus and extra-Christian claims to truth but also, though
perhaps less acutely and more subtly, between Jesus and the
Christian tradition as it has extended in time and space. The
communal tradition provides a certain continuum of words,
thought, feeling and behaviour, ritually focused in the
liturgy, and we have therefore more of an agreed 'scale'
on which to measure any particular variant of the Christian
vision against the original Jesus. History shows, however,
that distortions develop in the Christian vision, doubtless
because the original is demanding to live by; and naturally
the distortions are not easily seen to be such by those im-

mediately involved. Eventually 'reforming' figures emerge within the affected area, with appeal to scripture as the closest witness to the original. Or, in an ecumenical age, correction comes from other parts of the broader Christian tradition where a greater authenticity can be recognized in particular respects. If the name 'reformation' is perhaps better reserved for the more radical corrections brought to a distorted vision, nevertheless *ecclesia semper purificanda* [note 880]. The necessary corrigibility of the Christian vision in any of the forms it takes between Jesus and the final kingdom makes for a theologically grounded relativism, which is a recognition that the Christian community, with the rest of humanity, remains under the judgment of God. God's judgment is in fact written into the original vision as its shadow-side, the possibility of a failed vocation. Cultural variety appears to be part of the creator's purpose, and in so far as human beings respond positively to God's call to grow into his likeness, the varied forms of response must be substantially identical at heart. But failure to respond can occur in all cultures, whatever their relation to historic Christianity; and then cultural differences can take on the character of conflict, which is *eo ipso* contrary to the truth viewed as God's purpose to create a community of love.

The fourth point concerns participant observation [note 881]. At least since Heisenberg, the natural sciences have recognized that to observe is to affect the situation. The human sciences acknowledge, with greater or lesser reluctance, that some degree of both sympathetic and critical participation is necessary, if observers are to understand and interpret at all adequately the objects of their attention. Christianity affirms that the nature of its own vision is such that understanding can come only 'from within', i.e. it is given to faith. The vision is there for the catching in the liturgy, and it includes a practical component for living. Christianity yields its secret only to those who engage themselves existentially in worship and appropriate conduct. This is necessarily the case, since it is of the essence of the Christian vision to claim, or invite, the whole person. The sciences have tended to regard the observer's participation as a regrettable necessity, imposed by the nature of things. Christianity glories in the fact, the strict matter of fact, that reality can be known only by participation. Thus the epistemological principles of Christianity correspond better than the epistemology of much modern Western science to the place of human beings amid the reality of which they are a part and which they seek to know. Moreover, Christians gladly acknowledge that their knowledge is *relative* (to the knower) and, without falling into contradiction, claim that it is potentially *universal* (it is accessible to all human beings for their participation, since all humanity is included within God's purpose, according to the Christian vision) [note 882].

After those somewhat abstract remarks on epistemology we may return more concretely to historical Christianity [note 883]. With the help of examples drawn largely from the liturgy as the symbolic and ritual focus of the Christian faith, three types of question are to be faced concerning the relations between Christianity and culture. First, there is the question of how styles and forms of expression, which vary with culture, are related to any kind of persisting substantial identity which is claimed for Christianity. Second, there is the question of the relations between Christianity and particular cultures which are themselves shot through with the ideas and practices of other religions. Third, there is the question of the relations between Christianity and a Western culture in which Christianity itself has been the public religion.

2. *Pluralism of forms and identity of substance?*

There are certain areas of the liturgy in which stylistic and formal pluralism can easily be seen as a welcome manifestation of the abundant variety of humanity at the level of creation. The emotional and aesthetic feel of the cult may vary without any serious threat to its substantial constancy. In tracing some 'laws of liturgical evolution', Anton Baumstark detected a primary movement from 'austerity' to 'richness' [note 884]. As the ceremonies and prayers proliferated, it was natural that the expansions should take on local colouring and express the genius of the people. In a celebrated essay on 'the genius of the Roman rite', Edmund Bishop drew the contrast in style between roman and gallican prayers. Whereas the roman style is 'pregnant', 'precise', 'simple', 'sober', the gallican and mozarabic is 'elaborate', 'effusive', 'picturesque' [note 885]. If ceremonial honour is to be shown to the liturgical ministers or the eucharistic elements, it will appear culturally appropriate, and ideationally equivalent, that the Byzantines should have borrowed fans and lights and incense from the imperial court [note 886], while some modern Indian Catholics should have introduced the use of flowers and flames for honorific purposes in their new freedom to 'adapt' the Roman liturgy 'to suit the character and traditions of different peoples' (Vatican II, *Constitution on the Liturgy*, 37–40).

'Adaptation' has been the characteristic Catholic term [note 887], 'indigenization' the characteristic Protestant word, for a task which has imposed itself with increasing insistence in the case of a gospel and a faith brought in modern times to many parts of Africa and Asia in forms acquired over many centuries in the West. Special doctrinal problems arise when the Asian or African cultural forms into which Christianity might be translated are imbued with the spirit of other religions. Furthermore, there is the difficulty that all forms of human culture are liable to be affected by human sin. Questions in both these areas will be discussed in the next two sections of this chapter. Meanwhile we note the type of question which is raised by translation even on the plane of the natural variety provided in creation. Attention has often focused on the matter of the eucharistic elements. In Africa and Asia, there has been some call to replace the Mediterranean or European bread and wine by local food and drink [note 888]. It springs from the desire to make the worshippers feel 'at home' in the liturgy and to demonstrate the relevance of Christianity to everyday life in its local forms [note 889]. Biblical support may be sought in the fact that *lehem* bears not only the narrower meaning of 'bread' but also the wider meaning of 'food', and that palm-wine may serve as well as the fruit of the vine to 'make glad the heart of man' (Psalm 104:15). In terms of C. G. Jung's psychology, eating and drinking are the archetypal experiences or figures, and these may be concretized into a variety of ecologically conditioned symbolic and practical forms [note 890]. On the other hand, several factors favour the retention of bread and wine. First, the bread and wine keep clear the original reference to Jesus Christ, whom the New Testament presents as instituting the sacrament with these elements. Second, bread and wine carry forward a wealth of symbolic associations from scripture and tradition. Wine is the 'blood of grapes' (Genesis 49:11), and the vine and the vineyard provide images not only for the Old Testament but also for the gospels (Mark 12:1–9; John 15:1–11). The grains, the loaf, and the pieces allow the bread to gather up a number of ecclesiological themes concerning the one and the many (1 Corinthians 10:16f; Didache 9:4; Sarapion's anaphora; Cyprian and Augustine [note 891]). Third, the almost universal use of bread and wine in the Church up to now contributes a precious ecclesial bond in space and time.

The choice between bread and wine and locally variable food and drink is, I think, finely balanced. The use of water in baptism is less problematic. Even in arid deserts or frozen wastes, water manages with seasonal variations to keep more or less the full range of its significance as a medium of washing, an instrument of death and new life. Oil, and particularly olive oil, is less universal in its use and associations with healing, health, beauty, blessing, and appointment to office and honour. Could it be that the 'protestant' abandonment of its use in initiation, ordination and the sacrament of the sick was due at least in part to a Northern failure to appreciate the Mediterranean commodity? Nevertheless its scriptural resonance remains great: Genesis 8:11; Deuteronomy 6:11; 1 Samuel 10:1; 1 Kings 17:14; Psalms 23:5; 104:15; 133:2; Hosea 14:6; Luke 10:34; Romans 11:17–24; James 5:14; Revelation 11:4. It is as close to Christianity as the title given to Jesus, the Spirit-anointed Christ.

Similar questions arise in connexion with iconography [note 892]. In Africa, Jesus is rarely depicted as a middle-eastern Jew, except in the fancy-dress pictures of him introduced through Western 'religious' books and films of naturalistic intent and (usually) poor quality. Much more often, Jesus is presented as a European. It is understandable that African Christians should see Jesus in the guise of the Western missionaries who brought the gospel. It is no doubt part of the vulnerability of divine self-giving love that the figure of Jesus should also thereby have inevitably been compromised through association with the errors and failings of the Western missionaries and the crimes of their military and trading compatriots. The most serious pitch is reached when Africans are driven to acclaim 'new messiahs' who will be for their people 'what Jesus Christ is for the white man'. These dangers are reduced when, as sometimes happens, Jesus is represented as an African. In N'Kamba, the holy place of the Kimbanguists in Zaïre, there is a wood sculpture in which Jesus is portrayed in this way, with Simon Kimbangu filling the part of his namesake of Cyrene in carrying the Saviour's cross [note 893]. This is in line with the iconographic tradition which 'translates' Jesus to the artist's time and place, as happened in the middle ages and down to the seventeenth-century *calvaires* of Brittany. In the twentieth-century West, the most gripping pictorial representations of Jesus are those which rather universalize him in an archetypal style, with a minimum of concretion into particular cultural forms and symbols. One thinks of paintings by Georges Rouault and Bernard Buffet [note 894]. It is interesting that modern Western art should have been helped towards the 'universal-human' by the influence of traditional African sculpture at the beginning of this century. It may be that black Africa is the next *terrain d'élection* from which justice will best be done to the non-contradictory but tension-laden relation between the particularity and the universality of Jesus [note 895].

As was seen in chapter I, there is a close interweaving between religion and the arts. Anthropologically, it is clear that religion was the matrix of the arts. Theologically, Tillich affirmed that, conversely, a religious dimension remains present in all artistic creativity [note 896]. Because 'adaptation' of the Christian liturgy in Asia and Africa inevitably draws on art forms which have their origins in other religions, we shall return to the arts from that angle in the next section of this chapter. Meanwhile the discussion continues in terms of indigenization and cultural pluralism.

While indigenization is necessary on account of the relevance of the Christian gospel to *every* culture, a concomitant danger is that this particularization may be understood in such a way as to threaten the universal relevance of the gospel to *all* cultures. In face of the exclusivisms present in the negritude movement among artists in francophone black Africa, the Nigerian novelist and playwright Wole Soyinka remarked that the tiger was not for ever insisting on its tigritude. The recovery of their own cultural roots is vital to the dignity of peoples who have recently been, or still are, oppressed by people of other cultures. Especially on account of the universality inherent in the Christian vision, it would however be a pity if this particular concentration led, in anything but the shortest term, to a narrowing of the perspective such as marked, with less excuse, the Western churches at various times in the past. An amusing example of such cultural restriction of vision, albeit in a matter of theology rather than of art, is provided by 'the legend (in the Church of England) that the second Edwardine Prayer Book is largely the result of interference by foreigners in English ecclesiastical affairs' [note 897]. Since the break-up of the constantinian *corpus christianum*, it has become inappropriate to speak of the church of a nation or country. The missionary task is better reflected by talk of a church *in* and *for* a country. But this is to anticipate a discussion reserved for the next section but one.

In the question of adaptation, it would be a mistake to suppose that liturgical change could remain at the level of mere ornamentation. In modern mission history, some Westerners may at first have given a rather folkloristic impression of the indigenization which was eventually seen to be necessary. If African Christians appeared slow to begin the process of adaptation, it may have been because of their profound sense that, once started on, the way of indigenization would lead to such a far-reaching transformation of Christianity that its substantial identity might no longer be apparent to their Western fathers in the gospel. To use drum and dance in worship is to revive an entire spirituality, a whole style of mystical communion, where measurement against original and traditional Christianity might be difficult [note 898]. (A carol such as Sydney Carter's 'Lord of the dance', itself controversial among Western Christians, might allow some transcultural evaluation [note 899].) More generally, the 'independent churches' in Africa represent an ambiguous development. Some are easily recognizable as Christian in worship, doctrine and practice, others far less so [note 900]. One must hope that the independent churches and the churches which have remained closer to their Western denominational origins will together undertake the delicate task of sifting between genuine indigenization of the Christian faith and its substantial distortion.

Indigenization has been accused of antiquarianism. That accusation fails to appreciate the importance for many oppressed peoples of a return to their cultural roots, as already mentioned. But an important truth is contained in the programme of contemporary 'contextualization' which is proposed as a positive alternative to indigenization. The truth is that the Western influence of the colonial past cannot be undone, and (more positively) that African and Asian societies continue to evolve in a world context where the modern network of communications is making the earth, in M. McLuhan's phrase, a global village. It has even been suggested that the need is for a 'cosmopolitanization' of the liturgy [note 901]. The problem, however, lies again in the Western origin of the technical civilization which is in process of covering the earth. If we were as Westerners to assert that the spread of a technical civilization is a providential development of a planetary pattern which may help forward the diffusion of the gospel, we should immediately be exposed to the charges of neo-colonialism and cultural imperialism. A precedent might nevertheless be found in the earliest centuries of Christianity, when the spread of the gospel was facilitated alike by the military and commercial routes of the *imperium* and by the unifying conceptualities of Graeco-Roman culture [note 902]. In any case, no substantial superiority need be claimed for Western culture as such (its own relation to Christianity being problematical)—only the instrumental utility of its technical civilization for a unification of the world that *could* be informed by the love revealed in Christ. In such a teilhardian vision, what would be the theological and liturgical place left for the particular local cultures? There seems no reason why they should not continue to subsist within the universal framework as testimonies to the rich variety of God's work in human creation. More immediately, the politico-cultural 'context' in which African Christians are needing to work out appropriate liturgical forms—and appropriate is meant to cover both the affirmative and the critical dimensions to be discovered in the next two sections —is a complex one which includes tribalism, nationalism, panafricanism, and the desire to make a mark (whether in African or in Western terms is already a question) on the world scene, as well as the presence of old and new visitors from other continents.

The practice of contextualizing the Christian faith and liturgy is in fact written into the canonical scriptures. The particularization of a universal gospel in time and space is an original and permanent feature of Christianity. As the revelation of God and the exemplar of human response, Jesus himself was particular. As soon as the gospel spread beyond Galilee and Judaea, which were themselves multi-cultural areas to varying degrees, the forms of the message and the response changed in various ways with the cultural surroundings. These variations are reflected in the variety of the New Testament writings whose liturgical and homiletic connexions were observed in chapter V. Considerably over-simplifying, we can see already in the New Testament the transposition from a 'semitic' to a 'hellenistic' expression of Christianity, with perhaps 'hellenistic-jewish' Christians playing a mediating role. Harnack's 'acute hellenization' has roots in the New Testament itself [note 903]. Daniel von Allmen has shown how the hymns and liturgical formulas deposited and criticized in the New Testament illustrate canonically the process of cross-cultural translation: St Paul quotes material from the worship of hellenistic or semi-hellenistic churches which have already heard the message in some form, but the apostle takes care that the material is in line with the character and cross of Jesus [note 904]. The model suggests that the cultural transposition of Christianity today requires first the very provisional translation of the gospel for preaching into the new situations, then boldness of imagination in the primary response of worship and confession, and only in the third place the critical attention of the theologian. In areas of first-time evangelization, it may be possible to follow this temporal sequence; where it is rather a question of renewing the faith in Christian or post-Christian areas, the three 'moments' will be more obviously concurrent. The important thing is the religious primacy of the evangelist and of the creative response of the new believers, the latter especially taking poetic form in worship. Not having itself a directly originating or generative function (except perhaps in speculation, where it in its turn stands in need of controls), theology must beware of smothering fresh cultural expressions of the faith at birth. The theological evaluation is in any case an enterprise which requires collaboration between thinkers rooted in the 'transmitting' church and thinkers who emerge in the church of new believers.

One service which can be rendered by theology is the clarification of the issues at stake in the relations between Christianity and other religions, and in the view which is taken of human culture in general when the infection of sin is borne in mind. To these two sets of issues the next two sections are devoted.

3. *Relation to other religions?*

In the first centuries of Christianity, one of the forms taken by the objection to the 'scandal of particularity' was the question: If this is the true religion, why did it come so late? One line of defence adopted by Christian apologists consisted in the claim that Christianity was the fulfilment of the ancient prophecies of the Old Testament. Those prophecies themselves were seen to have a universal scope, as is shown by the frequent application to the Christian eucharist of Malachi's words (1:11):

From the rising of the sun to its setting my name is great among
the nations, and in every place incense is offered to my name,
and a pure offering; for my name is great among the nations,
says the Lord of hosts [note 905].

The apparently present tense of that 'prophecy' has given
food for thought to some modern exegetes of the Old Testament: could it be that even in his own time the prophet
admitted the existence of true worship outside Israel when the
worship of Israel itself had become debased [note 906]? In any
case, another tack taken by early Christian apologists was less
temporally aligned than the notion of prophecy and fulfilment:
Justin Martyr allowed the salvation of the good Greeks who
had lived 'according to the Logos' [note 907]. The question
of the relations between Christianity and other religions can
in fact arise both with respect to pre-Christian religions and
with respect to *extra*-Christian religions. The first situation
has continued to recur all along the Christian era, when the
gospel has been preached for the first time in a context
marked by another religion hitherto untouched by Christianity. The second situation obtains when Christianity needs
to relate itself to other religions which continue to exist
alongside Christianity and in mutual awareness with it.

Some historical examples may be taken to illustrate the
issues from the liturgy. Then some cases from the modern
missionary movement will lead into a more systematic
typology of Christian attitudes towards other religions, again
with concentration on the sphere of worship. A considerable
proportion of descriptive matter will be included, particularly
from Africa, since many readers will be unfamiliar with the
practices referred to [note 908].

The earliest period was marked by the gradual definition
of the Church over against Judaism. That issue was not
settled even by the close of the apostolic age. 'There was a
continuing relation between Christianity and Judaism which
involved both attraction and repulsion' (C. K. Barrett [note
909]). In the liturgical area, questions occur at a number of
points. What are we to make of the participation, recorded in
Acts, of the primitive Church in the worship of the Jerusalem

temple? Why do early Christian writers and liturgies mention Abel, Melchizedek, and Abraham, all figures from before the Mosaic legislation, as those who made acceptable sacrifices to God? [note 910]. Is L. Finkelstein right to look on the 'spiritualized' version of the *birkat ha-mazon* table-prayer in Didache 10 as a deliberate slur upon Judaism? [note 911]. Was the Sanctus borrowed from the synagogue and, if so, when and in what Christian liturgical context? A version of the Sanctus is found at Revelation 4:8 and 1 Clement 34 but not yet in the eucharistic prayer of *The Apostolic Tradition* [note 912]. How was the Christian Easter related to the Jewish Passover? The question is raised by 1 Corinthians 5:7 and by the quartodeciman controversy in the second century. What about the recurrent tendency among Christians to make the sabbath a liturgical day? [note 913]. What of the recourse to Old Testament circumcision for the timing and theological justification of infant baptism? Cyprian was asked whether baptism should be reserved for the eighth day after birth (he did not recommend the delay [note 914]), and much later Calvin and his followers defended the baptism of infants on the ground of the substantial 'oneness of the covenant' [note 915].

The Christian Church in fact lays claim to the Jewish Bible but treats it as the 'Old Testament', over against which the newness of the New has been variously defined. If Jesus, as the Christ, is 'the end of the Law' (Romans 10:4), is 'end' to mean abolition, or goal, or dialectical fulfilment? The answer 'abolition' fits too well with a history of endemic anti-semitism and periodic charges of deicide against the Jews. Theologically, it fails to recognize the 'holy and just and good' character which Paul recognized to the Law as a guide on the way of salvation. Dialogically, it excludes a meeting-ground with Judaism. On the other hand, the unequivocally positive answer of 'goal' might be favourably regarded by those modern Jews who are willing to (re)integrate Jesus into the Jewish tradition as a great prophet, even the greatest. But it would run counter to Paul's insight into the bankruptcy of the Law as a means of salvation. The answer must, I think, lie in dialectical fulfilment. Ironically, Jesus was put to death

by people who ostensibly upheld the (Jewish) Law—or the
(Roman) law. But to reject the God who approached humanity
in Jesus is in fact lawlessness, *anomia*, sin. Of the death of Jesus
we are all, as sinners, guilty: 'there is not one righteous, no,
not one' (Romans 3:9–18). It is therefore impossible to claim
salvation through having kept the Law. That is why the Law
cannot itself be a means of salvation. Yet the Law, as an
expression of God's will for humanity, can convict us of sin
and, having brought us to repentance, can resume its 'original'
and positive function as *torah*, a guide for the conduct of
those who are being saved. St Paul remained a Jew and hoped
for the salvation of his people. If his view of the Law has
just been rightly outlined, I do not see that it need be unacceptable to believing Jews [note 916].

Paul's view, moreover, corresponds to the fulfilment of
the Law—and the Prophets (as those who recalled the people
to the will of God)—which Jesus claimed to bring (Matthew
5:17–20). The Sermon on the Mount in fact so radicalizes
the Law as to make the unaided keeping of it impossible, and
yet all the values of God's kingdom become possible when
God gives his Spirit to those who seek his righteousness in
repentance and faith. May Jews still be brought to see Jesus
as the *eschatological* prophet, the prophet 'like Moses'? That
estimate of him finds positive representation in the New
Testament. In the eyes of some Jews, he burst even that
category, and they came to call him Lord [note 917].

It was not only in relation to Judaism that the early definition of Christianity took place: Christianity also defined itself,
not least in worship, over against pagan religion. In a passage
with a liturgical ring to it, St Paul confronts the gods many
and lords many with the one God and Father and the one
Lord Jesus Christ (1 Corinthians 8:4–6). The pagan deities
are dismissed, in the manner of the Old Testament, as idols.
In 1 Peter 1:2–5 (the whole epistle is closely associated with
baptism), the writer may be deliberately presenting the Christian initiatory rite as superior to the *taurobolium* of the Cybele
cult [note 918].

The Fathers of the second and third centuries look upon
the pagan rites as diabolical counterfeits of the Christian [note

919]. Justin writes in connexion with the eucharist: 'The evil demons have imitated this and ordered it to be done also in the mysteries of Mithras. For as you know or may learn, bread and a cup of water are used with certain formulas in their rites of initiation' [note 920]. In connexion with baptism, Tertullian speaks of 'the devil's imitations' whereby initiation into the cults of Isis or Mithras, for example, is by a washing, and people dip themselves in vain for regeneration and the remission of sins at the Apollinarian and Pelusian games [note 921]. Clement of Alexandria summoned the pagan devotee to come to the Church and find the *true* mysteries, and the same line was pursued into the fourth century by Julius Firmicus Maternus in his *de errore profanarum religionum* [note 922]. In the *contra Celsum*, Origen was already prepared to apply the words *mystēria, teletai, mystagōgia* to the Christian rites, though without diminishing his opposition to the pagan mysteries [note 923]. It was not, however, until the end of the fourth century, and then particularly in the East, that the Fathers started to use easily and freely the language of the mysteries in order to speak of the Christian rites. By that time, and with the 'conversion of the Empire', the pagan mysteries had ceased to be a serious overt rival to Christianity.

Morphologically, then, the similarities between the Christian and the pagan rites were admitted all along by the Christian writers, but in substance and power the Christian and the pagan rites were considered to be as opposed as truth and falsehood. We need therefore to make careful distinctions in time and evaluation, if we are to follow J. A. Jungmann's thesis that there was an 'impact of paganism upon Christian worship', and that Christianity adopted features from the surrounding religions into its liturgy in ways which eventually facilitated 'the transformation of pagan society' [note 924]. Elements instanced by Jungmann include the language and style of prayers, the symbols used in catacomb painting and sculpture [note 925], the kissing of holy objects, the use of milk and honey at baptism, the bridal crown, the funeral meal and *refrigerium*, the dates of processions and festivals. Discernment is necessary. Take the language and style of

25

prayers: it may have been very early that Christians picked up the Greek manner of addressing the Deity by an accumulation of alpha-privative epithets, and the Latin prayers of Christians may have been marked from the beginning by the 'juridical way of thinking' which characterized the Romans even in their religion; but both these features are problematic in relation to prayer directed to 'Abba' [note 926]. On the other hand, the use of milk and honey in Christian initiation, which dates at least from the time of Tertullian, Clement of Alexandria, and *The Apostolic Tradition*, was also probably borrowed from pagan birth and family practices, but it lent itself easily to a thoroughly Christian re-interpretation in terms of the promised land now entered on through baptism [note 927]. Tertullian objected to the use by Christians of the pagan wedding-wreath, whose purpose was to ward off evil spirits and perhaps also to betoken a religious vow; but by the time of Chrysostom the wreaths could be positively accepted as signifying the triumph of chastity preserved.

It is significant that the major calendrical borrowings from paganism began to take place in the fourth century. With the 'conversion of the empire', pagan feasts were there for the taking, the spoils of victory; the abandoned husks could be filled with Christian meaning. When the threat and the actuality of imperial persecutions ceased, the eschatological expectancy of the earlier period declined; and as the Church settled into the present world and made itself at home in history, a part was played in this 'sanctification of time' (G. Dix [note 928]) by the Church's take-over of pagan festivals and dates. The most famous example is Christmas. The date of 25 December for the celebration of Christ's birth is found in the Philocalian calendar at Rome in 354. After the year 274, the emperor Aurelian had introduced into Rome the oriental cult of 'the unconquered sun', and 25 December became a holiday as the *dies natalis solis invicti*. The emperor Constantine's religion, both before and after his conversion, appears to have contained a solar component, and it is not impossible that it was he who urged the adoption of the date for celebrating the nativity of Christ, 'the sun of righteousness' (it is interesting that the Roman rite took up the *tamquam sponsus* of Psalm 18/19:5 on this day). The sun-god's feast at the winter solstice probably lies behind the other celebration, more eastern in origin, of Christ's 'epiphany' on 6 January. The Light of the World manifests himself, and enlightens others (hence the feast's association with baptism, *phōtismos*). The water may derive from a tradition by which, on 5 January, certain springs yielded wine instead of water (hence also the liturgical association between Epiphany and the miracle at Cana, where Christ 'manifested his glory') [note 929]. A number of rather more recondite examples are also proposed by Jungmann [note 930]: he links the old *litania major* of 25 April, dropped from the calendar of 1969, with the Roman *robigalia* for the aversion of wheat rust; the procession of 2 February with an old Roman *amburbale* or sacrificial procession round the city; and the feast of the *cathedra Petri* on 22 February with an ancient Roman feast in honour of the dead, at which an empty chair was left.

It may be, however, that the pagan husks were not so empty. St Augustine records that the pagans of Hippo continued to keep their feast on Christmas day [note 931]. In 601, Gregory the Great sent advice to Augustine of Canterbury that the English converts should be allowed to keep their festive meals, provided that the 'many oxen' which they were accustomed to kill in sacrifice to demons should henceforth be slain to the praise of God [note 932]. Here was an attempt to transform a still vigorous reality from within. Again, at the level of European folk custom, the celebration of new life at the spring season was brought by the Church into the service of celebrating Christ's resurrection from the dead: witness the eggs and flowers of Easter [note 933]. That Christmas and Easter should in modern Europe have largely reverted to their *pagan* character, or acquired a *secular* character, as mid-winter and early-spring feasts, is perhaps an indication of the precariousness of Christianity's grasp on human culture; but more of that in the next section, when the adjacent question of Christianity's relation to 'natural religion' will also recur.

It is not only in the earlier history of the 'conversion of Europe' but also in the more modern history of Christian missionary activity that worship has provided test-cases for the relation of the Christian faith to established religions. Questions have usually arisen for the Church in two directions: whether Christian converts might continue to participate in the rites of the other religion; and whether the Christian liturgy might borrow features from the other cult. The answer to the first question has fundamentally been no, and the answer to the second has eventually inclined to yes; but the nuances have varied with circumstances.

The seventeenth and eighteenth centuries saw the long quarrel of the Chinese rites [note 934]. Some Catholic missionaries, particularly among the Jesuits, considered that many Chinese were being held back from conversion by the Christian prohibition against participation in traditional ceremonies in honour of Confucius and the ancestors. By exchanges of letters and visits between China and Rome, they sought to have this ban lifted. As is clearly seen in the contacts between the emperor K'ang-hi and the pope Clement XI, the debate turned on the religious character of the Chinese rites. If the pope did not allow himself to be persuaded that the rites were purely civil in character, and therefore allegedly non-religious, we can only admire his perspicacity in recognizing that political, social and religious elements were inextricably bound together in the composition of such a civilization. The final refusal to permit the participation of Christians in the Chinese rites may therefore faintly echo the early Christian rejection of the imperial cult: a Polycarp chose to be burnt at the stake rather than swear by the genius of Caesar. Civil religion is never far from idolatry, as we shall see in the next section and in chapter XII. The question of honouring the ancestors will recur presently in our discussion of African examples.

More recently, some Roman Catholics in Asia have made a determined bid to include elements from Indian religions in the Christian liturgy. Melodies, prayer-postures, greetings, and gestures of respect have made their way into the mass with relative ease. They are considered to find sanction in the approval given by Vatican II to cultural adaptation. But a Roman prohibition has fallen on certain bolder steps taken

in the experimental *New Orders of the Mass for India* published
by the National Biblical Catechetical and Liturgical Centre,
Bangalore (1974) [note 935]. After communion, the *japa* or
repetition of the name 'Jesu Om, Jesu Om' was proposed as
'an aid to concentration leading to silence and absorption in
the union with Christ'. But the greatest difficulty may have
come from the fact that the orders included a reading from
the Indian scriptures in the liturgy of the word, with this
justification: 'This inclusion does not imply that problems
concerning revelation in non-Christian religions and the
inspiration of the non-Christian scriptures have been solved
to everyone's satisfaction. . . . These problems stand a better
chance of a just solution if they are examined, not in the
abstract, but in the light of experience—experience of those
who have used these texts for reflection and prayer in the
context of the Bible. Besides, even if we recognize only the
"seeds of the Word" in these scriptures, the final manifestation
of the Word of God in Jesus Christ does not render the
"seeds" pointless and irrelevant. Jesus has come to fulfil,
not to destroy. . . . The non-Christian scriptures, even if
they represent only a cosmic revelation, still form part of the
dynamism of the Word and are better understood when
placed in this context. In the liturgy the non-Christian
scriptures are never read alone, but always in the context of
the Bible.' Again, the preface of the eucharistic prayer praised
God for his self-revelation in the religions of India. The
'cosmic covenant with all men' is applied to the Indian
context through successive mentions of the animistic religions
(with their worship of God as Power present in nature), of
the Hindu religion (with its three paths to salvation: *karma,
jnana, bhakti*), of Buddhism and Jainism together, and finally
of Islam:

> God of the nations,
> You are the desire and hope
> of all who search for you with a sincere heart.
> You are the Power almighty
> adored as Presence hidden in nature.
> You reveal yourself
> to the seers in their quest for knowledge,

to devout who seek you through sacrifice and detachment,
to every man approaching you by the path of love.
You enlighten the hearts that long for release
by conquest of desire and universal kindness.
You show mercy to those who submit
to your inscrutable decrees.

Beyond the earlier argument in terms of *praeparatio evangelica*,
it seems that some Indian Catholics may here be moving
towards the recognition of the teachings, and by implication
the teachers, of other religions *in their own right* [note 936].
Perhaps the historical fact of the Church's failure to convert
India is pointing Christian reflexion in this direction [note
937].

The situation is rather different in black Africa. Accompanied by the military and commercial might of the Western
nations, and meeting with a culture which was largely or
completely lacking in historical or literary monuments, the
historical religion of Christianity made great headway,
particularly in the nineteenth and twentieth centuries, among
peoples which had hitherto practised the primal religions of
Africa. The early call was to 'burn the fetishes' [note 938].
If some Christian converts continued to observe traditional
African rites, the practice was clandestine. But the official
rupture with traditional African religion and the widespread
'victory' of Christianity have more recently been succeeded
by a readiness on the part of some Christians, missionary as
well as local, both to re-evaluate African religion and also
to take features of African culture into the Christian liturgy.

African initiation rites constituted a test-case for Christian
participation in traditional customs with an inescapable
religious dimension. These socially vital rites were generally
forbidden to Christians by the Church authorities. But in
1967, at a time when traditional African initiation was already
in many places *en crise*, the Jesuit missionary J. Hallaire made
the following report on the experiment of allowing Catholics
among the Sara of southern Chad to go through the initiation
rite of their people [note 939]. Despite the fact that the *yondo*
normally includes certain elements of brutality and idolatry,

the Catholic mission decided in July 1966 to allow its catechumens and baptized members to share in the tribal initiation,
certain ceremonies excepted. The initiation was recognized
by the mission to possess educational, social and even
religious values. Hallaire observed that the atmosphere of
the *yondo* in 1966 was profoundly changed by the participation
of Christian boys, and he tells how several groups made a
witness by prefacing with an invocation of the Trinity the
dances which the newly initiated were to perform in the
villages. Hallaire himself remarked that an institution is not
'baptized' by a mere form of words, but he saw in this
experience an indication that the opposition between the
yondo and Christianity was not insurmountable.

   In his doctoral study of 1966, *Initiation africaine et initiation
chrétienne*, the Congolese Catholic C. Mubengayi Lwakale
proposed taking the ceremonies of traditional initiation into
the ambit of baptism or confirmation in the form of preparatory sacramentals [note 940]. Much is at stake here: it is a
question of the integration of a whole pattern of religious,
social and personal life, symbolized by the traditional initiation
rites, into the sphere of the gospel. The author believed that
this *can* be done, because the Church is welcoming towards all
genuine religious and human values which constitute *pierres
d'attente* for the gospel; and that it *must* be done, because the
whole activity of human beings must already be sanctified
in preparation for its final destiny of being assumed into the
eschatological kingdom. Two of the practical examples
given by the author are these: The first presentation of an
infant to the sun is seen as a consecration of the child to the
Creator who is symbolized by the sun. The later initiation
rites mime death and resurrection, death to infancy and
awakening to the status of adult. While the author finds this
to be 'astonishingly in harmony' with St Paul's doctrine of
baptism, we may wonder whether it does not rather dangerously obscure the idea, essential to Christianity, of death to
sin (cf. Romans 6) [note 941].

   The importance which black Africa attaches to the 'living
dead' ensures a corresponding importance for the continent's
funeral rites. Abbé G. Ilunga has described some traditional

rites of dying, death, burial and mourning, with their underlying meaning, in his native Katanga (Shaba) [note 942]. He
sifts them into three categories. First, practices which have
no religious incidence and which may be retained: the
establishment that death has taken place, its announcement,
and the *toilette mortuaire*. Second, frankly pagan practices
which many Christians still observe but which they must
abandon: consultation of the sorcerer on the cause of death;
the burial of hair and nails in the domestic precinct; certain
practices at the burial of twins or pregnant women; the
widow's carrying of a stick during mourning to represent her
husband; the sleeping with a leaf in the mouth, and the
eating of half a banana by the bereaved children, and of
chicken liver by the widow(er). Third, practices which can
be transposed into a Christian key: the summoning of the
community at the point of agony; the dying man's confession
and his reconciliation with estranged members of the family;
the vigil(s); the choice of friends as 'protectors' for the
bereaved during mourning; the taking and removing of
mourning garments.

Two further elements are so integral to traditional African
religion that the question inevitably arises concerning the
possibility of their transfer into Christianity. First, there is
the invocation of the ancestors. Here is a description given
by H. Sawyerr, from Sierra Leone [note 943]: 'The rites are
intended to keep alive the relationship of the living and dead
members of (the genealogical) line, and consist of regular
sacrifices during which prayers are offered for good crops,
fertility, good fortune or success. Sometimes, however, the
ancestors are invited to share in the family rejoicing as in the case
of the return home of a member of the family after a long absence,
or of a wedding. At other times, the rites are purely com-
memoratory, as on the anniversary of a death, or on festivals
celebrating the heroic exploits of the founding fathers.' How
far is this pattern of spiritual practice capable of transference
to Christian worship? How far are the ancestors able to cross
from the divine (for they are powers that sometimes need to
be propitiated) to the human side of the divine-human
relationship and 'become'—even though many of them will

have lived and died before the advent of the gospel message to their peoples—the Christian saints with whom the Church on earth forms a single community of intercession and rejoicing before the Father?

Second, sacrifice is integral to African traditional religion: the best parts of a chicken may be offered, a drink is poured out on the ground. Sawyerr believes that Christian worship ought to satisfy the spiritual needs for which an African is led by his traditional religion to expect satisfaction in worship. He argues that the pattern of spirituality associated with African sacrifice may be retained, though transformed, in an African understanding of the eucharist. He states that his solution is in harmony with 'the' traditional (Anglican) doctrine of the eucharist. Such a bold attempt to 'baptize' a pre-Christian spirituality needs perhaps to be more sensitive to the fact that if ecclesiastical tradition has constantly used sacrificial language in connexion with the eucharist, the understanding of sacrifice has been highly controversial (even within the single tradition of Anglicanism) [note 944].

Protestant churches remain particularly reticent in the question of integrating features from African culture into their worship. Nevertheless, African melodies, drums and dances are now being introduced into their liturgy also. Even here, however, it is more than a matter of mere ornamentation. The French Reformed sociologist and theologian Roger Mehl has suggested that the dislocation brought about by urbanization to older socio-religious complexes may be a factor in 'liberating' such elements of traditional pagan culture for insertion into a Christian context [note 945]. If that is so, the price of liberation has been high in terms of social disruption, and the association of Christianity with westernized cities can hardly have enhanced the faith in the eyes of thoughtful Africans. It would in any case be a mistake to suppose that, with the decline in outward observance of traditional religion in 'Christian' Africa, the associated psychological and spiritual patterns were no longer present. It is at this deeper level that the relation between Christian worship and traditional religion remains important. We still need to ask how far pre-Christian patterns may properly be transferred to Christian worship [note 946].

In some 'independent churches' in black Africa, it seems that Christianity has been so far assimilated to existing and recurrent patterns in African tradition that its own identity is threatened and even lost. Religious leaders are seen by themselves and others as 'black messiahs'. They take the place of Christ for their people, and elements of the Christian liturgy are transferred to them. This appears finally to be the case with Isaiah Shembe and the important Nazarite church in southern Africa, although the relationship between Shembe and Jesus takes on various nuances in the description given by Bengt Sundkler [note 947]. First, Jesus has a *typological* importance for Shembe. Sundkler expresses it so: 'What once happened through Jesus, among the Jews and for their salvation, is now being re-enacted through Shembe, among the Zulus and for their own salvation.' It is 'repeated revelation'. In illustration of this statement, Sundkler quotes an Epiphany hymn from the Nazarite hymn-book:

> They came, the wise men
> arriving from the East,
> Saying: Where is He,
> Who is the King of the Jews?
> *Chorus:* So it is also today
> On the hill-tops of Ohlange.

The 'hill-tops of Ohlange' are Ekuphakameni, the holy place of the Nazarites. Second, Shembe may be completely *identified* with Jesus. Sundkler records some of Shembe's followers as saying: 'Jesus came first as a white man. But now he has come as a black man, in the flesh, through Shembe.' Finally, Shembe may *replace* Jesus. When Sundkler asked a Nazarite woman what she thought of Jesus, she replied: 'Jesus! Him we have only seen in photos! But I know Shembe, and I believe in him. He is the one who created heaven and earth; he is God for us black people.' Pointing out that there are very few references to 'Jesus Krestu' in Shembe's hymn-book, Sundkler concludes that 'his place has been usurped by another'.

Similar attitudes towards their prophet may be detected among the wide-ranging Kimbanguist movement; and, as late as 1970, an official catechism of the Church of Jesus Christ on Earth by the Prophet Simon Kimbangu, which in 1969 had been admitted into membership of the World Council of Churches, contained the exchange:

Q. Whose contemporary is Simon Kimbangu?
A. He existed with God from the beginning (John 1:1-2).

Official Kimbanguist beliefs and worship have, however, been interpreted in an orthodox fashion by M. L. Martin [note 948]. She claims that the life of Jesus is seen to be 'recapitulated' in Simon Kimbangu, in whom the Holy Spirit dwelt with special richness. In Kimbanguist worship the trinitarian formula often takes the form '. . . and the Holy Spirit who spoke to us through the prophet Simon Kimbangu' or 'who acted through the prophet Simon Kimbangu' or 'who descended upon the prophet Simon Kimbangu'. This need be no less orthodox than the 'who spake by the prophets' of the Nicene Creed, but doctrinal suspicion must attach to the insistent singling out of the one man. Again, the name of Simon Kimbangu appears frequently in Kimbanguist prayers and songs. This may be something of a parallel to the mention of Mary in Catholic and Orthodox prayers and hymns: Simon Kimbangu is the channel by which Christ became a reality for Africa, and he is now close to God in heaven. There is no need to begrudge the Kimbanguists their special awareness of their saint's presence with them in worship, as long as he is not erected into an independent, or even divine, mediator.

Although it is difficult to consider as orthodox some of the official pronouncements of the present-day Kimbanguist church, let alone the extreme views that have sometimes been expressed by people who claim the name of Kimbangu, yet on the positive side I think it possible, as I have argued in detail elsewhere [note 949], that within Kimbanguism an African conception of Christ and of the Christian's relation to him may be struggling to find liturgical and theological expression, and indeed in a *potentially* orthodox way. If I am not mistaken, the idea that lies secretly at the back of Kimbanguist christology is that of Christ as the great founding Ancestor of the family. In each generation the Ancestor may 'come back' in (all) his descendants (but more powerfully in some), yet without quitting his position on the other side of death. After their own death, the descendants become even more integrated into the 'corporate personality' of the great Ancestor and themselves become ancestors. There are obvious dangers here. On the one hand, Christ may be made into a kind of intermediary demi-god, a 'powerful being' like an important African ancestor, and yet, like him also, limited, not 'one in essence' with God. And on the other hand, one of the great Ancestor's descendants, Simon Kimbangu by name, seems to have become so closely integrated with him that, by a kind of illegitimate extrapolation backwards, he shares his privilege of having been 'in the beginning with God'. Although an Ancestor-christology would have its dangers for the Christian faith, and although also it would entail some modification of the different African conceptions of the ancestor, yet the reasons should not be sufficient to prevent African theologians, qualified by psychology and culture to sense exactly what an ancestor is for Africans, from exploring its possibilities. It is well known that the christological titles used in the New Testament (Christ, Lord, Saviour, Son of God, Son of Man) came from their previous multiple backgrounds charged with associations not entirely appropriate to Jesus without transformation [note 950]; and no one would pretend that the Greek concepts of *ousia, hypostasis* and *physis* were immediately and unambiguously suited to Christian doctrine [note 951]. Both in the New Testament and in the Church of the Fathers, old terms and concepts had to be impregnated with Christian content; and this was done only through decades, and indeed centuries, of exploration and controversy. Without abandoning either the New Testament or the great doctrinal achievements of the patristic Church, may not something like that be allowed to happen in Africa?

Anticipating, adapting and extending H. Richard Niebuhr's

fivefold typology of the relations between Christ and culture which will be employed in the next section [note 952], we may now set out more systematically the various Christian attitudes towards other religions which have been adumbrated in the liturgical examples previously given. These attitudes sometimes appear in mixed form. Neither their factual adoption nor their theological appropriateness may be unrelated to particular moments or stages in the history of the Church, of local cultures and religions, and of human civilization in general.

Corresponding to Niebuhr's 'Christ against culture' is the attitude which totally rejects other religions. The opposition is between truth and falsehood, between worship and idolatry. In modern times, this has been the view of Karl Barth, for whom all 'religion' was a sinful attempt at self-salvation [note 953]. Although some have taken his view of the *Aufhebung* of religion to mean its temporary suspension but eventual assumption by Christ, Barth would in fact have no truck with the historical religions, so that in their case *aufgehoben* was really tantamount to abolished. Barth held that the Christian faith itself could degenerate into 'religion', but he then remained concerned for its reformation; he seems to have entertained no such concern for the living non-Christian religions as such. Although Barth himself, unlike some proponents of this view, alleviated its difficulty by his tendency towards the universality of ultimate salvation, the immediate problem is that it fails to value the signs of God's saving presence and of positive human response which pass the test of conformity to Jesus Christ, even though they occur outside historic Christianity. It would moreover be perverse to deny that at least some such signs occur through other religious systems and not *despite* them.

The counterpart of Niebuhr's 'Christ of culture' is the situation in which Christianity is absorbed, at least piecemeal, into another religion. This cannot be called a Christian attitude, but it is a fate which Christianity has sometimes suffered. It represents a tendency on the part of some Hindus sympathetic to Christianity, or at least to Jesus as they perceive him in the gospels. It emerges distinctly in the more extreme messianic groups of black Africa, which ought not properly to be called 'independent churches'.

Niebuhr's infelicitously designated 'Christ above culture' is matched, in respect of religion, by the notion of *praeparatio evangelica*. Pre-Christian religions belong to the nature which grace comes to perfect (Aquinas), and from which the Creator was never indeed absent. In the liturgical field, Odo Casel evaluated the pagan mysteries as preparations for the Christian sacraments. The danger here is that, despite the talk of a necessary purification, the distortions originally introduced by sin do not undergo a sufficiently radical correction when the old religion is assumed into Christianity. Nor in fact do the Asian religions show many signs of giving way to the gospel for which, on this view, they were supposed to prepare. If, on the other hand, the persistence of extra-Christian religions beyond the preaching of the gospel to their adherents is appreciated positively, the notion of preparation is hardly adequate to their recognized values.

Niebuhr called his fourth type 'Christ and culture in paradox'. The equivalent of this 'dualist' view sees non-Christian religions as a permanent and perhaps necessary foil to the Christian faith. They belong to the 'law' which, in Lutheran style, is seen solely in its contrast with the gospel and without appreciation of the positive relations which also exist between the two.

The fifth and final type in Niebuhr's classification is 'Christ the transformer of culture'. I consider this to be the most satisfactory of the five attitudes when applied to the religious question also. It is significant that the language of 'baptism' is often used in this connexion. This is best taken in the strong pauline sense of death and resurrection. As with the believer come to baptism, so also here it is a matter of conversion and rebirth, of judgment and renewal. The complex, indeed mysterious, fact of continuity and discontinuity is aptly expressed in terms of transformation or re-patterning (cf. Romans 12:1f).

To Niebuhr's five types there needs to be added, at least in respect of the religions, a sixth. This 'pluralist' attitude is a comparative newcomer among theologies which still intend to be Christian. It matches J. H. Hick's 'copernican revolution', whereby God replaces Christ at the centre of the 'universe of faiths' and Christianity becomes one of the circling planets [note 954]. The pluralist attitude may range from a cool indifferentism which scarcely goes beyond *Religionsgeschichte*, through the desire for peaceful coexistence, to a deliberate search for common components which may indeed finally lead to a single, though doubtless still variegated, religion for all humanity. Bearing in mind the perspective of the present book, it is interesting that Hick should quote from prayers and hymns in his attempts to establish 'the overlap and confluence of faiths' [note 955]. For my own part, I should find it difficult to allow Christian character to a theology which did not attribute to Jesus Christ at least the criteriological uniqueness for which I argued in chapter II.

It is at this point that a word must be said on the question of 'inter-faith worship'. The question may arise on occasions of inter-faith dialogue, but it occurs more commonly, in present-day Britain at least, in the 'civic' areas of local community relations, daily assembly in state schools, rallies for peace and justice, Commonwealth day, United Nations day, and so on. Specially composed prayers and songs, if they try to avoid rootage in a particular religion, run the risk of suggesting that 'religion' may have a genuine existence apart from its manifestation in the positive religions; at this stage it would be going much too far to hail such attempts as forerunners of a coming 'world-religion'. On the other hand, the selection of material from particular religions must tread between the unnecessary inclusion of elements which would cause strong offence to other believers and the avoidance of difficult features which may in fact be quite essential to the particular religion which is being drawn upon. An illustration of the difficulties can be found in a service broadcast by the BBC from a Birmingham secondary school [note 956]: a Muslim call to prayer was followed by the Our Father, whereas the Christian notion of God's fatherhood causes great difficulties for Islam. On the positive side, such clashes may offer opportunities for believers to explain themselves to one another in ways which could at least reduce misunderstandings.

4. *The way of the world?*

Consideration of the relations between Christianity and culture is bound to face the fact of sin, whose presence on the human scene it is impossible to deny. To concentrate on Western culture in this connexion has, in the case of a Western theologian, the advantage of allowing the discussion to take the form of self-criticism and thereby avoid the appearance of proffering condemnation from outside upon other cultures as such. Because for many centuries Christianity has had no positive religion as a serious religious rival in the West, the Western case has the added advantage of permitting an examination of the relations between Christianity, on the one hand, and 'natural' and 'civic religion', on the other, without the complicating factor of an interlacing between natural and civic religion and the particular non-Christian religions. For in such an interlacing it would be a delicate matter both to extricate the various strands and to evaluate them.

The truth in Karl Barth's depreciation of 'religion' consists in his recognition of the sharpness of the knife's edge that separates natural and civic religion from idolatrous worship given to the things of creation, to the forces of society—and ultimately to self [note 957]. Yet natural resources, human community, and human achievement are the stuff of culture. In these respects, it is the business of the Christian faith to indicate by word and example the proper place of the material world, social existence, and the efforts of men and women, in God's design and purpose for his creation. The Creator must be worshipped and his gifts well used, the community must find its identity in him, and human beings must grow in his moral and spiritual likeness: that is the culture of God's kingdom which is, for humanity, salvation.

In looking at Western culture, we take culture to comprise the total pattern of the particular society, with all its assumptions, values and forms, a 'whole way of life' (T. S. Eliot [note 958]); but we shall nevertheless, in accordance with a more restricted use of the word culture, devote special attention to the intellectual and artistic modes and achievements of our society, the philosophical, technical and aesthetic products that result from Western culture and in part constitute it. The discussion will be focused on the liturgy as a meeting-place between faith and culture, with historical and contemporary examples to illustrate the systematic questions [note 959]. Again we shall borrow, this time in a sense closer to Niebuhr's own use (though he was not himself interested in the liturgy as a focus of the cultural question), the fivefold typology according to which H. Richard Niebuhr arranged Christian attitudes towards culture. And again, as in the case of attitudes towards other particular religions, we shall find that recent developments may suggest, though problematically, an extension of Niebuhr's categories.

In Niebuhr's first type, which sets Christ against culture, culture is seen by Christians as belonging to 'the world' in the negative sense of that term that is characteristic of the First Letter of John. This was understandably the dominant attitude in the persecuted Church of the early centuries, when, torn and bleeding under the tortures of a hostile world, Christians cried out 'We worship God through Christ' (Tertullian [note 960]). To confess Jesus as Son of God and Lord was to stand out against the civic religion which deified the emperor and, by implication, idolatrously ascribed ultimate value to the state. Less dramatically, the hostility of the 'higher' ranges of Greco-Roman religion and culture towards Christianity was a recognition of the mortal threat posed to them by Swinburne's 'pale Galilean' [note 961]: their 'naturalistic' and 'humanistic' tendencies were radically challenged by the preaching of a God whose wisdom and power were demonstrated by the folly and weakness of the cross, and into whose kingdom of love one entered by the way of self-surrender. With the 'conversion of the Empire', other attitudes came into prominence, as we shall see. But the challenge to the culture of this world then continued to be represented by eschatological withdrawal into the monastic life of prayer [note 962]. A strong case could be made for seeing the Western Reformation as a protest, in the name of Christ, against a medieval culture in which Church and civil society had become so confused as to fall under the charge of a works-righteousness which came to liturgical expression in a distorted understanding and practice of the mass. The Reforma-

26

tion itself did not go far enough for the 'revolutionary left', and an element of political subversiveness always accompanied the cultically expressed programmes of minority Puritans, Independents, Baptists, and eventually Quakers. Later still, the rise of Pentecostal worship can be understood in part as vocalizing a social protest against the dominant values of Western culture, in Britain and the U.S.A. earlier this century and in Latin America now. Glossolalia would then be a reaction against the language of rationalism and materialism [note 963].

This first of Niebuhr's five types is clearly the appropriate attitude if society at large is totally dominated by values which run directly counter to God's kingdom. Even in an ostensibly Christian society, the witness of a critical minority may serve as a valuable corrective against an over-close identification between present achievement and the final kingdom. On the other hand, this first type or attitude can easily miss the signs of salvation present within the broad sweep of human life. In addition, it is open to the more subtle temptation of ignoring the degree to which even a Church which is called to holiness yet remains 'world' as long as sin stays unconquered in it and its members. Ironically, the champions of this first attitude towards culture may fall victim to the very self-righteousness which is for them the mark of the naughty world [note 964].

At the opposite extreme to 'Christ against culture' stands 'the Christ of culture'. If Christ-against-culture represents the 'manichean' temptation of Christianity, its opposite risks reducing Christ to a culture-hero. A chameleon Christ cannot criticize an idealized culture with which he has been too closely identified. The Emperor Constantine was hailed as 'the equal of the apostles', and the coronation of the ruler became the liturgical legitimation of the political and economic 'establishment' [note 965]. With the conversion of the Roman Empire, the European Church took the dress and the accoutre- ments of the magistracy into its worship: not only the bread and wine but the bishop himself, who was also a civil figure, received the accompaniment of lights and fans and incense. The Emperor Charlemagne could move to revise the Frankish

Church's liturgy [note 966]; and the worship of the Church of England has until recently remained subject to Parliament. While all this may represent a thrust towards the incarnation of faith in culture, the danger is that the Church will become too much wedded to the spirit of a particular age and society . . . and so blinded to its sins [note 967]. While the ancient liturgies properly prayed for travellers, and the pre-Vatican II Roman Ritual contained blessings for fire-engines, railways and aeroplanes [note 968], the sight of a bishop blessing a nuclear submarine, developed solely for military purposes, is disconcerting. As Karl Barth and the Barmen Declaration pointed out, the *deutsche Christen* had in effect abandoned the christological test provided by the second article of the Creed: isolated appeal to the first article and the 'ordinances of creation' left the door open to a pagan form of natural and civic religion—*Blut und Boden! Ein Volk, ein Reich, ein Führer!* [note 969]—in which the magistrates usurped the place of the God whose instruments they were supposed to be (cf. Romans 13). Hitler was baptized and confirmed [note 970]. If baptism and confirmation came for centuries to serve as the birth and puberty rites of Western society as a whole and still the kingdom tarried, it is not surprising that they should in the long run have forfeited their power as signs of conversion to God's rule. Now that the process of 'secularization' or 'dechristianization' (the appropriateness of these terms will be discussed later) has brought a decline in the natural and civic observance of baptism and confirmation, it is possible that they may soon recover with renewed clarity their function to signify entry into a Church whose witness should constitute a permanent challenge to the sin which continues to disfigure human life and society.

Between the extremes of 'Christ against culture' and 'the Christ of culture' Niebuhr discerns three mediating positions which attempt both to distinguish between Christ and culture and to relate them in a comprehensive view. We mention first the view which Niebuhr designates, rather unhappily, 'Christ above culture'. On this view, third in the list of five, Christ is not opposed to culture but neither is he absorbed into it. One may speak rather of a synthesis. Or there are two stages on the same way: the best in human culture, from which the Creator and his Logos are not absent, is a preparation for the gospel. This view may already be found in Clement of Alexandria, but its chief patron is Thomas Aquinas, from a time when the Church had become the guardian of Western culture. Grace comes not to destroy human culture but to perfect it by lifting it to a higher plane: and one instance of this elevation of human culture is the assumption of its artistic works into Christian worship. This was all the easier when artists and craftsmen shared the faith: Giselbertus sculpted the west front of Autun cathedral; Cimabue and Matthias Grünewald and El Greco painted altar-pieces; Palestrina and Bach wrote music for the mass. Even today, Sutherland's tapestry and Piper's glass adorn Spence's new cathedral at Coventry, and Benjamin Britten's works include a *Missa brevis*. These are examples of 'high' culture; but indigenous folk-tunes in all the countries of the West prove that popularity and aesthetic excellence are not necessarily contradictory, and the Church has often taken them, with more or less adaptation, into its worship [note 971]. Black American spirituals have gained wide acceptance in Western culture; the extent of the use of jazz in worship does not yet correspond to its increasing appreciation in society at large. Here the humble and meek begin to be exalted: what were in origin the counter-cultural idioms of an oppressed minority become vehicles of worship in the wider Church.

The attraction of this synthetic view of Christ and culture lies in its recognition of the present work of God for good in the breadth of human culture. The danger is that the provisional character of culture will be forgotten. The relative will be absolutized or the infinite reduced to the finite, if what the theologians of Vatican II called the *réalités terrestres* are too easily integrated into a single harmonious system with the divine. Proponents of the synthetic view will usually admit that cultural values must somehow be 'purified' in the process of being integrated into the realm of the gospel. This will eventually point us to a fifth view which is more satisfactory on this score than the synthetic view. But meanwhile we must look at a fourth view which, while not so extreme as 'Christ against culture', in that it knows that escape from culture is impossible, yet takes a more pessimistic attitude towards culture than the synthetic view and, unlike the fifth view, allows for no resolution.

The fourth view is designated by Niebuhr 'Christ and culture in paradox'. According to this 'dualist' view, human culture is entirely included under sin: 'the whole edifice of culture is cracked and madly askew' [note 972]. Yet both the kingdom of God *and* the kingdom of the world, Luther's *zwei Reiche,* are under God's control, though in different ways. The worldly kingdom is the work of 'God's left hand' (Luther), where God judges or, at best, preserves. The danger in making such a sharp distinction is that a division may appear even in God: his left hand may seem to ignore what his right hand is doing. Or the worldly realm, in its paradoxical autonomy from the sphere of the gospel, may get out of hand altogether in a process of secularization understood as decline from God.

If the arts, as products of human culture, are relegated by Christianity to the secular sphere, they may assert themselves as a rival religion. The sociologist R. Bocock considers that the development of secular arts and entertainment in the West 'has probably been much more significant in affecting church attendance than the growth of science as an alternative belief system' [note 973]. Bocock blames historical Christianity for neglecting the values of the senses and the beauty of the human body and its movement. We should, however, note that medieval drama developed at least on the fringes of worship, despite the suspicion which attached to it. But in so far as Bocock's reproach is accurate, it may then be said that the 'natural religion' of the *sacer ludus* has returned with a vengeance in the modern theatre and cinema. Pornography worships the creature in place of the creator, and human beings are thereby de-humanized because they are thus failing their vocation. Or again: it may be that the failure of the Church's worship to provide a persuasive model of play bears some responsibility for the idolatrous and murderous features of modern sport as a degenerate form of civic religion. In any case, the divorce which the dualist view always tends to encourage between Christian worship and all contemporary cultural forms is bound to weaken, even for believers, the practical ethical incidence of a liturgy which ought rather to resume and inform daily life. We need a better framework of theological understanding and action. This is provided, I suggest, by Niebuhr's fifth view: 'Christ the transformer of culture'.

Of the views so far examined, the 'Christ above culture' synthesis leans towards the 'Christ of culture' extreme, while the dualism of 'Christ and culture in paradox' tends towards the 'Christ against culture' end of the range. The fifth view, 'Christ the transformer of culture', appears to me to occupy a central position which includes the strengths of the two sides without their weaknesses. It rests on a positive doctrine of creation and the incarnation, while yet admitting the radical corruption of humanity. Corruption is perversion of the good, not intrinsic evil. Conversion and rebirth are needed. That is more radical than the 'purification' which the synthetist will admit, but it is not a question of 'replacement'. The pattern of death and resurrection displayed by the incarnate Christ means, when repeated in history through dying to sin and living to God, at least the beginnings of a transformation of existing human life and culture. The reality of this transformation makes it impossible to remain dualistically within the *simul justus et peccator* as a strict and irresolvable paradox. The primary liturgical model of the transformist view is the sacrament of (believer's) baptism, which is no easy integration and which, if it is purification, is so only by the radical route of death and resurrection, a conversion and rebirth. The secondary model of formal or informal 'penance', as a re-appropriation of baptism, points to the continuing need to struggle against sin but keeps admitted lapses within the perspective of a genuine growth in holiness [note 974].

The precariousness of cultural transformation towards God's rule is illustrated by the phenomenon of secularization or dechristianization in the modern West [note 975]. If secularization is defined as passage from the control of the institutional Church, its occurrence in recent Western history is incontrovertible. Whether the West may properly be said to be in process of dechristianization will depend in part on the relation which is theologically held to obtain between Christ and the institutional Church. But even according to what some will regard as the insufficiently institutional criterion of the 'christological pattern' as outlined in chapter IV, it appears undeniable that there has been an overall decline, despite the many humanitarian achievements of the Welfare State, from the God of Jesus Christ and the values of his kingdom. What help can a transformist view offer the Church's understanding and action at this historical juncture?

On its more stringent side, the ecclesiology proposed in chapter IV recognizes the world's need of a committed Christian community to bear explicit witness to the christological pattern. It is by bearing this witness that the Church has the chance to become an agent in the transformation of human culture towards God's kingdom. On a transformist view, the Church is considered to be the Church *for* a place. (In the 'Christ of culture' view and, less unacceptably, in the synthetist view, it appears as the Church *of* a place. In the 'Christ against culture' and the dualist views, it appears simply as the Church *in* a place.) This obligation of the Church to bear witness for the sake of human salvation means that the Church cannot be theologically satisfied with the 'sixth' position represented by some both within and outside the Church: they suggest that the Christian community in the modern West should see itself rather neutrally as one voluntary body among many within a pluralist society. While the Church should certainly respect the freedom of others to reject or ignore the Christian message, it cannot without infidelity to God renege on its missionary task of proclamation. The teleological and eschatological orientation implied in being the Church *for* the place in fact starts to provide assistance for the Western Church's present self-understanding and action in the tension between its own past and the future.

To transfer, then, from spatial to temporal categories. Being the Church *for* the place, as on the transformist view, is part of *inaugurated eschatology*. ('Christ of culture' and 'Christ and culture in synthesis' correspond to a heavily *realized* eschatology, with the emphasis on the 'already'. 'Christ against culture' and 'Christ and culture in paradox' correspond to a *futurist* stress in eschatology, with the 'not yet' very much in evidence still.) According to an inaugurated eschatology, the Church in the West can properly rejoice in the positive fruits of Christianity in Western civilization in the past centuries. When Revelation 20:22–27 pictures the treasures of the nations being brought into the holy city, there is some biblical support for the conviction that cultural achievements are somehow eternalized by God in such a way as to allow, say, Karl Barth to enjoy the music of Mozart in the heaven of the definitive kingdom [note 976]. In earthly history, the intellectual, artistic, technical, social and religious achievements of the past remain as a heritage to be appropriated and extended by successive generations. These gifts of God through human achievement are not imposed on us but are offered for free reception. In so far as the Christian basis and dimension of Western culture is at stake, a refusal of the gifts will be tantamount to apostasy: and that remains possible as long as the rule of God has not been incontestably established and human salvation brought to completion. In matters of grace, we always have to do with the delicate interplay between God's persuasive love and the liberty of human response. The *post*-Christian situation, which many consider to have already arrived in the West, is scarcely precedented, and it may be that new areas will appear as the privileged places of God's rule and human salvation. The thesis has been put forward that the decline of early North African Christianity was due in the first place to its own lack of evangelistic outlook, much earlier than the Church's disappearance in the face of advancing Islam [note 977]. In carrying out its task of continuing to proclaim the gospel, the committed Christian community in the modern West needs a twofold policy: on the one hand, it must capitalize on what remains of Christianity in the whole of Western culture, for these things were signs of the kingdom and they may still function transhistorically as such; on the other hand, it must also find contemporary ways of making the Christian witness in face of the creature-worship which perennially threatens true religion. Can the smouldering flax still be fanned into flame? Or must the surroundings become altogether darker before the light of the gospel is again perceived to shine? [note 978].

These are the questions faced by the institutional Church when it celebrates the official liturgy of Christianity in the twilight of an apparently declining Christendom. What to do about the inherited practice of generalized infant baptism, the demand for which is diminishing but which still produces in large numbers the 'baptized unbelievers' characteristic of Western society over the past two hundred years? [note 979]. Church weddings pose problems in a society where divorce has become common and sexual and family ethics are in disarray. What does the Church say at the funeral and memorial services of people known to have rejected or ignored the gospel? It is not only the *rites de passage* which are now problematical after the many centuries in which the Church more or less successfully 'baptized' into Christ the natural and civic religion of the Western nations. The rhythms of the year also enter in the matter. Has Christmas disappeared and the mid-winter festival 'reverted to nature'? The British parliament has decreed a spring bank-holiday independently of Whitsuntide, which has thus forfeited its previous festal status in society. In Sweden, the theme of midsummer has waxed while that of John the Baptist's birth has waned, and the Swedish Church is trying to recapture 24th June as a feast of creation. In England, the nineteenth-century harvest festival, in which christological themes are not particularly prominent, remains one of the most popular services among occasional participants in public worship [note 980]. In the civic area, socialist parties have taken over the pre-Christian May-day as the festival of labour, and Pius XII's attempt to claim it as the feast of St Joseph the Worker has been scarcely more successful than if, with the Anglicans, he had left it to St Philip and St James [note 981].

Clearly the Western experience makes it impossible to hold the transformist view in the form of a simple linear progress of culture towards the kingdom of God and human salvation [note 982]. Human freedom and its abuse in sin render regression possible at the level of culture just as it is at the

level of individual Christian existence. Backsliding remains
as absurd as St Paul's rhetorical question makes it appear:
Shall we continue in sin, that grace may abound? But, after
its early rigorism, the Church came to believe that the mercy
of God allows renewed repentance and fresh achievement.
And the Christian hope is that God in his grace will continue
to give signs of his saving presence and purpose in this or
another part of humanity, and that whatever has been
achieved of value will be taken up into his definitive kingdom.
Hope for history and for eternity will be a fairly implicit
motif in the next chapter and a more explicit theme in the
conclusion of this book.

XII

Ethics

1. (In)sincerity? (In)effectiveness?

LITURGY has both ethical presuppositions and ethical
consequences. If positive correspondence is lacking
between the vision and values celebrated in worship and
the practical attitudes and behaviour of the worshippers
before and after the liturgy, then either practical ethics must
have progressed beyond the conscious and formulated ideal,
or else, and in the much more likely other direction, a
question-mark is put against the sincerity and effectiveness
of the worship. Or, if that way of putting it appears unacceptably moralistic: failure of correspondence between liturgy
and ethics amounts to an undesirable separation between the
sacred and the secular. Let us look at the problem according
to the two formulations in turn.

Because of evolution in society and culture outside the
liturgy, it is possible that a gap may arise between the life
situations envisaged in the liturgical, most importantly
scriptural, texts (the cult is, phenomenologically speaking,
notoriously conservative) and the life situations which the
latter-day worshippers actually experience. In so far as this
gap is formal, the task is to *apply* the constant essential values
in the new contexts in ways that are as appropriate to those
contexts as the original applications were in the social and
cultural contexts in which the fundamental values were
canonically enunciated. But as in the case of beliefs, which
was examined in chapters VI and XI, so also in ethics: the
impossibility of a complete separation between essence and
forms means that translation across cultures must always
take place in a tension between identity and change. How
can the same love which the scriptures teach and the liturgy

celebrates be expressed in the ever changing circumstances of human history? Yet however delicate the task of trans-cultural application may be, it is inconceivable for the Christian that humanity should ever outgrow the value of *agapé*, so integral is this to the character and activity of God and therefore to the advancement of humanity into God's likeness. The problem, then, will never be that Christians have in practice progressed beyond the conscious ideal proclaimed in scripture and liturgy. Failure in essential, as distinct from formal, correspondence between liturgy and ethics will be due to shortfall on the ethical side. Such short-fall raises the moral problem of the (in)sincerity of worship and the theological problem of its (in)effectiveness. The two problems are in fact closely related.

As H. H. Rowley showed [note 983], the heart of sacrifice in the Old Testament was its expression of the worshippers' self-surrender to God: 'The ritual was believed to be effective only when it was the organ of the spirit. It is true that many in Israel thought its efficiency lay in the due performance of the ritual act, and there were sacrifices which encouraged such a notion. But it is also true that the efficacy of the ritual act was believed to depend on its being the expression of the spirit of the offerer. . . . It must be the organ of the approach of men to God in the sincerity of their confession before it could be the organ of God's approach to them in delivering them from their iniquity and in restoring them to righteous-ness, . . . the organ of the spirit of the offerer before (it could be) the organ of God's blessing upon him.'

To concentrate first on the theme of sincerity. Surrender to God implies obedience towards his will in behaviour. When the Old Testament prophets denounce Israel's worship, it is because the people's worship is belied by the people's conduct. It is not sacrifice as such which is being rejected in Hosea 6:6:

> I desire steadfast love and not sacrifice,
>   the knowledge of God, rather than burnt offerings.

The idiom implies: Your sacrifices are unacceptable *unless*

you practise steadfast love. Knowledge of God includes the
doing of his will [note 984]. The sacrifices are refused because
they come from evildoers, as the context in Hosea makes
clear. The social dimension of Israel's iniquity is apparent in
the thunderous phrases of Amos:

> I hate, I despise your feasts,
>   and I take no delight in your solemn assemblies.
> Even though you offer me your burnt offering and
>   cereal offerings,
>   I will not accept them,
> and the peace offerings of your fatted beasts
>   I will not look upon.
> Take away from me the noise of your songs;
>   to the melody of your harps I will not listen.
> But let justice roll down like waters,
>   and righteousness like an everflowing stream.
>   (5:21–24)

Similarly in Isaiah 1:10–17. The Lord is weary with the
people's worship, but the remedy lies in their own hands:

> Wash yourselves; make yourselves clean;
>   remove the evil of your doings from before my eyes;
> cease to do evil,
>   learn to do good;
> seek justice,
>   correct oppression;
> defend the fatherless,
>   plead for the widow.

The prophetic theme is carried over into the reported and
reflected teaching of Jesus. The house of prayer is desecrated
when it is made a den of robbers (Mark 11:17; cf. Jeremiah
7:11). To make an offering of what ought to have gone to
father or mother is to break God's commandment (Mark
7:9–13). An offering should not be made to God before
peace has been made with the brother (Matthew 5:23f). Love
of God is a lie without love of the brother (1 John 4:20f).
Love of God includes love of the neighbour: that is the
implication of the 'double commandment' and of the parable
of the Good Samaritan (Luke 10:25–37) [note 985].

In the Christian liturgy, the ancient kiss of peace, which had declined to a vestige but which recent practice has revitalized, is a sign that the eucharist is for those who are, in the phrase of the Anglican Prayer Book, 'in love and charity with their neighbours'. In terms of the larger social structures, a prophetic act is being performed by those Catholic priests of Latin America who renounce the cultic priesthood *until* justice has been attained in Church and society. The most famous example was the Colombian Camilo Torres, who said in explaining his request for laicization [note 986]:

> Within the present structure of the Church, it has become impossible for me to continue acting as a priest in the external aspects of our religion. . . . The Mass which is at the centre of the priesthood, is fundamentally communal. But the Christian community cannot worship in an authentic way unless it has first effectively put into practice the precept of love for fellow man. . . . I believe that the revolutionary struggle is appropriate for the Christian and the priest. Only by revolution, by changing the concrete conditions of our country, can we enable men to practise love for each other. Throughout my ministry as priest, I have tried in every way possible to persuade the laymen, Catholic or not, to join in the revolutionary struggle. In the absence of a massive response, I have resolved to join the revolution myself, thus carrying out part of my work of teaching men to love God by loving each other. . . . I forfeit one of the privileges I deeply love—the right to officiate as priest at the external rites of the Church. But I do so to create the conditions that will make these rites more authentic. . . . I have given up the duties and privileges of the clergy, but I have not ceased to be a priest. I believe that I have given myself to the revolution out of love for my fellow man. I have ceased to say Mass in order to practise love for my fellow man in the temporal, economic, and social spheres. When my fellow man has nothing against me, when he has carried out the revolution, then I will return to offering Mass, God permitting.

A Spanish theologian has gone so far as to say that 'where there is no justice, there is no eucharist' [note 987]. In what sense the creation of justice may require revolution, is a question to be faced later in this chapter.

To take up now the point of the liturgy's (in)effectiveness: Rowley's (correct) interpretation of the Old Testament understanding of sacrifice supplies the beginnings of an answer to any who should question the effectiveness of worship. It is only when a rite expresses the worshipper's devotion to God that it may be expected to mediate the divine blessing. To obviate the danger of *do-ut-des*, as though God gave a gift in return for the gift a man offered him, we may make the point in this way: openness to God is the condition for being transformed by him into his likeness in and through worship. This openness requires, I think, something more than 'not putting an obstacle'. In conjunction with the principle of *ex opere operato*, the principle of *non ponens obicem*, traditional in Catholic theology of the sacraments, is a safeguard against a donatist or a pelagian view that sacramental efficacy depends upon the worthiness of the minister or the autonomous effort of the recipient (although to advance the principle in justification of infant baptism is, in my opinion, to go too far) [note 988]. But the reception of God's grace requires, as I see it, an active engagement on the part of the recipient. In so far as the sacraments, or any form of worship, fail to produce appropriate fruit in the lives of the participants, the failure is due to a lack or refusal on the human side of the encounter with God. This is said in full awareness of the delicate questions of grace, freedom and faith discussed in chapters II and III. To abandon setting God and humanity in competition in the matter of salvation means that the human contribution can be acknowledged and required without detracting from the divine initiative and enablement. On the other hand, no tolerable doctrine of God could place the blame on the divine side: where the fruits fail, the responsibility is ours alone. St Paul teaches that 'unworthy' participation is in fact counter-productive. By abusing the Lord's supper, the Corinthians had brought upon themselves the judgment of sickness, weakness and death. Unless they mended their ways, they were on the road to final condemnation (1 Corinthians 11:17–34).

The active human engagement required by the baptismal life is expressed by St Paul in Romans 6. Certainly the 'baptismal aorists' in the passive voice may be held to reflect God's action towards the baptized: we *were baptized* into Christ Jesus; we *were buried* with him by baptism into death; our old self *was crucified* with him. These have their counterparts, however, in the *active* aorists, no doubt equally baptismal, of Galatians 5:24 and Colossians 3:9: those who belong to Christ Jesus *have crucified* the flesh; you *have put off* the old nature. And in Romans 6 itself, the imperatives make clear the continuing active engagement that is required: yield yourselves to God (vv. 11–13; 19). Newness of life is for 'walking in' (v. 4).

Absurdly (Romans 6:1f), Christians do, however, in fact continue to sin. That is why their address to God must still include the moment of confession and prayer for forgiveness. They repeat the psalmist's prayer in Psalm 51 for mercy, pardon and cleansing. Like him, they pray to be taught, recreated, renewed, restored, upheld. They know that their capacity to praise God and offer acceptable sacrifices is dependent on God himself (vv. 14–19). They know equally their own responsibility for making worship and behaviour match. To deny that need is to fall into antinomianism.

Because the preceding paragraphs will nevertheless have seemed to some to commit the contrary error of moralism, the question of the correspondence between liturgy and ethics will now be taken up again, this time from the angle of the sacred and the secular.

2. *Sacred or secular?*

Ernst Käsemann cannot be accused of the antinomianism to which Lutherans have sometimes seemed prone. In a sensitive exegesis of Romans 12:1f, he shows himself well aware of the ethical dimension of faith and displays a fine appreciation of the 'divine service' to which Christians are called in their daily lives in the world: *Gottesdienst im Alltag der Welt* [note 989]. Unfortunately, however, Käsemann feels obliged to set up, at least implicitly, an *opposition* between the service of God in daily living and the service of God in the liturgy (the most usual sense of *Gottesdienst* in ordinary German is liturgical). Certainly Käsemann cannot abide a special holiness of times and places, what he pejoratively calls 'the cult'. He considers the whole of the Christian life as already a strictly eschatological existence lived *coram Deo*. For my part, I suspect that the 'unlimited and unceasing glorification of the divine will' belongs only to heaven and the final kingdom: 'I saw no temple in the city, for its temple is the Lord God the Almighty and the Lamb' (Revelation 21:22). How strange that such an ardent champion of the *theologia crucis* as Käsemann should thus expose himself to an accusation of *theologia gloriae*! A sound eschatology, and, as we shall see, an anthropology governed by it, both demand that we should in the present have the sacred liturgy or 'cult' as a symbolic focus of all our service of God [note 990].

Some kind of distinction is still necessary between the 'sacred' and the 'secular' or 'profane' [note 991]. Secular here means 'belonging to this world' still, and profane carries the etymology of 'outside the temple'. The eschatological *reserve* requires the distinction between sacred and secular or profane. The eschatological *hope* promises that the distinction will prove to have been temporary. The eschatological *gift* already forbids an absolute separation between sacred and secular or profane and provokes even now their interpenetration.

To take up each of those three points, bringing out the anthropological nuance and considering the liturgy as the sacred *par excellence*. First: humanity is still on the way to the divine kingdom. As long as this world has not given way to the next, it appears that our vision and behaviour need a periodic concentration such as the symbols of the liturgy provide. We cannot yet bear the direct and uninterrupted vision of God, and our own behaviour is correspondingly diffuse and broken, only fragmentarily in accordance with God's will. The high moments of worship are necessary in order to clarify our vision and renew us in appropriate patterns of behaviour. The liturgy inevitably enjoys a sacred character both as compared with the state of affairs 'outside the temple' and as an anticipation, while yet amid 'this world', of the age to come. The distinction between sacred and secular or profane is necessary, because 'in this world' some things can be brought 'into the temple' only as the objects of confession of sin, intercession, or prayer for transformation.

Second: the ultimate hope is for the dissolution of the distinction between sacred and secular or profane. In the heavenly city there will be 'no' temple, because its 'temple' will be the Lord God Almighty and the Lamb (Revelation 21:22). When God is all in all (1 Corinthians 15:28), nothing will be 'outside the temple' precisely because of the all-embracing saving presence of God and the subjection of all things to his will. The kingdom 'of this world' will have become the kingdom of God and of his Christ (Revelation 11:15). Every human being and the whole human race in the totality of their individual and corporate existence are called to a final destiny which will be both the service of God and *eo ipso* their own salvation: to 'glorify God and enjoy him for ever'. Then sacraments will cease, because their anticipatory and *pars-pro-toto* character will have given way to fulfilment in universal reality.

Third: the sacraments, and Christian worship as such, are the gift and opportunity of new life in anticipation of the final kingdom. Where the gift is accepted and the chance taken, they are moments in the transformation and growth of humanity into the likeness of God. An absolute separation between the sacred and the secular or profane is impossible when it is the same human beings who are seeking the transformation of the whole of their lives through the grace of participation in the liturgical rites. The sacraments are meant both to resume and to inform existence as a whole. There will thus be interpenetration between sacred and secular or profane, when the rites serve their purpose as a recreative paradigm for the human attitudes and behaviour appropriate to a divine kingdom which intends to be total in scope and quality, and which is simultaneously the worship of God and the salvation of humanity.

So far I have been trying to establish the proper relationship between sacred and secular in our period of overlap between the ages (cf. 1 Corinthians 10:11). But there is no doubt that sacred and secular can be falsely related, both in theory and in practice. On the side of the sacred, there is the danger of an ideological sacralization which may fail in various ways to respect the reality of the secular. Three examples may be given. First: at the level of speculative theology I detect this danger in the teilhardian vision adopted in G. Martelet's *Résurrection, eucharistie et genèse de l'homme* [note 992]. The eucharist is there rightly seen as an agency of transformation towards glory in the Church, the world and the universe. But the unsatisfactory model of transubstantiation is projected from the liturgy onto the whole universe, so that the goal seems to be some kind of pantheistic identification between Christ and the 'transubstantiated' universe as his body. The Anglican Articles of Religion declare that transubstantiation 'overthroweth the nature of a sacrament' (article XXVIII): its magnification to the universal scale writes large the annihilation of created reality [note 993]. The second example is from comparative ecclesiology. The charge of sacralization is brought by V. Subilia against the Orthodox churches in connexion with their political quietism: the Waldensian theologian accuses them of fleeing from history into liturgy, of 'abdicating from their immediate Christian responsibility and taking refuge in the atemporal sphere of the rite' [note 994]. Whatever the truth of that particular allegation in the case of the Orthodox, liturgical escapism is certainly one of the forms taken by the temptation to sacralism. The sacred can be isolated as an area of escape from the life which still needs to be lived in the world. The third example of sacralization concerns the sociological structure of the Church. Exaggeration of the sacred is accompanied by the over-potentation of the ritual experts. Clericalism then devalues the work and witness of lay Christians in the daily world.

Tendencies to sacralization may provoke a reaction in favour of the secular. Secularization can be a healthy corrective, but it runs the risk of degenerating into ideological secularism. To take up again the previous three examples, this time in reverse order. First: one of the great achievements of the Reformation was to recover the dignity of the lay man and woman in their vocation, *beruf*. The invigorated exercise of the universal priesthood in the secular sphere was, however,

accompanied by the general impoverishment of ritual sense
in Protestantism. In some cases there even occurs an ideological opposition to 'the cult'. Stress on the lay vocation can
degenerate into the prizing of worldly success, which is
dangerous even, or especially, when interpreted as a sign of
divine favour. Second: political activism, if unsupported by
the liturgy, is threatened by the loss of two dimensions
essential to the kingdom: grace and ultimacy. Without the
initiative and continuing help of God, which the liturgy
celebrates and entreats, human salvation cannot be achieved.
Achievements in this world are in any case destroyed by time
and death unless they are taken up into the eternal and
definitive kingdom, of which the liturgy is the promise and
taste. The more humane among the Marxists are now feeling
after transcendence. Third: an anti-pantheist emphasis on
the relative autonomy of the created order should not pass
over into a claim for its absolute autonomy. That is the way
of deism and finally atheism. In its extreme form, secularization becomes not simply the (justified) overthrow of clericalism, nor the (already more problematic) abandonment of the
institutional Church, but decline from God.

Returning to positive statements, we may conclude this
section by developing a little the notion of the liturgy as
the symbolic *focus* of all our service of God. A two-way
movement is possible and necessary. One may start from the
focal point and move out into the wider area where the vision
of the kingdom requires to be translated from the language
of symbol into practical action. One may also begin with
the moral questions and opportunities of everyday life and
bring them to the liturgy for sharper definition in the concentrated mode appropriate to conscious encounter between
us and God. The first is by and large the approach adopted
by the Catholic moral theologian Bernard Häring in his
book on *The sacraments in a secular age: a vision in depth on
sacramentality and its impact on moral life* [note 995]. The 'positive
challenge' afforded by a 'secular age' consists in a challenge
to see how Christ, himself the great Sacrament, is already
savingly at work throughout creation and humanity. To
that end, the sacraments, in the plural, are signs to sharpen

our vision of the divine presence in the world; further, they are gifts enabling us to shape our will and our action conformably with God's, in configuration with Christ, in the opportunities of everyday living to God's glory. It is as men and women find, with the help of the liturgy, their 'centre of gravity and of value' in God that they are able to orient their lives, as themselves a kind of sacrament of the divine love, towards the welfare of all persons created in the image of God and called to his likeness. Thus Häring seeks to synthesize the whole of moral theology in a sacramental key [note 996].

Another Catholic moral theologian, Enda McDonagh, has argued that there may be advantage, particularly in a time of secularization, in adopting the reverse procedure and moving from 'morality' to 'prayer' [note 997]. Pointing to the slowness of both the liturgical and the charismatic movements to inspire and sustain a wider reform of society, the Irishman recalls 'the secular cultural context which has made God, the transcendent and religious dimension of life, unnecessary or irrelevant or at any rate much more remote and obscure. It has made the traditional prayer concepts, formulae and structures, however renewed, strangers to one's daily thinking and living. A lack of inner connexion which threatens a lack of inner conviction can sometimes be discerned even among those with a firm desire to maintain and develop their prayer life.' McDonagh proposes to begin rather in the concrete situation of human relationships, where moral experience is the mutual obligation to recognize, respect and respond to the other person as also an inviolable 'creative centre of knowing and loving, deciding and acting'. 'It is by considering morality in terms of this analysis of human relationships,' says McDonagh, 'and understanding what our moral responses as between people involve, first at the genuinely moral and human level, that I believe our awareness of God, our prayer-life can be enriched and expanded.' In the Christian understanding, human otherness derives from the final other we call God: 'so the moral response to the human other can and should by its own inherent dynamism expand into a response to the ultimate other; it can and should expand into prayer.' If response to the penultimate other is not to stop short at an idolatrous humanism, direct and explicit attention must be paid to the ultimate other in prayer. It then becomes possible to see and treat the human other as also made in God's image and sharing with oneself in the call to divine sonship.

Oscillation between worship and ethics is, I judge, both proper and required. In recognition of this, the next and the next-but-two sections will illustrate the movement from liturgy to life [note 998], while the next-but-one and the next-but-three sections will swing from life to liturgy. In the third part of this book all the section-headings so far have been in the interrogative, in order to comply with the perspective of 'contextual questions'. Although the questioning perspective continues, I now shift to the affirmative form in section-headings, in order to match the positive nature of the Christian hope and the positive contribution of ethics to the proclamation of the gospel.

3. *Freedom and service*

St Paul wrote to the Corinthians: 'You were washed, you were sanctified, you were justified in the name of the Lord Jesus Christ and in the Spirit of our God' (1 Corinthians 6:11) [note 999]. The reference to baptism seems unmistakable: apart from the mention of washing we note also that the verbs are in the aorist tense (for a single event in the past), that baptism was performed 'in the name of the Lord Jesus Christ' (clear in Acts), and that the Holy Spirit was closely associated with baptism (e.g. Acts 2:38; Titus 3:5; John 3:5). This verse, then, lays the apostolic base for the traditional view of baptism as the sacrament of justification: 'you were justified'. In the apostle's thought, justification is part of a complex of images which includes also redemption and liberation. God has emancipated us from the slavery of sin. Christ 'has set us free for freedom' (Galatians 5:1, aorist): 'you were called to freedom, brethren' (Galatians 5:13, aorist again). The contexts in 1 Corinthians 6 and Galatians 5 make it clear that Christian freedom is not a licence for 'the flesh', which includes among its works 'immorality, impurity, licentiousness, idolatry, sorcery, enmity, strife, jealously, anger, selfishness, dissension, party spirit, envy, murder, drunkenness, carousing, and the like'. Indulgence in these would in fact be a return to slavery. Christian freedom is freedom to serve God and the neighbour:

> You are not your own; you were bought with a price. So glorify God in your body.   (1 Corinthians 6:19f)

> Do not use your freedom as an opportunity for the flesh, but through love be servants of one another. For the whole law is fulfilled in one word, 'You shall love your neighbour as yourself.'
>   (Galatians 5:13f)

In Romans 6 St Paul writes to the baptized:

> Do not yield your members to sin as instruments of wickedness, but yield yourselves to God as men who have been brought from death to life, and your members to God as instruments of righteousness. . . . Thanks be to God, that you who were once slaves of sin have become obedient from the heart to the standard of teaching to which you were committed, and, having been set free from sin, have become slaves of righteousness. . . . Just as you once yielded your members to impurity and to greater and greater iniquity, so now yield your members to righteousness for sanctification. . . . Now that you have been set free from sin and have become slaves of God, the return you get is sanctification and its end, eternal life. For the wages of sin is death, but the free gift of God is eternal life in Christ Jesus our Lord.

Justification, of which baptism is the sacrament, must be viewed stereoscopically. Out of sheer grace God has declared us righteous in our faith-union with Christ. His word will come to fruition as, by his enablement, we yield ourselves to righteousness. To 'walk in newness of life' is the beginning of eternal life in Christ. St Paul is unhappy with his own talk of slavery to God (Romans 6:18f). Two chapters later, he corrects himself and speaks rather of sonship, to which the worshipper's cry of 'Abba! Father!' testifies (8:15–17; cf. Galatians 4:6f). Our service is not the forced labour of slavery but the free co-operation of sons. Sonship means being led by the Spirit of God (8:14; cf. Galatians 5:16, 25): the contexts in Romans 8:1ff and Galatians 5:16ff again make clear that attitudes and behaviour are at issue; to be children of God means to share the Father's character as revealed in his Son (cf. Matthew 5:44f; Ephesians 4:17–5:2). Final liberation into manifest sharing of God's glory in conformity with Christ is still to come (Romans 8:17–25; cf. Colossians 3:1–4; 1 John 3:1–3).

By himself justifying us instead of leaving us unsuccessfully to attempt our own justification, God sets us free from our selves, in our capacity as the old Adam, and begins making new persons of us through participation in Christ, the new Adam [note 1000]. This 'new creation' (2 Corinthians 5:17) means the service of God and of our fellow human beings, the love of God and of neighbour. Baptism is the sacrament of all this, gathering the whole process proleptically into a single sign. It is an eschatological sign, because it anticipates the last judgment and the final kingdom. Our repeated *reditus ad baptismum* (Luther) is a 'return' only because the end was already signified in the beginning. Recourse to baptism should in fact be progress in the reality which it signified and which will be fully achieved when God's rule is complete. The symbolic focus of our deliberate *reditus ad baptismum* is the liturgy. That is why the Lutheran theologian G. Ebeling can speak of 'the necessity of Christian worship', and in terms appropriate to the fact and experience of justification: in worship God graciously addresses us at the personal root of all our works; the hearing of the Word in faith liberates us for service in the world [note 1001].

It would be possible to develop a whole Christian ethic from the figures associated with baptism. Only hints can be given here. *Death and resurrection* is basic (Romans 6) [note 1002]. The baptismal life is a sharing in Christ's total self-surrender to the Father. It means dying to sin and living for God. This *change in allegiance* is indicated by the baptismal seal (cf. 2 Corinthians 1:21f; Ephesians 1:13f; 4:30). In the patristic period, sealing commonly meant the tracing of the sign of the cross on the forehead in oil after baptism, marking the baptized person for the God of Jesus Christ as a slave was branded for his owner and a soldier tattooed for his emperor. The change in allegiance is a *re-orientation of the person*. This is dramatized in the Byzantine apotaxis and syntaxis just before baptism: the candidate turns to the west, the place of darkness, in order to renounce Satan, and then turns eastwards, towards the light, in order to profess adherence to his new Lord [note 1003]. *Personal transformation* is expressed in the change of clothing. The believer strips off 'the old man' and dons 'the new man' who is Christ (Galatians 3:27; Colossians 3:9f). Undressing and dressing before and after baptism soon acquired a symbolic meaning. The clothing of the newly baptized in white garments is attested by Cyril of Jerusalem and by Ambrose [note 1004]. In the Byzantine rite, the baptized is 'clothed with the tunic of righteousness'. *New life* is received when the old is abandoned. The newness of the life which God gives and to which the believer is called is such that the language of regeneration and rebirth may be used in connexion with baptism: Titus 3:5; John 3:5.

Christians are, then, sons and daughters of God, *filii in Filio* (Galatians 3:26f, 4:4–6). Baptism 'into Christ' sets one into a community, a family expected to love one another as brothers and sisters (Romans 12:10). Romans 12 and 1 Corinthians 12 picture the community as a body, in which the many members should respect one another for their varied contributions, all of them God's gifts, to the common good. The sacramental ground of their common life is baptism: 'In one Spirit we were all baptized into one body' (1 Corinthians 12:13). Baptism into Christ radically removes all discrimination among Christians on grounds of history, culture, social status, or sex: 'There is neither Jew nor Greek, there is neither slave nor free, there is neither male nor female; for you are all one in Christ Jesus' (Galatians 3:27f; cf. 1 Corinthians 12:13; Colossians 3:11). The gift of life in the one body is a call to mutual forgiveness, love and peace (Colossians 3:12–15). Because the Father's purpose for humanity is all-embracing, the stranger in need and even the enemy are potentially brothers and sisters for the Christian [note 1005].

The previous two paragraphs have shown how a baptismal

ethic is relevant to humanity both in its more direct relation to God and as social being. The third aspect of the 'image' which we discovered in chapter I, namely the relation of humanity to creation, may also be illuminated by baptism. The key theme here is royal priesthood [note 1006]. Baptism is a sign of participation in Christ, the anointed king and priest (note the word-play in 2 Corinthians 1:21; 1 Peter 2:9; Revelation 1:6; 5:10). The development of a post-baptismal anointing rite is one of the most complicated stories in liturgical history, but there is no doubt that a part was played in it by the notion of participation in the Christ. Furthermore, all the Eastern rites apart from the Byzantine include a coronation of the newly baptized, perhaps in anticipation of the eschatological victory and reward (1 Corinthians 9:25; 2 Timothy 4:8; 1 Peter 5:4; Revelation 2:10); in any case, the crowning naturally attracts royal and priestly ideas [note 1007]. Even without the benefit of a coronation in his baptismal rite, the American Orthodox theologian Alexander Schmemann interprets the post-baptismal procession to the altar as entrance into the kingdom, having already in connexion with chrismation brought out the significance of Christian participation in the royal priesthood of Christ [note 1008]. It is Orthodox writers who are most sensitive to the cosmic dimension of the royal priesthood to which the human creature is called as creation's king and priest [note 1009]. Ethically, this means that our attitudes and behaviour in respect of the material creation should match up to the human responsibility of serving as God's steward towards the world and the spokesman of the world towards God. Some practical implications of man's place at the articulation between God and the world were outlined in chapter I.

A first journey outward from liturgy to life is now complete. The treatment of baptism under the rubric of freedom and service kept landing us in an area where it becomes convenient to take the triple theme of liberty, equality and fraternity as our secular departure for a passage back towards Christian ritual. The arrival ground this time will tend to be eucharistic.

4. *Liberty, equality, fraternity*

Liberté, égalité, fraternité: the slogan of the French Revolution sums up the best aspirations of modern western secular humanism. The difficulty of their attainment also illustrates the human predicament. The threefold ideal demands the end of contradictions which, in the world as it is, set individual and society in mutual opposition. Individuals have a positive need of their fellows in order to be human. Man is a social being and is constituted in the personal interchange of giving and receiving. Yet social forces easily oppress or diminish particular individuals: society may impose itself on an individual without receiving his intended contribution, or it may take things from him by force while failing to answer his own legitimate expectations. But should the individual be surprised if society on its own scale writes large the self-assertiveness which, as the caricature of his personal dignity, also distorts his own being?

Liberté, égalité, fraternité expresses the ideal of a community in which individualism and collectivism are transcended: on the basis of their equal dignity all human beings have their freedom recognized by their fellows as inviolable and in turn recognize their bond with their fellows in fraternal solidarity. But how is the ideal related to the actual? Do not the perceived interests of particular individuals, or of particular individuals and society at large, clash? But clashes of interest are also clashes of liberty. What kind of equality is to be affirmed when individuals are manifestly unequal in physical and mental capacity and, in every known culture, social circumstance? Is not fraternity as likely to find expression in fratricide as in mutual support? Various attitudes are found towards the gap between the actual and the ideal. A facile optimism expects its historical closure, even though technical progress does not appear to be accompanied by moral progress. On the other hand, a nihilistic despair does not do justice to the positive possibilities which human beings are at least able to conceive. A moderate attitude might consider the triple ideal as a utopia which served to stimulate human effort, and to which humanity might approximate asymptotically. If the utopia, however, is not to be illusory, it must be guaranteed by a divine transcendence. It requires a benevolent creator who sets these values of liberty, equality and fraternity for humanity, who aids human beings to achieve them, and who eternalizes them in a human society beyond the temporal death of individuals, generations, and even the whole race. The Christian tradition, on which revolutionism drew and on which revolutionism remained parasitic even in its own decline into deism and atheism, preaches such a God [note 1010]. Moreover, by its realistic recognition of sin the Christian faith is able to give some account of the present gap between the ideal and hard experience. Before looking at liberty, equality and fraternity in the light of the Christian faith, and focally of its liturgy, we need to tackle more generally the question of the political realm according to the Christian understanding.

In praying for civil rulers, the Anglican Book of Common Prayer lists among the duties of their 'godly and quiet' government 'the punishment of wickedness and vice' and 'the maintenance of true religion and virtue'. There are echoes here of three New Testament passages in particular. First: Romans 13:1–7, where St Paul sees the civil authorities as divinely instituted servants of God and stresses their deterrent and, by implication, protective functions in the face of crime [note 1011]. Second: 1 Timothy 2:1–7, where the apostolic injunction to pray for rulers is closely connected with the spread of the gospel:

> First of all, then, I urge that petitions, prayers, intercessions, and thanksgivings be offered for all men; for sovereigns and all in high office, that we may lead a tranquil and quiet life in full observance of religion and high standards of morality. Such prayer is right, and approved by God our Saviour, whose will it is that all men should find salvation and come to know the truth. For there is one God, and also one mediator between God and men, Christ Jesus, himself man, who sacrificed himself to win freedom for all mankind, so providing, at the fitting time, proof of the divine purpose. Of this I was appointed herald and apostle, to instruct the nations in the true faith.

Third: 1 Peter 2:13–17, which contains the clearest statement that the business of the civil authority is not only to 'punish criminals' but also to 'commend those who do right'.

These scriptural passages have the pre-constantinian empire in view. It is not simply 'all Christian kings, princes and governors', to borrow Prayer Book language, who carry these responsibilities and merit this respect. Traditionally, the Christian understanding has been that civil rulers *as such* have a divinely appointed role in the 'order of preservation', which may be defined as 'that disposition of the world and human society by which God maintains "fallen" humanity in earthly existence'. Their prime job, corresponding to 'the first use of the law', is to regulate society in face of the tendency to anarchy and chaos which expresses the self-centredness and self-assertion characteristic of humanity when it is failing its vocation [note 1012]. They are expected to carry out their task by the 'impartial administration of justice', to modernize a Prayer Book phrase. The resultant tranquillity serves 'true religion and virtue' at least in making opportunity for the preaching of the gospel, as the Reformers emphasized in their support of the existing social order. This in turn may help the civil rulers to go beyond the 'commendation of those who do right' and actually promote, by their own policy and manner of government, the establishment of the values proper to God's kingdom and human salvation. Karl Barth proposed a principle of 'analogy', whereby the civil community should express in an 'exterior' and 'provisional' way the 'interior' and 'definitive' freedom, justice, peace and humanity of the gospel [note 1013]. This is almost to translate into the civil sphere 'the third use of the law', which is as guidance for evangelical living. Clearer expectations in this direction may rightly be entertained of rulers and societies which claim to have accepted the gospel. In so far as saving grace is held to operate beyond the bounds of historic Christianity, there should be a corresponding extension of human responsibility in the matter of giving positive shape to the values of God's kingdom. In section 6 of this chapter we shall face the questions which arise when civil authorities fail in their divinely appointed duties. May and must not God's law itself, in its 'second use', be turned against its defaulting servants in order to bring them to repentance?

To turn now to liberty, equality and fraternity in the light of the Christian faith, and focally of its liturgy. First, liberty [note 1014]. When Yahweh through Moses first told Pharaoh to 'let my people go', it was in order that the people might celebrate a feast to the Lord (Exodus 5:1; cf. 3:18; 8:21). Freedom and worship continued to be associated in Israel's commemoration of its deliverance from the slavery of Egypt. Passover was a meal at which the participants reclined, adopting the posture of free men [note 1015]. The Christian eucharist took over the eschatological expectations from the Jewish paschal meal [note 1016]. The eucharist prefigures and anticipates the messianic banquet under which is pictured the glorious liberty of God's children in his kingdom. Because salvation concerns men and women as integral beings, the freedom they taste in the liturgy may set up a dynamic towards the attainment and preservation of liberty in the political sphere. In return, a vital test of political liberty is freedom of belief and worship, even where these may directly or indirectly amount to social criticism. Practical, even if not always constitutional, restrictions imposed in these areas by communist régimes are matter for charges as serious as those which Marx and Lenin brought against Christianity for diverting the oppressed from an action-provoking awareness of their misery. The question of the stabilizing or subversive function of Christian ritual will recur in the next section but one.

Now, equality. Unafraid of charges of individualism, Wolfhart Pannenberg has advanced the unfashionable thesis that one of the greatest contributions of Christianity to humanity has been the sense of individual dignity [note 1017]. The only ground and meaning for the fundamental and ultimate equality of human beings lies in the love of the God who creates, redeems and sanctifies them all. Their value is constituted by the fact that they are precious in his eyes. James Cone has movingly described the realization of individual worth in the assembly of black american Christians [note 1018]:

The black church congregation is an eschatological community that lives as if the end of time is already at hand. The difference between the earliest Christian community as an eschatological congregation and the black church community is this: The post-Easter community expected a complete cosmic transformation in Jesus' immediate return because the end of time was at hand; the eschatological significance of the black community is found in the people believing that the Spirit of Jesus is coming to visit them in the worship service each time two or three are gathered in his name, and to bestow upon them a new vision of their future humanity. This eschatological revolution is not so much a cosmic change as it is a change in the people's identity, wherein they are no longer named by the world but named by the Spirit of Jesus. . . . The Holy Spirit's presence with the people is a liberating experience. Black people who have been humiliated and oppressed by the structures of white society six days of the week, gather together each Sunday morning in order to experience a new definition of their humanity. The transition from Saturday to Sunday is not just a chronological change from the seventh to the first day of the week. It is rather a rupture in time, a *kairos*-event which produces a radical transformation in the people's identity. The janitor becomes the chairperson of the Deacon Board; the maid becomes the president of Stewardess Board Number 1. Everybody becomes Mr and Mrs, or Brother and Sister. The last becomes first, making a radical change in the perception of self and one's calling in the society. Every person becomes somebody, and one can see the people's recognition of their new found identity by the way they walk and talk and 'carry themselves'. They walk with a rhythm of an assurance that they know where they are going, and they talk as if they know the truth about which they speak. It is this experience of being radically transformed by the power of the Spirit that defines the primary style of black worship. This transformation is found not only in the titles of Deacons, Stewardesses, Trustees, and Ushers, but also in the excitement of the entire congregation at worship. To be at the end of time where one has been given a new name requires a passionate response with the felt power of the Spirit in one's heart.

It would take an insensitive fool to tax with 'escapism' or 'other-worldliness' the following prayer which Cone reports:

And now, Oh, Lord, when this your humble servant is done
down here in this low land of sorrow; done sitting down and
getting up; done being called everything but a child of God; Oh,
when I am done, done, done, and this old world can afford me a
home no longer, right soon in the morning, Lord, right soon,
meet me at the River of Jordan, bid the waters to be still, tuck
my little soul away in your chariot, and bear it away over yonder
in the third heaven where every day will be a Sunday and my
sorrows of this old world will have an end, is my prayer for
Christ, my Redeemer's sake, and Amen and thank God [note 1019].

Cone quotes religiously-inspired slave-insurrections to show
that historical immobilization does not inevitably result from
this compound of liturgically realized eschatology and the
belief in a 'home over yonder':

To be sure, black religion is not a social theory that can be a
substitute for scientific analysis of societal oppression. But it is
a spiritual vision about the reconstruction of a new humanity
wherein people are no longer defined by oppression, but by
freedom. This vision can serve as an important force for organiz-
ing people for the transformation of society. Because black
people know that they are more than what has been defined for
them, this knowledge of the 'more' requires that they struggle to
realize in the society the freedom they experience in their worship
life.

It is only the hope of heaven which truly liberates people for
action in history and sustains them in the struggle:

Black religion, while accepting history, does not limit salvation
to history. As long as people are bound to history, they are bound
to law and thus death. If death is the ultimate power and life has
no future beyond this world, then the rulers of the state who
control the military are in the place of God. They have the future
in their hands, and the oppressed can be made to obey the law of
injustice. But if the oppressed, while living in history, can see
beyond it, if they can visualize an eschatological future beyond
this world, then the 'sigh of the oppressed creature', to use
Marx's phrase, can become a revolutionary cry of rebellion
against the established order. It is this revolutionary cry that is
granted in the resurrection of Jesus. Salvation then is not simply

freedom *in* history; it is freedom to affirm that future which is *beyond* history. . . .

The 'otherness' of salvation, its transcendence beyond history, introduces a factor that makes a difference. The difference is not that we are taken out of history while living on earth—that would be an opiate. Rather it is a difference that plants our being firmly in history because we know that death is not the goal of history. The transcendence-factor in salvation helps us to realize that our fight for justice is God's fight, too, and Jesus' resurrection already defines what the ultimate outcome will be. It was this knowledge that enabled black slaves to live in history but not to be defeated by their limitations in history. . . . Because the slaves knew or believed that death had been conquered in Jesus' resurrection, they could also transcend death and interpret salvation as a heavenly, eschatological reality.

It would have been possible to make many of the same points concerning equality and dignity in a calm exposition of the implications of the eucharist; but I have preferred on this occasion to give the passionate word to James Cone, who speaks from a tradition which is not 'liturgical' in the narrow sense.

Finally, fraternity [note 1020]. The fratricidal tendencies of humanity need to be mastered. The psychic energies spent on hatred need transmutation into love. 'Do not be overcome by evil, but overcome evil with good' was St Paul's exhortation to the Christians in Rome (Romans 12:14–21). The apostle was echoing the teaching of Jesus which St Matthew reports in the Sermon on the Mount. The Christian liturgy provides an opportunity and a pattern for forgiveness, reconciliation and mutual love. Eucharistic rites traditionally include the confession of sins against others, prayers of intercession for people, the exchange of peace, and the sharing of the one bread and the one cup in table fellowship. Early Methodist worship expressed and engendered a strong sense of mutual solidarity, as is obvious from Charles Wesley's hymns. Note particularly the following, from the Methodist Hymn Book:

Blest be the dear uniting love   (No. 712)
Let us join—'tis God commands   (No. 713)

Thou God of truth and love (No. 716)
Help us to help each other, Lord (No. 717)
Christ, from whom all blessings flow (No. 720)
Jesus, united by Thy grace (No. 721)
All praise to our redeeming Lord (No. 745).

These hymns mingle praise, prayer and exhortation. Brotherly and sisterly love is seen both to require human effort and to depend for its origin and continuance on divine grace.

5. *Grace and gratitude*

Having in the last section moved from the secular to the sacred, we shall now travel yet again in the reverse direction from liturgy to life.

Grace and gratitude are linguistically related, as were *charis* and *eucharistia* in Greek [note 1021]. In worship we receive the self-giving love of God, and the test of our thankfulness is whether we reproduce that pattern of self-giving in our daily relationships with other people. Of course, the test already begins with our attitudes and behaviour as brothers and sisters in the liturgical assembly; and of course, the grace of God accompanies us into our daily living. Liturgy appears once more as the focal expression of facts which embrace the whole of our existence [note 1022].

The liturgies provide many examples of what may be called eucharistic ethics. Take first the ancient prayer from 'the Malabar liturgy', well known in the translation by C. W. Humphreys and P. Dearmer (English Hymnal No. 329):

Strengthen for service, Lord, the hands
That holy things have taken;
Let ears that now have heard thy songs
To clamour never waken.

Lord, may the tongues which 'Holy' sang
Keep free from all deceiving;
The eyes which saw thy love be bright,
Thy blessèd hope perceiving.

The feet that tread thy holy courts
From light do thou not banish;
The bodies by thy Body fed
With thy new life replenish.

With less detailed correspondence to the liturgical action, the heart of the matter is nevertheless expressed in the bishop's address to those being ordained to the priesthood in the Roman Catholic church:

> Realize what you are doing. Imitate what you handle. In as much as you celebrate the mystery of the Lord's death and resurrection, endeavour to mortify all sin in your members and to walk in newness of life [note 1023].

Roman prayers make clear that the same is expected of all who receive baptism and communion. The propers of the Easter season include the following petitions [note 1024]:

> Grant that your servants may keep in their lives
> to the baptism they have received in faith.

> Grant that the sacraments we have received at Easter
> may continue to live in our minds and hearts.

> Grant that we may imitate and achieve
> what we celebrate and profess.

> Grant that we who have celebrated the Easter ceremonies
> may hold to them in life and conduct [note 1025].

Not wishing to leap from the frying-pan of works-righteousness into the fire of antinomianism, the Reformers sought to make Christian conduct the thankful response to God's grace. Ethics were grounded in gratitude. Christian deeds were the proper fruit of Christian faith. Sanctification was in fact the continuing work of God in the believer. Its human subjects glorified God in their lives. This complex of themes comes to expression in the two post-communion prayers of the English *Book of Common Prayer*:

> O Lord and heavenly Father, we thy humble servants desire thy fatherly goodness mercifully to accept this our sacrifice of praise and thanksgiving. . . . And here we offer and present unto thee,

O Lord, ourselves, our souls and bodies, to be a reasonable, holy, and lively sacrifice unto thee; humbly beseeching thee, that all we, who are partakers of this holy Communion, may be fulfilled with thy grace and heavenly benediction. And although we be unworthy, through our manifold sins, to offer unto thee any sacrifice, yet we beseech thee to accept this our bounden duty and service; not weighing our merits, but pardoning our offences. . . .

Almighty and ever-living God, we most heartily thank thee, for that thou dost vouchsafe to feed us, who have duly received these holy mysteries, with the spiritual food of the most precious Body and Blood of thy Son our Saviour Jesus Christ; and dost assure us thereby of thy favour and goodness towards us; and that we are very members incorporate in the mystical body of thy Son, which is the blessed company of all faithful people. . . . And we most humbly beseech thee, O heavenly Father, so to assist us with thy grace, that we may continue in that holy fellowship, and do all such good works as thou hast prepared for us to walk in. . . .

Like St Paul in Romans 12:1f, whom he echoes, Cranmer ethicalizes the notion of sacrifice. Yet for all the attacks made by the Reformers on the sacrifice of the mass, Cranmer at least was aware that the ethical sacrifice, because of its doxological dimension, allowed and required a ritual focus for itself in the liturgy, if only in a post-communion prayer of self-oblation and not in any offering of the elements. The Prayer Book themes are taken up and strengthened in the fifth section of the Wesleys' *Hymns on the Lord's Supper*: 'Concerning the sacrifice of our persons'. The Methodist brothers are bold enough to claim that the offering of ourselves, sinners though we are, is 'conjoined' to the all-sufficient sacrifice of Christ. The dominant prayer and desire is for conformation to the Christ-pattern.

In the words of the American Methodist liturgist James F. White: 'Doxological living is the overflowing of the praise begun in worship into all of one's activities' [note 1026]. Contemporary eucharistic revision in the Church of England makes explicit the movement out from liturgy into life:

Almighty God,
we thank you for feeding us
with the body and blood of your Son
   Jesus Christ.
Through him we offer you
   our souls and bodies
to be a living sacrifice.
Send us out
in the power of your Spirit
to live and work
to your praise and glory [note 1027].

6. *Justice and peace*

Having thus been pitched out into the world, we shall find ourselves in this section driven back to prayer. The fact is: the world is not an easy place in which to live doxologically.

If the kingdom of God consists in justice, peace, and joy in the Holy Spirit (so Romans 14:17), our world displays many counter-signs of oppression, war and sorrow. True peace, *shalom*, includes justice. But temporary tranquillity is often purchased at the price of injustice. Failure in justice and peace is a major cause of grief. It is the Christian understanding that, within the order of preservation, the civil authorities have the principal responsibility for justice and peace. Because of the human propensity to sin, the justice of this world is bound to be somewhat rough and ready. But it is also the Christian understanding that worldly justice must nevertheless approximate to the divine justice which, as the will of God, is a mark of his kingdom. If justice becomes intolerably distorted, whether between nations or within a single nation, then the human or the national community as a whole has the right, and even the duty, to bring correction to bear on existing civil authorities, even to the point of overthrowing them if they otherwise fail to 'repent'. This will upset the temporary tranquillity. If force is used as a 'last resort', *ultima ratio*, the arguments just advanced will constitute the fundamental case for a 'just war' or for a 'just revolution', as tyrannicide is now usually called [note 1028]. At this point, the hardest question for the Christian and for the Church is whether they can *ever* initiate, support or even condone the

use of physical force. Is such force not excluded by the teaching and example of 'the pacific Christ' [note 1029]?

Light may be shed on this whole question yet again by the liturgy. Anthropologists and sociologists usually emphasize the stabilizing function of ritual: coronations serve to legitimate the political order. Historically, it must be admitted that sometimes, as in Charlemagne's empire [note 1030] or again in sixteenth- and seventeenth-century England, political authorities have also had an interest in the establishment of liturgical uniformity for the sake of reinforcing the unity of the realm. While a 'godly prince', to use the Reformation terminology, may sometimes be needed in order to purify a corrupt church, secular interference in worship, even by Christian rulers, is not usually desirable: it can too easily infringe the religious liberty which Christianity, on its own deepest principles, should foster [note 1031]. Nevertheless, for all the risks involved in a close association with the civil government, the official liturgies of the Church, in freely praying for rulers, have been following the insight, recognized as we saw in the New Testament, that the 'magistrate' has a divinely appointed function in the order of preservation. Where tendencies to anarchy are posing an intolerable threat to life and limb, the Church may even have the duty of supporting what in political terms will probably be called a 'revolution of the right'. In happier circumstances, the Church will encourage a good government in its attempts to approximate more positively to the justice and peace which mark God's kingdom.

Yet the anthropologists and the sociologists, if they stressed only the stabilizing function of ritual, would be distorting the picture as far as Christianity is concerned. In the Christian understanding, this world is, at best, never more than penultimate [note 1032]. Even relatively good governments are exposed to critique by the absolutely good rule of God in his kingdom. By keeping open the vision of a divine kingdom which transcends anything yet achieved, the Christian liturgy is to that extent subversive of all *installation dans le provisoire* [note 1033]. Christian worship may incite to what in political terms will probably be called a 'revolution of the left'. Worshipping Christians hear the 'prophetic perfects' of the Magnificat and may be expected to align themselves with the revolutionary action of God for the universal implementation of the inaugurated kingdom:

> My soul doth magnify the Lord. . . .
> He hath put down the mighty from their seat,
>   and hath exalted the humble and meek;
> He hath filled the hungry with good things,
>   and the rich he hath sent empty away.
>
>   (Luke 1:46, 52f)

The eucharist, properly celebrated, is a sign of that generous justice by which God invites the hungry and the thirsty to his table (Isaiah 55:1; Luke 6:21) [note 1034]. As the creative prefiguration of the feast which God is preparing for all peoples beyond the conquest of death (Isaiah 25:6–9), the Lord's meal should prompt Christians, who have themselves been welcomed equally to the sacrament, towards a fair distribution of the divine bounties at present made tangible in the earth's resources. For, as was expressed in Vatican II's constitution on the Church in the modern world, and the principle has been developed by the Roman Catholic international theological commission [note 1035]: there is a teleologically positive correspondence between human welfare on earth and final salvation in heaven, between the historical future and the eschatological kingdom. In God's intention, the values of the kingdom are already seeking penultimate embodiment in forms appropriate to our present existence [note 1036].

But how are Christians to judge the most appropriate forms of justice and peace at any particular historical juncture? And may Christians *fight* for justice and, paradoxically, peace? Worship again helps us in the search for answers.

Bearing in mind the politically engaged prophets of the Old Testament, G. Müller-Fahrenholz has advocated a 'dialogue with God' in which worshippers seek to discern the divine *oikonomia* amid the ambiguities of history and so the concrete will of God for them to act on in their own time and place [note 1037]. The ability to distinguish spirits

(1 Corinthians 12:10; 1 John 4:1) is a gift needed not only on the obviously doctrinal plane but also on the ethical plane: where do justice and injustice operate? what course of action is required in order to establish the one and put an end to the other? Specific decisions can only be taken in present reliance upon the Holy Spirit, and that is why direct prayer is called for at every point. In so far as the world is open to transformation towards God's kingdom, new steps can in this way be taken for the victory of divine values in human society. But since God operates through the 'givens' of past experience and present situations, the cult is an occasion for claimed prophetic insights to be tested against scriptures and tradition and against the *sensus fidelium* in this time and this place. The last test in particular may have to be dialectical, for prophetic figures must sometimes exercise criticism within and 'against' the Church (cf. 1 Peter 4:17). Granted the faithfulness of God, authentic prophecy will eventually show itself to have been a recovery and promotion of God's will and purpose as definitively revealed in Jesus Christ.

May, then, *Christians* fight for justice and, paradoxically, peace? Archbishop Anthony Bloom considers that 'the act of prayer is a more essential, final act of rebellion against slavery than taking up arms' [note 1038]. Already Origen had written on 'militant' prayer for a righteous cause and against the forces of evil [note 1039]. When Christians pray with sincerity 'Thy kingdom come, thy will be done on earth as it is in heaven', they are at the least, by their own *disponibilité*, increasing the powers for righteousness in the world. But should their commitment be backed by a willingness to take up arms?

The Christian writers of the early centuries generally considered military service incompatible with membership of the Church [note 1040]. The *Apostolic Tradition* stipulates: 'If a catechumen or one of the faithful wishes to become a soldier (i.e. a volunteer), let him be rejected, for he has despised God.' One reason was the idolatrous practices required of soldiers by the imperial religion, and Christians must always continue to resist the absolutizing of the state or of society. A second reason, however, was the 'pacific' teaching and example of Jesus Christ. Thus Tertullian: 'Is it right to occupy oneself with the sword, when the Lord proclaims that he who uses the sword shall perish by the sword? And shall the son of peace, for whom it is unfitting even to go to law, be engaged in a battle?' With the conversion of the empire under Constantine and Theodosius, a different historical situation obtained. From then on, the implementation of the order of preservation on its political side could no longer be left to a pagan civil authority while Christians kept their hands clean. Prayer for civil order had now to be matched by the assumption of governmental responsibilities. The general opinion has been that in the exercise of police duties, whether nationally or internationally, force may properly be used by Christians when it is a case of life and death. Judgments differ as to when that point is reached in particular cases. Some Christians refused to fight against Hitler. But it is hard to see how a Christian, or indeed anyone with a spark of humanity, could decline to intervene, with whatever force he or she can muster, if a child is being molested. But to intervene, at *risk to one's own life*, on behalf of a *third party*, in an *emergency situation*, is a far cry from using force to assert one's own claimed rights [note 1041]. Where does the possible use of force in a just revolution come in?

People not themselves suffering grave injustice and oppression have little or no existential standing to pronounce on the rightness or wrongness of the use of force in favour of justice and genuine peace. Where Christians see fellow human beings suffering grave injustice, they have a primary duty to pray for them. Intercessory prayer will be sincere when it is accompanied at least by social and political agitation aimed to correcting the injustice. At this point in world history, many Christians will further find themselves in a position to acknowledge their own share of responsibility in the active promotion of, or at least the passive acquiesence in, systemic injustice. This is certainly the case of Christians in the ex-imperialist and neo-colonialist countries of the West in relation to the peoples of the 'third world'. The liturgy may here teach us to hope for a threefold pattern.

First: we must be brought to repentance. The sincerity of our repentance will be shown in its fruits (cf. Matthew 3:8). The fruits may include an ascetic renunciation of material advantages, expressing and promoting our own release from the grip of material*istic* values. The true Christian 'possesses' this world's goods 'as though he did not possess them' (1 Corinthians 7:29–31; cf. Matthew 6:19–21, 24–34, and the parable of the rich fool, Luke 12:13–21). Fasting, for instance, is an exercise of freedom which prevents one's proper bodily appetites from passing into greed. Sacrificial giving prevents the laying up of treasures on earth: it is an entry into the movement of Jesus, who, though he was rich, yet for our sake became poor (St Paul introduces this christological remark while talking of the collection for the needy in Jerusalem, 2 Corinthians 8:9). Such a true ascesis, if undertaken by all Christians who have the opportunity to do so, could help in the revolutionary redistribution of the earth's resources which is necessary if the fast of many other human beings is to become the voluntary renunciation of available food, rather than the enforced lack of any food at all: starvation can be no proper part of either the order of preservation or the order of salvation. Another fruit of repentance will be direct political action towards a more just world order. Meanwhile, oppressors have no cause for complaint if their victims turn violence round against them. According to the book of Jeremiah, social oppression and injustice within the nation were part of Israel's unfaithfulness to Yahweh (2:34; 5:28; 7:5f; 21:12; 22:3, 13–17): and for this the people were to submit, said the prophet, to the Babylonian invasion as to divine judgment (21:1–10; 37–38). Within our present world community, revolutionary action on the part of the oppressed classes and peoples should be understood as divine judgment on the oppressing classes and peoples.

Second: it may nevertheless happen that the oppressed show *forgiveness* to their oppressors. We have no right to expect this, even if we repent. But where forgiveness is granted, we have a sure sign of the salvific presence and action of God—at the deepest level—among the forgiving. People who forgive thereby manifest their conformation to the character of God himself, who forgives undeserving sinners. To be forgiving is to grow in grace. Compare Matthew 6:12 = Luke 11:4; Matthew 18:21–35; Ephesians 4:32. Third, it may then be that *reconciliation* occurs. The oppressor must beware of crying 'reconciliation' too soon, lest it be his own final attempt at avoiding the depths of repentance and softening the demands of his own radical conversion. But when his victim graciously offers forgiveness, he must promptly enter into the proffered reconciliation. Both parties may then experience joy in the Holy Spirit, which is also a mark of God's kingdom. The Christian eucharist may seal the reconciliation, articulate the joy, and keep the values of justice henceforth clear.

7. *Ethics as witness*

Christian ethics is the confession of faith in praxis. This twelfth chapter has been the pendant to the sixth, in which our concern was with verbal confessions of faith. At the end of chapter VI, which marked the mid-point of the book, we drew the threads of worship, doctrine and life more closely together. The same manoeuvre can be undertaken now, to compact the strands again into a confessional node. At the end of chapter VI, attention fell on confession in its direction towards God. Now we concentrate on confession before the world. Christian behaviour is part of the Church's apostolic task.

God has called Christians out of darkness into his marvellous light (1 Peter 2:9). One of the ways in which they are to declare his wonderful works and proclaim his praises, *tas aretas exangellein*, is by their 'good conduct among the Gentiles' (2:12). Their 'good deeds' will cause the Gentiles to 'glorify God on the day of visitation'. We may hope that the conversion of unbelievers to the worship of God by means of this ethical witness may be as much part of 'realized eschatology' as the immediate conversion which St Paul can envisage the visitor undergoing as a result of 'prophecy' in the Christian assembly (1 Corinthians 14:21–25). If Christians, as a holy and royal priesthood, are expected to 'offer spiritual sacrifices acceptable to God through Jesus Christ' (1 Peter 2:5, 9a), their offering will thus unite their own behaviour and the faith of their converts.

Certainly St Paul speaks of his work of evangelism in cultic terms. By bringing the nations to the obedience of faith, he was 'making an offering of the Gentiles': God gave him grace 'to be a minister of Christ Jesus to the Gentiles in the priestly service of the gospel of God, so that the offering of the Gentiles might be acceptable, sanctified by the Holy Spirit' (Romans 15:16) [note 1042]. As the minister of this sacrifice, Paul also spent himself sacrificially, 'poured as a libation upon the sacrificial offering of your faith' (Philippians 2:17). As his own ministry drew to a close, the apostle charged Timothy: 'Endure suffering, do the work of an evangelist, fulfil your ministry. For I am already on the point of being sacrificed; the time of my departure has come' (2 Timothy 4:5f) [note 1043]. The dimension of witness before the world will thus be present also when St Paul summons all Christians 'to present your bodies as a living sacrifice, *thusia*, holy and acceptable to God, which is your spiritual worship, *logikē latreia*. Do not be conformed to this age but be transformed by the renewal of your mind, that you may prove what is the will of God, what is good and acceptable and perfect' (Romans 12:1f). Service in love, for which the apostle invokes no less a model than the one who 'though he was rich, yet for your sake became poor' (2 Corinthians 8:9), is an eminent expression of self-surrender: the liberality which St Paul urged towards the needy in Jerusalem 'and all others' has its part to play in the transformation of the world into a place where thanksgiving, *eucharistia*, abounds to God:

> You will be enriched in every way for great generosity, which through us will produce thanksgiving to God; for the rendering of this service, *hē diakonia tēs leitourgias tautēs*, not only supplies the wants of the saints but also overflows in many thanksgivings to God. Under the test of this service, you will glorify God by your obedience in confessing [note 1044] the gospel of Christ, and by the generosity of your contributions, *koinōnia*, for them and for all others; while they long for you and pray for you, because of the surpassing grace of God in you. Thanks be to God for his inexpressible gift!   (2 Corinthians 9:11–15) [note 1045]

Where divine grace is met by human gratitude, the gratitude is truly expressed in free service to brother, sister and neighbour, and the chorus of thanksgiving resounds to the glory of God at the approach of his kingdom of justice, peace and joy in the Holy Spirit.

It may not be inappropriate to end this final chapter in directly doxological mode, first with a hymn and second [note 1046] with a story. Charles Wesley's hymn expresses the whole life of the Christian in cultic terms:

> O Thou who camest from above
>   The pure celestial fire to impart,
> Kindle a flame of sacred love
>   On the mean altar of my heart!
>
> There let it for Thy glory burn
>   With inextinguishable blaze;
> And trembling to its source return,
>   In humble prayer and fervent praise.
>
> Jesus, confirm my heart's desire
>   To work, and speak, and think for Thee;
> Still let me guard the holy fire,
>   And still stir up Thy gift in me.
>
> Ready for all Thy perfect will,
>   My acts of faith and love repeat,
> Till death Thy endless mercies seal,
>   And make the sacrifice complete.
>
>   (MHB 386)

The story brings out the witnessing quality of a life lived in the divine love. It must stand as a single shining example of what Herbert Butterfield meant when he said that it is impossible to measure the vast difference that ordinary Christian piety has made to the last two thousand years of history [note 1047]. The story comes from a country in which Christians have experienced centuries of suffering, and from a Church which knows that its worship is surrounded by a cloud of martyred witnesses:

A Turkish officer raided and looted an Armenian home. He killed the aged parents and gave the daughters to the soldiers, keeping the eldest daughter for himself. Some time later she escaped and trained as a nurse. As time passed, she found herself nursing in a ward of Turkish officers. One night, by the light of a lantern, she saw the face of this officer. He was so gravely ill that without exceptional nursing he would die. The days passed, and he recovered. One day, the doctor stood by the bed with her and said to him, 'But for her devotion to you, you would be dead.' He looked at her and said, 'We have met before, haven't we?' 'Yes,' she said, 'we have met before.' 'Why didn't you kill me?' he asked. She replied, 'I am a follower of him who said "Love your enemies" '[note 1048].

CONCLUSION

Rewards

1. *Open systems*

I T is tempting to let this book remain without a conclusion. Most of its chapters have been left so unprovided. Readers were thereby implicitly invited to continue their thinking in that perspective without the sense that the answers to genuine questions were already decided in all details. It seemed valuable nevertheless to draw the threads rather more closely together at the end of the sixth and twelfth chapters, in order to indicate a fair measure of coherence in the overall pattern which was being presented. All this is meant as a formal correspondence to the notion of open systems which I hold to be an appropriate way of considering theology, the life of the Church, human existence, and indeed the divine kingdom. The conclusion, for temptations are to be resisted, seeks to apply the model of open systems substantially in those four areas. My belief in open systems is both grounded in and confirmed by my experience of Christian liturgy, with its stable structures that give room for improvisation, its regularities that allow adaptation to circumstance, its familiarities that permit the new to be recognized. Biologically, a closed system is moribund if not quite dead; yet the vital openness can be predicated only of a cohesive system. Spiritually, life and thought require both order and freedom for their flourishing [note 1049].

My modest hope is that this book will have begun to exemplify some of the rewards to be found in doing theology in a liturgical perspective. It is in and through the worshipping community that most believers catch the Christian vision. By this means of tradition the theologian is presented with a body of material which it is his specific duty to reflect on.

The inherited matter will have been shaped by liturgical use and experience. In my judgment, the rites, prayers and formulas which have figured in this book as significant samples present a constant core of substance sufficient to give Christianity a discernable diachronic identity. Even so, the texture of what has been transmitted remains open both on account of the historically varied expressions and understandings and also on account of temporary conflicts, some of which are indeed still awaiting resolution. It stays true, however, that *consistency* of elements and patterns will suitably predominate in our reception of the past, if we hold, as seems to be implied in the practice of worship and prayer, even a minimal doctrine of God's guidance in the life and history of the Church. On the other hand, the main factor of openness will be the questions addressed by the ecclesiastical and socio-cultural context. This does not mean that the inherited system must allow itself to be punctured by any and every sniper's bullet fired from a shifting base. Only those challenges will be accepted which are capable of positive integration into the system. Otherwise the risk is that a vision to which commitment has been given as fundamentally truthful will be altered beyond recognition or even totally destroyed [note 1050].

In those complex ways, the liturgy's own past and its present human surroundings contribute system and openness, whether we have in mind the liturgy itself or the second-order activity of theological reflexion upon it. Even more characteristically, the liturgy is the place in which open systems are maintained in vigour from the inseparable sources of God and his future. As a guide to understanding, Vatican I declared that all the divine mysteries are connected with one another and with man's last end: the implication appears to be that the reference of all doctrines is more or less directly to God, and that a doctrine may be measured against the final destiny he intends for humanity [note 1051]. This dual principle is *a fortiori* applicable to the first-order activity of worship. In one of those superficially surprising coincidences that are more profoundly signs of Christian identity, Vatican I was rejoining the Westminster Assembly and its Presbyterian catechism: the chief end of man is to glorify God and enjoy him for ever.

Worship embodies, and doctrine subserves, the divine kingdom and human salvation. In their present exercise, the future is coming into existence as the achievement of God's intention for humanity. In the liturgy, and correspondingly in theology, we seek to be open not only to our human environment but also, fundamentally and ultimately, to God. We want God to shape and transform our vision and our entire being. Stressing the intellectual aspect, T. F. Torrance writes: 'Worship is the exercise of the mind in the contemplation of God in which wonder and awe play an important part in stretching and enlarging our vision, or in opening up our conceptual forms to take in that which by its nature far outruns them' [note 1052]. If worship is thus, in M. Polanyi's phrase, 'heuristic vision' [note 1053], our improved understanding may also be expected to benefit our character and conduct. The more clearly we behold the Lord's glory, the more brightly should we reflect it in our living (2 Corinthians 3:18) [note 1054]. If as persons we are growing in the moral and spiritual likeness of God, our actions will congruously make us fellow-workers with God in the establishment of his kingdom. A function of the liturgy is by word and sacrament, by image and rite, to evoke the future in which God's kingdom and our salvation will be firmly achieved [note 1055]. In its light we are enabled to appreciate our inheritance from the past for what it has contributed towards the attainment of the twin goal, with the chance of building upon those positive features; and we can also be set free from whatever is restrictive and false in the tradition, with a renewed liberty to attempt intelligent co-operation in the construction of a future conceived by God as including human salvation. The part of theology may be to assist in the translation of vision into effect, the transformation of reality towards its goal. In this sense we may endorse Walter Kasper's statement that truth is what *will be* [note 1056]. Worship enlivens our hope of reaching it.

In many respects, what has been said about open systems in theology could be written large and applied to the official teaching activity of the Church. We shall discuss the matter more precisely as the question of fallibility and infallibility.

Better: the recent shift to the terminology of defectibility and indefectibility betokens a renewed awareness that truth includes life as well as doctrine [note 1057]. Worship, as the symbolic focus of both doctrine and life, will once again concentrate and illuminate our discussion.

2. *Travelling companions*

On several occasions already we have needed to say that the Christian vision supposes at least a minimal belief in God's providential guidance of the Church. This was the case with the composition of the scriptures and the establishment and definition of the scriptural canon. These scriptures, which by their liturgical reading are a principal means of transmitting the Christian faith, themselves speak much of God's fidelity. The God of the Bible is faithful to his purpose, which includes human salvation [note 1058]. Eucharistic prefaces celebrate what the Byzantines call the divine 'philanthropy' by reciting the series of God's mighty acts from creation to the sending of his Son. Every eucharistic gathering is a present claim upon the promises contained in what the Lutherans call the *verba testamenti* [note 1059]. The eucharistic communion is received as what Aquinas and the council of Trent called 'a pledge of our future glory', *pignus futurae nostrae gloriae* [note 1060]. All Christian worship explicitly or implicitly invokes the Holy Spirit who, according to the johannine Christ, will lead believers into all the truth (John 16:13) [note 1061].

Yet God's fidelity is often met by human infidelity. A recurrent burden of the prophetic message in the Old Testament was that Israel went whoring after strange gods. Only a remnant remained, when the divine judgement fell. These things 'are written for our warning' (1 Corinthians 10:11). St Paul tells gentile Christians that branches which have been grafted into the good olive tree may still be removed just as the first branches were not spared 'for their unbelief' (Romans 11:17ff). 'If a man does not abide in me, he is cast forth as a branch and withers' (John 15:6). Changing the image from the horticultural to the pastoral: the English *Book of Common Prayer* confesses that in fact 'we have erred and strayed from thy ways like lost sheep' [note 1062]. All the historic Christian liturgies make direct or oblique confession of sin. Because of the inseparability of faith and life, we may not assume that sin leaves our perception of the truth unaffected. Both the 'faith which believes' and the 'faith which is believed' can be disrupted and spoilt by sin. Before communion in the Roman rite, Christ is prayed to 'look not on our sins but on the faith of your Church'. In my judgment, it would be wrong both to distance Christians and 'the Church' and to posit too readily the existence of a faith adequate to and worthy of its object. The prayer is better seen as the prayer made by a Church of believing Christians for help in their continuing battle against sin. The request aims at 'the peace and unity of your kingdom' [note 1063]. I shall return in a moment to the relation between unity and truth, but let us first examine the eschatological prospect set by the kingdom.

The Bible and the liturgy testify both to divine fidelity and to human faith and faithlessness. They also bear witness that the living God is inexhaustibly God, and they proclaim that the achievement of his sovereign purpose is sure. What this may mean for any of his free creatures which refuse his fellowship, is a question which will re-emerge in the last two sections of this conclusion. Positively, the triumph of God's will appears to imply the ultimate indefectibility of his Church. For it is inconceivable that God in his faithfulness should abandon those who put their trust in him and walk in his ways. In their generation they are his witnesses before the world [note 1064]. However, the problem may well be where, if anywhere, to *locate* the Church at any given moment in history. Certainly St Paul, according to Romans 9–11, considered that Israel had committed corporate apostasy, and we should not consider his comparable warnings to the Church superfluous, though we shall want the apostle's figures of 'the potter's clay' and 'vessels of wrath' in Romans 9:18–24 to be qualified by other pauline, biblical and liturgical evidence concerning the integrity, freedom and responsibility of God's human creatures [note 1065]. Because he holds that 'the gifts and the call of God are irrevocable' (Romans 11:29), St Paul entertains hope for the eventual re-conversion of Israel, if only from jealousy at the inclusion of the Gentiles; but the apostle would assuredly not have located truth with (temporarily) apostate Israel. Nor indeed, as his epistles make clear, did he consider that even believing Christians enjoyed an unruffled perception of God's truth. And for all his confidence in his own apostolic authority and 'his' gospel [note 1066], St Paul included himself among those who still see only 'through a glass darkly'. The liturgies know that sacraments veil as well as reveal.

This eschatological reserve calls, I think, for caution on the part of any ecclesial community claiming infallibility for its carriage of the Christian truth through history [note 1067]. It should seek to remain open to the witness of prophetic and reforming remnants within or even beyond its own bounds. It should recognize the threat and perhaps, with hindsight, the actuality of distortions in its own perception of the truth. It is the Roman Catholic church which has most strongly and centrally institutionalized its claim to infallibility, yet even some moderately conservative theologians in its midst are now willing to admit that certain official expressions of the faith may have been at least 'one-sided', 'incomplete' [note 1068]. Perhaps the 1870 definition of infallibility may itself—and thereby—be included in that category. The Orthodox churches are also persuaded of their own infallibility, even though the organs of its exercise may be more diffuse. The potential spanner for loosening the works in this case is the traditional insistence by the Orthodox themselves that conciliar decisions must (continue to) be 'received' by the faithful. For their part, Protestants should take the *simul justus et peccator* seriously enough to realize that the purity of the gospel is likely to be represented in their own preaching only dialectically or with some adulteration. Nor should Protestants be allowed to dismiss all expansion as extravagance or to confuse simplicity with parsimony. We should open ourselves to the possibilities of J. M. R. Tillard's principle that 'the non-essential is necessary' [note 1069].

The discussion has been moving towards the question of unity and truth. In our eschatological perspective, the historical Church is definitely *in via*, though not yet *in patria* [note

1070]. More appropriate than a statically conceived infallibility or a hopeless fallibility lacking all confidence in divine guidance is the model of ecclesial communities as travelling companions on the journey towards a kingdom whose prince has come ahead and promised to escort us on the way. Let us discuss some of the issues more formally.

The first question is to know who our travelling companions are. We must take some rough-and-ready decisions. Our company comprises those who provisionally appear to be taking the same direction as we believe ourselves guided to pursue. At this stage, there is no need for a church to abandon its own ecclesiology, even if its ecclesiology includes some special claim on behalf of that particular community. In this way, the Orthodox churches have not relinquished their self-understanding as the one true Church upon joining the World Council of Churches, which in the Toronto statement of 1950 declared its own ecclesiological neutrality and thereby sought to allay also some Protestant fears about the creation of one great 'super-Church' [note 1071]. It is nevertheless interesting that thirty or forty years' experience of a certain fellowship in study and practice, and, whatever the difficulties and reservations, in worship and prayer, has led the separate churches to detect a certain ecclesial quality in their relationships which may be considered as at least 'pre-conciliar' [note 1072]. Even without the benefit of membership in the wcc, the Roman Catholic church has begun to modify an earlier exclusivist ecclesiology as a result of a new ecumenical awareness on its own part [note 1073]. On the other hand, many Protestants will have felt it as an approximation to Orthodoxy when, at the New Delhi assembly in 1961, the 'basis' of the wcc became explicitly trinitarian and doxological [note 1074], and, when, at the Nairobi assembly in 1975, the revised constitution stated that the wcc's purpose is to help the churches to advance to 'visible unity in one faith and in one eucharistic fellowship' [note 1075]. Again, the main Protestant churches now recognize, as a result of their developing relations with the Roman Catholic church, that the 'petrine ministry' is part of the ecumenical agenda [note 1076].

Having begun to discover our travelling companions, we can now ask what kinds of mutual help are to be expected. At this point it is worth recalling the earlier testimonies of experienced ecumenists concerning the creative part played by shared worship and prayer in the progress towards consensus in doctrine [note 1077]. For worship not only supplies the atmosphere in which the churches can make the eschatological journey together into all God's truth: it is even now a provisional expression of that truth, and the divine kingdom and human salvation consist in the true worship of God by his creatures. By a joint examination of their common and distinct liturgical pasts, and by the present sharing of worship and prayer, the churches may expect to find mutual support, correction and completion in their perception of the truth. In terms of open systems, the core substance of Christianity will be confirmed by the joyful discovery of common elements and common patterns, while the openness of the communities to one another is likely to bring both challenge and enrichment. No church should insist on the indispensability of a particular feature or the binding character of a particular configuration unless and until it has won the other churches to a positive appreciation of that feature or configuration. On the other hand, churches should be willing to reckon with their own possible blind spots and to allow for a possible revision of their attitudes towards this or that element or pattern. Where tensions remain, they are best faced within a fellowship of worship in which the opposing poles, and perhaps the tensions themselves, can be most deliberately referred to the God whose glory is being sought, and most immediately assessed for the contribution they make to human salvation.

That brings us to the final issue in connexion with fallibility and infallibility, defectibility and indefectibility, or simply the perception and practice of the truth: whether and how God is present with his people to bring them to his kingdom and their salvation. If God is not focally present in worship, then the game is not worth the candle. But that would be to deny two thousand years of Christian experience. The how of God's presence is a question as to both the manner and the character. The norm for the manner of God's presence is set by his presence in the man Jesus. It is, in one sense or another, an incarnational presence. Most obviously, it is mediated by human beings, ministers, preachers, people, human words, human symbols, human rites. The presence, and therefore the truth, of God are thereby mediated in so far, and only in so far, as these human bearers of them are conformed to Jesus Christ, the definitive revelation of God. Less obviously but more fundamentally, the Lord Jesus Christ himself, in the Holy Spirit, is present in the midst of those who assemble in his name as those to whom he has promised his companionship to the end of the age (Matthew 18:20; 28:20). Such, at least, is the testimony borne by worshipping Christians down the centuries, whether they have spoken of the Lord visiting his people or of their own hearts being uplifted to the Lord. That transcendent presence, still incarnational, is also transforming, and so Christians rightly have good hope that their minds are being renewed and their personalities shaped in such ways that they may know and do the will of God (cf. Romans 12:2). God's gracious action requires, as St Paul makes clear in the previous verse, that Christians place themselves at God's disposal. The delicate interplay between grace and freedom has to be considered in the matter of our apprehension of the truth. We are thereby brought to the character of God's presence in worship [note 1078].

Christian worship establishes and expresses the personal character of the relations between God and humanity. The character of Christian worship is that of an encounter in which God speaks to us and gives us the tokens of his love, and in which we offer him our praise and thanks, seek his forgiveness and renew our commitment, ask his help and entrust our future to him. Our knowledge of God is therefore 'personal knowledge' [note 1079]. This in no way precludes our talking *about* him or even indulging in 'propositional theology' on the basis of reflexion upon our experience of him. We may properly speak of his nature, his activity, his purposes, as we have perceived them in the context of worship. Yet the personal character of Christian worship constitutes a threefold reminder: of God's freedom to give himself or to withhold [note 1080]; of the only partial adequacy of human language to express personal relationships; and of our own failures in fidelity towards God. It is in the context of God's faithfulness and these limitations that discussion of fallibility and infallibility, defectibility and indefectibility, must take place. Its proper register is that of hope: *tēi gar elpidi esōthēmen* (Romans 8:24).

3. *Life through death*

'We have been saved in hope': St Paul's sentence characterizes also the existence of the individual Christian in the present age. The aorist verb and the future orientation of the noun mark the tension between the already and the not-yet of Christian existence. The passive voice implies that salvation is God's doing, while hope in the New Testament usually connotes active expectation on our part. These tensions distinguish what Nicholas Lash calls the 'more complex affirmations of eschatological hope' in the creeds: 'I believe in . . . the resurrection of the body, and the life everlasting', 'I look for the resurrection of the dead, and the life of the world to come' [note 1081]. This longest section of our conclusion [note 1082] will examine the relations between life and death in the light of Christian funeral liturgy and of baptism and eucharist as the sacraments in which these two themes figure principally [note 1083]. Special attention will be devoted to martyrdom as the event in which rite, reality and reward are most indissolubly joined.

Burial liturgies meet in the clearest possible way the requirement that worship and doctrine be referred to God and keep the final end of man in view. Burial prayers envisage God as the universal creator and judge, the merciful redeemer and re-creator. The implication is, first, that his authority as judge is grounded in his initial creative activity: it is because he is 'maker of all things' that he is 'judge of all men' [note 1084]. The second implication is that God's redemptive mercy is the moral condition of his exercise of recreative power: the 'comfortable words' are that 'Christ Jesus came into the world to save sinners', and that 'so God loved the world, that he gave his only-begotten Son, to the end that all that believe in him should not perish, but have everlasting life' [note 1085]. In the burial service of the English *Book of Common Prayer*, God is 'God most mighty', 'holy and merciful Saviour', 'most worthy Judge eternal', 'Father of our Lord Jesus Christ, who is the resurrection and the life, in whom whosoever believeth shall live, though he die, and whosoever liveth, and believeth in him, shall not die eternally' [note 1086]. The themes of creation and judgment, mercy and forgiveness, redemption and resurrection find expression in a beautiful Coptic burial prayer:

> O God eternal, who knowest the hidden things before they are, who didst bring all things into being out of nothing, in whose hands is the authority of life and death. . . . A mystery of thine is the creation of man, O Master, and the dissolution of thy temporal creation, and their eternal resurrection. To thee is rendered thanksgiving for all things, and for entry into the world, and for departures out of it in hopes of resurrection. We bless the coming of thy Christ, and the sonship thou hast given us in him, who condescended to our troubles and did raise us with himself into freedom from sufferings. Receive, O Lord, in thy holy charge, this soul of thy servant *N*, and keep it in rest until the resurrection and the appearing of Christ, in the bosom of our holy fathers, Abraham and Isaac and Jacob, whence sorrow and trouble and sighing flee away. And if he have committed any sins against thee as man, forgive him and pardon him, and let all his chastisements pass away, for thou didst not form man unto destruction but unto life. And give him rest in that place; and on us, too, here have mercy, and make us worthy to serve thee with freedom from care. . . . For thou art a merciful God and pitiful, and unto thee we offer up glory and honour and worship, Father, Son, and Holy Ghost, now and ever. Amen [note 1087].

To put these things in the style adopted in this book. First, to call God creator is to say that all life depends fundamentally, permanently and ultimately on him. Second, to call God judge is to imply that he has a will and purpose for his creation, and that human beings for their part have been given freedom and responsibility. Third, to call God redeemer is to give thanks that he has himself, in the person of 'his Son', borne the cost of human failures to rise to the divine vocation. Fourth, to call God the agent of resurrection and re-creation is to hope for his final victory which will include a human salvation wrought out of death and defeat.

Having laid the liturgical epithets under contribution for the doctrine of God as he relates to his creatures, we must now draw on Christian burial for doctrine concerning humanity in relation to God. The first point is that 'natural' life itself is a gift of God. 'The Lord gave, and the Lord has taken away. Blessed be the name of the Lord': the book of *Job* is much used in the liturgy of death [note 1088]. Human beings are free to reject an existence which they were simply 'given', but that is apparently to reject the very stuff out of which salvation might be shaped. That is doubtless the reason for the medieval prohibition, still found in the English *Book of Common Prayer*, against the use of the burial office for suicides as well as the unbaptized or excommunicate; more will be said later about the issues at stake here [note 1089]. The second point is that burial liturgies show an awareness of the enhanced life to which human beings are called, the 'more abundant' life of which the johannine Christ speaks (John 10:10). Psalm 42 figures prominently in funeral psalmody:

> My soul thirsts for God,
> for the living God.
> When shall I come and behold
> the face of God?

Natural life is but the sub-structure for a life of communion with God. It is the high vocation of humanity which makes the mortal predicament correspondingly more profound.

Our third point from the liturgies is in fact the association they make between death and sin. The Old Testament patriarchs died with honour and 'full of years', Enoch and Elijah were 'translated' into God's presence, and Abraham, Isaac and Jacob came to be pictured as the chief guests at the heavenly table; yet the more common fate was a descent into Sheol, where 'the dead do not praise the Lord' (Psalm 115:17; cf. Isaiah 38:18). St Paul sharpens the point: death is 'the wages of sin' (Romans 6:23), sin is 'the sting of death'

(1 Corinthians 15:56). And because of the universality of sin (Romans 3:9–18, 23; 5:12), human death as such is the symbol, the threat, and maybe the actuality, of separation from God. Refusal of God's fellowship means, as it were, a 'second death', a spiritual death of which physical death is the outward and visible sign [note 1090]. On account of this association between sin and death, the burial even of Christians became an occasion for summoning the surviving to repentance. In the *Ecclesiastical Hierarchy* of pseudo-Denis the Areopagite, the penitents, unlike the catechumens, are not to be dismissed from the funeral rites, 'for this spectacle teaches them clearly the uncertainty of the hour of death, the rewards promised to the good by the infallible Scriptures, and the punishment without end with which they threaten the wicked' [note 1091]. The medieval West produced the *Dies irae*, whose original liturgical use was as a sequence for the first Sunday in Advent but which was widely adopted for the mass of the dead (where it figures in the missal of Pius V). The Reformers continued the *memento mori* theme: John Knox's *Book of Discipline* recommends that 'the dead be committed to the grave with such gravity and sobriety as those that be present may seem to fear the judgments of God, and to hate sin which is the cause of death' [note 1092]. The 'art of dying' had been much cultivated in the later middle ages. The mortally sick monk might be laid on a hair-shirt and sprinkled with ashes [note 1093]. A much earlier date may be given to the more humane practice of including in burial prayers petitions for the forgiveness of any sins which the departed might have committed. Funeral offices have often used Psalm 51, doubtless recited vicariously on behalf of the dead person, just as the plea of the penitent thief was sometimes put into his mouth: 'Lord, remember me when thou comest into thy kingdom.'

The fourth point concerns the note of confident hope, even joy, which was struck in early Christian funeral rites, never became completely silenced, and has regained strength in some modern liturgical revisions. This is not to make light of the grief which separation causes the bereaved [note 1094]. At the least, however, the departed brother or sister has been released from the temptations and sorrows of the sin-ridden world: that thought, which is not without parallel in pagan antiquity, is clearly present in the more pessimistic Fathers of the Church [note 1095]; it is the earthly shadow-side of the long traditional prayers that the departed may find a place of refreshment, light and peace [note 1096]; it is expressed in the English Prayer Book thanksgiving 'that it hath pleased thee to deliver this our brother out of the miseries of this sinful world'; and it continues as far as the popularity of E. H. Bickersteth's 'Peace, perfect peace, in this dark world of sin?' as a funeral hymn in the Free churches. In terms of their ultimate destiny, those who die in the faith may more positively be held to have already passed safely beyond the final judgment. Certainly the area around John 5:19–30 is the most common source of gospel readings in the older funeral rites, with verse 24 at its heart:

> Truly, truly, I say to you, he who hears my word and believes him who sent me, has eternal life; he does not come into judgment, but has passed from death to life!

That same passage, however, contains a futurist strain:

> The hour is coming when all who are in the tombs will hear his (the Son's) voice and come forth, those who have done good, to the resurrection of life, and those who have done evil, to the resurrection of judgment.

The final ground of Christian hope is therefore in Jesus Christ as the one who will raise believers up to life at the last day: 'I am the resurrection and the life' is a favourite funeral antiphon. It may be this orientation towards Christ's role in the ultimate future which causes traditional burial rites to make noticeably little use of St Paul's themes concerning his own wish to be 'away from the body and at home with the Lord' (2 Corinthians 5:8), 'my desire is to depart and be with Christ, for that is far better' (Philippians 1:23). The immediate and intermediate state of the faithful departed is more readily pictured in the liturgies as the bosom of

Abraham, Isaac and Jacob, or as the gardens of paradise. A different prayer, from the Armenian rite, nevertheless merits quotation:

> Bring near his spirit, which thou hast consigned and committed into the hand of thy angel, unto the throne of thy holy glory, in company with the other shining souls to rejoice and exult and circle in the dance around thy royal throne, until the day of thy second coming from heaven in the glory of the Father and of all the holy angels, when thou shalt come again to renew and set up afresh thy image [note 1097].

Many such expressions of Christian hope raise questions about present and future, or even time and eternity, and to these we shall return in the very last section of the conclusion. Meanwhile we must look at another, though not unrelated, question raised by the funeral prayers: body and soul.

Traditional Christian burial liturgies distinguish between the soul, which is commended on its journey to God, and the body, which is entrusted to the earth in expectation of the final resurrection. For our purposes there is no need to seek background or parallels in the history of religions: it suffices that this distinction matches the twofold testimony of the New Testament. On the one hand, the pauline texts mentioned in the preceding paragraph are joined by the word of Jesus to the penitent thief, 'Today you will be with me in paradise' (Luke 23:43), and by the apocalyptic picture of Revelation 6:9–11: 'I saw under the altar the souls of those who had been slain for the word of God and for the witness they had borne' (martyrdom, as we shall discover, has always been considered as an immediate gateway to heaven). On the other hand, several New Testament texts envisage, doubtless with variations of detail, that believers will share in a general resurrection at the end of the world: so, for instance, 1 Thessalonians 4:16; 1 Corinthians 15:20–24; Acts 24:15; John 5:28f; 6:40, 44, 54. While it would be unscriptural to maintain the 'natural' immortality of a quasi-divine soul which was released at death from the prison of the body, modern biblical scholars have probably exaggerated the alleged inseparability of body and soul in the interest of seeing human beings as a psychosomatic unity [note 1098]. The gospel word is clear:

> Do not fear those who kill the body but cannot kill the soul; rather fear him who can destroy both soul and body in hell.
> (Matthew 10:28; cf. Luke 12:4f)

More positively put, certain psalms had already adumbrated a fellowship with God which death was powerless to destroy [note 1099], and St Paul declared his overwhelming confidence that not even death 'will be able to separate us from the love of God in Christ Jesus our Lord'—the Christ whom God had already, as it were by anticipation, raised from the dead (Romans 8:11, 28–39). While I am not able to *imagine* human existence without bodily support, human self-consciousness points to a transcendence unsatisfied by all biochemical reductionism and suggests at least a potential or incipient personality which grace may come to realize or perfect. That is the natural (created, not divine) object towards which God's saving love may be directed.

I will return in a moment to the bodily basis, but I must first make one final point concerning the soul as it is distinguished in funeral liturgies. Whereas the earlier Christian prayers concentrated, as the East continued to do, on the place of refreshment, light and peace into which God was asked to admit the faithful soul, the augustinian West, magnifying the simple early petitions for the soul's forgiveness, developed an emphasis on purgatorial cleansing which came to dominate popular appreciation of the liturgy of the dead and eventually outcropped in a pile of multiplied masses and peddled indulgences [note 1100]. Against this distorted understanding of God, man and salvation, the Reformation protested [note 1101]. It was doubtless by reaction that the Reformers largely contented themselves with speaking of the believer's condition between death and resurrection as a state of sleep. Where the English Prayer Book of 1549 still prayed that the departed 'may ever dwell in the region of light, with Abraham, Isaac, and Jacob, in the place where is no weeping, sorrow or heaviness', the Prayer

Book of 1552 simply stated, in a phrase borrowed from Hermann's *Consultation,* that 'it hath pleased almighty God of his great mercy to take unto himself the soul of our dear brother here departed' [note 1102].

To return to the bodily basis of human existence. In *Christianity at the Centre,* John Hick sketched arguments showing that the 'embodied' and the 'mental' or 'spiritual' views of the eschatological condition were equally respectable from a religious-philosophical angle (no doubt the unbeliever would say equally unconvincing) [note 1103]. In this light, I am myself prepared to let 'the Empty Tomb' remain among questions left undecided by historical investigation, provided two thousand years of liturgical testimony to the continuing personal presence of the living Lord Jesus be allowed to shape the core of Christianity [note 1104]. Whether it be the general resurrection or the resurrection of Jesus as the anticipation of that [note 1105], belief that the body is somehow concerned in the affair appears to me to indicate a number of truths which can also be stated in a moderately demythologized fashion. Let me first, however, present some ritual data from Christian burial which emphasize the significance of the body. First: although a few traces remain of the notion that contact with the corpse is a source of impurity (itself perhaps a 'natural' testimony to the value of life), a major factor in the shaping of Christian burial ritual was care for the dead body (and there is no sign of the primitive fear lest failure in this respect cause the offended spirit to visit the survivors for their neglect). Second: the medieval custom was to bury the dead with their head to the west and their feet (sometimes shod!) to the east, so that they might immediately stand erect at the appearance of Christ on his return in the East [note 1106]. Third: although the Reformed tradition was to make little ceremony of death and burial, Calvin saw burial itself (and the biblical usage of ointment and spices) as witnessing, against pagan denials, to the resurrection and the 'new life prepared for the bodies laid away' [note 1107]. Fourth: for all the unseemliness and superstition which have distorted the cult of relics, the long tradition of building altars over the remains of saints and

martyrs testifies to a high view of the body as a temple of
the Holy Spirit.

The cardinal point seems to me this: the physical or
biochemical sub-structure of the body, its particular location
in human history and culture, and the prospect of bodily
death, all together supply the necessary constraints within
which identifiable human personalities can take systemic
shape. This anthropological fact has consequences in several
areas of theology. Christologically, it makes 'the quest of
the historical Jesus' indispensable: it matters *which* human
being was crucified and raised; the character and conduct of
Jesus of Nazareth belong to the core of Christianity. Soteriologically, the lineaments of a personality developed in the
course of an earthly life will enduringly characterize the
subject in the divine kingdom: although salvation implies
for sinners a purification and a transformation which continue
through death, and even beyond, yet the personal continuity
of the beneficiary from beginning to end is everywhere
supposed by Christian funeral prayers and practices; it is the
soul of *this* person which is being commended and *his or her*
body which is being buried in hope of the resurrection.
Ethically, behaviour in our earthly span is invested with
eternal seriousness:

> For we must all appear before the judgment seat of Christ, so
> that each one may receive good or evil, according to what he
> has done in the body.   (2 Corinthians 5:10)

From what has been said earlier it will be obvious that when
I thus point out the constraints necessary to the systemic
constitution of human personality, I am not wishing to forget
the concomitant necessity of openness to fellow human beings
and to God, if the human personality is to have a future.
This complementary theme of openness will gradually receive
a compensating emphasis. The way will be by considering
on a sacramental basis both the paradox and the strange
continuity implied in the notion of life through death [note
1108].

'He became obedient unto death, even death on a cross'

(Philippians 2:8): the death of Jesus was the culminating point of a life of obedience to God (Hebrews 5:8), a final surrender to the Father (Mark 14:36; Luke 23:46). Whatever 'theory of the atonement' be used to conceptualize it, the Christian faith sees the death of Christ as marking *potentialiter* the end of human sinning. In terms of Romans 6, baptism is a sacrament of participation in Christ's death and therefore constitutes, in the modes of both gift and task, an end to sin. The living God raised faithful Jesus to a life in which death has no more dominion. In Christ, believers are called and enabled to 'walk in newness of life', in anticipation of a final conformation to him in resurrection. Our 'old self has been crucified with him'. To live not unto self but unto God spells righteousness, sanctification, and ultimately 'life eternal'. All this is a free gift of God, needing only to be appropriated. In this baptismal perspective, death is the gateway to life [note 1109]. Christian burial liturgies can look on death as the 'completion' of baptism. So paschal psalms, such as psalms 42–43, 114 and 116, are common to Easter, baptism and burial. The palm and olive branches of the funeral procession described by John Chrysostom [note 1110] evoke both the passover of Jesus and Christian baptism. In the *Ecclesiastical Hierarchy*, Denis connected the anointing of the corpse at the end with the anointing of the body at the beginning of baptism [note 1111]. The Western sprinkling of the bier with holy water recalls baptism, just as the *Asperges* has done at Sunday mass.

The eucharist itself is a paschal sacrament, the memorial of Christ's death and resurrection. Ignatius of Antioch called it 'a medicine of immortality, an antidote against death and for life in Jesus Christ for ever' [note 1112]. In the dual perspective of the Fourth Gospel, the eucharist is both the sacrament of eternal life already begun and also the promise of resurrection by Jesus at the last day (John 6). In correspondingly bold language, Cyril of Alexandria called the body received in communion 'a life-giving seed', 'a seed of immortality' [note 1113]. Burial is the opportunity for germination (John 12:24). Some delay is envisaged before flowering and fruit (James 5:7f). Whatever the meaning and extent of the resurrection wait [note 1114], the transformation of the

30

Christian is already under way. And, with yet another change in imagery [note 1115], final communion before bodily death is taken as a *viaticum*, provision for the soul's journey [note 1116]. The eucharistic life will be crowned by the banquet of the kingdom: 'he was nourished with your body and blood; grant him a place at the table in your heavenly kingdom' is a thoroughly traditional request in the new US Episcopal *Book of Common Prayer* (1976/77). It is to this joy feast of the Master that the burial liturgies pray the 'good and faithful servant' may be admitted [note 1117].

Rite, reality and reward are wonderfully concentrated in martyrdom [note 1118]. As she stood in the arena, Thecla threw herself into the water with the words 'In the name of Jesus Christ I baptize myself for the last day' (*Acts of Paul and Thecla*, 34). There are echoes of baptism in Polycarp's confession 'Eighty-six years I have served Christ, and he has done me no wrong: how then can I blaspheme my king who saved me?' The old bishop cast his final prayer in the form of a *eucharistia*:

> Lord God almighty, Father of thy beloved and blessed child Jesus Christ, through whom we have received knowledge of thee, God of angels and powers and of all creation and of the whole race of the righteous who live before thy face: I bless thee for granting me this day and hour, so that I may be numbered among the martyrs and given a share in the cup of Christ, to the resurrection of eternal life, in both soul and body, in the incorruption of the Holy Spirit. May I be welcomed among them this day before thy face as a rich and acceptable sacrifice, as thou didst prepare and reveal it beforehand and hast accomplished it, thou the faithful and true God. For this and for all things I praise thee, I bless thee, I glorify thee through the eternal and heavenly high priest Jesus Christ thy beloved child, through whom to thee [with him and the Holy Spirit] be glory now and for the ages to come.   Amen [note 1119].

Blandina, one of the martyrs at Lyons, is said to have been 'clothed with Christ'; as she was tied to the stake in prayer, her fellow-Christians saw in their sister the crucified Lord; when she was at last thrown to the wild beasts, she went 'like one bidden to a marriage supper' [note 1120]. The 'baptism of blood' [note 1121] was in fact popularly held to give immediate access to the heavenly feast [note 1122]: Agathonica perceives that she too has been invited to the 'glorious feast' to which Papylus and Carpus have already been called; James and Marianus are promised by a boy martyr that this very evening they too will be dining at the *convivium* of Agapius and the other martyred friends. The earthly eucharist was experienced as the foretaste of the heavenly banquet: that is why the martyrs of Abitinae in the time of Diocletian made *sine dominico non possumus* their watchword, 'we cannot do without the Lord's supper'.

The fellowship of martyrdom points up the corporate nature of the Church as the body of Christ into which all believers are baptized and which they become in and through eucharistic communion [note 1123]. Surrender to God in Christ opens people to mutual love: God's love is shed abroad in our hearts by the Holy Spirit (Romans 5:5). Martyrs are prize examples of the indwelling Spirit of love. That is why they are attractive to the rest of us: from early times the local churches kept the anniversaries of their martyrs' deaths, their 'birthdays' to the life of heaven; an old Western funeral antiphon prays that the departed may be welcomed by the martyrs and led by them into the holy city of Jerusalem [note 1124]; traditional eucharistic liturgies commemorate the martyrs and ask that we may share with them in the divine kingdom. The witness of the martyrs in their self-offering proves historically to be the inspiration of faith and love in others. According to Tertullian, the martyrs were the secret of the early Church's growth: 'The blood of the martyrs is the seed of the Church' [note 1125]. Tales of the martyrs have been a source of courage to many. Liturgical recognition of martyrs has often transcended the lines drawn by schism, so that the martyrs have been channels of peace between divided communities. Out of their deaths has come life in these various ways. Their passion has united and conformed them to Christ, through whom the life of God reaches us.

With that we come close to the heart of the paradox and strange continuity of life through death. Death allowed Jesus

Christ to love his friends 'to the end' (John 13:1). His body was given and his blood was shed for them and for the many, in fact for the life of the world (Mark 14:22–24; Luke 22:19f; 1 Corinthians 11:23–25; John 6:51). Therein he demonstrated the love of God who sought the human race for friendship even while it was at enmity with him: 'God shows his love for us in that while we were yet sinners Christ died for us' (Romans 5:6–10). When death is encompassed by the living God, it becomes the expression of self-giving love [note 1126]. The divine self-giving passed through creation, incarnation, crucifixion: finding human reciprocation in Jesus it returned to enrich the Godhead through the exaltation of the man who, lifted up, becomes a point of attraction for all. (I shall seek to justify the idea of 'enriching the Godhead' in the next and final section.) We now have the chance of entering into the movement of Jesus' self-giving: 'Whoever would save his life will lose it: and whoever loses his life for my sake and the gospel's will save it' (Mark 8:34–38). To love the God of Jesus Christ is also to love one's fellow human beings without distinction (Matthew 5:43–48). Renunciations receive ample reward in the kingdom (Matthew 19:29). The reward of love is to find one's identity in a community of ever-broadening and ever-deepening love. Equally intrinsic is the reward of failure to open oneself, in gift and receipt, to the others and to the Other: the *cor in se incurvatum*, the heart turned in upon itself, is moribund [note 1127].

4. *The divine kingdom*

It remains to thematize three matters which, because they bear most directly on God himself and touch man's destiny in the most final sense, are at once among the most important and the most difficult questions in all theology. They bring together the divine kingdom and human salvation and ask first about their advent, second about their scope, and third about their reciprocal relation. Not much new material will be introduced. Rather questions will be formulated, to which the re-reading of the book would furnish the adumbration of answers, but which readers are invited to carry with them into their own theological reflexion. My conviction, as throughout, is that the liturgical perspective will once more illuminate the issues, and my wish is that readers will pursue their thinking in this light.

First, the *advent* of the divine kingdom and human salvation. The question is that of the relation between present and future. Behind that stands the question of time and eternity. What God's eternity means for God in himself, God alone knows. Can it properly equated with 'sempiternity', being without beginning or end? 'Everlasting' and 'eternal' appear as liturgical variants. Some modern theologians certainly let being include becoming, even in the case of God. Our own experience, not least in worship, with memory and anticipation, *anamnesis* and *prolepsis* [note 1128], suggests that successiveness may not be without the possibility of an integration into simultaneity. Yet some would consider that such views threaten the sovereignty of God over time which Augustine's doctrine of creation *cum tempore* and not *in tempore* was designed to safeguard. The idea that temporality is a function of creation may be a pointer to all that we as creatures may know, or need to know, about time in relation to God. Whatever may be the case with God in himself, his decision, by an irreducible act of will, to create a temporally structured universe means that he must, in Brian Hebblethwaite's words, 'relate himself to it in a mode appropriate to its temporality. This is part of God's self-limitation, his *kenosis*, in creation' [note 1129]. If God is prepared to do that, there appears to be no cause for shame in the human use of time language in connexion with the coming of God's kingdom and the attainment of our own salvation.

The classical liturgies speak of the first and the second or final advent of Christ. They thereby express the tension between the already and the not-yet of the divine kingdom and human salvation. There appears to be both a qualitative and a quantative gap between what is and what will be, between what we know and what we hope for. The advent of Christ in our historical worship is with a view to advancing God's inaugurated kingdom and man's inchoate salvation by enabling a deeper and a wider human response to the divine self-gift. 'Blessed is he who came and who will come' is a

Syrian greeting to Christ in his eucharistic coming. J. J. von Allmen sees the Church's worship and mission as 'un pro-phétisme sacramentel', in and through which God's future becomes graciously present: 'Il y a sacrement là où l'éon à venir élit, atteint, exorcise (ou pardonne), occupe et consacre un élément de l'éon actuel et donc s'y rend present. Le sacrement est une répercussion de la première et un gage de la seconde venue de Jésus-Christ, luiquiest le sacrement par excellence. Le sacrement est prophétique en ce sens qu'il est pour l'éon présent à la fois une menace et une promesse, lui signifie sa fin et son avenir, l'appelle à la repentance et à l'espoir' [note 1130]. This age is renewed by being, in Olivier Clément's image, 'porous' to the age to come [note 1131]. Although the definitive character of the world to come appears to be such that the kingdom will be incontestably established and salvation inamissibly enjoyed, there is no reason to think that this means an end of open systems: the inexhaustible riches of God will allow for continuing growth in the relations between him and his perfected creatures [note 1132].

Second, the *scope* of the divine kingdom and human salva-tion. It is a question here of the quantitative and qualitative dimensions which God's kingdom and man's salvation may be expected to attain. Drawing on the praise of divine love in Ephesians 3:17–19 [note 1133], Charles Wesley took length and breadth to signify the comprehensiveness of its range, and height and depth the completeness of its achievement:

> What shall I do my God to love,
>   My loving God to praise?
> The length, and breadth, and height to prove,
>   And depth of sovereign grace?
>
> Thy sovereign grace to all extends,
>   Immense and unconfined;
> From age to age it never ends;
>   It reaches all mankind.
>
> Throughout the world its breadth is known,
>   Wide as infinity;
> So wide it never passed by one,
>   Or it had passed by me.

My trespass was grown up to heaven;
     But far above the skies,
In Christ abundantly forgiven,
     I see Thy mercies rise.

The depth of all-redeeming love
     What angel tongue can tell?
O may I to the utmost prove
     The gift unspeakable.

Deeper than hell, it plucked me thence;
     Deeper than inbred sin,
Jesus's love my heart shall cleanse
     When Jesus enters in.

Come quickly, gracious Lord, and take
     Possession of Thine own;
My longing heart vouchsafe to make
     Thine everlasting throne.

Assert Thy claim, maintain Thy right,
     Come quickly from above;
And sink me to perfection's height,
     The depth of humble love [note 1134].

Less ecstatically, the issues are those of universalism and perfection.

That God wills the salvation of all is not a thesis which depends simply on formal traffic in isolated scriptural texts, as for example 1 Timothy 2:3f: 'God our Saviour . . . desires all men to be saved and to come to the knowledge of the truth'. The substantial argument resides in the inconceivability of the opposite intention towards any of his creatures on the part of a Creator whose motive in creation is irreducibly love. A love which took self-giving to the point of suffering crucifixion is likely to be deep enough to persist while ever there is any chance of response. God's grace may then be expected to assume and develop even the slightest human motion towards love. Considerations of theodicy will point to particular divine care for those individuals whose own capacity for love has been intolerably restricted by nature or society. It may be that the only way to fail salvation is by wilful refusal. Programmatic universalism would be a totalitarian threat to the freedom which must characterize any human response in kind to the love of God towards us. Deliberate closure to the love of God to the point of irretrievability spells death. That such death should be subjectively experienced, permanently and eternally, makes no sense. Hell will be empty, though God may continue to bear in his heart the wounds he incurred through taking the risk of love in creation.

This vision matches, I think, the liturgical practice of the Church. Prayer is made for the whole human race in all its needs and in the hope that all people will come to enjoy salvation in the divine kingdom. Christians take the eucharist as a sacramental foretaste of the banquet in the final kingdom, in keeping with the already and the not-yet of salvation. The traditional prayer that communion may serve us for salvation and not for condemnation—Syrian anaphoras take delight in depicting the glorious return of Christ to exercise judgment [note 1135]—shows an awareness that heaven is not yet inamissibly ours but rather beckons us on towards perfection (cf. Philippians 3:10–21). Excommunication, where practised, is a more dramatic call to perseverance, always with the prospect that the chastised may be restored, preferably in this life but at least in the end (cf. 1 Corinthians 5:5) [note 1136]. The ancient admission of catechumens to the service of the word and their dismissal before the eucharist proper exemplifies the truth that the gospel is meant for all people and awaits the committed response of which baptism is the sacramental sign. In all of this, Church and sacraments are non-exclusive promises in the sense in dicated in chapter IV §9.

It is the sacraments which point to the extension of salvation beyond the human community. They suggest how the rest of creation may be included within the scope of God's intended kingdom. As we saw in chapter I in connexion with the earthly task of humanity, sacramental action is a paradigm in which the material creation is allowed to serve the purpose of human communion with God in a most explicit way. S. W. Sykes writes that we should not, as 'aristocrats of the mind', scorn the suggestion that 'new heavens and a new earth will bear a relationship to the physical environment of our present life'. Heaven becomes 'the future of that in us and in our interaction with the world which is of ultimate worth; that, in other words, which has become part of the completion of the will of God in time, and which may not, therefore, be allowed "to slip away from Him into futility or nothingness" ' [note 1137]. What that would mean object- ively for any parts of creation standing in no significant interaction with humanity or with any other personal beings, and what it would mean subjectively even for the sub-human creation directly around us, are matters that would take present speculation beyond useful limits.

As already hinted, the scope of salvation is also a matter of quality. There is the question of perfection or the completeness of achievement. John Wesley preached 'entire sanctification' or 'perfect love' [note 1138]. The perfection which he believed attainable in this earthly life was limited. Negatively formu- lated, it was the condition in which no sinful attitude or action was deliberately entertained or committed. While person and will and act must never be separated, psychology and sociology now suggest that some of the features which Wesley allowed as remaining 'frailties' are more constitutively related to human personality than an overly voluntarist or individualist view would recognize. Positively formulated, perfection meant for Wesley the pure love of God and neighbour. Here he himself recognized the room left for increase. Prolonging the perfectionist thrust of Wesley beyond the ending of earthly life, we may look for continuing personal growth in the nearer presence of God. Despite the insistence of Nicholas Cabasilas that it is a case of thanksgiving being offered 'for' the saints when they are commemorated in the liturgy [note 1139], it may be that a nuance of supplication still attaches to the preposition *pro* or *huper* even at the mention of the saints: certainly some Syrian and Armenian prayers read in that way, and the explanation given is that the saints them- selves have not yet quite reached perfection [note 1140]. We may here have a clue why the second advent of Christ and the final resurrection are still 'awaited'. Because of the communal nature of humanity and salvation, none is perfect until all are perfect. The kingdom will (have) come only when each and all of its beneficiaries have been irreversibly transformed into the moral and spiritual likeness of God. Even in this definitive condition, progress will still be possible on account of the inexhaustibility of God. But human lapses will be a thing of the past. The abstract quibbler may scent here a loss of liberty: existentially it will rather be a case of mature persons finding their perfect freedom in the service of a God who calls us not servants but friends (cf. John 15:15).

We thus reach the third and final question: briefly, the *reciprocal relation* between the divine kingdom and human salvation. A reciprocal relationship between God and humanity is both the condition and the content of Christian worship. Once God, by an irreducible act of will and for the irreducible motive of love, brings a responsive creature into being, he is seeking to draw such a creature into a communion with himself which will be both the creature's salvation and the realization of his own purpose. In worship we take in the outpouring of God's creative and redemptive love, and we offer in return our thanks and supplications. In this personal exchange we are coming into the moral and spiritual likeness of our Lover. This transformation is our glorification in both the objective and the subjective senses: by grace we are being made partakers of the divine nature, and in humility God is being enriched by the requital of his love on the part of his creatures. Our being changed from glory into glory is itself for the greater glory of God [note 1141].

At its own provisional conclusion a systematic theology may open into direct prayer for the unfettered circulation of glory which will be both God's kingdom and our salvation:

> Finish then Thy new creation,
>   Pure and spotless let us be;
> Let us see Thy great salvation,
>   Perfectly restored in Thee;
> Changed from glory into glory,
>   Till in heaven we take our place,
> Till we cast our crowns before Thee,
>   Lost in wonder, love, and praise.

NOTES

1. Theologians in the past have usually been male. For policy on the use of masculine and feminine language in this book, see note 870.

2. A. Jeffner, *Kriterien christlicher Glaubenslehre: eine prinzipielle Untersuchung heutiger protestantischer Dogmatik im deutschen Sprachbereich*, Uppsala: Almqvist & Wiksell, 1977, pp. 138–45; and, less directly, *The Study of Religious Language*, London: SCM, 1972, especially pp. 128–31. I also feel a certain affinity with T. W. Jennings, although our books are very different: see his *Introduction to Theology: an Invitation to Reflection upon the Christian Mythos*, Philadelphia: Fortress, 1976, and London: SPCK, 1977.

3. In his *Theology in Reconstruction*, London: SCM, 1965, T. F. Torrance suggests that the Greek way of thinking was a kind of seeing, whereas the Hebrew, Biblical and Reformation way of learning and knowing was through 'listening and responding, serving and obeying' (pp. 14f, 20f). In view of the prominence of visual imagery in the present book, I can only plead at the outset that the prophets could also 'see' the 'word' of the Lord (Amos), and that my vision includes strong practical, ethical and, in Torrance's term (p. 72f), 'kinetic' components. Physiologically, psychologically and aesthetically, I have a sharper visual than auditory awareness.

4. See, briefly, the critiques made of Freud, Marx and Durkheim in D. W. D. Shaw, *The Dissuaders*, London: SCM, 1978.

5. There is force in Marx's refusal to let us escape into an ideal Christianity distinct from our historical manifestation and function: see P. Frostin, *Materialismus, Ideologie, Religion: die materialistische Religionskritik bei Karl Marx*, Munich: Kaiser, 1978.

6. In the earliest evidence for creeds, there is some tension between threefoldness and fivefoldness, although the ecclesiological and eschatological references usually find themselves integrated in one way or another into the pneumatological 'third article'. Explaining the five loaves of the feeding miracle, the second-century *Epistula Apostolorum* states that Christian belief is in the Father, in Jesus Christ, in the Holy Spirit, in the holy Church, and in the forgiveness of sins. The third baptismal question in the Latin version of *The Apostolic Tradition* reads 'Credis in Spiritu sancto et sanctam ecclesiam et carnis resurrectionem?' Cyprian testifies to the baptismal interrogation 'Do you believe in remission of sins and life eternal through the holy Church?' (*ep.* 69, 7, CSEL p. 756). The creed in the Dêr Balyzeh papyrus should be similarly construed: 'and in the Holy Spirit, and in the resurrection of the flesh in the holy catholic church'. Note, finally, P. Nautin, *Je crois à l'Esprit saint dans la sainte Église pour la résurrection de la chair*, Paris: Cerf, 1947. On the whole question of the early

structures and forms, see the opening chapters of J. N. D. Kelly, *Early Christian Creeds*, London: Longmans, 1972³. We shall ourselves be finding considerable interweaving of pneumatology, ecclesiology and eschatology in chapters III and IV.

7. J. H. Newman, *Essay on the Development of Christian Doctrine*, 1878 edition, chapter 1, section 1.3: 'Christianity is dogmatical, devotional, practical all at once.' Newman's triads are not always the same. In the 1877 preface to the Lectures on the Prophetical Office of the Church (in *Via Media*), the three are: (1) philosophy, theology or doctrine; (2) religion, worship or rite; (3) polity, rule or government.

8. N. Smart, *The Religious Experience of Mankind*, New York: Scribner, 1969, and London: Collins, 1971.

9. 'Cultic' categories figure very prominently in B. Welte's *Religionsphilosophie*, Freiburg: Herder, 1978.

10. The biblical basis of his work is manifest in his Fernley-Hartley lecture of 1953: A. R. George, *Communion with God in the New Testament*, London: Epworth, 1953.

11. At Queen's, Birmingham, our developed practice in the formation of candidates for the 'non-stipendiary ministry' has been to teach liturgy as a foundation course, in order to begin at the place where most students have appropriated the Christian faith.

12. Although I know of no other complete systematic theology written from a liturgical perspective, there exist several theologies of worship, which it is my secondary purpose to supply also in this book. The following may be mentioned: J. J. von Allmen (Swiss Reformed), *Worship: its theology and practice*, London: Lutterworth, 1965; L. Bouyer (Roman Catholic), *La vie de la liturgie: une critique constructive du mouvement liturgique* (ET *Liturgical Piety*, Notre Dame: University Press, 1955, and *Life and Liturgy*, London: Sheed & Ward, 1956), and *Le rite et l'homme: sacralité naturelle et liturgie*, Paris: Cerf, 1962 (ET *Rite and Man: Natural Sacredness and Christian Liturgy*, Notre Dame: University Press, and London: Burns & Oates, 1963); P. Brunner (Lutheran), 'Zur Lehre vom Gottesdienst der im Namen Jesu versammelten Gemeinde' in K. F. Müller and W. Blankenburg (eds.), *Leiturgia: Handbuch des evangelischen Gottesdienstes*, vol. 1, Kassel: Stauda, 1952, pp. 83–364 (ET *Worship in the Name of Jesus*, St Louis: Concordia, 1968); F. W. Dillistone (Anglican), *Christianity and Symbolism*, London: Collins, 1955; W. Hahn (Lutheran), *Die Mitte der Gemeinde: zur Frage des Gottesdienstes und des Gemeindeaufbaus*, Gütersloh: Mohn, 1959 (ET *Worship and Congregation*, London: Lutterworth, 1963); J. A. Kay (Methodist), *The Nature of Christian Worship*, London: Epworth, 1953; E. J. Lengeling (Roman Catholic), articles 'Kult' and 'Liturgie' in H. Fries (ed.), *Handbuch theologischer Grundbegriffe*, Munich: Kösel, 1962–63, vol. 1, pp. 865–80, vol. 2, pp. 75–97; A. Schmemann (Orthodox), *Introduction to Liturgical Theology*, Portland, Maine: American Orthodox Press, and Leighton Buzzard: Faith Press, 1966; E. Underhill (Anglican), *Worship*, London: Nisbet, 1936; C. Vagaggini (Roman

Catholic), *Il senso teologico della liturgia*, Rome: Edizioni paoline, 1965[4] (ET *Theological Dimensions of the Liturgy*, Collegeville, Minn.: Liturgical Press, 1976); P. Verghese (Syrian Orthodox), *The Joy of Freedom: Eastern Worship and Modern Man*, London: Lutterworth, 1967; A. Verheul (Roman Catholic), *Einführung in die Liturgie*, Freiburg: Herder, 1964 (ET *Introduction to the Liturgy*, London: Burns & Oates, 1968, and Wheathampstead: Anthony Clarke, 1972); World Council of Churches, *Report on Worship*, Faith and Order Paper no. 39, Geneva, 1963. Among theologies of the sacraments the following may be noted: N. Clark (Baptist), *An Approach to the Theology of the Sacraments*, London: SCM, 1956; J. D. Crichton (Roman Catholic), *Christian Celebration: The Sacraments*, London: Chapman, 1973; D. L. Gelpi (Roman Catholic), *Charism and Sacrament*, New York: Paulist Press, 1976, and London: SPCK, 1977; B. Häring (Roman Catholic), *The Sacraments in a Secular Age*, Slough: St Paul Publications, 1976; B. Leeming (Roman Catholic), *Principles of Sacramental Theology*, London: Longmans, 1960[2]; F. J. Leenhardt (Swiss Reformed), *Parole visible: pour une évaluation nouvelle du sacrement*, Neuchâtel: Delachaux & Niestlé, 1971; O. C. Quick (Anglican), *The Christian Sacraments*, London: Nisbet, 1927; J. L. Segundo (Roman Catholic), *The Sacraments Today*, Maryknoll: Orbis, 1974; and (I note with special pleasure the Fernley lecture of 1927) C. Ryder Smith (Methodist), *The Sacramental Society*, London: Epworth, 1927. To give titles on the individual sacraments and other rites would prolong this list unduly, but see notes 182, 184, 187, 190, 192, 194, 195. Bibliographical information on baptism and the eucharist can be found in my *Christian Initiation* (1969), *Eucharist and Eschatology* (1971), and 'Recent thinking on Christian beliefs: baptism and eucharist' in *Expository Times* 88 (1976–77), pp. 132–37.

13. On the prominence of 'anthropology' in modern theology, and with essays on Bultmann and Barth, see H. Fischer (ed.), *Anthropologie als Thema der Theologie*, Göttingen: Vandenhoeck & Ruprecht, 1978.

14. K. Rahner's position is stated resumptively in his *Grundkurs des Glaubens*, Freiburg: Herder, 1976 (ET *Foundations of Christian Faith*, New York: Seabury, and London: DLT, 1978). See also F. Greiner, *Die Menschlichkeit der Offenbarung: die transzendentale Grundlegung der Theologie bei Karl Rahner*, Munich: Kaiser, 1978.

15. For the *imago Dei* theme in the history of theology, see D. Cairns, *The Image of God in Man*, London: SCM, 1953, revised edition Collins, 1973, and G. C. Berkouwer, *De mens het bild Gods*, Kampen: Kok, 1957 (ET *Man the Image of God*, Grand Rapids: Eerdmans, 1962).

16. The echo here is of Romans 1:18–32.

17. Throughout this chapter and book I am assuming a fundamental and final unity of the human race, grounded in the creative intention of God and aimed towards a destiny of salvation in the divine kingdom. This does not exclude a positive and no doubt permanent diversity at the level of nature, nor the negative divisions which will last (only) as long as sin persists. These questions emerge explicitly in chapter XI under the

heading Culture. Meanwhile we note that the universal vision of Christianity concerning humanity is given striking liturgical expression when the eucharistic president speaks on behalf of the whole race in the Alexandrine anaphora of *St Gregory Nazianzen*: 'As the lover of man, thou didst create me as a man. Thou hadst no need of my service, though I had need of thy lordship. Of thy mercy thou didst bring me into existence, thou didst establish the heavens above me as a roof, thou didst make the earth firm for me to walk upon: for my sake thou didst confine the sea: for my sake thou didst give life to animals in their kinds: thou didst put all things under my feet, nor didst thou permit me to lack any of the things of thy love. It is thou who didst fashion me and lay thy hand upon me, thou didst inscribe in me the image of thy power, thou didst endue me with the gift of *logos*, thou didst open paradise for my delight, thou didst bestow on me the instruction of the knowledge of thyself, thou didst reveal to me the tree of life, didst make known to me the thorn of death. From one tree thou didst debar me that I might not eat of it: I ate it, I rejected thy law, I neglected thy commandment, I brought on myself the sentence of death. Thou, Lord, didst convert my punishment (into salvation). . . . Thou who didst ever exist, camest on earth for us who were ignorant, didst enter the Virgin's womb, albeit God that cannot be contained. Thou didst not think it robbery to be equal with God, but thou didst empty thyself and take on thee the form of a servant, didst bless my nature in thyself, didst fulfil thy law for me. . . . Thou didst go forth like a sheep to the slaughter, didst manifest thy solicitude for me on the Cross, didst slay my sin in thy sepulchre, didst take my firstfruits up into heaven, didst reveal to me thy second advent wherein thou shalt come to judge the quick and the dead and to give to every one according to his deeds. I offer to thee, Lord, the symbols of this my free service: my actions are a copy of thy word. It is thou who hast given me this mystic share in thy flesh in the bread and wine. For in the night in which thou didst give thyself up. . . .' (A. Hänggi and I. Pahl, eds., *Prex eucharistica*, Fribourg: Éditions universitaires, 1968, pp. 360–65; my ET adapted from J. M. Rodwell).

18. On God as 'object' and 'subject', see G. van der Leeuw, ET *Religion in Essence and Manifestation*, London: Allen & Unwin, 1938, p. 23.

19. A strong presentation of Christian worship from the angle of the Creator-creature relationship is made by the Lutheran V. Vajta, 'Creation and worship' in *Studia Liturgica* 2 (1963), pp. 29–46. This is in fact a characteristically Lutheran approach: see also Vajta's *Die Theologie des Gottesdienstes bei Luther*, Stockholm: Svenska Kyrkans Diakonistyrelses Bokförlag, and Göttingen: Vandenhoeck & Ruprecht, 1954[2] (abbreviated ET *Luther on Worship*, Philadelphia: Muhlenberg, 1958).

20. A useful study, within its limits, is W. Dürig, *Imago: ein Beitrag zur Terminologie und Theologie der römischen Liturgie*, Munich: Zink, 1952.

21. In seeking to discern 'the foundations of Christian *morality*' in the notion of humanity's being made in 'the divine image', K. Ward enumerates

the same three themes. His subject matter favours the reverse order: 'The rationale of the Christian view is that men are created for community, dependent co-operation with God's purposes, and delight in God's being.' But he can also list them in the order suited to my liturgical approach: 'Christian morality is a constant pursuit of a fuller realization in oneself of contemplative delight, creative striving, and fellowship with all rational creatures' (*The Divine Image*, London: SPCK, 1976, p. 75). I am pleased to find my threefold interpretation confirmed also by H. J. Kraus, a Reformed dogmatician who had half a career as an Old Testament scholar behind him and who makes the notion of *imago Dei* the basis of his own systematic doctrine of man: *Reich Gottes, Reich der Freiheit: Grundriss systematischer Theologie*, Neukirchen: Erziehungsverein, 1975, pp. 141–49. He stresses the character of the *imago* as a promise and a destiny (*Bestimmung*).

22. The scriptural 'proofs' advanced are Romans 11:36, 1 Corinthians 10:31, and Psalm 73:25–28, to which the Longer Catechism adds John 17:21–23.

23. See my *Eucharist and Eschatology*, pp. 102–104; and M. Steinheimer, *Die* ΔΟΞΑ ΤΟΥ ΘΕΟΥ *in der römischen Liturgie*, Munich: Zink, 1951.

24. Feuerbach's reductionist aphorism is brilliantly re-developed by A. Schmemann in *The World as Sacrament*, London: DLT, 1965 (published variously in the USA as *For the Life of the World* and *Sacraments and Orthodoxy*).

25. On word as the sign and medium of both distinction and communion, see T. F. Torrance, *God and Rationality*, London: OUP, 1971, pp. 156–58.

26. Some indications are given in D. Crystal, *Linguistics, Language and Religion*, New York: Hawthorn, 1965; H. A. P. Schmidt, 'Language and its function in Christian worship' in *Studia Liturgica* 8 (1971–72), pp. 1–25; A. C. Thistleton, *Language, Liturgy and Meaning*, Bramcote: Grove, 1975; and several articles in the February 1973 number of *Concilium*, notably in this connexion J. Ladrière, 'The performativity of liturgical language' (pp. 50–62). More broadly: J. Macquarrie, *God-Talk: an examination of the language and logic of theology*, London: SCM, 1967; and L. Bejerholm and G. Hornig, *Wort und Handlung: Untersuchungen zur analytischen Religionsphilosophie*, Gütersloh: Mohn, 1966.

27. In the Old Testament, *dabar* can be used in cases where we might say 'thing', 'action', 'event', rather than 'word'.

28. J. R. Lucas, 'The philosophical background to eucharistic theology' in I. T. Ramsey and others, *Thinking about the Eucharist: Essays by members of the Archbishops' Commission on Christian Doctrine*, London: SCM, 1972, pp. 1–13; F. J. Leenhardt, *Parole visible*. Notice the wide-ranging study —well aware of the religious dimension—by Marcel Jousse, *L'anthropologie du geste*, 3 volumes, Paris: Gallimard, 1974–78.

29. Ninian Smart says that 'the language of worship begins with the

vocative' (*The Concept of Worship*, London: Macmillan, 1972, p. 11). He does not go so far as Martin Buber on the addressability but non-expressibility of the divine Thou (ET *I and Thou*, Edinburgh: T. & T. Clark, 1937). I. T. Ramsey wrote: 'We plot and map out theological phrases with reference to a characteristically religious situation—one of worship, wonder, awe. Without such an empirical anchorage all our theological thinking is in vain, and where there is controversy and argument we are to look for their resolution where they are fulfilled in worship' (*Religious Language*, London: SCM, 1957, p. 89, cf. p. 185).

30. It is John Macquarrie who speaks of 'architectonic' and 'critical' reasoning in theology: *Principles of Christian Theology*, London: SCM, revised edition 1977, pp. 15–18.

31. In reverse, the praise of God is called *theologia* in the approach to the Sanctus in the liturgies of St Mark and St Basil (A. Hänggi and I. Pahl, eds., *Prex eucharistica*, pp. 110, 234).

32. N. A. Nissiotis, 'La théologie en tant que science et en tant que doxologie' in *Irénikon* 33 (1960), pp. 291–310. Modern Orthodox writers still reveal that the doxological dimension of theology is usually more explicit in the Eastern than in the Western tradition: see, for instance, P. Evdokimov, *L'orthodoxie*, Neuchâtel: Delachaux & Niestlé, 1959; V. Lossky, ET *The Mystical Theology of the Eastern Church*, London: J. Clarke, 1957, and ET *In the Image and Likeness of God*, New York: St Vladimir's, 1974, and Oxford: Mowbray, 1975. In the contemporary West, the tide may be rising. It is interesting that the great Dominican systematician Edward Schillebeeckx should conclude his monumental two volumes on 'Jesus' and 'Christ and the Christians' with summaries in the doxological forms of a homily, a creed, and a eucharistic prayer: *Jezus, het verhaal van een levende*, and *Gerechtigheid en liefde, genade en bevrijding*, Bloemendaal: Nelissen, 1974 and 1977. Note already Schillebeeckx's brief section on 'the doxological character of theological interpretations' in his *Geloofsverstaan*, Bloemendaal; Nelissen, 1972 (ET The *Understanding of Faith*, London: Sheed & Ward, 1974, pp. 17–19). An awareness is also discernible in the German Catholic Walter Kasper: for instance, in his *Dogma unter dem Wort Gottes*, Mainz: Grünewald, 1965, pp. 33, 47–51; in 'The relationship between gospel and dogma: an historical approach' in *Concilium*, January 1967, pp. 73–79; and in 'Geschichtlichkeit der Dogmen' in *Stimmen der Zeit* 179 (1967), pp. 401–16, especially 'Das Dogma als Doxologie': 'Das Dogma ist gedachte Liturgie, die Liturgie gebetetes Dogma' (p. 407). Note also the following articles: P. E. Fink, 'Towards a liturgical theology' in *Worship* 47 (1973), pp. 601–9; G. M. Lukken, 'The unique expression of faith in the liturgy' in *Concilium*, February 1973, pp. 11–21, and 'La liturgie comme lieu théologique irremplaçable' in *Questions liturgiques et paroissiales* 56 (1975), pp. 97–112; D. Power, 'Two expressions of faith: worship and theology' in *Concilium*, February 1973, pp. 95–103. By contrast, we find Hans Küng, at the conclusion of his *Christsein*, Munich: Piper, 1974, p. 642 (ET *On being a Christian*, London:

Collins, 1977), lamenting that his appearance before the Holy Office had not left him time to deal with worship in his 700-page book.

33. See p. 22f and then again chapter II. My own christology is both high and kenotic: see especially notes 102 and 176.

34. J. Jeremias, *The Prayers of Jesus*, London: SCM, 1967; and elsewhere.

35. On the criteria of dissimilarity and multiple attestation, see N. Perrin, *Rediscovering the Teaching of Jesus*, London: SCM, 1967, chapter 1. The criteria have been subjected to scrutiny by R. S. Barbour, but the general direction of his criticisms is certainly not to *reduce* the amount of Jesus-material: *Traditio-historical criticism of the gospels*, London: SPCK, 1972.

36. Second collect, morning prayer, in the Church of England's *Book of Common Prayer*.

37. On the Methodist covenant service, see D. H. Tripp, *The Renewal of the Covenant in the Methodist Tradition*, London: Epworth, 1969.

38. Historically, see R. J. Daly, *The Origins of the Christian Doctrine of Sacrifice*, Philadelphia: Fortress, and London: DLT, 1978, and, with a more direct hermeneutical effort for today, Frances M. Young, *Sacrifice and the Death of Christ*, London: SPCK, 1975.

39. See also, with an emphasis on Jesus' human growth in God-enabled prayer, Justin Kelly, 'Prayer and the incarnation: an approach to the identity of Jesus through religious experience' in *The Way*, supplement no. 34, autumn 1978, pp. 3–25.

40. G. von Rad, Genesis-commentary, *ad* 1:26–28.

41. N. Young, *Creator, Creation and Faith*, London: Collins, 1976. Young does not fall into the nature-mysticism against which T. S. Derr warns: *Ecology and Human Need*, Philadelphia: Westminster, 1975.

42. G. von Rad, Genesis-commentary, *ad* 1:3–5.

43. On the new *Missale Romanum* of 1969–70, see especially J. D. Crichton, *Christian Celebration: The Mass*, London: Chapman, 1971, and L. Sheppard (ed.), *The New Liturgy: a comprehensive introduction*, London: DLT, 1970.

44. J. M. van Gangh, *La multiplication des pains et l'eucharistie*, Paris: Cerf, 1975; A. Heising, *Die Bostchaft der Brotvermehrung*, Stuttgart: Katholisches Bibelwerk, 1966.

45. See chapter XII.

46. Note Ecclesiasticus 38:31–34, and the ambiguous last sentence: 'Their prayers are about their daily work' or 'Their daily work is their prayer'. N. Smart holds that the 'primary concept of worship' is 'superimposed' from 'Sunday' onto the secondary 'sweeping' (*The Concept of Worship*, pp. 3–5). I prefer to see Christian worship as a ritual focus within a broader field, which includes everyday work; and I shall be using the method of oscillation between ritual and various parts of the broader field (see particularly chapter XII). The cultural anthropologist B. Malinowsky stressed the integration—which is not to say confusion—of ritual and technology among primitive peoples: both technical skills and

31

ritual performance went into the making of a canoe ('Magic, science and religion' in J. Needham, ed., *Science, Religion and Reality*, London: Sheldon, 1926², pp. 19–84, in particular pp. 29–34).

47. Note the shift in emphasis in monasticism: 'If in the first early Christian view every undertaking could become a prayer, a ministry, a creating of and bearing witness to the kingdom, in monasticism prayer itself now became the sole undertaking, replacing all other tasks' (A. Schmemann, *Introduction to Liturgical Theology*, p. 107). Schmemann understands the rise of monasticism as an 'individual-eschatological' protest against the threatened loss by the total Church of its own 'other-aeon' character in the constantinian world.

48. N. D. O'Donoghue, 'Creation and participation' in R. W. A. McKinney (ed.), *Creation, Christ and Culture* (T. F. Torrance *festschrift*), Edinburgh: T. & T. Clark, 1976, pp. 135–48.

49. *Homo orans, laborans, collaborans*: the triad is exploited with sensitivity to the liturgical and eschatological perspectives by G. Vahanian, *Dieu et l'utopie*, Paris: Cerf, 1977, pp. 142–47.

50. J. Huizinga, *Homo ludens: proeve eener bepaling van het spel-element der cultuur*, Haarlem: Tjeenk Willink, 1938 (ET *Homo ludens: a study of the play-element in culture*, London: Routledge & Kegan Paul, 1949); cf. H. Rahner, 'Der spielende Mensch' in *Eranos-Jahrbuch 1948*, Zürich: Rhein-Verlag, 1949, pp. 11–87 (ET *Man at Play*, London: Burns & Oates, 1965).

51. It may be because worship is related to both work and rest that W. Rordorf can envisage with equanimity the secularization of Sunday into a workday provided Christians continue to worship on it, while Beckwith and Stott favour the retention of Sunday's constantinian status as a day of rest as well as Christian worship: W. Rordorf, *Der Sonntag: Geschichte des Ruhe- und Gottesdiensttages im ältesten Christentum*, Zürich: Zwingli-Verlag, 1962 (ET *Sunday*, London: SCM, 1968); R. T. Beckwith and W. Stott, *This is the Day: the Biblical Doctrine of the Christian Sunday in its Jewish and Early Christian Setting*, London: Marshall, Morgan and Scott, 1978.

52. R. Guardini, *Vom Geist der Liturgie*, Freiburg: Herder, 1918 (ET *The Spirit of the Liturgy*, London: Sheed & Ward, 1930). It is, of course, 'serious' play, like children's games: Guardini quotes the old entrance-prayer of the mass, 'Introibo ad altare Dei: ad Deum qui *laetificat juventutem meam*'.

53. J. J. von Allmen, 'Worship and the Holy Spirit' in *Studia Liturgica*, 2 (1963), pp. 124–35, and *Prophétisme sacramentel*, Neuchâtel: Delachaux & Niestlé, 1964, pp. 287–311.

54. H. Cox, *The Feast of Fools*, Cambridge, Mass.: Harvard, 1969.

55. The theme of play runs through J. Moltmann's *Die ersten Frei-gelassenen der Schöpfung*, Munich: Kaiser, 1971 (ET, with an extended introduction by D. E. Jenkins, *Theology and Joy*, London: SCM, 1973), although the liturgical implications remain strangely subjacent. (There were hints of an anti-liturgical or anti-sacramental streak in Moltmann's *Theology of*

Hope and *Crucified God,* but he showed a greater appreciation of worship by the time he got to *Kirche in der Kraft des Geistes,* Munich: Kaiser, 1975, ET *The Church in the Power of the Spirit,* London: SCM, 1977.) See further now the interesting book by the Dutch Remonstrant G. J. Hoenderdaal, *Riskant spel: liturgie in een geseculariseerde wereld,* The Hague: Boekencentrum, 1977; and J. G. Davies, *New Perspectives on Worship Today,* London: SCM, 1978, especially chapters 1 ('Play and worship') and 6 ('Laughter and worship').

56. In a thin bibliography, note A. C. Bridge, *Images of God,* London: Hodder, 1960, and H. U. von Balthasar's 'theological aesthetics', *Herrlichkeit,* Einsiedeln: Johannes, 1961ff. See also two important essays by the Catholic poet and painter David Jones, in his *Epoch and Artist,* London: Faber, 1959: 'The preface to *The Anathemata*', and 'Art and sacrament', with the appended note on 'The utile'.

57. P. Tillich, *Theology of Culture,* New York: OUP, 1959, p.v: 'The religious dimension . . . is never absent in cultural creations even if they show no relation to religion in the narrower sense of the word.' In his *Systematic Theology* (3 volumes in one; Digswell Place: Nisbet, 1968), Tillich characteristically sees idolatry as making something that is not ultimate into an ultimate concern; it then becomes an enslaving demon.

58. M. Argyle, *Bodily Communication,* London: Methuen, 1975.

59. See the chapter on 'eucharistic symbolism and man's condition' in G. Martelet, *Résurrection, eucharistie et genèse de l'homme,* Paris: Desclée, 1972 (ET *The Risen Christ and the Eucharistic World,* London: Collins 1976), and C. Vagaggini, 'Caro salutis est cardo: corporcità, eucaristia e liturgia' in *Miscellanea liturgica in onore di S. E. il cardinale G. Lercaro,* vol 1, Rome: Desclée, 1965 (ET *The Flesh, instrument of salvation: a theology of the human body,* Staten Island, N. Y.: Alba House, 1969).

60. A. R. Johnson, *The One and the Many in the Israelite Conception of God,* Cardiff: University of Wales, 1961²; A. W. Wainwright, *The Trinity in the New Testament,* London: SPCK, 1962.

61. L. Hodgson, *The Doctrine of the Trinity,* London: Nisbet, 1943.

62. K. Barth, *Kirchliche Dogmatik,* III/1, pp. 207–20 (ET pp. 191–206).

63. G. Dix and H. Chadwick, *The Treatise on the Apostolic Tradition of St Hippolytus of Rome,* London: SPCK, revised edition, 1968, p. 47 (chapter 26:9 in Dix's numbering; chapter 28 in B. Botte's edition, *La Tradition apostolique de saint Hippolyte,* Münster: Aschendorff, 1963). A brief note on the complex question of *The Apostolic Tradition* is to be found in C. Jones, G. Wainwright and E. Yarnold (eds.), *The Study of Liturgy,* London: SPCK, and New York: OUP, 1978, pp. 57–59.

64. J. F. Keating, *The Agapé and the Eucharist in the Early Church,* London: Methuen, 1901.

65. F. Baker, 'Love feast' in J. G. Davies (ed.), *A Dictionary of Liturgy and Worship,* London: SCM, 1972, pp. 247–50.

66. On Zwingli's theology of the sacraments, see J. Courvoisier *Zwingli:*

a Reformed Theologian, Richmond, Va.: John Knox, 1963, and London: Epworth, 1964, pp. 63–78.

67. Karl Marx rightly saw work and social relationships as constitutive of humanity: compare our sections on 'the earthly task' and 'social being'. In his critique of false transcendence, he was rightly aiming at idolatry. Unfortunately he was unable to distinguish the true transcendence which liberates and enables: for the Christian the vocation to 'communion with God' is the *primary* constitutive factor of humanity.

68. For the Old Testament theology, and with a lively awareness of the dangers even within Christianity, see H. J. Kraus, *Reich Gottes, Reich der Freiheit*, pp. 117–19.

69. The heart of the icondules' case is presented by St John of Damascus in this way: 'I do not worship matter, I worship the Creator of matter, who for my sake became matter, and accepted to dwell in matter, and through matter wrought my salvation. I will not cease reverencing matter, for it was through matter that my salvation was effected' (*On Ikons*, I. 16, PG 94, 1245).

70. N. Smart, *The Concept of Worship*, p. 41f.

71. K. E. Kirk, *The Vision of God*, London: Longmans, 1931.

72. O. Clément, *Transfigurer le temps*, Neuchâtel: Delachaux & Niestlé, 1959.

73. M. Luther, *Lectures on Romans* (1515–16), Weimar edition, vol. 56, p. 356. See V. Vajta, *Die Theologie des Gottesdienstes bei Luther* (abbreviated ET *Luther on Worship*), especially part one, chapter 1: 'Worship and idolatry' (pp. 3–42; ET pp. 3–25). John Macquarrie writes powerfully of idolatry as 'the root sin'. The *aversio a Deo et conversio ad creaturam* may take the form either of thing-idolatry (the sins of indulgence and greed) or of self-idolatry (the sins of pride): *Principles of Christian Theology*, 1977[2], pp. 259–62. Worship of self is probably the basic form, for 'one's own self is the last idol' (p. 318f).

74. 'Christus tamen futurus fuerit homo': J. Calvin, *Inst.* I, 15, 3. For Jesus as the 'epiphany' of the *imago Dei*, see H. J. Kraus, *Reich Gottes, Reich der Freiheit*, p. 286f.

75. J. A. T. Robinson, *Honest to God*, London: SCM, 1963, chapter 4, and *The Human Face of God*, London: SCM, 1973.

76. E. Schillebeeckx, *Jezus, het verhaal van een levende*, part IV, section 3.

77. For Orthodox theology of the ikon, see L. Ouspensky and W. Lossky, *Der Sinn der Ikonen*, Bern: Urs Graf-Verlag, 1952 (ET *The Meaning of Icons*, Boston: Book and Art Shop, 1969); and P. Evdokimov, *L'orthodoxie*, pp. 216–38: 'Initiation à l'icone'.

78. N. Smart, *The Concept of Worship*, pp. 6–10.

79. The difference between this and arianism on the one hand or adoptionism on the other will, I hope, become clear in chapter II and, in a subsidiary way, in chapter VI§7 and chapter X§5.

80. *Katoptron* is a mirror, and the verb in 2 Corinthians 3:18 may mean either to behold or to reflect. My explanation in the text combines the two.

See further N. Hugedé, *La métaphore du miroir dans les épîtres de saint Paul aux Corinthiens*, Neuchâtel: Delachaux & Niestlé, 1957.

81. E. Schillebeeckx, *Christus, sacrament van de Godsentmoeting*, Bilthoven: Nelissen, 1960³ (ET *Christ the Sacrament of Encounter with God*, London: Sheed & Ward, 1963).

82. The terminology of the numinous was introduced into the modern discussion by R. Otto, *Das Heilige*, Gotha: Klotz, 1917 (ET *The Idea of the Holy*, London: OUP, 1923).

83. Augustine, *Confessions* I.1, 1.

84. N. Smart, *The Concept of Worship*, p. 27.

85. ET from A. Linton, *Twenty-five Consecration Prayers*, London: SPCK, 1921, p. 44f.

86. N. Smart talks of 'going off the top of the word-scale' (*The Concept of Worship*, p. 29).

87. There can be a 'filled silence': see the 'prayers and sermons' of K. H. Miskotte, *Gevulde stilte*, Kampen: Kok, 1974. Note the essays of G. Steiner, *Language and Silence*, London: Faber, 1967, especially pp. 30–54 ('The retreat from the word'), pp. 55–74 ('Silence and the poet').

88. J. P. Audet, 'Esquisse historique de genre littéraire de la "bénédic-tion" juive et de l'"eucharistie" chrétienne' in *Revue biblique* 65 (1958), pp. 371–99.

89. From the general thanksgiving in the Church of England's *Book of Common Prayer*.

90. J. A. Jungmann, *The Early Liturgy*, Notre Dame: University Press, 1959, London: DLT, 1960, p. 300.

91. The interweaving of thanksgiving, proclamation and confession of faith can be illustrated terminologically from liturgical history. J. A. Jungmann adduces examples of *praedicatio* and *exhomologesis* being used of the great eucharistic prayer, while the creed may be called a *eucharistia*: *Missarum sollemnia*, part 3, chapter 2, section 8; and part 4, chapter 2, section 3. Jungmann's great work on the history of the mass exists in several editions and translations. I have therefore preferred to make references in this way rather than give page numbers. Over the years I have usually worked either from *Missarum sollemnia: eine genetische Erklär-ung der römischen Messe*, Vienna: Herder, 1949², or from *Missarum sollemnia: explication génétique de la messe romaine*, Paris: Aubier, 3 volumes, 1956–58.

92. Intercessory prayer raises in one form the question of interaction between God and the world, which will tend to recur in this book under the guise of the 'intervention' and 'immanence' issues but also in the shape of discussion on 'grace'. See J. D. Crichton, *Christian Celebration: The Prayer of the Church*, London: Chapman, 1976, chapter 8 ('The intercessions'); G. Greshake, 'Theologische Grundlagen des Bittgebets' in *Theologische Quartalschrift* 157 (1977), pp. 27–40. For some philosophical discussion of intercession and petition, see: P. Baelz, *Prayer and Providence*, London: SCM, 1968; E. J. Bicknell, *In Defence of Christian Prayer*, London: Long-mans, 1925; H. H. Farmer, *The World and God*, London: Nisbet, 1935,

chapters 8 and 15; F. Heiler, *Das Gebet*, Munich: Reinhardt, 1919² (ET *Prayer*, London: OUP, 1932); L. Hodgson, *For Faith and Freedom*, vol. 2, Oxford: Blackwell, 1957, chapter 8; H. D. Lewis, *Our Experience of God*, London: Allen & Unwin, 1959, chapters 16 and 17; J. R. Lucas, *Freedom and Grace*, London: SPCK, 1976, chapter 5 ('Rogationtide queries'); H. Meynell, *God and the World*, London: SPCK, 1971, chapter 5; D. Z. Phillips, *The Concept of Prayer*, London: Routledge, 1965; I. T. Ramsey, *Our Understanding of Prayer*, London: SPCK, 1971; B. H. Streeter and others, *Concerning Prayer*, London: Macmillan, 1916.

93. G. Wainwright, *Eucharist and Eschatology*, London, Epworth, 1971.

94. For the theme of 'God's absence' in twentieth-century theology, whether 'the sense of the absence of God' or 'the absence of the sense of God,' see H. Döring, *Abwesenheit Gottes*, Paderborn: Bonifacius, 1977. See also W. Kasper, 'Unsere Gottesbeziehung angesichts der sich wandelnden Gottesvorstellung' and 'Möglichkeiten der Gotteserfahrung heute' in his *Glaube im Wandel der Geschichte*, Mainz: Grünewald, 1970, paperback 1973, pp. 103–26, 127–56; and K. H. Miskotte, *Als de goden zwijgen*, Amsterdam: Holland, 1956 (enlarged ET *When the Gods are silent*, London: Collins, 1967).

95. J. H. Hick, *Evil and the God of Love*, London: Macmillan, 1966, chapter 14, section 7; and, more generally, *Faith and Knowledge*, Ithaca, N. Y.: Cornell, 1966², and London: Macmillan, 1967².

96. D. Bonhoeffer, ET *Letters and Papers from Prison*, London: SCM, 1953, revised and enlarged 1967, letter of 16 July 1944.

97. In his *Jesus* book (ET *Jesus and the Word*, New York: Scribner, 1934), R. Bultmann interpreted the tension between the presence and the futurity of God and his kingdom in terms of God's nearness and remoteness. God is distant, in his otherness but particularly in his justice, from his creatures who have 'departed' from him in their sin. God is close in providence and salvation. It is God's forgiveness of the sinner which binds the two together. Note also T. F. Torrance's view of space as 'relation' rather than 'receptacle' and the important consequences of this for conceiving the eucharistic presence: *Space, Time and Incarnation*, London: OUP, 1969.

98. R. Barthes and others, *Analyse structurale et exégèse biblique*, Neuchâtel: Delachaux & Niestlé, 1972, in particular p. 37. Barthes himself is not using 'scandal' in a theological sense; he is referring, at the level of the 'structure' of the story, to a bold departure from the structure usual in such stories as analysed by V. Propp.

99. R. Martin-Achard remarks that Jacob comes out of the adventure wounded but blessed; he has lost something but has received something more valuable in exchange (in *Analyse structurale et exégèse biblique*, pp. 53, 55). Is there a hint here of the *felix culpa* theme? 'O happy fault that merited such and so great a Redeemer' is how the Fall is spoken of in the *Exsultet* of the Roman paschal vigil.

100. M. F. Wiles, *The Remaking of Christian Doctrine*, London: SCM,

1974; *Working Papers in Doctrine*, London: SCM, 1976, chapters 3 ('In defence of Arius'), 4 ('The doctrine of Christ in the patristic age'), 5 ('The nature of the early debate about Christ's human soul'), 9 ('The unassumed is the unhealed'), 10 ('Does Christology rest on a mistake?'), 14 ('The criteria of Christian theology'); *Explorations in Theology*, London: SCM, 1979, chapters 2 and 3. J. H. Hick, *God and the Universe of Faiths*, London: Macmillan, 1973, chapters 7–12 ('The reconstruction of Christian belief', 'The essence of Christianity', 'The copernican revolution in theology', 'The new map of the universe of faiths', 'Christ and incarnation', 'Incarnation and mythology'); *The Centre of Christianity*, London: SCM, 1977 (revised edition of *Christianity at the Centre*, London: Macmillan, 1968). G. W. H. Lampe, *God as Spirit*, Oxford: Clarendon, 1977. Wiles and Hick contributed to the symposium *The Myth of God Incarnate* (ed. J. H. Hick, London: SCM, 1977), with whose general direction I take issue at several points in chapters II and VI of this book.

101. Wiles borrows the phrase 'doctrinal criticism' from a seminal essay by G. F. Woods, in F. G. Healey (ed.), *Prospect for Theology*, Digswell Place: Nisbet, 1966, pp. 73–92. Wiles wishes to bring to the creeds and to traditional doctrines the same kind of critical scrutiny as modern 'biblical criticism'—now widely acceptable in the Church after initial resistance—has brought to the scriptures: *Working Papers in Doctrine*, chapter 12 ('Looking into the Sun'). In his *Explorations in Theology*, related chapters are 1, 2 and 5.

102. M. F. Wiles, *The Remaking of Christian Doctrine*, pp. 17–19. An informed defence of a (kenotically conceived) incarnation and of the uniqueness of Christ may be found in B. Hebblethwaite's article, 'Incarnation—the essence of Christianity?' in *Theology*, March 1977, pp. 85–91. My own christology is of a kenotic stamp, although I shall not enter into the details of its relationship to the various versions of kenoticism current in nineteenth and early twentieth century theology in both Germany and Britain. I intend the word broadly in the sense of the divine self-limiting and self-giving in creation and salvation. See, e.g., pp. 22, 205–10, 351f.

103. On worship in the New Testament Church see G. Delling, *Der Gottesdienst im Neuen Testament*, Berlin: Evangelische Verlagsanstalt, 1952 (ET *Worship in the New Testament*, London: DLT, 1962); F. Hahn, *Der urchristliche Gottesdienst*, Stuttgart: Katholisches Bibelwerk, 1970 (ET *The Worship of the Early Church*, Philadelphia: Fortress, 1973); R. P. Martin, *Worship in the Early Church*, London: Marshall, Morgan & Scott, 1974[2]; C. F. D. Moule, *Worship in the New Testament*, London: Lutterworth, 1961.

104. J. D. G. Dunn puts it thus: 'As with the continuation of the common meal, so in prayer, the first Christians were not merely doing as Jesus did, but doing it in conscious reference to and continuing dependence on Jesus' (*Jesus and the Spirit*, London: SCM, 1975, p. 187; cf. his *Unity and Diversity in the New Testament*, London: SCM, 1977, pp. 124–73).

105. For recent New Testament scholarship concerning the title 'Lord',

see C. F. D. Moule, *The Origin of Christology*, Cambridge: University Press, 1977, pp. 35–46.

106. On the acts of obeisance, see A. W. Wainwright, *The Trinity in the New Testament*, p. 103f, and C. F. D. Moule, *The Origin of Christology*, p. 175f.

107. On Philippians 2:5–11, see R. P. Martin, *Carmen Christi: Philippians 2:5–11 in recent interpretation and in the setting of early Christian Worship*, Cambridge: University Press, 1967.

108. A. M. Hunter, *Paul and his Predecessors*, London: SCM, 1961², p. 82.

109. If that statement was largely historical in tenor, H. E. W. Turner immediately prolongs the thought in systematic vein: 'This is the starting-point of Christology, not the goal which the theologian hopes to reach' (*Jesus the Christ*, Oxford: Mowbray, 1976, p. 1). Vincent Taylor summed up the result of his own work on *The Names of Jesus* (London: Macmillan, 1953, note especially p. 172f): 'The names and titles ... carry us back to a time when doctrinal motives were only beginning to be operative. ... They are both the foreshadowing and the precipitate of primitive Christian christology. In their formation and use, liturgical and devotional influences were as strongly operative as the attempt to define the person of Christ' (*The Person of Christ in New Testament Teaching*, London: Macmillan, 1958, p.v).

110. M. F. Wiles, *The Making of Christian Doctrine*, Cambridge: University Press, 1967, p. 64f. We shall have to question later the systematic attitude which Wiles adopts in the face of these admitted historical data.

111. R. E. Brown, *Jesus God and Man*, Milwaukee: Bruce, 1967, and London: Chapman, 1968. He highlights the liturgical linkage of such cases (pp. 34–8).

112. On the beginning of St John's gospel, see, resumptively, A. Feuillet, *Le prologue du quatrième évangile*, Paris: Desclée de Brouwer, 1968.

113. The word 'psalm' in the New Testament may sometimes refer to hymns composed by Christians. Nevertheless, the psalms of the Old Testament were well known in the early Christian assembly. See pp. 210–212.

114. B. M. Metzger, 'The punctuation of Rom. 9:5' in B. Lindars and S. S. Smalley (eds.), *Christ and Spirit in the New Testament* (C. F. D. Moule *festschrift*), Cambridge: University Press, 1973, pp. 95–112.

115. Pliny's letter to Trajan, *Epp.* X, 96.

116. On this question, see R. S. Barbour, 'Creation, Wisdom and Christ' in R. W. A. McKinney (ed.), *Creation, Christ and Culture*, pp. 22–42.

117. See note 107. Other studies of hymns embedded in the New Testament include R. Deichgräber, *Gotteshymnus und Christushymnus in der frühen Christenheit*, Göttingen: Vandenhoeck & Ruprecht, 1967; J. T. Sanders, *The New Testament Christological Hymns: their historical religious background*, Cambridge: University Press, 1971; G. Schille, *Frühchristliche Hymnen*, Berlin: Evangelische Verlagsanstalt, 1965; K. Wengst, *Christologische Formeln und Lieder des Urchristentums*, Gütersloh: Mohn, 1972. Note

already the article by D. M. Stanley, ' "Carmenque Christo quasi deo dicere . . ." ' in *Catholic Biblical Quarterly*, 20 (1958), pp. 173–91.

118. Kirsopp Lake commented in the Loeb edition of the Apostolic Fathers: 'The metaphor is probably from the chorus or choir which gathered round the altar in heathen ceremonial, and sang a sacrificial hymn.'

119. R. Deichgräber, *Gotteshymnus und Christushymnus in der frühen Christenheit.*

120. The fullest study is J. Kroll, *Die christliche Hymnodik bis zu Klemens von Alexandria*, Darmstadt: Wissenschaftliche Buchgesellschaft, revised reprint 1968.

121. M. F. Wiles, *The Making of Christian Doctrine*, p. 67f.

122. On the whole question of 'orthodoxy' and 'heresy' in the first centuries, see W. Bauer, *Rechtgläubigkeit und Ketzerei im ältesten Christentum*, Tübingen: Mohr, 1934 (enlarged ET *Orthodoxy and Heresy in Earliest Christianity*, Philadelphia: Fortress, 1971, and London: SCM, 1972), and the critique and counter-thesis in H. E. W. Turner, *The Pattern of Truth: a study in the relations between orthodoxy and heresy in the early Church*, London: Mowbray, 1954.

123. In this paragraph I continue to follow Wiles's historical account.

124. Eusebius, *Church History*, VII, 30, 10.

125. Eusebius, *Church History*, V, 28, 5.

126. For Origen's understanding, see especially his *de oratione* and his *contra Celsum*, V, 4; VIII, 13 and 26.

127. For example, Athanasius, *ad Adelphium*, 3, PG 26, 1074–7.

128. I now follow the historical development further than Wiles takes it.

129. This is the case over a long stretch of the Armenian anaphora of St Gregory Nazianzen, including the institution narrative ('Thou didst take bread . . .'), and is common practice at the 'anamnesis' in Syrian Jacobite anaphoras: see A. Hänggi and I. Pahl (eds.), *Prex eucharistica*, pp. 264–309, 327–31. The Ethiopian anaphora of St Athanasius is also addressed to Christ in part, again including the institution narrative; Ethiopian anaphoras are a wild growth and may sometimes address the Blessed Virgin Mary (Hänggi and Pahl, pp. 142–203).

130. After the council of Chalcedon, the patriarchate of Antioch inserted the phrase 'who was crucified for us'. The anti-chalcedonian origin of this incision caused it to be rejected by the Orthodox on suspicion of monophysitism, and the *Trishagion* has since been addressed by them to the whole Trinity. See I. H. Dalmais, *Les liturgies d'Orient*, Paris: Fayard, 1959, p. 68. This hymn found its way from the East into mozarabic and gallican liturgies.

131. The part addressed to Christ may have been the original core of the hymn. The arianizing or strongly subordinationist author of *Apostolic Constitutions* turns the whole address to the Father of Christ. See J. Lebreton, 'La forme primitive du *Gloria in excelsis*, prière au Christ, ou

prière à Dieu le Père?' in *Recherches de science religieuse* 13 (1923), pp. 322–9, and 'Le désaccord de la foi populaire et de la théologie savante dans l'Église chrétienne du IIIe siècle' in *Revue d'histoire ecclésiastique* 19 (1923), pp. 481–506, and 20 (1924), pp. 5–37; B. Capelle, 'Le texte du *Gloria in excelsis*' in *Revue d'histoire ecclésiasitque* 44 (1949), pp. 439–57; M. F. Wiles, *The Making of Christian Doctrine*, p. 76f. Lebreton's second article contains important matter on Origen's treatise *On Prayer*.

132. On the *Te Deum* as the preface, Sanctus and post-sanctus of an old Latin (perhaps North African) paschal liturgy, see E. Kähler, *Studien zum Te Deum und zur Geschichte des 24. Psalms in der alten Kirche*, Göttingen: Vandenhoeck & Ruprecht, 1958. Kähler places the original text before the middle of the fourth century. He argues that there is nothing in the texts to prove its association with Nicetas of Remesiana, either as author or as editor. The third section, which is often thought to be later, addresses 'the Lord'. Kähler considers it original, being prayers for those baptized in the paschal vigil.

133. The next chapter will, for instance, say something of the trinitarian doxologies.

134. M. F. Wiles, *The Making of Christian Doctrine*, p. 93.

135. M. F. Wiles, *The Making of Christian Doctrine*, p. 164.

136. M. F. Wiles, *The Making of Christian Doctrine*, p. 168.

137. D. von Allmen, 'Die Geburt der Theologie: das Problem einer "einheimischen" Theologie im Lichte des Neuen Testaments' in *Evangelische Missions-Zeitschrift* 27 (1970), pp. 57–71, 160–76. He invokes the articles of E. Schweizer, 'Die Kirche als Leib Christi in den paulinischen Antilegomena' and 'The Church as the missionary body of Christ' from Schweizer's *Neotestamentica*, Zürich: Zwingli-Verlag, 1963, pp. 293–316, 317–29.

138. Here von Allmen follows R. C. Tannehill, *Dying and Rising with Christ*, Berlin: Töpelmann, 1967.

139. On Paul's critique of Corinthian worship, see E. Jüngel, 'Zur Kritik des sakramentalen Verständnisses der Taufe' in F. Viering (ed.), *Zu Karl Barths Lehre von der Taufe*, Gütersloh: Mohn, 1971, pp. 25–43. And see below, p. 253.

140. For Wiles, see J. H. Hick (ed.), *The Myth of God Incarnate*, p. 8f; his own contribution to M. F. Wiles and others, *Christian Believing: The Nature of the Christian Faith and its Expression in Holy Scripture and Creeds: A Report by the Doctrine Commission of the Church of England*, London: SPCK, 1976, in particular pp. 126, 131f; and his *Explorations in Theology*, pp. 24–27. For Hick, see *The Myth of God Incarnate*, pp. 177–9, 183; his *God and the Universe of Faiths*, pp. 172–9; and his *The Centre of Christianity*, p. 31f ('That Jesus is my Lord and Saviour is language like that of the lover for whom Helen is the sweetest girl in the world').

141. For Wiles and Hick, see the previous note.

142. See meanwhile chapter VI also. For *The Myth of God Incarnate*, see note 100.

143. On God the Father as 'fount of deity' in the Cappadocian Fathers, see J. N. D. Kelly, *Early Christian Doctrines*, London: Black, 1977[5], pp. 258–69.

144. See R. Bultmann's essay on the original 'basis' of the WCC ('a fellowship of churches which accept our Lord Jesus Christ as God and Saviour'), in *Glauben und Verstehen*, vol. 2, Tübingen: Mohr, 1952, pp. 246–61, 'Das christologische Bekenntnis des Oekumenischen Rates' (ET in R. Bultmann, *Essays Philosophical and Theological*, London: SCM, 1955, pp. 273–90).

145. For Athanasius, see J. N. D. Kelly, *Early Christian Doctrines*[5], pp. 243–47.

146. On the old antiochene and (see later, p. 71) alexandrine schools in christology, see R. V. Sellers, *Two Ancient Christologies*, London: SPCK, 1940, and *The Council of Chalcedon*, London: SPCK, 1953, pp. 132–81. The classical Antiochenes accepted the pre-existence of Christ, although their adoptionist 'predecessors' had not done so. There is a rough correspondence between the alexandrine tendency and H. E. W. Turner's 'christology from the side of God' (contrast 'from the side of man'—see *Jesus the Christ*), and between the antiochene tendency and W. Pannenberg's 'christology from below' (contrast 'from above'). Pannenberg's 'from below' is primarily a noetic or methodological movement. The outcome in the order of reality is still apparently an 'eternal' Christ, who entered time 'from the eschaton', the predestined anticipation of the consummation: see W. Pannenberg, *Grundzüge der Christologie*, Gütersloh: Mohn, 1964 (ET *Jesus: God and Man*, London: SCM, 1968). One might almost say that in 'giving his only Son' God was staking his own future: the obedience of Jesus (graced and free: here, of all places, there must be no opposition or competition between God and man) ensured God's future, i.e. the coming of the kingdom.

147. One function of the *homoousion* in the Nicene Creed is to make clear that God was giving *himself* to the world in Jesus Christ: 'God's presence, and his very self, and essence all-divine' (Newman: 'Praise to the holiest in the height'). Over the central range of Christian tradition this has not been felt either to diminish Christ's humanity (Newman's 'in man, for man': no competition-thinking) or to exhaust the 'fount of godhead'.

148. In connexion with the *dia*-formula, I find no need to follow the sharp distinction made by W. Kramer between 'sovereign power', which he considers original, and 'high-priestly meditation': *Christos, Kyrios, Gottessohn*, Zürich: Zwingli-Verlag, 1963, sections 15–19 (ET *Christ, Lord, Son of God*, London: SCM, 1966, in particular pp. 82f, 87–90).

149. J. A. Jungmann, *Die Stellung Christi im liturgischen Gebet*, Münster: Aschendorff, 1962[2] (ET *The Place of Christ in Liturgical Prayer*, Staten Island, N.Y.: Alba, and London: Chapman, 1965).

150. J. A. Jungmann, *The Early Liturgy*, Notre Dame: University Press, 1959, and London: DLT, 1960, p. 195.

151. T. F. Torrance, 'The mind of Christ in worship: the problem of apollinarianism in the liturgy' in his *Theology in Reconciliation*, London: Chapman, 1975, pp. 139–214.

152. J. Dowden showed how already the English *Book of Common Prayer* changed the address of some older prayers from Christ to the Father: *The Workmanship of the Prayer Book*, London: Methuen, 1904², pp. 127–9, and *Further Studies in the Prayer Book*, London: Methuen, 1908, pp. 286–95.

153. J. D. Crichton presents a strongly mediatorial view of Christ in his *Christian Celebration: The Prayer of the Church*. He happily uses the imagery of Clement of Alexandria which makes Christ the choir-leader, *chorēgos*, of the Church's worship (pp. 24, 33). He would even welcome the 'restoration' of the *Gloria patri* at the end of the psalms to the form 'Glory be to the Father, through the Son/Christ, in the Holy Spirit' (p. 85).

154. *The Methodist Service Book*, London: Methodist Publishing House, 1975.

155. Augustine, *In Joan. Ev.*, tr. 6, 7, PL 35, 1428.

156. G. Wainwright, *Eucharist and Eschatology*.

157. D. G. Attfield, 'Can God be crucified? A discussion of J. Moltmann' in *Scottish Journal of Theology* 30 (1977), pp. 47–57.

158. On the Cross as the proper theological starting-point for trinitarian doctrine, see E. Jüngel, *Gottes Sein ist im Werden*, Tübingen: Mohr, 1966² (ET *The Doctrine of the Trinity: God's Being is in Becoming*, Edinburgh: Scottish Academic Press, 1976), and *Gott als Geheimnis der Welt*, Tübingen: Mohr, 1977. To say that God is love is, according to Jüngel, to say that he is a 'unity of life and death to the advantage of life'. Perhaps one could say that it is by inexhaustibly giving himself away that God is and remains the source of all else and brings creation to its destiny. The integrity and relative autonomy which he wills for creation as his free partner mean that his purpose can be achieved only at painful cost to himself.

159. See pp. 208–10.

160. Note the fine book—sensitive to worship and prayer—by J. A. Baker, *The Foolishness of God*, London: DLT, 1970.

161. This against one argument advanced by Frances Young in her contribution—the best in the book—to *The Myth of God Incarnate* (ed. J. H. Hick): 'A cloud of witnesses', in particular p. 27, argument (i). The heart of her chapter is that 'God is to be understood as a suffering God, at least in the same sense as we can talk of him as loving' (p. 37).

162. Gregory Nazianzen, *ep.* 101. Even this principle has been subjected to critical probing by M. F. Wiles, although hardly with a view to reducing Christ's humanity: *Working Papers in Doctrine*, chapter 9.

163. L. Goppelt, *Typos: die typologische Deutung des Alten Testaments im Neuen*, Gütersloh: Bertelsmann, 1939; J. Daniélou, *Sacramentum futuri: études sur les origines de la typologie biblique*, Paris: Beauchesne, 1950; G. W. H. Lampe and K. Woollcombe, *Essays in Typology*, London: SCM,

1957; A. T. Hanson, *Jesus Christ in the Old Testament*, London: SPCK, 1965.

164. This question recurs in different contexts in chapters III, IV and XI.

165. Justin Martyr, *Apol.* I. 46.

166. R. Panikkar, *The Unknown Christ of Hinduism*, London: DLT, 1964. K. Rahner returns to the theme of anonymous Christianity several times in his *Schriften zur Theologie*, Einsiedeln: Benzinger, 1954ff (ET *Theological Investigations*, London: DLT, 1961ff): 'Anonymous Christians' (in vol. 6), 'Atheism and implicit Christianity' (in vol. 9), 'Anonymous Christianity and the missionary task of the Church' (in vol. 12), 'Observations on the problem of the "anonymous Christian"' (in vol. 14). The thing itself, though not the name, permeates his *Grundkurs des Glaubens* (ET *Foundations of Christian Faith*).

167. J. H. Hick, *God and the Universe of Faiths*.

168. J. H. Hick, *Evil and the God of Love*, chapter 14, section 7, and chapter 17.

169. John 13:1, *eis telos*. 'His own' are, in the broadest perspective, the whole of humanity.

170. G. W. H. Lampe, *God as Spirit*, p. 164f.

171. The original title of Schillebeeckx's book was *De Christusontmoeting als Sacrament van de Godsontmoeting*. The title adopted in the English translation dates from the third edition: *Christ the Sacrament of Encounter with God*.

172. Leo the Great, *serm.* 74, 2, PL 54, 398.

173. For examples from the patristic period, see W. H. Bates, 'The background of Apollinaris's eucharistic teaching' in *Journal of Ecclesiastical History* 12 (1961), pp. 139–54; H. Chadwick, 'Eucharist and christology in the Nestorian controversy' in *Journal of Theological Studies*, new series 2 (1951), pp. 145–64. For examples from the Reformation: P. C. Empie and J. I. McCord (eds.), *Marburg Revisited: a Re-examination of Lutheran and Reformed Traditions*, Minneapolis: Augsburg, 1966; F. Wendel, *Calvin, sources et évolution de sa pensée religieuse*, Paris: Presses universitaires de France, 1950, pp. 166–9, 263–9 (ET *Calvin*, London: Collins, 1963, pp. 221–5, 345–52); J. S. Whale, *Christian Reunion: historic divisions re-considered*, London: Lutterworth, 1971, pp. 56–96. A modern book which multiplies correspondences between christology and the eucharist, the eucharist and christology, is G. Martelet, *Résurrection, eucharistie et genèse de l'homme* (ET *The Risen Christ and the Eucharistic World*).

174. See note 146.

175. Thus Schillebeeckx introduces a qualifying *aliquo sensu* when he reports, approvingly, that 'the Greek patristic view of the eucharistic change was *in a sense* an extension of the "hypostatic union", the incarnation': *The Eucharist* (as in note 195), p. 68.

176. A kenotic christology also fits well with the positions of such an intentionally 'orthodox' New Testament scholar as R. E. Brown concerning the limitations of Jesus' knowledge and the indirectness of the christological evidence: see his *Jesus God and Man*, and his *Biblical Reflections*

on Crises facing the Church, New York: Paulist Press, and London: DLT, 1975, chapter 2: ' "Who do men say that I am?"—a survey of modern scholarship on Gospel christology'.

177. Y. Congar, 'L'idée de sacrements majeurs ou principaux' in *Concilium* no. 31 (January 1968), pp. 25–34.

178. According to Augustine, Christ is the minister of baptism (see note 155). Even if Christ is seen as the element or sphere 'into' which the candidate is baptized, nevertheless the imagery remains 'external', whereas in communion Christ is 'internalized'.

179. In my judgment, the best modern book on the work of Christ is F. W. Dillistone's *The Christian Understanding of Atonement,* Digswell Place: Nisbet, 1968. The same author's sacramental awareness is evident from his *Christianity and Symbolism.* See also H. R. Weber, *Kreuz und Kultur: Deutungen der Kreuzigung Jesu in neutestamentlichen Kulturen der Gegenwart,* Geneva: WCC, 1975. In its more commercial editions this study has been robbed of its chapters on verbal, pictorial and practical translation across cultures: *Kreuz: Überlieferung und Deutung der Kreuzigung Jesu im neutestamentlichen Kulturraum,* Stuttgart: Kreuz, 1975 (ET *The Cross: Tradition and Interpretation,* London: SPCK, 1979).

180. The baptismal 'institution narrative' of Matthew 28:19 comes under the same suspicion as attaches to all post-resurrection material in modern critical scholarship. The eucharistic institution risks being (pejoratively) classed as an aetiological cult-legend: see, for instance, (despite his denial of the term) W. Marxsen, *Das Abendmahl als christologisches Problem,* Gütersloh: Mohn, 1965[2] (ET *The Lord's Supper as a Christological Problem,* Philadelphia: Fortress, 1970), where the origin of the Lord's Supper is seen to reside more generally in the meals of Jesus' ministry *rather than* in an institution at a Last Supper. On the other hand, the basic historicity of the institution at the Last Supper is presupposed by J. Jeremias, *Die Abendmahlsworte Jesu,* Göttingen: Vandenhoeck & Ruprecht, 1960[3] (ET *The Eucharistic Words of Jesus,* London: SCM, 1966), and by many others.

181. For baptism, there are the gospel accounts of Jesus' own baptism and the important sayings of Mark 10:38f and Luke 12:50. As to the eucharist, meal-words and meal-deeds abound in the gospels: see G. Wainwright, *Eucharist and Eschatology,* pp. 25–42.

182. A select bibliography on baptism must include the following titles, the very abundance of which is an indication that many crucial questions come to a focus in Christian initiation: K. Aland, *Die Säuglingstaufe im Neuen Testament,* Munich: Kaiser, 1961 (ET *Did the Early Church baptize infants?* London: SCM, 1963), *Die Stellung der Kinder in den frühen christlichen Gemeinden—und ihre Taufe,* Munich: Kaiser, 1967, and *Taufe und Kindertaufe, zugleich eine Auseinandersetzung mit Karl Barths Lehre von der Taufe,* Gütersloh: Mohn, 1971; K. Barth, *Die kirchliche Lehre von der Taufe,* Zürich: Evangelischer Verlag, 1943 (ET *The Teaching of the Church regarding Baptism,* London: SCM, 1948), and *Kirchliche Dogmatik* IV/4, Zürich:

EVZ, 1967 (ET *Church Dogmatics* IV/4, Edinburgh: T. & T. Clark, 1969); M. Barth, *Die Taufe, ein Sakrament?* Zürich: Evangelischer Verlag, 1951; G. R. Beasley-Murray, *Baptism in the New Testament,* London: Macmillan, 1962; A. Benoit, B. Bobrinskoy, and F. Coudreau, *Baptême, sacrement d'unité,* Tours: Mame, 1971; D. Boureau, *L'avenir du baptême,* Lyons: Chalet, 1970; D. Bridge and D. Phypers, *The water that divides,* London: Inter-Varsity Press, 1977; O. Cullmann, *Die Tauflehre des Neuen Testaments,* Zürich: Zwingli-Verlag, 1948 (ET *Baptism in the New Testament,* London: SCM, 1950); G. Delling, *Die Zueignung des Heils in der Taufe,* Berlin: Evangelische Verlagsanstalt, 1961, and *Die Taufe im Neuen Testament,* Berlin: Evangelische Verlagsanstalt, 1963; J. D. G. Dunn, *Baptism in the Holy Spirit,* London: SCM, 1970; S. J. England, *The One Baptism,* St Louis: Bethany, 1960; T. M. Finn, *The Liturgy of Baptism in the Baptismal Instructions of St. John Chrysostom,* Washington, D.C.: Catholic University of America, 1967; J. D. C. Fisher, *Christian Initiation: Baptism in the Medieval West,* London: SPCK, 1965, and *Christian Initiation: The Reformation Period,* London: SPCK, 1970; W. F. Flemington, *The New Testament Doctrine of Baptism,* London: SPCK, 1948; N. Gäumann, *Taufe und Ethik: Studien zu Römer 6,* Munich: Kaiser, 1967; A. George and others, ET *Baptism in the New Testament,* London: Chapman, 1964; A. Gilmore, *Baptism and Christian Unity,* London: Lutterworth, 1966; A. Gilmore (ed.), *Christian Baptism: a fresh attempt to understand the rite in terms of scripture, history, and theology,* London: Lutterworth, 1959; A. Hamman, *Le baptême et la confirmation,* Paris: Desclée, 1969; H. Hubert, *Der Streit um die Kindertaufe,* Bern: Lang, 1972; P. J. Jagger, *Christian Initiation 1552–1969: rites of baptism and confirmation since the Reformation period,* London: SPCK, 1970; J. Jeremias, *Die Kindertaufe in den ersten vier Jahrhunderten,* Göttingen: Vandenhoeck & Ruprecht, 1958 (revised ET *Infant Baptism in the first four centuries,* London: SCM, 1960), and *Nochmals: die Anfänge der Kindertaufe,* Munich: Kaiser, 1962 (ET *The Origins of Infant Baptism: a further reply in answer to Kurt Aland,* London: SCM, 1963); E. Jüngel, *Karl Barths Lehre von der Taufe,* Zürich: EVZ, 1968; W. Kasper (ed.), *Christsein ohne Entscheidung, oder Soll die Kirche Kinder taufen?* Mainz: Grünewald, 1970; H. Kirsten, *Die Taufabsage: eine Untersuchung zu Gestalt und Geschichte der Taufe nach den altkirchlichen Taufliturgien,* Berlin: Evangelische Verlagsanstalt, 1960; G. Kretschmar, 'Die Geschichte des Taufgottesdienstes in der alten Kirche' in K. F. Müller and W Blankenburg (eds.), *Leiturgia,* vol. 5, Kassel: Stauda, 1970, pp. 1–348; G. W. H. Lampe, *The Seal of the Spirit,* London: SPCK, 1967[2]; F. J. Leenhardt, *Le baptême chrétien, son origine, sa signification,* Neuchâtel: Delachaux & Niestlé, 1944; P. C. Marcel, ET *The Biblical Doctrine of Infant Baptism,* London: Clarke, 1953 (from 'Le baptême, sacrement de l'alliance de grâce' in *La revue réformée,* 1950); L. L. Mitchell, *Baptismal Anointing,* London: SPCK, 1966; D. Moody, *Baptism: Foundation for Christian Unity,* Philadelphia: Westminster, 1967; B. Neunheuser, *Taufe und Firmung,* Freiburg: Herder, 1956 (ET *Baptism and Confirmation,* Freiburg: Herder, 1964); C. H. Ratschow, *Die eine christliche Taufe*, Gütersloh: Mohn, 1972; H. M. Riley, *Christian Initiation*, Washington, D.C.: Catholic University of America, 1974; E. Schlink, *Die Lehre von der Taufe*, Kassel: Stauda, 1969 (ET *The Doctrine of Baptism*, St. Louis: Concordia, 1972); A. Schmemann, *Of Water and the Spirit*, New York: St. Vladimir's, 1974, London: SPCK, 1976; R. Schnackenburg, *Das Heilsgeschehen bei der Taufe nach dem Apostel Paulus*, Munich: Zink, 1950 (ET *Baptism in the Thought of St. Paul*, Oxford: Blackwell, 1964); Scotland, Church of, *The Biblical Doctrine of Baptism*, Edinburgh: St. Andrew Press, 1958; A. Stenzel, *Die Taufe: eine genetische Erklärung der Taufliturgie*, Innsbruck: Rauch, 1958; F. Viering (ed.), *Zu Karl Barths Lehre von der Taufe*, Gütersloh: Mohn, 1971; E. C. Whitaker, *Documents of the Baptismal Liturgy*, London: SPCK, 1970², and *The Baptismal Liturgy: an Introduction to Baptism in the Western Church*, London: Faith Press, 1965; R. E. O. White, *The Biblical Doctrine of Initiation*, London: Hodder, 1960; J. Ysebaert, *Greek Baptismal Terminology: its origins and early development*, Nijmegen: Dekker & Van de Vegt, 1962. Many references to articles in periodicals will be found in my book *Christian Initiation*, London: Lutterworth, 1969, and in my article 'Développements baptismaux depuis 1967' in *Études théologiques et religieuses* 49 (1974), pp. 67–93.

183. As to re-orientation or conversion (*shub* in Hebrew; *epistrephein* in Greek): in some Eastern rites of baptism, the candidate, having faced west to renounce Satan (the *apotaxis*), turns east, towards the place of the rising sun, in order to profess allegiance to Christ (the *syntaxis*). This and similar baptismal themes will recur in other connexions: in chapter IV§4 (holiness), IV§7 (justification by faith), XII§3 (freedom and service).

184. Many of the baptismal books mentioned in note 182 deal also with confirmation. In addition: J. P. Bouhot, *La confirmation, sacrement de la communion ecclésiale*, Lyons: Chalet, 1972; L. A. van Buchem, *L'homélie pseudo-eusébienne de pentecôte: l'origine de la 'confirmatio' en Gaule méridionale et l'interprétation de ce rite par Fauste de Riez*, Nijmegen: Janssen, 1967; G. Dix, *Confirmation, or the Laying on of Hands?* London: SPCK, 1936, and *The Theology of Confirmation in relation to Baptism*, Westminster: Dacre, 1946; J. D. C. Fisher, *Confirmation then and now*, London: SPCK, 1978; L. Ligier, *La confirmation: sens et conjoncture oecuménique hier et aujourd'hui*, Paris: Beauchesne, 1973; A. J. Mason, *The Relation of Confirmation to Baptism*, London: Longmans, 1891; L. S. Thornton, *Confirmation: its place in the baptismal mystery*, Westminster: Dacre, 1954; M. Thurian, *La confirmation, consécration des laïcs*, Neuchâtel: Delachaux & Niestlé, 1957; L. Vischer, *Die Geschichte der Konfirmation*, Zürich: Evangelischer Verlag, 1958; E. C. Whitaker, *Sacramental initiation complete in baptism*, Bramcote: Grove, 1975. To explain the association about to be made with a *Christus victor* soteriology, I recall that the phrase of Faustus of Riez concerning confirmation as a 'strengthening for the fight', *robur ad pugnam*, had a long and successful history in the West. The tap given by the bishop to the candidate's cheek—probably in origin a form of the kiss of peace—was later interpreted along the same lines.

185. G. Aulén, ET *Christus Victor*, London: SPCK, 1931.

186. The language here is that of Luther's *Ein' feste Burg* and of Thomas Carlyle's translation. In the original, Christ is simply equated with 'der Herr Zebaoth'. Luther's contempt for the devil is shown by the fact that even God's 'little Word' can slay him: 'Ein Wörtlein kann ihn fällen'.

187. J. D. Crichton, *The Ministry of Reconciliation: a commentary on the 'Ordo paenitentiae'* 1974, London: Chapman, 1974; J. Fitzsimons (ed.), *Penance: virtue and sacrament*, London: Search, 1969; J. Gunstone, *The Liturgy of Penance*, London: Faith Press, 1966; J. A. Jungmann, *Die lateinischen Bussriten in ihrer geschichtlichen Entwicklung*, Innsbruck: Rauch, 1932; H. R. Mackintosh, *The Christian Experience of Forgiveness*, London: Nisbet, 1927; R. C. Mortimer, *The Origins of Private Penance in the Western Church*, Oxford: Clarendon, 1939; A. Nocent, *Le sacrement de la réconciliation dans l'Église d'occident*, Rome: S. Anselmo, 1972; P. F. Palmer, *Sacraments and Forgiveness: History and Doctrinal Development of Penance, Extreme Unction and Indulgences*, Westminster, Md.: Newman, 1959, and London: DLT, 1960; B. Poschmann, *Busse und letzte Oelung*, Freiburg: Herder, 1951; O. D. Watkins, *A History of Penance*, 2 volumes, London: Longmans, 1920. *La Maison-Dieu* no. 117 (1974) was devoted to 'Pénitence et réconciliation', and *Concilium*, January 1971, contained a survey by F. Funke on recent writing on penance.

188. Justin Martyr's *First Apology*, 61 and 65, shows enlightenment to have been a baptismal term. Christologically and soteriologically, Jesus Christ is 'the light of the world' (Luke 2:32; John 1:4-9; 8:12; 2 Cor. 4:4), and the image is used in connexion with Christian witness (Matthew 5:14-16) and conduct (Eph. 5:7-13). Ephesians 5:14 is sometimes considered to be a baptismal hymn: it belongs to the category of *Weckrufe* (G. Schille, *Frühchristliche Hymnen*, pp. 94-101).

189. R. C. Moberly, *Atonement and Personality*, London: Murray, 1901.

190. A. Chavasse, *Étude sur l'onction des infirmes dans l'Église latine*, Lyons: Sacré Coeur, 1942; E. Frost, *Christian Healing*, Oxford: Mowbray, 1949[2]; C. W. Gusmer, *The Ministry of Healing in the Church of England: an ecumenical liturgical study*, Great Wakering: Mayhew-McCrimon, 1974; M. T. Kelsey, *Healing and Christianity in ancient thought and modern times*, New York: Harper & Row, and London: SCM, 1973; P. F. Palmer, *Sacraments and Forgiveness*, part 2: 'Extreme unction', and pp. 394-8; B. Poschmann, *Busse und letzte Oelung*, pp. 125-38; F. W. Fuller, *Anointing of the Sick in Scripture and Tradition*, London: SPCK, 1904.

191. M. Wilson, *The Church is healing*, London: SCM, 1966, and *Health is for people*, London: DLT, 1975.

192. Orders is a highly controversial field, made particularly difficult by the combination of professional and existential interests on the part of theologians who, at least in the West, have usually been ordained ministers. On the theology of the ordained ministry, I pick out the following: J. J. von Allmen, *Le saint ministère selon la conviction et la volonté des Réformés du XVIe siècle*, Neuchâtel: Delachaux & Niestlé, 1968; R. E. Brown, *Priest*

and Bishop: Biblical Reflections, Paramus: Paulist Press, 1970, and London: Chapman, 1971; B. Cooke, *Ministry to Word and Sacraments*, Philadelphia: Fortress, 1976; A. T. Hanson, *The Pioneer Ministry*, London: SCM, 1961; K. E. Kirk (ed.), *The Apostolic Ministry: Essays on the History and Doctrine of Episcopacy*, London: Hodder, 1946; A. Lemaire, *Les ministères dans l'Église*, Paris: Centurion, 1974 (ET *Ministry in the Church*, London: SPCK, 1977); J. Line, *The Doctrine of the Christian Ministry*, London: Lutterworth, 1959; T. W. Manson, *The Church's Ministry*, London: Hodder, 1948, and *Ministry and Priesthood: Christ's and ours*, London: Epworth, 1958; B. Minchin, *Every Man in his Ministry*, London: DLT, 1960; R. C. Moberly, *Ministerial Priesthood*, London: Murray, 1910² (reprinted SPCK, 1969); R. S. Paul, *Ministry*, Grand Rapids: Eerdmans, 1965; W. Telfer, *The Office of a Bishop*, London: DLT, 1962. From the boundless literature on the narrow subject of the 'validity' of Anglican orders, I simply mention the irenical studies of J. J. Hughes, *Absolutely Null and Utterly Void: an account of the papal condemnation of Anglican orders 1896*, London: Sheed & Ward, 1968, and *Stewards of the Lord: a reappraisal of Anglican orders*, London: Sheed & Ward, 1970. On the liturgical history of ordination, see M. Andrieu, *Les Ordines romani du haut moyen âge*, vols. 3 and 4, Louvain: Spicilegium Sacrum Lovaniense, 1951 and 1956; P. F. Bradshaw, *The Anglican Ordinal: its history and development from the Reformation to the present day*, London: SPCK, 1971; B. Kleinheyer, *Die Priesterweihe im römischen Ritus*, Trier: Paulinus, 1962; H. B. Porter, *The Ordination Prayers of the Ancient Western Churches*, London: SPCK, 1967; and C. Jones, G. Wainwright, and E. Yarnold (eds.), *The Study of Liturgy*, pp. 289–349. Note also P. van Beneden, *Aux origines d'une terminologie sacramentelle: 'ordo', 'ordinare', 'ordinatio' dans la littérature chrétienne avant 313*, Louvain: Spicilegium Sacrum Lovaniense, 1974.

193. Some New Testament scholars see Mark 10:45b as an addition to the pericope.

194. P. Adnès, *Le mariage*, Tournai: Desclée, 1963; J. J. von Allmen, *Maris et femmes d'après saint Paul*, Neuchâtel: Delachaux & Niestlé, 1951 (ET *Pauline Teaching on Marriage*, London: Faith Press, 1963); D. S. Bailey, *The Man-Woman Relation in Christian Thought*, London: Longmans, 1959; J. Dominian, *Christian Marriage*, London: DLT, 1967; P. Evdokimov, *Sacrement de l'amour: le mystère conjugal à la lumière de la tradition orthodoxe*, Paris: Épi, 1962²; E. Schillebeeckx, ET *Marriage: secular reality and saving mystery*, London: Sheed & Ward, 1965; O. D. Watkins, *Holy Matrimony*, London: Rivington, 1895.

195. A select bibliography on the eucharist: J. J. von Allmen, *Essai sur le repas du Seigneur*, Neuchâtel: Delachaux & Niestlé, 1966 (ET *The Lord's Supper*, London: Lutterworth, 1969); J. de Baciocchi, *L'eucharistie*, Tournai: Desclée, 1964; R. Bornert, *Les commentaires byzantins de la divine liturgie*, Paris: Archives de l'Orient chrétien, 1966; L. Bouyer, *L'eucharistie: théologie et spiritualité de la prière eucharistique*, Tournai: Desclée, 1966 (ET *Eucharist*, Notre Dame: University Press, 1968); Y. Brilioth, *Nattvarden i*

evangeliskt gudstjänstliv, Stockholm: Svenska Kyrkans Diakonistyrelses Bokförlag, 1951² (ET *Eucharistic Faith and Practice: Evangelical and Catholic*, London: SPCK, 1930); R. F. Buxton, *Eucharist and Institution Narrative: a study in the Roman and Anglican traditions of the consecration of the eucharist from the eighth to the twentieth centuries*, Great Wakering: Mayhew-McCrimon, 1976; F. Clark, *Eucharistic Sacrifice and the Reformation*, Oxford: Blackwell, 1967²; J. P. de Jong, *De eucharistie, symbolische werkelijkheid*, Hilversum: Gooi & Sticht, 1966 (enlarged French translation *L'eucharistie, réalité symbolique*, Paris: Cerf, 1972); J. Delorme and others, ET *The Eucharist in the New Testament*, London: Chapman, 1964; G. Dix, *The Shape of the Liturgy*, Westminster: Dacre, 1945; F. X. Durwell, *L'eucharistie, présence du Christ*, Paris: Éditions ouvrières, 1971; L. Dussaut, *L'eucharistie, pâques de toute la vie*, Paris: Cerf, 1972; B. Forte, *La chiesa nell'eucaristia*, Naples: D'Auria, 1975; J. Jeremias, *Die Abendmahlsworte Jesu* (ET *The Eucharistic Words of Jesus*); E. J. Kilmartin, *The Eucharist in the Primitive Church*, Englewood Cliffs: Prentice-Hall, 1965; N. Lash, *His Presence in the World*, London: Sheed & Ward, 1968; P. Lebeau, *Le vin nouveau du royaume*, Paris: Desclée de Brouwer, 1966; J. Lécuyer, *Le sacrifice de la nouvelle alliance*, Le Puy: Mappus, 1962; F. J. Leenhardt, *Le sacrement de la sainte cène*, Neuchâtel: Delachaux & Niestlé, 1948, and *Ceci est mon corps*, Neuchâtel: Delachaux & Niestlé, 1955 (ET in O. Cullmann and F. J. Leenhardt, *Essays on the Lord's Supper*, London: Lutterworth, 1958); H. Lietzmann, *Messe und Herrenmahl*, Berlin: de Gruyter, 1955³ (ET *Mass and Lord's Supper*, Leiden: Brill, in fascicles from 1953); S. McCormick, *The Lord's Supper: a Biblical Interpretation*, Philadelphia: Westminster, 1966; J. H. McKenna, *Eucharist and Holy Spirit: the eucharistic epiclesis in twentieth-century theology*, Great Wakering: Mayhew-McCrimon, 1975; E. L. Mascall, *Corpus Christi*, London: Longmans, 1965²; P. Neuenzeit, *Das Herrenmahl: Studien zur paulinischen Eucharistieauffassung*, Munich: Kösel, 1960; E. Schillebeeckx, *Christus tegenwoordigheid in de eucharistie*, Bilthoven: Nelissen 1967 (ET *The Eucharist*, London: Sheed & Ward, 1968); H. J. Schulz, *Die byzantinische Liturgie: vom Werden ihrer Symbolgestalt*, Freiburg: Lambertus, 1964; D. Stone, *History of the Doctrine of the Holy Eucharist*, 2 volumes, London: Longmans, 1909; T. Süss, *La communion au corps du Christ: études sur les problèmes de la sainte cène et les paroles d'institution*, Neuchâtel: Delachaux & Niestlé, 1968; M. Thurian, *L'eucharistie: mémorial du Seigneur, sacrifice d'action de grâce et d'intercession*, Neuchâtel, Delachaux & Niestlé 1959 (ET *The Eucharistic Memorial*, 2 volumes, London: Lutterworth, 1960–1); J. M. R. Tillard, *L'eucharistie, pâque de l'Église*, Paris: Cerf, 1964; G. Wainwright, *Eucharist and Eschatology*.

196. Examples could be multiplied to show how the eucharist attracts to itself all the soteriological themes already mentioned in association with the other sacraments. The following allusions must suffice: death and resurrection, mortification of sin and birth to new life (see J. M. R. Tillard, *L'eucharistie, pâque de l'Église*, throughout); the battle ('O salutaris hostia/quae caeli pandis ostium/bella premunt hostilia/da robur, fer

auxilium'—from *Verbum supernum prodiens*); forgiveness and reconciliation (*eis aphesin hamartiōn*, Matthew 26:28; and the kiss of peace); healing ('the medicine of immortality and the antidote to death', Ignatius of Antioch; and the *remedia* of the Roman post-communion prayers); free service ('Qui cumque traderetur voluntariae passioni', *Apostolic Tradition*; and 'Hanc igitur oblationem servitutis nostrae', Roman canon; self-giving love ('the marriage-feast of the Lamb', Rev. 19:9; and 'his closest love', Wesley's *Hymns on the Lord's Supper*, no. 60). The most characteristic imagery of the eucharist is, of course, feeding ('our *epiousion* bread', *panem crastinum*):

> Author of life divine,
>   Who hast a table spread,
> Furnished with mystic wine
>   And everlasting bread,
> Preserve the life Thyself hast given,
> And feed and train us up for heaven.
>
> Our needy souls sustain
>   With fresh supplies of love,
> Till all Thy life we gain,
>   And all Thy fulness prove,
> And, strengthened by Thy perfect grace,
> Behold without a veil Thy face.
>
> (Charles Wesley, MHB No. 764)

197. So in the old anaphora of Basil of Caesarea ('In these last days you have manifested to us who sat in darkness and the shadow of death your only-begotten Son, our Lord and God and Saviour, Jesus Christ'), in the Byzantine liturgy of St John Chrysostom ('Holy are you . . . for you so loved the world that you gave your only-begotten Son that all who would believe in him should not perish, but have eternal life'), and in the English *Book of Common Prayer* ('Almighty God, our heavenly Father, who of thy tender mercy didst give thine only Son Jesus Christ to suffer death upon the cross for our redemption . . .'): texts from R. C. D. Jasper and G. J. Cuming, *Prayers of the Eucharist: Early and Reformed*, London: Collins, 1975, pp. 30, 80, 187.

198. 'Through Christ our Lord you give us all these gifts. You fill them with life and goodness, you bless them and make them holy' (ICEL translation, taken from *The Sunday Missal*, London, Collins: 1975). The original reference is to seasonal fruits, which were blessed at this point: see J. A. Jungmann, *Missarum sollemnia*, part 4, chapter 2, section 18.

199. R. Bultmann in H. W. Bartsch (ed.), *Kerygma und Mythos*, Hamburg: Reich, vol. 1, 1948, pp. 19f, 23, note 2; vol. 2, 1952, pp. 181–4 (ET *Kerygma and Myth*, London: SPCK, 1953, pp. 6f, 10, note 2; the ET omits the article from which the third reference is taken).

200. In *The Divine Relativity: a Social Conception of God* (New Haven: Yale University Press, 1964²), C. Hartshorne argues that his (whiteheadian) view has a far higher degree of continuity with the 'naive forms of religious speech', 'the God of worship', than has the absolutistic conception of deity of an earlier metaphysics. He quotes Whitehead's dictum that a deity's 'power is the worship he inspires'.

201. T. F. Torrance, *Theological Science*, London: OUP, 1969.

202. For John Macquarrie, see chapter X§5, where Process Theology is also taken up again.

203. M. Plathow, *Das Problem des 'concursus divinus'*, Göttingen: Vandenhoeck & Ruprecht, 1976.

204. N. Smart, *The Concept of Worship*, p. 39f. The printed text contains typographical dislocations, and these have been corrected according to information supplied by Professor Smart.

205. Smart, p. 11f. Smart's picture is at least as old in Christian theology as Irenaeus, with his notion of the 'limitlessness' of God: see R. A. Norris, *God and World in Early Christian Theology*, New York: Seabury, 1965, p. 86 (London: Black, 1966, p. 69f). As Norris shows (pp. 89–97, British edition pp. 72–80), it is all tied up with Irenaeus' appreciation of the *creatio ex nihilo* and of the goodness of creation.

206. M. F. Wiles also argued for a personalist view of the sacraments in 'Grace in Church and sacrament', in *Theology*, October 1969, pp. 451–59; cf. already 'The Holy Spirit in Christian theology' in *Theology*, June 1963, pp. 233–7 (now reprinted in his *Explorations in Theology*). Professor Wiles tells me that he is writing a book on the relations between his 'remade' Christian doctrine and Christian worship: note the questions raised earlier in chapter II and again in chapter VI.

207. Note Charles Wesley's hymn (MHB, No. 761):

> Jesus, we thus obey
> Thy last and kindest word;
> Here in Thine own appointed way,
> We come to meet Thee, Lord.

208. See, for example, G. Greshake, *Geschenkte Freiheit: Einführung in die Gnadenlehre*, Freiburg: Herder, 1977; B. Lonergan, *Grace and Freedom: Operative Grace in the Thought of St Thomas Aquinas*, London: DLT, 1971; P. S. Watson, *The Concept of Grace*, London: Epworth, 1959.

209. P. Schoonenberg has been a sharp critic of 'competition-thinking': see, for instance, the chapter 'God or man: a false dilemma' in his ET *The Christ*, London: Sheed & Ward, 1972. Note also K. Rahner's dictum that 'God is not diminished by our becoming greater' ('Nature and grace', in ET *Theological Investigations*, vol. 4, London: DLT, 1966, pp. 165–88, in particular p. 177).

210. 'Full' pelagianism is not here meant to be contrasted with what became known as semi-pelagianism, where the human will, though weakened by original sin, was held to be capable of taking the first steps of faith unaided. I am intending to exclude naked pelagianism throughout

the relationship between God and humanity. On Augustine, pelagianism and semi-pelagianism, see chapter VII and B. Lohse's excellent handbook, *Epochen der Dogmengeschichte,* Stuttgart: Kreuz, 1974³, pp. 105–34 (ET *A Short History of Christian Doctrine,* Philadelphia: Fortress, 1978).

211. The marriage partners are the ministers of the sacrament to each other. It is doubtless this stress on human freedom which chiefly causes the sacramental nature of marriage to be opposed by those Protestants who understand the *sola gratia* to exclude human co-operation in the matter of salvation. Further: if one were to follow out the hints scattered on pp. 73–79 to the effect that there is a certain correspondence between particular sacraments and particular theories of the atonement, then marriage would most obviously be matched, among traditional atonement theories, by the abelardian or 'subjective'; and this is a theory with which classical Protestants have shown little sympathy. Note, however, the Wesleys' *Hymns on the Lord's Supper,* no. 60:

> Who seek redemption through his love,
> His love shall them redeem;
> He came self-emptied from above,
> That we might live through Him.

212. G. Philips, *L'union personnelle avec le Dieu vivant: essai sur l'origine et le sens de la grâce créée,* Gembloux: Duculot, 1974. A piquant detail in the history is that the scholastics saw in the *habitus* of charity a safeguard against pelagianism—whereas it is precisely the notion of the *habitus* which was to strike Protestants as proof of the pelagianism of Catholicism.

213. D. M. Baillie, *God was in Christ,* London: Faber, 1955².

214. In his Cadbury lectures given in the University of Birmingham, 1978, S. W. Sykes exploited W. B. Gallie's notion of 'the essentially contested concept' in order to show that controversy belonged to the very identity of historical Christianity. Sykes argued that disputes among Christians about the truth need to be set within the containing context of communal worship, where all parties are open to God and his power to transform. For W. B. Gallie, see *Philosophy and the Historical Understanding,* London: Chatto & Windus, 1964, especially pp. 157–91. Professor Sykes's lectures will be published under the title *The Identity of Christianity.* His views on the function of communal worship to 'conserve riches' matched my own arguments in chapter X concerning liturgical and doctrinal revision.

215. W. R. Matthews, *The Problem of Christ in the Twentieth Century,* London: OUP, 1950, p. 70f.

216. *Qui fecit nos sine nobis, non salvabit nos sine nobis*: John Wesley liked to quote this (uncharacteristically?) augustinian phrase: see, for instance, the sermon *On Working out our own Salvation,* I, 1.

217. I. T. Ramsey, *Models for Divine Activity,* London: SCM, 1973,

p. 13: 'Discourse about the Spirit is a way of being articulate about God's initiating activity and our responsive activity.'

218. See A. Heron, 'Logos, Image, Son: some models and paradigms in early christology' in R. W. A. McKinney (ed.), *Creation, Christ and Culture*, pp. 43–62.

219. On the pneumatological clauses, whose presence in our Nicene Creed is due to their adoption by the council of Constantinople in 381, see J. N. D. Kelly, *Early Christian Creeds*[3], pp. 338–44. The *filioque* is a later Western addition, whose introduction has continued to offend the East as much on account of the lack of ecumenical consultation as on account of its content. Anti-arian motives were at work in favour of its introduction in the West, but the Orthodox East, even on the substantial question, prefers the idea of 'through the Son', in order to save the monarchy of the Father (see Kelly, *op. cit.*, pp. 358–67). The question of the *filioque* recurs on p. 305 and in notes 452 and 733.

220. This line is followed in G. W. H. Lampe, *God as Spirit*, and in M. F. Wiles, *Explorations in Theology*, chapter 6: 'The Holy Spirit in Christian theology'.

221. C. F. D. Moule points out that it is less accurate to say that the Spirit 'takes the place' of Christ than that, in both the Fourth Gospel and Acts, 'the Spirit communicates and extends the presence of Christ': *The Origin of Christology*, p. 104f.

222. A. W. Wainwright, *The Trinity in the New Testament*, pp. 15–40.

223. A stimulating exegetical essay on this passage is found in E. Käsemann, *Paulinische Perspektiven*, Tübingen: Mohr, 1969, pp. 211–36: 'Der gottesdienstliche Schrei nach der Freiheit' (ET in *Perspectives on Paul*, London: SCM, 1971, pp. 122–37). According to Käsemann, Paul critically re-interprets glossolalic prayer by linking it with the *groanings* of creation for deliverance and with the *continuing struggle* of believers for free obedience as children of God.

224. The verb *krazein* is used to introduce the Sanctus at 1 Clement 34, 6.

225. Note also Jude 20: 'Pray *en Pneumati hagiōi*.'

226. In the tradition, 'being made to drink of the one Spirit' is sometimes given a baptismal interpretation, sometimes a eucharistic: see G. Wainwright, *Eucharist and Eschatology*, p. 115f.

227. 'Sealing' was understood sacramentally in the early Church, whether of baptism or of 'confirmation': see G. W. H. Lampe, *The Seal of the Spirit*. J. D. G. Dunn's anti-sacramental interpretation of such Spirit-references in the New Testament is eccentric: *Baptism in the Holy Spirit*.

228. I am indebted to A. W. Wainwright, *The Doctrine of the Trinity in the New Testament*, pp. 224f, 227–30.

229. Nor, I think, by papyrus 46, which reads ΟΙ ΠΝΕΥΜΑΤΙ ΛΑΤΡΕΥΟΝΤΕϹ, omitting 'God'.

230. The Greek would have needed to repeat the definite article *ton*

in order to make the sense adjectival. The lack of the definite article in Latin allows the ambiguity which led Augustine astray.

231. A. W. Wainwright refers to H. Lietzmann, *I Korintherbrief*, p. 29.

232. This and the following three ordination prayers are taken, with slight adaptations of the translation, from H. B. Porter, *The Ordination Prayers of the Ancient Western Churches*, pp. 20f, 26f, 34f, 74f.

233. The puzzling greeting 'The Lord be with you: And with thy spirit' seems to belong to this first pneumatological pattern of divine Spirit/human spirit.

234. J. A. Jungmann, *Die Stellung Christi im liturgischen Gebet*[2], pp. 130ff, 178ff.

235. The Church of England's Series 1, 2 and 3 'alternative services' in the 1960s and 1970s were authorized for limited periods as part of the build-up to the *Alternative Service Book* (1980), into which they should, with some modification, be taken. For an account of the process of liturgical revision in the Church of England, with its inner-anglican doctrinal incidences, see C. O. Buchanan's succession of booklets *Recent Liturgical Revision in the Church of England*, Bramcote: Grove Booklets on Ministry and Worship Nos. 14, 14A, 14B, 14C, 1973–78. It is not intended to abolish the use of the *Book of Common Prayer* ('1662').

236. Basil, *On the Holy Spirit*, 3, PG 32, 72. See J. A. Jungmann, *Die Stellung Christi im liturgischen Gebet*[2], pp. 155ff, 172ff; M. J. Lubatschiwsky, 'Des hl. Basilius liturgischer Kampf gegen den Arianismus' in *Zeitschrift für katholische Theologie* 66 (1942), pp. 20–38.

237. Basil did not know the so-called *Apostolic Tradition* of Hippolytus, where the doxology is made *Patri et Filio cum Spiritu sancto*, but the authenticity of this formulation is not above suspicion.

238. See C. L. Feltoe (ed.), *The Letters and other remains of Dionysius of Alexandria*, Cambridge: University Press, 1904, p. 198.

239. G. Kretschmar, *Studien zur frühchristlichen Trinitätslehre*, Tübingen: Mohr, 1956.

240. Justin, *Apology* I, 65; 67.

241. Basil, *On the Holy Spirit*, 74, PG 32, 208.

242. Aphraates, *Homily* 23, (PS 2, 128, 14–17, ed. Parisot).

243. Theodore is recorded in Nicetas, *Thesaurus* 5, 30 (PG 139, 1390). There is confirmatory evidence in Philostorgius, *H.E.* 3, 13, PG 65, 501. See H. Thurston, 'The "Gloria Patri"' in *The Month* 131 (1918), pp. 406–17. In a doctrinally divided Antioch, bishop Leontius was driven to mumbling the doxology, raising his voice only at 'world without end' (Theodoret, *H.E.* 2. 19, PG 82, 1057–60).

244. Cf. R. H. Connolly (ed.), *Didascalia Apostolorum*, Oxford: Clarendon, 1929, p. 204f.

245. W. Wright, *Apocryphal Acts of the Apostles*, vol. 2, London: Williams and Norgate, 1871, p. 268.

246. R. H. Connolly, *The Liturgical Homilies of Narsai*, Cambridge: University Press, 1909, pp. 23, 59, 67 (where note 1 may be misleading).

247. E. C. Whitaker, 'The history of the baptismal formula' in *Journal of Ecclesiastical History* 16 (1965), pp. 1–12. By 'declaratory formula' I mean the 'performative' pronouncement by the ministers: *Ego te baptizo* ... or *Baptizetai*. ... The earlier 'form' appears to have been the baptismal interrogations and responses themselves.

248. *The Making of Christian Doctrine*, pp. 80, 87. I draw several of my examples from Wiles. Wiles' own historical presentation would perhaps have been more nuanced if he had known Kretschmar's work. Certainly Kretschmar insists on the prime importance of the baptismal locus, but his thesis is much more widely based in the whole liturgical life of the Church.

249. Tertullian, *Against Praxeas*, 26, PL 2, 213. Athanasius, *Letters to Serapion*, I, 29f, PG 26, 597–600. Basil, *On the Holy Spirit*, 24–36, PG 32, 109–33.

250. *Apostolic Constitutions* V, 7 (cf. III, 17).

251. G. R. Beasley-Murray, *Baptism in the New Testament*, p. 91, quotes a sixfold example from Strack-Billerbeck, *Kommentar zum Neuen Testament aus Talmud in Midrash*, vol. 1, 1922, p. 1054f.

252. M. Barth, *Die Taufe, ein Sakrament?* p. 552: 'Die "Taufe auf Jesus Christus" ist immer eine Taufe auf den vom Vater erwählten Sohn: auf den "Gesalbten", der mit dem Heiligen Geist tauft.'

253. Justin, *Apology* I, 61.

254. It is in the context of the (saving and judging) power of the Spirit that Nicetas of Remesiana could write: 'He (the Spirit) can be no stranger to the divine nature, who is no stranger to the divine activities. It is idle to refuse to him the name of God or the worship due to God, when you cannot deny that he has the power of God. I will therefore adore Father, Son, and Holy Spirit with one and the same religious worship; not separately, as the heathen worship their "gods many", but as one God. When worship is paid to the Spirit, it is paid to him whose Spirit he is' (*On the Holy Spirit*, quoted by H. B. Swete, *The Holy Spirit in the Ancient Church*, London: Macmillan, 1912, p. 312f).

255. It is interesting that when the deistically inclined M. F. Wiles wrote on the Holy Spirit (*The Remaking of Christian Doctrine*, chapter 5), he met with most approval from Jesuits and from (Arminian) Methodists; their theology of (universal) grace is furthest removed from coercion.

256. Cf. Augustine's reserve concerning the word *persona*—'We speak only in order not to say nothing' (*de Trinitate*, V, 9, 10)—and, more broadly, the whole apophatic strand in Eastern Orthodox theology.

257. Basil, *On the Holy Spirit*, 16–21, PG 32, 93–105.

258. It is largely with this 'economic' aspect that two modern trinitarian studies are concerned: C. W. Lowry, *The Trinity and Christian Devotion*, London: Eyre & Spottiswoode, 1946; J. E. L. Newbigin, *The Relevance of Trinitarian Doctrine for Today's Mission*, London: Edinburgh House, 1963. Bishop Newbigin's great work of ecclesiology, *The Household of God*, London: SCM, 1953, is also trinitarian in conception.

259. In the co-ordinated doxology, whether in the form of 'with' or in the form of 'and', normal liturgical practice is to name the Father first: here is further testimony to the persistent sense of the divine monarchy.

260. *Acts of Thomas*, 27, cf. 50; E. Hennecke and R. McL. Wilson, *New Testament Apocrypha*, vol. 2, London: Lutterworth Press, 1965, pp. 456f, 470, and G. Bornkamm's commentary, *ibid.*, p. 438f.

261. L. Hodgson, *The Doctrine of the Trinity*, pp. 232–4.

262. In dependence on C. C. J. Webb's *God and Personality*, Hodgson writes: 'The idea of personality implies a plurality of persons. We cannot think of any life as truly personal unless it be a life of intercourse between persons. . . . The doctrine of creation, in orthodox Christianity, asserts that the created universe is not necessary to the being of God. It is entirely dependent upon God for its being, but God has no need of it in order to be entirely himself in all the rich fulness of his Godhead. The doctrine of the Trinity implies that in the eternal being of God, quite apart from creation, there exist all the elements necessary for a fully personal life. It enables us to believe that the life of God is essentially and eternally personal without denying the implications of the doctrine of creation' (p. 190).

263. B. Bobrinskoy, 'Le Saint-Esprit dans la liturgie' in *Studia Liturgica* 1 (1962), pp. 47–60. Note also the ecumenical symposium introduced by A. M. Triacca, *Le Saint-Esprit dans la liturgie* (Conférences Saint-Serge, XVIe semaine d'études liturgiques, 1969), Rome: Edizioni liturgiche, 1977.

264. ET from E. C. Whitaker, *Documents of the Baptismal Liturgy*[2], p. 80f.

265. U. Zwingli, *De canone missae epicheiresis* (1523).

266. The hymns are accessible in J. E. Rattenbury, *The Eucharistic Hymns of John and Charles Wesley*, London: Epworth, 1948.

267. *Hymns on the Lord's Supper*, No. 16 (MHB No. 765). The prayer in *Apostolic Constitutions* VIII reads: 'And we beseech you . . . to send down your Holy Spirit upon this sacrifice, the witness of the sufferings of the Lord Jesus, that he may make this bread body of your Christ, and this cup blood of your Christ; that those who partake may be stengthened to piety, obtain forgiveness of sins, be delivered from the devil and his deceit, be filled with Holy Spirit, become worthy of your Christ, and obtain eternal life, after reconciliation with you, almighty Lord' (ET from Jasper and Cuming, *Prayers of the Eucharist*).

268. I take the memorial to be both Godward and manward: see my *Eucharist and Eschatology*, pp. 60–8. This is controversial exegetically but appears to me, in this connexion, to fit the 'linking' role of the Spirit.

269. See earlier pp. 67–70.

270. D. E. Jenkins 'defines' man as 'the potential worshipper who has the capacity to fall in love': *What is Man?* London: SCM, 1970, p. 123.

271. This clear evidence of the tradition needs re-affirmation against all, whether charismatics or Kimbanguists, who reduce Christian water-baptism to 'the baptism of John'. On the worship of the Church of Jesus

Christ on Earth through the Prophet Simon Kimbangu, see M. L. Martin, *Kirche ohne Weisse*, Basel: Reinhardt, 1971 (ET *Kimbangu: an African Prophet and his Church*, Oxford: Blackwell, 1975); and see pp. 365, 383f.

272. J. Macquarrie writes: 'In the first place, the Spirit proceeds, he comes forth from God to move through all creation. But having penetrated the creation, he strives in it and with it to bring it to union with God. There is, as it were, a double movement of the Spirit—he proceeds and he returns' (*Thinking about God*, London: SCM, 1975, p. 127; in traditional terminology, 'procession' is more usually reserved for the inner relation between the Spirit and the Father, while 'mission' is used for the Spirit's relation to creation).

273. *Ho de katergasamenos hyēmas*: the New English Bible translates 'God himself has *shaped* us for this very end'.

274. A positive reflexion on the matter by a modern Protestant is found in P. Y. Eméry, *L'unité des croyants au ciel et sur la terre*, Taizé, 1962 (ET *The Communion of Saints*, London: Faith Press, 1966).

275. N. Smart, *The Concept of Worship*, p. 48.

276. When the Christians desired to remove the martyred Polycarp's body and 'touch his holy flesh', the Jews at Smyrna suspected that they would 'abandon the Crucified and begin worshipping this one'. The authors of *The Martyrdom of Polycarp* replied: 'We can never forsake Christ, who suffered for the salvation of the whole world of those who are saved, the faultless for the sinners, nor can we ever worship any other. For we worship this one as the son of God, but we love the martyrs as disciples and imitators of the Lord, deservedly so, because of their unsurpassable devotion to their own King and Teacher. May it be also our lot to be their companions and fellow disciples' (17). See K. Donovan in C. Jones, G. Wainwright and E. Yarnold, *The Study of Liturgy*, pp. 421–4. Note also the fine theological comments of J. Macquarrie, *Principles of Christian Theology*, 1977[2], p. 400f.

277. G. Wainwright, *Eucharist and Eschatology*, pp. 117–19.

278. Chapters 48–49: see J. M. Hussey and P. A. McNulty, *Nicholas Cabasilas: a Commentary on the Divine Liturgy*, London: SPCK, 1960, pp. 106–14.

279. For this interpretation of the *communicantes* paragraph, see J. A. Jungmann, *Missarum sollemnia*, part 4, chapter 2, section 9, and on the *nobis quoque pecatoribus*, ibid., section 17.

280. MHB No. 824. On the *communio sanctorum* theme in Methodism, see R. N. Flew, 'Methodism and the Catholic Tradition' in N. P. Williams and C. Harris (eds.), *Northern Catholicism*, London: SPCK, 1933, pp. 515–30.

281. The source of the *mot* escapes me. Perhaps it was not Karl Rahner. Certainly Rahner himself has worked contructively at individual eschatology: see, resumptively, *Grundkurs des Glaubens*, pp. 414–29 (ET *Foundations of Christian Faith*, pp. 431–47).

282. Saints can also be prized for having discerned, taught and transmitted what is held to be the saving faith in its true form. The commemoration of the doctors of the Church brings dogma self-consciously to the very heart of the eucharistic anaphora in the liturgy of the ('monophysite') Orthodox Syrian Church of the East (India): 'Again we remember those who have before us fallen asleep in holiness and taken repose in the abode of the saints, and who maintained and delivered and entrusted to us the one apostolic and uncorrupt faith. We also acknowledge those three synods, sacred, holy and ecumenical; namely that in Nicea, that in Constantinople, and that in Ephesus; and our illustrious and divine holy Fathers and Doctors, who participated in them; the venerable St James, the first archbishop of Jerusalem, apostle and martyr; and Ignatius, Clement, Dionysius, Athanasius, Julius, Baselius, Gregorius, Dioscorus, Timothy, Philoxenus, Antimus and Ivanius; and mentionable especially by name is St Cyril, that exalted and veritable tower of knowledge, who expounded the doctrine of the incarnation of God the Word, our Lord Jesus Christ, declaring and showing clearly that he became incarnate. We remember also our patriarch St Severus, the crown of the Syrians, the eloquent mouth, the pillar and the doctor of the holy Church of God as a whole; the meadow abounding in blossom, who preached all the time that St Mary was undoubtedly the God-bearer; and our venerable and holy Father Mor Jacob Baradaeus, the upholder of the Orthodox Faith; and Mor Ephrem and Mor Jacob and Mor Isaac and Mor Balaeus and Mor Bar Soumas, the chief among the mourners; and Mor Simeon the Stylite, and Mor Abahai the elect one; and those before them, and with them, and after them, who have kept and handed down and entrusted to us the one genuine and undefiled faith. May their prayers be a stronghold to us. Let us beseech the Lord' (*The Service Book of the Holy Qurbana*, Kottayam, 1970²).

283. On these categories, see J. L. Leuba, *L'institution et l'événement: les deux modes de l'oeuvre de Dieu selon le Nouveau Testament, leur différence, leur unité*, Neuchâtel: Delachaux & Niestlé, 1950 (ET *New Testament Pattern*, London: Lutterworth, 1953).

284. E. G. C. F. Atchley, *On the Epiclesis of the Eucharistic Liturgy and in the Consecration of the Font*, London: OUP, 1935.

285. Some scholars have seen the *quam oblationem* (before the institution narrative) or the *supra quae* and *supplices te rogamus* (after the institution narrative) as equivalent to the Eastern epiclesis, but the Roman prayers do not mention the Holy Spirit.

286. E. Bishop, 'The moment of consecration' in R. H. Connolly, *The Liturgical Homilies of Narsai*, Cambridge: University Press, 1909, pp. 126–63.

287. See the most important essay of G. A. Michell, *Eucharistic Consecration in the Primitive Church*, London: SPCK, 1948, which called attention particularly to the Jewish *berakah* form (see earlier, note 88; and later note 373), and to the text of 1 Timothy 4:3–5. J. A. Jungmann, *Missarum*

sollemnia, part 4, chapter 2, section 13, declares that the primitive conception of consecration through the whole eucharistic prayer persisted in many cases into the middle ages.

288. T. Klauser calls the post-tridentine period the age of 'rubricism': *Kleine abendländische Liturgiegeschichte*, Bonn: Hanstein, 1965[5] (ET *A Short History of the Western Liturgy*, London: OUP, 1969). See again later, p. 263.

289. On the new Roman eucharistic prayers, see the books mentioned in note 43, and the following: O. Jordahn, 'The ecumenical significance of the new eucharistic prayers of the Roman Liturgy' in *Studia Liturgica* 11 (1976), pp. 101–17; B. Kleinheyer, *Erneuerung des Hochgebets*, Regensburg: Pustet, 1969; H. C. Schmidt-Lauber, 'The eucharistic prayers in the Roman Catholic church today' in *Studia Liturgica* 11 (1976), pp. 159–76; and several articles in *La Maison-Dieu* no. 94 (1968). An important preparatory study was C. Vagaggini, *Il canone della messa et la riforma liturgica*, Torino: ElleDiCi, 1966 (ET *The Canon of the Mass and Liturgical Reform*, London: Chapman, 1967).

290. Justin, *Apology* I, 67.

291. The broad outline of a 'service of word and sacrament' may be reflected already in the New Testament: note especially Luke 24:27–30 and Acts 20:7–11. C. P. M. Jones has suggested that the 'word' may at first have followed the 'sacrament' in the manner of a *symposion* (compare 1 Corinthians 11–14), whereas John 6, and then the whole structure of chapters 13–20 (discourses, high-priestly prayer, sacrifice, Spirit), already reflects the 'reversal' into Justin's sequence of word and sacrament: 'The eucharist: the New Testament' in C. Jones, G. Wainwright and E. Yarnold, *The Study of Liturgy*, pp. 148–69.

292. See, in other contexts, pp. 254, 349.

293. See the 'Acts of Uniformity' of 1549, 1552, 1559, 1662.

294. D. L. Gelpi, *Charism and Sacrament*, as in note 12.

295. D. L. Gelpi, *Charism and Sacrament*, pp. 146, 203f.

296. Anglican/Roman Catholic International Commission: *Ministry of Ordination* (1973) makes this a major category.

297. A. E. Harvey, *Priest or President?* London: SPCK, 1975. See also T. Lloyd (ed.), *Lay Presidency at the Eucharist?* Bramcote: Grove Books, 1977. As I perceive the question of liturgical priesthood, the president voices the great prayer of the priestly people of God: 'Let us give thanks to the Lord our God'.

298. The recovery of the eschatological dimension has been a prominent feature of twentieth-century theology: see my *Eucharist and Eschatology*, chapter 1. Eschatology is said to be a 'confusing' (J. Carmignac, 'Les dangers de l'eschatologie' in *New Testament Studies* 17, 1970–1, pp. 365–90) and 'slippery' word (I. H. Marshall, 'Slippery words: I. Eschatology' in *Expository Times* 89, 1977–8, pp. 264–9). But in this it does no more than match the biblical concept of 'kingdom of God', to which it corresponds and which is far more complex and subtle than Carmignac allows (Marshall is more sympathetic, and sees the word's usefulness as well as its dangers).

The word is expressly defended by D. E. Aune in his *The Cultic Setting of Realized Eschatology in Early Christianity*, Leiden: Brill, 1972.

299. On sign-language in the liturgy, see J. P. de Jong, *De eucharistie, symbolische werkelijkheid*; R. Grainger, *The Language of the Rite*, London: DLT, 1974; several essays in J. P. Jossua and Y. Congar (eds.), *La liturgie après Vatican II*, Paris: Cerf, 1967; J. M. Powers, *Eucharistic Theology*, New York: Herder, 1967, and London: Burns & Oates, 1968, chapters 3 and 4. There are interesting insights in Mary Douglas, *Purity and Danger*, London: Routledge, 1966, and *Natural Symbols*, London: Barrie & Rockliff, 1970, and, somewhat indirectly, in I. and P. Opie, *The Lore and Language of Schoolchildren*, London: OUP, 1959. Note already Susanne K. Langer, *Philosophy in a New Key: a study in the symbolism of reason, rite, and art,* Harvard: University Press, 1942. Finally the symposium edited by J. Shaughnessy, *The Roots of Ritual*, Grand Rapids: Eerdmans, 1973.

300. See also the writings of E. O. James, notably *Christian Myth and Ritual: a historical study*, London: Murray, 1933.

301. For this paragraph, see B. Malinowsky, 'Magic, Science and religion' (as in note 46), particularly pp. 37–41, 61, 76–8; M. Eliade, *Myth and Reality*, New York: Harper & Row, 1963, London: Allen & Unwin, 1964. For the world of classical antiquity, see B. A. van Gronigen, *In the Grip of the Past*, Leiden: Brill, 1953.

302. According to N. H. Snaith, time as 'circular' (seasonal) and time as 'horizontal' (the *passage* of the years) are proper and natural human ways of thinking about time, both inside and outside the Bible. Specific to the Bible is 'vertical' time, the 'now' in which God 'invades' both circular and horizontal time. See 'Time in the Old Testament' in F. F. Bruce (ed.), *Promise and Fulfilment* (S. H. Hooke *festschrift*), Edinburgh: T. & T. Clark, 1963, pp. 175–86. Although Snaith's article was given short shrift in the revised edition of James Barr's *Biblical Words for Time* (London: SCM, 1969²), Snaith appears to me substantially right (I should not be so concerned as he is to *limit* 'vertical' time to the Bible, and I should want to put in an 'immanenist' balance to his 'invasion'), and his general picture is not dependent on the narrowly lexical methods which Barr had been savaging in the first edition of his own book (1962) and in *The Semantics of Biblical Language* (London: OUP, 1961).

303. J. J. von Allmen, 'The theological frame of a liturgical renewal' in *Church Quarterly* 2 (1969–70), pp. 8–23.

304. The whole material for the controversy about Novatianist baptism is found in Cyprian's letters 69–75 (CSEL numbering), and in the anonymous *de rebaptismate*.

305. Augustine, *de baptismo contra Donatistas*.

306. Pure preaching of the gospel and right administration of the sacraments are found as constituent marks of the congregation in Lutheran (*Augsburg Confession*, 7), Anglican (*XXXIX Articles*, 19), and Reformed (*Scots Catechism* 18 & 25) teaching. The Reformed characteristically add the mark of 'discipline'.

307. (Ana)baptists are an exception at the level of the rite, but they do not usually question the substance of faith where it exists in those who had the misfortune to be baptized only as infants.

308. Interpretations of *subsistit in* range from 'is identical with' through 'is most clearly seen in' to 'is present in the Roman Catholic church among others'. On the varied ecclesiological tendencies of the Vatican II documents, see A. Dulles, 'The Church, the Churches, and the Catholic Church' in *Theological Studies* 33 (1972), pp. 199–234, and *Models of the Church*, Garden City, N. Y.: Doubleday, 1974, and Dublin: Gill & Macmillan, 1976.

309. So Firmilian (Cyprian, *ep.* 75). B. Leeming has argued, however, that this is a misrepresentation of Stephen's position due to the fact that Cyprian and Firmilian never grasped that in refusing to (re)baptize heretics or schismatics Stephen was already acting, even if he did not advance the argument in so many words, upon the later Roman Catholic distinction between validity and fruitfulness (*Principles of Sacramental Theology*[2], pp. 189–93).

310. DS 870, 875. This claim was made in face of political rulers but also in face of the Greek Church. The claim was repeated in a directly ecclesiastical context by the council of Florence, to the exclusion of 'heretics and schismatics' (DS 1351).

311. DS 1617.

312. G. Baum, *That they may be one: a study of papal doctrine (Leo XIII—Pius XII)*, Westminster, Md.: Newman, and London: Aquin, 1958, and *The Quest for Christian Unity*, London: Sheed & Ward, 1963 (American edition: *Progress and Perspectives: the Catholic quest for Christian unity*, New York: Sheed & Ward, 1962).

313. John of Damascus, *On the Orthodox Faith*, IV, 9, PG 94, 1120.

314. Baptisms performed in an *emergency* by an infidel have been recognized by the Roman Catholic church. Most churches have also held, as against the Donatists, that the personal unworthiness of the minister does not detract from a baptism. These are cases in which the 'benefit of the doubt' is allowed for the sake of the recipient. No conclusions should be drawn for *normal* understanding and practice.

315. On the plurality of creedal formulations, see N. Lash, *Voices of Authority*, London: Sheed & Ward, 1976, pp. 35–42, and our own chapter VI.

316. For further discussion of baptism and unity in the positive context of ecumenism, see chapter IX.

317. A triadic, practically trinitarian, pattern is found in several modern ecclesiological treatises: L. Bouyer, *L'Église de Dieu, corps du Christ et temple de l'Esprit*, Paris: Cerf, 1970; H. Küng, *Die Kirche*, Freiburg: Herder, 1967, section C (ET *The Church*, London: Search, 1968); and, unbeatably, J. E. L. Newbigin, *The Household of God*.

318. On 1 Corinthians 6:11, see chapter XII§3.

319. C. F. D. Moule, 'The judgment theme in the sacraments' in W. D.

Davies and D. Daube (eds.), *The Background of the New Testament and its Eschatology* (C. H. Dodd *festschrift*), Cambridge: University Press, 1956, pp. 464–81.

320. E. Käsemann, 'Anliegen und Eigenart der paulinischen Abendmahlslehre' now in his *Exegetische Versuche und Besinnungen*, vol. 1, Göttingen: Vandenhoeck & Ruprecht, 1960, pp. 11–34 (ET *Essays on New Testament Themes*, London: SCM, 1964, pp. 108–35).

321. H. Karpp, *La pénitence: textes et commentaires des origines de l'ordre pénitentiel dans l'Église ancienne*, Neuchâtel: Delachaux & Niestlé, 1970.

322. For a non-western example, see E. Carr, 'Penance among the Armenians: notes on the history of its practice and theology' in *Studia Liturgica* 11 (1976), pp. 65–100.

323. The authors of the 1549 and 1552 English Prayer Books apparently had such reservations concerning the holiness of the Church that they dropped the adjective 'holy' from the Nicene Creed's qualification of the Church.

324. This is a hall-mark of Lutheran theology. Some accounts of Luther's theology available in English are: G. Ebeling, *Luther: Einführung in sein Denken*, Tübingen: Mohr, 1964 (ET *Luther: an introduction to his thought*, Philadelphia: Fortress, and London: Collins, 1970); W. von Loewenich, *Luthers Theologia Crucis*, Witten: Luther-Verlag, 1967[5] (ET *Luther's Theology of the Cross*, Belfast: Christian Journals, 1976); E. G. Rupp, *The Righteousness of God*, London: Hodder, 1953; P. S. Watson, *Let God be God!* (Fernley-Hartley lecture 1947), London: Epworth, 1947. Good systematic theologies by modern Lutheran theologians are: G. Aulén, *Den allmännelig akristna tron*, Lund: Svenska Kyrkans Diakonistyrelses Bökforlag, 1957[3] (ET *The Faith of the Christian Church*, Philadelphia: Muhlenberg, 1960, and London: SCM, 1961), and R. Prenter, *Skabelse og genløsning*, Copenhagen: Gads, 1955[2] (ET *Creation and Redemption*, Philadelphia: Fortress, 1967).

325. An Orthodox theologian would probably object that in this section I have become individualistically lost in the sin of Church *members*, while neglecting the fact that the *Church* itself remains holy. My reply is that I refuse an ideal Church *apart from* its members: the ideal Church is the ideal *of* its members, what they are called to *become*. Because vision of God and revision of life are so closely related, the emphasis in this section concerning the holiness of the Church could fall on ethics, while the chapter in part three which corresponds to the second 'note' of the Church will concentrate on the liturgy: 'Revision' (chapter X). The linkage between liturgical holiness and ethical holiness is stressed again, not only at the end of that chapter (X§7), but also in chapter XII as part of the Church's apostolic witness before the world.

326. J. Jeremias, *Die Abendmahlsworte Jesu*[3], pp. 171–4, 218–24 (ET 1966, pp. 179–82, 225–31).

327. On the universal scope of the eucharistic invitation, see J. C.

Hoekendijk, *The Church Inside Out*, London: SCM, 1967, pp. 102–106, 148–66, and my *Eucharist and Eschatology*, pp. 128–35.

328. There is a valuable *status quaestionis* from the New Testament angle by R. Schnackenburg, 'Apostolicity: the present position of studies', in *One in Christ* 6 (1970), pp. 243–73. That whole issue of *One in Christ* (vol. 6, no. 3) is devoted to the joint study between the WCC and the Roman Catholic church on 'Catholicity and Apostolicity'. In addition to the report of the joint theological commission, the following individual contributions are reproduced: J. N. D. Kelly, ' "Catholic and apostolic" in the early centuries'; E. Lanne, 'The local church, its catholicity and apostolicity'; J. D. Zizioulas, 'The eucharistic community and the catholicity of the Church'; J. Bosc, 'The catholicity of the Church'; A. Ganoczy, 'Ministry, episcopacy, primacy'; J. Witte, 'Some theses about the sacramentality of the Church in connection with catholicity and apostolicity'; W. Pannenberg, 'The significance of eschatology for the understanding of the apostolicity and catholicity of the Church'; E. Lanne, 'Pluralism and unity: the possibility of a variety of typologies within the same ecclesial allegiance'.

329. In the sixteenth century, the Church of England intended to maintain the ministerial succession while greatly reforming the doctrine and practice of the Church. On the other hand, while political factors were certainly present (there also), it is arguable that the Church of Denmark deliberately abandoned the old succession as part of the Reform. For some modern Protestant views on continuity and discontinuity, see G. A. Lindbeck, 'A Protestant view of the ecclesiological status of the Roman Catholic church' in *Journal of Ecumenical Studies* 1 (1964), pp. 243–70; J. J. von Allmen, 'The continuity of the Church according to Reformed teaching', *ibid.*, pp. 424–44, criticized by A. C. Cochrane, 'The mystery of the continuity of the Church: a study of Reformed symbolics', *ibid.*, 2 (1965), pp. 81–96. A Roman Catholic theologian, Nicholas Lash, has made some irenically intended comments on the mutual and necessary complementarity of lineal succession and present church life in the adjudication of ecclesial and ministerial authenticity: *His Presence in the World*, pp. 182–94.

330. The apostolic message will cut no ice where it is not matched in practice by the transformed life which it preaches. That is why the chapter in part three which corresponds to the fourth 'note' of the Church can be headed 'Ethics' (chapter XII). Already here we may suggest that testing for apostolic authenticity ought to include ethical factors as well as the examination of doctrine and church order. Priggishness should be excluded by the fact that it is *tension towards* achievement which will be the likely measure, not yet perfection (cf. Philippians 3:12).

331. W. F. Flemington, *The New Testament Doctrine of Baptism*.

332. See the academic dogfight between Jeremias and Aland over the scraps, in the writings mentioned in note 182.

333. This must be maintained against such Lutheran dogmaticians as

E. Schlink, *Die Lehre von der Taufe*, and C. H. Ratschow, *Die eine christliche Taufe*.

334. M. Luther, *Von der Wiedertaufe* (1528), Weimar edition, vol. 26, pp. 156, 169.

335. See Augustine, *ep.* 98, PL 33, 359–64.

336. J. Duplacy, in A. George and others, *Baptism in the New Testament*, pp. 115–58.

337. John Macquarrie puts it thus: 'Man is saved only in so far as he responds to and appropriates into his existence the saving activity that is directed toward him' (*Principles of Christian Theology*, revised edition 1977, p. 316). Note again the (uncharacteristically?) augustinian phrase borrowed by John Wesley: 'He who made us without ourselves will not save us without ourselves' (as in note 216).

338. See E. C. Whitaker, 'The baptismal interrogations' in *Theology*, March 1956, pp. 103–12.

339. G. Wainwright, 'The need for a Methodist service for the admission of infants to the catechumenate' in *London Quarterly and Holborn Review* 191 (1968), pp. 51–60.

340. J. Gelineau, *Voices and Instruments in Christian Worship*, London. Burns & Oates, 1964, pp. 22–4.

341. N. Afanassieff, 'Le sacrement de l'assemblée' in *Internationale kirchliche Zeitschrift* 46 (1956), pp. 200–13. Note also the ecumenical symposium introduced by A. M. Triacca, *L'assemblée liturgique et les différents rôles dans l'assemblée* (Conférences Saint-Serge, XXIIIe semaine d'études liturgiques, 1976), Rome: Edizioni liturgiche, 1977.

342. On Lefebvre and Lash, see later, pp. 247–49.

343. The phrase 'global village' is M. McLuhan's: *Understanding Media*, New York: McGraw-Hill, 1964, chapter 10.

344. See earlier, page 125 and note 310, for the political and ecclesiastical circumstances of this claim. When the Roman claim to exclusive salvation was repeated by the council of Florence, pagans were explicitly consigned, along with Jews, heretics and schismatics, to eternal fire (DS 1351, quoting the augustinian Fulgentius of Ruspe, *de fide, ad Petrum*, 38–39, 79–80, PL 65, 704).

345. See earlier, p. 68, for Justin, Rahner and Panikkar.

346. J. H. Hick, *God and the Universe of Faiths*.

347. On the 'definitiveness' of Jesus Christ, see, from very varied angles, H. Berkhof, *Christus de zin der geschiedenis*, Nijkerk: Callenbach, 1959³ (ET *Christ the Meaning of History*, London: SCM, 1966); J. Macquarrie, *Principles of Christian Theology*, revised edition 1977, especially pp. 303–5, 443f; J. Pelikan, *The Finality of Jesus Christ in an Age of Universal History: a dilemma of the third century*, London: Lutterworth, 1965; K. Rahner, *Grundkurs des Glaubens*, e.g. pp. 161f, 247f (ET *Foundations of Christian Faith*, pp. 157f, 250f); Choan-Seng Song, 'From Israel to Asia: a theological leap' in *Ecumenical Review* 28 (1976), pp. 252–65.

348. See p. 68f, also p. 106, and again p. 359f.

349. Although that precise phrase is not, I think, found in Vatican II's Dogmatic Constitution on the Church, it is used by Roman Catholic theologians who contributed much to the ecclesiological thinking of the Council.

350. G. Parrinder, *Worship in the World's Religions*, London: Faber, 1961, Sheldon, 1974²; N. Smart, *The Religious Experience of Mankind*; J. H. Hick, *God and the Universe of Faiths*, chapter 10; J. S. Mbiti, *Concepts of God in Africa*, London: SPCK, 1970, and *Prayers of African Religion*, London: SPCK, 1975. Parrinder rightly emphasizes (p. 13) the vital links between the way in which the deity is conceived and the way in which he is worshipped and prayed to. On this question see also J. D. Crichton, *Christian Celebration: The Prayer of the Church*, especially chapters 1, 5 and 8.

351. I. H. Dalmais, 'Rites et prières accompagnant les lectures dans la liturgie eucharistique' in B. Botte and others, *La Parole dans la liturgie*, Paris: Cerf, 1970, pp. 107–21. More generally, J. A. Lamb, 'The place of the Bible in the liturgy' in P. R. Ackroyd and C. F. Evans (eds.), *The Cambridge History of the Bible*, vol. 1 (from the beginning to Jerome), Cambridge: University Press, 1970, pp. 563–86; S. J. P. van Dijk, 'The Bible in liturgical use' in G. W. H. Lampe (ed.), *The Cambridge History of the Bible*, vol. 2 (The West from the Fathers to the Reformation), Cambridge: University Press, 1969, pp. 220–51; S. L. Greenslade (ed.), *The Cambridge History of the Bible*, vol. 3 (The West from the Reformation to the present day), Cambridge: University Press, 1963, pp. 479–86 (by the editor).

352. These three levels of sacramental action were first clearly formulated with regard to the eucharist by Hugh of St Victor, *Summa sententiarum*, tr. 6, ch. 3, PL 176, 140.

353. Systematic theologians enjoy the professional privilege of a half or a whole generation's delay behind biblical scholars. This has the advantage of allowing the results of biblical scholarship to settle.

354. G. von Rad, *Das formgeschichtliche Problem des Hexateuchs*, 1938 (ET *The Problem of the Hexateuch, and other essays*, Edinburgh: Oliver & Boyd, 1966). I am not unaware of the criticisms made against his thesis, particularly in respect of his initial separation of the Sinai and the Settlement traditions. See, for instance, A. Weiser, *Einleitung in das Alte Testament*, Göttingen: Vandenhoeck & Ruprecht, 1957⁴, § 13 (ET *Introduction to the Old Testament*, London: DLT, 1961, pp. 81–99), and O. Kaiser, *Einleitung in das Alte Testament*, Gütersloh: Mohn, 1970², § 7 (ET *Introduction to the Old Testament*, Oxford: Blackwell, 1975, pp. 66–77). It does not really matter whether 'the Yahwist' was an individual (as von Rad pictures him) or a group (perhaps with cultic functions).

355. The fact that it was a covenant renewal festival might explain why the Sinai inauguration did not need to be mentioned in the credo: 'on ne récite pas une rubrique, on l'exécute,' as P. Benoit said about the use of the eucharistic institution narrative: 'Le récit de la cène dans Lc. xxii, 15–20' in *Revue biblique* 48 (1939), pp. 357–93, in particular p. 386.

356. S. Mowinckel, *Psalmenstudien, II: Der Thronbesteigungsfest Jahwäs und der Ursprung der Eschatologie*, Kristiania (Oslo): Jacob Dybwad, 1922, pp. 54–65; H. J. Kraus, *Gottesdienst in Israel*, Munich: Kaiser, 1954[1], pp. 125–8; G. von Rad, *Theologie des Alten Testaments*, vol. 2, Munich: Kaiser, 1960, pp. 112–25; H. Zirker, *Die kultische Vergegenwärtigung der Vergangenheit in den Psalmen*, Bonn: Hanstein, 1964.

357. Josephus, *Bell. Jud.* V, 98ff; VI, 290–95. There are hints to that effect in the New Testament: John 6:4, 15; Matthew 26:5; Luke 13:1–3; 23:19; on which see J. Jeremias, *Die Abendmahlsworte Jesu*[3], p. 199, note 4 (ET *The Eucharistic Words of Jesus*, p. 207, note 4). For the Jewish material see R. Le Déault, *La nuit pascale*, Rome: Institut biblique pontifical, 1963.

358. G. Wainwright, *Eucharist and Eschatology*, pp. 22–4.

359. G. Wainwright, *Eucharist and Eschatology*, passim.

360. G. Hölscher, *Die Profeten*. Leipzig: Hinrichs, 1914; S. Mowinckel, *Psalmenstudien, III: Die Kultprophetie und prophetische Psalmen*, Kristiania (Oslo): Jacob Dybwad, 1923; A. R. Johnson, *The Cultic Prophet in Ancient Israel*, Cardiff: University of Wales, 1944; 1962[2].

361. Recent commentaries often group these books together and treat them in this liturgical perspective: so, for instance, J. H. Eaton, *Obadiah, Nahum, Habakkuk, Zephaniah*, London: SCM, 1961, and J. D. W. Watts, *Joel, Obadiah, Jonah, Nahum, Habakkuk and Zephaniah*, Cambridge: University Press, 1975. This is not the place to list more specialist studies on the individual books.

362. See H. J. Kraus, *Psalmen*, Neukirchen: Erziehungsverein, 1961[2], vol. 1, pp. xxxvii–lvi; A. Weiser, *Die Psalmen*, Göttingen; Vandenhoeck & Ruprecht, 1963[3], pp. 12–68 (ET *The Psalms*, London: SCM, 1962, pp. 20–101).

363. S. Mowinckel, *Psalmenstudien, II*.

364. For a survey of Christian use: J. A. Lamb, *The Psalms in Christian Worship*, London: Faith Press, 1962.

365. Even some of the problematic psalms might come into their own again in worship along the lines of the third chapter of Dorothee Soelle's *Leiden*, Stuttgart: Kreuz, 1973 (ET *Suffering*, London: DLT, 1975): 'Suffering and Language'.

366. His phrase is 'der älteste erhaltene Predigtband der Kirche': W. Marxsen, *Das Neue Testament als Buch der Kirche*, Gütersloh: Mohn, 1966 (ET *The New Testament as the Church's Book*, Philadelphia: Fortress, 1971)·

367. In a very popular survey concerning 'die Erforschung der synoptischen Evangelien', R. Bultmann wrote in chapter 6: 'One may designate the final motive by which the gospels were produced as the *cultic* (that is, the needs of common worship), if one considers that the highpoint of Christian life was the gathering of the community for worship, when the figure of Jesus, his teaching as well as his life, was set forth before the eyes of the faithful, and when accordingly the gospels served for public reading. . . . The preacher as a rule led up to his words about Jesus'

suffering, death and resurrection by a review of his work. Out of such preaching grew the gospels, as gradually the single fragments of tradition, which told of Jesus' words and deeds, were drawn into this framework. . . . The gospels proclaim Jesus Christ, and were meant to be read as proclamations' (ET in F. C. Grant, ed., *Form Criticism*, new edition, New York: Harper & Row, 1962).

368. Pliny, *epp.* X, 96.

369. For 'confessing' *Kyrios Kaisar* and cursing Christ, see also the *Martyrdom of Polycarp*, 8, 2.

370. From fourth-century descriptions of the rites of initiation we know that the creed was 'delivered' to the candidates some time before their baptism and was then 'rendered' by them shortly before it. The creed was a summary of the faith which it was the bishop's duty as principal teacher to receive, safeguard and transmit. More will be said about creeds in chapter VI.

371. H. Conzelmann, *Grundriss der Theologie des Neuen Testaments*, Munich: Kaiser, 1968², pp. 81–3 (ET pp. 62–4).

372. See p. 49f and note 117.

373. See G. Dix, *The Shape of the Liturgy*, pp. 52ff, 78ff, 83ff, 215ff; G. A. Michell, *Eucharistic Consecration in the Primitive Church*; J. P. Audet, as in note 88; L. Ligier, 'From the Last Supper to the eucharist' in L. Sheppard (ed.), *The New Liturgy*, pp. 113–50, and 'The origins of the eucharistic prayer' in *Studia Liturgica* 9 (1973), pp. 161–85; and some criticisms in T. J. Talley, 'The eucharistic prayer of the ancient Church according to recent research: results and reflections' in *Studia Liturgica* 11 (1976), pp. 138–58.

374. Concerning the opening greeting and blessing or thanksgiving, G. Delling considers it probable that 'an exchange of influence took place between the beginnings of letters and the introductory formulae of the worship service' (*Der Gottesdienst im Neuen Testament*, p. 55; ET p. 39). On the conclusion of letters in relation to the service of worship, see later p. 164 and note 389.

375. See note 180. Jeremias allows liturgical influence to have affected the historical kernel.

376. R. Perdelwitz, *Die Mysterienreligion und das Problem des I. Petrusbriefes*, Geissen: Töpelmann, 1911; W. Bornemann, 'Der erste Petrusbrief —eine Taufrede des Sylvanus' in *Zeitschrift für die neutestamentliche Wissenschaft* 19 (1919–20), pp. 143–65.

377. H. Preisker's revised edition of H. Windisch, *Die katholischen Briefe*, Tübingen: Mohr, 1951, pp. 156–62. F. L. Cross, *I Peter, a paschal liturgy*, London: Mowbray, 1954.

378. Tertullian, *adversus Marcionem* I, 14; *de corona*, 3; Clement of Alexandria, *Paid.*, I, 6 and 34ff; Hippolytus, *Ap. Trad.*, 23, 2 (Dix), 21 (Botte). For Rome, see texts as late as John the Deacon's letter to Senarius, 12, and the Blessing of milk and honey in the baptismal mass for Pentecost in the Leonine sacramentary. For certain complications, note J. Crehan,

Early Christian Baptism and the Creed, London: Burns, Oates and Washbourne, 1950, pp. 171–5. See also, later, p. 374.

379. On 1 *Peter*, see further M. E. Boismard, 'Une liturgie baptismale dans la *Prima Petri*' in *Revue biblique* 63 (1956), pp. 182–208, and 64 (1957), pp. 161–83.

380. J. C. Kirby, *Ephesians, Baptism and Pentecost*, London: SPCK, 1968.

381. A. T. Hanson has detected 'elements of a baptismal liturgy' in Titus 2–3: *Studies in the Pastoral Epistles*, London: SPCK, 1968, chapter 7. Note also G. Friedrich, 'Ein Tauflied hellenistischer Judenchristen: 1 Thess. 1:9f' in *Theologische Zeitschrift* 21 (1965), pp. 502–16.

382. A. Guilding, *The Fourth Gospel and Jewish Worship*, London: OUP, 1960.

383. M. D. Goulder, *Midrash and Lection in Matthew*, London: SPCK, 1974, and further, *The Evangelists' Calendar*, London: SPCK, 1978. According to Goulder, *Mark* is a book of 'gospels' following the readings of the Jewish calendar for both the festal and sabbath cycles, from New Year (1st Tishri) to Easter. *Matthew* is a midrashic 'rewriting' of *Mark*, extended to provide 'gospels' for a whole year from after Easter round to Easter, with special emphasis on the Jewish Christian festivals. *Luke* is a midrashic 'rewriting' of both *Mark* and *Matthew*, also running from after Easter round to Easter, but developing the 'fulfilments' of the sabbath cycle. Dr Goulder is also working on the Fourth Gospel, which he sees as a series of catechetical 'gospels' for a Quartodeciman church, covering the fifty days up to Easter Week.

384. W. D. Davies, 'Reflections on Archbishop Carrington's *The Primitive Christian Calendar*' in W. D. Davies and D. Daube (eds.), *The Background of the New Testament and its Eschatology*, pp. 124–52 (the reference is to P. Carrington, *The Primitive Christian Calendar*, Cambridge: University Press, 1952); L. Morris, *The New Testament and the Jewish Lectionaries*, London: Tyndale, 1964.

385. The danger of 'pan-liturgism' is adverted to by W. C. van Unnik, 'Dominus vobiscum: the background of a liturgical formula', in A. J. B. Higgins (ed.), *New Testament Essays* (T. W. Manson memorial volume), Manchester: University Press, 1959, pp. 270–305. J. D. G. Dunn uses the phrase accusingly, in *Unity and Diversity in the New Testament*, pp. 141–8.

386. G. W. Anderson, *A Critical Introduction to the Old Testament*, London: Duckworth, 1959, p. 16. In the Christian context, Augustine argued for the canonicity of the book of *Wisdom* on the grounds that it had long been read and heard in the Church as being of divine origin: *de praed. sanct.* 14, 27, PL 44, 980; cf. *de doctrina christ.* II, 8, 12–13, PL 34, 40–1.

387. The New Testament is a collection of writings which in the first place were read and loved in the churches and only then combined into a 'canon': so A. Jülicher, *Einleitung in das Neue Testament*, Tübingen: Mohr, 1901⁴, pp. 362–451 (note especially section 36).

388. Justin, *Apol.* I, 67.3; cf. 66.3.

389. G. J. Cuming, 'Service-endings in the Epistles' in *New Testament Studies* 22 (1975–6), pp. 110–13. Several scholars had earlier suggested that the ending of 1 Corinthians formed an introduction or transition to the eucharist: H. Lietzmann, *Messe und Herrenmahl*[3], p. 229 (bringing together 1 and 2 Cor., Rom. 16, and 1 Thess. 5); G. Bornkamm, *Das Ende des Gesetzes*, Munich: Kaiser, 1952, pp. 123–32; J. A. T. Robinson, 'Traces of a liturgical sequence in 1 Cor. 16:20–24' in *Journal of Theological Studies* n.s. 4 (1953), pp. 38–41.

390. I am picking up—somewhat against the sense in which the author used the phrases from the Book of Job—the celebrated ending of R. H. Lightfoot's *History and Interpretation in the Gospels* (London: Hodder, 1935): 'It seems, then, that the form of the earthly no less than of the heavenly Christ is for the most part hidden from us. For all the inestimable value of the gospels, they yield us little more than a whisper of his voice; we trace in them but the outskirts of his ways. Only when we see him hereafter in his fulness shall we know him also as he was on earth. And perhaps the more we ponder the matter, the more clearly we shall understand the reason for it, and therefore shall not wish it otherwise. For probably we are at present as little prepared for the one as for the other.'

391. E. Käsemann (ed.), *Das Neue Testament als Kanon*, Göttingen: Vandenhoeck & Ruprecht, 1970, p. 410.

392. A typical statement of Käsemann on the 'irreconcilability' of Paul and James is found in 'Begründet der neutestamentliche Kanon die Einheit der Kirche?', in his *Exegetische Versuche und Besinnungen*, vol. 1, in particular p. 220 (ET *Essays on New Testament Themes*, p. 102).

393. Cyril of Jerusalem, *Catecheses* IV, 36, PG 33, 500.

394. As in note 392, in particular p. 215 (ET p. 96).

395. E. Käsemann, 'Das Problem des historischen Jesus', in *Exegetische Versuche und Besinnungen*, vol. 1, pp. 187–214 (ET in *Essays on New Testament Themes*, pp. 15–47); see also 'The problem of a New Testament theology' in *New Testament Studies* 19 (1972–3), pp. 235–45. Some obvious steps towards mitigating the apparent problems are indicated by C. F. D. Moule, 'The influence of circumstances on the use of eschatological terms' in *Journal of Theological Studies* n.s. 15 (1964), pp. 1–15, and by G. B. Caird, 'Les eschatologies du Nouveau Testament' in *Revue d'histoire et de philosophie religieuses* 49 (1969), pp. 217–27.

396. C. F. D. Moule, *The Birth of the New Testament*, London: Black, 1966[2], p. 9. Compare the work of Moule's pupil, J. D. G. Dunn, *Unity and Diversity in the New Testament*, 1977, but by now the 'unifying strand' has become very narrow and there is a käsemannian stress on a broad diversity.

397. H. Küng, 'Der Frühkatholizismus im Neuen Testament als kontroverstheologisches Problem' in *Theologische Quartalschrift* 142 (1962), pp. 385–424 (ET in H. Küng, *The Living Church*, London: Sheed & Ward, 1963, pp. 233–93).

398. Note the comment of Harold W. Turner, a student of African Christianity: 'We recall Luther's judgment on James as an "epistle of straw" and place that against the fact that both independent and older African churches which I have investigated on this point all make a greater use of James than of most other parts of the New Testament, and certainly greater use than we make of it.' This point of difference is then set within a broader context in a paragraph which, though still rather undeveloped in its factual basis, opens up exploratory perspectives in connexion with our own third and fourth points: 'When it comes to the differential use of Scripture, which exists in all sections of the Christian Church, it is interesting to discover that something of a common pattern probably runs through both the West and Africa. My limited inquiries in both areas indicate, for instance, that Gen. 1–11 is used much more than Gen. 12–50, and more than most of the rest of the Old Testament; that John's Gospel rivals that of Matthew in usage, with Mark used least of the four; and that the Acts of the Apostles is used very little. If something of a common pattern in the differential use of Scripture extends even to such apparently "way out" sections of the Church as the African independents (in spite of their own special quirks at some points) we have new evidence of the way the Bible actually functions across the Christian world, and the exciting possibility of being able to establish broad lineaments of a world Christian norm for the differential use of Scripture' (in M. E. Glasswell and E. W. Fasholé-Luke, eds., *New Testament Christianity for Africa and the World: Essays in honour of Harry Sawyerr*, London: SPCK, 1974, p. 171).

399. B. S. Childs, *Biblical Theology in Crisis*, Philadelphia: Westminster, 1970.

400. The importance of the salvation-historical vista is stressed by J. D. Crichton, *Christian Celebration: The Prayer of the Church*, chapter 6 ('The lectionaries'). In the Catholic tradition of the divine office, the perspective is prolonged by the patristic and hagiographical readings. See B. de Gaiffier, 'La lecture das actes des martyrs dans la prière liturgique en Occident' in *Analecta bollandiana* 72 (1954), pp. 134–66; H. Urner, *Die ausserbiblische Lesung im christlichen Gottesdienst: ihre Vorgeschichte und Geschichte bis zur Zeit Augustins*, Göttingen: Vandenhoeck & Ruprecht, 1952. The post-Vatican II *Liturgy of the Hours* extends the range of reading right into the present.

401. According to Karl Barth, Israel was a mirror presented to the nations for them to recognize themselves in (*Kirchliche Dogmatik* IV/1, p. 187, ET p. 171f).

402. A. D. Nock, *Conversion*, Oxford: Clarendon, 1933, presents 'the general view of antiquity' thus (p. 237): 'It was easy enough for an ancient to think of this mortality putting on immortality, but the reverse process was not envisaged. Humanity, in its essential nature and quality, was regarded as a liability rather than an asset.' Nock quotes the *Corpus hermeticum* X, 25: 'None of the heavenly gods will leave the bounds of

heaven and come down on earth.' Two further texts are adduced by C. H. Talbert, *What is a Gospel?* Philadelphia: Fortress, 1977, and London: SPCK, 1978, p. 77f: Celsus, in Origen, *contra Celsum*, V, 2; and Justin, *Dialogue with Trypho*, 60: 'No one with even the slightest intelligence would dare to assert that the Creator and Father of all things left his super-celestial realms to make himself visible in a little spot on earth.' Justin lands us in the middle of the problem and opportunities of what became trinitarian theology. The climax of the difficulties—and of the glory—is reached with the *death* of Jesus: it was with the *crucifixion* of 'our Maker' in view that Charles Wesley could sing of the 'God of unexampled grace' (MHB No. 191).

403. See pp. 69, 106, 145.

404. An optional reading from Indian scriptures was included in the experimental *New Orders of the Mass for India* produced by the National Biblical Catechetical and Liturgical Centre, Bangalore: see, later, p. 377. The use of these orders has now been prohibited by Rome, perhaps because of qualms on the part of Indian opponents.

405. See G. Siegwalt, *La Loi, chemin du salut*, Neuchâtel: Delachaux & Niestlé, 1971.

406. *Sacrificium laudis*, Roman canon; 'sacrifice of praise and thanksgiving', *Book of Common Prayer*; '*thusia aineseōs*', Byzantine liturgy of St John Chrysostom, before the anaphora.

407. Christian lectionaries rightly pay little attention to *Leviticus*: these forms of sacrifice have been superseded. Yet the best of the Old Testament recognized that the heart of sacrifice lay in ethical obedience: H. H. Rowley, *Worship in Ancient Israel*, London: SPCK, 1967, pp. 111–43 ('The forms and meaning of sacrifice'). See again, chapter XII§1.

408. The connected questions of law and gospel, Old Testament and New, Judaism and Christianity, recur particularly on pp. 370-72 within the broader context of the relations between Christianity and other religions. This is not to deny that the relationship with Judaism is a special one.

409. Liturgical use is also a motive for *translating* the scriptures: see B. Botte, 'Les traductions liturgiques de l'Écriture' in B. Botte and others, *La Parole dans la liturgie*, pp. 81–105; F. C. Grant, *Translating the Bible*, Edinburgh: Nelson, 1961, for example, pp. 16f, 51f, 105.

410. The complex weaving of scriptural threads into the liturgical tapestry is well illustrated in respect of patristic theology by J. Daniélou, *Bible et liturgie*, Paris: Cerf, 1958² (ET *The Bible and the Liturgy*, Notre Dame: University Press, 1956).

411. See A. Miller, 'Schriftsinn und liturgischer Sinn' in *Benediktinische Monatschrift* 16 (1934), pp. 407–13, though this brief treatment has its problematic features.

412. J. Barr, *The Bible in the Modern World*, London: SCM, 1973, especially the chapter entitled 'The Bible as literature'; the quotation is taken from p. 58f.

413. C. F. Evans, 'Hermeneutics' in *Epworth Review*, January 1975, pp. 81–93; the quotation is taken from p. 87f.

414. For J. Barr, see *The Bible in the Modern World*, especially the chapter entitled 'The Bible and interpretation'. C. F. Evans touches on some of the issues in *Is 'Holy Scripture' Christian?* London: SCM, 1971. And, with radical intent, D. Nineham, *The Use and Abuse of the Bible: a study of the Bible in an age of rapid cultural change*, London: Macmillan, 1976.

415. On liturgical preaching in the early Church, see A. Olivar, 'Quelques remarques historiques sur la prédication comme action liturgique dans l'Église ancienne' in *Mélanges liturgiques offerts au R. P. Dom B. Botte, o.s.b.*, Louvain: Abbaye du Mont César, 1972, pp. 429–43. Modern theologies of preaching include: J. J. von Allmen, 'La prédication' in *Verbum caro* 9 (1955), pp. 110–57 (ET *Preaching and Congregation*, London: Lutterworth, 1962); R. E. C. Browne, *The Ministry of the Word*, London: SCM, 1976[2]; R. H. Fuller, *What is Liturgical Preaching?* London: SCM, 1957; T. H. Keir, *The Word in Worship*, London: OUP, 1962; J. Knox, *The Integrity of Preaching*, New York: Abingdon, 1957; P. Milner (ed.), *The Ministry of the Word*, London: Burns & Oates, 1967.

416. Translation from H. Ott, *Theology and Preaching*, London: Lutterworth, 1965, pp. 22, 28. See also W. Kasper, *Die Methoden der Dogmatik—Einheit und Vielheit*, Munich: Kösel, 1967 (ET *The Methods of Dogmatic Theology*, Shannon: Ecclesia Press, 1969), especially chapter 3.

417. Augustine, *In Jo. ev.*, tract. 30, 1, PL 35, 1632. Quoted by A. Squire, *Asking the Fathers*, London: SPCK, 1973, p. 121. In the patristic age the primary sense of *lectio divina* was the public reading of the scriptures. Fr Squire gives the example of St Anthony to illustrate what such reading might mean for a hearer: 'It is no accident of history that it was in church, during the public reading, that Anthony the Great heard the words which gave him his special vocation, as St Athanasius tells us. Anthony had, apparently, been reflecting nostalgically upon the simple communal life of the early Christians, as described in the Acts of the Apostles, and it was upon these thoughts that the Gospel being read seemed suddenly to make a direct comment. "As though God had put him in mind of the saints and as though the reading had been directed especially to him, Anthony immediately left the church and gave to the townsfolk the property he had from his forebears." It is God, then, who suggests the thought taken, we must not fail to note, from Anthony's previous knowledge of the Scriptures, and upon this thought the liturgical reading makes an observation in which Anthony believes that God is addressing him personally. It is, no Christian can doubt, the fact that it is God who, in a very special sense, speaks in the Scriptures that enables them to address us directly in a way no other books can, when our minds and hearts are properly attuned.'

418. A. Squire, *Asking the Fathers*, p. 121f.

419. Origen, *In Exod.*, hom. 13, 3, PG 12, 391.

420. Rupert of Deutz, *Commentary on Joshua*, PL 167, 1017.

421. On classical Protestantism, see T. Süss, 'Bible, parole de Dieu, prédication' in B. Botte and others, *La Parole dans la liturgie*, pp. 123–43. Notice the 'real presence' in the Second Helvetic Confession (1566): 'Praedicatio verbi divini est verbum divinum.'

422. Karl Barth, *Kirchliche Dogmatik* I/1.

423. See J. Macquarrie, *Principles of Christian Theology*, 1977², pp. 435f, 447–58. Note also 1 Thessalonians 2:13: 'We thank God constantly for this, that when you received the word of God which you heard from us, you accepted it not as the word of men but as what it really is, the word of God, which is at work in you believers.' The apostolic idiom should not, of course, mislead us into thinking that human words were not the medium.

424. For 'extension of personality' in the Bible, see A. R. Johnson, *The One and the Many in the Israelite Conception of God*, and *The Vitality of the Individual in the Thought of Ancient Israel*, Cardiff: University of Wales, 1949, p. 8f. For a characteristically modern exploration of personal presence, see briefly R. Mehl, 'Structure philosophique de la notion de présence' in *Revue d'histoire et de philosophie religieuses* 38 (1958), pp. 171–6.

425. H. von Campenhausen emphasizes the decisively christological content of the primitive Christian confession, in 'Das Bekenntnis im Urchristentum', *Zeitschrift für die neutestamentliche Wissenschaft* 63 (1972), pp. 210–53: 'Das christliche Bekenntnis ist ursprünglich keine Aufzählung der dem Glauben wesentlichen Überlieferungsstücke und Lehrwahrheiten, ... sondern die ebenso kurze wie unmissverständliche Bezeichnung des einen göttlichen Gegenübers, dessen Bejahung den einzelnen Christen zum Christen macht und von jedem Nichtchristen unterscheidet, also der Person Jesu' (p. 211). He returns to its missionary purpose in a supplementary note in *ZNW* 66 (1975), pp. 127–29.

426. See pp. 156–58.

427. C. H. Dodd, *The Apostolic Preaching and its Developments*, London: Hodder, 1936.

428. *The Apostolic Tradition*, 21. The version given is largely borrowed from G. J. Cuming, *Hippolytus: a text for students*, Bramcote: Grove Books, 1976, p. 19. Whatever the difficulties in reconstructing the text, the substantial point about the use of the creed *during* baptism remains.

429. The edition by J. Wilkinson, *Egeria's Travel Diary*, London: SPCK, 1971, contains much parallel liturgical material from other places.

430. G. Every, *The Baptismal Sacrifice*, London: SCM, 1959.

431. Irenaeus, *adversus haereses* III, 4, 1-2. On the rule of faith and its degrees of fixity, see J. N. D. Kelly, *Early Christian Creeds*³, pp. 6–29, 62–88.

432. But note H. von Campenhausen, 'Das Bekenntnis Eusebs von Caesarea (Nicea 325)' in *Zeitschrift für die neutestamentliche Wissenschaft* 67 (1976), pp. 123–39. He argues that Eusebius' confession was not the local baptismal creed of Caesarea but the confession of an 'individual theologian' proving his orthodoxy; it may, with other such individual

submissions, have been used in the drafting of the conciliar 'creed'. To my mind, von Campenhausen's whole presentation depends on too sharp a division between the *regula fidei* (supposed to be chiefly anti-heretical in intent) and the baptismal confessions of faith. With greater probability, Kelly holds that the creed of Nicaea was based on a local baptismal creed, though not that of Eusebius from Caesarea: *Early Christian Creeds³*, pp. 211–30. See again later, p. 258.

433. J. N. D. Kelly, *Early Christian Creeds³*, pp. 296–331, 339–44.

434. Curiously, the Gelasian sacramentary and the Ordo Romanus VII reveal that the Nicene-Constantinopolitan Creed was used for some time in catechetical instruction at Rome, though the baptismal interrogations kept the 'old Roman' form which was the nucleus of the Apostles' Creed. See J. N. D. Kelly, *Early Christian Creeds³*, pp. 346–8.

435. J. N. D. Kelly, *Early Christian Creeds³*, pp. 351–7.

436. In the Byzantine ordination of a bishop, the bishop-elect recites the Nicene Creed, followed by a long profession of faith elaborating on his orthodoxy concerning the Trinity and Christ. On 'Orthodoxy Sunday', the first Sunday in Lent, Romans 16:17–20 and Matthew 18:10–18 are read in a special 'Office of Orthodoxy', the true faith is celebrated, and anathemas are launched at heretical positions.

437. J. N. D. Kelly, *Early Christian Creeds³*, pp. 348–57. Antioch may have been the place of its first introduction into the eucharist, slightly earlier, under the monophysite patriarch Peter the Fuller; there is, however, doubt about the report to that effect in Theodore the Reader.

438. It is the bishop or the presbyter who thus 'teaches the mysteries' to the people. See J. Cooper and A. J. Maclean, *The Testament of our Lord*, Edinburgh: T. & T. Clark, 1902, pp. 84–9 (I. 28).

439. On the Nicene Creed and the eucharist, see also p. 258f.

440. Augustine, *serm.* 58, 11, PL 38, 399–400, quoted by J. N. D. Kelly, *Early Christian Creeds³*, p. 370.

441. R. C. D. Jasper, *Prayer Book Revision in England 1800–1900*, London: SPCK, 1954. See also G. J. Cuming, *A History of Anglican Liturgy*, London: Macmillan, 1969, pp. 176, 178, 180 (Wesley was notoriously busy), 200–2, 215, 225.

442. There is a story that the professedly *ex animo* recitation of the creeds by one modernist was interpreted by some to mean that he said them *cum grano salis*. See, perhaps, A. M. Ramsey, *From Gore to Temple*, London: Longmans, 1960, pp. 84–6.

443. *Doctrine in the Church of England: the Report of the Commission on Christian Doctrine appointed by the Archbishops of Canterbury and York in 1922*, London: SPCK, 1938, pp. 37–9.

444. The Doctrine Commission of the Church of England, *Christian Believing: The Nature of the Christian Faith and its Expression in Holy Scripture and Creeds*, London: SPCK, 1976.

445. The Anglican contributors to the symposium edited by J. H. Hick were D. Cupitt, M. Goulder, L. Houlden, D. Nineham and M. Wiles.

446. N. Lash, 'Credal affirmation as a criterion of Church membership' in J. Kent and R. Murray (eds.), *Intercommunion and Church Membership*, London: DLT, 1973, pp. 51–73. See also, later, p. 304f.

447. On plausibility structures, see P. L. Berger and T. Luckmann, *The Social Construction of Reality*, Garden City, N.Y.: Doubleday, 1966, and Harmondsworth: Lane, 1967; P. L. Berger, *The Sacred Canopy*, Garden City, N.Y.: Doubleday, 1967 (British edition *The Social Reality of Religion*, London: Faber, 1969); P. L. Berger, *A Rumour of Angels*, Garden City, N.Y.: Doubleday, 1969, Harmondsworth: Lane, 1970.

448. M. F. Wiles, *Working Papers in Doctrine*, p. 150. Wiles speaks of 'a basic outline of doctrine': the context makes clear that he has the creeds in mind. See also his essay in the report of the Church of England Doctrine Commission, *Christian Believing*, 1976, pp. 125–32; and his *Explorations*, chapter 1.

449. E. Schillebeeckx, *Jezus, het verhaal van een levende*, IV, 1, 1. On this subject note also N. Lash, *Change in Focus*, London: Sheed & Ward, 1973.

450. Schillebeeckx is reticent on the 'scarcely changing' character of the deep structures. In the matter that concerns theologians, I imagine (though one cannot be sure from outside the situation; and that such a situation should ever arise, may God forbid!) that a profound shift would have to be admitted if it ceased to be *possible* to think a transcendent origin, support and goal of the universe.

451. See G. Steiner, *After Babel: Aspects of Language and Translation*, New York and London: OUP, 1975.

452. The only addition to the Nicene-Constantinopolitan Creed as confirmed at Chalcedon has been the Western *filioque*: see already note 219 and again p. 305. The Apostles' Creed had practically achieved its final form by the fifth century, and the *textus receptus* has held sway since the middle ages (though Lutherans read 'Christian' for 'catholic'): see J. N. D. Kelly, *Early Christian Creeds³* pp. 368–434.

453. On the status of 'alternative services' in the Church of England, see note 235.

454. The United Church of Canada includes the text in its service books. Background material, and other modern statements of faith, are contained in *Creeds: a report of the committee on Christian faith*, first printed in 1969 and revised in 1975.

455. K. Rahner recognizes the legitimacy and need of 'brief creedal statements', contemporary and plural, albeit not *replacing* the Apostles' Creed; but it could hardly be said that the samples he offers at the end of his *Grundkurs des Glaubens* (ET *Foundations of Christian Faith*) lend themselves to liturgical use.

456. Observe in John Hick's preface to *The Myth of God Incarnate*: 'The later conception of Jesus as God incarnate, the Second Person of the Holy Trinity living a human life, is a mythological or poetic way of expressing his significance for us' and ' "Orthodoxy" is a myth, which can and often does inhibit the creative thinking which Christianity sorely

needs today'. On 'theology' as a politicians' swear-word, see P. Howard, *New Words for Old*, London: Hamish Hamilton, 1977, pp. 109–11.

457. Augustine, *enarratio in ps. cxlviii*, 17, PL 37, 1947–8.

458. On the *Agnus Dei*, see J. A. Jungmann, *Missarum sollemnia*, part 4, chapter 3, section 7.

459. The Wesley hymns are MHB nos. 386 and 264; and 'Come, let us join our friends above', mentioned in the next sentence, is no. 824 (see earlier p. 111f).

460. J. Gelineau, *Voices and Instruments in Christian Worship*, p. 118f, and 'Music and singing in the Liturgy' in C. Jones, G. Wainwright and E. Yarnold (eds.), *The Study of Liturgy*, pp. 440–54.

461. The music is recorded on *La messe à Yaoundé* (Arion ARN 30 B 147).

462. D. Martin, *Sociology of English Religion*, London: SCM, 1967, p. 88.

463. See chapter IV§8.

464. A. Harnack, *Die Mission und Ausbreitung des Christentums in den ersten drei Jahrhunderten*, Leipzig: Hinrich, 1924[4], p. 394f.

465. For the early centuries, see J. Kroll, *Die christliche Hymnodik bis zu Klemens von Alexandria*.

466. The point could cut both ways: the 'heretical' Paul of Samosata complained of the 'modern' hymns which ascribed divinity to Christ. See earlier p. 52.

467. For a re-examination of Arius' hymns and theology, see G. C. Stead, 'The *Thalia* of Arius and the testimony of Athanasius' in *Journal of Theological Studies* n.s. 29 (1978), pp. 20–52.

468. Ambrose wrote hymns with the deliberate intention of spreading orthodox teaching in face of arianism: K. Federer (as in note 523), pp. 43–54.

469. Methodism includes the first four volumes of John Wesley's sermons among its 'doctrinal standards', thereby re-inforcing the doxological nature of its 'confessional basis'.

470. H. Bett, *The Hymns of Methodism*, London: Epworth, 1945[3]; R. N. Flew, *The Hymns of Charles Wesley: a study of their structure*, London: Epworth, 1953; B. L. Manning, *The Hymns of Wesley and Watts*, London: Epworth, 1942; J. E. Rattenbury, *The Evangelical Doctrines of Charles Wesley's Hymns*, London: Epworth, 1941, and *The Eucharistic Hymns of John and Charles Wesley*, London: Epworth, 1948; J. W. Waterhouse, *The Bible in Charles Wesley's Hymns*, London: Epworth, 1954. Also: A. M. Allchin and H. A. Hodges, *A Rapture of Praise*, London: Hodder, 1966; J. A. Kay, *Wesley's Prayers and Praises*, London: Epworth, 1958; and D. A. Davie, *Purity of Diction in English Verse*, London: Routledge, 1967[2], pp. 70–81.

471. A study of the 1933 Methodist Hymn Book is A. S. Gregory, *Praises with understanding*, London: Epworth, 1949[2].

472. C. Northcott, *Hymns in Christian Worship*, London: Lutterworth, 1964, p. 19.

473. *English Hymnal*, Nos. 317, 326, 330.

474. Some of the doctrinal hymns of Wesley remain very 'objective': for example, 'Hail! holy, holy, holy Lord!' (MHB No. 37), 'Father, in whom we live' (39), 'Father, whose everlasting love' (75: a powerful declaration of the universal scope of the atonement), 'Let earth and heaven combine' (142), 'Christ the Lord is risen today' (204).

475. For 'ecstatic reason', see Paul Tillich, *Systematic Theology*, 3 volumes in one, Digswell Place: Nisbet, 1968, I, p. 60 and the recurrent use of 'ecstasy'. Note also Paul van Buren's location of religious language, along with poetry and love-talk, on the linguistic borders or frontiers: *The Edges of Language*, New York: Macmillan, and London: SCM, 1972. It is not certain what are the ontological implications of this in van Buren's own eyes, remembering the fierce anti-transcendentalism of his *Secular Meaning of the Gospel*, New York: Macmillan, and London: SCM, 1963.

476. The phrase *sub contraria specie* is characteristic of Luther.

477. J. M. Neale, *Hymns of the Eastern Church*, fourth edition, with verifications, various readings, and prose translations by S. G. Hatherly, London: Hayes, 1882, pp. 62–79.

478. J. A. Kay, *Wesley's Prayers and Praises*, p. 103.

479. The reading is as early as Justin, *Dialogue with Trypho*, 73, and Tertullian, *Against Marcion*, III, 19.

480. The hymn has always been popular in Lutheranism, and there is a good German translation. The quoted verse reads:

> Vor dem die Sterne neigen sich,
> Du kamst ins Fleisch demütiglich,
> Darin zu leiden williglich;
> Im tiefsten Schmerz dein Leib erblich.

The English translation by Ray Palmer, 'O Christ, our King, Creator Lord', is less successful (*Poetical Works*, London: Dickinson, 1876, p. 105f).

481. For Gregory Nazianzen, see J. N. D. Kelly, *Early Christian Doctrines*, p. 298. The reference is to *orat*. 45, 29, PG 36, 661, and the phrase is *theos stauroumenos*, 'a God hanging on a cross'. For Luther, see W. von Loewenich, ET *Luther's Theology of the Cross*, p. 30. The reference is to the Weimar edition, vol. 1, p. 614: *crucifixus et absconditus deus*.

482. Note A. N. Whitehead's dictum quoted in note 200. For the definition of a god as 'a proper object of worship', see N. Smart, *The Concept of Worship*, especially pp. 31f, 51f. In a sense the definition is analytic, but it does, as Smart points out, 'suffer some sea change at the end of an exploration, for it is in the whole context of ritual, numinosity, etc., that one can see that a god is to be worshipped'. The Christian would certainly wish to add the divine love to 'the whole context'.

483. For Luther, see Weimar edition, vol. 40/3, p. 337, quoted with other passages in G. Ebeling, *Luther*, ET p. 235. For a strong modern Lutheran statement on the *Deus incarnatus, Deus humanus*, with explicit

sacramental incidences, see R. W. Jenson, 'The body of God's presence' in R. W. A. McKinney (ed.), *Creation, Christ and Culture*, pp. 82–91, and his *Visible Words: The Interpretation and Practice of Christian Sacraments*, Philadelphia: Fortress, 1978. I should myself want to take Luther's point in a 'criteriological' and consequently 'non-exclusive' sense as in chapters II and IV.

484. E. Jüngel, *Gott als Geheimnis der Welt*. See earlier note 158.

485. From Isaac Watts: 'We give immortal praise/To God the Father's love' (MHB No. 40).

486. J. D. G. Dunn, *Jesus and the Spirit*, p. 238f, speaks of a 'charismatic hymnody'.

487. Tertullian speaks of singing to God 'de scripturis sanctis vel *de proprio ingenio*' (*Apol.*, 39); cf. *Against Marcion*, V, 8; and see J. Kroll, *Die christliche Hymnodik*, p. 24.

488. B. Fischer, *Die Psalmenfrömmigkeit der Martyrerkirche*, Freiburg: Herder, 1949. Fischer's position is criticized by J. D. Crichton, *Christian Celebration: The Prayer of the Church*, pp. 59–61.

489. On the history of the divine office, see in outline the contributions of J. D. Crichton, G. J. Cuming and W. J. Grisbrooke to C. Jones, G. Wainwright and E. Yarnold (eds.), *The Study of Liturgy*, pp. 350–95. Also J. D. Crichton, *Christian Celebration: The Prayer of the Church*. Fr Crichton is sensitive to the doctrinal incidences of the liturgy.

490. On the psalms at the eucharist and elsewhere, see J. A. Lamb, *The Psalms in Christian Worship*.

491. In the strictest Reformed worship, the only sung matter allowed was scriptural paraphrases.

492. C. H. Dodd, *According to the Scriptures*, London: Nisbet, 1952; B. Lindars, *New Testament Apologetic: the doctrinal significance of Old Testament quotations*, London: SCM, 1961.

493. B. Fischer has shown how early were the twin interpretative principles, *psalmus vox Christi* and *psalmus vox ad Christum*: 'Le Christ dans les psaumes' in *La Maison-Dieu* no. 27 (1951), pp. 86–109, and 'Les psaumes, prière chrétienne: témoignages du IIe siècle' in Bishop Cassien and B. Botte (eds.), *La prière des heures*, Paris: Cerf, 1963, pp. 85–99.

494. L. Brou, *The Psalter Collects*, London: Henry Bradshaw Society, vol. 83, 1949. Brou takes three series of collects, African, Spanish, and Roman, from fifth to sixth century sources. Texts and French translations also in P. Verbraken, *Oraisons sur les 150 psaumes*, Paris: Cerf, 1967.

495. Text from L. Brou, p. 181. We may translate: 'Lead us, Lord, by the gentle reins of your law, that we may reach your eternal dwelling and there drink our fill from your generous cup.'

496. J. Gelineau and others, *Le Psautier de la Bible de Jérusalem*, Paris: Cerf, 1961, p. 83f.

497. Quoted by B. L. Manning, *The Hymns of Wesley and Watts*, p. 80. See also H. Escott, *Isaac Watts, hymnographer*, London: Independent Press, 1962.

498. On the Lucan canticles, see, with bibliographies, J. Mc Hugh, *The Mother of Jesus in the New Testament,* London: DLT, 1975, and R. E. Brown, *The Birth of the Messiah,* Garden City, N.Y.: Doubleday, and London: Chapman, 1977.

499. The revised Roman *Liturgy of the Hours* appeared in 1971. Other New Testament 'canticles' taken from the epistles include Colossians 1:12–20, Ephesians 1:3–10, 1 Timothy 3:16, and 1 Peter 2:21–24. See J. D. Crichton, *Christian Celebration: The Prayer of the Church,* pp. 67f, 87–9.

500. There is no doubt a more intense *psychological* presence of a particular element in the christological mystery at particular festivals: Christ's birth at Christmas, his resurrection at Easter, and so on. This is the part of truth in Odo Casel's theory concerning the particular seasonal presence of distinguishable christological mysteries (plural): see O. Casel, *Das christliche Kultmysterium,* Regensburg: Pustet, 1960⁴ (ET *The Mystery of Christian Worship,* London: DLT, 1962). *Theologically,* however, the mystery of God in Christ is a single totality, the same yesterday, today and forever. This is the truth towards which the 'puritan' suspicion of special seasons points. Casel himself recognizes this 'wholeness' of the mystery and its presence (pp. 90–9). On the broad outlines of the Christian calendar, from the historical point of view, see A. A. McArthur, *The Evolution of the Christian Year,* London: SCM, 1953.

501. See the double issue of *Studia Liturgica* (volume 10, 1974, no. 3/4) devoted to 'Common prayer'.

502. Literally: 'law of praying, law of believing'.

503. See H. Ott, 'Theologie als Gebet und als Wissenschaft' in *Theologische Zeitschrift* 14 (1958), pp. 120–32.

504. Notice the reticence as late as J. A. Jungmann, *Die Stellung Christi im liturgischen Gebet,* 1962², p. 244, note 48.

505. E. Renaudot, *Liturgiarum orientalium collectio,* revised edition, Frankfort: Baer, 1847, vol. 1, pp. i–lxxv: 'Dissertatio de liturgiarum orientalium origine et autoritate'.

506. J. A. Assemani, *Codex liturgicus ecclesiae universae,* vol. 3, Rome: Rotili, 1750, pp. xviii–xxx: 'De authoritate liturgiarum'. Their authority is to be sought *ex usu Ecclesiarum.*

507. F. A. Zaccaria, *Bibliotheca ritualis,* vol. 1, Rome: Monaldini, 1776, pp. lv-lxxxviii: 'De usu librorum liturgicorum in rebus theologicis', in particular p. lx. He adds that in general Western books are to be preferred to Eastern, while the books of the Roman church are best of all. Zaccaria goes on to 'prove' several doctrines—some of them controversial—from the liturgical books (*confirmare, demonstrare, comprobare, ostendere, evincere* are among the verbs he uses).

508. The case against Meaux in polemically presented by Dom Prosper Guéranger, *Institutions liturgiques,* vol. 3, Paris: Julien & Lanier, 1851, pp. 469–513. With the definition of Mary's immaculate conception as part of the historical setting, note also Dom M. Bouix, *Tractatus de jure*

liturgico, Paris: Lecoffre, 1853 (1873³), particularly part 1, chapter 7: 'De valore dogmatico liturgiae' (pp. 12–79(88)³).

509. G. Tyrrell, *Through Scylla and Charybdis, or the old theology and the new*, London: Longmans, 1907, chapter 3: 'Lex orandi, lex credendi', in particular p. 104f.

510. Compare the willingness of contributors to *The Myth of God Incarnate* to continue using the traditional words in worship.

511. See later pp. 294, 335ff.

512. For Casel, see note 500. Another important writing by O. Casel was 'Das Mysteriengedächtnis der Messliturgie im Lichte der Tradition' in *Jahrbuch für Liturgiewissenschaft* 6 (1926), pp. 113–204. L. Bouyer (ET *Liturgical Piety/Life and Liturgy*, p. 89) reports that Casel, a while before his death, acknowledged some words of Pius XII in *Mediator Dei* (encyclical of 20 November 1947) as the exact statement of the thought he wished to proclaim: *Id agit quod jam in cruce fecit*, '(Our Lord) does that (in the mass) which he did on the Cross'. For a *status quaestionis*, see I. H. Dalmais, 'Liturgy and the mystery of salvation' in *The Church at Prayer: Introduction to the Liturgy*, New York: Desclée, 1968, pp. 190–211 (partial English adaptation of A. G. Martimort, ed., *L'Église en prière*, Tournai: Desclée, 1965³).

513. On the notion of mystery in the Fathers, see further P. M. Gy, 'La notion chrétienne d'initiation' in *La Maison-Dieu* no. 132 (1977), pp. 33–54.

514. Pius XII, *Mediator Dei*, in *Acta apostolicae sedis* 39 (1947), pp. 521–95, here p. 544 (ET *Christian Worship*, London: Catholic Truth Society, n.d., here p. 28f, paragraphs 62–3; the paragraphs are not numbered in the original).

515. 'Archeologism' is how the translator renders the pope's phrase, *insana antiquitatum cupido* (p. 546; ET p. 30, paragraph 68).

516. *Mediator Dei*, in *AAS* 39 (1947), p. 545f (ET p. 29f, paragraphs 65–7).

517. *Mediator Dei*, in *AAS* 39 (1947), p. 540 (ET p. 25, paragraph 49).

518. *Mediator Dei*, in *AAS* 39 (1947), p. 540f (ET p. 25f, paragraph 51).

519. *Mediator Dei*, in *AAS* 39 (1947), p. 541 (ET p. 26, paragraph 52).

520. Ibid.: 'Supremo Ecclesiae Magisterio subicitur'.

521. *Mediator Dei*, in *AAS* 39 (1947), p. 540 (ET p. 25, paragraph 51): 'Liturgia igitur omnis catholicam fidem continet, quatenus Ecclesiae fidem publice testatur.'

522. See pp. 238–40. Here is a select bibliography of Catholic writing from around the time of *Mediator Dei* and, with a longer run-up, the definition of Mary's assumption in *Munificentissimus Deus*: K. Adam, 'Les bases dogmatiques de la liturgie' in *Questions liturgiques et paroissiales* 22 (1937), pp. 3–18, 75–92, 147–58; R. Aubert, 'Liturgie et magistère ordinaire' in *Questions liturgiques et paroissiales* 33 (1952), pp. 5–16; J. Brinktrine, 'Die Liturgie als dogmatische Erkenntnisquelle' in *Ephemerides liturgicae* 43 (1929), pp. 44–51, and 'Der dogmatische Beweis aus der Liturgie' in *Scientia sacra* (K. J. Schulte *festschrift*), Cologne: Bachem, and Düsseldorf: Schwann, 1935, pp. 231–51; M. Cappuyns, 'Liturgie et

théologie' in *Questions liturgiques et paroissiales* 19 (1934), pp. 249–72; A. Eguiluz, 'Lex orandi, lex credendi' in *Verdad y vida* (Mexico) 6 (1948), pp. 47–65; J. de Castro Engler, 'Lex orandi, lex credendi' in *Revista eclesiástica brasileira* 11 (1951), pp. 23–43; K. Federer, *Liturgie und Glaube* (as in note 523); M. Pinto, *O valor teológica da liturgia* (as in note 523); P. Renaudin, 'De auctoritate sacrae liturgiae in rebus fidei' in *Divus Thomas* 13 (1935), pp. 41–54; H. A. P. Schmidt, 'Lex orandi, lex credendi in recentioribus documentis pontificiis' in *Periodica de re morali canonica liturgica* 40 (1951), pp. 5–28, and *Introductio in liturgiam occidentalem*, Rome: Herder, 1960, pp. 131–9; T. Vaquero, 'Valor dogmático da liturgia ou relações entre a liturgia e a fé' in *Revista eclesiástica brasileira* 9 (1949), 346–63; A. Vonier, 'The doctrinal power of the liturgy in the Catholic church' in *Clergy Review* 9 (1935), pp. 1–8; W. de Vries, 'Lex supplicandi —lex credendi' in *Ephemerides liturgicae* 47 (1933), pp. 48–58. Later: I. H. Dalmais, 'La liturgie comme lieu théologique' in *La Maison-Dieu* no. 78 (1964), pp. 97–105, and 'The liturgy and the deposit of faith' in *The Church at Prayer: Introduction to the Liturgy*, New York: Desclée, 1968, pp. 212–19 (partial English adaptation of A. G. Martimort, ed., *L'Église en prière*, Tournai: Desclée, 1965³). With these, we arrive at the period of the writings listed in note 32, where the style is post-Vatican II, i.e. less *kontroverstheologisch*, more ecumenical.

523. PL 51, 205–12. The early history is traced, from Prosper backwards, by K. Federer, *Liturgie und Glaube: eine theologiegeschichtliche Untersuchung*, Freiburg in der Schweiz: Paulus-Verlag, 1950. On the question of Prosper's authorship, Federer refers to M. Cappuyns, 'L'origine des Capitula pseudo-célestiniens contre le semi-pélagianisme' in *Revue bénédictine* 41 (1929), pp. 156–70. I am indebted to Federer's work at many points in the ensuing pages. Note also B. Capelle, 'Autorité de la liturgie chez les Pères' in *Recherches de théologie ancienne et médiévale* 21 (1954), pp. 5–22. There is much historical material in M. Pinto's systematic study, *O valor teológico da liturgia*, Braga: Cruz, 1952.

524. *De vocatione omnium gentium*, I, 12, PL 51, 664–5 (partly quoted later, note 527); see M. Cappuyns, 'L'auteur du "De vocatione omnium gentium" ' in *Revue bénédictine* 39 (1927), pp. 198–226.

525. Prosper, *contra Collatorem*, 12, 3, PL 51, 245: 'Aut quod Ecclesia quotidie pro inimicis suis orat, id est, pro his qui necdum Deo crediderunt, numquid non ex Spiritu Dei facit? Quis hoc dixerit, nisi qui hoc non facit, aut qui putat fidem non esse Dei donum? Et tamen quod pro omnibus petitur, non pro omnibus obtinetur. Nec est iniquitas apud Deum, qui saepe postulata non tribuit, quae postulare donavit.' On the early prayers of intercession in the West, see P. de Clerck, *La 'prière universelle' dans les liturgies latines anciennes: témoignages patristiques et textes liturgiques*. Münster: Aschendorff, 1977. A treatment of some theological issues in connexion with intercessions particularly at the eucharist is found in W. J. Grisbrooke, 'Intercession at the eucharist' in *Studia Liturgica* 4 (1965), pp. 129–55, and 5 (1966), pp. 20–44.

526. 'Ex Spiritu Dei': PL 51, 245 (as in note 525).

527. Compare PL 51, 664: 'De hac ergo doctrinae apostolicae regula, qua Ecclesia universalis imbuitur, ne in diversum intellectum nostro evagemur arbitrio, quid ipsa universalis Ecclesia sentiat, requiramus. . . . Quam legem supplicationis ita omnium sacerdotum, et omnium fidelium devotio concorditer tenet, ut nulla pars mundi sit in qua huiusmodi orationes non celebrentur a populis christianis.'

528. Augustine, *contra Julianum*, VI.4, 10–5, 14, PL 44, 827-31; and *opus imperf. contra Julianum*, II, 181, PL 45, 1220; cf. *ep*. 194, 43, PL 33, 889.

529. Augustine, *serm*. 174, 7–9, PL 38, 943–5; cf. *ep*. 194, 44-6, PL 33, 889–91; *opus imperf. contra Julianum*, II.30, PL 45, 1154. In the modern debate on infant baptism, E. Jüngel has sharply called into question the appeal to existing practice, however traditional the practice and the appeal to it. He says that a systematic doctrine of baptism has to *choose* between a pauline understanding of baptism and the hellenistic, massively 'sacramental' practice which antedated Paul and which, despite Paul's criticism, continued its way and was invoked and reinforced by Augustine: 'Zur Kritik des sakramentalen Verständnisses der Taufe' in F. Viering (ed.), *Zu Karl Barths Lehre von der Taufe*, pp. 25–43.

530. Augustine, *de dono perseverentiae* 23, 63–5, PL 45, 1031-3; *ep*. 217, PL 33, 978-89.

531. Augustine, *serm. frag*. 1, 3, PL 39, 1721.

532. Augustine, *de civitate Dei* XXI, 24, 1f, PL 41, 737-8; *serm*. 159, 1, PL 38, 868; *serm*. 172, 2, PL 38, 936-7; *serm*., 297, 2, 3, PL 38, 1360; *de haeresibus*, 53, PL 42, 40; *enchiridion*, 110, PL 40, 283; *de cura pro mortuis*, 1, 3, PL 40, 593.

533. See W. Roetzer, *Des heiligen Augustinus Schriften als liturgiegeschichtliche Quelle*, Munich: Hueber, 1930, pp. 38-43. Many of my references to Augustine were found through this book.

534. Many examples are to be found in W. Roetzer, op. cit.

535. Note *de catechizandis rudibus*, 26, 50, PL 40, 344-5.

536. Augustine, *ep*. 55, 13, PL 33, 210–11; *ep*. 55, 21, PL 23, 214; *ep*. 55, 34, PL 33, 221.

537. Augustine, *ep*. 54, 6, PL 33, 202-3; *ep*. 55, 34-5, PL 33, 221-2.

538. English translations in E. Yarnold, *The Awe-inspiring Rites of Initiation*, Slough: St Paul, 1972.

539. Chrysostom explains baptism in advance, but his catecheses do not include the explanation of the eucharist.

540. Modern examples of fundamental doctrinal teaching based on the liturgy are C. Davis (Roman Catholic), *Liturgy and Doctrine*, London: Sheed & Ward, 1960, and *The Making of a Christian*, London: Sheed & Ward, 1964; H. McCabe, o.p., *The New Creation: Studies on living in the Church*, London: Sheed & Ward, 1964; and A. Schmemann (Orthodox), *The World as Sacrament*. Teaching at a more detailed level is found in L. Bouyer's exposition of the rites of Holy Week, *Le mystère pascal*, Paris:

Cerf, 1957³ (ET *The Paschal Mystery*, London: Allen & Unwin, 1951). I understand that the French Catholic bishops, meeting at Lourdes in October 1978, decided to take eucharistic prayer IV in the 1970 Roman missal as a basis for catechesis in the whole Christian faith.

541. Ambrose, *de mysteriis*, 5, 28.

542. See earlier p. 96f.

543. G. Mercato, *Antiche reliquie liturgiche ambrosiane e romane, con un excursus sui frammenti dogmatici ariani del Mai* (Studi e Testi, 7), Rome: Typografia vaticana, 1902, pp. 45–71.

544. Ambrose, *de fide ad Gratianum*, I.2, 12f, PL 16, 554.

545. Jerome, *dial. contra Luciferianos*, 8, PL 23, 172. Among the 'other things' are the threefold immersion of the head in baptism, the milk and honey, and the prohibition of both kneeling and fasting during the Easter season.

546. Augustine, *de baptismo contra Donatistas*, IV, 24, 31, PL 43, 474; cf. II.7, 12, PL 43, 133; *ep.* 54, 1, 1, PL 33, 200.

547. On Optatus, see Federer, pp. 54–8.

548. Cyprian, *ep.* 69, 7 and 12 (CSEL, pp. 756, 760f).

549. Cyprian, *ep.* 63, 14 (CSEL, p. 712); 71, 3 (p. 773); 73, 13 (p. 787); 74, 9 (p. 806f).

550. Cyprian, *ep.* 63, 14 (p. 712).

551. 'Consuetudo sine veritate vetustas erroris est' (*ep.* 74, 9; p. 806).

552. Cyprian, *ep.* 70, 1–2 (pp. 767–9). Cyprian's principal point is that 'heretics and schismatics' cannot perform the baptismal rites because they have neither Spirit nor priesthood nor altar.

553. Cyprian, *de catholicae ecclesiae unitate*, 17 (CSEL, p. 226).

554. Cyprian, *ep.* 69, 13 (CSEL, p. 762f).

555. Cyprian, *ep.* 69, 11 (CSEL, p. 760); 70, 3 (p. 769); 73, 6 (p. 783); 74, 5 (p. 802f).

556. On Tertullian, see Federer, pp. 75–93.

557. Tertullian insists on the *truth*. In his *de virginibus velandis*, written in his montanist period, he says that old custom is heretical if it is contrary to the truth. A usage may be passed on by custom from a good beginning; but a practice may also have its source in ignorance (PL 2, 937–8).

558. Tertullian, *adversus Marcionen*, IV.40, PL 2, 490–3. 'The bread which he took, and divided among his disciples, he made into his body, saying, *This is my body*, that is, the figure of my body. Now there could have been no figure, unless it had been a veritable body; for an empty thing, which a phantasm is, would have been incapable of figure. Or else, if you suppose he formed bread into a body for himself because he felt the lack of a veritable body, then it was bread he ought to have delivered up for us. . . . So also at the reference to the cup, when establishing the covenant sealed with his own blood, he affirmed the reality of his body: for there can be no blood except from a body which is flesh' (ET by E. Evans, *Tertullian: Adversus Marcionen*, Oxford: Clarendon, 1972, pp. 493–5).

559. Tertullian, *adversus Marcionem*, I, 14, PL 2, 587.

560. Tertullian, *de resurrectione carnis*, 8, PL 2, 852.

561. Irenaeus, *adversus haereses* IV. 18, 4, PG 7, 1026–7.

562. Irenaeus, *adversus haereses*, V. 2, 3, PG 7, 1125–7.

563. Irenaeus, *adversus haereses* IV. 18, 5, PG 7, 1028.

564. On the resurrection of the body, see the conclusion of this book, pp. 449-54.

565. See note 287.

566. An early Roman, indeed papal, grounding for this is furnished by Innocent I in his reply to enquiries about rites from Decentius, bishop of Gubbio: 'If the bishops of the Lord would observe the Church's institutions fully as the blessed apostles bequeathed them to us, there would be no diversity or variety in either the ceremonies or the sacramental prayers. But as each one thinks it right to abide by what seems good to him rather than by tradition, differences in the observances and celebrations appear in different places and churches. This is a scandal for the people, who, no longer knowing the ancient traditions now corrupted by the presumption of men, either believe that the churches are no longer in agreement among themselves or think that it was the apostles and their immediate successors who brought in the contradiction. Who could ignore or despise what was left to the Roman church by Peter, prince of the apostles, and has always been observed there, and should be observed by all without adding anything unauthorized or after non-Roman models? For it is clear that in the whole of Italy, Gaul, Spain, Africa, Sicily and the islands, no church was founded by any other persons than those sent to them as bishops by the venerable apostle Peter or his successors' (*ep.* 25, 1f, PL 20, 551–2). It was not yet a question of imposing fully organized liturgical books; it was a matter of various ritual points to do with the moment to give the peace at mass and to recite the diptychs, the giving of 'confirmation' by bishops only, the Saturday fast, the bringing of the *fermentum* to presbyteral churches (see my 'Conciliarity and eucharist' in *One in Christ* 14, 1978, in particular pp. 40–2), exorcism, penance, unction of the sick. Later, pope Vigilius (537–55) was consulted by Profuturus, bishop of Braga, on ritual questions, and his reply is found in *ep.* 1, PL 69, 15–19. Both these cases are treated, with bibliography, in E. Dekkers, 'Créativité et orthodoxie dans la *lex orandi*' in *La Maison-Dieu* no. 111 (1972), pp. 20–30. Dekkers hints at certain problems of authenticity in the letter of Innocent I: certainly its 'phrases incisives feront la joie des canonistes'.

567. Alcuin, *adversus Felicem*, VII.13, PL 101, 226–7.

568. Alcuin, *adversus Elipandum*, II.9, PL 101, 266–7.

569. In the eleventh-century controversy on the eucharistic presence, both Berengar and his opponents Lanfranc and Witmund lay claim to the post-communion prayer from the Gelasian and Gregorian sacramentaries: 'Perficiant in nobis, quaesumus, Domine, tua sacramenta quod continent, ut quod nunc specie gerimus, rerum veritate capiamus.' See PL 149, 1467–8, and PL 150, 436.

570. Trent, session VI, decree on justification, chapter 10, DS 1535.

571. A doctrinal *locus* is a place from which teaching may be drawn. The Spanish Dominican Melchior Cano (1509–60) listed ten, of which the first seven are *loci proprii*, and the remainder *loci alieni*: scripture, dominical and apostolic traditions, the Catholic Church, councils, the Roman church, the Fathers, the scholastic theologians; natural reason, philosophers, human history. The liturgy might be seen as related to all of these, in various ways. I should myself want to consider the liturgy as a doctrinal locus in its own nature and right. The relative weighting and interplay among the *loci* is of course the problem to which the whole second part of this book is addressed.

572. Trent, session XXII, on the sacrifice of the mass, chapter 4 and canon 6, DS 1745 and 1756.

573. J. Brinktrine, 'Die Liturgie als dogmatische Erkenntnisquelle' in *Ephemerides liturgicae* 43 (1929), pp. 44–51, and 'Der dogmatische Beweis aus der Liturgie' in *Scientia sacra* (K. J. Schulte *festschrift*), Cologne: Bachem, and Düsseldorf: Schwann, 1935, pp. 231–51.

574. Thomas Aquinas, commentary on 1 Corinthians, chapter 11, lectio 6.

575. J. Brinktrine, in the articles mentioned in note 573, is embarrassed by a number of doctrinally awkward rubrics, notably one in the communion of the sick according to the thirteenth-century Roman pontifical which 'expressed the erroneous opinion that the unconsecrated wine was changed into the blood of Christ through contact with the consecrated host'. He has to plead that the doctrine had not been officially clarified at the time, and that the saving efficacy of communion was not diminished since the communicant received the whole Christ under the single species of bread. The upshot is to reduce the value of the liturgy to a *probable* source in matters as yet undefined by the magisterium.

576. J. B. Bossuet, *États d'oraison*, book 6, in Œuvres, ed. Migne, 1856, vol. 4, p. 115. Bossuet's notion that the liturgy is 'the principal instrument of the Church's Tradition' is taken up by Y. Congar in the theological half of his massive study on *Tradition and Traditions* (ET London: Burns & Oates, 1966, pp. 427–35).

577. Bernard of Clairvaux, *ep.* 174, 5 (to the canons of Lyons), PL 182, 334.

578. Thomas Aquinas, *Summa theologiae* III, 27, 1.

579. For a bibliography, see earlier notes 508 and 522.

580. Text in *Pii IX pontificis maximi Acta*, Typographia Bonarum Artium, ?1855, pp. 597–619; the passages quoted are on pp. 598–601. See again, later, p. 259f.

581. Pope Sixtus IV (1471–84) gave approval to the feast. The office of the immaculate conception was introduced into the breviary during the reign of Pius V (1566–72). Clement XI (1700–21) made the feast obligatory in the universal Church.

582. '. . . atque adeo lex credendi ipsa supplicandi lege statueretur.'

583. There was certainly a popular mid-August 'commemoration of Mary' by the early fifth century, when interest had already begun to be taken in her *transitus*; but it may be a century or two before a distinguishable feast of her 'dormition' yet emerged.

584. In the bull promulgating the Assumption, *Munificentissimus Deus*, Pius XII quotes this prayer from the (Gregorian) sacramentary 'which our predecessor Hadrian I sent to the emperor Charlemagne' (*Acta apostolicae sedis* 42 (1950), pp. 753–73, in particular p. 759).

585. F. Suarez, *In III partem divi Thomae*, disputatio 21, sect. 2, paragraphs 5 and 9 (*Opera omnia*, vol. 19, Paris: Vivès, 1860, p. 317f).

586. P. Oppenheim, *Principia theologiae liturgicae*, Turin: Marietti, 1947. The passages quoted are from his contribution on 'Maria in der lateinischen Liturgie' to P. Sträter (ed.), *Katholische Marienkunde: Maria in der Offenbarung*, Paderborn: Schöningh, 1952², in particular p. 184f.

587. In *Munificentissimus Deus* itself, Pius XII cited the liturgical evidence of the feast of the Dormition or Assumption and quoted prayers from the Gregorian sacramentary, a Gallican source, and the Byzantine liturgy. The pope stressed that the Church's liturgy did not generate the Catholic faith but was rather its fruit: nevertheless he recalled that his predecessors Sergius I (687–701), Leo IV (847–55), and Nicholas I (858–67), in order to strengthen the faith of believers, had elevated the feast of the Assumption in dignity. Pius XII further appealed to the mystery of the Assumption in the rosary 'whose recitation this Apostolic See has so greatly recommended'. The passage appealing to the liturgy is found in *AAS* 42 (1950), pp. 758ff. The summary statement is that the truth of Mary's Assumption 'sacris litteris innititur, *christifidelium animis penitus est insista, ecclesiastico cultu inde ab antiquissimis temporibus comprobata*, ceteris revelatis veritatibus summe consona, theologorum studio, scientia ac sapientia splendide explicata et declarata' (p. 769). In return, 'the collect of the new mass for the feast of the Assumption (15 August) introduces the actual wording of the dogma, as does the collect for December 8 (the Immaculate Conception)—an indication that both are new "dogmatic" feasts': so R. Peil, (enlarged ET) *A Handbook of the Liturgy*, Freiburg: Herder, 1960, p. 233. With perhaps a hint of things that then appeared still to come, J. de Castro Engler was in 1951 calling attention to the fact that an office and mass of the Blessed Virgin Mary 'mediatrix of all graces' (decree of the Sacred Congregration of Rites, 12 January 1921), though not imposed on the whole Church, had been conceded to many congregations and dioceses, and that a prayer invoking the 'Blessed Virgin, co-redemptrix of the human race' had been indulgenced by Pius X: 'Lex orandi, lex credendi' in *Revista eclesiástica brasileira* 11 (1951), in particular p. 29f.

588. The marian examples figure in J. M. R. Tillard's rich article on 'Sensus fidelium', in *One in Christ* 11 (1975), pp. 2–29. Tillard writes of the proper complementarity but frequent tension between 'popular faith' and 'educated faith'. On the one hand, 'the non-essential is necessary', if the

faith is meant to take concrete form in the whole human *humus*. On the other hand, spontaneous movements have to be tested for their 'genuineness' in relation to 'the data of Revelation'. It is just this testing which is problematic, and our next section will be devoted to the problems. On the substantive issue of marian piety and belief, a Catholic priest and theologian whom I greatly respect speaks of the 'devotional impossibility' of thinking of Mary as a sinner in any way. Note what appears by now to be the rather 'maximalist' study by R. Laurentin, *Notre Dame et la messe*, Paris: Desclée de Brouwer, 1954 (ET *Our Lady and the Mass*, Dublin: Clonmore & Reynolds, 1959); also the sympathetically critical work of the Waldensian G. Miegge, *La Vergine Maria: saggio di storia del dogma*, Torre Pellice: Claudiana, 1959, who says in this connexion that the *lex orandi, lex credendi* principle 'non è cosi assoluto come si vuole, poichè vi sono espressioni della pietà che non si traducono mai in rigorose proposizioni dottrinali: la poesia è sempre un po' al di là della teologia, e la sua responsabilità dogmatica non deve essere esagerata' (p. 11).

589. N. A. Nissiotis, 'Worship, eucharist and "intercommunion": an Orthodox reflection' in *Studia Liturgica* 2 (1963), pp. 193–222, in particular p. 201.

590. In P. Brunner's *Zur Lehre vom Gottesdienst der im Namen Jesu versammelten Gemeinde* (ET *Worship in the Name of Jesus*), the chapter on 'worship as the service of God to the congregation' precedes the chapter on 'worship as the congregation's service before God'. See already H. Asmussen, *Die Lehre vom Gottesdienst*, Munich: Kaiser, 1937, and E. Schlink, *Der kommende Christus und die kirchlichen Traditionen*, Göttingen: Vandenhoeck & Ruprecht, 1961, part II, chapter 4 (ET *The Coming Christ and the Coming Church*, Edinburgh: Oliver & Boyd, 1967, pp. 132–43). In V. Vajta, *Die Theologie des Gottesdienstes bei Luther*, 'worship as the work of God' precedes 'worship as the work of faith'. W. Hahn arranges his book *Worship and Congregation* in two parts: 'God's service to us', 'The service we render God in worship'. In *The Knowledge of God and the Service of God according to the Teaching of the Reformation*, London: Hodder, 1938, Karl Barth puts 'The Church service as divine action' before 'The Church service as human action'. In the work which he edited, *The Church at Prayer*, the Catholic A. G. Martimort certainly recognizes the initiative of God in 'the dialogue between God and his people' (part 1, chapter 6), but it is perhaps significant that the later chapter (8) on 'the twofold movement of the liturgy' takes the sequence 'worship of God and sanctification of man'.

A graphic statement of Luther's views is supplied by the following passage apropos of the Magnificat: 'Now, no one is God's servant unless he lets Him be his God and perform His works in him, of which we spoke above. Alas, the word "service of God" has nowadays taken on so strange a meaning and usage that whoever hears it thinks not of these works of God, but rather of the ringing of bells, the wood and stone of churches, the incense pot, the flicker of candles, the mumbling in the churches, the gold, silver, and precious stones in the vestments of choirboys and celebrants, of chalices and monstrances, of organs and images, processions and churchgoing, and most of all, the babbling of lips and the rattling of rosaries. This, alas, is what the service of God means now. Of such service God knows nothing at all, while we know nothing but this. We chant the Magnificat daily, to a special tone and with gorgeous pomp; and yet the oftener we sing it, the more we silence its true music and meaning. Yet the text stands firm. Unless we learn and experience these works of God, there will be no service of God, no Israel, no grace, no mercy, no God, though we kill ourselves with singing and ringing in the churches and drag into them all the goods in the world' (*Commentary on the Magnificat*, 1521; ET from J. Pelikan (ed.), *Luther's Works*, St Louis: Concordia, 1956ff, vol. 21, p. 350).

591. See V. Vajta, *Die Theologie des Gottesdienstes bei Luther* (abbreviated ET *Luther on Worship*), part 1, chapter 2: 'Beneficium and sacrificium' (pp. 43–113; ET pp. 27–63).

592. Vincent of Lérins, *Commonitorium*, 2 (ET *The 'Commonitorium against Heresies' of Vincentius Lerinensis*, London: Elliot Stock, 1879). For the argument that *Augustine*, though unnamed, is the target of the 'semi-pelagian' Vincent, see B. Lohse, *Epochen der Dogmengeschichte*[3]. p. 129 (ET *A Short History of Christian Doctrine*).

593. J. H. Newman, *Essay on the Development of Christian Doctrine* (1845; revised 1878).

594. It was in the form of 'letters to a member of the Society of Friends' that F. D. Maurice originally wrote *The Kingdom of Christ* (1838; 1842[2]), dealing with baptism, creeds, forms of worship, the eucharist, the ministry, and the scriptures, as 'signs of a spiritual society'. He has interesting things to say on many of the themes which are occupying us in the second part of this book.

595. On the relations between liturgy and ethics, see in detail chapter XII.

596. It may have been an 'enthusiastic' understanding of the sacraments in the sense of an over-realized eschatology which prompted the ethical disorders addressed by Paul in Romans 6 and 1 Corinthians 10 and 11. In the epistles, the apostolic 'magisterium' intervenes in order to correct understanding and practice.

597. The positive need (as distinct from inconvenient necessity) for re-interpretation is increasingly recognized in Roman Catholic theology. See even the generally 'conservative' statement on *Authority in the Church* agreed by the Anglican/Roman Catholic International Commission ('Venice 1976'), paragraph 15. Oswald Loretz has argued that Vatican II sanctions the end of the 'absolute inerrancy' doctrine of scripture and offers the chance of a fresh start in understanding the Bible as genuinely human witness—through which God still speaks—to the 'truth' of God's salvation (for the Bible itself, the opposite of truth is not error but 'the lie'): *Das Ende der Inspirationstheorie: Chancen eines Neubeginns*, Stuttgart:

Katholisches Bibelwerk, 2 vols., 1974 and 1976. The collapse of inerrancy and the recognition of cultural limitations in respect of *scripture* is seen by Loretz to underlie the current acknowledgment of the historical condition-edness of *all dogma* which renders the old 'inerrancy' view of the infallibility of the ecclesiastical magisterium inappropriate. Here too the question is not whether the documents of the magisterium may contain errors; the question is, what in them is true.

598. The quotation is from an ordination address given by archbishop Lefebvre on 29 July 1976. ET from Y. Congar, *Challenge to the Church: the case of Archbishop Lefebvre*, London: Collins, 1977, p. 29f (original: *La crise dans l'Église et Mgr Lefebvre*, Paris: Cerf, 1976).

599. Y. Congar, ET *Challenge to the Church*, p. 30f. Congar himself has shown how strong the Tradition is—when it was not being anti-Protestant—on the exercise by the faithful of their baptismal priesthood: 'L' 'ecclesia' ou communauté chrétienne, sujet intégral de l'action liturgique' in J. P. Jossua and Y. Congar (eds.), *La liturgie après Vatican II*, pp. 241–82.

600. N. Lash, *Voices of Authority*, London: Sheed & Ward, 1976, pp. 43–54.

601. On the issue of doctrinal development, see (by Roman Catholics) Y. Congar, *La tradition et les traditions*, 2 vols., Paris: Fayard, 1961–63 (ET *Tradition and Traditions*, London: Burns & Oates, 1966); J. R. Geiselmann, *Die heilige Schrift und die Tradition*, Freiburg: Herder, 1962 (partial ET *The Meaning of Tradition*, Freiburg: Herder, and London: Burns & Oates, 1966); G. B. Gilmore, 'J. A. Möhler on doctrinal development' in *Heythrop Journal* 19 (1978), pp. 383–98; J. P. Jossua, 'Immutabilité, progrès ou structurations multiples des doctrines chrétiennes?' in *Revue des sciences philosophiques et théologiques* 52 (1968), pp. 173–200 (especially p. 192f on the mass); N. Lash, *Change in Focus: a study of doctrinal change and continuity*, London: Sheed & Ward, 1973, and *Newman on Development: the search for an explanation in history*, London: Sheed & Ward, 1975; H. de Lubac, 'Le problème du développement du dogme' in *Recherches de science religieuse* 35 (1948), pp. 130–60; K. Rahner, ET 'The development of dogma' and 'Considerations on the development of dogma' in *Theological Investigations*, vol. 1 (1961), pp. 39–77, and vol. 4 (1966), pp. 3–35; E. Schillebeeckx, several chapters in his *Openbaring en theologie*, Bilthoven: Nelissen, 1966[2] (ET *Revelation and Theology*, London: Sheed & Ward, 1967); M. Schmaus (ed.), *Die mündliche Überlieferung*, Munich: Hüber, 1957 (essays by H. Bacht, 'Tradition und Lehramt in der Diskussion um das Assumpta-Dogma', by H. Fries, 'J. H. Newmans Beitrag zum Verständnis der Tradition', and by J. R. Geiselmann, 'Das Konzil von Trient über das Verhältnis der heiligen Schrift und der nicht geschriebenen Traditionen'); J. H. Walgrave, *Unfolding Revelation: the nature of doctrinal development*, London: Hutchinson, and Philadelphia: Westminster, 1972; (and by Protestants) O. Chadwick, *From Bossuet to Newman: the idea of doctrinal development*, Cambridge: University Press,

1957; G. A. Lindbeck, 'The problem of doctrinal development and contemporary Protestant theology' in *Concilium*, January 1967, pp. 64–72; J. Pelikan, *Development of Christian Doctrine*, New Haven: Yale University Press, 1969, and *Historical Theology: Continuity and Change in Christian Doctrine*, London: Hutchinson, and New York: Corpus, 1971; M. F. Wiles, *The Making of Christian Doctrine*, and *The Remaking of Christian Doctrine*, chapter 1. Note also the WCC 'Montreal report' on *Tradition and traditions*, Faith and Order paper no. 40, Geneva, 1963.

602. The text of the Anglican/Roman Catholic International Commission on *Authority in the Church* ('Venice 1976') declared: 'Although the categories of thought and the mode of expression may be superseded, restatement always builds upon, and does not contradict, the truth intended by the original definition' (paragraph 15). On the other hand: if not 'definitions', then at least 'customs, accepted positions, beliefs, formulations and practices, as well as innovations and re-interpretations, may be shown to be inadequate, mistaken, or even inconsistent with the gospel' (paragraph 18).

603. Poets are notoriously sensitive. John Wesley wrote: 'Many Gentlemen have done my Brother and me (although without naming us) the honour to reprint many of our hymns. Now they are perfectly welcome so to do, provided they print them just as they are. But I desire they would not attempt to mend them—for they really are not able. None of them is able to mend either the sense or the verse. Therefore, I must beg of them one of these two favours: either to let them stand just as they are, to take them for better for worse; or to add the true reading in the margin, or at the bottom of the page; that we may no longer be accountable either for the nonsense or for the doggerel of other men.' It was only on his deathbed that John Keble sanctioned the change to 'As in the hands' in the Gunpowder Plot Day hymn in *The Christian Year* (see G. Battiscombe, *John Keble*, London: Constable, 1963, p. 111f):

> Oh, come to our Communion Feast,
> There present in the heart,
> Not in the hands, th'eternal Priest
> Doth His own Self impart.

Hymnal compilers soon get out their daggers and double daggers to alter the verses of dead authors, though not all of them are polite enough to use such a typographical convention to signify changes.

604. H. Lietzmann's thesis was presented in *Messe und Herrenmahl* (1926). A fresh emphasis on the importance of Jesus' post-Resurrection meals in eucharistic foundations was made by O. Cullmann: 'La signification de la sainte cène dans le christianisme primitif' in *Revue d'histoire et de philosophie religieuses* 16 (1936), pp. 1–22 (ET in O. Cullmann and F. J. Leenhardt, *Essays on the Lord's Supper*, London: Lutterworth, 1958, pp. 5–23); and *Urchristentum und Gottesdienst* (ET *Early Christian Worship*, London: SCM,

1953). For the argument that death and resurrection were equiprimordial in the primitive eucharist, see E. Schweizer, 'Das Abendmahl eine Vergegenwärtigung des Todes Jesu oder ein eschatologisches Freudenmahl?' in *Theologische Zeitschrift* 2 (1946), pp. 81–101.

605. See G. Bornkamm, 'Abendmahl und Kirche bei Paulus' in *Zeitschrift für Theologie und Kirche* 53 (1956), pp. 312–49; E. Käsemann, 'Anliegen und Eigenart des paulinischen Abendmahls' in *Exegetische Versuche und Besinnungen*, vol. 1, pp. 11–34 (ET *Essays on New Testament Themes*, pp. 108–35); P. Neuenzeit, *Das Herrenmahl*, pp. 170–2, 221–5; B. Reicke, *Diakonia, Festfreude und Zelos in Verbindung mit der altchristlichen Agapenfeier*, Uppsala/Wiesbaden, 1951, pp. 252–93.

606. On the Lord's prayer in the early Church, see G. W. H. Lampe, ' "Our Father" in the Fathers' in P. Brookes (ed.), *Christian Spirituality* (E. G. Rupp *festschrift*), London: SCM, 1975, pp. 9–31; W. Rordorf, ' "Wie auch wir vergeben *haben* unsern Schuldern" (Matth. VI, 12b)' in *Studia Patristica X* (Texte und Untersuchungen, 107), Berlin: Akademie-Verlag, 1970, pp. 236–41. Rordorf suggests that the variant Eastern reading 'as we have forgiven' reflects the fact that the pre-commuion recitation already presupposed the pre-anaphoral kiss of peace, whereas 'as we forgive' corresponds to the Western *pax* exchanged *after* the Lord's prayer ('as we in our turn forgive . . .').

607. For the idea that the Lord's prayer was used as a eucharistic consecration prayer, see J. Schousboe, 'La messe la plus ancienne' in *Revue de l'histoire des religions* 96 (1927), pp. 193–256; and cf. A Schweitzer, *Die Mystik des Apostels Paulus*, Tübingen: Mohr, 1930, p. 268 (ET *The Mysticism of Paul the Apostle*, London: Black, 1931).

608. See p. 159 and notes 88, 373, 911.

609. R. P. C. Hanson, 'The liberty of the bishop to improvise prayer in the eucharist' in *Vigiliae christianae* 15 (1961), pp. 173–6; also L. Bouyer, 'L'improvisation liturgique dans l'Église ancienne' in *La Maison-Dieu* no. 111 (1972), pp 7–19.

610. Chapter 10, ed. Dix-Chadwick, p. 19 (as corrected on erratum slip); translation compared with Botte's (chapter 9).

611. Origen, *Conversation with Heracleides*.

612. Cyprian, *de catholicae ecclesiae unitate*, 17 (CSEL, p. 226).

613. E. Dekkers, 'Créativité et orthodoxie dans la *lex orandi*' in *La Maison-Dieu* no. 111 (1972), pp. 20–30.

614. P. G. Cobb summarizes thus: 'It was the duty of the bishop, the privilege of a priest, to preach in the liturgy. By the fourth century it had become the general practice in the East that all priests present who wished to do so should preach and, after them, the bishop himself (*Ap. Const.*, 2.57.9; *Egeria* 25.1). In the West the danger of heresy led to priests being forbidden to preach (Socrates, *HE*, 5.22, PG 67.640; Sozomen, *HE*, 7.19, PG 67.1476; Celestine I, *ep.* 21, PL 50. 528–30) but exceptions were made, of Augustine when he was a priest, for example. This was acceptable in North Africa and Italy, where dioceses were small, but north of

the Alps, where they were large, it was intolerable. In Gaul the council of Vaison in 529, at the instance of St Caesarius, gave priests the right to preach (canon 2; Mansi, 8.727)' (in C. Jones, G. Wainwright and E. Yarnold (eds.), *The Study of Liturgy*, p. 187).

615. Tertullian, *de carne Christi*, 17, PL 2, 826.

616. Eusebius, *H.E.* VII. 30.

617. For the hymns of Arius, see p. 201 and note 467. Sozomen's report is in *H.E.* VIII. 8, PG 67, 1536–37.

618. Eusebius, *H.E.* VII. 30.

619. Irenaeus, *adversus haereses*, V. 1, 3, PG 7, 1122–3; cf. Clement of Alexandria, *Paid.* II, 2, PG 8, 409–12.

620. Justin uses the word *krama* ('mixture'). It was an ordinary custom in Greek antiquity to mix water with wine. The council in Trullo—which in 692 condemned the Armenian refusal about to be mentioned in the text—believed the practice of the mixture to be apostolic (canon 32).

621. On the Armenian practice and the persistent controversy, see J. M. Hanssens, *Institutiones liturgicae de ritibus orientalibus*, vols. 2 and 3: *De missa rituum orientalium*, Rome: Pontifical Gregorian University, 1930–32, in particular vol. 2, pp. 250–71.

622. Cyprian, *ep.* 63, 13 (CSEL, p. 711).

623. Luther, *Formula missae*, 16.

624. Trent, session XXII, chapter 7 and canon 9 (DS 1748 and 1759).

625. Another symbolism, with various theological applications, associates the water and the wine with the water and the blood from Christ's pierced side (John 19:34). This is already found in Ambrose, *de sacramentis* V. 1, 4. It characterizes a prayer at the addition of water to the chalice in the Ambrosian, Lyonese and Carthusian rites: D. Buenner, *L'ancienne liturgie romaine: le rite lyonnais*, Lyons: Vitte, 1934, p. 229f.

626. L. Duchesne, *Le Liber pontificalis*, vol. 1, Paris: Thorin, 1886, pp. 239, 241.

627. See J. A. Jungmann, *Die Stellung Christi im liturgischen Gebet* (ET *The Place of Christ in Liturgical Prayer*); *The Early Liturgy*, especially chapter 15; and *Liturgisches Erbe und pastorale Gegenwart*, Innsbruck: Tyrolia, 1960 (bad ET in *Pastoral Liturgy*, Tenbury Wells: Challoner, 1962), pp. 3–86: 'Die Abwehr des germanischen Arianismus und der Umbruch der religiösen Kultur im frühen Mittelalter'.

628. See, earlier, chapters II and III, particularly pp. 52f, 63, 96f, and again p. 305.

629. From a study on 'The blessing of the baptismal font in the Syrian rite of the fourth century', in *Theological Studies* 7 (1946), pp. 309–13, J. Quasten concluded that 'here as elsewhere the third person of the Trinity becomes more and more prominent. The theology of the Logos, which attributed the incarnation, the inspiration of the prophets, and the consecration of the eucharistic bread, as well as the sanctification of the baptismal font, to Christ, now gives way to theology of the Holy Spirit'. The general claim needs a little nuancing if, on the one hand, B. Botte

is right to consider 'Sarapion's Euchologion', with its Logos-epiclesis, the work of a fifth-century Arian ('L'euchologe de Sérapion est-il authentique?' in *Oriens christianus* 48 (1964), pp. 50–56); and if, on the other hand, an early fourth-century date is allowed to the 'Alexandrine anaphora of St Basil', with its Spirit-epiclesis (see, for instance, A. Houssiau, in L. Sheppard (ed.), *The New Liturgy*, pp. 228–43).

630. G. Kretschmar comments on these liturgical incidences of the council of Constantinople's pneumatological doctrine and suggests that 'common patterns of rite shared by different regions of the Church are by no means always a sign of great antiquity, for they may be the result of a conformity introduced later in the wake of new theological insights' ('Recent research on Christian initiation', in *Studia Liturgica* 12 (1977), in particular p. 92f).

631. For a masterly unravelling of the tangled Syrian evidence concerning anointing and the Spirit, see E. J. Yarnold, in C. Jones, G. Wainwright and E. Yarnold, *The Study of Liturgy*, pp. 105–8.

632. Fourth council of Toledo (633), quoting advice given by Gregory the Great to Leander of Seville. The same point is made by Ildefonsus, *de cognitione baptismi*, 117, PL 96, 160. See J. D. C. Fischer, *Christian Initiation: Baptism in the Medieval West*, p. 91, and E. C. Whitaker, *Documents of the Baptismal Liturgy*[2], pp. 115, 224.

633. Quoted by J. D. C. Fisher, op. cit., p. 50.

634. J. D. C. Fisher, op. cit., p. 51; E. C. Whitaker, *Documents*[2], p. 212.

635. See the note in F. Procter and W. H. Frere, *A New History of the Book of Common Prayer* (1901 and many reprints), London: Macmillan, 1958, p. 317f.

636. On the question of the base(s) of the Nicene Creed, see J. N. D. Kelly, *Early Christian Creeds*[3], in particular chapters 7 and 10; though also the article by H. von Campenhausen mentioned in note 432.

637. See, in an earlier context, p. 186f.

638. J. A. Jungmann, *Missarum sollemnia*, part 3, chapter 2, section 8.

639. See p. 238f.

640. See Y. Brilioth, *Eucharistic Faith and Practice: Evangelical and Catholic*, pp. 86–90.

641. See, for instance, E. Schillebeeckx, *Christus tegenwoordigheid in de eucharistie* (ET *The Eucharist*).

642. The observance of Corpus Christi originated in the vision of an Augustinian nun, in Liège in 1246. Urban IV had been archdeacon of that city.

643. Already John Wyclif had written in his *de eucharistia*: 'They are worse than heathens, believing that the consecrated host is their god.' J. A. Jungmann writes: 'The holiest of the Church's possessions remained, it is true, the centre of genuine piety. But alas, the clouds and shadows surrounding this centre brought matters to such a pass that the Institution of Jesus, that well of life from which the Church had drawn for 1500 years, became an object of scorn and ridicule and was repudiated as a

horrible idolatry by entire peoples' (*Missarum sollemnia*, part 1, section 12);
cf. 'Der Stand des liturgischen Lebens am Vorabend der Reformation' in
Liturgisches Erbe und pastorale Gegenwart, pp. 87–107 (bad ET in *Pastoral
Liturgy*).

644. J. A. Jungmann, 'Liturgisches Leben im Barock' in his *Liturgisches Erbe und pastorale Gegenwart* (bad ET in *Pastoral Liturgy*).

645. Pius XI, *Quas primas* in *Acta apostolicae sedis* 17 (1925), pp. 593–610.

646. For an early example, see note 566.

647. Constance, session XIII, decretum de communione sub panis
tantum specie (DS 1198–1200); Trent, session XXII, canons 7, 8, 9
(DS 1757, 1758, 1759).

648. H. A. P. Schmidt, *Liturgie et langue vulgaire: le problème de la langue
liturgique chez les premiers Réformateurs et au concile de Trente* (Analecta
Gregoriana 53), Rome: Gregorian University, 1950, p. 135.

649. Pius XII, *Mediator Dei* in *Acta apostolicae sedis* 39 (1947), p. 545 (ET
Christian Worship, p. 29, paragraph 64).

650. The Swiss Catholic H. J. auf der Maur bewails the fact that even
since Vatican II 'the final judgment on the liturgical expression of the
faith was entrusted to the Congregation for the Doctrine of the Faith.
With its one-sided understanding of orthodoxy, this Congregation is
readily disposed to be suspicious of, and to put the brake on, living
expressions in liturgy. Of course, there will always be a need for the
critical function of theology vis-à-vis the spontaneous growth of the
expression of faith in worship; but this encounter ought to take the form
of a dialogue. Any language for prayer and worship that was imposed by
an ivory-tower theology or a timorous orthodoxy, any content of worship
and liturgy decreed by a supervisory court, could not but have the most
devastating effect on communal prayer and celebration in the future' ('The
difficulties of common prayer today' in *Studia Liturgica* 10 (1974), pp.
167–88).

651. T. Klauser, *Kleine abendländische Liturgiegeschichte* (ET *A Short
History of Western Liturgy*); J. A. Jungmann, article quoted in note 644.
Yet, even then, the mass was not entirely unchanging, as J. D. Crichton
amusingly shows against the latter-day conservatives: *The Once and the
Future Liturgy*, Dublin: Veritas, 1977, chapter 1.

652. H. O. Old, *The Patristic Roots of Reformed Worship*, Zürich:
Theologischer Verlag, 1975.

653. On the Augsburg documents, see J. Pelikan, *Obedient Rebels*, New
York: Harper & Row, and London: SCM, 1964, p. 30f.

654. Note the wise remark of W. H. Frere in his largely historical and
phenomenological study, *The Principles of Religious Ceremonial*, London:
Mowbray, 1928[2]: 'No one can hope to judge fairly of matters of ceremonial
who does not see that the reason why they cause such heat of controversy
is that they signify so much' (p. 9).

655. On the Prayer Book of 1559, see H. Gee, *The Elizabethan Prayer
Book and Ornaments*, London: Macmillan, 1902. The Prayer Book, and

more, is contained in W. K. Clay (ed.), *Liturgical Services: Liturgies and Occasional Forms of Prayer set forth in the Reign of Queen Elizabeth* (Parker Society edition), Cambridge: University Press, 1847.

656. The 'post-consecratory' elevation of the elements spread from France in the thirteenth century. Devotionally, it became a surrogate communion.

657. J. Pelikan, *Obedient Rebels*, p. 151.

658. As recently as the Lambeth conference of 1978, the Anglican bishops could say: 'In order to find out what characterizes Anglican doctrine, the simplest way is to look at Anglican worship and deduce Anglican doctrine from it' (*The Report of the Lambeth Conference 1978*, London: Church Information Office, 1978, p. 99). For a recent discussion, see S. W. Sykes, *The Integrity of Anglicanism*, Oxford: Mowbray, 1978. The part played by the *Book of Common Prayer* in the spread of Anglicanism is described by M. A. C. Warren, 'The missionary expansion of Ecclesia anglicana' in M. E. Glasswell and E. W. Fasholé-Luke (eds.), *New Testament Christianity for Africa and the World*, pp. 124–40. It is perhaps noteworthy that contemporary Anglicanism most readily expresses its identity among the 'world confessional families' in terms of 'the Anglican *communion*'. The eucharistic texts of Anglicanism up to about 1960 can be found in B. J. Wigan, *The Liturgy in English*, London: OUP, 1964[2]. Historical studies covering the range of offices are: F. Procter and W. H. Frere, *A New History of the Book of Common Prayer* (1901); G. J. Cuming, *A History of Anglican Liturgy* (1969); and, for the American stream, E. L. Parsons and B. H. Jones, *The American Prayer Book: its origins and principles*, New York: Scribner, 1937; J. W. Suter and G. J. Cleaveland, *The American Book of Common Prayer: its origins and development*, New York: OUP, 1949; and M. E. Shepherd, Jr., *The Oxford American Prayer Book Commentary*, New York: OUP, 1950.

659. Eucharistic texts from the recent bloom of liturgical revisions are found in two collections by C. O. Buchanan, *Modern Anglican Liturgies 1958–1968*, London: OUP, 1968, and *Further Anglican Liturgies 1968–1975*, Bramcote: Grove, 1975. Accounts of recent baptismal revision can be found in articles by R. C. D. Jasper, L. Weil and D. Holeton in *Studia Liturgica* 12 (1977), no. 2–3.

660. Luther's *Taufbüchlein* of 1523 contained both a pre-baptismal and a post-baptismal anointing, but these disappeared from the 1526 book. A similar change took place between Zwingli's rites of 1523 and 1525. The Anglican Prayer Book of 1552 dropped the post-baptismal anointing that the book of 1549 had retained.

661. J. D. C. Fisher, *Christian Initiation: The Reformation Period*, p. 116f.

662. In his *Disputation with Friar Arbuckill* (1547), John Knox wrote of ceremonies: 'Such as God has ordained we allow, and with reverence we use them. But the question is of those that God has not ordained, such as, in baptism, are spittle, salt, candle, cuide (except it be to keep the bairn from cold), hands, oil, and the rest of the papistical inventions.'

35

And in his *Answers to some Questions concerning Baptism* (1556): 'The baptism now used in the Papistry is not the true baptism which Christ Jesus did institute, and command to be used in his kirk. . . . That it is adulterate, and so consequently profane, is evident: first, for many things be added, besides Christ's institution; and all men's addition in God's perfect ordinance, especially in his religion, are execrable and detestable before him. Secondly, the promises of salvation in Christ Jesus are not in the papistical baptism lively and truly explained to the people; the word is not preached; yea, that which they read is not understood. The end and use of a true sacrament is not considered, but rather are the people led to put their confidence in the bare ceremony. . . . Yea, farther, who offereth their children to the papistical baptism, offereth them not to God, nor to Christ Jesus his Son, but to *the devil, chief author and inventor of such abominations.*' From Fisher, op. cit., p. 118.

663. A. H. Couratin, 'Liturgy' in J. Daniélou, A. H. Couratin and J. Kent, *Historical Theology*, vol. 2 of the Pelican Guide to Modern Theology, Harmondsworth: Penguin, 1969, in particular p. 231.

664. E. C. Ratcliff, 'The liturgical work of archbishop Cranmer' reprinted in his *Liturgical Studies*, edited by A. H. Couratin and D. H. Tripp, London: SPCK, 1976, pp. 184–202. For the place of some creative figures within the general 'anonymity' of the history of worship, see J. F. White, *Christian Worship in Transition*, Nashville: Abingdon, 1976, chapter 5 ('Individuality and liturgy').

665. W. de Vries, s.j., 'Lex supplicandi—lex credendi' in *Ephemerides liturgicae* 47 (1933), pp. 48–58.

666. I am of course using (later) labels to characterize the Reformers' positions. For the continental Reformers, see A. Barclay, *The Protestant Doctrine of the Lord's Supper: a study in the eucharistic teaching of Luther, Zwingli and Calvin*, Glasgow: Jackson & Wylie, 1927. A recent study on Luther, by a Roman Catholic, is W. Schwab, *Entwicklung und Gestalt der Sakramententheologie bei Martin Luther*, Frankfort: Lang, 1977. The interpretation of Cranmer's eucharistic theology is highly controversial. There is a calm account in P. Brooks, *Thomas Cranmer's Doctrine of the Eucharist: an essay in historical development*, London: Macmillan, 1965. Rather more *engagés* are M. Davies (conservative Roman Catholic), *Cranmer's Godly Order: The Destruction of Catholicism through Liturgical Change*, Chawleigh: Augustine, 1976, and C. O. Buchanan (evangelical Anglican), *What did Cranmer think he was doing?* Bramcote: Grove, 1976.

667. See *Die Bekenntnisschriften der evangelisch-lutherischen Kirche*, Göttingen: Vandenhoeck & Ruprecht, 1956³, p. 418.

668. English translations of Luther's, Zwingli's, Bucer's and Calvin's texts are found in B. Thompson, *Liturgies of the Western Church*, Cleveland: Collins, 1962. Studies in W. D. Maxwell, *An Outline of Christian Worship*, London: OUP, 1936, pp. 72ff, and *The Liturgical Portions of the Genevan Service Book*, London: Faith Press, 1965² (original: Edinburgh: Oliver & Boyd, 1931). Apart from the standard works by Procter and Frere and

by Cuming mentioned in note 658, valuable historical material on Cranmer's work is found in the old studies of J. Dowden, *The Workmanship of the Prayer Book in its literary and liturgical aspects*, and *Further Studies in the Prayer Book*.

669. For Cranmer's skilful retention of older phraseology in a new interpretative context, see G. Dix, *The Shape of the Liturgy*, pp. 640–74.

670. For Gardiner's 'catholic misinterpretations', see R. T. Beckwith, in C. Jones, G. Wainwright and E. Yarnold, *The Study of Liturgy*, p. 265f. The directness of Bucer's influence on Cranmer is difficult to assess: see G. J. Cuming, *A History of Anglican Liturgy*, p. 100f, and E. C. Whitaker, *Martin Bucer and the Book of Common Prayer*, Great Wakering: Mayhew-McCrimmon, 1974.

671. F. Clark, *Eucharistic Sacrifice and the Reformation*, London: DLT, 1960, Oxford: Blackwell, 1967[2].

672. N. Lash, *His Presence in the World*, pp. 126–37, in particular p. 127f. Lash also quotes from J. F. McCue, 'Luther and Roman Catholicism on the mass as sacrifice' in *Journal of Ecumenical Studies* 2 (1965), pp. 205–33: 'When theologians who defend the sacrificial concept of the Mass seem not to be disturbed by the development of a sub-Christian understanding of sacrifice within Roman Catholic piety, then there is at least some justification for thinking that the piety does express the doctrine. It is a very natural assumption, though in a surprising number of cases it turns out to be false, that practice and doctrine will agree, and that the meaning of the latter is best understood by means of the former.... Among Roman Catholics, the liturgical movement has taken seriously the responsibility of making practice express doctrine' (p. 233). The whole passage is interesting for our theme of the two-way interplay between worship and doctrine.

673. See pp. 336–39.

674. For Dussaut, see again p. 339.

675. M. Luther, *Ein Sermon von dem neuen Testament* (1520), Weimar edition, vol. 6, p. 369. Quoted in an important article by Irmgard Pahl, 'Das eucharistische Hochgebet in den Abendmahlsordnungen der Reformationskirchen' in *Questions liturgiques et paroissiales* 53 (1972), pp. 219–50.

676. From the Calvinist A. M. Toplady's hymn, 'Rock of Ages, cleft for me'. Note the modern Danish Lutheran R. Prenter (as in note 681): 'Le sacrifice, qualifié par la prière eucharistique d'action de grâces, ce n'est que les mains vides tendues par les pécheurs vers le Dieu riche et miséricordieux, afin qu'il les remplisse' (pp. 60–8).

677. Cyril of Alexandria, *In Joannis Evangelium*, ad 16:26f, PG 74, 464–65: *proaleitai tēn tou mesiteuontos aitēsin*. Expounded by T. F. Torrance, *Theology in Reconciliation*, p. 184f.

678. E. Jüngel, *Gott als Geheimnis der Welt*, pp. 430–53. See earlier, note 158 and p. 210.

679. D. Bonhoeffer, ET *Christology*, London: Collins, 1966.

680. Bonhoeffer does not make this linguistic distinction between

Geschichte and *Historie*: I think it became popular only later. But the reality of the distinction is certainly there in Bonhoeffer.

681. R. Prenter, *Connaître Christ*, Neuchâtel: Delachaux & Niestlé, 1966.

682. R. Prenter sets out more formally his understanding of the proper relations between worship and doctrine in 'Liturgie et dogme', in *Revue d'histoire et de philosophie religieuses* 38 (1958), pp. 115–28, and in 'Liturgy and theology', in his *Theologie und Gottesdienst: gesammelte Aufsätze*, Aarhus: Aros, 1977, pp. 139–51. He writes with the understanding that 'la liturgie est la forme corporelle du dogme et le dogme est l'âme de la liturgie'.

683. J. McIntyre, *The Shape of Christology*, London: SCM, 1966, chapter 2.

684. D. Cupitt, 'The Christ of Christendom' in J. H. Hick (ed.), *The Myth of God Incarnate*, pp. 133–47.

685. The confession of Mark's *centurion* at the foot of the Cross, '*This man was filius Dei*', is a subversion of Caesar's imperium (Mark 15:39; cf. 10:42–45).

686. In a brilliant review of *The Myth of God Incarnate* (in *New Blackfriars*, August 1977), the Dominican Herbert McCabe rightly taxes Cupitt with supposing an intolerable antithesis between God and man, although it is perhaps debatable whether McCabe is correct in fathering this opposition on classical Protestantism.

687. For these two criteria, see M. F. Wiles, *The Remaking of Christian Doctrine*, chapter 1.

688. Another Anglican to show historical awareness of the interaction between worship and belief, liturgy and doctrine, is R. P. C. Hanson, in his perceptive introduction to volume 2 of the Pelican Guide to Modern Theology: *Historical Theology*, pp. 16–20. As with Hanson, the sociocultural dimension of the interplay is recognized in the brief observations of the Reformed theologian, Roger Mehl, in his *Traité de sociologie du protestantisme*, Neuchâtel: Delachaux & Niestlé, 1966, pp. 78–81 (ET *The Sociology of Protestantism*, London: SCM, 1970, pp. 80–5).

689 E. Schlink, 'Die Struktur der dogmatischen Aussage als ökumenisches Problem' in *Kerygma und Dogma* 3 (1957), pp. 251–306, reprinted in *Der kommende Christus und die kirchlichen Traditionen* (ET *The Coming Christ and the Coming Church*, pp. 16–84). There is a sympathetic Catholic echo to Schlink in A. Dulles, 'Dogma as an ecumenical problem' in *Theological Studies* 29 (1968), pp. 397–416.

690. Influenced by Schlink, M. Plathow makes a distinction between theological reflexion and doxological confession, seeing the two as a complementary pair in his treatment of *Das Problem des concursus divinus* (Göttingen: Vandenhoeck & Ruprecht, 1976). Plathow's concluding recommendation is that the descriptive reflexion which starts from the duality of God and man—whether beginning with the majesty of God (Thomists; Reformed) or with the independence and integrity of the creature (Molinists; Lutherans)—needs to learn from the faith-confession of God's almighty work in creation, preservation, rule, and new creation;

while this approach by way of doxological confession, characteristic of Augustine, Luther and Barth, in turn needs to devote more serious theological reflexion to the value of the creature in its own being and work. I should myself want to point out a route not sufficiently clarified by Plathow: to move into theological reflexion from the liturgical experience less of the overwhelmingness and all-operativeness of God than of the 'non-competitiveness' between God and humanity, although I recognize that the 'synergism' which is the positive face of non-competitiveness is likely to raise some Protestant hackles; see earlier, p. 83f. Properly pursued, I think this path could take us beyond the difference still seen—albeit in a mutually complementary way—between Protestant ('existential' or 'confessing') and Catholic ('sapiential' or 'objectivizing') ways of thinking about justification by O. H. Pesch, *Die Theologie der Rechtfertigung bei Martin Luther und Thomas von Aquin*, Mainz: Grünewald, 1967, pp. 935–48. Feed-back of doctrine into worship is horribly exemplified in the Westminster Directory's instructions for the *eucharistia*: the whole calvinistic doctrine of double predestination is fed in characteristically didactic style into the liturgy when the minister is told to give thanks 'for this Sacrament in particular, by which Christ, and all His benefits, are applied and sealed up unto us, which, notwithstanding the denial of them to others, are in great mercy continued unto us, after so much and long abuse of them all' (text in R. C. D. Jasper and G. J. Cuming, *Prayers of the Eucharist: Early and Reformed*, pp. 173–8).

691. In the US Lutheran/Roman Catholic statement on *Eucharist and Ministry* (1970), the Lutherans neatly, even cheekily, invoke liturgical evidence to prove the 'orthodoxy' of Roman Catholicism concerning the heart of the gospel: 'Lutherans are well aware that Roman Catholics pray the same Sunday collects that Lutherans pray (including those that stress man's helplessness and salvation by grace alone, such as those for Sexagesima Sunday, the Second Sunday in Lent, Laetare Sunday, Easter Day, and the First, Third, Eighth, Twelfth, Fourteenth, Sixteenth, and Eighteenth Sundays after Trinity). They know too that the Roman Catholic Church affirms the gospel in unmistakable terms in many other places of its liturgy—for example the *Exsultet* in the Easter Eve office and the *Veni, Sancte Spiritus*, in Whitsuntide. *Augsburg Confession*, 20, 40, recalls that "the Church sings: *Sine tuo numine/Nihil est in homine, Nihil est innoxium*": "Without (the action of) your godhead, there is nothing in a human being, there is nothing that is not destructive", from the *Veni, Sancte Spiritus*' (from *Lutherans and Catholics in Dialogue*, vol. 4, eds. P. C. Empie and T. A. Murphy, Washington, D.C.: United States Catholic Conference, 1970).

692. The so-called Athanasian Creed figures in the Western monastic office of prime and passed from there into occasional use in Anglican morning prayer. On its controversial place in the Anglican service, see earlier p. 188f. Note the study of its origins, history and theology by J. N. D. Kelly, *The Athanasian Creed*, London: Black, 1964.

693. We shall return to Schlink in chapter IX: Ecumenism.

694. W. Pannenberg, 'Analogie und Doxologie' in W. Joest and W. Pannenberg (eds.), *Dogma und Denkstrukturen* (E. Schlink *festschrift*), Göttingen: Vandenhoeck & Ruprecht, 1963, pp. 96–115 (ET in Pannenberg's *Basic Questions in Theology*, vol. 1, London: SCM, 1970, pp. 211–38; cf. pp. 202–10, the last part of an essay on 'What is a dogmatic statement?').

695. In addition to Bonhoeffer, Prenter, Schlink and Pannenberg, one more Lutheran theologian to show an interest in our worship and doctrine question is W. Elert. In his *Der christliche Glaube: Grundlinien der lutherischen Dogmatik*, Hamburg: Furche, 1956³, pp. 355f, 360, he argues that doctrine on baptism and on the Lord's supper must neither be 'deduced' from other parts of dogmatics (whether the doctrine on creation, christology, pneumatology or soteriology) nor start out from a general notion of 'sacrament'. Rather, baptism and supper are *primary* in the factual givenness of their institution by Christ and their performance in the Church. Understanding of them should begin from those facts. Indeed, if a contradiction should appear between doctrine (at any point, but especially the doctrine of the Church) and those facts, the first assumption must be that the doctrine is in need of correction. For Elert, see further note 711.

696. Although they are usually aware of some tensions in the relations between worship and doctrine, these theologians concentrate on how the relationship 'ought to be'. It is curious that they do not in these contexts pay much attention to the fact that Luther's reformation was a dogmatic protest against distorted liturgy. I have myself judged that Protestants are more likely to be persuaded of the positive importance of worship for doctrine if full weight continues to be given—simultaneously and dialectically—to doctrine as a critical control upon liturgy. Not, of course, that doctrine itself is exempt from error.

697. On the issues in the early Church, see W. Elert, in the works mentioned in note 711; S. L. Greenslade, *Schism in the Early Church*, London: SCM, 1964²; K. Hein, *Eucharist and Excommunication: a study in early Christian doctrine and discipline*, Bern: Lang, 1973; M. F. Wiles, *Explorations in Theology*, London: SCM, 1979, chapter 9 ('Sacramental unity in the early Church').

698. On the varying understandings of 'economy', see F. J. Thompson, 'Economy: an examination of the various theories of Economy held within the Orthodox Church, with special reference to the economical recognition of the validity of non-Orthodox sacraments' in *Journal of Theological Studies* n.s. 16 (1965), pp. 368–420.

699. For Orthodox exceptions, see N. Zernov, *The Reintegration of the Church: a study in intercommunion*, London: SCM, 1952, particularly pp. 51–75; H. Symeon, 'De l'eucharistie comme sacrement de l'unité' in *Contacts* 16 (1964), pp. 126–46= 'The eucharist as the sacrament of unity' in *Sobornost* 4 (1964), pp. 637–50; N. A. Nissiotis, *Die Theologie der Ostkirche im ökumenischen Dialog*, Stuttgart: Evangelisches Verlagswerk, 1968, pp. 137–9 (in material added to an essay which originally appeared as

'Worship, eucharist and "intercommunion": an Orthodox reflection' in *Studia Liturgica* 2 (1963), pp. 193–222); J. Klinger, in M. Thurian, J. Klinger and J. de Baciocchi, *Vers l'intercommunion*, Tours: Mame, 1970, pp. 69–118. Klinger, a Polish Orthodox, argued that the aim of the ancient canons in forbidding communion with heretics and schismatics was to safeguard the unity of the Church in a centrifugal age; the same cause of unity would be served in our own centripetal age by permitting communion with the non-orthodox. The stricter Orthodox position is restated by K. T. Ware, 'Church and eucharist, communion and intercommunion' in *Sobornost* 7 (1978), pp. 551–67.

700. V. Subilia, *Il problema del cattolicesimo*, Turin: Claudiana, 1962, pp. 222–31 (ET *The Problem of Catholicism*, London: SCM, 1964, pp. 175–82).

701. V. Subilia, *I tempi di Dio*, Turin: Claudiana, 1970.

702. V. Subilia, *Presenza e assenza di Dio nella coscienza moderna*, Turin: Claudiana, 1976, p. 23f.

703. Subilia has set out his understanding of Catholic 'sacramentalism' in his study of Vatican II, *La nuova cattolicità del cattolicesimo*, Turin: Claudiana, 1967, pp. 79–87, 137–47.

704. On the Liturgical Movement, see pp. 221f and 335ff.

705. Note particularly E. Schillebeeckx's influential *Christ the Sacrament of Encounter with God*.

706. N. Ehrenström, *Confessions in Dialogue: a survey of bilateral conversations among world confessional families 1959–1974*, Geneva: WCC, 1975[3]. These personal testimonies are important in view of the fact that on the one occasion—Uppsala 1968—when a full assembly of the WCC devoted itself thematically to the subject of worship, the matter proved highly controversial; but that was at the height of the 'secular sixties': see 'The Uppsala Report on Worship', introduced by D. L. Edwards and commented on by J. J. von Allmen, in *Studia Liturgica* 6 (1969), pp. 66–78; J. M. R. Tillard, 'The Uppsala Document on Worship' in *One in Christ* 5 (1969), pp. 151–68; J. Sullivan, 'The current status of worship reflection in the WCC' in *One in Christ* 12 (1976), pp. 58–82. R. E. Davies captures the flavour of classical ecumenism when he writes that 'the Ecumenical Movement happens when separated Churches, through their appointed representatives, come together, *in an atmosphere of shared prayer and worship*, to make known to and discuss with one another their traditions of faith and worship and thought and order, in the conviction that they have something to impart and to receive from one another, with a view to eventual, however long delayed, organic union within the restored wholeness of the Body of Christ': *Religious Authority in an Age of Doubt* (Fernley-Hartley lecture of 1968), London: Epworth, 1968.

707. See also Y. Congar, 'Théologie de la prière pour l'unité' in *Verbum caro* no. 82 (1967), pp. 1–13 (ET in *One in Christ* 3 (1967), pp. 262–73).

708. Another example from an Orthodox theologian is B. Bobrinskoy, 'Fondements théologiques de la prière commune pour l'unité in *Verbum*

caro no. 82 (1967), pp. 14–31 (ET in *One in Christ* 3 (1967), pp. 274–290).

709. Faith and Order Paper No. 73, Geneva: WCC, 1975.

710. A detailed study of the Arnoldshain Theses by a Jesuit will be found in W. L. Boelens, *Die Arnoldshainer Abendmahlsthesen: die Suche nach einem Abendmahlskonsens in der Evangelischen Kirche in Deutschland 1947–1957 und eine Würdigung aus katholischer Sicht*, Assen: Van Gorkum, 1964. See also T. F. Torrance, 'Doctrinal consensus on Holy Communion: the Arnoldshain theses' in *Scottish Journal of Theology* 15 (1962), pp. 1–35.

711. Lutherans in particular have felt difficulty in establishing church-fellowship even with other Protestants. There can be no church-fellowship without doctrinal agreement: this point is highlighted by the Lutheran dogmatician Werner Elert in his study of the early Church: *Abendmahl und Kirchengemeinschaft in der alten Kirche hauptsächlich des Ostens*, Berlin: Lutherisches Verlagshaus, 1954 (ET *Eucharist and Church Fellowship in the First Four Centuries*, St Louis: Concordia, 1966). Elert had the contemporary situation very much in mind: he contributed to *Koinonia: Arbeiten des Oekumenischen Ausschusses der Vereinigten Evangelisch-Lutherischen Kirche Deutschlands zur Frage der Kirchen- und Abendmahlsgemeinschaft*, Berlin: Lutherisches Verlagshaus, 1957, in particular pp. 57–78: 'Abendmahl und Kirchengemeinschaft in der alten Kirche'. An English version of the Leuenberg text can be found in *Lutheran World* 20 (1973), pp. 347–53.

712. How *problematic* differences in liturgical forms could be, is still seen in *Ways of Worship: the Report of a Theological Commission of Faith and Order*, edited by P. Edwall, E. Hayman and W. D. Maxwell, London: SCM, 1951. See further W. Hahn, 'Prolegomena to the ecumenical discussion on the liturgy' in *Studia Liturgica* 2 (1963), pp. 2–7.

713. Briefly, J. H. Strawley, *The Liturgical Movement: its origin and growth*, Oxford: Mowbray, 1954, and H. E. Chandler, 'Liturgical Movement' in J. G. Davies (ed.), *A Dictionary of Liturgy and Worship*, pp. 216–22. See earlier p. 221f, and again pp. 335ff.

714. A. Haquin, *Dom Lambert Beauduin et le renouveau liturgique*, Gembloux: Duculot, 1976.

715. This is emphasized in L. Bouyer's *Liturgical Piety/Life and Liturgy*, which gives a theological history of the Liturgical Movement.

716. See pp. 335ff.

717. N. Clark and R. C. D. Jasper (eds.), *Initiation and Eucharist: essays on their structure by the Joint Liturgical Group*, London: SPCK, 1972. An early statement of the understanding(s) of worship represented in the group is found in R. C. D. Jasper (ed.), *The Renewal of Worship*, London: OUP, 1965.

718. R. C. D. Jasper (ed.), *The Calendar and Lectionary*, London: OUP, 1967.

719. W. J. Grisbrooke, 'Anaphora' in J. G. Davies (ed.), *A Dictionary of Liturgy and Worship*, pp. 10–17.

720. Whether in the first or in the second half of the twentieth century,

liturgical revision has brought out the considerable tensions among catholics, evangelicals and liberals in the Church of England. For the story of the attempted revision of the Prayer Book in 1927–8, see G. K. A. Bell, *Randall Davidson, Archbishop of Canterbury*, London: OUP, 1952³; and note the writings of the leading Anglican liturgiologist of the day, W. H. Frere, both *Some Principles of Liturgical Reform*, London: Murray, 1911, and R. C. D. Jasper (ed.), *Walter Howard Frere: his correspondence on liturgical revision and construction*, London: SPCK, 1954. The process in the 1960s and 70s in the Church of England is chronicled in the booklets by C. O. Buchanan mentioned in note 235. Observe the generally sympathetic presentation in R. C. D. Jasper (ed.), *The Eucharist Today: Studies on Series 3*, London: SPCK, 1974. Yet the revisions have been attacked by conservative evangelicals (e.g. R. Beckwith, 'A turning point in Prayer Book revision' in *The Churchman* 89 (1975), pp. 120–9), by anglo-catholics (e.g. M. Moreton, *Consecrating, Remembering, Offering: Catholics and Series 3, 2, and 1, and 1662*, London: Church Literature Association, 1976), and by liberals (e.g. J. L. Houlden, himself a member of the Liturgical Commission, in *The Eucharist Today*, pp. 168–76). The revision of the eucharist in the world-wide Anglican communion is presented and interpreted by C. O. Buchanan in the two collections mentioned in note 659: we witness the conflicting trends of increasing diversification and the emergence of new 'family patterns'.

721. Transubstantiation is relegated to a footnote: 'The word transubstantiation is commonly used in the Roman Catholic Church to indicate that God acting in the eucharist effects a change in the inner reality of the elements. The term should be seen as affirming the *fact* of Christ's presence and of the mysterious and radical change which takes place. In contemporary Roman Catholic theology it is not understood as explaining *how* the change takes place.'

722. F. J. Leenhardt, 'Le pain et la coupe' in *Foi et vie* 46 (1948), pp. 509–26; *Le sacrement de la sainte cène*, 1948; *Ceci est mon corps*, 1955; 'La présence eucharistique' in *Irénikon* 33 (1960), pp. 146–72.

723. The early Dutch debate can be followed in J. M. Powers, *Eucharistic Theology*, New York: Herder, 1967, and London: Burns & Oates, 1968, chapter 4, and in E. Schillebeeckx, ET *The Eucharist*. P. Schoonenberg and L. Smits represented positions that E. Schillebeeckx considered inadequate as restatements of the doctrine enshrined in 'transubstantiation'. For the continuing discussion, see *Zeitschrift für katholische Theologie* 97 (1975), no. 4.

724. L. Vischer, *A Documentary History of the Faith and Order Movement 1927–63*, St Louis: Bethany Press, 1963, p. 10.

725. For the history of 'reservation', see A. A. King, *Eucharistic Reservation in the Western Church*, London: Mowbray, 1965.

726. T. T. Rowe, *The Communication Process*, London: Epworth, 1978.

727. N. Lash, *His Presence in the World*, pp. 134–7. See also earlier, p. 190f.

728. K. Rahner, in his remarks on Hans Küng's book, *Justification*:

see Rahner, ET *Theological Investigations,* vol. 4, London: DLT, 1966, pp. 195–7.

729. It would be foolish, and perhaps dishonest, to isolate the liturgy from its dogmatic context and see it as the sole-sufficient area in which doctrinal agreement is needed. A Protestant may not forget that a simple commemoration of Mary in the Catholic liturgy *connotes* the marian dogmas; a Catholic may rightly question the weight of a sacrificial phrase in a Protestant liturgy if the Protestant dogmatic context is unacceptably anti-sacrificial. For all that, the creative possibilities of liturgical agreement will continue to be emphasized in the next section.

730. For Schlink, see earlier pp. 279-82.

731. N. Lash, 'Credal affirmation as a criterion of Church membership' in J. Kent and R. Murray (eds.), *Church Membership and Intercommunion,* pp. 51–73. Note also J. M. R. Tillard, 'How do we express unity of faith?' in *One in Christ* 14 (1978), pp. 318–27

732. By 'hierarchy of truths', the council means that truths 'vary in their relation to the foundation of the Christian faith' (*Unitatis redintegratio,* 11). Conservative exegesis stresses that it is still a hierarchy of *truths,* and that to move one stone is to affect the shape and solidarity of the building.

733. On the *filioque,* see already notes 219 and 452. The question has been under discussion in the Anglican/Orthodox conversations: see K. T. Ware and C. Davey (eds.), *Anglican–Orthodox Dialogue: The Moscow Statement agreed by the Anglican–Orthodox Joint Doctrinal Commission 1976 with introductory and supporting material,* London: SPCK, 1977, pp. 13, 34, 43, 62–8, 87f. The Episcopal Church in the USA seemed set fair to drop the clause from its liturgy but it reappeared in the 1977 text of *The Book of Common Prayer.* The matter is also being studied in the Faith and Order Commission of the WCC.

734. True, polemicists have magnified the differences. But a substantial reconciliation can be achieved through the proposition *dia.* Or the two positions can be seen as differences in accent. At this point of speculative penetration into the mystery of God, some degree of reticence is in any case prudent. I recall Ninian Smart's observation that a certain 'gingerly' approach is proper in worship (*The Concept of Worship,* p. 66).

735. J. P. Jossua, 'Signification des confessions de foi' in *Istina* 17 (1972), pp. 48–56. See also: A. Hamman, 'Du symbole de la foi à l'anaphore eucharistique' in P. Granfield and J. A. Jungmann (eds.), *Kyriakon* (J. Quasten *festschrift*), vol. 2, Münster: Aschendorff, 1970, pp. 835–43; and E. Vilanova, 'The development of the expression of faith in the worshipping community: the post-apostolic age' in *Concilium,* February 1973, pp. 29–39.

736. F. Probst, *Lehre und Gebet in den drei ersten christlichen Jahrhunderten,* Tübingen: Laupp, 1871, pp. 56–8; cf. *Liturgie des 4. Jahrhunderts und deren Reform,* Münster: Aschendorff, 1893, pp. 6of, 114.

737. See W. H. Frere, *The Anaphora or Great Eucharistic Prayer,* London: SPCK, 1938 (the thesis is unveiled in chapter 3 and then demonstrated);

L. Bouyer, *Eucharistie*, chapter 8 (with reservations concerning 'schématisme'); L. Ligier, in L. Sheppard (ed.), *The New Liturgy*, especially pp. 145–9.

738. The precise form, not to say presence, of the epiclesis in *The Apostolic Tradition* is controversial, but G. J. Cuming fairly comments: 'As an invocation on behalf of the worshippers, not specifying the effect on the elements, it seems quite credible' (*Hippolytus: a text for students*, p. 11). Technical treatments include: B. Botte, 'L'épiclèse de l'anaphore d'Hippolyte' in *Recherches de théologie ancienne et médiévale* 14 (1947), pp. 241–51; L. Bouyer, *Eucharistie*, pp. 170–7; R. H. Connolly, 'The eucharistic prayer of Hippolytus' in *Journal of Theological Studies* 39 (1938), pp. 350–69; G. Dix-H. Chadwick, *The Apostolic Tradition*, pp. 75–9; E. C. Ratcliff, 'The Sanctus and the pattern of the early anaphora' in his *Liturgical Studies*, pp. 18–40.

739. Justin, *Apol.* I, 65, 3; 67, 2. On triadic understandings and patterns, see earlier p. 257f.

740. H. J. Schulz, *Ökumenische Glaubenseinheit aus eucharistischer Überlieferung*, Paderborn: Bonifacius, 1976. Schulz is the author of an earlier liturgico-dogmatic study of the Byzantine liturgy: *Die byzantinische Liturgie: vom Werden ihrer Symbolgestalt*.

741. For recent critical reflexion on the relation between eucharistic doctrine and the Roman canon, see R. A. Keifer, 'Liturgical text as primary source for eucharistic theology' in *Worship* 51 (1977), pp. 186–96 and, behind that, his 'The unity of the Roman canon' in *Studia Liturgica* 11 (1976), pp. 39–58. Examples of individual Catholic theologians examining and even expounding particular doctrines on a liturgical base are: I. Herwegen, 'Das Königtum Christi in der Liturgie' in his *Alte Quellen neuer Kraft*, Düsseldorf: Schwann, 1922², pp. 80–116; P. Oppenheim, 'Christi persona et opus secundum textus liturgiae sacrae' in *Ephemerides liturgicae* 49 (1935), pp. 367–83, and 50 (1936), pp. 224–42; H. Engberding, 'Maria in der Frömmigkeit der östlichen Liturgien', and P. Oppenheim, 'Maria in der lateinischen Liturgie', both in P. Sträter (ed.), *Katholische Marienkunde: Maria in der Offenbarung*, Paderborn: Schöningh, 1952², pp. 119–36, 183–267; G. M. Lukken, *Original Sin in the Roman Liturgy: research into the theology of original sin in the Roman sacramentaria and the early baptismal liturgy*, Leiden: Brill, 1973; A. Thaler, *Das Selbstverständnis der Kirche in den Gebetstexten der altspanischen Liturgie*, Bern and Frankfort: Lang, 1975.

742. See also, though not explicitly in the perspective of unity, I. H. Dalmais, 'The expression of the faith in the Eastern liturgies' in *Concilium*, February 1973, pp. 77–85.

743. The ecumenical canon is included in R. C. D. Jasper (ed.), *The Daily Office revised*, London: SPCK, 1978, pp. 11–13.

744. E. Schillebeeckx, ET *Mary, Mother of the Redemption*, London: Sheed & Ward, 1964, p. 149. Schillebeeckx accuses Protestantism of holding an 'extrinsicalist' view of reality throughout, with ill effects not only in christology and mariology but also in ecclesiology, the doctrine

of grace and of the sacraments, and eschatology: *The Eucharist*, pp. 76–86.

745. See my 'Mary in relation to the docrinal and spiritual emphases of Methodism' in *One in Christ* 11 (1975), pp. 121–44.

746. Note further, from *A Collection of Hymns for the Use of the People called Methodists* (1780/1877), no. 413:

> Thou who didst so greatly stoop
> To a poor virgin's womb,
> Here Thy mean abode take up;
> To me, my Saviour, come!
> Come, and Satan's works destroy,
> And let me all Thy Godhead prove,
> Filled with peace, and heavenly joy,
> And pure eternal love.

747. See further, on the whole question, D. H. Tripp, 'Hymns as ecumenical liturgy' in *One in Christ* 10 (1974), pp. 267–75. Tripp concludes by quoting from the compilers of the 1889 *Methodist Free Church Hymns*: hymns which 'have originated from minds whose doctrinal beliefs are wide asunder' are nevertheless 'animated by a catholicity of thought and love for the great verities of the Christian religion that have . . . strengthened the hope and intensified the prayer for the coming of the time when the whole Christian Church shall "keep the unity of the Spirit in the bond of peace".'

748. N. Lash, 'Credal affirmation as a criterion of Church membership' in J. Kent and R. Murray (eds.), *Church Membership and Intercommunion*, p. 72.

749. Note already the discussion on baptism in chapter IV§3.

750. See B. Leeming, *Principles of Sacramental Theology*, especially chapters 14–15.

751. According to Firmilian and Cyprian, this was already the position of Stephen of Rome in the third century, but they may have been misinterpreting the pope: see earlier note 309.

752. See G. Baum, *That they may be one: a study of papal doctrine (Leo XIII–Pius XII)*.

753. Avery Dulles, s.j., 'The Church, the Churches, and the Catholic Church' in *Theological Studies* 33 (1972), pp. 199–234.

754. See my article 'Christian initiation in the ecumenical movement' in *Studia Liturgica* 12 (1977), pp. 67–86.

755. In favour of variety of understanding and practice at the *eucharist*, see M. F. Wiles, 'Eucharistic theology: the value of diversity' in I. T. Ramsey and others, *Thinking about the Eucharist: papers by members of the Church of England Doctrine Commission*, pp. 115–22.

756. E. Schlink, 'Gottes Handeln durch die Taufe als ökumenisches Problem' in *Pluralisme et oecuménisme en recherches théologiques: mélanges offerts au R. P. Dockx, o.p.*, Gembloux: Duculot, 1976, pp. 119–36.

757. Already at the time of the Lund Faith and Order conference in 1952, T. F. Torrance argued for intercommunion partly on the basis of 'the one baptism'—which he presupposed at that time but whose recognition still needs in fact to be achieved: 'Eschatology and the eucharist' in D. M. Baillie and J. Marsh (eds.), *Intercommunion*, London: SCM, 1952, pp. 303–50.

758. J. Willebrands, 'Moving towards a typology of churches' in *Catholic Mind*, April 1970, pp. 35–42.

759. The uniat churches, which preserve their 'rites', sprang at different times from the Eastern churches between which and Rome a separation still exists: see the Vatican II decree on the Catholic Eastern churches, *Orientalium ecclesiarum*. Even in separation, the Vatican II decree on ecumenism, *Unitatis redintegratio*, could already refer warmly to the Eastern patrimony in the *Orthodox* churches, which should be maintained and fostered as necessary unity is restored. For the view that different rites can be complementary expressions of a single vitality, see I. H. Dalmais, 'Signification de la diversité des rites au regard de l'unité chrétienne' in *Istina* 7 (1960), pp. 301–18.

760. Note also the exploration—sensitive both to the *difficulties* of 'uniatism' and to the issue of *doctrinal* pluralism—by the Benedictine E. Lanne, 'Pluralism and unity: the possibility of a variety of typologies within the same ecclesial allegiance' in *One in Christ* 6 (1970), pp. 430–51.

761. The idea was taken up in the Roman Catholic/Presbyterian-Reformed conversations in the USA, where the statement of May 1975 on 'The unity we seek' speaks of the shape of future unity as 'a communion of communions (*communio communiorum*), a Church of churches (*ecclesia ecclesiarum*)': see *One in Christ* 13 (1977), pp. 258–79.

762. N. Goodall (ed.), *The Uppsala Report 1968*, Geneva: WCC, 1968, p. 17. See L. Vischer, ' "A genuinely universal council. . . "?' in *Ecumenical Review* 22 (1970), pp. 97–106.

763. W. A. Visser 't Hooft (ed.), *The New Delhi Report*, London: SCM, 1962, pp. 116–35.

764. The report of the Salamanca consultation is found in *Ecumenical Review* 26 (1974), pp. 291–303.

765. In this and the next four paragraphs I am drawing on arguments presented more fully in my article 'Conciliarity and eucharist', *One in Christ* 14 (1978), pp. 30–49, and *Midstream* 17 (1978), pp. 35–53; and, behind that, in 'L'intercommunion, signe et issue de l'impasse œcuménique', *Nouvelle revue théologique* 92 (1970), pp. 1037–54, and my book, *Eucharist and Eschatology*, particularly pp. 135–46.

766. See the Vatican II decree on ecumenism, *Unitatis redintegratio*, 3.

767. Innocent III, *de sacro altaris mysterio*, IV, 36, PL 217, 879.

768. Augustine, *serm.* 57 (PL 38, 389), 227 (PL 38, 1099–1101), and 272 (PL 38, 1247–8).

769. My ecclesiology corresponds to the 'eschatological' in Dulles' typology (as in note 753). I believe that eucharistic sharing provides

orientation and sustenance to Christian communities which are 'on the way' to the unity of the Church.

770. See my 'The ecclesiological significance of interchurch marriage' in M. Hurley (ed.), *Beyond Tolerance: The Challenge of Mixed Marriage*, London: Chapman, 1975, pp. 104–9. Reciprocal intercommunion between mixed marriage partners is already authorized among Catholics and Protestants, in Strasbourg and in Switzerland. Wedding rites for mixed marriages have been composed in German-speaking Switzerland (the use of *Ökumenische Trauung*, 1973, is officially permitted by the Roman Catholic, Protestant and Old Catholic churches) and in Germany (the Roman Catholic archdiocese of Freiburg and the Protestant church in Baden published in 1974 a common order of service under the title *Gemeinsame kirchliche Trauung: Formular C*, and its use has been approved by the Old Catholic church and by the Moravian and Methodist regional authorities).

771. In connexion with eucharistic sharing, J. C. Hoekendijk powerfully argued that Christians are *always* in an emergency situation: the 'urgent' is the 'normal' for the Christian. See *The Church Inside Out*, pp. 148–66 ('Safety last').

772. In England, the idea of a covenant on the basis of 'ten propositions' was put forward by the Churches' Unity Commission, 1974–8. The Churches' Council for Covenanting pursues the matter.

773. 'Vigilance and unity' is to take up the twin theme of the Groupe des Dombes statement on episcopal ministry in the *local* church: *Le ministère épiscopal: réflexions et propositions sur le ministère de vigilance et d'unité dans l'église particulière* (Presses de Taizé, 1976).

774. J. E. L. Newbigin, 'All in one place or all of one sort?' in R. W. A. McKinney (ed.), *Creation, Christ and Culture* (T. F. Torrance *festschrift*), pp. 288–306. Newbigin engages in critical discussion with cardinal Willebrands but particularly with J. Macquarrie's book, *Christian Unity and Christian Diversity* (London: SCM, 1975).

775. On the complexity of the idea of 'place', see the report *In Each Place: Towards a Fellowship of Local Churches Truly United*, Geneva: WCC, 1977.

776. The place of the papacy in Christian unity is receiving increased attention as Catholics and Protestants meet. An individual reflexion: J. J. von Allmen, *La primauté de l'église de Pierre et de Paul: remarques d'un protestant*, Fribourg: Éditions universitaires, 1977. A private symposium: P. J. McCord (ed.), *A Pope for all Christians? An inquiry into the role of Peter in the modern Church*, New York: Paulist Press, 1976, and London: SPCK, 1977. Official conversations: Lutheran/Roman Catholic dialogue in the USA, and notably R. E. Brown, K. P. Donfried and J. Reumann (eds.), *Peter in the New Testament*, Minneapolis: Augsburg, 1973, and London: Chapman, 1974, written in preparation for *Papal Primacy and the Universal Church*, vol. 5 of *Lutherans and Catholics in Dialogue*, Minneapolis: Augsburg, 1974.

777. The question of persisting *confessional* identity appears to be

particularly important to Lutherans: see Harding Meyer, ' "Einheit in versöhnter Verschiedenheit"—"konziliare Gemeinschaft"—"organische Union": Gemeinsamkeit und Differenz gegenwärtig diskutierter Einheits-konzeptionen' in *Ökumenische Rundschau* 27 (1978), pp. 377–400. In the thinking of WCC Faith and Order, 'conciliar fellowship' is not intended as an *alternative* to 'organic union' but as its *form*; whereas the notion of 'reconciled diversity' current in the discussions among 'world confessional families' appears to remain structurally within the stage of what the Salamanca Faith and Order consultation called 'pre-conciliar fellowship', despite increasing doctrinal 'convergence' among the confessional bodies. Harding Meyer himself admits that 'organic union' may be right in 'mission countries'; nor does he exclude the possibility of a future fusion of traditions even in the areas of origin; but meanwhile he stresses the need for continuing institutions to carry the confessional traditions forward.

778. See N. Ehrenström (ed.), *Confessions in Dialogue*, 1975³. A valuable *Workbook of Bibliographies for the Study of Interchurch Dialogues*, edited by J. Puglisi, was published by the Centro pro Unione, Rome, 1978.

779. B. Sundkler, *The Church of South India: the Movement towards Union 1900–1947*, London : Lutterworth, 1954.

780. See T. S. Garrett, *Worship in the Church of South India*, London: Lutterworth, 1965².

781. See my *Christian Initiation*, pp. 65–9.

782. For supporting arguments, see G. Wainwright, *Christian Initiation*, pp. 66–9.

783. B. Fischer, 'Formes de la commémoration du baptême en Occident' in *La Maison-Dieu* no. 58 (1959), pp. 111–34.

784. D. H. Tripp, *The Renewal of the Covenant in the Methodist Tradition*, London: Epworth, 1969.

785. See pp. 269ff.

786. See for general background, though without particular attention to language, J. G. Davies, *Every Day God: Encountering the Holy in World and Worship*, London: SCM, 1973. More directly: L. Gilkey, *Naming the Whirlwind: The Renewal of God-Language*, Indianapolis: Bobbs-Merrill, 1969, and, briefly, 'Addressing God in faith' in *Concilium*, February 1973, pp. 62–76; D. B. Stevick, *Language in Worship: Reflections on a Crisis*, New York: Seabury, 1970; H. A. P. Schmidt, 'Faith and its confession in an a-religious world' in *Concilium*, February 1973, pp. 117–33. See also the literature mentioned in note 840.

787. For a historical survey, see C. Korolevsky, *Liturgie en langue vivante*, Paris: Cerf, 1955 (English adaptation *Living Languages in Catholic Worship*, London: Longmans, 1957).

788. In first-century Aramaic-speaking Palestinian Jewry, the language of Bible reading and liturgical prayer was Hebrew. J. Jeremias detects numerous semitisms behind the New Testament texts of the eucharistic institution narratives and thinks transmission may have taken place in

both Hebrew and Aramaic, leaving open the question which was original: see *Die Abendmahlsworte Jesu*[3], pp. 153–95 (ET *The Eucharistic Words of Jesus*, 1966, pp. 160–203).

789. It did not take place without hesitation. T. Klauser suggests that pope Damasus was bold enough to take the step, following the example of Milan and even perhaps borrowing the Latin mass-canon from St Ambrose: 'Der Übergang der römischen Kirche von der greichischen zur lateinischen Liturgiesprache' in *Miscellanea Giovanni Mercati*, vol. 1 (Studi e Testi, 121), Vatican City: Biblioteca Apostolica Vaticana, 1946, pp. 467–82.

790. A gap between the language of worship and the language of society could come about in earlier times in three different ways. First, linguistic evolution: the liturgy remained fixed in patristic Greek; in Ethiopia, Ge'ez turned into Amharic, but the liturgy was left behind; as the modern Slav languages developed, the liturgy continued to be cele-brated in Staroslav or 'Church Slavonic'; Latin was still used in church, while the people began to speak Italian, Spanish and French. Second, political and military changes: despite the spread of Arabic by conquests, the churches of the Levant and Egypt maintained, to varying degrees, Greek, Syriac, or Coptic as their liturgical language. Third, importation: Syriac was taken to the Malabarese in India; with a few exceptions (some of them in the peculiar circumstances of Eastern Europe), the ordinary Roman practice from medieval times up to Vatican II was for its mission-aries and representatives abroad to introduce the Roman rite in the Latin tongue (this was already the case in the evangelization of the German nations, where the military, political, and cultural prestige of the *imperium* also helped in the introduction of Latin; for the agonizing story of the struggle for the use of Mandarin Chinese, see F. Bontinck, *La lutte autour de la liturgie chinoise aux XVIIe et XVIIIe siècles*, Louvain: Nauwelaerts, 1962).

791. For evidence of this practice, see the references given in J. H. Srawley, *The Early History of the Liturgy*, Cambridge: University Press, 1947[2], p. 234 (cf. pp. 124, 155).

792. Justin, *Apol.* I, 67, 3.

793. G. Dix, *The Shape of the Liturgy*, p. 18.

794. E. Bishop, in R. H. Connolly, *The Liturgical Homilies of Narsai*, pp. 92–7.

795. J. A. Jungmann, *The Early Liturgy*, p. 197f.

796. W. D. Maxwell, *An Outline of Christian Worship*, pp. 74, 112–19, where references are given.

797. G. Dix, *The Shape of the Liturgy*, p. 18f.

798. P. Benoit, 'Le récit de la cène dans Luc xxii, 15–20' in *Revue biblique* 48 (1939), in particular p. 386.

799. For recent developments in the study of the anaphora of Addai and Mari, see P. G. Cobb, in C. Jones, G. Wainwright and E. Yarnold (eds.), *The Study of Liturgy*, pp. 176–9.

800. H. O. Old, *The Patristic Roots of Reformed Worship*.

801. Zwingli knew Ambrose's *de sacramentis* and used its quotations from the eucharistic prayer in order to prove the variability of liturgical forms over against an absolutely unchangeable 'canon' (H. O. Old, op. cit., p. 106). The Byzantine liturgies of *St Chrysostom* and *St Basil* were just starting to become known in the West, and (less easily) *St James* and the 'Clementine liturgy' (*Apostolic Constitutions* VIII); but the evaluation and appreciation of them had scarcely begun; see F. A. Gasquet and E. Bishop, *Edward VI and the Book of Common Prayer*, London: Hodges, 1891³, p. 186f, and J. Dowden, *The Workmanship of the Prayer Book²*, pp. 47–56, 147f.

802. Note the sub-title of J. D. C. Fisher's *Christian Initiation: Baptism in the Medieval West*: 'a study in the disintegration of the primitive rite of initiation'. How primitive 'confirmation' was, is of course disputed (the evidence is set out with scrupulous fairness in Fisher's later book, *Confirmation then and now*). But it is certain that big changes occurred between (let us say) the 'early patristic' and the medieval period. A. H. Couratin saw here an example of the interaction between doctrine and practice: 'The accidental postponement of confirmation led to a new doctrine of the sacrament, and in turn the new doctrine gradually brought about the abandonment of infant confirmation' (in J. Daniélou, A. H. Couratin and J. Kent, *Historical Theology*, p. 209).

803. The Catholic writer H. Hubert, in his book *Der Streit um die Kindertaufe*, has argued that it is only Protestants who experience infant baptism as *problematic*, the reasons lying in the *sola scriptura*, the *sola fide*, and the 'theology of the Word'. Catholics, by contrast, accept 'developing Tradition', and by their use of other sacraments (confirmation, penance, eucharist), they avoid that 'over-loading' of baptism which is characteristic of Protestant (especially Lutheran) theology and which poses so many problems in the case of *infant* baptism. Hubert argues that, historically, 'infant baptism is the constant and the theology of it the variable'. That even Catholics are now starting to find infant baptism problematic is shown, for instance, by Daniel Boureau's book, *L'avenir du baptême*, and by P. Schoonenberg's contribution to *Christsein ohne Entscheidung?* (ed. W. Kasper).

804. See earlier p. 140 and note 334.

805. What, even now, is the weight of 'their parents or someone from their family shall speak for them' in *The Apostolic Tradition*? Tertullian speaks of the *promissiones* of the sponsors involving their own responsibility. See D. S. Bailey, *Sponsors at Baptism and Confirmation*, London: SPCK, 1952, pp. 1–10. Luther rejected the idea of *fides aliena*: so Karl Barth, ET *The Teaching of the Church regarding Baptism*, p. 45f. Luther's two *Taufbüchlein* retained the inherited Roman practice of addressing the baptismal interrogations directly to the infant.

806. Concerning believers' baptism, Zwingli admitted in 1525: 'This error misled me also some years ago, so that I thought it much better to

36

baptize children after they have come to a riper age.' See W. M. S. West, 'The Anabaptists and the rise of the Baptist movement' in A. Gilmore (ed.), *Christian Baptism*, pp. 225–48. On the *corpus christianum* connexion, see also K. Barth, ET *The Teaching of the Church regarding Baptism*, p. 52f, and *Kirchliche Dogmatik* IV/4, p. 185 (ET p. 168).

807. The defensiveness was accompanied by a certain positive attempt at purification, as we shall admit in a moment: see T. Vismans, 'Het concilie van Trente en de liturgie' in *Tijdschrift voor liturgie* 46 (1962), pp. 109–22.

808. Uniats retained their language, and there were some very exceptional cases of the popular tongue being used in the 'Latin' rite in Eastern Europe. In the West, it was apparently long forbidden to translate the mass at all, even for private reading by the laity. See C. Korolevsky, ET *Living Languages in Catholic Worship*. Bilingual rituals became a feature of the earlier Liturgical Movement, before Vatican II.

809. Trent, session XXII, chapter 4 and canon 6 (DS 1745; 1756).

810. See C. Howell, in C. Jones, G. Wainwright and E. Yarnold (eds.), *The Study of Liturgy*, p. 242. Again, for the *partial* success of the 'restoration' in connexion with the divine office, see J. D. Crichton, ibid., p. 384. The *Institutio generalis Missalis romani* of 1969–70 sees the post-Vatican II missal of Paul VI as being in a better position to achieve the aims of the post-Trent missal of Pius V concerning the return to 'the norms of the early Fathers': ET *General Instruction on the Roman Missal*, London: Catholic Truth Society, 1973, paragraphs 6–9.

811. So powerfully were the moths attracted to the Roman light that some institutions failed to claim their right to their own tradition. On the 'lesser' Western rites, see A. A. King, *Liturgies of the Primatial Sees* (Lyons, Braga, Milan, Toledo), 1957; *Liturgies of the Religious Orders* (Carthusians, Cistercians, Premonstratensians, Carmelites, Dominicans), 1955; and *Liturgies of the Past* (Aquileia, Beneventum, Gallican, Celtic, medieval England, Nidaros/Trondheim), 1959. All were published by Longmans, London.

812. W. J. Grisbrooke, *Anglican Liturgies of the Seventeenth and Eighteenth Centuries*, London: SPCK, 1958.

813. R. F. Buxton, *Eucharist and Institution Narrative*, chapters 8 and 9.

814. G. Donaldson, *The Making of the Scottish Prayer Book of 1637*, Edinburgh: University Press, 1954.

815. W. Nagel, *Geschichte des christlichen Gottesdienstes*, Berlin: de Gruyter, 1962, pp. 146–51. I am grateful to David Tripp for pointing me to this and the book mentioned in the following note.

816. A. L. Mayer, *Die Liturgie in der europäischen Geistesgeschichte*, Darmstadt: Wissenschaftliche Buchgesellschaft, 1971, pp. 185–245 ('Liturgie, Aufklärung und Klassizismus').

817. R. C. D. Jasper, *Prayer Book Revision in England 1800–1900*. The broader English story is told in the series by Horton Davies on *Worship and Theology in England* (Princeton, N.J.: University Press, and London:

OUP, 1961–75): vol. 1, *From Cranmer to Hooker, 1534–1603*; vol. 2, *From Andrewes to Baxter and Fox, 1603–1690*; vol. 3, *From Watts and Wesley to Maurice, 1690–1850*; vol. 4, *From Newman to Martineau, 1850–1900*; vol. 5, *The Ecumenical Century, 1900–1965*.

818. On the Athanasian Creed, see earlier p. 188f and note 692.

819. J. F. White, *The Cambridge Movement: The Ecclesiologists and the Gothic Revival*, Cambridge: University Press, 1962.

820. See, very briefly, A. R. Vidler, *The Church in an Age of Revolution*, Harmondsworth: Penguin, 1961, chapter 14 ('Ritualism and Prayer Book revision').

821. Newman's *Tract XC*: 'Our present scope is merely to show that while our Prayer Book is acknowledged on all hands to be of Catholic origin, our Articles also, the offspring of an un-Catholic age, are, through God's good providence, to say the least, not un-Catholic, and may be subscribed by those who aim at being Catholic in heart and doctrine.' The exploitation of ambiguities and loopholes, found necessary by Newman with respect to the Articles, had appeared necessary and possible to Stephen Gardiner with respect even to the 1549 Prayer Book.

822. For the Anglican *theological* background, see M. E. Stewart's Belfast Ph.D. thesis, *Anglican Eucharistic Theology in the Twentieth Century*, 1975.

823. See earlier pp. 294ff.

824. H. Cox, *The Seduction of the Spirit*, New York: Simon & Shuster, 1973, and London: Wildwood House, 1974, p. 214.

825. A. Haquin, *Dom Lambert Beauduin et le renouveau liturgique*.

826. For bibliography on the new Roman Catholic eucharistic prayers, see earlier notes 43 and 289.

827. See J. D. Crichton, *Christian Celebration: The Sacraments*, chapters 3–6.

828. For the interaction between liturgy and doctrine on the question of infant baptism all along the course of Church history, see together two chapters in W. Kasper (ed.), *Christsein ohne Entscheidung?*: W. Breuning, 'Die Kindertaufe im Licht der Dogmengeschichte' (pp. 72–95), and A. Stenzel, 'Die Kindertaufe im Licht der Liturgiegeschichte' (pp. 96–107). Stenzel also wrote on 'Zeitgebundenes und Überzeitliches in der Geschichte der Taufe' in *Concilium*, February 1967, pp. 96–102. Note my 'The rites and ceremonies of Christian initiation: developments in the past' in *Studia Liturgica* 10 (1974), pp. 2–24.

829. Melchior Cano, in his *De locis theologicis*, took infant baptism as an example of how the Church's traditions are the only sure guide by which the true meaning of scripture may be discerned: see J. McHugh's important introduction on scripture and tradition, in his *The Mother of Jesus in the New Testament*, pp. xxiii–xlviii.

830. See earlier p. 222.

831. See G. Wainwright, *Eucharist and Eschatology*, pp. 60–8, and notes for bibliography.

832. J. Jeremias, *Die Abendmahlsworte Jesu*[3], pp. 229–46: 'Damit Gott meiner gedenke' (ET *The Eucharistic Words of Jesus*, 1966, pp. 237–255).

833. G. Wainwright, *Eucharist and Eschatology*, pp. 68–70.

834. See earlier p. 272 and note 195. Dussaut makes interesting use of structuralist techniques in his exegesis. For one of his key theses he can claim the support of Thomas Aquinas in his commentary on 1 Corinthians: 'Corpus Christi repraesentat mysterium incarnationis . . . sed sanguis Christi in sacramento directe repraesentat passionem.'

835. For some theological background, see the full sweep of articles published in *Studia Liturgica* vol. 2 (1963), no. 2, and written in preparation of the Montreal report on *Worship* (WCC Faith and Order Paper No. 39, 1963): R. Prenter, 'Worship and creation'; H. Riesenfeld, 'Worship and the Cross and Resurrection of Christ'; B. Bobrinskoy, 'Worship and the Ascension of Christ'; J. J. von Allmen, 'Worship and the Holy Spirit'. Roman Catholic devotion had so settled on the Cross as to leave undervalued such references to the Resurrection as there were in the rite of the mass: see W. B. McGrory, *The Mass and the Resurrection*, Rome: Catholic Book Agency, 1964. In Protestantism the ritual concentration on the Cross was almost complete.

836. See P. Lebeau, *Le vin nouveau du royaume*, and my *Eucharist and Eschatology*, chapter 2: 'Antepast of heaven'.

837. J. M. R. Tillard, 'L'eucharistie et le Saint-Esprit' in *Nouvelle revue théologique* 90 (1968), pp. 363–87.

838. J. L. Houlden, 'Liturgy and her companions: a theological appraisal' in R. C. D. Jasper (ed.), *The Eucharist Today: Studies on Series 3*, pp. 168–76. A more general treatment, but still with a side-swipe at liturgiographers on p. 2f, is found in Houlden's little book, *Patterns of Faith: a study in the relationship between the New Testament and Christian doctrine*, London: SCM, 1977. In *Theology*, May 1976, pp. 129–31, J. Drury contrasted the Series 3 communion service unfavourably with the Church of England Doctrine Commission's report on *Christian Believing*. Whereas the latter shows 'a temperate and vivid sense of common search and faith which makes good spiritual reading', the former has the following characteristics pejoratively predicated upon it: 'a striking fondness for dogmatic pronouncements', obtrusive and obsessional christocentricity, out-of-context use of 'abstruse fragments of New Testament documents', 'atavism', making an 'arrangement of ancient formulations', the 'recitation of doctrines'.

839. It is this combination of factors which allows T. G. A. Baker both to tax the liturgical revisers with biblicism ('the pepper-pot use of biblical texts') and to say that 'the influence of New Testament scholarship on the (new) liturgy has been marginal': *Questioning Worship*, London: SCM, 1977. He argues that the revisers' inadequacies are both exegetical (harmonizing biblical diversities) and hermeneutical (ignoring the shift in world-views), resulting perhaps from a crypto-fundamentalistic

identification between the Bible and the Word of God. The present dean of Worcester would like to hear much less scripture in worship.

840. For the question of *worship* and modern western 'secularization': R. Panikkar, *Worship and secular man: an essay on the liturgical nature of man, considering secularization as a major phenomenon of our time and worship as an apparent fact of all times; a study towards an integral anthropology*, Maryknoll, N.Y.: Orbis, and London: DLT, 1973; E. Schillebeeckx, *God the Future of Man*, London: Sheed & Ward, 1969, chapter 3 ('Secular worship and Church liturgy'); W. Vos (ed.), *Worship and Secularization*, Bussum: Brand, 1970 (=*Studia Liturgica*, vol. 7, nos. 2–3). See further chapter XI§4.

841. Note—though the emphasis here is more on the synchronic and less on the diachronic aspects of the problem—the WCC Faith and Order study of the 1970s on the unity of the Church and the unity of humankind (Faith and Order Papers nos. 72 and 77); also the related symposium edited by O. H. Pesch, *Einheit der Kirche, Einheit der Menschheit: Perspektiven aus Theologie, Ethik und Völkerrecht*, Freiburg: Herder, 1978.

842. One author among many, the Argentine Methodist José Míguez Bonino: *Doing Theology in a Revolutionary Situation*, Philadelphia: Fortress, = *Revolutionary Theology Comes of Age*, London: SPCK, 1975; and *Christians and Marxists: The Mutual Challenge to Revolution*, London: Hodder, and Grand Rapids: Eerdmans, 1976.

843. See the indications in J. M. Lochman, *Marx begegnen*, Gütersloh: Mohn, 1975 (ET *Encountering Marx: Bonds and Barriers between Christians and Marxists*, Belfast: Christian Journals, 1977); and Max Horkheimer, *Die Sehnsucht nach dem ganz Anderen: ein Interview mit Kommentar von Helmut Gumnior*, Hamburg: Furche, 1970. A sensitive Christian commentary on the whole question is found in H. Gollwitzer, *Krummes Holz, aufrechter Gang: zur Frage nach dem Sinn des Lebens*, Munich: Kaiser, 1970.

844. Simply, in R. Bultmann, *Jesus Christ and Mythology*, New York: Scribner, 1958, chapter 5.

845. J. Killinger, *Leave it to the Spirit: commitment and freedom in the new liturgy*, New York: Harper & Row, and London: SCM, 1971. Review by A. C. Bridge, in *Theology*, March 1972, p. 163f. In August 1972 the reviewer defended himself against a letter charging him with unfairness on account of his combination of items from four different services envisaged by the author.

846. Epiphanius, *Panarion* 52.1.1. to 52.3.8. Reference in D. E. Aune, *The Cultic Setting of Realized Eschatology in Early Christianity*, p. 179.

847. H. Gunkel, *Schöpfung und Chaos in Urzeit und Endzeit*, Göttingen: Vandenhoeck & Ruprecht, 1895, especially pp. 367–79.

848. The prayer-collections of Oosterhuis include *Bid om vrede*, Utrecht: Ambo, 1966 (ET *Your Word is Near*, New York: Paulist, 1968); *In het voorbijgaan*, Utrecht: Ambo, 1968 (ET *Prayers, Poems and Songs*, and *Open Your Hearts*, New York: Herder, 1970 and 1971); *Zien soms even*, Utrecht: Ambo, 1972 (ET *At Times I See*, New York: Seabury, 1974). I am much

indebted to the sensitive studies of Oosterhuis by J. B. Ryan in *The Eucharistic Prayer: a study in contemporary liturgy*, New York: Paulist Press, 1974, and 'Eucharistic prayers for contemporary men and women' in *Studia Liturgica* 11 (1976), pp. 186–206.

849. Another Catholic poet of the liturgy, the Canadian André Gignac, writes of his experiments in 'Une expérience de création eucharistique' in *Liturgie et vie chrétienne* no. 89 (1974), pp. 262–68. More theoretically: J. P. Manigne, 'The poetics of faith in the liturgy' in *Concilium*, February 1973, pp. 40–50. Issue no. 111 of *La Maison-Dieu* (1972) was devoted to 'Créativité et liturgie'.

850. See earlier p. 25 and again p. 414.

851. Something of the complexity of this problem can be deduced from the writings of the educationalist B. Bernstein, notably *Class, Codes and Control*, expanded edition, St Albans: Paladin, 1973.

852. See earlier p. 253f. On 'variation and fixity' at the eucharist, see also G. Every, *Basic Liturgy: a study in the structure of the eucharistic prayer*, London: Faith Press, 1961, *in nuce* pp. 6–8, 10–17. Further: L. Ligier, 'La struttura della preghiera eucaristica: diversità e unità' in *Ephemerides liturgicae* 82 (1968), pp. 191–215.

853. This should be taken in tandem with the 'emerging theological consensus' in the areas of ecclesiology, doctrine and worship produced by COCU in 1976: *In Quest of a Church of Christ Uniting*.

854. For earlier material concerning the relations between the conception of God, on the one hand, and worship and prayer, on the other, see W. Dürig, *Pietas liturgica: Studien zum Frömmigkeitsbegriff und zur Gottesvorstellung der abendländischen Liturgie*, Regensburg: Pustet, 1958; also A. Buckel, *Die Gottesbezeichnungen in den Liturgien der Ostkirchen*, Würzburg: Triltsch, 1938.

855. Whitehead and Hartshorne are more philosophers, Cobb and Ogden more theologians. By Cobb, note for instance *A Christian Natural Theology based on the thought of Alfred North Whitehead*, Philadelphia: Westminster, 1965, and London: Lutterworth, 1966. By Ogden, *The Reality of God, and other essays*, New York: Harper & Row, 1966, and London: SCM, 1967.

856. N. Pittenger, *Life as Eucharist*, Grand Rapids: Eerdmans, 1973. More generally, 'Further thoughts on Christian "re-conception" today', in *Church Quarterly* 3 (1970–1), pp. 117–24.

857. See, for instance, several of the articles collected in Macquarrie's *Thinking about God*, London: SCM, 1975.

858. J. Macquarrie, *Thinking about God*, p. 146.

859. J. Macquarrie, *Principles of Christian Theology*, revised edition 1977, chapters 4 and 5.

860. J. Macquarrie, *Thinking about God*, p. 145f.

861. See N. Young, *Creator, Creation and Faith*, London: Collins, 1976, pp. 41–3, 124–7.

862. J. Macquarrie, *Principles of Christian Theology*, revised edition 1977,

chapters 6, 19 and 20, and his *Paths in Spirituality*, London: SCM, 1972.

863. On creation, incarnation and crucifixion as part of a single movement of *kenosis* on God's part, see J. Macquarrie, *Principles of Christian Theology*, revised edition 1977, pp. 256, 302f.

864. See, for example, Sharon Neufer Emswiler and Thomas Neufer Emswiler, *Women and Worship: a guide to non-sexist hymns, prayers, and liturgies*, New York: Harper & Row, 1974; and a report adopted by the 187th General Assembly, May 1975, of the United Presbyterian Church in the USA: *Language about God: Opening the Door.*

865. *Churches on the Way to Consensus: a survey of the replies to the agreed statements 'One Baptism, One Eucharist and a Mutually Recognized Ministry'*, Geneva: WCC Secretariat on Faith and Order, typescript FO/77:3, revised June 1977, p. 241.

866. 'Advocate' is sometimes the third name. There is difficulty in that, biblically and traditionally, creation is predicated also of the second and even of the third persons of the Trinity; that Redeemer is a name given also to the first person; and that Advocate is a title ascribed also to the second person, at least in his human nature.

867. J. Macquarrie, *Thinking about God*, p. 130f.

868. J. Macquarrie, *Thinking about God*, p. 131.

869. For the maternal quality of God's love, see Jeremiah 31:3, Hosea 11:1f; Isaiah 49:15f.

870. My own policy in this book has been to avoid, where possible, the use of masculine language in generic references to humanity, although I have occasionally recoiled in face of the intolerable clumsiness to which such avoidance would have given rise in the present unconverted state of the English tongue. I have used male language of God in the absence of a satisfactory alternative tradition.

871. J. J. von Allmen speaks of a vital rhythm of *sustolē* and *diastolē: Essai sur le repas du Seigneur*, pp. 111–16, 120.

872. J. G. Davies, *Worship and Mission*, London: SCM, 1966.

873. For the various stages in the Church of England's liturgical revision, see note 235.

874. Notably, Voltaire's *L'ingénu*. The visitors may simply come from a *different* culture, as in Montesquieu's *Lettres persanes*.

875. See note 17.

876. In an adjacent context, B. Lonergan adopts the axiom 'whatever is received, is received after the manner of the receiver': *The Way to Nicea*, London: DLT, 1976, pp. 7, 12.

877. G. Kittel, in G. K. A. Bell and A. Deissmann, *Mysterium Christi*, London: Longmans, 1930, p. 31–49: 'das Ärgernis der Einmaligkeit' is the German phrase.

878. See p. 69; also pp. 106, 145.

879. By a positive understanding of 'relativity' I may appear to be coming close to E. Troeltsch, *Die Absolutheit des Christentums und die*

Religionsgeschichte, Tübingen: Mohr, 1929³ (ET *The Absoluteness of Christianity and the History of Religions*, London: SCM, 1972). But I should probably be accused by Troeltsch of 'reverting' to Schleiermacher, since my christology is at least as 'high' as Schleiermacher's. A recent Catholic discussion, from several angles, is edited by W. Kasper, *Absolutheit des Christentums*, Freiburg: Herder, 1977. The chapters are as follows: K. Lehmann, 'Absolutheit des Christentums als philosophisches und theologisches Problem'; E. Senger, 'Jahwe, Abraham und das Heil aller Völker—ein Paradigma zum Thema Exklusivität und Universalismus des Heils'; G. Lohfink, 'Universalismus und Exklusivität des Heils im Neuen Testament'; H. Bürkle, 'Der christliche Anspruch angesichts der Weltreligionen heute'; W. Breuning, 'Jesus Christus als universales Sakrament des Heils'; H. U. von Balthasar, 'Die Absolutheit des Christentums und die Katholizität der Kirche'.

880. Vatican II, dogmatic constitution on the Church, *Lumen gentium*, I.8.

881. On the themes of this paragraph, see T. F. Torrance, *Theological Science*, London: OUP, 1969, and *God and Rationality*, London: OUP, 1971.

882. The theme of cultural unity and diversity, both diachronic and synchronic, has been explored at the 'secular' level of linguistic translation in a brilliant book by George Steiner, *After Babel*. It is a matter of what he calls elsewhere 'the possibilities of and constraints on translation both within and between human tongues, the mystery of imperfect or ready understanding' (G. Steiner, *Heidegger*, London: Collins, 1978, p. 21). The director Peter Brook has been investigating these questions in the forms of the theatre, in work centred on Les Bouffes du Nord, Paris. A book with interesting sidelight to cast on the liturgy is his *The Empty Space*, London: McGibbon & Kee, 1968. Note also the writings on intercultural questions of the renowned Bible translator E. A. Nida, as for example *Message and Mission: The Communication of the Christian Faith*, New York: Harper, 1960.

883. The *historical* conditioning—i.e. largely the diachronic question—of dogmatic statements has come to the fore as a theme in recent Roman Catholic theology. Apart from work done in connexion with the notion of development (see note 601), notice the writings of Walter Kasper (for example, *Glaube im Wandel der Geschichte*, Mainz: Grünewald, 1970); distinctly on the conservative side, L. Scheffczyk, *Schwerpunkte des Glaubens*, Einsiedeln: Johannes, 1977 (especially 'Kirche und Theologie unter dem Gesetz der Geschichte?', 'Gibt es bleibende Wahrheiten?', 'Die Einheit des Dogmas und die Vielfalt der Denkformen', 'Christentum an der Schwelle der Selbstauflösung?'); and, perhaps more 'liberal', E. Schillebeeckx, *God the Future of Man* (chapter 1, 'Towards a Catholic use of hermeneutics'), *Geloofsverstaan* (ET *The Understanding of Faith*), and, directly on the eucharist and still in favour of 'transubstantiation' over against the alleged adequacy of transsignification and transfinalization,

The Eucharist. The theme keeps recurring in K. Rahner's *Theological Investigations*: for instance, 'The development of dogma' (in vol. 1); 'Considerations on the development of dogma' (in vol. 4); 'What is a dogmatic statement?' (in vol. 5); 'The historicity of theology' (in vol. 9); 'The teaching office of the Church in the present-day crisis of authority' and 'Heresies in the Church today?' (in vol. 12); and the first five essays in volume 14.

884. A. Baumstark, *Vom geschichtlichen Werden der Liturgie*, Freiburg: Herder, 1923; revised by B. Botte, *Liturgie comparée: principes et méthodes pour l'étude historique des liturgies chrétiennes*, Chevetogne, 1953; English adaptation by F. L. Cross, *Comparative Liturgy*, London: Mowbray, 1958, pp. 15–30.

885. E. Bishop, 'The genius of the Roman rite' in *Liturgica Historica*, Oxford: Clarendon, 1918, pp. 1–19.

886. For the procession bringing the elements to the altar, see R. F. Taft, *The Great Entrance: a history of the transfer of the gifts and other pre-anaphoral rites of the liturgy of St John Chrysostom* (Orientalia christiana analecta, 200), Rome: Pontifical Oriental Institute, 1975.

887. 'Adaptation' tends now to be replaced by 'incarnation': see A. Shorter, *African Christian Theology—adaptation or incarnation?*, London: Chapman, 1975.

888. Already in the nineteenth century, the Bible Christian (Methodist) missionary Sam Pollard was using tea in China: R. E. Kendall, *Eyes of the Earth*, London: Cargate, 1954, pp. 138, 140, 146. Tea was the everyday drink, rice wine being used for parties and traditional religious rites.

889. The importance of 'feeling at home' in the liturgy and 'worshipping with understanding' has been stressed by the Nigerian theologian, E. Bolaji Idowu, *Towards an Indigenous Church*, London/Ibadan: OUP, 1965, pp. 26–38.

890. For the use of Jung in liturgical connexions, see G. Cope, *Symbolism in the Bible and the Church*, London: SCM, 1959.

891. Cyprian, *ep.* 69, 5 (CSEL, p. 753f), cf. 63, 13 (CSEL, p. 712). Augustine, *serm.* 227 (PL 38, 1100), 272 (PL 38, 1247–8).

892. For India, see R. W. Taylor, *Jesus in Indian Paintings*, Madras: Christian Literature Society, 1975.

893. For a sympathetic account of the Kimbanguist church, including some description of its theology and worship, see M. L. Martin, ET *Kimbangu*, in particular pp. 140–84. The dust-jacket reproduces the wood sculpture.

894. The new Vatican Museum of Religious Art contains several canvases by Rouault and Buffet.

895. See further E. Mveng, *L'art d'Afrique noire: liturgie cosmique et langage religieux*, Tours: Mame, 1964, and *Art nègre, art chrétien?*, Rome: Les amis italiens de Présence africaine, 1969.

896. P. Tillich, *Theology of Culture*, New York: OUP, 1959.

897. R. F. Buxton, *Eucharist and Institution Narrative*, p. 159. Buxton

quotes (p. 164) Charles Wheatly in the eighteenth century: 'BUT *Bucer* being called in to give his Opinion of it, this momentous and principal Office of our Liturgy had the Misfortune to suffer great Alterations. Some Amendment in the Method it might possibly have born; But the practice of foreign Churches, and not Primitive Liturgies, being always with him the Standard of Reformation, the most ancient Forms and Primitive Rites were forced to give way to modern Fancies.'

898. In the small chapel of the National Biblical Catechetical and Liturgical Centre, Bangalore, a wrought-iron window-frame depicts Christ in the shape of Shiva, the dancing god.

899. See the symposium on *Worship and Dance*, Birmingham: University Institute for the Study of Worship and Religious Architecture, 1975.

900. Accounts of worship in independent churches can be found in C. G. Baëta, *Prophetism in Ghana*, London: SCM, 1962, and in H. W. Turner's two-volume study of the Nigerian-founded 'Church of the Lord (Aladura)' (which, he concludes, 'should be classified as a Christian church'), *African Independent Church*, vol. 2, Oxford: Clarendon, 1967.

901. Augustinus Schnijder, 'Cosmopolitization of mankind and adaptation of the liturgy' in *Studia Liturgica* 8 (1971–2), pp. 169–84.

902. I am not of course denying that Greco-Roman culture was a highly *complex* unity. See, for instance, H. Chadwick, *Early Christian Thought and the Classical Tradition*, Oxford: Clarendon, 1966; C. N. Cochrane, *Christianity and Classical Culture: a study of thought and action from Augustus to Augustine*, Oxford: Clarendon, 1940; A. D. Nock, *Conversion: the old and the new in religion from Alexander the Great to Augustine of Hippo*, Oxford: Clarendon, 1933; R. A. Norris, *God and World in Early Christian Theology*; L. G. Patterson, *God and History in Early Christian Thought: a study of themes from Justin Martyr to Gregory the Great*, New York: Seabury, and London: Black, 1967.

903. A. Harnack, *Lehrbuch der Dogmengeschichte*, vol, 1, Freiburg: Mohr, 1886, pp. 372–662 (ET *History of Dogma*, vol. 2, London: Williams & Norgate, 1896, pp. 169ff).

904. D. von Allmen, article mentioned in note 137. Taking the example of the hymn in Philippians 2:5–11, von Allmen points out elements of continuity with the Jewish and Jewish Christian tradition: the clear allusion to Isaiah 45:25f, and possibly the theme of (Jesus as) the Servant of Yahweh (Isaiah 52–53; Mark 10:42–45). 'Yet this last theme has been profoundly modified in the hymn, in function of an idea which is not in fact Jewish. For in the hymn it may be seen that the term *slave* is explained by the term *man*. This is clear from the parallelism of the stanzas. Slavery is every man's condition, and therefore Jesus' in his incarnation. This goes much further than Jesus' own use of the image. For the Jewish and Jewish Christian tradition, man is not a slave. It is for the Greeks, particularly at this late date, that man is a slave, bound hand and foot in submission to all-powerful Destiny (see for example P. Wendland, *Die hellenistisch-römische Kultur*, Tübingen,

1912. pp. 104–6). Likewise, it would be possible to find in the hymn a number of other expressions which find their closest equivalent in the gnostic myths of the Original Man: "the divine estate", "the equal of God" (see on this point the commentary of J. Gnilka, *Der Philipperbrief*, Freiburg, 1968, pp. 131–47). But none of this constitutes a dangerously syncretistic undertaking, open to accusations of heresy. For in the hymn it is no longer a matter of a mythical Original Man losing his divine form and assuming a human appearance. The vocabulary remains, but it is used to sing the praise of Jesus of Nazareth who entered history as a man of flesh and blood. Nor, unlike certain gnostic poems, does the hymn sing of the way of salvation for every soul now lost in slavery to "matter", needing to have its divine origin recalled to it in order that through "knowledge" it may rediscover its true identity. Rather, the hymn sings of the mighty activity of God in the death and resurrection of Jesus of Nazareth. We must see in this hymn an interesting, and indeed successful, attempt to express the mystery of the condescension of Christ in a characteristically Greek vocabulary.' 'Even death on a cross' and 'in heaven and on earth and under the earth' are probably pauline *re-inforcements* of the hymn. In the hymn of Colossians 1:15–20, von Allmen sees Paul as making the *critical* additions of 'the head of the body, *that is the Church*' (verse 18) and *'by the blood of the cross'* (verse 20); see earlier, p. 56. Von Allmen presents his exegesis of the hymns from Philippians and Colossians in more detail in his *L'évangile de Jésus Christ: naissance de la théologie dans le Nouveau Testament*, Yaoundé: CLE, 1972, pp. 112–33. See also J. D. G. Dunn, *Unity and Diversity in the New Testament*, pp. 134–7, 294f.

905. *Didache*, 14; Justin, *Dialogue w th Trypho*, 41 and 116–17; Irenaeus, *adversus haereses* IV, 17, 5f; Hippolytus, *Commentary on Daniel*, 4:35; Eusebius, *Demonstration of the Gospel*, I.10; Aphraates, *Demonstrations* 16, 3 (PS 1, 768); Zeno of Verona, *Tract* I.15, 4 (PL 11, 364).

906. The Hebrew is enigmatic. Some of the difficulties can be seen from the discussion by J. G. Baldwin in her *Haggai, Zechariah, Malachi*, Leicester: Inter-Varsity Press, 1972, pp. 227–30, and also in commentaries on the same books by D. R. Jones (London: SCM, 1962, p. 186f) and R. Mason (Cambridge: University Press, 1977, p. 144f). The main possibilities for exegesis were already set out by J. M. P. Smith in the International Critical Commentary (1912).

907. Justin brings forward this second line of argument when he is addressing a pagan: *Apol.* I, 46 (see earlier pp. 68, 144). He uses the argument from fulfilment of prophecy when he is in dialogue with Trypho the Jew: there are hints that the eucharist, as the 'memorial' of Christ's self-sacrifice, fulfils not only Malachi 1:11 but also the Old Testament sacrificial system (see chapter 41 for the reference to the 'offering of fine flour' of Leviticus 14:10, and chapter 116 for the reference to the priesthood of Zechariah 3).

908. I am not myself a great admirer of 'theology by anecdote', but

the champions of 'narrative theology' may perhaps see some slight concession to their position here.

909. C. K. Barrett, *The Gospel of John and Judaism*, London: SPCK, 1975, p. 69.

910. Ambrose, *de sacramentis* IV, 27; the Roman canon; the Alexandrine anaphora of St Mark; mosaics in San Vitale, Ravenna. A. H. Couratin suggests that the selection of *pre*-Mosaic figures may go back into the second century, when 'Christians were in acute controversy with the Jews' (in J. Daniélou, A. H. Couratin and J. Kent, *Historical Theology*, p. 196). Later, Aaron and Samuel will be included in the Byzantine liturgy of St James, and Moses also in the Byzantine St Basil: F. E. Brightman, *Liturgies Eastern and Western*, Oxford: Clarendon, 1896, pp. 41, 319f.

911. L. Finkelstein, 'The *birkat ha-mazon*' in *Jewish Quarterly Review* n.s.19 (1928–9), pp. 211–62. For the Jewish *birkat ha-mazon* as the model of the Christian *eucharistia*, see L. A. Ligier, in L. Sheppard (ed.), *The New Liturgy*, pp. 113–50, and in *Studia Liturgica* 9 (1973), pp. 161–85. See, earlier, pp. 159, 253f, and notes 88 and 373.

912. Nor is the Sanctus found in the anaphora of *Testamentum Domini* or in a fragmentary anaphora of St Epiphanius (on which see B. Botte, in *Le Muséon* 73, 1960, pp. 311–15). E. C. Ratcliff argued that the anaphora in *The Apostolic Tradition* originally concluded in the Sanctus (see 'The Sanctus and the pattern of the early anaphora' in his *Liturgical Studies*, pp. 18–40), and that the Sanctus in the anaphora of Addai and Mari, *in its present placing*, was an 'intrusion' ('The original form of the anaphora of Addai and Mari: a suggestion', ibid., pp. 80–90).

913. A. A. McArthur, *The Evolution of the Christian Year*, pp. 22–8, On the whole Sabbath/Sunday question, see R. T. Beckwith and W. Stott, *This is the Day*.

914. Cyprian, *ep.* 64 (CSEL, pp. 718–21).

915. Calvin, *Inst.*, book IV, chapters 14–16; H. H. Wolf, *Die Einheit des Bundes: das Verhältnis von Altem und Neuem Testament bei Calvin*, Neukirchen: Erziehungsverein, 1958.

916. The latest major work on the relation of Paul to Judaism is E. P. Sanders, *Paul and Palestinian Judaism*, London: SCM, 1977. According to Sanders, Paul's view of the law is that 'its requirement is just, in itself it aims aright. But the requirement is fulfilled only in Christ, and the aim, life, is accomplished only in Christ' (p. 497). If the law is 'abolished', its 'dethronement' is due to the fact that the *one* way of salvation which God has now provided for *all*, whether Jew or Gentile, is participation in the body of Christ. On the roles of grace and works as the ground and condition of salvation, Paul and rabbinic Judaism are in agreement: the difference is whether or not they are located in Christ (pp. 515–18; 543–52). The '(new) covenantal nomism' which W. D. Davies predicated upon Paul (*Paul and Rabbinic Judaism*, London: SPCK, 1958²) is held by Sanders to be the pattern into which the Church *later* settled, a relapse

from the novelty of Paul's pattern of participatory union with Christ the universal Lord as the beginning of eschatological transformation (pp. 511–515). I am not sure that the difference between Paul's and the 'later' pattern is as great as Sanders now argues.

917. On the theological question of the relation of Christianity to Judaism, see pp. 172-5, and on the 'uses of the law', see p. 417f and note 1012.

918. This line is taken by R. Perdelwitz (see note 376). In his commentary on *The First Epistle of Peter* (Oxford: Blackwell, 1947, p. 17), F. W. Beare summed up the argument as follows: 'For this fearful ceremony (of the *taurobolium*), the candidate was lowered into a pit with a grating over him; above this a bull was slaughtered, and the blood allowed to pour down over his whole body. On emerging, he was hailed as one "reborn for eternity" (*renatus in aeternum*); he was crowned with a wreath of laurel; and his bloody garment was stored away for him in the temple against the time when the ceremony would have to be repeated, twenty years later; for we meet the curious notion to which numerous inscriptions bear witness, that the "eternity" thus acquired was secure for only twenty years. Against this background, Perdelwitz now sets the language of the Epistle. Here again we have the thought of a regeneration accomplished through a cultic act—in this case, baptism. But the life thus conferred is not limited to a span of twenty years; it is *aphthartos* (incorruptible, truly immortal). The Christian's inheritance is laid up for him in heaven, not in any earthly temple; and it is no garment stained with blood, but a treasure *amiantos* (undefiled). After the ceremony the mystes is given a crown of laurel, which must soon wither; but that which the Christian receives is *amarantos* (unfading).'

919. For this paragraph, see P. M. Gy, 'La notion chrétienne d'initiation' in *La Maison-Dieu* no. 132 (1977), pp. 33–54.

920. Justin, *Apol.* I, 66.4.

921. Tertullian, *de baptismo*, 5. For explanatory details, see the edition by R. F. Refoulé, *Tertullien: Traité du baptême* (Sources chrétiennes, 35), Paris: Cerf, 1952, p. 72.

922. Clement of Alexandria, *Protrepticus* 12, 119–20; Julius Firmicus Maternus, *de errore profanarum religionum*, 19, PL 12, 1022–25.

923. For example, Origen, *contra Celsum* III. 59–60.

924. J. A. Jungmann, *The Early Liturgy to the time of Gregory the Great*, especially chapters 11–13.

925. See, for example, P. du Bourguet, ET *Early Christian Painting*, London: Weidenfeld, 1965; M. Gough, *The Origins of Christian Art*, London: Thames & Hudson, 1973; W. Weidlé, *The Baptism of Art: Notes on the Religion of the Catacomb Paintings*, Westminster: Dacre, n.d.

926. On the widest question of the Church's search for a language in the second century, see S. Laeuchli, *The Language of Faith: an introduction to the semantic dilemma of the early Church*, New York: Abingdon, 1962.

927. See p. 162 and note 378.

928. G. Dix, *The Shape of the Liturgy*, chapter 11.

929. On Christmas and Epiphany, see also A. A. McArthur, *The Evolution of the Christian Year*, pp. 31–69.

930. J. A. Jungmann, *The Early Liturgy*, pp. 145–47.

931. J. A. Jungmann, *The Early Liturgy*, p. 148.

932. Gregory the Great, *epp.* XI, 76, PL 77, 1215–16.

933. On Easter eggs, see E. O. James, *Christian Myth and Ritual*, pp. 290–92.

934. See E. Preclin and E. Jarry, *Les luttes politiques et doctrinales aux XVIIe et XVIIIe siècles* (vol. 19 of A. Fliche and V. Martin, *Histoire de l'Église*), Paris: Blond & Gay, 1955, pp. 173–92.

935. Some of the background thinking, and a regrettably truncated text of the mass itself, is presented by the director of the Bangalore centre, D. S. Amalorpavadass, 'Indigenization and the liturgy of the Church' in *International Review of Mission* 65 (1976), pp. 164–81.

936. In the Dharmaram seminary chapel, Bangalore, the altar is flanked by two mosaics portraying, on the right, the Last Supper and, on the left, the symbols of the religions: the lotus, the swastika, the crescent moon, the star. Buddhist, Hindu, Islamic and Jewish symbols recur in the wrought iron work of the chapel also.

937. Even in more Protestant contexts in India, the question is raised of adopting, adapting and transforming 'certain Hindu festivals which have become mainly social in character', for example *onam* in Kerala and *pongal* in Tamilnad (both harvest festivals), or *dipvali* (a festival of lights), or *pooja* (dedication of tools, of learning, etc.): see J. R. Chandran and W. Q. Lash (eds.), *Christian Worship in India*, Bangalore: CLS, 1961.

938. This was the message of Prophet Harris as he swept along the Ivoirian lagoon. There are books about him by W. J. Platt (*An African Prophet*, 1934), M. Musson (*Prophet Harris*, 1950), and G. M. Haliburton (*The Prophet Harris*, 1971).

939. J. Hallaire, 'Chrétiens africains face à l'initiation ancestrale' in *Études*, April 1967, pp. 482–94.

940. C. Mubengayi Lwakale, *Initiation africaine et initiation chrétienne*, Léopoldville (Kinshasa): Éditions du C.E.P., 1966.

941. See further B. Bürki, 'Traditional initiation in Africa' in *Studia Liturgica* 12 (1977), pp. 201–6. A Swiss Reformed who teaches liturgics at Yaoundé, Cameroon, Bürki is also the author of *La case des chrétiens: essai de théologie pratique sur le lieu de culte en Afrique*, Yaoundé: CLE, 1973, and *L'assemblée dominicale: introduction à la liturgie des églises protestantes d'Afrique*, Supplements to Neue Zeitschrift für Missionswissenschaft 25, Immensee, 1976.

942. G. Ilunga, 'Rites funéraires et christianisme en Afrique' in *Jeunes églises* no. 21 (October 1964), pp. 1–11.

943. H. Sawyerr, *Creative Evangelism: towards a new Christian encounter with Africa*, London: Lutterworth, 1968, especially chapter 5 ('A fresh liturgical approach').

944. The portmanteau character of the notion of sacrifice is well brought out by J. L. Houlden, 'Sacrifice and the eucharist' in I. T. Ramsey and others, *Thinking about the Eucharist*, pp. 81–99.

945. R. Mehl, *Traité de sociologie du protestantisme*, p. 162f (ET *The Sociology of Protestantism*, p. 179).

946. For recent developments in Catholic Africa, see B. Luykx, *Culte chrétien en Afrique après Vatican II*, Supplements to Neue Zeitschrift für Missionswissenschaft 22, Immensee, 1974.

947. B. Sundkler, *Bantu Prophets in South Africa*, London: OUP 1961², in particular, pp. 278–94, 328–30.

948. M. L. Martin, *Kirche ohne Weisse* (ET *Kimbangu*).

949. G. Wainwright, 'Theological reflections on "The Catechism concerning the Prophet Simon Kimbangu" of 1970' in *Orita* 5 (1971), pp. 18–35.

950. For Jesus as 'the man who bursts all categories', see E. Schweizer, *Jesus Christus im vielvältigen Zeugnis des Neuen Testaments*, Munich and Hamburg: Siebenstern, 1968 (ET *Jesus*, London: SCM, 1971).

951. See the exemplary study by G. C. Stead, *Divine Substance*, Oxford: Clarendon, 1977.

952. H. Richard Niebuhr, *Christ and Culture*, New York: Harper & Row, 1951.

953. K. Barth, *Kirchliche Dogmatik* I/2 (ET pp. 280–361). See also H. Kraemer, *The Christian Message in a non-Christian World*, London: Edinburgh House, 1938.

954. J. H. Hick, *God and the Universe of Faiths*; see earlier pp. 68, 144f.

955. Especially chapter 10 of *God and the Universe of Faiths*.

956. Reported on by T. T. Rowe, in *The Times Educational Supplement*, 13 December 1974. I have seen the script of the broadcast.

957. B. Lonergan remarks (*The Way to Nicea*, p. 5f): 'Those who in secular matters are most religious, in the sphere of religion are most prone to idolatry.' The undifferentiated consciousness is unable to distinguish between the symbol and the transcendent reality. Thus Lonergan dismisses 'the romantic notion that undifferentiated consciousness is the religious consciousness *par excellence*'.

958. T. S. Eliot, *Notes towards the Definition of Culture*, London: Faber, 1962², pp. 31, 41, 120.

959. A fascinating series of studies from the area of Germanic culture, made by a Catholic scholar over a period from 1925 to 1955, is found in Anton L. Mayer, *Die Liturgie in der europäischen Geistesgeschichte* (edited and introduced by E. von Severus, 1971). Mayer's titles are sufficient to indicate the richness and range of the collection: 'Altchristliche Liturgie und Germanentum', 'Die Liturgie und der Geist der Gotik', 'Renaissance, Humanismus und Liturgie', 'Liturgie und Barock', 'Liturgie, Aufklärung und Klassizismus', 'Liturgie, Romantik und Restauration', 'Die Stellung der Liturgie von der Zeit der Romantik bis zur Jahrhundertwende', 'Die geistesgeschichtliche Situation der liturgischen Erneuerung in der

Gegenwart', 'Der Wandel des Kirchenbildes in der abendländischen Kulturgeschichte'. Historical and contemporary examples of the interaction between worship and culture abound in A. G. Herbert, *Liturgy and Society*, London: Faber, 1935. For the very broad perspective, see also H. Butterfield, *Christianity in European History*, London: Collins, 1952. For serious theological reflexion on the relations between liturgy and contemporary American culture, see: W. J. Burghardt, 'A theologian's challenge to liturgy', J. F. White, 'Worship and culture: mirror or beacon?', J. Gallen, 'American liturgy: a theological locus', all in *Theological Studies* 35 (1974), pp. 233–48, 288–301, 302–11; M. Collins, 'Liturgical methodology and the cultural evolution of worship in the United States' in *Worship* 49 (1957), pp. 85–102; and the booklet of the United Methodist Church, *Ritual in a New Day*, Nashville: Abingdon, 1976.

960. Tertullian, *Apology*, 21, PL 1, 462.

961. 'Thou hast conquered, O pale Galilean/The world has grown grey from thy breath.'

962. A. Schmemann, *Introduction to Liturgical Theology*, pp. 101–13.

963. On glossolalia, see W. J. Samarin, *Tongues of Men and Angels: The Religious Language of Pentecostalism*, New York; Macmillan, 1972.

964. On the subject of the last two paragraphs, see D. Martin, 'Christianity, civic religion, and three counter-cultures' in his *The Dilemmas of Contemporary Religion*, Oxford: Blackwell, 1978, pp. 1–19. His three typical counter-cultures are those of the medieval monk, the Protestant dissenter, and the contemporary radical. In the counter-cultures, choice and commitment are emphasized over against 'the biological continuities of generation'.

965. On the constantinian and medieval pattern, see W. Pannenberg, *Die Bestimmung des Menschen: Menschsein, Erwählung und Geschichte*, Göttingen: Vandenhoeck & Ruprecht, 1978, chapter 4: 'Das christliche Imperium und das Phänomen einer politischen Religion im Christentum' (ET *Human Nature, Election, and Destiny*, Westminster: Philadelphia, 1977, pp. 62–82). Whereas it is modish to insist on the problems which cultural change has made for Christian identity, Pannenberg makes the reverse emphasis that the continuity of the Christian tradition is the ground of the unity of Western culture (especially chapter 5).

966. For Charlemagne, see note 1031.

967. Official liturgical compositions give little recognition to our technical age, although there is a spin-off from the American space-programme in the popular eucharistic prayer II C of the 1977 *Book of Common Prayer* of the Episcopal Church in the U.S.A.: 'At your command all things came to be: the vast expanse of interstellar space, galaxies, suns, the planets in their courses, and this fragile earth, our island home.' Astronaut Frank Borman's reading of the opening of *Genesis* from Apollo VIII will be remembered. At another level, B. D. Spinks has argued that the Church of England's liturgical revision is precisely the product of a technocratic society, in 'Christian worship or cultural incantations?', *Studia Liturgica*

12 (1977), pp. 1–19: it is the work of 'experts'; the liturgical commissions are themselves 'classless' (there must be irony in Spinks's use of classless); the cross-denominational similarities of the new liturgies may be 'less a triumph for ecumenism and the liturgical movement than for modern mass production and egalitarianism'; the Series 3 eucharist was preceded by 'opinion polls' and 'fact-finding missions' among the consumers.

968. The Latin was quaint: benedictio machinae ad exstinguendum incendium; benedictio viae ferrae et curruum; benedictio machinae itineri aerio destinatae. . . .

969. There had been the *Kulturprotestantismus* of the late nineteenth and early twentieth centuries. But God's support was not, of course, limited to one side in the First World War:

> God heard the embattled nations sing and shout
> 'Gott strafe England!' and 'God save the King!'
> God this, God that, and God the other thing—
> 'Good God,' said God, 'I've got my work cut out.'
>
> (J. C. Squire)

See A. Wilkinson, *The Church of England and the First World War*, London: SPCK, 1978.

970. For Hitler's baptism I rely on Karl Barth, who adds Stalin and Mussolini to boot (ET *The Teaching of the Church regarding Baptism*, p. 59f). I have not checked on their confirmation: for the Orthodox baby Josef it may be presumed, nor do I imagine Catholic schoolboys Adolf and Benito to have escaped.

971. Note, more generally, Raymond Williams' socialist goal of a genuine 'common culture' (*Culture and Society 1780–1950*, London: Chatto & Windus, 1958; *The Long Revolution*, London: Chatto & Windus, 1961). This influenced the Roman Catholic writer B. Wicker, in his *Culture and Liturgy*, London: Sheed a Ward, 1963. 'In the contemporary world, particularly in the advanced industrial societies', Wicker saw the liturgy of the Catholic church as 'almost the only living cultural tradition which is still in direct contact with *all* parts of the population' (p. 46). 'To be a Catholic is necessarily to try to be, in the true and unsnobbish sense, a cultured person' (p. 47). For Wicker (p. 148), hope for the growth of a Christian society lay in the intersection between Williams's 'culture is ordinary' and the notion that 'liturgy is ordinary' (drawing on C. Davis, *Liturgy and Doctrine*, p. 9: 'It is paradox to say it of so great a mystery, but essentially the liturgy is an ordinary affair for Christians. It forms the centre of the ordinary life of the Church').

972. H. Richard Niebuhr, *Christ and Culture*, p. 155.

973. R. Bocock, *Ritual in Industrial Society: a sociological analysis of ritualism in modern England*, London: Allen & Unwin, 1974, pp. 150–2, 163–5. For the medieval history, to which I shall advert in a moment

37

see O. B. Hardison, Jr., *Christian Rite and Christian Drama ine th Middle Ages*, Baltimore: Johns Hopkins, 1965.

974. A basically 'transformist' viewpoint is represented by B. Wicker, *Culture and Liturgy*: In the liturgical assembly, the supernatural reality of the Church becomes partly visible—and, to that extent, directly encounterable by a world in need of conversion; the liturgical assembly is also the foundation for the social and cultural relations of the community of the faithful outside the liturgical assembly—and hence shapes their everyday witness to the world and affects the quality of that witness. In the reverse direction, and in a complementary movement: the liturgy, by using outside cultural forms for the Church's supernatural purpose, plays its part in 'baptizing' the outside culture and 'raising it to Christ'. The liturgical assembly is the 'paradigm', 'model', 'prototype' of a truly Christian, and human, society. Again (p. 181): 'The liturgy lies in that midway region . . . between the high generalities of the visionary and the practical problems of the ordinary man. In trying to make the liturgy live, in a city suburb or an African village, the Church is tackling the problem of mediating the ideal of a Christian society to the prosaic world which lies around it. Moreover . . . it is doing this by the medium of art. In the design of the church, in the performance of music, in the reading of biblical poetry or biography, in the representation of the drama of salvation, and in the social life which all this should generate among those participating in the action—in all these ways the Church is using art to translate vision into actuality. It is here, then, that the place for a return of art to the people can be realized and the social results of this renewal of culture be achieved. But they can only be fulfilled through the participation of all those involved, and through a deep concern with the cultural values through which the vision is to be mediated.'

975. On secularization, see, among many others, R. Gill, *Social Context of Theology*, Oxford: Mowbray, 1975; and D. Martin, *A General Theory of Secularization*, Oxford: Blackwell, 1978. Note further the discussion in chapter XII§2.

976. There is a wonderful appreciation of Mozart by Karl Barth in *Kirchliche Dogmatik* III/3 (ET pp. 297-9). As to the 'immortal Marlene Dietrich . . . I don't know where she will have a mention in the *Dogmatics*. Perhaps in eschatology, because she is such a borderline case?' (E. Busch, ET *Karl Barth*, London: SCM, 1976, p. 312). I look forward to introducing some German theologians to the delights of cricket.

977. The thesis spread from C. P. Groves, *The Planting of Christianity in Africa*, London: Lutterworth, 1948. It needs some modification in the light of I. P. Ellis, 'In defence of early North African Christianity' in M. E. Glasswell and E. W. Fasholé-Luke (eds.), *New Testament Christianity for Africa and the World*, pp. 157-65.

978. W. Pannenberg (as in note 965) holds that modern Western culture is a 'Christian culture' in rather a special sense. The fundamentally Christian idea of individual freedom has been spread throughout society;

'secularization' has freed people from clerical control; the persistence, whether admitted or unadmitted, of Christian elements has been enough to prevent a dangerous re-sacralization, which would have happened because of the necessarily 'religious' basis of society; secularization is dangerous, however, in that liberty is ambiguous and can take the shape of self-idolatrous liberal*ism*, individual*ism*.

979. The Church of England's figures are revealing. The number of infant baptisms per 1,000 live births in the total population dropped from 602 in 1956, to 531 in 1962, to 428 in 1976. Confirmations fell from 190,000 in 1960 to 94,000 in 1976 (from 34.2 to 14.7 per 1,000 population aged 12–20 years). Of a total population of 46,620,000 in 1976, 27,214,000 persons had been baptized in the Church of England, 8,993,000 had been confirmed, and the number of Easter communicants was 1,681,000.

980. In the earlier West, harvest themes were integrated into the mass by the blessing of seasonal produce towards the end of the canon; see note 198. In the Byzantine Church, harvest is linked with the christological feast of the Transfiguration (6 August): in the Mediterranean region the firstfruits of the grape harvest are presented; elsewhere other crops are brought according to geographical circumstances.

981. Pius XII instituted the feast in 1955: see *Acta apostolicae sedis* 47 (1955), p. 406. The liturgical texts are in *AAS* 48 (1956), pp. 226–37.

982. The ambiguities of the situation in society at large can be illustrated from the following paragraph by a non-Christian humanist, S. Körner: 'My own conjecture is that at least one important cause of (the churches') continuing loss of influence on the personal and social life of their members is the desperate attempt by many churchmen to prove the relevance of Christianity to modern life by receiving some of its most trivial features into Christian doctrine and praxis. Approval of shows like *Godspell*, a funeral service conducted in the language of Bingo, sloppy 'thoughts for the day' transmitted by the BBC at breakfast time, allowing the use of Christian ritual to people whose words and deeds show their contempt for the faith of their ancestors, and countless other trivializations of Christian ontology and ethics cause sadness not only to all sincere Christians, but also to many humanists who are aware of the indebtedness of our culture to the thought of Christian theologians and the deeds and sufferings of the Christian saints' (*Epworth Review*, January 1976, p. 75).

983. H. H. Rowley, 'The forms and meaning of sacrifice' in his *Worship in Ancient Israel*, pp. 111–43.

984. See F. G. Downing, *Has Christianity a Revelation?* London: SCM, 1964, for emphasis on the practical ethical component of knowledge of God.

985. For the exegesis that the two loves, of God and neighbour, are not merely juxtaposed, see K. Rahner, 'Reflections on the unity of the love of neighbour and the love of God' in ET *Theological Investigations*, vol. 6, London: DLT, 1974², pp. 231–49; resumptively, *Grundriss des Glaubens*, pp. 301f, 437f (ET *Foundations of Christian Faith*, p. 309f, 456f).

This view also characterizes the thought of the Irish moral theologian, Enda McDonagh: note particularly *Invitation and Response*, Dublin: Gill & Macmillan, 1972, chapter 4: 'The primacy of charity' (pp. 59–78; cf. p. 26).

986. *Revolutionary Priest: the complete writings and messages of Camilo Torres*, Harmondsworth: Penguin, 1973, pp. 333–6, 373–5.

987. José M. Castillo, 'Donde no hay justica no hay eucaristía' in *Estudios eclesiásticos* 52 (1977), pp. 555–90. Note also G. Gutiérrez, ET *A Theology of Liberation*, Maryknoll, N.Y.: Orbis, 1973, London: SCM, 1974, p. 137: 'The Latin American Church is sharply divided with regard to the process of liberation. Living in a capitalist society in which one class confronts another, the Church, in the measure that its presence increases, cannot escape—nor try to ignore any longer—the profound division among its members. Active participation in the liberation process is far from being a uniform position of the Latin American Christian community. The majority of the Church continues to be linked in many different ways to the established order. And what is worse, among Latin American Christians there are not only different political options within a framework of the free interplay of ideas; the polarization of these options and the extreme seriousness of the situation have even placed some Christians among the oppressed and persecuted and others among the oppressors and persecutors, some among the tortured and others among the torturers or those who condone torture. This gives rise to a serious and radical confrontation between Christians who suffer from injustice and exploitation and those who benefit from the established order. Under such circumstances, life in the contemporary Christian community becomes particularly difficult and conflictual. Participation in the eucharist, for example, as it is celebrated today, appears to many to be an action which, without an authentic Christian community underlying it, becomes an exercise in make-believe.' On pp. 262–5, Gutiérrez writes positively on the implications of the eucharist for 'the building up of a real human brotherhood'.

988. In controversial theology, *ex opere operato* became for many Protestants a swear-word associated with 'Catholic magic'. In fact, however, the point is to emphasize the 'work done' by *Christ in his life, death and resurrection and* when the sacraments are celebrated in obedience to him. For a brief modern statement of Catholic understanding of *ex opere operato*, see K. Rahner, *Grundkurs des Glaubens*, pp. 398–400 (ET *Foundations of Christian Faith*, pp. 413–15). Rahner admits that his account 'prescinds from sacraments which are administered to those who have not come of age'.

989. E. Käsemann, 'Gottesdienst im Alltag der Welt' in his *Exegetische Versuche und Besinnungen*, vol. 2, Göttingen: Vandenhoeck & Ruprecht, 1964, pp. 198–204 (ET *New Testament Questions of Today*, London: SCM, 1969, pp. 188–95).

990. In his *Principles of Christian Theology*, revised edition 1977, p. 376f, John Macquarrie recalls Voltaire's Candide, who found no temples in

the land of Eldorado but was told that their worship was constituted by their daily work. Macquarrie comments: 'But what might be true "at the end" or true for man if he were, as Voltaire and many of his contemporaries supposed, capable of leading a purely "rational" existence, is not true of man as he actually lives in world history, and to pretend that it is would be a strange kind of angelism. To try to escape or bypass historical institutions is impossible for two reasons—man's embodiment, and also his sin.'

991. A more balanced view than Käsemann's, and with sensitivity to the eschatological nuances, is presented by E. Schillebeeckx in 'Secular worship and Christian liturgy', chapter 3 of his *God the Future of Man*. Note also, more generally, his 'God, society and human salvation' in M. Caudron (ed.), *Geloof en maatschappij*, Gembloux: Duculot, 1978, pp. 87–99.

992. G. Martelet, *Résurrection, eucharistie et genèse de l'homme* (ET *The Risen Christ and the Eucharistic World*).

993. Although that account of the matter had not been preferred by St Thomas (*Summa theologiae* III. 75. 3), the council of Trent left open the annihilation account of transubstantiation, whereby the substance of the bread and wine was destroyed and replaced by the substance of Christ; and this view remains tenable today in Roman Catholicism after its long grip on Catholic thinking. Even a more modest theory of the conversion of the substance of the bread and wine into the substance of Christ appears to threaten the integrity or relative autonomy of the creature. Certainly I expect there to be no *opposition* between God and the creature in the eschatological condition (which the eucharist may properly be seen to anticipate), but I expect their distinction to be maintained. This appears to me to correspond even, or precisely, to the vision of 1 Corinthians 15:24–28, where 'God will be all in all' (for the exegesis of this passage, see my *Eucharist and Eschatology*, pp. 94f, 102–10). Galatians 2:19f cannot be interpreted to mean that Paul has *ceased to be* Paul and become 'substantially' Christ. Christians are being transformed into the *moral and spiritual likeness* of God.

994. V. Subilia, *Presenza e assenza di Dio nella coscienza moderna*, p. 110.

995. See note 12.

996. Compare also John Macquarrie, who views worship as the focal 'concentration' of life: it is 'continuous with all of life', and its 'pattern' must 'spread out into all the concerns of life' (*Principles of Christian Theology*, revised edition 1977, especially pp. 151, 490f, 502f, 512f).

997. E. McDonagh, 'Morality and prayer' in R. W. A. McKinney (ed.), *Creation, Christ and Culture* (T. F. Torrance *festschrift*), pp. 187–203. The christological pivot of McDonagh's thinking is made especially clear in chapters 4 and 5 of his *Gift and Call: Towards a Christian Theology of Morality*, Dublin: Gill & Macmillan, 1975: 'Morality and Jesus Christ' (pp. 67–95), and 'The Church, a learning community' (pp. 98–106).

998. This is the direction taken by Enda McDonagh himself in the

chapter on 'Liturgy and Christian living' in his *Invitation and Response,* pp. 96–108. That we have already seen him arguing for the reverse movement lends support to my case for an oscillatory procedure. A certain oscillation is perhaps characteristic also of J. L. Segundo, *The Sacraments Today.* It follows, too, from R. Panikkar's dictum that 'worship does not claim anything else than to be the very quintessence of human life' (*Worship and Secular Man,* pp. 59–62).

999. On baptism, see earlier pp. 127ff and 138ff.

1000. In his commentary on Luther's tract concerning 'the freedom of a Christian man', E. Jüngel makes clear how for the Reformer the believer is a person still 'under construction' (*noch im Bau*): *Zur Freiheit eines Christenmenschen: eine Erinnerung an Luthers Schrift,* Munich: Kaiser, 1978. Luther brings out the *apparent* paradox between freedom and service: see Jüngel, p. 55f.

1001. G. Ebeling, 'Die Notwendigkeit des christlichen Gottesdienstes' in *Zeitschrift für Theologie und Kirche* 67 (1970), pp. 232–49. For a previous generation of Lutherans, note A. Allwohn, *Gottesdienst und Rechtfertigungsglaube,* Göttingen: Vandenhoeck & Ruprecht, 1926. Many of our themes are interwoven—and given a strong social orientation—in the final course of lectures taught by such a deliberately 'Reformation' theologian as Helmut Gollwitzer, *Befreiung zur Solidarität: Einführung in die Evangelische Theologie,* Munich: Kaiser, 1978: Word, grace, gratitude, freedom, faith, prayer, discipleship in the struggles of this world, the tasks of justice and peace, kingdom.

1002. N. Gäumann, *Taufe und Ethik: Studien zu Römer 6.*

1003. For the *apotaxis* and *syntaxis,* see earlier p. 40 and note 183.

1004. Cyril of Jerusalem, *Myst. cat.* IV, 8; Ambrose, *de mysteriis,* 7, 34.

1005. V. Codina, 'Dimension social del bautismo' in *Estudios eclesiásticos* 52 (1977), pp. 521–54.

1006. See earlier pp. 25 and 348.

1007. See Paul Verghese (a Syrian Orthodox from India), *The Joy of Freedom: Eastern Worship and Modern Man,* pp. 66–75. Hebrew kings and high priests wore crowns (*nēzer*). Greek victors received wreaths. On the crown as an eschatological symbol, see J. Daniélou, ET *Primitive Christian Symbols,* London: Burns & Oates, 1964, pp. 14–24.

1008. A. Schmemann, *Of Water and the Spirit.*

1009. Again, A. Schmemann, *The World as Sacrament.*

1010. In *Dieu et l'utopie,* Paris: Cerf, 1977, the French Protestant theologian G. Vahanian seeks to 'articulate the transcendence of God upon utopia'—rather than upon nature or history as in traditional theologies. But it is not clear that the God of Vahanian, who was an early death-of-God theologian in the 1960s, is recognizably the God of the Christian tradition. Holding a much more traditional doctrine of God, H. Gollwitzer has argued that the individual, in his search for meaning in life, cannot be finally satisfied unless there is hope for him in a permanent society of persons which transcends death. The eternal kingdom of God is necessary if the human struggle to find meaning in life is ever to come to a final resolution. See H. Gollwitzer, *Krummes Holz, aufrechter Gang: zur Frage nach dem Sinn des Lebens.*

1011. Paul also sees the civil authorities as instruments of divine *retribution* upon criminals. But since my concern here is with the social function of civil authorities rather than with the relations between the individual and God, I need not tackle this difficult notion.

1012. In Reformation theology, there are three 'uses of the law' (though the third is more Calvinist than Lutheran). The first use, best called the political, is to regulate society in the face of human sin. The second, usually called theological, is to bring people to conviction of their sin in order that, repentant, they may accept the gospel of salvation. The third use, which may be called didactic, is for ethical guidance within the Christian life. Little is available in English on this matter of the three uses of the Law, but see A. R. Vidler, *Christ's Strange Work*, London: Longmans, 1944, and London: SCM, 1962². There is a fine study by G. Siegwalt, *La loi, chemin du salut*, Neuchâtel: Delachaux & Niestlé, 1971. For the Reformation origins, see briefly G. Ebeling, 'Zur Lehre vom triplex usus legis in der reformatorischen Theologie' in his *Wort und Glaube*, vol. 1, Tübingen; Mohr, 1960, pp. 50–68 (ET *Word and Faith*, London: SCM, 1963, pp. 62–78).

1013. K. Barth, *Christengemeinde und Bürgergemeinde*, Munich: Kaiser, 1946 (ET in *Against the Stream*, New York: Philosophical Library, 1954). W. Pannenberg (as in note 965) sees it as the Church's nature and function to be the effective-symbolic representative of the kingdom of God—not to do the political job but to embody the values of the divine kingdom before the world in 'sacramental' actions and declarations; he is sensitive to the doxological and liturgical dimensions of this service—and also to the provisionality of all human political achievement (chapter 2).

1014. The February 1974 issue of *Concilium* is devoted to 'Politics and liturgy' and contains a number of generally 'liberationist' articles: H. A. P. Schmidt, 'Lines of political action in contemporary liturgy'; H. B. Meyer, 'The social significance of the liturgy'; J. Navone, 'Evil and its symbols'; J. Llopis, 'The message of liberation in the liturgy'; J. Moltmann, 'The liberating feast'; D. Power, 'The song of the Lord in an alien land'; J. Gelineau, 'Celebrating the paschal liberation'; H. A. P. Schmidt, 'Political symbols, poems and songs'. See also the pamphlet by T. Cullinan, *Eucharist and Politics*, published by the Catholic Institute for International Relations, London, n.d. A forthcoming book known to me only from the publisher's blurb is Tissa Balasuriya (a Roman Catholic priest from Sri Lanka), *The Eucharist and Human Liberation*, Maryknoll, N.Y.: Orbis, and London: SCM, 1979.

1015. J. Jeremias, *Die Abendmahlsworte Jesu*³, p. 42f (ET p. 48f).

1016. G. Wainwright, *Eucharist and Eschatology*, pp. 22–4.

1017. W. Pannenberg, *Die Bestimmung des Menschen: Menschsein, Erwählung und Geschichte* (ET *Human Nature, Election and History*), chapter 1.

1018. J. H. Cone, 'Sanctification, liberation, and black worship' in *Theology Today* 35 (1978–9), pp. 139–52. Theological interpretation of black American worship materials figures prominently in two of Cone's books: *The Spirituals and the Blues*, New York: Seabury, 1972, and *God of the Oppressed*, New York: Seabury, 1975, and London: SPCK, 1977.

1019. Quoted by Cone from Langston Hughes and Arna Bontemps, *Book of Negro Folklore*, New York: Dodd, Mead, & Co., 1958, p. 256f.

1020. See J. M. R. Tillard, L'eucharistie et la fraternité' in *Nouvelle revue théologique* 91 (1969), pp. 113–35. The theme is prominent in N. Lash, *His Presence in the World: a study in eucharistic worship and theology.*

1021. The themes of grace and gratitude are closely interwoven in B. Häring, *The Sacraments in a Secular Age.*

1022. In part IV/4 of his *Church Dogmatics*, Karl Barth was intending to present 'Christian ethics' in terms of obedient and faithful response to God's work and word—and to do this by a treatment of baptism, the Lord's prayer, and the Lord's supper: E. Busch, ET *Karl Barth*, London: SCM, 1976, p. 443f. Note also A. C. Cochrane, *Eating and Drinking with Jesus: an ethical and biblical enquiry*, Philadelphia: Westminster, 1974.

1023. Quoted from the Roman Pontifical of 1968, *de ordinatione presbyterorum*, 14, where the resurrection references are new additions. The striking *imitamini quod tractatis*, 'imitate what you handle', dates from older versions of the ordinal, back to Durandus of Mende in the thirteenth century.

1024. This point is made, and samples are given, by both B. Häring, *The Sacraments in a Secular Age*, p. 13, and G. Martelet, ET *The Risen Christ and the Eucharistic World*, pp. 190–4. Because the translations are inadequate to the rich density of the Latin, I give also the originals: *Deus, qui ecclesiam tuam novo semper foetu multiplicas: concede famulis tuis, ut sacramentum vivendo teneant, quod fide perceperunt* (collect of Easter Tuesday); *Concede, quaesumus omnipotens Deus: ut paschalis perceptio sacramenti, continua in nostris mentibus perseveret* (post-communion of Easter Tuesday); *Omnipotens sempiterne Deus, qui paschale sacramentum in reconciliationis humanae foedere contulisti: da mentibus nostris, ut quod professione celebramus, imitemur effectu* (collect of Easter Friday); *Praesta, quaesumus omnipotens Deus: ut qui paschalia festa peregimus, haec, te largiente, moribus et vita teneamus* (collect of Sunday after Easter, *in albis*). These are given in the wording and distribution found in the missal of Pius V. The material is redistributed in the missal of Paul VI.

1025. By a feed-back process, the personal conversion signified by baptism is proposed by some patristic writers as a model for understanding the transformation of the eucharistic bread and wine: Ambrose, Augustine and a remarkable passage from an Easter sermon of Faustus of Riez (PL 67, 1053) are quoted by G. Martelet, ET *The Risen Christ and the Eucharistic World*, p. 114f. See also earlier note 993.

1026. J. F. White, *The Worldliness of Worship*, New York: OUP, 1967, pp. 119–26.

1027. Church of England, Series 3 eucharist. On the stages of liturgical revision in the Church of England, see earlier note 235.

1028. F. H. Russell, *The Just War in the Middle Ages*, Cambridge: University Press, 1975.

1029. I use with positive intent the epithet that was used rather ironically by S. G. F. Brandon, *Jesus and the Zealots*, Manchester: University Press, 1967, chapter 6. According to Brandon, 'the pacific Christ' was an invention of the primitive Church seeking to whitewash Jesus and curry favour with the Roman authorities. I remain unpersuaded by recent attempts to show Jesus' sympathy with the military policy of the Zealots. See, for a decisive rebuttal, O. Cullmann's book, *Jesus und die Revolutionären seiner Zeit*, Tübingen: Mohr, 1970 (ET *Jesus and the Revolutionaries*, New York: Harper & Row, 1970).

1030. For Charlemagne, see J. D. Crichton, in C. Jones, G. Wainwright and E. Yarnold (eds.), *The Study of Liturgy*, p. 375.

1031. Charlemagne's attempts to impose liturgical uniformity met with resistance even on the part of people who supported the political unity of the empire: see G. Kretschmar, 'Die Geschichte des Taufgottesdienstes in der alten Kirche' in K. F. Müller and W. Blankenburg (eds.), *Leiturgia*, vol. 5, in particular p. 327f.

1032. St Thomas Becket put his allegiance to the king and all claims of the State under the qualification 'saving the honour of God' (D. H. Tripp, in C. Jones, G. Wainwright and E. Yarnold, eds., *The Study of Liturgy*, p. 530).

1033. 'Les autorités romaines reprochaient (au christianisme) de fomenter, en fait, un utopisme politique qui contrecarrait et sapait l'ordre des choses, le *statu quo*, parce qu'il se fondait sur une conception eschatologique de l'homme': G. Vahanian, *Dieu et l'utopie*, p. 137.

1034. Notice R. F. Buxton's information and comment concerning the canons intended to accompany the Scottish episcopal Prayer Book of 1637: 'Any of the consecrated elements remaining at the end of the celebration are to be distributed to poor communicants for them to eat and drink before they leave the church, presumably for their physical nourishment—an interesting combination of sacramental observance and charitable provision for the poor' (*Eucharist and Institution Narrative*, p. 105f.

1035. Meeting in 1976. Papers and conclusions in K. Lehmann (ed.), *Theologie der Befreiung*, Einsiedeln: Johannes, 1977.

1036. See G. Martelet, ET *The Risen Christ and the Eucharistic World*, notably the last chapter: 'The eucharist and the genesis of man' (pp. 180–96), which presupposes the earlier chapter on 'Eucharistic symbolism and man's condition' (pp. 30–59).

1037. G. Müller-Fahrenholz, *Heilsgeschichte zwischen Ideologie und Prophetie*, Freiburg: Herder, 1974, in particular pp. 221–33. The following paragraph is not dependent on Müller-Fahrenholz.

1038. A. Bloom, *Living Prayer*, London: DLT, 1966, p. 23.

1039. Origen, *contra Celsum*, VIII, 73.

1040. R. H. Bainton, *Christian Attitudes toward War and Peace: a historical survey and critical re-evaluation*, New York: Abingdon, 1960, and London: Hodder, 1961.

1041. A. Hastings fails to make this distinction in 'The moral choice of violent revolution', in his *Mission and Ministry*: Sheed & Ward, 1971, pp. 59–68.

1042. The words *leitourgos, hierourgein* and *prosphora* are used. In *Der urchristliche Gottesdienst*, pp. 34–7, 52–4, F. Hahn shows that cultic vocabulary is characteristically used in the New Testament Church in connexion with evangelism and charitable service. It is in this perspective that liturgy, ethics and the Church's apostolic task are brought closely together by J. G. Davies, *Worship and Mission*.

1043. The whole context, from 2 Timothy 3:10 to 4:8, presents the ministry of evangelism in broadly sacrificial terms. Note also Philippians 2:25–30: 'I have thought it necessary to send you Epaphroditus my brother and fellow worker and fellow soldier, and your messenger and minister to my need. . . . He nearly died for the work of Christ, risking his life to complete your service (*leitourgia*) to me.'

1044. The word is *homologia*.

1045. On the high theological significance of the aid to Jerusalem, see K. P. Nickle, *The Collection*, London: SCM, 1966. Another case of liturgical language being used in this connexion is Romans 15:26f (*koinōnia, leitourgein*).

1046. Despite note 908!

1047. H. Butterfield, *Christianity and History*, London: Bell, 1949, chapter 7. Butterfield's arguments provide a framework in which to give some answer to the kind of indictment made against historical Christianity in, say, J. Kahl, *Das Elend des Christentums*, Hamburg: Rowohlt, 1968 (ET *The Misery of Christianity*, Harmondsworth: Penguin, 1971). Kahl's charges serve to remind us how much 'world' remains within the Church, and how the history of Christianity still stands under the eschatological proviso.

1048. I give the story as I heard it in Dr Peter Stephens' address to the devotional session of the Methodist Conference, 1978: *Christians Conferring*, London: Epworth, 1978.

1049. On 'open systems', see E. Busch, ET *Karl Barth*, p. 283f; J. Moltmann, in R. W. A. McKinney (ed.), *Creation, Christ and Culture*, p. 124; T. F. Torrance, *Theological Science*, p. 240 and elsewhere. The notion chimes with the very broad movement of thought labelled 'structuralism': see J. Piaget, *Le structuralisme*, Paris: Presses universitaires de France, 1968 (ET *Structuralism*, London: Routledge & Kegan Paul, 1971).

1050. While I believe Christianity as a whole to have sorted out challenges well enough to retain a consistent identity of its own, I recognize that some individuals have been led away from the faith by outside critiques and alternative world-views.

1051. DS 3016: 'Ac ratio quidem, fide illustrata, cum sedulo, pie et sobrie quaerit, aliquam Deo dante mysteriorum intelligentiam eamque fructuosissimam assequitur tum ex eorum, quae naturaliter cognoscit, analogia, tum *e mysteriorum ipsorum nexu inter se et cum fine hominis ultimo.*' In his treatise on God as one and as triune, J. Auer aptly begins his opening section on 'the living God as the goal of the doctrine of God, *der lebendige Gott, das Ziel der Gotteslehre*' with the statement: 'The God whom our theological reflexion seeks is the God to whom our prayer, our petition and thanks and praise, our worship is addressed.' (*Gott der Eine und Dreieine*, vol. 2 of a nine-volume *Kleine Katholische Dogmatik*, eds. J. Auer and J. Ratzinger, Regensburg: Pustet, 1978, p. 21f.)

1052. T. F. Torrance, *God and Rationality*, p. 204f. Note also the important seventh chapter on 'the epistemological relevance of the Spirit': 'Theological statements operate, then, with what we may call *open concepts*—concepts which, to be sure, must be closed on our side, for we have to formulate them as carefully and exactly as we can, but which on God's side are open (and therefore apposite) to the infinite objectivity and inexhaustible reality of the divine Being. That is to say, the kind of conceptuality with which we operate in theology is one in which our acts of cognition are formed from beyond them by the reality disclosed so that the content of what is revealed constantly bursts through the forms we bring to it in order to grasp it. This can happen only under the power of the Spirit, as He presses upon us from the side of the divine Being. The Spirit is thus the act of God upon us which keeps our concepts or cognitive forms open, so that our thoughts and speech are stretched out beyond themselves toward the inexhaustible nature of the divine Being. Apart from this impact of the Spirit upon us, the forms of our thought and speech become quite obscure and indeed may even become a form of obstruction to the divine revelation or a means of suppressing the truth through the transmutation of knowledge into our own constructs' (p. 186f). It is worship which keeps the epistemological process personal.

1053. M. Polanyi, *Personal Knowledge*, London: Routledge & Kegan Paul, 1958, pp. 279–86.

1054. See earlier, p. 36 and note 80.

1055. See my *Eucharist and Eschatology*.

1056. W. Kasper, *Dogma unter dem Wort Gottes*, pp. 65–84, and 'Kirche und Theologie unter dem Gesetz der Geschichte' in *Glaube im Wandel der Geschichte*, pp. 39–62. Sympathetic presentation and critique in H. Döring, *Abwesenheit Gottes*, pp. 420–8.

1057. The watershed was H. Küng's *Unfehlbar?*, Mainz: Benziger, 1970 (ET *Infallible?*, London: Collins, 1971). 'Indefectible' could also be given dynamic associations over against the static flavour that had attached to 'infallible'. It is not so much that the one word is intrinsically better than the other: rather a terminological change was needed to mark an attempted reinterpretation and renewal of a concept.

1058. 'Covenant' is a key word of biblical theology in this connexion.

Note also the association of fidelity and truth in the *'āman* and *'emeth* vocabulary.

1059. H. C. Schmidt-Lauber, *Die Eucharistie als Entfaltung der verba testamenti: eine formgeschichtlich-systematische Einführung in die Probleme des lutherischen Gottesdienstes und seiner Liturgie*, Kassel: Stauda, 1957.

1060. For Thomas Aquinas: the antiphon of the *Magnificat* on Corpus Christi. For Trent: DS 1638. The idea of pledge is frequent in the early sacramentaries (see my *Eucharist and Eschatology*, p. 53), and also in the Wesleys (*ibid.*, p. 56f).

1061. See earlier chapter III, especially §§ 4-6.

1062. Confession at morning and evening prayer.

1063. The whole prayer reads: 'Lord Jesus Christ, you said to your apostles: I leave you peace, my peace I give you. Look not on our sins, but on the faith of your Church, and grant us the peace and unity of your kingdom where you live for ever and ever' (ICEL text).

1064. Acts 14:15–17 suggests that *à la rigueur* God can do without human witnesses, the natural creation sufficing (cf. Romans 1:18ff). But he evidently values those men and women who do bear him witness (Hebrews 12:1, 23).

1065. Doctrines of predestination extrapolate from historical 'result' to protological purpose. This is acceptable as a movement of thanksgiving for salvation: 'the God who is saving us must always have intended our salvation'. But it is quite a different matter to make God's fore-ordaining directly responsible for human loss. We are here involved in delicate questions of divine grace and human freedom (see earlier, for example, p. 83f and notes 208–11), and of time and eternity (see the whole of the last section of this conclusion). The crucial point is that God's sovereignty be interpreted kenotically: 'he reigned from a tree' (see p. 208).

1066. For 'my' gospel, see Rom. 2:16; 16:25; 2 Tim. 2:8 (cf. Gal. 1:6–24).

1067. This eschatological reserve is the principal theological ground of the recent moderation in Roman Catholic claims; see H. Küng, *Unfehlbar?* (as in note 1057); D. L. Gelpi, *Charism and Sacrament*, pp. 219–24. P. Chirico, *Infallibility* (as in note 1078).

1068. Note even the declaration of the Congregation for the Doctrine of Faith, *Mysterium Ecclesiae*, of 5 July 1973 against an unnamed Hans Küng.

1069. See note 588.

1070. For the importance of ritual pilgrimage, see J. Sumption, *Pilgrimage: an image of medieval religion*, London: Faber, 1975, and V. Turner and E. Turner, *Image and Pilgrimage in Christian Culture*, New York: Columbia University Press, and Oxford: Blackwell, 1978.

1071. The 'Toronto Statement' of the WCC central committee was entitled *The Church, the Churches and the World Council of Churches: The Ecclesiological Significance of the World Council of Churches.* See also W. A.

Visser 't Hooft, 'The Super-Church and the Ecumenical Movement' in *Ecumenical Review* 10 (1957–8), pp. 365–85.

1072. See already *The Fourth World Conference on Faith and Order: Montreal 1963*, London: SCM, 1963, p. 48f; and thereto W. A. Visser 't Hooft, 'Die Bedeutung der Mitgliedschaft im Oekumenischen Rat der Kirchen' in *Oekumenische Rundschau* 12 (1963), pp. 229–36, and H. H. Wolf, 'Oekumenische Erneuerung im Verständnis des Oekumenischen Rates und der römisch-katholischen Kirche' in *Materialdienst des Konfessions-kundlichen Instituts* 15 (1964), pp. 61–5. Note further the development of the theme of conciliar fellowship at the Salamanca consultation of Faith and Order in 1973: *Ecumenical Review* 26 (1974), pp. 291–302.

1073. See A. Dulles, 'The Church, the Churches, and the Catholic Church' in *Theological Studies* 33 (1972), pp. 199–234, and Dulles' two books, *Models of the Church*, Garden City, N.Y.: Doubleday, 1974, Dublin: Gill and Macmillan, 1976, and *The Resilient Church*, Garden City, N.Y.: Doubleday, 1977, Dublin: Gill and Macmillan, 1978.

1074. The 1948 basis was: 'The WCC is a fellowship of Churches which accept our Lord Jesus Christ as God and Saviour.' In 1961 the basis became: 'The WCC is a fellowship of Churches which confess the Lord Jesus Christ as God and Saviour according to the Scriptures and therefore seek to fulfil together their common calling to the glory of the one God, Father, Son and Holy Spirit.' See W. J. Hollenweger in *Expository Times* 86 (1974–75), pp. 324–8.

1075. *Breaking Barriers: Nairobi 1975*, London: SPCK, 1976, p. 317f.

1076. In addition to the studies mentioned in note 776, see A. D. Falconer, 'Contemporary attitudes to the papacy: Protestant and Orthodox perspectives' in *The Furrow* 27 (1976), pp. 3–19.

1077. See pp. 289–92.

1078. In P. Chirico's *Infallibility: The Crossroads of Doctrine*, Kansas City: Sheed, Andrews and McMeel, 1977, the notion of the risen Christ's 'presence in power' is, I think, vital to the possibility of infallibility in matters of faith. The author is also aware that christologies which reduce Christ to the exemplary and symbolic stand in contradiction to 'the two thousand year old faith experience of the Roman Catholic Tradition'. It is all the more surprising that he does not draw more directly on the Church's liturgical experience in his own argumentation for infallibility in matters of faith. Chirico's paragraph on the eucharist (pp. 91–7) is concerned in a more general way with the existence, graspability and expressibility of universal meanings, which seems to me, in terms of the author's thesis, a necessary early, but not a finally sufficient, condition of ecclesial infallibility in matters of faith.

1079. M. Polanyi, as in note 1053.

1080. The Augsburg Confession declares that the Holy Spirit produces faith by the word and the sacraments 'where and when God pleases', *ubi et quando visum et Deo* (article V). It would be unthinkable to attribute arbitrariness or even fickleness to God. I suggest that the proper context of understanding is the depths of God's personality and his resourcefulness in seeking to achieve his purpose through the inclusion and enhancement of human freedom and integrity rather than by their suppression.

1081. N. Lash, 'Credal affirmation as a criterion of Church membership' (as in note 446), p. 70.

1082. I will not apologize for the rather detailed nature of the discussion. With the apostle I hold that 'if in this life only we have hope in Christ, we are of all men most miserable' (1 Cor. 15–19, AV). I therefore share the opposition of S. W. Sykes, in the article mentioned in the next note, to any trend to play down the importance of 'eternal life'.

1083. On Christian funeral rites, see B. Bürki, *Im Herrn entschlafen: eine historisch pastoraltheologische Studie zur Liturgie des Sterbens und des Begräbnisses*, Heidelberg: Quelle & Meyer, 1969; and G. Rowell, *The Liturgy of Christian Burial*, London: SPCK, 1977. It is from those two books that I draw many examples of prayers and ceremony in the following discussion. On the theological side, see L. Boros, *Mysterium mortis: der Mensch in der letzten Entscheidung*, Olten: Walter, 1962 (ET *The Moment of Truth: Mysterium Mortis*, London: Search Press, 1965); J. H. Hick, *Death and Eternal Life*, London: Collins, 1976; E. Jüngel, *Tod*, Stuttgart: Kreuz, 1971 (ET *Death: the riddle and the mystery*, Edinburgh: St Andrew, 1975); J. Pelikan, *The Shape of Death: Life, Death, and Immortality in the Early Fathers*, New York: Abingdon, 1961, and London: Macmillan, 1962; K. Rahner, *Zur Theologie des Todes*, Freiberg: Herder, 1959² (ET *On the Theology of Death*, London: Burns & Oates, 1965²); S. W. Sykes, 'Life after death: the Christian doctrine of heaven' in R. W. A. McKinney (ed.), *Creation, Christ and Culture*, pp. 250–71. Note also the inter-disciplinary study edited by G. Cope, *Dying, Death and Disposal*, London: SPCK, 1970, and in particular the fine chapter by W. J. Grisbrooke, 'Towards a liturgy of committal' (pp. 57–84). In the philosophically oriented debate between N. Lash and B. Hebblethwaite in *The Heythrop Journal* 19 (1978) and 20 (1979), my money is on Hebblethwaite: N. Lash, 'Eternal life: life "after" death?' (July 1978, pp. 271–84); B. Hebblethwaite, 'Time and eternity and life "after" death' (January 1979, pp. 57–62); Lash (January 1979, p. 63f); Hebblethwaite (April 1979). See further, note 1129.

1084. It is no accident that these phrases come from the *confession of sin* in the communion service of the English *Book of Common Prayer*. The Reformers inherited the medieval Western use of death and burial as an opportunity to call the living to amendment of life. Here, then, is a feedback of the burial liturgy upon the communion office.

1085. Again the English communion office (see previous note), taking up 1 Timothy 1:15 and John 3:16.

1086. The first three phrases are borrowed from the medieval sequence, *Media vita*.

1087. Quoted from G. Rowell, *The Liturgy of Christian Burial*, p. 54f.

1088. Favourite texts in *Job* are 1:21; 14:1; 19:25–27. In the *Rituale romanum* of 1614, lessons from *Job* figure prominently in the office of the dead.

1089. See the paragraphs on the scope of the divine kingdom and human salvation in the last section of this conclusion.

1090. I am not here claiming to make a direct interpretation of Revelation 2:11; 20:6; 21:8.

1091. D. Rutledge, *Cosmic Theology: The Ecclesiastical Hierarchy of Pseudo-Denys*, London: Routledge & Kegan Paul, 1964, p. 191 (PG 3, 587).

1092. *The Book of Discipline*, 1560, quoted by G. Rowell, *The Liturgy of Christian Burial*, p. 82.

1093. Instances are quoted by G. Rowell, *The Liturgy of Christian Burial*, p. 64f.

1094. Much attention has been devoted to bereavement in recent pastoral theology: note C. M. Parkes, *Bereavement: Studies of Grief in Adult Life*, London: Tavistock, 1972; Y. Spiegel, *Der Prozess des Trauerns*, Munich: Kaiser, 1973 (ET *The Grief Process*, London: SCM, 1978); D. K. Switzer, *The Dynamics of Grief*, Nashville: Abingdon, 1970. The early Coptic burial prayer, already quoted on page 445, includes the following petitions before the final doxology: 'Them that are troubled comfort. Them that survive console. Them that are orphaned maintain. And them that are gathered together and share in their trouble—have mercy upon them and bless them. Give unto them an heavenly reward in the world to come and for ever and ever.' In the article mentioned in note 1083, W. J. Grisbrooke writes: 'In order to reflect adequately the paschal character of Christian death, the liturgy of committal must be at once triumphant and penitential, confident and suppliant, exultant and restrained. And this is not only theologically necessary: it accords also with both the spiritual and the psychological needs of the bereaved' (p. 61). I shall come later to an explicit discussion of 'the paschal character of Christian death'.

1095. See J. Pelikan, *The Shape of Death* (as in note 1083).

1096. More will be said in a moment about prayers for the immediate well-being of the departed soul.

1097. Quoted by G. Rowell, *The Liturgy of Christian Burial*, p. 39.

1098. See O. Cullmann, *Immortality of the Soul or Resurrection of the Dead? The Witness of the New Testament*, London: Epworth, 1958.

1099. For example, psalms 16, 23, 37, 63, 73.

1100. Masses 'for the dead' have their roots as far back as Tertullian's *Exhortation to Chastity*, 11 (PL 2, 926) and *On monogamy*, 10 (PL 2, 942). A fairly wide range of meaning may attach to the preposition 'for': see later p. 461 and note 1140.

1101. Rowell quotes a Lutheran text of 1526 forbidding mention of purgatory, 'for it is only by faith that God purges and cleanses his church from sin' (*The Liturgy of Christian Burial*, p. 74f). Not all notions of purification and progress after death are excluded by this principle. For recent

Roman Catholic reflexion on eschatological questions, see J. Ratzinger, *Eschatologie: Tod und ewiges Leben*, Regensburg: Pustet, 1977 (vol. 9 of the *Kleine Katholische Dogmatik* referred to in note 1051).

1102. Bucer had written: 'I know that this custom of praying for the pious dead is most ancient but, as it is our duty to prefer the divine to all human authority and since scripture nowhere teaches us by word or example to pray for the departed ... I wish that this commendation of the dead and prayer for them be omitted.' In the Swedish service of 1529, the Lutheran Olavus Petri hedged his bets by building conditions into the prayers: 'if this our departed brother ... be in such an estate that our prayers can avail for his good', and 'if the estate of the departed permits'. See G. Rowell, *The Liturgy of Christian Burial*, pp. 87 and 78f.

1103. J. H. Hick, *Christianity at the Centre*, 1968 edition, pp. 107–18 (cf. pp. 47–9). In Hick's major work on *Death and Eternal Life*, London: Collins, 1976, the perspectives have changed and Hick inclines to a view of the ultimate estate as 'probably not embodied and probably not in time', but also 'beyond the existence of separate egos' (p. 463f).

1104. An example of conservative biblical exegesis is A. M. Ramsey, *The Resurrection of Christ*, London: Collins, 1961²; and an example of liberal exegesis is W. Marxsen, *Die Auferstehung Jesu von Nazareth*, Gütersloh: Mohn, 1968 (ET *The Resurrection of Jesus of Nazareth*, London: SCM, 1970). Various moderate positions are found, for instance, in R. E. Brown, *The Virginal Conception and Bodily Resurrection of Jesus*, New York: Paulist Press, and London: Chapman, 1973; C. F. Evans, *Resurrection and the New Testament*, London: SCM, 1970; R. H. Fuller, *The Formation of the Resurrection Narratives*, New York: Macmillan, 1971, and London: SPCK, 1972. In this delicate matter, exegesis and hermeneutics are always closely intertwined. A sensitive and explicitly hermeneutical study is provided by P. Selby, *Look for the Living: The Corporate Nature of Resurrection Faith*, London: SCM, 1976. W. Künneth's much reprinted dogmatic study, *Theologie der Auferstehung*, Munich and Hamburg: Siebenstern, 1968⁵, remains staunchly conservative.

1105. On the expected general resurrection as the interpretative framework for the resurrection of Jesus, see W. Pannenberg, *Grundzüge der Christologie*, chapter 3 (ET *Jesus: God and Man*, especially pp. 74–88). As with other current expectations, the fulfilment brought by Jesus could involve transmutation in this case also.

1106. Hildebert of Lavardin, *serm.* 121, PL 171, 896. Durandus of Mende, *Rationale divinorum officiorum* VII. 35, 38.

1107. J. Calvin, *Inst.* III, 25, 5–8

1108. The notions of paradox and strange continuity are deliberately picked up from VI§7. Our present theme is of a piece with the divine *kenosis* in incarnation and crucifixion which was treated in that earlier section.

1109. B. Bürki, *Im Herrn entschlafen*, pp. 7–27.

1110. See G. Rowell, *The Liturgy of Christian Burial*, p. 25.

1111. D. Rutledge, *Cosmic Theology: The Ecclesiastical Hierarchy of Pseudo-Denys*, p. 199: 'After the kiss of peace the bishop anoints the body of the dead with holy oil. You will remember that in the ceremony of birth from God it is, before baptism, by anointing with holy oil that the initiate is permitted for the first time to participate in the sacred symbols, immediately after he has been stripped of his former dress. Now, on the contrary, it is at the end of all that holy oil is poured out over the dead. Then the sacred anointing summoned the initiate to a holy warfare; now the pouring of the oil signifies that in this combat he has fought to victory' (PG 3, 565).

1112. Ignatius, *ad Eph.* 20, 2.

1113. For Cyril of Alexandria, see PG 72, 912 and PG 73, 581.

1114. On the resurrection wait, see p. 461f.

1115. For the range of imagery in this connexion, see my *Eucharist and Eschatology*, pp. 110–14.

1116. On the eucharist as *viaticum*, see B. Bürki, *Im Herrn entschlafen*, pp. 69–86.

1117. For 'the Master's Joy' as meaning a feast in Matthew 25:21, 23, see J. Jeremias, *Die Abendmahlsworte Jesu*[3], p. 225 (ET p. 234).

1118. B. Bürki, *Im Herrn entschlafen*, pp. 27–47. Notice also the WCC Faith and Order text on 'Witness unto death' (from the Bangalore meeting 1978, in Faith and Order paper no. 92). Similarities between the Faith and Order text and my own are due to self-plagiarism.

1119. *Martyrdom of Polycarp*, 14. The fuller form of the doxology is inauthentic: see J. A. Jungmann, *Die Stellung Christi im liturgischen Gebet*, p. 127f. For the issues involved, see earlier pp. 96–98.

1120. The letter recounting the martyrdoms at Lyons and Vienne in A.D. 177 is found in Eusebius, *Church History*, V, 1, 3ff.

1121. For the *baptisma sanguinis*, see B. Bürki, *Im Herrn entschlafen*, pp. 39–41.

1122. For detailed references to the *acta martyrum* containing the three episodes about to be mentioned, see my *Eucharist and Eschatology*, p. 124f.

1123. Cyril of Jerusalem (*Myst. cat.* IV, 1 and 3) and Cyril of Alexandria (*In Jo. evang.* XI, 11, PG 74, 560) both say that eucharistic communion makes Christians 'concorporal', *sussōmoi*, with Christ. Augustine says that communicants 'are what they receive', namely the body of Christ (*serm.* 57, 7, PL 38, 389).

1124. With slight variants the antiphon runs: 'In paradisum deducant te angeli, in tuo adventu suscipiant te martyres, et perducant te in civitatem sanctam Hierusalem' (see G. Rowell, *The Liturgy of Christian Burial*, pp. 17, 61, 72, 109).

1125. I quote the tag in its familiar form. The Latin is slightly different. 'Plures efficimur quotiens metimur a vobis; semen est sanguis Christianorum': 'The oftener we are mown down by you, the larger grow our numbers; the blood of Christians is a seed' (Tertullian, *Apology*, 50, PL 1, 535).

38

1126. For the last time I will recall E. Jüngel's description of love—and God—as 'Einheit von Tod und Leben zugunsten des Lebens' (see earlier note 158 and pp. 210 and 273.

1127. An examination of the teaching of Jesus according to the synoptic gospels is found in W. Strawson, *Jesus and the Future Life* (Fernley-Hartley lecture 1959), London: Epworth, 1970².

1128. See my pages on 'in remembrance of him till he come' in *Eucharist and Eschatology*, pp. 60–93.

1129. B. Hebblethwaite (as in note 1083), p. 61f. Hebblethwaite continues: 'Moreover, if we take the doctrine of the Incarnation seriously, we are to suppose that God, in taking humanity into himself, has taken time into himself as well. Certainly Christ's risen humanity is not to be construed simply as a prolongation of his earthly life. His risen life at the right hand of the Father is certainly transformed, no longer corruptible and mortal. But in some sense we must surely say that the life of the risen Christ whom we encounter in prayer and in the eucharist comes "after" the short span of his life on earth. Nor can this just be an accommodation to the fact that *we* now live at a time long after the early years of the first century A.D. For if God takes his creation seriously, as we know from the Incarnation that he does, its temporal structure must matter to him. Surely for God too, commerce with us through the risen Christ comes "after" his commerce with Peter and John through Jesus of Nazareth. If then there is a sense which "before" and "after" must continue to be predicated of the life of the risen Christ, we must go on to say that even from God's point of view "before" and "after" must have real application to our own lives. We too are to be raised with Christ. Much may be said of the qualities of eternal life in which we are to participate by adoption into Christ's body during our earthly pilgrimage. But we cannot ignore the promise of our ultimate resurrection, transformation, completion, consummation—call it what you will. . . . If Christ is risen, the dead *shall* live; and however marked the break in temporal continuity, however radical the transformation, we cannot give up the idea that in some sense the consummation of all things, in which *all* men are to participate, comes *after* our earthly life and *after* the span of human history.'

1130. Composite quotation from J. J von Allmen, *Prophétisme sacramentel*, chapter 1 (pp. 9–53).

1131. O. Clément, 'Le dimanche et le Jour éternel' in *Verbum caro* no. 79 (1966), in particular p. 112.

1132. See J. Macquarrie, *Principles of Christian Theology*, 1977 edition, pp. 359, 365f.

1133. 'May Christ dwell in your hearts through faith, that you, being rooted and grounded in love, may have power to comprehend with all the saints what is the breadth and length and height and depth, and to know the love of Christ which surpasses knowledge, that you may be filled with all the fulness of God' (Eph. 3:17–19).

1134. MHB 77, though the sixth and the eighth verses are there omitted;

see R. N. Flew, *The Hymns of Charles Wesley*, pp. 21–4. MHB 75 ('Father, whose everlasting love') is Charles Wesley's war-cry against 'limited atonement': 'Lift up the standard of Thy Cross,/And all shall own Thou diedst for all.' See Flew, *op. cit.*, pp. 48–51; J. E. Rattenbury, *The Evangelical Doctrines of Charles Wesley's Hymns*, pp. 117–36.

1135. For examples see A. Hänggi and I. Pahl (eds), *Prex Eucharistica*, pp. 279, 283, 287, 290, 301f.

1136. Even the most ferocious of doctrinal anathemas, as in 'The Office of Orthodoxy' (see note 436), may be seen as admonitory rather than finally condemnatory: 'Following the sacred scriptures, and holding the traditions of the primitive Church, we reject and anathematize all those who oppose His truth, if while awaiting their conversion and repentance, they refuse to repent to the Lord.'

1137. S. W. Sykes (as in note 1083), p. 271. He refers to W. A. White-house, 'New heavens and a new earth?' in G. B. Caird and others, *The Christian Hope*, London: SPCK, 1970, pp. 83–101. See also J. J. von Allmen, *Prophétisme sacramental*, pp. 44–51.

1138. For J. Wesley's teaching on this matter, see R. N. Flew, *The Idea of Perfection in Christian Theology*, London: OUP, 1934, pp. 313–41; H. Lindström, *Wesley and Sanctification*, London: Epworth, 1950; C. W. Williams, *John Wesley's Theology Today*, Nashville: Abingdon, and London: Epworth, 1960, pp. 167–90. Also J. E. Rattenbury, *The Evangelical Doctrines of Charles Wesley's Hymns*, pp. 298–307.

1139. J. M. Hussey and P. A. McNulty, *Nicholas Cabasilas: a Commentary on the Divine Liturgy*, pp. 108–14 (chapter 49 of the commentary).

1140. See J. A. Jungmann, *Die Stellung Christi im liturgischen Gebet*, pp. 234–8.

1141. It is scarcely necessary to say that this reciprocal relation between God and humanity renders inadequate the notion of a (merely) 'objective immortality' whereby we should be preserved in God's memory without the subjective experience of salvation on our part. The 'objective immortality' view is found in some parts of modern Protestantism. It may represent a concession to the 'plausibility structures' of contemporary Western Culture (see note 447), but its apologetic value is not obvious. From our angle, its fundamental fault is that it runs counter to the language of vision, knowledge, praise and feasting by which the scriptures and the liturgies strive to express a definitive human salvation which is already anticipated in earthly worship.

POSTSCRIPT

At proof stage I note that the Lutheran G. Ebeling's new dogmatics takes prayer as 'the key to the doctrine of God': *Dogmatik des christlichen Glaubens*, vol. I, Tübingen: Mohr, 1979, pp. 192–244. This /harmonizes with my whole approach. Ebeling's work could be added to the bibliographical references in such places as notes 503 and 1051.

Bibliography

BOOKS and articles can be traced through the names of their authors or editors in the index of persons. Full bibliographical details are given at the first mention of a study in the text or notes. Where I know a book to have been published first in the U.S.A., I have tried, in the case of original works though not of translations, to give the place, publisher and date of the American edition. Details are also given of the British edition, which is the edition I have myself most often used. Publishers sometimes while away the transatlantic journey by altering the pagination (see, for example, note 205), and I apologize for cases in which the page references do not fit the edition which I did not consult.

In order to avoid devoting an indecent number of footnotes to the writings in which I have either anticipated or elaborated on certain positions adopted in this book, I have gathered the other publications here into a single list of supportive studies.

'The baptismal eucharist before Nicaea' in *Studia Liturgica* 4 (1965), pp. 9–36.

'The need for a Methodist service for the admission of infants to the catechumenate' in *London Quarterly and Holborn Review*, January 1968, pp. 51–60.

Christian Initiation, London: Lutterworth Press, and Richmond, Va.: John Knox, Ecumenical Studies in History No. 10, 1969, 108 pp.

'Culte et culture: l'africanisation de la liturgie dans une perspective théologique' in *Flambeau* No. 21 (February 1969), pp. 11–22.

'Quelques principes sous-jacents au catholicisme romain' in *Flambeau* No. 22 (May 1969), pp. 75–84.

'L'intercommunion, signe et issue de l'impasse oecuménique' in *Nouvelle revue théologique* 92 (1970), pp. 1037–54.

'Scripture and tradition: a systematic sketch' in *Church Quarterly* 3 (1970–1971), pp. 17–28.

Eucharist and Eschatology, London: Epworth Press, 1971, third impression 1978, 238 pp.

'Dieu est-il à l'oeuvre hors des limites ecclésiatiques?' in *Flambeau* No. 29 (February 1971), pp. 18–25.

'Les sacrements' in *Manuel de théologie pratique*, Yaoundé: Editions CLE, 1971, pp. 57–72.

'Theological reflections on "The Catechism concerning the Prophet Simon Kimbangu" of 1970' in *Orita* 5 (1971), pp. 18–35.

'The localization of worship' in *Studia Liturgica* 8 (1971–2), pp. 26–41.

'The risks and possibilities of liturgical reform' in *Studia Liturgica* 8 (1971–72), pp. 65–80.

Le baptême, accès à l'Église, Yaoundé: Editions CLE, 1972, 136 pp.

'The Anglican/Roman Catholic Statement on the Eucharist' in *The Clergy Review* 57 (1972), pp. 258–60.

'La théologie systématique en Grande-Bretagne' in *Études théologiques et religieuses* 47 (1972), pp. 431–52.

'La théologie protestante allemande aux XIXe et XXe siècles: faut-il l'étudier en Afrique?' in *Flambeau* No. 36 (November 1972), pp. 220–37.

'Autour de la notion de civilisation chrétienne' in *Revue de théoligie et de philosophie* 22 (1972), pp. 413–30.

'Mt. xxii.11–13: une controverse primitive sur l'admission à la sainte cène' in *Studia Evangelica VI* (Texte und Untersuchungen 112), 1973, pp. 595–8.

'Développements baptismaux depuis 1967' in *Études théologiques et religieuses* 49 (1974), pp. 67–93.

'The rites and ceremonies of Christian initiation: developments in the past' in *Studia Liturgica* 10 (1974), pp. 2–24.

'The 1973 Anglican/Roman Catholic Statement on Ministry and Ordination: a Methodist comment' in *The Clergy Review* 59 (1974), pp. 205–11.

'The ecclesiological significance of inter-church marriage' in M. Hurley (ed.), *Beyond Tolerance*, London: Geoffrey Chapman, 1975, pp. 104–9.

'Mary in relation to the doctrinal and spiritual emphases of Methodism' in *One in Christ* 11 (1975), pp. 121–44.

'The New Testament as canon' in *Scottish Journal of Theology* 28 (1975) pp. 551–71.

'The Methodist Service Book 1975' in *Epworth Review*, January 1976, pp. 110–18.

'The eucharist as an ecumenical sacrament of reconciliation and renewal' in *Studia Liturgica* 11 (1976), pp. 1–18.

'The nature of the eucharistic prayer' in *Studia Liturgica* 11 (1976), pp. 208–211.

'Revolution and quietism: two political attitudes in theological perspective' in *Scottish Journal of Theology* 29 (1976), pp. 535–55.

'Recent thinking on Christain beliefs: baptism and the eucharist' in *Expository Times* 88 (1976–7), pp. 132–7.

'Christian worship and Western culture' in *Studia Liturgica* 12 (1977), pp. 20–33, and in *Epworth Review*, September 1977, pp. 102–15.

'Authority in the Church: a Methodist comment' in *One in Christ* 13 (1977), pp. 195–200.

'Christian initiation in the ecumenical movement' in *Studia Liturgica* 12 (1977), pp. 67–86.

'Recent foreign theology: historical and systematic' in *Expository Times* 89 (1977–78), pp. 40–6.

'The periods of liturgical history', 'Recent eucharistic revision', 'The language of worship', 'The understanding of liturgy in the light of its history'—all in C. Jones, G. Wainwright and E. Yarnold (eds.), *The Study of Liturgy*, London: SPCK, and New York: OUP, 1978, pp. 33–8, 280–8; 465–73; 495–509.

'Conciliarity and eucharist' in *One in Christ* 14 (1978), pp. 30–49, in *Midstream* 17 (1978), pp. 135–53, and in *Churches in Conciliar Fellowship?* (Conference of European Churches, occasional paper 10), Geneva, 1978, pp. 74–96.

'Recent foreign theology: historical and systematic' in *Expository Times* 90 (1978–9), pp. 87–93.

Index of Persons

Bibliographical references to works with more than one author/editor will be found under the first named author or editor.

In general, only initials are given, except where a first name or other identifying detail seems desirable. The following abbreviations are used:

(A)bp.   (Arch)bishop
ed(s).   editor(s)
Patr.   Patriarch
St.   Saint

Non-bibliographical references in the notes are differentiated by the use of italics.

For authors of books of the Bible and for biblical characters, see the Subject Index.

J.A.V.

Abelard, P., 68, 84
Ackroyd, P. R. and Evans, C. F. (eds.), note 351
Adam, K., note 522
Adnès, P., note 194
Afanasiev, N., 143; note 341
Aland, K., notes 182, *332*
Alcuin, 235–6; notes 567, 568
Allchin, A. M. and Hodges, H. A., note 470
Allmen, D. von, 56, 368; notes 137, 138, 904
Allmen, J. J. von, 27, 122, 458; notes 12, 53, 192, 194, 195, 303, 329, 415, 706, 776, 835, 871, 1130, 1137
Allwohn, A., note 1001
Amalorpavadass, D. S., note 935
Ambrose, St., of Milan, 201, 228–9, 327, 413; notes *468*, 541, 544, 625, *789*, *801*, 910, 1004, *1025*
Anderson, G. W., note 386
Andrieu, M., note 192

Ant(h)ony, St., of Egypt, note *417*
Aphraates, 97; notes 242, 905
Apollinarius, 255
Aquinas, see Thomas Aquinas
Areios, 200
Argyle, M., note 58
Arius, 52, 201, 255; notes *467*, *617*
Artemon, 52
Asmussen, H., note 590
Assemani, J. A., 220; note 506
Atchley, E. G. C. F., note 284
Athanasius, 52, 58–9, 98, 99, 201; notes 127, *129*, 249
Attfield, D. G., note 157
Aubert, R., note 522
Audet, J. P., notes 88, 373
Auer, J., note 1051
Auer, J. and Ratzinger, J. (eds.), note 1051
Augustine, St., of Hippo, 225, 280, 329, 375; notes 83, *133*, *614*, *690*
  baptism, 65, 124, 227, 244; notes 155, *178*, 335

Subject Index

baptism—*continued*
    'renewal' of, 322–3
    and salvation, 144–5
    sign of freedom, 142, 410–14
    'Spirit-baptism', 107, 108; note 271
    threefold formula, 98–100, 353; note
        247
    and unity, 116, 123–7
    unrepeatable, 232, 309, 322
    use of water, 364
Baptists, 31, 310–11, 321–2, 330–1, 390;
    note 307
    see also baptism, believer's
Barmen Declaration, 391
bereavement, note 1094
Bible: *see* Scripture
'black rubric', 264–5
Bobbio Missal, 140, 258
body:
    ascesis, 28
    resurrection of, 17, 232–3, 234, 444,
        449–54; note 564
Bossey, Ecumenical Institute, 290
Brittany, 365
Buddhism, 377
burial rites, 211, 397, 444, 446–51, 453
    African, 379–80
Byzantine Christianity:
    baptism, 40, 258, 413, 414
    eucharist, 53, 113, 186, 187
    liturgies, 111, 143, 149, 202, 326, 333;
        note 910
    ordination, note 436
    see also Eastern Church(es); Orthodoxy

calendar, pagan influences on, 374
Calvinism: *see* Reformed tradition
Canada, United Church of, 197; note 454
canticles, 213
catechisms, 329
ceremonies, Protestant attitude to, 263–7
Chad, Africa, 378–9
Chalcedon, Council of, 53, 186; note 130
    Definition of, 80, 281
Chalcedonian theology, 60, 64, 71, 256,
    278
Chinese rites, dispute, 376
chrismation, 309
Christ: *see* Jesus Christ
Christ the King, feast of, 261
Christianity:
    novelty of, 174–5
    and other religions, 359–60, 369–87
    relevance to modern life, 394–8, 404–10;
        note 982
Christmas, 397
    date of, 228, 374–5
Church, 7, 118–46
    alter Christus, 288
    apostolic, 135–8, 226
    authority, 137, 198, 226; liturgy and,
        240–50, 252
    catholicity, 132–5, 231

community nature, 142–3, 455
creedal identity, 189–94
eschatological community, 43, 118–22,
    438–44; note 1047
establishment, 390
holiness, 127–32, 245; notes 323, 325
(in)defectibility, 438, 439
(in)fallibility, 231, 249–50, 251, 283,
    437, 440
limits of, 143–6, 439–42; note 344
mission, 143–6, 355–6, 395; note 1013
national churches, 366
semper purificanda, 361
transmission of vision, 2, 3–4
unity, 122–7, 132, 190–1, 320; Churches
    Unity Commission, note 772
Western institutional view of, 113, 395
Church of England:
    anglo-catholicism, 334
    Articles, 261, 407; note 306
    creeds, 188–9
    doctrine: *Christian Believing*, 189; notes
        140, 444, 448, 755, 838; *Doctrine in
        the Church of England*, 189; note 443
    Lambeth Conference (1978), note 658
    liturgical revision, 328–34; note 720;
        Alternative Service Book, note 235;
        Series 2, 196–7, 355; Series 3, 95,
        296, 341; notes 838, 967, 1027
    and Parliament, 391
    statistics, note 979
    see also Common Prayer
circumcision, and baptism, 371
civil authorities, 416–17, 426, 428–9
Clementine Liturgy, 105
clericalism, 407
Colossians, Epistle to, 56
Common Prayer, Book of, 93, 111, 140,
    188, 269, 416, 423–4, 445, 446, 448;
    notes 36, 89, 152, 197, 235, 323, 406,
    660, 821, 1084
    1549 book, 266, 332, 450
    1552 book, 264, 328, 330, 366, 451
    1559 book, 264
    1662 book, 264, 266, 332
    1928 book, 189, 334
    American, 349, 454

communicatio idiomatum, 66, 205, 209
communion with God, 16–23
concomitance, principle of, 331
concursus divinus, 80
confession of faith, 39–40, 182–3, 303,
    431–4
    exhomologein, 39; note 91
    homologein, 156, 157
    see also creeds
confession of sin, 39, 75, 131, 439
    see also penance
confirmation, 74–5, 93, 108
    baptism and, 330; note 802
    decline of, 391
    Orthodox chrismation and, 309